Readings in Language Development

Wiley Series on Communication Disorders

Thomas J. Hixon, Advisory Editor

This collection of books has been developed by John Wiley & Sons to meet some of the needs in the field of communication disorders. The collection includes books on both normal and disordered speech, hearing, and language function. The authors of the collection have been selected because they are scientific and clinical leaders in their field and, we believe, are eminently qualified to make significant and scholarly contributions to the professional literature.

Language Development and Language Disorders
Lois Bloom and Margaret Lahey

Readings in Language Development
Lois Bloom

Readings in Childhood Language Disorders
Margaret Lahey

Elements of Hearing Science: A Programmed Text
Arnold M. Small

Readings in Language Development

Lois Bloom, Editor
Teachers College, Columbia University

JOHN WILEY & SONS
New York Santa Barbara Chichester Brisbane Toronto

Copyright © 1978, by John Wiley & Sons, Inc.

All rights reserved. Published simultaneously in Canada.

Reproduction or translation of any part of this work beyond
that permitted by Sections 107 or 108 of the 1976 United States
Copyright Act without the permission of the copyright owner
is unlawful. Requests for permission or further information
should be addressed to the Permissions Department, John
Wiley & Sons, Inc.

Library of Congress Cataloging in Publication Data

Main entry under title:
Readings in language development.

(Wiley series on communication disorders)
1. Children—Language—Addresses, essays, lectures.
2. English language—Semantics—Addresses, essays, lectures. I. Bloom, Lois. II. Series.

LB1139.L3R384	401'.9	77-10717

ISBN 0-471-08221-x

Printed in the United States of America

10 9 8 7 6 5 4 3

CONTRIBUTORS

Beatrice Beebe, Yeshiva University
Stephen Bennett, Harlem Hospital
  Department of Child Psychiatry
Lois Bloom, Teachers College,
  Columbia University
Melissa Bowerman, University of
  Kansas
Martin Braine, New York University
Roger Brown, Harvard University
Robin Chapman, University of
  Wisconsin
Eve Clark, Stanford University
John Delack, University of British
  Columbia, Canada
Jill de Villiers and Peter de Villiers,
  Harvard University
Peter Eimas, Brown University
Catherine Garvey, Johns Hopkins
  University
Jean Berko Gleason, Boston University
Lila Gleitman, University of
  Pennsylvania
Paul Guillaume
Michael Halliday, University of Sydney,
  Australia
Lois Hood, Rockefeller University
Joseph Jaffe, College of Physicians and
  Surgeons, Columbia University
Peter Jusczyk, Dalhousie University,
  Canada
Werner Leopold, Professor Emeritus,
  Northwestern University
Patsy Lightbown, Concordia University,
  Canada
John MacNamara, McGill University,
  Canada
Jon Miller, University of Wisconsin
Peggy Miller, Teachers College,
  Columbia University
Elizabeth Shipley, University of
  Pennsylvania

v

PREFACE

In the study of language development there are many issues and ideas that bear on the nature of language in general, and on the nature of mind and mental development. Moreover, the data for studying language development are abundant; virtually all small children are learning to talk. As a result, the study of child language has been the subject of considerable interest and research in the last century. However, different investigators have observed and described the data of language development differently, and have asked different questions of the data.

A representation of the literature in child language that would be adequate to answer most questions and speak to most issues having to do with language development is not possible. Inevitably, "collections" of almost anything reflect the interests and, for better or worse, the biases of the collector. The readings presented here were selected with two principal interests in mind—first, to complement and expand the text of *Language Development and Language Disorders*, by Lois Bloom and Margaret Lahey, John Wiley, and second, to provide a core of readings for advanced undergraduate and graduate students interested in language development, language disorders, psycholinguistics, and special education in particular, and in developmental psychology, education, and linguistics in general.

With only a few exceptions, the readings presented here are reports of empirical research that present, describe, and interpret actual data of children's language behavior. The readings essentially follow the plan of the first half of the text of *Language Development and Language Disorders:* (1) Describing Children's Language; (2) Origins of Language Content, Form and Use in Infancy; (3) Development of Language Content/Form in the Acquisition of Vocabulary; (4) Development of Language Content/Form in the Acquisition of Semantic-Syntactic Structure; and Variation and Complexity in Development of Language Content/Form; (6) Development of Language Use in Relation to Content and Form; (7) Developmental Interaction Between Understanding and Speaking; and (8) Processes in Learning Language.

Lois Bloom

ACKNOWLEDGMENTS

There are a number of persons who were kind enough to review the list of potential contributions to this volume and offer comments on the relevance of one or another selection, or suggest other possible selections. My thanks go to Margaret Lahey, Lois Hood, Karin Lifter, Lorraine Rocissano, John Broughton, Lila Ghent Braine and Eve Clark. Denise and Diane Lahey assisted in assembling the manuscript, and Pam Maffei and Barbara Kennedy took care of the correspondence to obtain permissions to reprint. This book presents the work of other persons and I thank them, in particular, for sharing in coordinating the effort to describe and understand children's language development.

L.B.

CONTENTS

Readings in Language Development

Part 1
DESCRIBING CHILDREN'S LANGUAGE

The readings presented here provide a historical perspective and give important examples of some of the different methodologies that have been used to describe children's language. Until the 1950s, there were two main types of research in language development—the longitudinal diary studies of individual children, as represented here by the excerpts from *Werner Leopold's (1939) diary*, and the cross-sectional studies of large numbers of children. The greatest effort in this period of time was devoted to normative studies of large groups of children, who varied in age, social class, sex, birth position, and so forth. These studies were comprehensively reviewed in McCarthy (1954) and have come to be called "count" or normative studies. It is interesting that the count studies came about in reaction to the diary studies that had begun to appear in the literature at the turn of the century. The swing toward behaviorism and the striving for scientific rigor in psychology in the 1930s and 1940s resulted in a disparagement of information, however detailed and minutely recorded, gathered by a parent-investigator, who, it was presumed, was necessarily biased in what he or she chose to record, and in what was overlooked as well.

The typical normative, "count," studies described certain properties of the form of children's speech; for example, the average length, parts of speech, and numbers of different words in a representative number (usually 50 to 100) of a child's utterances. The principal result was the specification of linguistic developmental milestones that allowed comparison among individual children or groups of children. These milestones provide only a very general and gross index of development, and, more seriously, they ignore the notion of development as continuous *change* over time. Thus, important differences in behavior that occur within a particular developmental milestone, and the ways in which the different milestones are actually interrelated and interdependent, were easily overlooked in the cross-sectional developmental studies of the 1930s and 1940s.

The count studies are represented here by the study by *Madorah Smith (1933)*. In addition to being an example of the count studies of the 1930s, Smith's study has another historical distinction—it was one of the earliest empirical attempts to obtain evidence that child language was systematic and rule-governed. Inferences about the underlying regularities in children's language could be made by observing the "errors" children made in their spontaneous speech.

An altogether different approach to uncovering the regularities in children's linguistic knowledge was the experimental study by *Jean Berko Gleason (1958)*. This study is representative of the reaction to the count studies of children's utterances that began in the 1950s. People began to seek different kinds of information about children and began asking different kinds of questions in language development research. Most important, there was a turn away from descriptions of the form of speech in an effort to discover what children *know* about language at any given time. Researchers in the 1950s, for example, Brown (1957) and Berko (1958), began to inquire into the knowledge that underlies the ability to speak and understand—the "productive system . . . that [the child] employs in the creation of new forms" (Berko and Brown, 1960).

The new questions required the development of experimental techniques for observing children's response to the manipulation of certain kinds of language and situation variables. Such research generally involved fewer children than was typical of the earlier cross-sectional count studies, but was designed to obtain more basic kinds of information. This era in psycholinguistic research has been very amply summarized and described in a number of reviews (for example, Berko & Brown, 1960; Miller & Ervin, 1964; and Ervin-Tripp, 1966). These studies convincingly demonstrated that children do not learn all of the sounds, words, and possible sentences in a language. Instead, what the child learns is an underlying linguistic system that is, itself, never directly available to the child, or the adult. The studies of Berko (1958, reproduced here) and Brown (1957) made this point most explicitly and most elegantly. Whereas Smith had earlier described children's spontaneously occurring language behavior, Berko Gleason "interfered" and presented children with specific tasks to elicit particular language behaviors. Her study, in addition to being a methodological innovation, answered the question of whether children's language was systematic and rule-governed with a definite *yes*, and the search for the "underlying system" of rules for children's language was launched.

The fact that children learned phonological and morphological rule systems had long been suspected by the earlier diarists and other linguists (see, for example, Jakobson, 1968, and Jesperson, 1922). Linguistic field research had generally emphasized discovery procedures in the phonology and morphology of languages. The study of syntax or grammar was quite another matter. It was not at all clear how one could discover the grammar of a language and it was even less clear how much of a grammar existed in early child language. However, with the advent of the theory of generative transformational grammar (Chomsky, 1957), the search for grammar became the goal of language development research in the 1960s, evolving in a very natural way from the interest in underlying knowledge that began in the 1950s. In short, attempts to discover what a child knows were pursued in the 1960s as a search for grammar or the description of the rule systems that could account for the use of sentences.

Again going back to the spontaneous language behavior of children, *Martin Braine (1963)* described the regularities in the ways in which three children combined words in their earliest sentences, and made inferences about the kinds of rules children might be learning in order to say sentences. Research such as the study of Braine that is included here, and the comparable studies by Brown and Fraser (1963) and Miller and Ervin, (1964) was concerned with a still smaller population of subjects.

Continuing in the tradition of describing the regularities in samples of the spontaneous speech of a few children, Cazden (1968) was able to provide an account of the sequence in which three American-born children acquired noun and verb inflections. This study was later extended in two methodologically important ways. First, Brown (1973) compared the results of Cazden's longitudinal descriptive study with the results of other similarly descriptive studies of noun and verb inflections in the literature and reported a consensus among them. In the study presented here, *Jill de Villiers and Peter de Villiers (1974)* used the resulting description of the sequence of acquisition of grammatical morphemes as an *etic* scheme for testing the acquisition of grammatical morphemes in a cross-sectional study of the speech of a large number of children.

There is a continuity in the studies by Leopold, Braine, and Cazden in that they were describing children's language behavior directly, and a continuity in the studies by Smith and Berko Gleason in that they were using the adult model language as a standard or yardstick for describing children's language behavior. Whereas Smith had described children's "errors" or deviations from the model language in spontaneous speech, Berko Gleason used an experimental task to examine the regularities and the errors children made when asked to add word endings to nonsense forms.

Together, these five readings in the first section provide a historical perspective as well as an overview of methods for describing children's language. Research into the nature of child language in general, and the development of morphology in particular, is represented here by three studies that approached the problems of obtaining and interpreting evidence differently: painstakingly recording all of the speech behaviors in the first two years (Leopold), observing speech errors (Smith), experimentally manipulating children's language behavior (Berko Gleason), observing regularities in samples of naturally occurring speech events to obtain an emic scheme (Braine) and, then, using an emic scheme as an etic plan (de Villiers and de Villiers).

Essentially, with the exception of Werner Leopold and other diarists, most research in language development before the 1970s was primarily concerned with describing the *form* of child language. However, all of the same methodologies, and others as well, have since been used for research that has explored the origins of language form, content, and use in infancy, and the intersection of form, content, and use in language learning that begins in the second year.

Speech Development of a Bilingual Child
Werner F. Leopold

METHODS OF PROCEDURE

A diary was kept uninterruptedly from the child's eighth week on, in great detail until the end of the seventh year; thereafter only striking features were recorded. The observations were written down as they were made, usually in daily entries. From 1;7 on they became too numerous for this procedure; they were then entered on slips in my pocket and transferred in systematic order into the diary at infrequent intervals, usually every Sunday. I relied almost exclusively on my own observations, because phonetic exactness was deemed essential, especially during the first two years, and her mother's ear was not sufficiently trained. Data not checked by my own observation were used very sparingly and with great caution. I had to make use of her mother's notes during a period of six weeks (first days of July to August 11, 1932; E 1;11–2;1) when I was away in New York to fill a summer teaching appointment. The notes were then entered from frequent reports by letter in their approximate phonetic form, but were eventually disregarded in the phonetic evaluation.

After the middle of January, 1932 (1;6), words which she repeated only on demand were no longer taken into consideration, but only such as had become an active part of her vocabulary. Otherwise every word was recorded through 2;0. After that, progress became so rapid that the entries had to be restricted to new acquisitions of typical importance, still rather detailed, but no longer complete. Comparative notes about the child's general (non-linguistic) development were occasionally inserted, but were not the main purpose of the investigation; however, a "baby book" was carefully kept by the mother and resorted to for the sketch of the general development given in the final chapter of this volume. The author realizes the importance of the general physical and psychological development as a setting for the unfolding of speech; but the difficulty of publishing a comprehensive study made limitations necessary. He consoles himself with the thought that his study will be no more defective on the psychological side than those of psychologists are on the linguistic side. The training which he has had in psychology as a student (G. E. Müller was one of his teachers), and extensive reading in psychology in four languages guarantee at least that he is not unaware of the psychological background.

Baby talk was not used by the adults speaking to the child—without pedantry,

From Werner F. Leopold, *Speech Development of a Bilingual Child, A Linguist's Record*. Volume I, Vocabulary Growth in the First Two Years. Published originally by Northwestern University Press, Evanston, Illinois, 1939. Reprinted with permission of AMS Press, New York.

however; there were a few instances in which here "cute" forms became fixed for a time by adoption on the part of her environment. Her mother did use the third person in speaking of herself for a time subsequent to the first two years, a practice which, curiously enough, never took root in Hildegard's speech habits. As a rule, the child's language has been allowed to develop subconsciously; her utterances were not corrected formally.

We succeeded in keeping the fact that her speech was being studied from entering her consciousness. Her occasional question in later years, "What are you writing?" was easily answered, "I am taking notes for my work." She is so used to seeing her father write all the time that she has apparently never suspected that he was studying her speech. I have never noticed any self-consciousness produced by my taking notes.

The indexing of words and linguistic facts up to the end of the second year was begun and carried to an advanced stage immediately after the end of this period, during my sojourn in New York in the summer of 1932. That was important, because the distinction between words surviving to the end of that period and those inactive by that time could be made only at that time, since the diary did not show the continued use of a word after its initial appearance had been recorded, unless changes of its form, other phenomena of linguistic importance, or its occurrence in sentences warranted reptition. For other data, the diary remained a dependable source of information, which could be tapped again and again in the following years.

The speech of her sister Karla, born six years after Hildegard, was not recorded in the same detail; but I took many comparative notes on it, which are here given as footnotes. I was working on the text of this study particularly when Karla was 1;7–1;11 old, a stage of many new words. A good number of footnotes about Karla's speech could be added on that occasion. The bilingual procedure with Karla was the same as with Hildegard. But the English environment was still stronger in her case. The number of German words which Karla used was therefore much smaller. But she also understood nearly everything I said to her in German.

THE FIRST YEAR

During the first few weeks, the only sounds produced were cries of dissatisfaction. The crying consisted of front vowels between [æ] and [a], usually [a]. During the first week it was clearly [ʔaˡʔaːː], later as a rule simple long [ʔaː].

The child also began early to stretch lustily upon awakening, holding her breath until her face turned red. She allowed the air to escape gradually, interrupted by laryngeal stops, usually with her mouth closed, therefore with nasal resonance.

0;1. The seventh and eighth weeks brought considerable progress: the forehead became visibly higher, the eyes had brilliancy and expression, and smiling as a sign of recognition developed, unmistakably from the third day of the eighth week (E 0;1). The development of a personality began.

At the same time, the sounds ceased to be purely incidental.[1] She uttered more

---

[1] The sixth to the ninth week is the normal time for the beginning of cooing. See the conspectus in Decroly, p. 26.

arbitrary sounds of satisfaction, all of them formed in the back of the mouth—supposedly "difficult" sounds, but well known to be the property of all children at the beginning stage of their linguistic development. They were as a rule clearly expiratory fricatives produced preferably at the rear velum and at the uvula, sometimes so far back that they seemed to come from the larynx. Occasionally the fricative was introduced by the stop of the same position, resulting quite commonly in such "difficult" affricates as [kχ]; not infrequently they took the form of [ʀ].

Apparently, the front part of the tongue was not yet very flexible, although in crying the whole rim of the tongue was visibly turned up, the mouth forming almost a horizontal rectangle.

I imitated these sounds, partly in order to study them, partly in order to amuse the child. During the seventh week, she turned toward these sounds with a puzzled expression and a day or two later sometimes reacted with a happy smile. Her attention for acoustic impressions was at that stage still irregular, less general than for visual ones. It seemed that she preferred female voices, but that impression was not definite.

During the same (seventh) week, she also began to utter occasionally a new kind of vocalic sounds during rest stops while drinking, sounds resembling short [œ] or [ʌ]. Once, while she was lying on the dressing-stand, a two-syllable combination was heard consisting of a half-high front vowel with some velar timbre, followed by a strongly velar voiced stop or fricative and ending in back [ɑ], something like [æ'γɑ:] or [æ'gɑ:];[2] the velar timbre of the first vowel appeared to the ear as [l], but it was not clearly an [l]. The quality of these early sounds is so indistinct and unconventional that they defy transcription and almost description. Similar combinations were repeated during the eighth week once or twice, always playfully and without any intention or consciousness of achievement.

Loud speaking in her immediate neighborhood still frightened her like other sharp noises. But low, friendly words, whether German or English, attracted her attention, which was presumably directed toward timbre and intonation.

On the last day of the second month, she repeatedly produced fully-voiced sounds in addition to the usual obtuse laryngeal and velar fricatives during her bath. As a rule the tongue was at rest, but once the tongue tip approached the gums, resulting in a combination which sounded very much like [hɪldə], the [ə] tending toward [a], as if she were saying her name, Hilda. That was pure accident, since she was not addressed by this form. Labial vibrating sounds appeared rarely. Once a palatal click was observed.[3] But on the whole, back sounds still prevailed. On the same day, when she was in a specially good mood, also during her bath, a two-syllable combination was heard, the second part of which was clearly [ʀu:]. This was the first [u]; the back of the tongue was being lifted higher.

Cooing as an articulated expression of feelings of satisfaction was therefore well established by the end of the second month, having begun before the middle of it.

0;2. In the first days of the third month, both smiling and the production of ar-

---

[2] Romanes (p. 122) reports that one of his children, a very late speaker, once said "Ego" very distinctly, M 1;2.

[3] Grégoire (p. 387) observed palatal clicks at 0;8.

ticulated sounds increased. When fully awake and in a happy mood, especially during her bath and between 5 and 6 p.m., before her dinner, she liked to "speak' in monologues—a valuable exercise of the speech organs for the impending task. The basis was shifting toward the front; velar sounds no longer prevailed; labials became more frequent[4]—probably on account of a growing flexibility of the tongue and the lips rather than under the influence of speech sounds heard from those around her. But on the whole, sounds were still incoherent, interrupted by silent kicking and voiceless laryngeal panting. The combinations [uk'χu:], with very strong rounding of the lips, and [agɔbw:] were observed, [bw:] being a vibrating labial with velar timbre.[5] Clicks again occurred twice, with the mouth completely closed.[6] Several times the upper lip showed very strong protrusion and rounding so as almost to reach up to the nose;[7] the possibility of muscular modification of the lips had been discovered and was being practised.[8] The vowels [ɛ], [ə], [ʌ], [u], [ʊ] had been added to the [a] sounds. Most effective for her entertainment was the production of clicks and especially of velar affricates without a vowel.

0;3. In the following weeks, the development did not progress very much linguistically, but the unfolding of the intelligence showed itself in a more and more vivid attention for the environment. The existence of linguistic plateaus is well known[9]— periods in which the speech-development falls behind the physical or intellectual progress. But I have, on the other hand, observed other periods when striking progress in speech coincided with a rapid general development. It seems that at times the energy of acquisition must be restricted to one field, whereas at other times it is so great that it works in all fields equally, physical, intellectual, and linguistic. At any rate progress is clearly uneven; periods of rapid development alternate with periods of rest and consolidation.

At this stage her eyes and ears followed all happenings with untiring attention.[10] Objects had evidently been recognized for weeks. In unaccustomed surroundings, she would restlessly look around and fix her attention on certain objects. Smiling was frequently supplemented by loud laughing.[11] She was now especially amused by funny sounds, more than by funny faces.[12] Velar fricatives still served best to entertain her; recognition of her own productions may have had something to do with her satisfaction. She did not yet play spontaneously at this stage. She would rattle her toy for a while when it was put into her hand; but that was probably only an accidental

---

[4] Karla had a game of smacking her lips at B 0;4.

[5] Pavlovitch (§ 73) describes this " 'roulement' provoqué par les lèvres" (0;8) as a variety of [r], although he realizes that it is not an imitation of [r].

[6] Karla the same way at the same time.

[7] This was not observed with Karla.

[8] Karla later, B 0;4, strikingly at M 0;4.

[9] Stern, p. 163.

[10] Pavlovitch (§ 34) describes a similar concentrated attention, but with no clear indication of time.

[11] Karla not until first half of 0;4.

[12] Karla by both, at the same time.

result of the violent movements of the arms which she made for exercise.[13] The noise itself was interesting to her, but not agreeable; she winced, which meant that she was slightly afraid of it.

"Speaking" became often more continuous, without improvement of articulation. It occurred most commonly in the morning between 7 and 8, when she was in good humor[14] after feeding and a good night's sleep; for more than two months she had been used to sleeping without disturbance from 6 to 6 o'clock. But she also babbled at other times without special motivation. Intentions of communication could not be assumed, although sometimes it looked as if she answered or meant to say something.[15] Nor did she understand anything spoken to her in German or English as far as reactions are a test; but she was receptive for timbre of voices and strength of sounds. A vigorous [hɛı!] would put a stop of surprise to her crying, unless her trouble was too great.[16]

0;6. For several months thereafter, progress was limited to physical and intellectual phenomena, every week bringing new observations. Linguistically the development seemed at a standstill, if not in actual retrogression. For months she babbled much less.[17] Instead, she amused herself for a time by producing high screeching laryngeal sounds,[18] which later alternated with "speaking" exercises.[19] The screeching was then softened into very gentle, melodious and pleasing tones, for which I could find no designation. At this period the well-known expiratory bilabial vibrating sound [bw:][20] became a favorite sound, which it remained for months. It was frequently an expression of protest and preceded crying; but even more often it was produced simply for amusement.

At the end of the seventh month, on January 27, 1931, she babbled more than usually, and both parents independently observed that the sounds were much clearer than before, a striking difference. Even in the course of the day, a development in this respect seemed noticeable. In especially good humor all day, she smiled and laughed surprisingly much and did not cry, except for a half-hour in the afternoon, when a lady of our acquaintance was visiting. Somehow she did not approve of this visitor and

---

[13] Karla rattled toys consciously at M 0;4.

[14] Karla likewise babbled most when she was in good humor.

[15] Same observation with Karla.

[16] Karla reacted in the same manner to any vigorous speaking and to singing, to which she was always very receptive.

[17] Same observation with Karla.

[18] During the whole fourth month and beyond, Karla produced high joyful sounds, in the beginning with inspiratory articulation, which could best be described by the German term "Jauchzen" (or "Krähen," which Ronjat however retains within his French text for a different purpose). This stage was much reduced with Hildegard. Alternation of these sounds with babbling exercises fell for Karla in the beginning of the fifth month. The softening into melodious tones was observed from M 0;4 to E 0;6, by that time predominantly with expiratory articulation.

[19] Same observation with Karla.

[20] Preyer (p. 117) describes "the labial *brrr*, the so-called 'coachman's *R'*'" for 1;1.—Karla also liked labial sounds M 0;4; she used [bw:] constantly M 0;4, rarely 0;6, again E 0;6.

cried with an entirely new sound, which perhaps indicated fear, for an unknown reason; that was a new observation, too. The distinctive feature of progress was the appearance of more definite consonants. Up to that day her sounds had usually been vowels interrupted by rather indefinite movements of the tongue.[21] Now the tongue began to move in a much more energetic manner in the front part of the mouth; some of these motions were clearly visible. They resulted in sounds between [d] and palatal [g]. On account of insufficient practice and the absence of teeth, the consonants were not always well defined in place and manner of articulation. The closure of stops was not complete in the beginning of the day, but improved in the course of the afternoon so as to result in some fairly accurate productions of the consonants [d] and palatal [g]. Once on the same day, a single syllable was produced perfectly distinctly, namely [sa], a short [a] preceded by normal voiceless [s], the first [s] that occurred and for a long time the only one.

During these days she often amused herself by producing repeated glottal stops (expiratory, like all her sounds).[22] The effect was that of coughing, and may have been an imitation of it; but it was articulated intentionally.[23] After a few days, this practice disappeared. All games, including the linguistic ones, commanded her attention only for limited periods.[24]

0;7. The eighth month brought little progress. On February 14 she said distinctly and repeatedly [dada] and [baba], with front [a]; but these "words" remained for a long time without meaning for the unprejudiced observer. Most babbling sounds continued to be vocalic, prevalently ranging from [a] to [ɛ], long, without many tongue movements. The consonants that did occur resembled [d] and [g].[25] [b] was heard only once before the day mentioned, except for the bilabial vibrating affricate [bw:], which maintained its amusement value for her and was developed to inimitable mastery. She liked to produce it while eating,[26] with malice toward none, but with disastrous effect. On the same day, [ʔæːʔæː] and [hæːhæː] were heard, but these combinations were not new.

She reacted to speaking when she felt like it. Actual understanding was limited to her own name, Hildegard. At least from February 1 (E 0;6) it usually induced her to turn her head expectantly toward the speaker. There was no doubt that she referred these sounds in some way to herself.[27]

---

[21] Karla had only vowel sounds to the second half of 0;3; consonants began E 0;3. But vowels also predominated decisively until E 0;6.

[22] Preyer (p. 106, 117) emphasizes the same fact for 0;5 and 1;1: "I have not once observed an attempt to form sounds while drawing in the breath."—Hildegard's clicks, suction sounds, can hardly be considered as inspiratory.—But cf. the note on Karla's inspiratory sounds, p. 19. —Grégoire reports the production of inspiratory vowels for several months from E 0;3 on, and playful inspiratory consonants until 1;0 (p. 386).

[23] Not observed with Karla.

[24] Same observation with Karla.

[25] Karla the same way 0;6; [g] more frequent than [d].

[26] Same observation with Karla.

[27] Pavlovitch (§ 24) records this stage of development at a much earlier period, 0;3. But cf. Stern p. 18 (0;10?) and p. 83 (M 0;11).—Karla, less certain, at E 0;6.

0;8. The ninth month was important in Hildegard's linguistic development. In the
first half, her physical progress was more marked than the intellectual growth. She
learned few new sounds. Understanding was not visibly improved. The most frequent
babbling-combinations were [dæ] and [d ɪ].[26] Every combination ended in a vowel.
[28] For her own entertainment she often produced a vigorous click formed between
the tongue and the upper lip.[29] She had two lower teeth at this stage, which did not
affect pronunciation. While sucking her finger—an incurable habit defying all attempts at correction even to this day (age 9)—she would utter at that time a strong
sound produced by vibration of the vocal cords, with a rhythmical increase and
decrease in intensity;[30] it was possible to check on her habit at a distance by listening
to this tone. The game of producing the labial vibrating sound had subsided; it
occurred only occasionally. On March 13, she uttered an [r] sound, which resembled
uvular [ʀ] so much that her mother, imitating it, succeeded for the first time in her
life in pronouncing the German [ʀ]. Just the same, upon listening more closely, I discovered it to be a velar vibrant sound produced by forming a narrow opening between the back tongue and the velum with the aid of saliva. The sound remained
ephemeral.[31]

In the second half of the ninth month she took a decisive step forward: both
speaking and understanding began.[32] It was speaking in a very rudimentary sense.
She had a strong desire for receiving attention. She contrived a means for attaining
this aim by uttering a short, sharp scream (first reported on March 13), especially
when I was sitting at some distance from her.[33] This utterance was in form farther
removed from standard speech than many of her babbling combinations. But it was
distinguished from them by an important addition: the intention of communication,
which must be considered the chief criterion of language.[34] Encouraged by the
result, she used this sound very often during the following week, and it assumed the
more articulate form [ʔaǃ], very short and vigorous. The intention of communication
was beyond doubt, though its content varied. At the same time, a more primitive form

---

[26] Same observation with Karla.

[28] It may well be a widely valid law of infant speech that every syllable should end in a vowel.
The English nursery word "daddy" could be derived from babbling combinations, but "dad" is
more likely an adult back-formation.—Hildegard never used either "daddy" or "dad" for her
father up to 2;0. She must have heard these words frequently, but support for "papa" was much
stronger. Karla also used "papa" regularly, but tried [dadi] at 1;7; [dæːdi] 1;8.

[29] Karla rarely, accidentally.

[30] Not observed with Karla. She was also a finger-sucker, but a less determined one.

[31] I observed it with Karla at E 0;6 and E 0;9 as palatal "spit-bubble" [r]. I have not found this
sound described anywhere.

[32] According to McCarthy, p. 6, O'Shea counts the babbling stage until E 0;7, Sully until
second half of first year to first quarter of second year. Sully's description is better, because
babbling stage and speaking stage overlap.

[33] Same observation with Karla, E 0;6. Karla had at this stage several sounds, which were
strikingly short and controlled by her will. They were no longer purely sounds of self-expression,
nor did they contain an objective communication as yet; but they were meant as a game of
conversation with others—a preparatory stage for communicative speaking.

[34] Cf., among many others, E. Sapir, *Language*, New York, 1921, p. 17.

of communication was used when she indicated dissatisfaction with the state of her diapers by crying.[35] Though this form of utterance is primarily self-expressive, it cannot be omitted, because it developed into communication by producing the desired reaction.

About March 19 or 20, her mother thought she noticed that the word "daddy" made her pay attention, stop crying, and look around. A similar reaction to the standardized disapproval by "no, no!" was also observed; but the impression was not definite beyond doubt.[36] All doubt that understanding (apart from her name, which in the first half of 0;8 she understood even when it was spoken with ordinary voice, without emphasis[37]) had begun was removed in the last days of March. On the wall there was a picture of herself which she liked very much, perhaps because the curved glass over it produced plesant reflections. By repeatedly saying the word "baby" in front of it, her mother had succeeded in building up a strong association between the word and the object. Upon hearing the question, "Where is the baby?" she would turn all the way around in the high-chair to see the picture, and laugh with joy when she succeeded. The same reaction was achieved by the German question, "Wo ist das Baby?", because the association was clearly with the noun. On March 29, her chair was in a different place. Upon hearing the well-known question, she turned around to the right as she had learned to do. There her glance fell on a young colleague calling on us, much to the amusement of the company present. But she immediately corrected her mistake by turning around to the left. The association with the object was stronger than that with the motion. When the chair was placed back in the old position, the process of learning to change the motion repeated itself.

The question, "Where is daddy?" tended to produce the same reaction. The acoustic difference between "baby" and "daddy" was not great enough, and the question as a whole had been too strongly associated with a certain reaction. The term "daddy" was therefore abandoned by us and replaced by the bilingual "papa."

The diary at this point reveals my astonishment at the course which the development took. From the literature on child-language I had expected a stage of mechanical sound-imitation, with later induction of meanings for the words thus acquired.[38] Undoubtedly this stage plays a rôle with other children, although it is agreed that the understanding of words and sentences generally comes much earlier than speaking.[39] In Hildegard's case, the phase of mechanical imitation was completely lacking; meanings were always developed before sound-forms. The impulse for any kind of imitation was strikingly weak in this child.[40] At later stages, too, she avoided saying a word before she understood it.

---

[35] Karla much earlier.

[36] Similarly uncertain, E 0;6–M 0;8, with Karla, who however reacted definitely to the stimulus "patsch, patsch!" at 0;7.

[37] Not so Karla by M 0;8.

[38] Decroly (p. 97) cites Meumann, Compayré, Sully, and Stern as authorities for the opinion that sound-imitation precedes real speaking as a preparatory stage, with Preyer dissenting.

[39] Cf. for instance Decroly, p. 87. Preyer (pp. 93 and 215f.) also strongly believes in the priority of understanding over speaking.

[40] Karla was much more willing to imitate words from direct presentation and, especially at 1;8, learned many in fairly good phonetic form in this manner. But mechanical echolalia was

Her sounds had decreased rather than increased. She did not practice much. Perhaps the consonants had become clearer. [g] was no longer heard; [d] was less frequent; [bababa] was the most common combination.[41] Voiceless consonants were absent, likewise [m] and [n]. That was again a surprise, as I had expected [mama] to be the first mechanical combination[42] uttered by children.[43]

0;9. During the tenth month, the number of sounds increased, and understanding progressed considerably. On the first day, the first voiceless consonant was heard in the combination [tæ tæ], which alternated with [dæ dæ][44] [da da da] developed two meanings: in ordinary tone, it expressed satisfaction,[45] in a loud tone it was clearly scolding.[46] The click recurred in the [t] position after the "invention" of the [t] at the alveoles or front palate, and developed into a game. A few days later, new fricatives appeared: [baβa], [jɛjɛ], [dja] (all vowels short). [aɪ] was the first diphthong observed. In the second half of the month [ɲɛɲɛ], [çɛ] and other fricatives similar to [ç] were heard. [ji] was new with regard to both sounds; they remained rare. The first [k] appeared in [kə]. The long expected [mamama] was finally introduced, without meaning.

The understanding extended to several set phrases. The "baby" game remained the most entertaining exercise, but her interest spread to other pictures, and she reacted correctly to the question, "Wo ist das Bild?" where no baby was in the picture. Upon "Wie gross bist du?" (only in German) she learned to put both hands on her head, smiling—her own modification of the standard reaction of holding up the arms.[47] Upon "patticake" she put both hands together. The corresponding German "Backe,

---

not common with her either until 1;9, when it became quite conspicuous.

[41] Karla 0;8 [g], [d], and [b].

[42] Cf. F. Tracy, *The psychology of childhood*, Boston, 1896, p. 159. He calls the syllable "ma" "that sound which is, in the majority of cases, the first articulation."

[43] In Karla's speech, too, [mama] did not occur up to M 0;8, although she already produced an occasional [u], [w], and [gega]. The opinion that syllables like [ma], [pa], [ta] are the first used by infants, which is frequently found in linguistic and psychological literature, is certainly not borne out by the observations made on my children. The psychoanalytical explanation of the first labials as "a prolongation of the act of sucking" (cf. for instance Spielrein, Intern. Zs. f. Psychoanal. 6, p. 401; quoted by Piaget, *Language and Thought of the Child*, p. 3f.) seems far-fetched in the light of my experience. Cf. also notes to the word [mama] in the following vocabulary. Generalized statements of this kind make the need for a greater number of exact scientific records like the present very apparent. Even the existing material should have sufficed to warn against such generalizations.

[44] Karla said [(ha)ta], with voiceless vowels and unaspirated [t], E 0;7, [hata] aloud on the next day, frequently; [dædæ] second half 0;7.

[45] Wundt (third edition, vol. 1, p. 295) also registers "da-da" as indicating comfort.

[46] Karla scolded [giŋ(giŋgiŋ)] 0;6, [dɪdɪ] M 0;8.

[47] Karla with certainty 0;11; she raised her arms correctly. The trick, with the same words, was reported by Tiedemann as early as 1787 (cf. English ed., p. 35). It is probably much older than that. No traditions are more stable than those of the nursery, witness the English children's rhymes, which survive unchanged although the vocabulary and setting of old rural England are largely meaningless to modern American city children.

backe Kuchen" immediately produced the same reaction, with no building-up of an association, perhaps by accident. But the latter response was still often confused with the former. "Peek-a-boo" and "Guck, guck (Kuckuk)" were learned; she liked to do this hiding game on her own accord with a blanket, etc., but silently, with no attempt at sound-imitation. The hopping reaction to "hopp, hopp, hopp!" was learned in a baby swing,[48] but soon simulated in any position without fail.

The speaking progress, aside from the babbling sounds mentioned before, was slight. [ʔa!] was addressed not only to persons, but also to distant objects and escaped toys. At the end of the month, the new combination [bi] was heard with reference to a picture (Bild).[49] The identity was doubted at the time of entry; but later developments make it probable that this was indeed the first reproduction of a standard word, a German one. This word, however, was ephemeral at its first appearance.[50]

0;10. At the end of the eleventh month, her active vocabulary consisted of two words, both of which were new. The first one made its appearance in the first days of the month while she was spending a week in Milwaukee with her mother and heard only English spoken. It was "pretty," a surprisingly difficult word for the beginnings of a child's vocabulary,[51] it was taught her by her relatives. It remained active after her return to Evanston and turned out to be the most stable part of her early vocabulary. It was articulated slowly and distinctly, sound by sound, usually in a whisper, but occasionally with full voice. Its recorded form was at first[ˈprəti], at the end of the month [prɪti]. The articulation was surprisingly clear for this stage of development and for such a difficult word. The only sound which showed variation was the [r]. At the first recording, it is expressly described as a brief rolled tongue-tip [r], which was never used otherwise. But it was frequently replaced by a fricative varying between [ç], [ʃ], and [s], later also [w]. The word was usually whispered and accompanied by pointing. It was correctly used as an expression of admiration, especially when pointing toward a picture; sometimes admiration was merged with a desire to have the object. The latter was not necessarily objectively "pretty"; a concentration of her interest on it was a sufficient incentive for the use of the word. Sometimes it was heard, when she was at play and in good humor, in the rudimentary form [pr] or its equivalent.

The second word was [dɛ], with a short vowel, later varied [dɪ:] and [de:], a demonstrative interjection uttered while pointing with her right hand at objects, also usually

---

[48] Karla second half 0;7; not clearly distinguished from "patsch, patsch!" M 0;8.

[49] Pavlovitch (§ 48) records the first [i] at 1;1.

[50] In the second half of 0;9, Karla said rather clearly [bebi] for a doll; she understood Karla, Hildegard, Papa, Ticktack, and Bonnie (name of our dog). Sounds: [nβnβ], [nana], [mæ(mæ)], [ma(ma)]; occasionally a click, and [w] followed by a vowel. She imitated a [b]-like sound produced by sliding the tongue rapidly to and fro between the lips.

[51] Karla also acquired it, at 0;9, at first as monosyllabic [pyi], voiceless, with a falling diphthong. It became more perfect in form (whispered [p'ɤt'i] 0;11) and a constantly used favorite word from 0;11 to 1;3; in her case soon usually pronounced aloud, although she also began it in whispered form.—I have heard of other children acquiring the word early doubtless because of its frequent use by the environment. Karla's first word was "by-by," second half 0;8. Ronjat and Pavlovitch observe the beginning of active speaking also at 0;8.

pictures.[52] It appeared first as the answer to a question about a picture, accompanied by an expression of astonishment and satisfaction. Her mother immediately understood it as "there"; I tried to identify it was "da"; but the later history made it probable that it represented the English adverb.

Aside from these two definite words, her continual prattling[53] contained more diversified sounds and gave the impression of real speaking; but no other meanings were associated with sound-groups. The non-standard [ʔa], short, to arouse attention continued. Her palatal click was put into the service of calling squirrels; she used it upon the direction, "Call the squirrel." [mama], [mama] and [mamama] occurred frequently.[54] Her mother referred it to herself, but I observed it only repeatedly at the sight of her food, and without any reference while she was playing. It did not become a word until much later. Once the striking combination [mama papa] was heard in isolation; but it was never repeated and did not have any meaning. Her sound games were coming closer to standard sounds, but were still part of the preparatory playful stage. Understanding, on the other hand, progressed again. For German stimuli it was lost temporarily during her stay in Milwaukee, but returned rapidly. "Wie gross bist du?" "Backe, backe Kuchen," and "Patticake" brought the fixed reactions whenever she felt like performing. She had now reached the creeping stage, and warnings were often necessary; she understood the falling intonation of "No, no!" and "Nein, nein!" and obeyed. Upon "Gib *mir* das" she willingly gave her toy,[55] the extended hand being as much an incentive as the words. Often an open hand was extended to her so that she might clap it with her own (command: "Patsch, patsch!"),[56] naturally these two reactions were often confused.

Her speaking progress was hampered by the lack of an impulse for imitation.[57] As a rule she repeated neither sounds nor motions of others.[58] She did sometimes imitate hand-clapping and familiar sounds like bilabial vibration [bw:] or palatal clicks, but without showing marked interest or interrupting her games. On the other hand, she liked to repeat sounds and motions of her own which produced an amusing reaction in the hearer, like screeching, which was received with simulated fright, and hitting herself in order to hear the sympathetic "Au, au!" For the latter purpose she would pitilessly hit her own head with her hand or a toy, but she never tried to say [ʔau] herself. She could not be induced to imitate new sounds. I let her hear such

---

[52] Karla did not use this word in the first year, and rarely in the second.

[53] It is a matter of course that stages of development overlap; meaningless sound exercises continue after intelligent words have begun. Cf. for instance Compayré, p. 293.

[54] Karla second half 0;9.

[55] Karla began this E 0;9.

[56] Karla second half 0;7.

[57] Decroly (pp. 85–105) has a detailed study of different types of imitation, from two months up to sixteen months, including (p. 94f.) Guillaume's system of four stages. "Immediate imitation" without understanding (echolalia) is what is here as usually meant by the term. "Deferred imitation" (metalalia according to Stern, p. 135) of course played a considerable part in Hildegard's development. Ronjat gives no observations on imitation. Decroly (p. 95, note) realizes that echolalia does not occur with all children.

[58] Karla imitated motions and sounds at 0;8. Same notation for E 1;1.

combinations as [gra], [bra], [bam] in clear enunciation and constant repetition. She was attentive and amused, but did not make a single attempt to imitate them. I concentrated later on the simple combination [bambam]; the reaction remained equally passive.[59] It seemed she had to find her own way without help, a characteristic which was frequently observed later on.

For the sake of comparison, it is of interest to note that at the same stage she showed remarkable persistence at solving a mechanical problem. I showed her how to push a sliding lid on a square medicine box. She grasped the problem immediately and tried it again and again, without result on that day; the operation was too difficult for the clumsy little fingers and the untrained eyes; but on the next day she returned to the task when alone and worked for about half an hour on it, until she finally succeeded. By that time there was not much left of the box.

0;11. During the last month of the first year, understanding again showed a significant development, whereas speaking was not improved appreciably. "Papa" was identified at the beginning, but "Mama" not until the end of the month,[60] she continued to say the meaningless syllables [mama], whereas accidental combinations like [baba] had become rare. The identification of "Opa," her grandfather, was added in Germany (her first trip to Germany occurred in this month). The persistent attempt to make her say [bam] failed as before. The word [tɪktak], presented to her while she was looking at my watch was assimilated. When I asked her, without preparation, "Wo ist die Ticktack?" she turned around to look at my wristwatch.[61] She learned on her own initiative to raise her arms to help the process of undressing her; the command "Hoch, hoch!" soon led to the same reaction. On the train to New York I accompanied a drinking motion of hers with the word "Prost!" Immediately she took up the suggestion as a game and reacted to this word by tilting back her head and making a gesture of drinking, not only with her cup, but with any object she happened to have in her hand. Once learned, such associations would remain fixed. She understood "Komm her!" and "Come here" and crept near when her own plans permitted.[62] In Hamburg she usually reacted by running away on hands and feet, with a roguish squeal, challenging people to catch her—a game which gave negative confirmation of the fact that she understood.[63] She invariably obeyed the warning "Nein, nein!"[64] "Finger aus dem Mund!" she understood,[64] but rarely obeyed, because of a firmly intrenched conviction to the contrary. She had less objection to

---

[59] Preyer (pp. 108f., 112, 118, 123, 131, 133) reports similar failure of deliberate imitation at E 0;9 and very limited success at 0;10 and 1;1–2. His child, on the other hand, also liked to repeat his own syllables. Preyer (pp. 86, 147, 164, 182, 185) however definitely found echolalia present, that is, repetition of final syllables or words of a sentence, or of the whole sentence, but without meaning.

[60] Karla both 0;11.

[61] Karla 0;11.

[62] Karla understood "Komm zu Papa," M 0;11.

[63] Karla understood and obeyed 0;11; later she also liked to run away with mischievous glee.

[64] Karla 0;11.

[64] Karla 0;11.

following the direction not to put objects in her mouth, "Nicht in den Mund!"[65] Having the companionship of two canary birds in the house, she answered the direction, "Call the birdie," with her click, first learned for squirrels and also still applied to the English word "squirrel." Surprisingly the same reaction took place upon "Ruf den Vogel!" which had not been practised. A few days later, she understood the question, "Wo ist der Vogel?" which proved that the noun had been assimilated. The word "Look" made her pay attention. "By-by" was answered with a waving motion of the arm, less dependably so the German equivalent "winke, winke."[66] Toward the end of the month, she reacted to the question, "Wo ist die Ticktack?" also by looking at a clock, the selection of either my watch or the clock apparently depending on the most recent visual impression.

Most striking was the progress with regard to words that had not been learned by means of a fixed association between stimulus and reation. When dressing her, her mother used to speak informally about the articles of clothing she was putting on. When she once asked, "Where are your shoes?" Hildegard put her hands on them. I tested the unexpected reaction by asking again, "Wo sind deine Schuhe?" The success was the same. This was the first instance that an association had been built up in the natural way, without being taught artificially, and at the same time the first case of analytical understanding of a word in a nonstereotype connection.

This occasion showed how much the task of bilingual training was facilitated by the fact that English and German are so closely related. The process would be quite different in the case of two less similar languages. I tried the same question in Spanish: "Hildegard, ¿ dónde están tus zapatos?" There was no reaction whatever. Intonation alone does not suffice in such a case; at least the key-word must be formally assimilated, minor divergences being still negligible.[67]

This experience belonged to the last days in America. During the first week in Germany, a similar occurrence showed even more clearly how words began to be understood within an unfamiliar context. A lady of the household, who spoke very distinctly and loud, used in the course of a conversation the word "gross." Hildegard, who was sitting close by, immediately raised both arms: she had recognized the key-word for this reaction ("Wie gross bist du?") in a different connection.

As to speaking, the two most active words during the first two weeks in Germany remained the demonstratives particle [dɛ][68] and the term of admiration and sometimes of desire, [ˈprtɪ], whispered.[69] A clue to the approximate pronunciation can be found in the fact that members of the household, on the occasion of her next visit four years later, had preserved this characteristic word as a nick-name for her in the form Pütti, [pʏti].

---

[65] Karla understood this 0;11, but obeyed it less well, whereas she was more willing to take the finger out of her mouth.

[66] Karla both, 0;11.

[67] P. Schäfer, Zeitschrift für pädagogische Psychologie 23 (1922), pp. 277 and 284f., gives experimental corroboration of the impression that only the phonetically stressed elements together with the "rhythm" of the stimuli are significant.

[68] Missing in Karla's speech 0;11.

[69] Karla likewise.

A few other words remained in the budding stage. Her physical needs were definitely communicated by means of crying. Once she seemed to repeat [pip] for "Piepvogel," which she often heard now. She was experimenting with the word "Ticktack," first in the form [tak], later [tɪktak], without voice, finally simplified into a double click. While playing she often said during the last few days of the month [jajajaja], but it could not be definitely established as a reflection of the German affirmative adverb.

Otherwise her development rather concentrated on a rapidly increasing physical skill, an astonishing mental receptiveness and an unmistakable interest in small practical problems.

1;0. With the moment that the child crosses the threshold of the second year, I abandon the chronological discussion of her linguistic development and replace it by a systematic analysis. A few significant observations from the beginning of the second year will close this chapter by way of transition.

In the very first days, understanding increased considerably, for directions and questions as well as for individual words identifying objects. She developed a great interest in music[70] and, with a serious, absorbed facial expression, called attention to it by raising the index finger of her right hand[71] and uttering a demonstrative sound, a high-pitched short [ʔɪ]. Any kind of music received the same reaction: piano, street musicians, singing, whistling, etc. Her active vocabulary consisted of three words: [dɑ], the German form, which had taken the place of the former [dɛ]; whispered [ˈprɑtɪ], the persistent English word; and whispered [ˈtˈɪ-tˈa], *Ticktack*, which is both German and English, but actually resulted from German presentation. During the month a few new words were learned, all of German origin, but the speaking remained very limited. Around the time of her first birthday she began learning to walk. At the end of the month it was observed for the first time that a direction understood in German ("Kannst du allein stehen?") was not also understood in English—the German environment was taking its effect. Understanding improved remarkably. Again and again we were surprised to notice that she understood what had never been practised with her and that she singled out individual familiar words from contexts in which they were not emphasized. She often played with a little music-box shaped like a fiddling frog. Her interest in it was so strong that it became annoying. In order to avoid the tell-tale designation "Frosch," I once spoke of it as "das musikalische Wassertier." She immediately pointed to where it was standing, high up, and expressed her ardent wish to have it. She had recognized the word "Musik" even in its unfamiliar adjective form with shifted stress! By the end of the month she followed complex directions like "Gib Klaus den Spiegel" or "Lass den Wauwau Papa beissen."[72] The stage was reached when it proved impractical to continue recording everything that she understood. Understanding, recognizing and combinative thinking (solving of practical problems) progressed rapidly, whereas speaking and walking developed slowly.

1;1. She did not reach the stage of walking without support until the second half

---

[70] Karla likewise.—Later Hildegard's musical ability turned out to be only average.

[71] Not observed with Karla.

[72] This seems very early. Preyer (p. 142) records the correct execution of simpler double commands ("Take the hat and lay it on the chair") for 1;8.

of the fourteenth month. At the same time a slightly increased tendency to repeat words spoken for her was observed. Once she fixed her attention on the lips of the speaker and moved her own as if forming the sounds, without on that occasion getting to the point of actual articulation; it remained the only observation of this kind until years later.[73]

1;2. During the fifteenth month she returned to America and had to re-learn English, which by that time had been forgotten, a process which took months. There had been very little understanding of English before the departure, whereas the understanding of German was quite well developed by the end of the summer in Germany.

VOCABULARY TO THE AGE OF TWO

All words used actively during the first two years (to E 1;11, or B 2;0) are listed alphabetically in phonetic spelling in the last form which they took, with their English or German standard equivalent in form. Under the head-form the history of the word is given. Words no longer active at B 2;0 are marked with an asterisk (*). The glottal stop [ʔ] is indicated, but disregarded in the alphabetical sequence.

Phonetic transcriptions are enclosed in brackets; but in the head-forms, all of which are in phonetic spelling, the brackets are omitted, both in the body of the vocabulary and in the alphabetical indexes of standard forms which follow it. The principles followed in the alphabetical order of phonetic symbols need not be explained, because words can be found with the help of the alphabetical indexes in standard spelling.

Words in parentheses in the standard versions of her sayings are added to explain the relationship of words from the point of view of standard syntax. This does not necessarily mean that the same syntactic arrangement was present in the child's mind.

*ʔa:, *andere* or *other;* both [ɑ] and [ʌ] yield [a], the glottal stop would point to German, the context to English. Only once 1;7: [ʔa: mɪ], *(the) other mitten.* She understood "andere" well, but never said it otherwise.[74]

ʔa, *all* (adjective and pronoun plural). 1;10 [ʔa bau], *all aboard,* imitated. 1;11 [ʔau bau da], *all balls (are) da;* [ʔa bebi], *all babies,* a translation of the German presentation "alle kleinen Kinder"; "all" was becoming more frequent as an adjective.[75] (Shortly after the 2;0 limit, the form changed to the more standard [ʔɔ:].)

ʔa, *all* (adverb, ="ganz"). 1;5 [ʔa:] with palms turned outward and thumbs sticking out, for "all gone." Replaced 1;7 by the German "alle." But [ʔa:] remained

---

[73] Preyer (p. 87) states that the hearing child uses mouth-reading less than is generally assumed, but reports instances of it from the observations of Humphreys (at 1;0; p. 258) and von Taube (at 0;9; p. 262).

[74] Karla understood "andere" at 1;7, but did not say it until 1;11:[ʔana ˈhænd], *(die) andere hand* (English noun). 1;11 also [oto], *other.*

[75] Karla early in [ʔa: bu], *all books,* from M 1;4, with an intonation of astonishment giving it the value of "So many books!" Rarely with other nouns.

for the adverb "all" in other combinations: 1;7 [ʔaːtiti], *all sticky* (shift of stress on the first of the three syllables must be due to presentation with a strong emotional pitch accent on "all"). 1;8 [ˡʔa ˡwe], *all wet;* [ʔau we] ([u] due to assimilation to following [w]). 1;10 [ʔɑ dɑʊ], *all gone;*[76] [ʔa wet']; once [ʔa naʃ], *all nass;* [ʔa daˈɪ], *all dry;* also with back [ɑ]. 1.11 with a greater variety of adjectives: "all through," "all gone," [ʔa biʃ bok'], *all broken (to)pieces;* front [a] still prevalent, but in [ʔɔ d ɔ], *all gone,* favored by assimilation, also [ɔ]. (2;1 standard vowel:[ɔː].)

*ʔɑ, *arme*. In emotional combinations like "der arme Wauwau!" understood since B 1;2, spoken 1;7: "(der) arme Wauwau," "(der) arme (Hampel) mann!" 1;10 replaced by [po], *poor,* with the same facial expression. Also front [a].

ʔā, always with front [a], German *an* and English *on,* only as adverbs. Frequent since 1;9. The word was always in stressed position; it generally expressed wishes, which were frequently uttered with interrogatory intonation. Most frequent use: "zieh an," "put on" (clothes, beads, etc.). Also for: "(put the lid) on" (the bottle) 1;9 (definitely English), "(turn the) radio, water on" 1;10, 1;11 (="stelle an," "drehe auf"); same meaning: "(Licht) an" 1;10 (definitely from German presentation), often also for the opposite, along with the correct [ʔauʃ], *aus.* In one instance the wish may have been faintly subordinated grammatically:1;11[ʔaʃ(ı) baba ʔā], *ask papa (to put it) on,* namely to put a pull-string into her under-wear after she had pulled it out; extended use of the adverb. Only once did the word contain no element of wish; 1;10 [baba dıt ʔā], *papa (turned) this on (yesterday),* an early example of wish-free narration; I had opened the shower faucet when she was in the bath-tub; the disagreeable surprise was vividly remembered. The word never repre-sented the preposition, because prepositions hardly occurred before 2;0. "I want to ride on papa's neck" for instance was expressed [haɪ baba nık] 1;10. There were cases in which its function seemed similar to a preposition: 1;11 [dı, ʔā, maɪ nık], *this on, my neck,* "hang this bell around my neck," and [baba ʔā miʔ], *Papa, (please put this) on (for) me;* they may be considered cases of transition, but the "on" probably still had more or less its full value. (The preposition "on" clearly appeared 2;1: [hek, baba, maɪ ˡʔautoˌbiə ʔā maɪ wiə], *Look, papa, my automobile on my wheel;* she was holding the toy against the wheel of the cart in which she was riding.)—Compare also [ma], *come on,* which was felt as one word, the connection with "on" not being appreciated.[77]

*ʔaʔa!, address to dogs, 1;0–2. The family called it "barking," but I doubt the

---

[76] Karla [ʔa daŋ] or, with reduplicating assimilation, [da daŋ] 1;1; obsolete B 1;4. B 1;6 [ʔaː], with palms turned outward, usually followed by the name of the object which was gone, especially [ˡʔaː ˌgaga], *all cracker*="food is all gone."

[77] Karla [an] 1;8, at once in a much more perfect form: [ti, an], *chair, on*—"I want to get up on the chair." [ā] also occurred, but less frequently.

onomatopoetic origin of it. It would rather seem to be a development from the early self-expressive sound [ʔa!] (here listed under its last form [ʔɔʔ]) which had at this time become less frequent in its original function of calling attention to something and was often replaced by [da] with pointing; the doubling of it may be due to primary or (more likely) imitative onomatopoeia. It appeared first E 1;0 in two-word form, [ʔa ʔa], short. At E 1;1 it was contracted into one word [ʔaʔa] with falsetto voice, used also with reference to dog-pictures and, by extension, to ask for the picture-book; at B 1;2 it served primarily for dogs, by extension for other animals, for instance cows; [wawa], *Wauwau*, also with falsetto voice, appeared E 1;1. After that this more standard form soon replaced it, and the interjectional sound was again restricted to its demonstrative function.

ʔaʔa, *A-a,* a standard word in German nursery language for announcing physical needs. The vowels are short. B 1;1 reproduced as a double voiced glottal stop, accompanied by unconventional pointing to the part of the anatomy involved; clearly distinguished from the simultaneous [ʔa, ʔa] used for shouting at dogs. E 1;3 it assumed the form [ˈʔa-ˈʔa], with a serious facial expression; rarely abused as "false alarm," to attract attention or to terminate undesirable conditions.[78] B 1;4 always with reduced voice, but very emphatic. By 1;6 it had reached the standard form, voiced. At 1;8, when she learned the adjective "big," she used it freely with different nouns and also said [bɪʔʔaʔa], which however did not indicate a distinction between the two kinds of physical needs; "big" was merely an intensive, but it was used only before nouns, whereas before that time [ʔaʔa] may well have had verbal character. During the same month it was also combined with the indefinite wish-word "bitte"; in this combination [ʔaʔa] functioned rather as a verb. At 1;11 she said [no ʔaʔa], meaning either "I do not want to make A-a" or "I have finished making A-a." She saw a roll of toilet paper in a store and invented her own name for it: [ʔaʔa bubu], *A-a paper.* Then (1;11) the verb "make" began to appear rarely: [mɔʔau mek ʔaʔa], *meow makes A-a;* from then on the word was definitely a noun, as in standard speech.

*ʔa.i, *Alex* 1;11,the name of her uncle in Milwaukee. Discontinued after her return to Evanston.

*ʔaˑi, *alley* 1;11.

ʔaɪ, *ei!* 1;4, an interjection which adults used while stroking her cheek gently. Probably first presented to her in Germany (0;11–1;2), absorbed slowly by her. At 1;4, when I talked with a lady about the peculiarities of the English diphthong [aɪ], her mother noticed that Hildegard stroked her own cheek. Then we became conscious of the fact that she also used

---

[78] Karla used [bʊ], *pooh,* often with pointing, for the same purpose. B 1;4. B 1;8 she had not learned "A-a," although it was used even by the English-speaking adults of the household. The adults adopted her "pooh." At B 1;9 she began to echo [ʔaʔa] in addition to saying [pˈu].

the word occasionally; but we had not realized before that it had a meaning. Another case recorded (1;7) also involved a misunderstanding. I asked her, "Hast du Ei?", whereupon she stroked her cheek.

ʔaɪ, *Ei*. At 1;7, she misunderstood the word "Ei" because of homonymy with "ei" and "eye." At E 1;8 she used[ʔaɪ] for an Easter egg of rubber, some weeks later for a real egg[79] while she was eating it (where shape would seem to be subordinated to substance), alternating with [ʔɛk], *egg;* apparently she said the German word to her father, the English to her mother. At 1;11, the egg-shaped ball was called[ʔek baʊ], *egg-ball,* but "Ei" also re-appeared in this combination, [ʔaɪ baʊ], *Ei-ball;* she heard it designated alternately as "egg-ball" and "Eiball."

ʔaɪ, *eye,* 1;7. On the occasion when she misunderstood "Ei" as "ei!" (see [ʔaɪ], *ei!),* she pointed to her eye, saying [ʔaɪ], as the next attempt to understand. When I acknowledged this interpretation by "Ja, das ist dein Auge," she repeated [ʔaʊ]. My diary carries at this point the sympathetic exclamation: "Poor child! How is a person expected to learn to speak under such circumstances!" However, at 1;8 she used the word correctly in a sentence: [wewe ʔaɪ], *(I have a) Wehweh (in my) eye =*"my eye hurts."[80]

ʔaɪ, *I,* 1;5. In the history of this word, a clear distinction must be made between an early mechanical imitation and the much later intelligent use of it. It first occurred unanalyzed in[ʔaɪˡiə], *I see you* (see separate entry), 1;5. Otherwise [ʔaɪ] was used regularly from 1;5 to 1;9 as an answer to questions which called for the first person pronoun as an answer. But the case shows very clearly that a mere record of the first use of a certain word is very misleading; psychological analysis of the meaning behind the form is imperative. During all these months, the answer "I" was nothing but a mechanical reaction to questions beginning with "Who wants to . . ." in a strikingly falling intonation. To be sure, the question itself was understood and the answer was meaningful to the extent that it expressed her enthusiasm for the suggestion. But it was for her not a personal pronoun. Once (1;8) she said [ʔaɪ! baɪbaɪ], with falling intonation, without the usual stimulus of a question. It would be tempting to construe this as a sentence, "I (want to go) by-by"; but it was really nothing more than a wishful "by-by" prefixed by the emotional affirmative wish-particle [ʔaɪ]. The idea of the first person pronoun was learned from about 1;8 on in the possessive relation, and from 1;10 on "I" was replaced by[maɪ], which then served as her first real personal pronoun. (See [maɪ], *mine.)* At 1;11 a new mechanical response to questions like "Who likes candy?" was taught her by her

---

[79] Karla E 1;8.

[80] Karla [ʔaɪ] 1;8. Although a monolingual English child is spared the confusion of "eye" with "Ei" and "ei," its task is not much easier since it may still confuse "eye" and "I"; cf. D. R. Major, *First Steps in Mental Growth,* New York, 1906, p. 309. Hildegard and Karla did not fall into this trap.

aunt: "I do," first with assimilation [ʔau du] then correctly [ʔaɪ du], with falling intonation. But shortly before that (1;11) the first real "I" had made its appearance in the combination [ʔaɪ biə . . .], *I spiel* . . . (At 2;1 "my" and "I" were in balance for the personal pronoun, with "I" gaining ground. The form was [ʔaɪ] or [ʔa], corresponding to the more or less careful pronunciations of the colloquial standard.) She almost never used her name instead of the first person pronoun (see [haɪta]).

*ʔaɪˡiə, *I see you.* Imitated in a game, 1;5. Ephemeral. Simultaneously a similar game-sentence, *[daːiːɛ], *da ist es,* 1;4–1;5. "See" did not occur otherwise[81] ("you" as [ju]>[ʒu] very frequently 2;1).

ʔaɪni,*ironing.* 1;8 repeated with understanding ("snowing" at the same time). 1;9: Her mother stated in a conversation, "Apricots contain lots of iron"; Hildegard reacted unexpectedly with [dada—ʔaɪni, ʔaɪŋi], *Carolyn (was,* or *did) ironing.* She had recognized the word "iron," but misinterpreted it in the meaning familiar to her ("plätten" instead of "Eisen").

ʔaɪ(ʃ),*eins,* in counting 1-2-3 (1;11); but "1" was more commonly skipped, because it was usually presented by me as the stimulus for the series.[82]

*ʔaɪʃ, *Eis* she repeated once 1;7; the final consonant was still unusual at that time. The English equivalent "ice" is of course practically identical in sound; but the word was actually presented in German.

aɪta, *high-chair* 1;5. The [t] was unaspirated, possibly sometimes voiced [d]—"Chair" and "Stuhl" did not become active.[83]

*ʔaɪte, *Eiskrem,* 1;9, the German terms used by me for the English "icecream"; it was at that time current in Germany (there later replaced by "Sahne-Eis"). It gave way (1;11) to the English original (see [ʔati]).

ʔalə, *alle* 1;7, only in the meaning of "gone," "empty." (The attributive adjective was used in its English form, see [ʔa].) One of her most frequent words from 1;7 to 2;0 and beyond. The English equivalent appeared first 1;5 in the very expressive form of [ʔaː], with the palms turned outward and thumbs sticking out, after presentation of "all gone" by the maid. I immediately proceeded to associate the German "alle" with it. At 1;7, she used the German [ʔalə], with an un-German velar [l]. The gesture of the spread palms was transferred to the new form. It was also used for persons: [mama ʔalə], *Mama alle,* where the English "gone" fits, but not the German "alle." Still, I would not assume English influence; such an extension of meaning was perfectly normal in her speech. At 1;8 she said [ʔajə ʔajə] for shutting off the radio, after presentation of "alle." At 1;9 she used it also in the combination "bath, bathing (is)

---

[81] Karla [tiʔ], *(Do you) see?* 1;10.

[82] Karla 1;10 [ʔaɪn], with reference to one piece of candy, from presentation "nur eins." 1;11 also [wʌn], *one.*

[83] Karla tried [tul] E 1;6, [tu] B 1;8 and said frequently [ti] since 1;7, which might come from "chair," but was more likely a transfer from "Tisch." She liked to play with a little chair and a small Japanese table; the latter she first called [ti], *Tisch.* At 1;10 "chair" was improved to [te]; [tu] continued also.

alle," where neither the German nor the English is suitable ("my bath is finished"). During this month the forms [ʔajɛ] and [ʔajə] were used, [j] was a little later a frequent substitute for [l]. But at 1;10 she returned to [ʔalə], now mostly with a clear, palatal German [l], the tongue movement being visible; the [j] was a transitory stage in the shift from velar to palatal [l], which was achieved in this frequent word sooner than in others. At 1;11, "all gone" began to be used, but less frequently than [ʔalə], the latter continued to be used also for persons, and not only in the meaning of "gone," but also of "not there," again a slight shift of meaning. The negative sense was clearly indicated by the gesture of shaking her head, which accompanied the statement, [meˡʔa wewe ʔal ə], *Mary Alice's Wehweh alle,* equivalent to: "Mary Alice has no pain (wound, illness) any longer." At this time, no connection between "alle" and the adjective "all," [ʔaʊ] seemed to be felt. In emphatic pronunciation, the [ə] appeared in full vowel form as [ɛ] or, with lip-rounding, as [œ], or [ʌ]. (During my prolonged absence from Evanston, the word disappeared together with many other German words; it was replaced by "all gone," see [ʔaː], *all,* 2;1.) The German synonym "weg" (see *[wek])* was used sporadically at 1;10.[84]

*ʔap, *ab.* Occurred only once (1;11) in a situation which suggested "Wisch ab": she wiped sand from a bench, saying at the same time [wiʃ ʔap]. She understood "Mund abwischen" from 1;3, but never said it in that connection. At least a crossing with "up" is likely; notice that "up" is frequently used in English in a similar function to "ab": "wipe up." However, all her uses of "up" were concrete, not figurative; and "wipe up" would not be possible in the situation where she first learned to understand the word, when the parallel presentation in English was "wipe your mouth off" (Germanism? "off"="ab"!).

ʔap, *up,* 1;4. (For a synonym see [ʔaʊχ], *auf.)* One evening (B 1;4) she said often and with enjoyment [ʔap], when she wanted to get up on the daven-port;[85] probably taught her by the maid. For months it remained the only word ending in a consonant. On the same evening, when I told her "aufstehen," she got up and said [ʔap], showing that the word was associated not only with the wish to get up on the sofa, but also with another upward motion; for both motions, the same expression ("get up") is used in English, but not in German ("hinauf" or "rauf" and "aufstehen"). Later in the month, "up" was used also for the opposite wish, [da], *down* being said only upon request. This does not mean that the directional sense of "up" was not well understood; the use of a

---

[84] Karla, who used less German vocabulary than Hildegard, did not learn "alle" before 2;0. She did try "weg" at 1;8, but in the sense of "wegtun," "put away"; usually "back back" < "put it back."

[85] Karla began to say [ʔap] in a similar situation, second half 1;7. For months before that time she refused to be taught the word and used "get down" instead. E 1;8 "up high," in a dynamic and a static application; at first definitely [hap haɪ].

word in the opposite sense is frequent in child language, and several examples of this phenomenon were observed in Hildegard's speech. Once (B 1;6) she said [ʔap] when she wished to have the lid of a cardboard box taken off. I interpreted it as "open, aufmachen," but this possibility was eliminated by the later experiences: from 1;4 to 2;0 she used the word consistently and very frequently in its standard meaning; (cf. also "auf" 1;6 in a similar situation); "open" appeared in 1;8 as [ʔabu], later [ʔapu], "auf(machen)" in the same situation (lid of can) later in the month (1;6) as [ʔaʊ] (see [ʔaʊχ]. Apparently she was really thinking of the upward movement to be performed with the lid, or she was translating the more fitting German "auf." The word continued during the following months in the function of a wish to have herself, another person, or an object perform an upward motion: 1;6 "I want to get up" (on a high place or out of bed); "Put the periodical up on the mantel"; 1;7 combined with "bitte" and in the combinations "way up" and "mehr up" = "higher up," "Mama up" = "Mama, get up." This latter command she addressed to her mother every morning at 1;8. But once she said it shortly after her mother had risen, pounding on the empty bed, thus making a factual statement with no wish implied; it was probably not in a past tense ("Mama has got up"), but rather in the present ("Mama is up"). From then on, "up" was frequently used as a statement devoid of wish, both for a condition at rest ("oben") and for an upward motion ("hinauf"): 1;9 looking at candy on the mantel, she said "way up," which was at that stage a current combination (see [weː]), in the intonation of a statement (the request followed); 1;11 "(I am going to take) this dolly up (to) bed"; "meow up (in the) Baum"; "(I am) up(stairs)" (answer to question, "Where are you?"); "wake up" = "I am awake," frequently, also in play. Other verbs in a standard combination with "up" came in at 1;11: "roll up," "cover up," "häng up" (in spite of German verb, cf. [he]); the earliest one was "pick up," 1;10 or even (a little doubtful) 1;9.

ʔapa, *apple*, B 1;5, immediately also for a picture of an apple; unaspirated [p] or voiceless [b]. Twelve days later clearly [ʔaba], with voiced [b] (assimilation). 1;8 [ʔapa]. The possibility of "Apfel" being the prototype is disregarded because the diary expressly lists "apple" as the model at the first occurrence, no doubt for some good reason. On account of the constant double presentation as "apple" and "Apfel," the German word must have had a supporting effect. But there is no other evidence for the treatment of [-pf-].[86]

ʔapu, *open*. 1;8 [ʔabu], expressing a wish, alongside the older [ʔaʊ] (see [ʔaʊχ], *auf*). At 1;10 the words of the finger-game, "This is the church, and this is the steeple; open the door, and see all the people" were imitated as [dɪ dʒʊɪ, ʔabo doɪ]. Transferred at once to reality, [ʔabo dɔ], *open (the)*

---

[86] Karla 1;10 [ʔapu] and [hapu], *apple;* B 1;11 [paɪnæpu], *pineapple.*—The form "apoo" is also listed by F. Tracy. *The psychology of childhood³*, Boston, 1896, p. 137.

door. 1;11 [ʔabo do], *open (the) door* and [do ʔabɔ], *(the) door (is) open* —statement (adjective) along with wish (imperative); [dɪ do ʔapu], *this door open.* [abu] re-appeared 2;1, now as an infinitive in a five-word sentence.) The difference between voiced and voiceless stops was not phonemic at this stage, so that assimilation to voiced surroundings could easily take place. [b] instead of [p] is the result of carrying the voice of the vowels right through the stop without interruption.[87]

*ʔat', ask. Two or three times B 1;11 in two different forms: [ʔaʃ(ı) baba ʔa], *(I shall) ask papa (to put it) on,* namely to put the drawstring, which she had pulled out, into her underwear (papa was expected to repair all damage she had done, although his real endeavors were restricted to repairing toys); [ʔat' mama dɪt ʔaʊ], *(I shall) ask mama this out (aus),* namely, "to take this off," modeled after the German "ausziehen."

ʔati, *ice-cream,* often 1;11. It took the place of the older German **[ʔaɪte]* 1;9, at first in the more nearly standard form [ʔaɪti][88] but soon and lastingly with simplification of [aɪ] to [a] due to dissimilation; notice that in the German **[aʔɪte]* with its different second vowel [aɪ] did not change to [a].

The following are a few of Leopold's conclusions concerning parts of speech and semantic development in Hildegard's first two years. Many of the observations that he made in 1939 have since been echoed in the contemporary literature of the 1970s, which not only lends reliability to the power of his descriptions, but also reaffirms the consistencies among different children learning different languages at different times in the century.

PARTS OF SPEECH

In this volume I do not deal with the syntax of the first two years; but since a great many observers classify the early words by parts of speech, a word must be said about that aspect at this point. In my own notes I tried to carry out such an analysis month by month, but I finally decided to discard the tabulation. Many writers on the subject[90] have pointed out that words in child language do not fall into the same categories as in adult language. Words which are nouns for adults may be something quite different to the child; they "really function not only as nouns, but as verbs, adjectives, interjections, and almost any part of speech that is needed in the situa-

---

[87] Karla [op'] 1;9, as imperative: "open this box for me" etc. Once B 1;10 she said first [ʔap], *up,* but with the meaning of German "auf," then [ʔop], *open,* when she wanted a drawer opened. 1;11 still [ʔop].

[88] Karla's form, B 1;9–11, was [ʔaːni]. M 1;11 [ˈʔaːni ˈkim].

[90] For instance Dewey, McCarthy (p. 18), Decroly (p. 108). Romanes (pp. 296–98) in 1889 quotes still older authors (Max Müller, Friedrich Müller) on the undifferentiated character of early words. P. Guillaume (Journal de Psychologie, v. 24 [1927] p. 9–10) is strongly opposed to analyzing the early vocabulary by parts of speech.

tion" (McCarthy). It is still better to say that no such grammatical analysis applies to child utterances. Words are grammatically undifferentiated. At the stage of the one-word sentence, the meaning is conveyed directly and implicitly; the thought or feeling is not yet cast into conventional patterns. John Dewey (p. 66) speaks of "the original protoplasmatic verbal-nominal-interjectional form," which is only "gradually differentiated into rigidity"; he draws his striking formulation from Romanes, who speaks of the "undifferentiated protoplasm of speech" (p. 295) and repeats the pet term "protoplasmatic," which is inspired by his biological background, in several places (*e.g.,* pp. 329, 358).

The separation of parts of speech is more meaningful at the stage when sentences become more complete or conventional, in our case from about 1;9 on. But even then the separation cannot be carried through clearly, since many words still waver between different categories.[91] This condition is never overcome completely, since even in the standard language such instances remain, especially in English with its facile transition of words from one category to another. It is also doubtful whether the child's grammatical thinking has changed as much as the perfected form seems to indicate. Max Müller[92] formulated this idea very well: "Even if a child learns to speak grammatically, it does not yet think grammatically; it seems, in speaking, to wear garments of its parents, though it has not yet grown into them." This clever metaphor probably distorts the underlying situation; the child is not likely to creep into his parents' clothes until he dimly perceives their physical and social usefulness. But it may be granted that the perception is dim in the beginning, and that grammatical categories do not become clear and well-defined all at once. Romanes (p. 328f.) objects that, although transfers of words to different parts of speech occur frequently in child language, this is due entirely to "the exigencies of expression." On the whole he thinks that "from the very first, there is a marked tendency to observe the distinctions which belong to the principal parts of speech," and gives plausible examples. It is true that the ungrammatical character of child speech should not be exaggerated. The process of approximation to standard speech, which goes on continually in child speech, operates in syntax as well as in sounds from the beginning. But the fact remains that this process is normally not sufficiently advanced by the end of the second year to make a classification by parts of speech valuable. It is correct that nouns prevail in the early stages and that verbs begin to increase at the end of the period under discussion;[93] also that adjectives are earlier than adverbs, etc. That corresponds to the successive interests on which the child's attention is centered. But it is not safe to go beyond such general statements; exact statistical data must be misleading. Dewey (p. 66) calls attention to the great individual differences in distribution of parts of speech, which for him point to interesting differences in individual psychology. There are such differences, no doubt, but I would not trust the statistics

[91] The grammatically unanalyzed complex of observation represented by the word "Wauwau" was well described long ago by H. Steinthal, *Einleitung in die Psychologie und Sprachwissenschaft,* Berlin, 1871, pp. 399–401.
[92] *Lectures on the Science of Language,* 2, p. 91f., quoted by Romanes, p. 296.
[93] Cf. *e.g.* McCarthy, p. 16; Decroly, p. 122.

to establish them; the diverging figures may be entirely due to the differences in assigning words to parts of speech.

To make this apparent, let me cite some examples from Hildegard's speech. At 1;8 she uttered a wish to have something opened by saying "open"; but at the same time she also used "auf" for the same purpose. The mechanical classifier would count the former as a verb, the latter as an adverb. Yet psychologically they were synonyms, and grammatically they were undifferentiated. The name of an object was rarely said as a dispassionate, objective statement; usually it was tinged with the wish to have it or with an emotional reaction to it. In the former case it resembled closely an imperative, that is a verb; in the latter, an interjection. Yet mechanically both usages would appear as nouns. As late as 1;11, "this door open" might be in her speech a statement, "open" being an adjective, or else a wish, "open" being an imperative (verb). Actually no such classification was probably present, even subconsciously. Also at 1;11 she used "wait" instead of the earlier "Augenblick!" This would appear in the statistics (if genetic aspects were taken into account at all) as a shift from a noun to a verb, whereas psychologically no more change occurred than the replacement of a German word by an English one. Again, when "come on" was substituted for "mit" (1;10), it did not mean a shift from an adverb to a verb plus adverb; "mit" stood for "komm mit" with a quite normal phonetic clipping, but few observers without linguistic training would recognize that. I think these examples suffice to substantiate my contention that a statistical classification of words by parts of speech is fruitless and misleading up to the level of two years. For older children the situation is quite different.

STRIKING GAPS

A word in passing should be devoted to striking gaps in the vocabulary; I have not found this negative aspect in other vocabulary studies. One might think that in the fairly extensive stock of words acquired by the end of the second year all important matters within the child's orbit would be represented. That is not the case. Taking haphazard examples of words missing in Hildegard's vocabulary, which were well within her range of experience, we find that such common nouns as "chair," "picture," "tongue," "yard," "garden," "street" were absent in both languages. "Chair" occurred only in the compound "high-chair." "Picture" was represented by "Bild" 0;9–1;4, but later went out of use. "Zunge," the German equivalent for "tongue," was tried, but it did not get out of the experimental stage, possibly because of its phonetic difficulty.[94] Imitation of the adjective "good" was not tried once. Its most important function, "tastes good," was represented by "m." But it would seem that there are enough other important meanings of "good"; yet it did not become active.[95] The

---

[94] E. S. Holden, Transactions of the American Philological Association 1877, p. 60: " . . . the ease of pronunciation, far more than the complexity of the idea, determines the adoption of a word."

[95] Charlotte Bühler (p. 149) lists the "value word" "gut" as early as 1;1 for her daughter Inge; for Bubi Scupin (p. 150) at 1;4. Karla had "good" at 1;10. She also used many of the other words here mentioned, before 2;0.

absence of "little" and "small" is even more surprising. Among verbs the following are conspicuous by their absence, even in the otherwise early imperative form: "see," "take," "haben," "jump"[96] (apart from the mysterious [daʃ], which took the place of "jump" in some of its applications). "Hug," "look," and "like" did not appear until 2;1. "Come" was missing except in the combination "come on." I have no explanation for the existence of such gaps. One would expect personal usefulness to be the guiding principle in the selection of words for active assimilation. The samples just given seem to indicate that there are restrictions to the validity of this assumption. The situation serves as a reminder of the fact that, although language-learning proceeds by imitation, there is considerable leeway for the children to display personal freedom and individual differences in the selection from the language-material presented and the order of its acquisition.[97] The interest of the child is no doubt the guiding principle; but it is not easy to look into the child's mind and to find out how this interest is determined. Usefulness as adults see it apparently does not yield a suffi-cient basis of explanation. All through life we learn only what recommends itself to us through a strong personal interest of one kind or another, and that is not alike for any two individuals. It is not surprising that the same individual differences should appear in the earliest learning processes of children.

SEMANTIC GROUPS

If a grammatical classification of early vocabulary yields no satisfactory results, a semantic grouping should be more revealing. It is certainly of interest to see how the words are distributed over the various fields of the child's life.[98] I have attempted such a classification, but must warn the reader beforehand that it gives only a rough picture of the situation. It is not easy in many instances to determine under which heading a word should be listed. A certain amount of arbitrariness is unavoidable; many words would fit as well in another classification, and a few of them are indeed listed twice. But even with this restriction, I deem the results not without interest. Where the classification seems queer, the reader should consult the main lists to compare the actual use of the words.

1. FOOD   0;10: *[mam :a]. 1;0: *[mjamjam], m. 1;5: apple (Apfel), mehr. 1;6: cake, cookies, milk (Milch). 1;7: *[kχ], cracker, juice, spoon, water, Brot. 1;8: *cocoa, egg. 1;9: bacon, toast (Toast), *Zwieback (zwieback), *Butter, Ei, *Eiskrem. 1;10: candy, drink, eat, meat, peas, *Kuchen. 1;11: *ba-nana (Banane), feed, fork, *glass (Glas), ice-cream, knife, *oatmeal, pudding (Pudding).
2. TOYS AND GAMES.   1;0: *Ball, *sch! 1;1: *bimbam!, *kiek!, *pieks!, Wauwau.

---

[96] Karla said [ha:m] and "jump" at 1;9.

[97] Cf. Karl Bühler, "Vom Wesen der Syntax." *Idealistische Neuphilologie, Festschrift K. Vossler*, 1922, pp. 54–84.

[98] William Boyd, Pedagogical Seminary 21 (1914), pp. 95–124, gives such a classification, subdividing the parts of speech.

1;4: peek-a-boo, *da ist es! 1;5: *klingelingeling!, *I see you. 1;6: box,
cake, dolly, duck, Bleistfit. 1;7: bear (Bär), block, choo-choo, mouse
(Maus). 1;8: paper (Papier), Fritzchen, *Hase, house (Haus), rollen. 1;9:
ball, beads, roll, bauen. 1;10: aboard, balloon, boat (Boot), church,
crash, hottey, *Mickey mouse (Mickey-Maus), *radio, sandbox, stick,
three, two, dicken, drei, zwei. 1;11: bake, bike, blow, knock, pail, piano,
slide, *story, throw, backe!, eins, *hacke!, *hoppe!, *klappert, *Löscher,
*patsch!, spielen, *watschel!

3. ANIMALS.   0;11: *piep piep! 1;0: *[ʔaʔa]. 1;1: *"quak quak!," Wauwau. 1;2: moo
(muh!). 1;3: *kitty. 1;6: duck, *natt-natt. 1;8: meow (miau). 1;10: bite,
hottey, *beissen, Katz (Dasch). 1;11: *dog, doggie, fly, scratch
(kratzen), *Miezi. Cf. also Toys. The list seems short, but for a city child,
animals are no longer a frequent phenomenon, and Wauwau was a
very frequent word, which for a long time did duty for several animals.

4. PERSONS.   1;0: papa (Papa), *Opa. 1;1: *Gertrud (Gertrude), *Tante. 1;2: baby
(Baby), Carolyn. 1;3: mama (Mama). 1;4: Marion. 1;5: man (Mann), Rita.
1;6: Dodo. 1;7: *Bates, *Jasper, Joey, *Mack, Frau. 1;8: boy, Grandpa,
*June, *Paul, Onkel (Oino). 1;9: Helen, *Jack. 1;10: *Alex, Florence,
Hildegard, *John, *Leona, Mary Alice, Theresa. Notice that the father
was the first person named, and that the mother was preceded by six
other persons, of whom five were designated by proper names.

5. PARTS OF BODY.   1;6: Bauch. 1;7: eye, knee (Knie), Auge. 1;8: ear, nose. 1;10:
feet, mouth, neck, Haar. 1;11: hair, hand (Hand), *nails, Fuss, *Zunge.
Notice the late start of this category, really at 1;7, because the item
of 1;6 was at first only part of a game. The terms had great stability.

6. CLOTHING, (UN)DRESSING, ETC.   1;1: *kritze! 1;3: bath (Bad, baden). 1;4: bed
(Bett). 1;5: brush, *mitten. 1;6: hat, out (aus), shoe (Schuh), toothbrush,
Nackedei. 1;7: bobby, stocking, Taschentuch. 1;8: wash (waschen).
1;9: bathe, *kimona, on (an). 1;10: button, comb, dress, *pocket, soap,
towel, Handschuh, Schnucks, *Tasche. 1;11: cover, forgot, petticoat,
*hoch!

7. OTHER HOME ROUTINE.   0;9: *Bild. 0;11: ticktock (Ticktack). 1;0: *Blumen. 1;1:
A-a 1;4: down, up. 1;5: high-chair, naughty, night, mehr. 1;6: away,
book (Buch), bottle, light, *more, oil, out (aus), sh!, auf, mine (mein). 1;7:
sticky, way wet, alle, Augenblick, my. 1;8: ironing, open, *pocket-book,
ride, rock this (dies), *wischen, nass, *Spiegel. 1;9: bite, broken, much,
pick (up), watch. 1;10: break, crash, cry, door, dry, go, gone, *measles,
noise, push, wake up, *beissen, kaputt, *lutscht, *weg. 1;11: bake, bell,
blow, buy, call, do, fall, fix, lie, make, money, new, piece, pillow, *pow-
der-puff, put, read, ring, room, scratch (kratzen), *spill, *that, through,
wait, write, abwischen, Brief, Hängen, *holen, *Nacht, *steht, zu
(closed).

8. OUTDOOR LIFE AND TRAFFIC.   1;3: by-by. 1;5: auto (Auto). 1;6: buggy, *snow,

*Schnee. 1;7: choo-choo, ice (Eis). 1;8: house (Haus), walk, wheel, Baum. 1;9: *outside. 1;11: airplane, alley, automobile (Automobil), beach, bug, flower, home, stone, street-car, sun-suit, train, tragen.

9. EMOTIONS.   0;8: *[ʔə?]. 0;9: *[dɪdɪdɪ]. 0;10: *[nenene], pretty, tsk tsk (t, t). 1;0: oh. 1;2: pooh (pfui). 1;4: ei! 1;5: *bäh! 1;6: *ätsch! 1;7: *[kχ], *arme, *huch! 1;8: all right, big, poor, au!, dunkel, Wehweh. 1;9: *bums! 1;11: *[buː:], *donnert. Note that the increase in interjections and other emotional terms does not keep step with other categories at the later stages. The percentage of terms of German origin is high. This is the group in which non-standard forms are most prominent, early and late.

10. SOCIAL RELATIONS.   1;3: thank you (danke), ja. 1;4: *yes. 1;5: hello, *hoohoo (huhu), bitte. 1;6: m-m, no, *nein. 1;8: hm?, *komm mit. 1;9: please. 1;10: come on. 1;11: *ask, dear, don't, kiss, *Kuss, *Liebling. The list is very incomplete. All imperatives and many other items could be listed here. Note that the affirmative sentence adverb starts at 1;3, the negative at 1;6, at once in three different forms.

11. GRAMMATICAL CLASSIFIERS.   1;4: *me. 1;5: I. 1;10: my (="I"). 1;11: *a, me, *of.

12. ABSTRACTS.   0;10: *there. 1;0: da. 1;4: hot. 1;5: all (adv.), heiss. 1;7: *other (andere). 1;8: far away, Milwaukee, now, dunkel. 1;9: here (hier), *weisser. 1;10: all (adj.), cold, *dark, in, nice, too, *why. 1;11: high, New York, not, right, where. This list is inadequate. Other more or less abstract terms are scattered in other categories. But it gives a few samples of local, temporal and general abstracts, accommodating at the same time some words which are difficult to classify.

Grammatical Errors in the Speech of Preschool Children

Madorah E. Smith

This study is an attempt to determine, through an examination of the extent and type of grammatical errors found in the speech of preschool children, the average age at which children are able to form sentences that are approximately correct and what are the most troublesome points in grammatical speech to a child.

The material used for this study consisted of 305 records of the spontaneous conversation of 220 different children, covering a total of 22,994 sentences or 99,289 running words. The age range was eighteen months to six years. For classification into age groups a child was counted two years old if his age fell within the limits of eighteen and twenty-nine months inclusive.

The children were drawn from English-speaking homes representing all social levels, although the number was greater from the upper classes. The average I.Q. of the children for whom test scores were available (a representative two-thirds of the number) was 110.

The study of their grammatical errors was approached from two angles: improvement in elimination of error with increase in age, and the particular types of errors most frequently found.

With these aims in mind, all errors in the material were carefully segregated. Tabulation was made according to age and according to type of error.

An index of the amount of error in each child's conversation was calculated by dividing the number of errors made by the number of words used. This gave a score of 1.00 for a baby using entirely one-word sentences, and of .00 for any record which contained no errors whatsoever. The 1.00 error index for one-word sentences resulted because, too much guesswork being required to complete them grammatically, they were included in the list of incomplete sentences. Although conceivably two or more omissions might have occurred, but one error was counted in such cases. In longer sentences, if more than one necessary word was omitted both omissions were counted as errors. Incomplete sentences were divided into two groups: those in which some form of the copula was omitted and those in which some other verb or object or subject was omitted. Neologisms, foreign words, baby words and slang were not counted as errors but were given separate consideration. The use of one

From *Child Development* **4,** pp. 183-190. The Society for Research in Child Development, 1933. Reprinted by permission of the Society for Research in Child Development.

Table 1   Frequency of Errors

	Age in Months				
	24	36	48	60	66–72
Number of records	65	74	75	75	5
Average error-index:					
Per child	58	21	7	5	6.5
Boys	67	19	7.4	4.6	4.5
Girls	50	23	7.5	6.1	
Errors per 1000 words:					
All types	363	152	73	50	55
Incomplete sentences:					
Copula omitted	38	15	4	1	1
Others	225	71	36	28	32
Articles	39	15	3	2	2
Verbs	30	24	17	12	11
Prepositions	11	8	5	2	4
Nouns and pronouns	6	4	2	1	1
Agreement	8	6	3	2	1
Confused parts of speech	3	5	1	1	½
Other errors	3	3	2	2	1
Age differences—years in	2–3	3–4		4–5	2–5
Average error-index	37 ± 7.6	14 ± 5.6		2 ± 3.9	53 ± 6.5

part of speech for another when the child did not know how to make the correct transformation was counted as an error.

NEOLOGISMS; FOREIGN AND BABY WORDS

In view of the number of very young children included, there were surprisingly few of such words. Sixty-seven of the records were of Honolulu children. In these records, it was found that 2 Hawaiian words appeared: "kaukau" for "food" used by two children and "pau" for "finished" or "enough" by six children. These words are both very frequently used by English-speaking adults in the Islands who know practically no other Hawaiian words.

The baby words used by more than one child were "choo-choo" or "too-too train" by 14 children, "bye-bye" by 7, "bow-wow" or "wow-wow" by 4, "hanky" by 4, and "tockies" by 2. "Uh-uh" and "um-hm" instead of "yes" and "no" were used by 27 and "huh?" for "What did you say?" by 33 children, but these are so common in colloquial speech that they were not included in the error index.

Among the neologisms and individual baby words or phrases were a number of duplicated sounds. A list of these, not including those mentioned above, follows.

Table 2   Types of Errors

Incomplete sentences			5,716
Omitted copula		683	
Others		5,033	
Verb errors			1,666
Use of auxiliary		680	
Got		360	
Ain't or hain't		138	
Other errors			
Conjugation		478	
Past tense regular	57		
irregular	188		
Participles present	12		
past	48		
Future tense	163		
Transitive and intransitive		10	
Errors of agreement			377
Subject-verb		335	
Others		42	
In use of noun and pronoun			227
Gender noun 1 pronoun 10 both		11	
Number 80 5		85	
Case 24 107		131	
In use of article			703
In prepositions			445
Sign of infinitive		168	
Other errors		277	
In use of negative			47
Other confusions parts of speech			175
In use of comparative			9
Relative or conjunction omitted			68
Other omissions			27
Redundancy			175
Errors in word order			37

"Me-me" for "come in," "gung-gung" for "grand-ma," "dup-dup dere" for "up there," "pup-pup high" for "up high," "go night-night" for "go to bed," "boo-boo boat" for "steamer," "chih-chih" for "chicken," "yum-yum" and "ninny" for "food," "ingun-gun" (?) and "dar-dar" (?). The last 2 were not mere babbling, for they were clearly used as words in the midst of otherwise intelligible sentences, but their meaning was not ascertained. All but the last 2 of these duplicated words were found in the records of the two-year-old children.

This tendency to repetition of sound in baby words is seen not only in the baby language of many nations; but also in the amount of repetition of words and phrases found in our records which amounted to 5 repetitions per hundred words for our entire group or fifteen per hundred at two years, five at three, two at four and one per hundred at five years.

Non-repetitive neologisms for which the meaning could be determined were "tat" for "what is that?" at two years, "ra" for "growl" and "lasser-noon" for "yesterday afternoon" at three years, "slobbing-side," "toppy-head" and "tigoo" all used as pet names to her baby brother by a four-year-old girl, "razor-bleezers" for "razor blades" also at four years, "squibbled" and "squirreled" for "crooked" and "twisted" and "dabbish" for "mussy-looking" "trackender" for "tractor" and "shorthander" for "one who writes shorthand" at five years. Most of these words can be explained as far-fetched mispronunciations or the fusion of 2 correct words. "Ra" used in the sentence "He would ra at him" is onomatopoeic.

ERRORS

There were 9531 errors found or about one error for every ten words.

INCOMPLETE SENTENCES

The most common type of error was the omission of an essential word or words leaving a distinctly incomplete sentence. For every hundred words spoken at two years, there were 26 omissions, 9 at three, 4 at four, and 3 at five years. The omission of the copula was so common that it was listed separately. At two years, it was omitted in 70 per cent of the sentences where it clearly belonged, at three years in 32, at four in 8 and at five in only 2 per cent of the cases where it should have been used. There were 4 such errors per hundred words at two years falling to 1 per thousand at five.

VERBS

Next in frequency were errors in the use of the verb. These errors occurred 4 times per hundred words at two years and were reduced to 12 per thousand at five. There were 1666 errors altogether in the use of the verb, not counting the omission of verb or copula nor errors of agreement nor the confusion of a verb with another part of speech, which are listed under other headings. Of these errors "got" was used erroneously 60 times and "ain't" or "hain't" 138 times.

The use of the proper auxiliary was the most frequent error found. Aside from its omission in the future tense, there were 680 such errors. The auxiliary was often omitted altogether and the most common error in choice of auxiliary was that of "can" for "may." Sixty-six per cent of the times an auxiliary should have been used it was omitted at two years, this per cent decreasing with increase of age to 7 per cent at five years.

Of the 478 errors in conjugated forms, 245 were made in forming the past tense. Of these, 188 were in conjugating irregular verbs. As soon as the child begins to use the past tense, he appears to generalize and tries to conjugate all verbs regularly using, for example, "catched" and "runned" instead of the irregular forms. This was the most common type of error in the use of the past tense but sometimes a participle was used instead of the correct form as "done" for "did" or "seen" for "saw." The 57 errors in the use of the past tense of the regular verbs were most frequently due to failure to conjugate at all rather than to using the wrong ending.

The next most troublesome tense was the future in the use of which 163 errors occurred. These were mostly through failure to use the form at all, the present tense taking its place. Forty-eight errors occurred in the use of the past, 12 in that of the present participle or 60 for all forms of the participle. The most common error in this group was "broke" for "broken" which occurred 10 times.

Only 6 errors were found in the use of the present tense, all at four and five years: "went" being used three times for "go," "be" for "are" twice and "lost" for "lose" once.

Ten errors occurred in using a transitive verb as an intransitive or vice-versa; "lay" for "lie" being the only pair of such words confused more than once.

All verb errors decreased in frequency with age except in the case of "got" and "ain't" which increased by 1 word per thousand each year from 3 per thousand at two years to six at five.

NOUNS AND PRONOUNS
Errors in the use of the noun numbered 105 and of the pronoun 122. Their frequency falls from 6 per thousand words at two years to 1 per thousand at five. The use of the correct number was the most troublesome point with nouns, 80 of the noun errors being of that type. The majority of these errors consisted in the wrong formation of the plural of nouns which have irregular plurals; examples are, "mans," "mens," "tooths," "foots." In other cases the plural ending was duplicated as in "biteses" or the singular was used instead of the plural and a few times the plural form for the singular. The possessive sign of the noun was omitted 24 times. The wrong gender was used once in the case of nouns and ten times in the case of pronouns.

Case was the most troublesome feature for pronouns, 107 such errors occurring altogether. Practically all the errors after fifty-four months are of case in pronouns or number in nouns, almost all the children by that age having mastered the use of the possessive in nouns, gender in either nouns or pronouns and the use of number in pronouns.

ARTICLES
The use of the article is learned relatively late. In these records, 703 errors in its use occurred, in almost all cases the error being one of omission. In a few cases however "a" and "an" were confused or the definite article confused with the indefinite. At two years 70 per cent of the times an article should have been used it was omitted, 30 per cent of the time at three years and 6 per cent at four while the oldest group still omitted or used articles wrongly 3 per cent of the time.

AGREEMENT
Of the 377 errors that fall into this class, 335 were in the wrong agreement of subject and verb of which "he," "she" or "it don't" numbered fifty-six. This last error, so common with adults, remains constant from three to six years while all other errors of agreement fall from 8 per thousand words at two years to 1 per thousand in our oldest age group.

PREPOSITIONS

Errors in the use of the preposition were divided into two groups: 168 of these errors consisted in the omission of the sign of the infinitive, 277 were errors, mostly of omission, though a few times a wrong preposition was chosen as "in" for "into." At two years, 42 per cent of the infinitive signs and 18 per cent of other prepositions were omitted; by four years these percentages had dropped to 8 and 5 respectively after which improvement was irregular.

PARTS OF SPEECH CONFUSED

One part of speech was used for another 175 times or 3 times per thousand words at two years, 5 times per thousand at three and less than once per thousand thereafter. The most frequent wrong use of this type was that of a noun (92 times) for the first person pronoun which is an error deliberately encouraged by parents who use their own and the child's name instead of pronouns in talking to babies. The other errors of this type are due to inadequate vocabulary, the child, for instance, using a verb he does know for the corresponding noun which he has not yet learned. Some such uses are found in the following examples: At three years; "the stir," "a making man," "give me the rub" (eraser). At four years; "I am down to the low" (bottom of page), the "bang" or "shoot" for "gun," "That sure is a pretty decorate," "Please, sharp the pencil." At five years; "The change stick." Other confusions were of adverb and adjective, such errors as are frequently found among older children.

MISCELLANEOUS ERRORS

The remaining errors taken altogether at no age exceeded 3 per thousand and numbered 222 in all. Sixty-eight of these were omissions of a relative or a conjunction when such a connective was essential, and 27 more were omissions of other parts of speech not discussed above where the word omitted was necessary for clearness or correctness of speech.

   Nine errors occurred in the comparison of adjectives or adverbs; for example "quicklier." These were all of regularly compared adverbs and adjectives as the irregular forms seem to be learned as separate words and one of them "more" is used quite frequently and correctly at two years. Thirty-four cases of redundancy occurred, most of which were the addition of unnecessary prepositions as in "He prints it up," "The airplane landed up." Forty-seven errors in the use of the negative were found. At two and three years, all of these were in the use of "no" for "not," but almost all the errors in the use of the negative by the older children were in using a double negative, an error occurring for the first time at three-and-a-half years.

WORD ORDER

This type of error occurred 37 times. It was seldom found singly in any child's record and the majority of even the youngest children's records were quite free from such errors. One small boy who was observed at different ages from eighteen months to five-and-a-half years was a particularly crooked talker at four years and ten of these errors occurred in records of his conversation taken at three years ten months and at four years four months. He was backward in talking and his earlier records consisted of only or mainly one-word sentences where word order errors would have small chance of occurring. At the time he started to print, he showed some tendency to mirror-writing and now, at almost twelve years, he reverses the order of letters in his spelling. Examples of word-order errors by this boy are: "Where you did hide?" "This I want." "See 'em dere in," and by others, "Eat soup warm."

ERROR INDICES

Averages of the error indices for the children at each age are given in table 1. The differences from two to five and from two to three years are decidedly significant and from three to four years, the chances are 994 in a thousand that the true difference is greater than its sigma.

As in other sex comparisons as to the development of language, the girls are better than the boys at two years but thereafter the advantage changes at each age level studied.

For 36 children repeated records from two to six each were available. Their average improvement for each successive half-year from eighteen months to six years is, in order, 17, 29, 15, 11, 4, 3, 0, 1½ and 1 per thousand. Improvement is greatest from two to two-and-a-half years then gradually less with very little gain after four-and-a-half.

By the time the child is six years old, most of his errors in speech have been eliminated except such as he commonly hears spoken by his elders. Not counting the verb errors, "he don't," "got," "ain't," and "can" for "may" the verb errors at five have decreased to 5 per thousand words and no other type of error except incomplete sentences occurs more than twice per thousand words. By this time the child would be able to speak correctly if he did but have a good example before him. Among the records of the 15 children from sixty-six to seventy-two months old, 2 were perfect. Both of these children came from homes of above average in social class and had well-educated parents. One child was a boy, the other a girl and both had high I.Q.'s. Only 1 of these fifteen children whose error index exceeded three came from a home where correct English was spoken and this child had for some time attended a kindergarten where the majority of the pupils came from bilingual homes. Considering the 4 children of this group who had attended such kindergartens, we find their error-indices to average 4.8, the 3 other children who came from homes of the upper social class averaged 1.0 and the remaining eight 6.2. At five years, these 3 groups averaged 4.6 for the 12 in the kindergarten attended also by bilingual children, 4.4 for the 45 others from the middle and upper social classes and 7.7 for the 18 children from the laboring class. As the children from the better homes averaged higher mentally that might be one reason for fewer errors especially at the younger ages so this comparison was not carried below five years by which time the child is capable of reasonably correct speech.

CONCLUSIONS

1. There is a strong tendency to rhythm in the vocalizations of very young children seen in the fact that the majority of their neologisms and corruptions of words and phrases contain duplication of sounds.
2. Children are able to generalize in the use of inflected words often before they

are three years old; this tendency being so marked that a high percentage of their errors of inflexion are due to the extending of rules for the formation of regular forms to other words irregularly inflected.

3. Although the immaturity of the child is responsible for the greater proportion of his errors at two and three years, the fact that at five and six years, the only errors occurring more than once per thousand words, are those that are among the commonest in the speech of adults would suggest that by the age of five the primary factor of incorrect speech in the child is the poor example set by those around him and with a good example, he would be capable of correct grammatical speech.

4. The earlier development of baby girls is again evidenced in the lower percentage of error in their speech at two years.

5. Omissions of different types and errors in inflection comprise a large majority of the errors found.

The Child's Learning of English Morphology

Jean Berko Gleason

In this study[1] we set out to discover what is learned by children exposed to English morphology. To test for knowledge of morphological rules, we use nonsense materials. We know that if the subject can supply the correct plural ending, for instance, to a noun we have made up, he has internalized a working system of the plural allomorphs in English, and is able to generalize to new cases and select the right form. If a child knows that the plural of *witch* is *witches*, he may simply have memorized the plural form. If, however, he tells us that the plural of *gutch* is *gutches*, we have evidence that he actually knows, albeit unconsciously, one of those rules which the descriptive linguist, too, would set forth in his grammar. And if children do have knowledge of morphological rules, how does this knowledge evolve? Is there a progression from simple, regular rules to the more irregular and qualified rules that are adequate fully to describe English? In very general terms, we undertake to discover the psychological status of a certain kind of linguistic description. It is evident that the acquisition of language is more than the storing up of rehearsed utterances, since we are all able to say what we have not practiced and what we have never before heard. In bringing descriptive linguistics to the study of language acquisition, we hope to gain knowledge of the systems and patterns used by the speaker.

In order to test for children's knowledge of this sort, it was necessary to begin with an examination of their actual vocabulary. Accordingly, the 1000 most frequent words in the first-grader's vocabulary were selected from Rinsland's listing.[2] This listing contains the most common words in the elementary school child's vocabulary, as taken from actual conversations, compositions, letters, and similar documents. This list was then examined to see what features of English morphology seem to be most commonly represented in the vocabulary of the first-grade child. From this we

---

From Word, **14,** 1958, The International Linguistic Association. Reprinted by permission of Johnson Reprint Corporation.

[1] This investigation was supported in part by a fellowship from the Social Science Research Council. During the academic year 1957–58 the writer completed the research while holding an AAUW National Fellowship. A dissertation on this subject was presented by the writer to Radcliffe College in April, 1958. I am indebted to Professor Roger W. Brown for his inspiration and his help in the conduct of this study.

[2] H. D. Rinsland, *A Basic Vocabulary of Elementary School Children* (New York: The Macmillan Company, 1945).

could decide what kind of extensions we might expect the child to be able to make. All of the English inflexional morphemes were present.

The areas that seemed to be most promising from this examination were the plural and the two possessives of the noun, the third person singular of the verb, the progressive and the past tense, and the comparative and superlative of the adjective. The pronouns were avoided both because of the difficulty involved in making up a nonsense pronoun, and because the pronouns are so few in number and so irregular that we would hardly expect even adults to have any generalized rules for the handling of new pronouns. Moreover, we do not encounter new pronouns, whereas new verbs, adjectives, and nouns constantly appear in our vocabularies, so that the essential problem is not the same. The past participle of regular or weak verbs in English is identical with the past tense, and since the regular forms were our primary interest, no attempt was made to test for the past participle. A number of forms that might suggest irregular plurals and past tenses were included among the nouns and verbs.

The productive allomorphs of the plural, the possessive, and the third person singular of the verb are phonologically conditioned and identical with one another. These forms are /-s ∞ -z ∞ -əz/, with the following distribution:

/-əz/ after stems that end in /s z š ž č ǰ/, e.g. *glasses, watches;*
/-s/ after stems that end in /p t k f θ/, e.g. *hops, hits;*
/-z/ after all other stems, viz. those ending in /b d g v ð m n ŋ r l/, vowels, and
     semivowels, e.g. *bids, goes.*

The productive allomorphs of the past are /-t ∞ -d ∞ -əd/, and they are also phonologically conditioned, with the following distribution:

/=əd/ after stems that end in /t d/, e.g. *melled;*
/-t/ after stems that end in /p k č f θ š/, e.g. *stopped;*
/-d/ after stems ending in voiced sounds except /-d/, e.g. *climbed, played.*

The progressive -*ing* and the adjective =*er* and -*est* do not have variants. It might also be noted that the possessive has an additional allomorph /-ø/; this occurs after an inflectional /-s/ or /-z/, so that if the form *boy* is made plural, *boys,* the possessive of that plural form is made by adding nothing, and indicated in writing only by the addition of an apostrophe: *boys'.*

The children's vocabulary at the first-grade level also contains a number of words that are made of a free morpheme and a derivational suffix, e.g. *teacher,* or of two free morphemes, e.g. *birthday.* The difficulties encountered in this area are many. First, it might be noted that there are not many contrasts, i.e., not many cases of the same derivational suffix being added to different bases to produce forms of like function. Although *beautiful* and *thankful* both appear on the list, it does not seem that these examples are numerous enough for us to expect a young child to be able to append -*ful* to a new noun in order to produce an adjective. Word derivation and compounding are furthermore often accompanied by changes in stress and pronunciation, so that the picture is additionally complicated. There seemed to be enough examples of the pattern   as in *bláckboârd* as against *black board,* and of the diminutive-affectionate -y, the adjectival -er, and the agentive -er to warrant testing for these forms.

So far as the general picture is concerned, all speakers of the language are constrained to use the inflectional endings and apply them appropriately to new forms when they are encountered. We are not so often called upon to derive or compound new words, although by the time we are adults we can all to some extent do this. From the children's actual vocabulary we were able to make an estimate of the kind of morphological rules they might be expected to possess, and from these items a test could be constructed. It was noted, moreover, that in the child's vocabulary there are a number of compound words, like *blackboard* and *birthday*. It is entirely possible to use a compound word correctly and never notice that it is made of two separate and meaningful elements. It is also possible to use it correctly and at the same time have a completely private meaning for one or both of its constituent elements. In order to see what kind of ideas children have about the compound words in their vocabularies, it was decided to ask them directly about a selected number of these words.

Within the framework of the child's vocabulary, a test was devised to explore the child's ability to apply morphological rules to new words. He was called upon to inflect, to derive, to compound, and, lastly, to analyse compound words.

MATERIALS AND PROCEDURE

In order to test for the child's use of morphological rules of different types and under varying phonological conditions, a number of nonsense words were made up, following the rules for possible sound combinations in English. Pictures to represent the nonsense words were then drawn on cards. There were 27 picture cards, and the pictures, which were brightly colored, depicted objects, cartoon-like animals, and men performing various actions. For reasons that will be discussed later, several actual words were also included. A text, omitting the desired form, was typed on each card. An example of the card to test for the regular plural allomorph in /-z/ can be seen in Figure 1.

This is a wug.

Now there is another one.
There are two of them.
There are two _____.

Figure 1.   The plural allomorph in /-z/.

The subjects included 12 adults (seven women and five men), all of whom were college graduates. Many of these adults had also had some graduate training. All were native speakers of English.

The child subjects were obtained at the Harvard Preschool in Cambridge and the Michael Driscoll School, in Brookline, Massachusetts. At the Preschool, each child was brought to the experimenter, introduced, and told that now he was going to look at some pictures. The experimenter would point to the picture and read the text. The child would supply the missing word, and the item he employed was noted phonemically. After all of the pictures had been shown, the child was asked why he thought the things denoted by the compound words were so named. The general form of these questions was "Why do you think a blackboard is called a blackboard?" If the child responded with "Because it's a blackboard," he was asked, "But why do you think it's called that?" The children at the preschool ranged between four and five years in age. Twelve girls and seven boys were asked all items of the completed test, and two groups, one of three boys and three girls and one of five boys and three girls, were each asked half of the inflexional items in preliminary testing.

At the Driscoll School, the experimenter was introduced to the class and it was explained that each child was going to have a turn at looking at some pictures. The procedure from this point on was the same as for the Preschool. All children in the first grade were interviewed. There were 26 boys and 35 girls in this group. Ages ranged from five and one half to seven years.

The following is the order in which the cards were presented. Included is a statement of what was being tested, a description of the card, and the text that was read. Pronunciation is indicated by regular English orthography; a phonemic transcription is included for first occurrences of nonsense words.

1. PLURAL.   One bird-like animal, then two. "This is a wug /wʌg/. Now there is another one. There are two of them. There are two ——."

2. PLURAL.   One bird, then two. "This is a gutch /gʌč/. Now there is another one. There are two of them. There are two ——."

3. PAST TENSE.   Man with a steaming pitcher on his head. "This is a man who knows how to spow /spow/. He is spowing. He did the same thing yesterday. What did he do yesterday? Yesterday he ——."

4. PLURAL.   One animal, then two. "This is a kazh /kæž/. Now there is another one. There are two of them. There are two ——."

5. PAST TENSE.   Man swinging an object. "This is a man who knows how to rick /rik/. He is ricking. He did the same thing yesterday. What did he do yesterday? Yesterday he ——."

6. DIMINUTIVE AND COMPOUNDED OR DERIVED WORD.   One animal, then a miniscule animal. "This is a wug. This is a very tiny wug. What would you call a very tiny wug? This wug lives in a house. What would you call a house that a wug lives in?"

7. PLURAL.   One animal, then two. "This is a tor /tɔr/. Now there is another one. There are two of them. There are two ——."

8. DERIVED ADJECTIVE.   Dog covered with irregular green spots. "This is a dog

with quirks /kwərks/ on him. He is all covered with quirks. What kind of dog is he? He is a —— dog."

9. PLURAL.   One flower, then two. "This is a lun /lʌn/. Now there is another one. There are two of them. There are two ——."

10. PLURAL.   One animal, then two. "This is a niz /niz/. Now there is another one. There are two of them. There are two ——."

11. PAST TENSE.   Man doing calisthenics. "This is a man who knows how to mot /mat/. He is motting. He did the same thing yesterday. What did he do yesterday? Yesterday he ——."

12. PLURAL.   One bird, then two. "This is a cra /kra/. Now there is another one. There are two of them. There are two ——."

13. PLURAL.   One animal, then two. "This is a tass /tæs/. Now there is another one. There are two of them. There are two ——."

14. PAST TENSE.   Man dangling an object on a string. "This is a man who knows how to bod /bad/. He is bodding. He did the same thing yesterday. What did he do yesterday? Yesterday he ——."

15. THIRD PERSON SINGULAR.   Man shaking an object. "This is a man who knows how to naz /næz/. He is nazzing. He does it every day. Every day he ——."

16. PLURAL.   One insect, then two. "This is a heaf /hiyf/. Now there is another one. There are two of them. There are two ——."

17. PLURAL.   One glass, then two. "This is a glass. Now there is another one. There are two of them. There are two ——."

18. PAST TENSE.   Man exercising. "This is a man who knows how to gling /gliŋ/. He is glinging. He did the same thing yesterday. What did he do yesterday? Yesterday he ——."

19. THIRD PERSON SINGULAR.   Man holding an object. "This is a man who knows how to loodge /luwdž/. He is loodging. He does it every day. Every day he ——."

20. PAST TENSE.   Man standing on the ceiling. "This is a man who knows how to bing /biŋ/. He is binging. He did the same thing yesterday. What did he do yesterday? Yesterday he ——."

21. SINGULAR AND PLURAL POSSESSIVE.   One animal wearing a hat, then two wearing hats. "This is a niz who owns a hat. Whose hat is it? It is the —— hat. Now there are two nizzes. They both own hats. Whose hats are they? They are the —— hats."

22. PAST TENSE.   A bell. "This is a bell that can ring. It is ringing. It did the same thing yesterday. What did it do yesterday? Yesterday it ——."

23. SINGULAR AND PLURAL POSSESSIVE.   One animal wearing a hat, then two. "This is a wug who owns a hat. Whose hat is it? It is the —— hat. Now there are two wugs. They both own hats. Whose hats are they? They are the —— hats."

24. COMPARATIVE AND SUPERLATIVE OF THE ADJECTIVE.   A dog with a few

spots, one with several, and one with a great number. "This dog has quirks on him. This dog has more quirks on him. And this dog has even more quirks on him. This dog is quirky. This dog is——. And this dog is the——."

25. PROGRESSIVE AND DERIVED AGENTIVE OR COMPOUND.   Man balancing a ball on his nose. "This is a man who knows how to zib /zib/. What is he doing? He is——. What would you call a man whose job is to zib?"

26. PAST TENSE.   An ice cube, then a puddle of water. "This is an ice cube. Ice melts. It is melting. Now it is all gone. What happened to it? It——."

27. SINGULAR AND PLURAL POSSESSIVE.   One animal wearing a hat, then two. "This is a bik /bik/ who owns a hat. Whose hat is it? It is the——hat. Now there are two biks. They both own hats. Whose hats are they? They are the——hats."

28. COMPOUND WORDS.   The child was asked why he thought the following were so named. (No pictures were used for these items.)

a. afternoon
b. airplane
c. birthday
d. breakfast
e. blackboard
f. fireplace
g. football
h. handkerchief
i. holiday
j. merry-go-round
k. newspaper
l. sunshine
m. Thanksgiving
n. Friday

It took between ten and fifteen minutes to ask a child all of these questions. Even the youngest children have had experience with picture books, if not actual training in naming things through pictures, and no child failed to understand the nature of the task before him. It was, moreover, evident that a great number of these children thought they were being taught new English words. It was not uncommon for a child to repeat the nonsense word immediately upon hearing it and before being asked any questions. Often, for example, when the experimenter said "This is a *gutch*," the child repeated, *"Gutch."* Answers were willingly, and often insistently, given. These responses will be discussed in the following section.

RESULTS

Adult answers to the inflectional items were considered correct answers, and it was therefore possible to rate the children's answers. In general, adult opinion was unanimous—everyone said the plural of *wug* was *wugs,* the plural of *gutch* was *gutches;* where the adults differed among themselves, except in the possessives, it was along the line of a common but irregular formation, e.g. *heaf* became *heaves* in the plural for many speakers, and in these cases both responses were considered correct. If a child said that the plural of *heaf* was *heafs* or *heaves* /-vz/, he was considered correct. If he said *heaf* (no ending), or *heafès* /-fəz/, he was considered incorrect, and a record was kept of each type of response.

SEX DIFFERENCES

The first question to be answered was whether there is a sex difference in the ability to handle English morphology at this age level. Since it seemed entirely possible that boys entering the first grade might be on the whole somewhat older than girls entering the first grade, it was necessary to equate the two groups for age.

The children were divided into seven age groups. Since at each of these levels there were more girls than boys, a random selection of the girls was made so that they would match the boys in number. The distribution of these ages and the number in each group can be seen in Table 1. This distribution was utilized only in comparing the performance of the boys with that of the girls; in all other instances, the responses of the entire sample were considered.

The groups of 28 boys and 28 girls thus selected were compared with one another on all inflectional items. The chi square criterion with Yates' correction for small frequencies was applied to each item, and on none was there a significant difference between the boys' and girls' performance; boys did as well as girls, or somewhat better, on over half the items, so that there was no evidence of the usual superiority of girls in language matters. From this it would appear that boys and girls in this age range are equal in their ability to handle the English morphology represented by these items.

Table 1   Distribution of Children at Each Age Level for Comparison of the Sexes

Age	Boys	Girls	Total
4	2	2	4
4:6	1	1	2
5	2	2	4
5:6	2	2	4
6	10	10	20
6:6	6	6	12
7	5	5	10
Total:	28	28	56

Table 2   Age Differences on Inflectional Items

Item	Percentage of Correct Preschool Answers	Percentage of Correct First Grade Answers	Significance Level of Difference
Plural			
glasses	75	99	.01
wugs	76	97	.02
luns	68	92	.05
tors	73	90	—
heafs	79	80	—
cras	58	86	.05
tasses	28	39	—
gutches	28	38	—
kazhes	25	36	—
nizzes	14	33	—
Progressive			
zibbing	72	97	.01
Past Tense			
binged	60	85	.05
glinged	63	80	—
ricked	73	73	—
melted	72	74	—
spowed	36	59	—
motted	32	33	—
bodded	14	31	.05
rang	0	25	.01
Third Singular			
loodges	57	56	—
nazzes	47	49	—
Possessive			
wug's	68	81	—
bik's	68	95	.02
niz's	58	46	—
wugs'	74	97	.02
biks'	74	99	.01
nizzes'	53	82	.05

AGE DIFFERENCES

Having ascertained that there was no difference between boys' and girls' answers, we combined the sexes and went on to compare the younger with the older children. The oldest children at the Preschool were five years old, and the youngest at the Driscoll School were five and one half years, so that the dividing line was made between the schools. Chi square corrected for small frequencies was again applied to all inflectional items. First graders did significantly better than preschoolers on slightly less than half of these. The differences can be seen in Table 2.

FORMATION OF THE PLURAL

The nature of the children's answers can best be seen through a separate examination of the noun plurals, the verbs, and the possessives. The percentage of all children supplying correct plural endings can be seen in Table 3. The general picture indicates that children at this age have in their vocabularies words containing the three plural allomorphs /-s ∿ -z ∿ -əz/, and can use these words. The real form *glasses* was included here because we knew from a pretest that children at this age generally did not make correct application of /-əz/ to new forms, and we wanted to know if they used this form with a common English word. Evidently they have at least one actual English model for this contingent plural. In uncomplicated cases children at this age can also extend the use of these forms to new words requiring /-s/ or /-z/, as indicated by the high percentage of right answers for *wug* and *bik*, a form used in the pretest and answered correctly by a correspondingly high number of children. For the items *wugs* and *glasses* there is, moreover, a significant difference between the younger and older groups. For *glasses* they progress from 75 per cent right to 99 per cent right in the older group, a change that is significant at the 1 per cent level. The few wrong answers in these cases were either a complete failure to respond, or a repetition of the word in its singular form.

Table 3   Percentages of Children Supplying Correct Plural Forms

Item	Allomorph	Per cent Correct
glasses	/-əz/	91
wugs	/-z/	91
luns	/-z/	86
tors	/-z/	85
heafs, -ves	/-s//-z/	82
cras	/-z/	79
tasses	/-əz/	36
gutches	/-əz/	36
kazhes	/-əz/	31
nizzes	/əz/	28

From this it is evident that however poorly children may do on extensions of the rule for forming the plural of *glass*, they do have this item in their vocabulary and can produce it appropriately. During the period from preschool to the first grade, those who do not have this item acquire it. They can also extend the rule for the addition of the /-s/ or /-z/ allomorph where the more general rules of English phonology dictate which of these forms must be used. During this period they perfect this knowledge.

The ability to add /-z/ to *wug and /-s/ to *bik does not alone prove that the child possesses the rule that tells which allomorph of the plural must be used: English phonology decrees that there cannot be a consonant cluster */-kz/ or */-gs/. The final consonant determines whether the sibilant must be voiced or unvoiced. The instances in English where there is a choice are after /l/ /n/ and /r/ and after a vowel or semivowel. Thus we have minimal pairs like: *ells: else; purrs: purse; hens: hence; pews: puce.* In forming the plural of *wug or *bik,* the child has only to know that a dental sibilant must be added; which one it is is determined by the invariant rules of combination that govern English consonant clusters. If, however, he is faced with a new word ending in a vowel, semivowel, /-l/, /-n/, or /-r/, he himself must make the choice, because so far as English phonology is concerned he could add either a /-z/ or an /-s/ and still have a possible English word. We would expect him, therefore, to have more difficulty forming the plural of a new word ending in these sounds than in cases where phonology determines the form of the sibilant. These problems are represented by the forms *cra, *tor,* and *lun.* As Table 3 indicates, the percentages correct on these items were respectively 79, 85, and 86. The difference between performance on *wug and *cra is significant at the 5 per cent level.

During the period from preschool to the first grade, they improved markedly in their handling of *cra and *lun. The differences between the younger and older groups were significant at the 5 per cent level. The case of adding /-s/ to these forms did not, however, arise. The child here, as in so many other stages of language-learning, answered complexity with silence: the wrong answers were invariably the unaltered form of the singular.

The only other case to be answered correctly by the majority of the children was *heaf. Since adults responded with both *heafs and *heaves /-vz/, both of these answers were considered correct. It must be noted that although 42 per cent of the adults gave *heaves as the plural of this item, employing what would amount to a morphophonemic change along the lines of: *knife: knives; hoof: hooves,* only three children out of a total of 89 answering this item said *heaves; 9 or 10 per cent added nothing, and an additional four formed the plural with the wrong allomorph, i.e. they said /hiyfəz/, treating the /-f/ as if it belonged to the sibilant-affricate series. /f/ is, of course, phonetically very similar to /s/, and one of the questions suggested by this problem was whether children would generalize in the direction of phonetic similarity across functional boundaries—/f/ is distinguished phonetically from /s/ only in that it is grave and /s/ is acute. It is, so to speak, no more different from /s/ than /z/ is, and it is as similar to /s/ as /ž/ is to /z/. It does not, however, so far as English phonology is concerned, function like /s š z ž č ǰ/, none of which can be immediately followed by another sibilant within the same consonant cluster. The high percentage of correct items indicates that /f/ had already been categorized as belonging to the consonant class that can be followed by /-s/, and the phonetic similarity between /f/ and the sibilants did not lead the children to generalize the rule for the addition of the /-əz/ allomorph in that direction. Nor could any irregular formation be said to be productive for children in this case, although for adults it apparently is.

The proportion of children's right answers suddenly drop when we come to the form *lass*. As Table 3 shows, 91 per cent of these children when given the form *glass* could produce the form *glasses*. When given the form *lass*, a new word patterned after *glass*, only 36 per cent could supply the form *lasses*. The picture becomes progressively worse with the other words ending in sibilants or affricates, and by the time we reach the form *niz*, only 28 per cent answered correctly. *Niz*, of these four, is the only one that ends in a sound that is also the commonest plural allomorph, /-z/, and the children did the worst on this item. What is of additional interest is that on these four items there was no significant improvement from the preschool to the first grade. The difference between performance on *cra*, the worst of the other items, and *tass*, the best of these, was significant at the 1 per cent level. Again, the wrong answers consisted in doing nothing to the word as given. It must be noted, however, that in these items, the children delivered the wrong form with a great deal of conviction: 62 per cent of them said "one *tass*, two *tass*" as if there were no question that the plural of *tass* should and must be *tass*. From this it is evident that the morphological rules these children have for the plural are not the same as those possessed by adults: the children can add /-s/ or /-z/ to new words with a great deal of success. They do not as yet have the ability to extend the /-əz/ allomorph to new words, even though it has been demonstrated that they have words of this type in their vocabulary.

Table 4   Percentages of Children Supplying Correct Verb Forms

Item	Allomorph	Percentage Correct
Progressive		
zibbing	/-iŋ /	90
Past Tense		
binged, bang	/-d ∿ æ ←(i)/	78
glinged, glang	/-d ∿ æ ←(i)/	77
ricked	/-t/	73
melted	/-əd/	73
spowed	/-d/	52
motted	/-əd/	33
bodded	/-əd/	31
rang	/æ ←(i)/	17
Third Singular		
loodges	/-əz/	56
nazzes	/-əz/	48

The form "kazh" /kæž/ was added here once again to see in what direction the children would generalize. /ž/, although it is in the sibilant-affricate group, is very rare as a final consonant in English: it occurs only in some speakers' pronunciation of *garage, barrage,* and a few other words. As Table 3 indicates, the children treated this word like the others of this group. It might also be noted here that for the forms *gutch* and *kazh,* some few children formed the plural in /-s/, i.e., /gʌčs/ and /kæzs/. Ten per cent did this for *gutch,* and 5 per cent for *kazh,* errors that indicate that the phonological rules may not yet be perfectly learned. What is clearest from these answers dealing with the plural is that children can and do extend the /-s/ and /-z/ forms to new words, and that they cannot apply the more complicated /-əz/ allomorph of the plural to new words.

VERB INFLECTIONS

The children's performance on the verb forms can be seen in Table 4. It will be observed that the best performance on these items was on the progressive, where they were shown a picture of a man who knew how to *zib* and were required to say that he was *zibbing.* The difference between *zibbing* and the best of the past tense items, *binged,* was significant at the 5 per cent level. The improvement from the younger to the older group was significant at the 1 per cent level; fully 97 per cent of the first graders answered this question correctly. Here, there was no question of choice; there is only one allomorph of the progressive morpheme, and the child either knows this *-ing* form or does not. These results suggest that he does.

The results with the past tense forms indicate that these children can handle the /-t/ and /-d/ allomorphs of the past. On *binged* and *glinged* the percentages answering correctly were 78 and 77, and the older group did significantly better than the younger group on *binged.*

Actually, the forms *gling* and *bing* were included to test for possible irregular formations. A check of English verbs revealed that virtually all in *-ing* form their past tense irregularly: *sing: sang; ring: rang; cling: clung,* and many others. The only *-ing* verbs that form a past tense in *-ed* are a few poetic forms like *enringed, unkinged,* and *winged,* and onomatopoeias like *pinged* and *zinged.* Adults clearly felt the pull of the irregular pattern, and 50 per cent of them said *bang* or *bung* for the past tense of *bing,* while 75 per cent made *gling* into *glang* or *glung* in the past. Only one child of the 86 interviewed on these items said *bang.* One also said *glang,* and two said *glanged*—changing the vowel and also adding the regular /-d/ for the past.

The great majority on these forms, as well as on *ricked* which requires /-t/, formed the past tense regularly. There was a certain amount of room for variation with the past tense, since there is more than one way of expressing what happened in the past. A number of children, for example said "Yesterday he was *ricking.*" If on these occasions the experimenter tried to force the issue by saying "He only did it once yesterday, so yesterday once he——?" The child usually responded with "once he was *ricking.*" Taking into account this possible variation, the percentages right on *rick, gling* and *bing* represent a substantial grasp of the problem of adding a phonologically determined /-t/ or /-d/.

With *spow* the child had to choose one or the other of the allomorphs, and the drop to 52 per cent correct represents this additional complexity. Several children here retained the inflectional /-z/ and said /spowzd/, others repeated the progressive or refused to answer. No child supplied a /-t/.

On *motted, the percentage correct drops to 33, although the subjects were 73 per cent right on the real word melted, which is a similar form. On *bodded they were 31 per cent right, and on rang only 17 per cent right. The older group was significantly better than the younger on rang and *bodded. What this means is that the younger group could not do them at all—not one preschool child knew rang—and the older group could barely do them. What emerges here is that children at this age level are not able to extend the rule for forming the past tense of melted to new forms. They can handle the regular /-d/ and /-t/ allomorphs of the past in new instances, but not /-əd/. Nor do they have control of the irregular past form rang, and consequently do not form new pasts according to this pattern, although adults do. They have the /-ed/ form in actual words like melled, but do not generalize from it. With ring, they do not have the actual past rang, and, therefore no model for generalization. In the children's responses, the difference between *spowd, the worst of the items requiring /-t/ or /-d/, and *molted, the best requiring /-əd/ is significant at the 2 per cent level. For *mot and *bod, the wrong answers, which were in the majority, were overwhelmingly a repetition of the present stem: "Today he *bods; yesterday he *bod." To the forms ending in /-t/ or /-d/ the children added nothing to form the past.

The third person singular forms require the same allomorphs as the noun plurals, /-s ~ -z ~ -əz/, and only two examples were included in the experiment. These were *loodge and *naz, and required the /-əz/ ending. Fifty-six per cent of the children supplied the correct form *loodges, and 48 per cent supplied *nazzes. The wrong answers were again a failure to add anything to the stem, and there was no improvement whatsoever from the younger to the older group on these two items.

FORMATION OF THE POSSESSIVE

The only other inflectional items statistically treated were the regular forms of the possessive. The percentages of children supplying right answers can be seen in Table 5. In the singular, the problem was the same as for the noun plurals, and the children's difficulty with the /-əz/ form of the allomorph is mirrored in the low percentage who were able to supply *niz's /-əz/ when told "This is a niz who owns a hat. Whose hat is it? It is the——?" For *bik's there was a significant improvement at the 2 per cent level between the younger and older groups. For *niz's the younger group did no worse than the older group.

In the plural possessives the problem is somewhat different: since these words are already regularly inflected, the possessive is formed by adding a morphological zero. The children did not add an additional /-əz/ to these forms, and in the case of *nizzes', they erred on the side of removing the plural -es, e.g. for the plural possessive they said simply *niz in those cases where they gave the wrong answers.

It was the adults who had difficulty with the plural possessives: 33 per cent of them said *wugses /-zez/ and *bikses /-sez/, although none said *nizeses /-əzəz/. This is undoubtedly by analogy with proper nouns in the adults' vocabulary, i.e., no adult would say that if two dogs own hats, they are the *dogses /-zəz/ hats. However an adult may know a family named Lyons, and also a family named Lyon. In the first instance, the family are the Lyonses /-zəz/ and if they own a house, it is the Lyonses' /-zəz/ house; in the second instance, the family are the Lyons and their house is the Lyons' /-nz/. The confusion resulting from competing forms like these is such that some speakers do not make this distinction, and simply add nothing to a proper noun

Table 5   Percentages of Children Supplying Correct Possessive Forms

Item	Allomorph	Percentage Correct
Singular		
wug's	/-z/	84
bik's	/-s/	87
niz's	/-əz/	49
Plural		
wugs'	/-∅/	88
biks'	/-∅/	93
nizzes'	/-∅/	76

ending in /-s/ or /-z/ in order to form the possessive—they say "it is Charles' /-ɪz/ hat." Some speakers seem also to have been taught in school that they must use this latter form. It seems likely that the children interviewed had not enough grasp of the /-əz/ form for these niceties to affect them.

ADJECTIVAL INFLECTION
The last of the inflectional items involved attempting to elicit comparative and super-lative endings for the adjective *quirky. The child was shown dogs that were increas-ingly *quirky and expected to say that the second sas *quirkier than the first, and that the third was the *quirkiest. No statistical count was necessary here since of the 80 children shown this picture, only one answered with these forms. Adults were unani-mous in their answers. Children either said they did not know, or they repeated the experimenter's word, and said "*quirky, too." If the child failed to answer, the experi-menter supplied the form *quirkier, and said "This dog is quirky. This dog is quirkier. And this dog is the——?" Under these conditions 35 per cent of the children could supply the -est form.

DERIVATION AND COMPOUNDING
The children were also asked several questions that called for compounding or deriving new words. They were asked what they would call a man who *zibbed for a living, what they would call a very tiny *wug, what they would call a house a *wug lives in, and what kind of dog a dog covered with *quirks is.

Adults unanimously said that a man who *zibs is a *zibber, using the common agentive pattern -er. Only 11 per cent of the children said *zibber. Thirty-five per cent gave no answer. 11 per cent said *zibbingmàn and 5 per cent said *zibmàn, com-pounds that adults did not utilize. The rest of the children's answers were real words like clown and acrobat.

For the diminutive of *wug, 50 per cent of the adults said *wuglet. Others offered little *wug, *wuggie, *wugette, and *wugling. No child used a diminutive suffix.

Fifty-two per cent of the children formed compounds like *báby *wùg, teény *wùg*, and *little *wùg*. Two children, moreover, said a little *wug is a *wig*, employing sound symbolism—a narrower vowel to stand for a smaller animal. For the house a *wug lives in, 58 per cent of the adults formed the asyntactic compound *wúghoùse*. Others said *wuggery, *wúgshoùse*, and *wúghùt*. Again, no child used a suffix. The younger children did not understand this question, and where the older children did, they formed compounds. Eighteen per cent of the first graders said *wughoùse*. Others suggested birdcage and similar forms. What emerges from this picture is the fact that whereas adults may derive new words, children at this stage use almost exclusively a compounding pattern, and have the stress pattern at their disposal: the adults unanimously said that a dog covered with *quirks* is a *quirky* dog. Sixty-four percent of the children formed the compound *quírk dòg* for this item, and again, no child used a derivational suffix.

ANALYSIS OF COMPOUND WORDS

After the child had been asked all of these questions calling for the manipulation of new forms, he was asked about some of the compound words in his own vocabulary; the object of this questioning was to see if children at this age are aware of the separate morphemes in compound words. The children's explanations fall roughly into four categories. The first is identity: "a blackboard is called a *blackboard* because it is a blackboard." The second is a statement of the object's salient function or feature: "a blackboard is called a *blackboard* because you write on it." In the third type of explanation, the salient feature happens to coincide with part of the name: "a blackboard is called a *blackboard* because it is black;" "a merry-go-round is called a *merry-go-round* because it goes round and round." Finally, there is the etymological explanation given by adults—it takes into account both parts of the word, and is not necessarily connected with some salient or functional feature: "Thanksgiving is called *Thanksgiving* because the pilgrims gave thanks."

Of the children's answers, only 13 per cent could be considered etymological. Most of their answers fell into the salient feature category, while the number of identity responses dropped from the younger to the older group. Many younger children offered no answers at all; of the answers given, 23 per cent were identity. Of the older children, only 9 per cent gave identity answers, a difference that was significant at the 1 per cent level.

As we might expect, the greatest number of etymological responses—23 per cent —was given for *Thanksgiving*, which is an item that children are explicitly taught. It must be noted, however, that despite this teaching, for 67 per cent of the children answering this item, Thanksgiving is called *Thanksgiving* because you eat lots of turkey.

The salient feature answers at first seem to have the nature of an etymological explanation, in those instances where the feature coincides with part of the name— 72 per cent of the answers, for instance, said that a fireplace is called a fireplace because you put fire in it. When the salient feature does not coincide with part of the name, however, the etymological aspects also drop out. For *birthday*, where to the child neither the fact that it is a day nor that it is tied to one's birth is important, the number of functional answers rises: it is called *birthday* because you get presents or eat cake. Only 2 per cent said anything about its being a day.

The child approaches the etymological view of compound words through those words where the most important thing about the word so far as the child is concerned coincides with part of the name. The outstanding feature of a merry-go-round is that it does, indeed, go round and round, and it is the eminent appropriateness of such names that leads to the expectation of meaningfulness in other compound words.

Although the number of etymological explanations offered by the children was not great, it was clear that many children have what amounts to private meanings for many compound words. These meanings may be unrelated to the word's history, and unshared by other speakers. Examples of this can be seen in the following.

"An airplane is called an *airplane* because it is plain thing that goes in the air."

"Breakfast is called *breakfast* because you have to eat it fast when you rush to school."

"Thanksgiving is called that because people give things to one another." (Things-giving?)

"Friday is a day when you have fried fish."

"A handkerchief is a thing you hold in your hand, and you go 'kerchoo'."

These examples suffice to give the general nature of the private meanings children may have about the words in their vocabulary. What is of additional interest, is that the last explanation about the handkerchief was also offered by one of the college graduate adult subjects.

We must all learn to handle English inflection and some of the patterns for derivation and compounding. So long as we use a compound word correctly, we can assign any meaning we like to its constituent elements.

CONCLUSION

In this experiment, preschool and first-grade children, ranging from four to seven years in age, were presented with a number of nonsense words and asked to supply English plurals, verb tenses, possessives, derivations and compounds of those words. Our first and most general question had been: do children possess morphological rules? A previous study of the actual vocabulary of first graders showed that they know real items representing basic English morphological processes. Asking questions about real words, however, might be tapping a process no more abstract than rote memory. We could be sure that our nonsense words were new words to the child, and that if he supplied the right morphological item he knew something more than the individual words in his vocabulary: he had rules of extension that enabled him to deal with new words. Every child interviewed understood what was being asked of him. If knowledge of English consisted of no more than the storing up of many memorized words, the child might be expected to refuse to answer our questions on the grounds that he had never before heard of a *wug, for instance, and could not possibly give us the plural form since no one had ever told him what it was. This was decidedly not the case. The children answered the questions; in some instances they pronounced the inflectional endings they had added with exaggerated care, so that it was obvious that they understood the problem and wanted no mistake made about their solution. Sometimes, they said "That's a hard one," and pondered a while before answering, or answered with one form and then corrected themselves. The answers were not always right so far as English is concerned; but they were consistent and orderly answers, and they demonstrated that there can be no doubt that children in this age range operate with clearly delimited morphological rules.

Our second finding was that boys and girls did equally well on these items. Sometimes the girls had a higher percentage of right answers on an item, and more often the boys did somewhat better, but no pattern of differences could be distinguished and the differences were never statistically significant. These findings are at variance with the results of most other language tests. Usually, girls have been shown to have a slight advantage over boys. In our experiment, girls were no more advanced than boys in their acquisition of English morphology. Since other language tests have not investigated morphology *per se,* it is easy enough to say that this is simply one area in which there are no sex differences. A reason for this lack of difference does, however, suggest itself: and that is the very basic nature of morphology. Throughout childhood, girls are perhaps from a maturational point of view slightly ahead of the boys who are their chronological age mates. But the language differences that have been observed may be culturally induced, and they may be fairly superficial. Some social factor may lead girls to be more facile with words, to use longer sentences, and to talk more. This can be misleading. A girl in an intellectual adult environment may, for instance, acquire a rather sophisticated vocabulary at an early age. This should not be taken to mean that she will learn the minor rules for the formation of the plural before she learns the major ones, or that she will necessarily be precocious in her acquisition of those rules. What is suggested here is that every child is in contact with a sufficiently varied sample of spoken English in order for him to be exposed at an early age to the basic morphological processes. These processes occur in simple sentences as well as in complex ones. Practice with a limited vocabulary may be as effective as practice with an extensive vocabulary, and the factors that influence other aspects of language development may have no effect on morphological acquisition. Since, moreover, this type of inner patterning is clearly a cognitive process, we might expect it to be related to intelligence more than to any other feature. Unfortunately, there were no IQ's available for the subjects, so that a comparison could not be made, and this last must remain a speculation.

Our next observation was that there were some differences between the preschoolers and the first graders. These were predominantly on the items that the group as a whole did best and worst on: since no child in the preschool could supply the irregular past *rang,* and a few in the first grade could, this difference was significant. Otherwise, the improvement was in the direction of perfecting knowledge they already had—the simple plurals and possessives, and the progressive tense. The answers of the two groups were not qualitatively different: they both employed the same simplified morphological rules. Since this was true, the answers of both groups were combined for the purpose of further analysis.

Children were able to form the plurals requiring /-s/ or /-z/, and they did best on the items where general English phonology determined which of these allomorphs is required. Although they have in their vocabularies real words that form their plural in /-əz/, in the age range that was interviewed they did not generalize to form new words in /-əz/. Their rule seems to be to add /-s/ or /-z/, unless the word ends in /s z š ž č ǰ/. To words ending in these sounds they add nothing to make the plural —and when asked to form a plural, repeat the stem as if it were already in the plural. This simplification eliminates the least common of the productive allomorphs. We may now ask about the relative status of the remaining allomorphs /-s/ and /-z/. For the items like *lun or *cra, where both of these sounds could produce a phonologically possible English word, but not a plural, no child employed the voiceless alternant /-s/. This is the second least common of the three allomorphs. The only places where this variant occurred were where the speaker of English could not say otherwise. So far as general English phonology is concerned a /-z/ cannot in the same cluster follow a /-k-/ or other voiceless sound. Once the /-k-/ has been said, even if the speaker intended to say /-z/, it would automatically devoice to /-s/. The only morphological rule the child is left with is the addition of the /-z/ allomorph, which is the most extensive: the /-əz/ form for him is not yet productive, and the /-s/ form can be subsumed under a more general phonological rule.

What we are saying here is that the child's rule for the formation of the plural seems to be: "a final sibilant makes a word plural." The question that arises is, should we not rather say that the child's rule is: "a voiceless sibilant after a voiceless consonant and a voiced sibilant after all other sounds makes a word plural." This latter describes what the child actually does. However, our rule will cover the facts if it is coupled with a prior phonological rule about possible final sound sequences. The choice of the voiceless or voiced variant can generally be subsumed under phonological rules about final sound sequences; the exceptions are after vowels, semivowels, and /l- n-r-/. In these places where phonology leaves a choice, /-z/ is used, and so the child's conscious rule might be to add /-z/. It would be interesting to find out what the child thinks he is saying—if we could in some way ask him the general question, "how do you make the plural?"

Another point of phonology was illustrated by the children's treatment of the forms *heaf and *kazh. It was demonstrated here that the children have phonological rules, and the direction of their generalizations was dictated by English phonology, and not simple phonetic similarity. /-z/ is a comparatively rare phoneme, and yet they apparently recognized it as belonging to the sibilant series in English, and they rarely attempted to follow it with another sibilant. The similarity between /f/ and the sibilants did not, on the contrary cause them to treat it as a member of this class. The final thing to be noted about *heaf if that several children and many adults said the plural was *heaves. This may be by analogy with *leaf: leaves*. If our speculation that the /-z/ form is the real morphological plural is right, there may be cases where instead of becoming devoiced itself, it causes regressive assimilation of the final voiceless consonant.

The allomorphs of the third person singular of the verb and the possessives of the noun are the same as for the noun plural, except that the plural possessives have an additional zero allomorph. These forms were treated in the same way by the children, with one notable exception: they were more successful in adding the /-əz/ to form possessives and verbs than they were in forming noun plurals. They were asked to produce three nearly identical forms: a man who *nazzes;* two *nizzes;* and a *niz's* hat. On the verb they were 48 per cent right; on the possessive they were 49 per cent right, and on the noun plural they were only 28 per cent right.

The difference between their performance on the noun plural and on the other two items was significant at the 1 per cent level. And yet the phonological problem presented by these three forms was the same. For some reason the contingent rule for the formation of the third person singular of the verb and for the possessive is better learned or earlier learned than the same rule for the formation of noun plurals. The morphological rule implies meaning, and forms that are phonologically identical may be learned at different times if they serve different functions. These forms are not simply the same phonological rule, Since their different functions change the percentage of right answers. Perhaps the child does better because he knows more verbs than nouns ending in /s z š ž č ǰ/, and it is possible that he has heard more possessives than noun plurals. It is also possible that for English the noun plural is the least important or most redundant of these inflections. This is a somewhat surprising conclusion, since nouns must always appear in a singular or plural form and there are ways of avoiding the possessive inflection: it is generally possible to use an *of* construction in place óf a possessive—we can say *the leg of the chair* or *the chair's leg,* or *the chair leg* although in cases involving actual ownership we do not say *of.* A sentence referring to *the hat of John* sounds like an awkward translation from the French. And no child said it was *the hat of the *niz.* The children's facility with these forms seems to indicate that the possessive inflection is by no means dying out in English.

Of the verb forms, the best performance was with the present progressive: 90 per cent of all the children said that a man who knew how to *zib* was *zibbing.* Undoubtedly, children's speech is mostly in the present tense, and this is a very commonly heard form. Explanations of what is happening in the the present all take this form. "The man is *running"*—or *walking* or *eating* or *doing* something. The additional point is that the *-ing* forms are not only very important; this inflection has only one allomorph. The rules for its application are completely regular, and it is the most general and regular rules that children prefer.

The children's handling of the past tense parallels their treatment of the plurals, except that they did better on the whole with the plurals. Again, they could not extend the contingent rule. Although they have forms like *melted* in their vocabulary, they were unable to extend the /-əd/ form to new verbs ending in /t d/. They treated these forms as if they were already in the pást. They applied the allomorphs /-d/ and /-t/ appropriately where they were phonologically conditioned, and only /-d/ to a form like *spow,* where either was possible. This suggests that their real morphological rule for the formation of the past is to add /-d/, and under certain conditions it will automatically become /-t/. Many adult speakers feel that they are adding a /-d/ in a word like *stopped;* this may be because of the orthography, and it may be because they are adding a psychological /-d/ that devoices without their noticing it.

Whereas the children all used regular patterns in forming the past tense, we found that for adults strong pasts of the form *rang* and *clung* are productive. Since virtually all English verbs that are in the present of an *-ing* form make their pasts irregularly, this seemed a likely supposition. Adults made *gling* and *bing* into *glang* and *bang* in the past. New words of this general shape may therefore be expected to have a very good chance of being treated according to this pattern—real words like the verb *to string* for instance, have been known to vacillate between the common productive past and this strong subgroup and finally come to be treated according to the less common pattern. The children, however, could not be expected to use this pattern since we could not demonstrate that they had the real form *rang* in their repertory. They said *ringed.* At one point, the experimenter misread the card and told the child that the bell *rang.* When the child was asked what the bell did, he said, "It *ringed."* The experimenter then corrected him and said, "You mean it *rang."* The child said that was what he had said, and when asked again what that was, he repeated, "It *ringed,"* as if he had not even heard the difference between these two allomorphs. Perhaps he did not.

The adults did not form irregular pasts with any other pattern, although a form was included that could have been treated according to a less common model. This was the verb *mot,* which was of the pattern *cut* or *bet.* There are some 19 verbs in English that form their past with a zero morpheme, but this group does not seem to be productive.

The cases of *gling,* which became *glang* in the past and *mot,* which became *motted* suggest some correlates of linguistic productivity. About nineteen verbs in English form their past tense with a zero allomorph. About 14 verbs form their past like *cling,* and seven follow the pattern of *ring.* Within these last two groups there are words like *win,* which becomes *won,* and *swim,* which becomes *swam.* We can also find words similar to *win* and *swim* that are quite regular in the past: *pin* and *trim.* But virtually all of the verbs that end in *-ing* form their past in *-ang* or *-ung.* There are approximately 10 of these *-ing* verbs.

The productivity of the *-ang* and *-ung* forms proves that new forms are not necessarily assimilated to the largest productive class. Where a small group of common words exist as a category by virtue of their great phonetic similarity and their morphological consistency, a new word having the same degree of phonetic similarity may be treated according to this special rule. *Ox : oxen* is not similarly productive, but probably would be if there were just one other form like *box : boxen,* and the competing *fox : foxes* did not exist. With *mot,* the zero allomorph is not productive because although it applies to more cases than are covered by the *-ing* verbs, it is not so good a rule in the sense that it is not so consistent. The final /-t/, which is the only common phonetic element, does not invariably lead to a zero allomorph, as witness *pit : pitted, pat : patted,* and many others.

Although the adults were uniform in their application of *-er* and *-est* to form the comparative and superlative of the adjective, children did not seem to have these patterns under control unless they were given both the adjective and the comparative form. With this information, some of them could supply the superlative.

Derivation is likewise a process little used by children at this period when the derivational endings would compete with the inflectional suffixes they are in the process of acquiring. Instead, they compound words, using the primary and tertiary accent pattern commonly found in words like *bláckboàrd.*

The last part of the experiment was designed to see if the children were aware of the separate elements in the compound words in their vocabulary. Most of these children were at the stage where they explained an object's name by stating its major function or salient feature: a blackboard is called a *blackboard* because you write on it. In the older group, a few children had noticed the separate parts of the compound words and assigned to them meanings that were not necessarily connected with the word's etymology or with the meaning the morphemes may have in later life. Not many adults feel that Friday is the day for frying things, yet a number admit to having thought so as children.

These last considerations were, however, tangential to the main problem of investigating the child's grasp of English morphological rules and describing the evolution of those rules. The picture that emerged was one of consistency, regularity, and simplicity. The children did not treat new words according to idiosyncratic pattern. They did not model new words on patterns that appear infrequently. Where they provided inflectional endings, their best performance was with those forms that are the most regular and have the fewest variants. With the morphemes that have several allomorphs, they could handle forms calling for the most common of those allomorphs long before they could deal with allomorphs that appear in a limited distribution range.

The Ontogeny of English Phrase Structure: The First Phase

Martin D. S. Braine

Students of infants and of language have long wondered over the fact that a structure of such enormous formal complexity as language is so readily learned by organisms whose available intellectual resources appear in other respects quite limited.[1] While a certain amount of work has been done on phonological development, and there has been much speculation about the acquisition of "meanings," development at the morphological and syntactic levels has been relatively little studied.[2] Yet it is perhaps the development at these levels that is the most striking and puzzling.

Before the question how the child learns can be broached, the question what the child learns has to be answered. The question "What is learned?" can be answered at two levels. The first answer has to be a description of the structure of the language at successive stages of development, and the task is purely one for structural linguistics. At a more interpretative level, the question "What is learned?" is answered by a statement of the nature of the stimulus attributes and relationships which the child

From *Language*, **39**, 1, 1963, Linguistic Society of America. Reprinted by permission of the Linguistic Society of America.

[1] I am deeply indebted to Dr. and Mrs. Chaim Shatan, Dr. Dorothy Kipnis, and Mrs. Harold L. Williams, parents of the children, for their careful record keeping and continuous cooperation over a long period. The investigation was supported in part by USPHS small research grant M-5116(A) from the National Institute of Mental Health, Public Health Service.

[2] D. McCarthy, "Language development in children," in *Manual of child psychology* (ed. L. Carmichael; New York, 1954), reviews a number of studies which employ traditional grammatical categories instead of treating the child's speech as sui generis. Of greater interest are a number of studies of children's knowledge of English inflexional rules, reviewed by J. Berko and R. W. Brown, "Psycholinguistic research methods," in *Handbook of research methods in child development* (ed. P. H. Mussen; New York, 1960); but these studies use subjects at least three or four years old, who have already mastered much of English phrase structure. Some corpora of utterances by children who seem somewhat more advanced than those reported here have been recently discussed by R. W. Brown and C. Fraser, "The acquisition of syntax," in *Verbal learning and verbal behavior* (ed. C. N. Cofer; New York, 1962), and also by W. Miller and S. Ervin, "The development of grammar in child language," in *The acquisition of language, Child development monographs* (ed. U. Bellugi and R. W. Brown; in press). Miller and Ervin's paper came to my attention after this article was written; they note some of the same phenomena discussed here. Their term "operator" appears to correspond to my term "pivot."

learns to distinguish; at this level the task is as much psychological as linguistic, and the answer should in some sense 'explain' why the grammar at a particular stage has the structure that it has.

The present paper reports and attempts to interpret the structural characteristics of the first word combinations uttered by three children followed by the writer from about 18 months of age. In the analysis of the data, the structural features of the corpora will first be described, then the sequence of development, and finally, from the description of structure an attempt will be made to infer what was learned.

To provide a common time scale for each child the month in which the first word combination (i.e. utterance containing two or more words) was uttered will be called the "first month"; this month will be taken as the starting point in all references to the time of an event, e.g. "first four months." The "first phase" in these children refers to the first four or five months on this time scale, and is defined statistically by a low rate of increase in the number of word combinations. In each child the number of different word combinations at first increased slowly and then showed a sudden upsurge around the fifth or sixth month. For example, the cumulative number of Gregory's recorded different word combinations in successive months was 14, 24, 54, 89, 350, 1400, 2500+, . . . , and undoubtedly the sampling was more complete in the earlier than the later months. In each child the upsurge in the number of different word combinations in the fifth and sixth months was accompanied by a marked increase in the structural complexity of utterances. The first phase appears to be fairly well delineated, being characterized not only by a particular temporal span and slow increase in the number of word combinations, but also by a typical and simple structural property which it is the purpose of this paper to describe.

PROCEDURE

GATHERING OF THE CORPORA.

In the case of two children, Gregory and Andrew, the mother or both parents maintained a seriatim written record of their child's spontaneous comprehensible utterances. A "spontaneous" utterance was defined as any utterance which was not a direct imitation or repetition of something said by another person in the previous few seconds. A "comprehensible" utterance was defined as any utterance which the parent could identify with considerable confidence as an attempt to say an English word or morpheme, or a string of English words or morphemes. The parents were instructed not to attempt to represent pronunciation, but merely to record in conventional spelling the word or sequence of words they heard the child say. In the case of word combinations the parents also recorded a paraphrase into ordinary English indicating what they understood by the child's utterance. The written record of utterances was started when the child had an estimated vocabulary of 10–20 single-word utterances (i.e. before the first word combination appeared).[3]

---

[3] No tape recordings were made of Gregory and Andrew in the early months because of the uneconomically large number of hours spent in recording and listening that would have been required to obtain the small number of word combinations at the child's command. A few tape

In addition to listing the utterances, the parents also recorded how often each utterance occurred (up to five times). The measure of frequency was included to provide an internal check on the accuracy of the record; it was assumed that utterances heard several times would be less likely to be erroneously recorded than those heard only once. Since the few word combinations that occurred only once did not differ from the others in any discernible way, no distinction will be made when discussing the corpora between utterances occurring once and those occurring many times.

In the case of the third child, Steven, a similar written record was soon abandoned, primarily because serious question arose whether certain sounds were properly identifiable as words. To resolve this question required investigation of phonetic regularities in Steven's speech. The entire corpus was therefore tape-recorded. The material discussed here was obtained in twelve play sessions of about four hours total duration, spaced over a four-week period during the fourth and fifth months. During the play sessions Steven's mother kept a running record of what she understood Steven to say; morpheme identifications were based on a comparison of her written record with the sounds on the tape, made in the light of what had been learned about the phonetic characteristics of Steven's speech.

The fact that the data on Steven were tape-recorded should not mislead the reader into thinking that the morpheme identifications are necessarily more reliable in his case. The major factor affecting the certainty with which a child's words can be identified is the clarity with which he speaks, and Gregory and Andrew spoke more clearly than Steven.

At the time of their first word combination two of the children were 19 months old and the third 20 months.[4]

"WORD" AND "WORD COMBINATION".

On the assumption that the morphological units of the child's speech might be longer, but would probably not be shorter than the morphemes of adult English, the following somewhat crude distributional criterion was adopted for a "word" (or 'morpheme'— no distinction between "word" and "morpheme" will be made for the child's language). Those segments are considered "words" which are the longest segments that cannot be divided into two or more parts of which both are English morphemes that

---

recordings were made in the fifth month, and after the sixth month a high proportion of each corpus was tape-recorded, the written record being eventually abandoned as no longer practicable. This later material is not discussed here. Comparison of the written record with tape recordings made at the same age revealed that constructions present in the one were always present in the other, and with about equal frequency, a fact which is evidence of the reliability of the written records.

[4] The procedure described leads to a lexical and not a phonemic representation of morphemes. With very young children there are reasons for not making a phonemic analysis preparatory to an investigation at the morphological and syntactic levels. For example, it is not easy to use the 21-month-old as an informant who gives same-different judgments to questions. Moreover, the contrasts that exist are not constant over time. The strong likelihood that a child may hear contrasts which he cannot produce not only means that partially separate analyses of receptive and productive functions would be necessary, but may also lead to a special situation in which phonemic strings would frequently have to be inferred from lexical ones.

occur in the corpus independently of the others. Thus ice cream and all gone are each classified as one word in Gregory's speech, since neither ice nor cream, nor all nor gone, occur in other contexts or alone. However, for Andrew all gone is classified as a combination of two words, since gone occurs by itself, and all occurs independently in all wet, all dressed, etc. In line with the criterion, the few expressions in which only one part occurs elsewhere (like English *cranberry*) are treated as single units.

In writing the children's utterances, the morphemic status will be indicated by spacing: where English words are run together (e.g., *howareyou*), they are not separate units by the above criterion.

GRAMMATICAL STRUCTURE

GREGORY.

Table 1 summarizes the 89 word combinations uttered by Gregory during the first four months. Over two-thirds contain one or another of a small group of words in first position. Thus, *byebye* occurs in 31 combinations, always in first position; *see* occurs in 15 combinations, always (except for the exclamatory *ohmy see*) in first position; similarly *allgone, big, my, pretty, more, hi,* and *nightnight* recur in first position in two or more combinations. These words will be called 'pivot' words, since the bulk of the word combinations appear to be formed by using them as pivots to which other words are attached as required. There is some communality among the words that follow the pivots: six of the words that follow *see* also occur after *byebye;* most or all of the words that follow *hi, my, big, pretty* are also to be found after *byebye,* and some after other pivot words. Although none of the five words that follow *allgone* occur after other pivots, this is probably accidental (cf. *allgone shoe* and *see sock, allgone lettuce* and *byebye celery, more melon, my milk*). The evidence suggests that the pivot words occupying utterance-initial position have essentially similar privileges of occurence. Accordingly, there is a basis for defining two primitive word classes: a class of pivots (P) to which a few frequently occurring words belong, and a complementary class which has many members, few of which recur in more than one or two different combinations (49 different words follow pivots, 34 of which occur in only one combination.) The latter class will be called the X-class.

Table 1   Gregory's Word Combinations, First Four Months

14 combinations with see (—), e.g.	my mommy	nightnight office	hi plane	allgone shoe
see boy	my daddy	nightnight boat	hi mommy	allgone vitamins
see sock	my milk			allgone egg
see hot		31 combinations	big boss	allgone lettuce
	do it	with byebye (—),	big boat	allgone watch
	push it	e.g.	big bus	
pretty boat	close it	byebye plane		20 unclassified, e.g.
pretty fan	buzz it	byebye man	more taxi	mommy sleep
	move it	byebye hot	more melon	milk cup, ohmy see

All words which occur in the frame P(—) also occur as single-word utterances, whereas some of the pivots do not occur alone. There is, therefore, a basis for identifying the X-class with the class of single-word utterances.

Of the 89 word combinations, 64 are PX sequences. Five of the remaining combinations have a recurring element in utterance-final position: *do it, push it, close it,* etc. These appear to exemplify the same kind of pivotal construction as the previous combinations discussed, except that now the pivot is in the final position. *Do, push, close,* etc., all occur as single-word utterances; *it* does not occur by itself. These five combinations may therefore be classified as XP sequences. The remaining 20 combinations appear to have no determinable structure. Some of them are greetings or exclamations (e.g. *hi howareyou*), some are English compound words (e.g. *mail man*), others may well be early cases of later developing forms.

There is no overlap between the 49 words occurring in the frame P(—) and the five words occurring in (—)P. This lack of overlap may be accidental (the fact that the five words which follow *allgone* fail to occur following other first-position pivots has already been assumed to be accidental). However, it is primarily English nouns and adjectives that occur in the context P(—), whereas the words occurring in (—)P are all English verbs; Gregory may be adumbrating a substantive-verb distinction within the X-class. Using subscripts to denote subclasses, the structures employed by Gregory may be summarized as P_1X, XP_2, or, if one chooses to credit him with the substantive-verb distinction, P_1X_1, X_2P_2.

ANDREW.

Andrew's word combinations during the first five months are listed in Table 2. About half the combinations contain *all, I, see, other, no,* or *more* in utterance-initial position; the pivotal mode of construction seems quite comparable to Gregory's, although the individual words are not the same. However, while there was only one second-position pivot in Gregory's corpus, Andrew seems to have several, one of which is a phrase which itself has internal positional structure (*there,* preceded by *down, in, on,* or *up*).

There is some overlap between the sets of words that follow the various first-position pivots, e.g. *all fix* and *no fix, all wet* and *no wet, all shut* and *I shut, hi màma* and *no mama;* but these are the only examples (cf. *other bread* and *more toast; other milk, more juice, no water*). There is one case of overlap between the words preceding the second-position pivots: *light off* and *light up there.* More substantial overlap is present between the sets of words preceding second-position pivots and following first-position pivots: 9 of the 19 words that occur in the context (—)P also occur in the context P(—), e.g. *pants off* and *other pants, water off* and *no water, hot in there* and *more hot, sit down there* and *I sit.* Andrew's pivotal constructions may therefore be summarized by the formulae P_1X and XP_2. All words occuring in either P_1(—) or (—)P_2 also occur as single-word utterances; as with Gregory, the X-class may be identified with the class of single-word utterances.[5] But unlike Gregory, there is

---

[5] Some of the pivots (e.g. *more*) occur as single-word utterances, others (e.g. *all*) do not. Those that occur alone seem also to occur as X-words in word combinations (e.g. *no more, more down there*); they can therefore properly be regarded as belonging to both classes.

Table 2   Andrew's Word Combinations, First Five Months

Pivotal Constructions

all broke	no bed	more car[d]	other bib	airplane by[f]
all buttoned	no down[a]	more cereal	other bread	siren by
all clean	no fix	more cookie	other milk	
all done	no home	more fish	other pants	mail come
all dressed	no mama[b]	more high[e]	other part	mama come
all dry	no more	more hot	other piece	
all fix	no pee	more juice	other pocket	clock on there
all gone	no plug	more read	other shirt	up on there
all messy	no water	more sing	other shoe	hot in there
all shut	no wet[c]	more toast	other side	milk in there
all through		more walk		light up there
all wet			boot off	fall down there
	see baby		light off	kitty down there
	see pretty	hi Calico	pants off	more down there
I see	see train	hi mama	shirt off	sit down there
I shut		hi papa	shoe off	cover down there
I sit			water off	other cover down there

Other Utterances

airplane all gone	byebye back	what's that	look at this
Calico all gone	byebye Calico	what's this	outside more
Calico all done[g]	byebye car	mail man	pants change
salt all shut	byebye papa	mail car	dry pants
all done milk	Calico byebye	our car	off bib
all done now	papa byebye	our door	down there
all gone juice		papa away	up on there some more
all gone outside[h]			
all gone pacifier			

[a] "Don't put me down."
[b] "I don't want to go to mama."
[c] "I'm not wet."
[d] "Drive around some more."
[e] "There's more up there."
[f] "A plane is flying past."
[g] Said after the death of Calico the cat.
[h] Said when the door is shut: "The outside is all gone."

nothing to indicate that Andrew is as yet developing anything like a substantive-verb contrast.

Of the 102 combinations, 73 are pivotal constructions. In a further 9 combinations a pivotal construction (*all* X) occurs as an immediate constituent of a longer utterance; these (and also *other cover down there*, listed among the pivotal constructions) seem to be early examples of more complex forms belonging to the next phase of development. The remaining 20 combinations have not been classified. Some of them may contain pivot words (e.g. *our car, our door*).[6]

STEVEN.

Table 3 lists Steven's identifiable word combinations, recorded in twelve play sessions during the fourth and fifth months. The corpus was tape-recorded because the phonetic characteristics of Steven's speech made the morphemic status of parts of his utterances uncertain. In discussing these characteristics, phonetic symbols will be used. Since no phonemic analysis was made to determine what contrasts he controlled, these symbols are to be understood as identifications by English-speaking listeners; they provide only an approximate indication of the sounds. The lack of a phonemic analysis also makes it impossible to distinguish clearly between allophonic and allomorphic variation.

Steven's pronunciation is extremely variable—much more so than either Gregory's or Andrew's. In particular the last consonant of *that* and *it* takes a variety of forms: [t, d, h, ?, ð, tš, ts, z, tz]. Much of this variation is probably allophonic, but a terminal sibilant also appears occasionally after *here* and *there*. Separate morphemic status is not assigned to the terminal sibilant, because forms with and without the sibilant are in free variation, and also because the terminal sibilant, present in the third and fourth months, disappears completely in the fifth and sixth months and reappears only when *is* occurs in other contexts in his speech. In addition to the allomorphs *it ~ its, here ~ heres*, etc., it is possible that *it* and *that* may not be independent morphemes, since there appear to be occasional intermediate forms, e.g. [het, ditz]. (In the latter case, Steven may be trying to say *this*.) The general character of the combinations listed in Table 3 would not be altered by treating *it* and *that* as allomorphs.

From a grammatical point of view the most interesting phonological feature of Steven's speech is the periodic occurrence, at the beginning or in the middle of utterances, of either a front-central vowel, or, somewhat less often, of [d] or [t] followed by a front or central vowel. Steven's family usually identified these as English words—as *a* or *the* before nouns, as *I* before *want, see, get*, as *to* in such contexts as *want* (—) *do*, as *it* in context *want* (—) *high* or *want* (—) *up*, and as *is* or *of* in appropriate other contexts. Before *that, there, Lucy*, etc., these phonetic entities could not be interpreted. One or another of these elements is present in over 40% of Steven's utterances. The tape-recordings indicate that these elements occur before any word, that their phonetic shape is not affected by the class of the following

---

[6] In deciding whether utterances containing infrequently occurring words were pivotal constructions, the writer was sometimes guided by the child's subsequent development. For example, although *mail* occurs three times in first position (*mail man, mail car, mail come*), it is not classified as a pivot because there are no further cases of *mail* in first position in subsequent weeks; on the other hand, although *come* only recurs twice in final position, the subsequent uses of it in final position suggest that it is a pivot. Similarly, in Gregory's corpus (Table 1), although *more* and *pretty* only occur twice, they are regarded as pivots because they recur frequently in initial position before X-words in the next month of Gregory's development.

morpheme and that utterances with and without them are in free variation. While it is quite likely that these elements are an interesting distillate of the unstressed and phonetically often obscure English articles, prepositions, and auxiliary verbs, there is no basis for giving them morphemic status at this stage of Steven's development (although it may be desirable at some later stage). The alternative course will be taken of regarding them as a periodic feature of the intonation pattern. Consistent with this decision is the fact that when these elements occur in utterances of three words or longer, they appear to separate immediate constituents; clearly defined junctures often appear at the same points. Thus, a vowel sometimes occurs at the marked point in *want* (—) *do* and *want* (—) *ride,* but in *want do pon* and *want drive car,* the vowel seems to shift forward: *want do* (—) *pon, want drive* (—) *car.* Similarly there is a vowel

Table 3   Steven's Word Combinations, Tape-Recorded Sample at End of Fourth Month

Pivotal Constructions

want baby	it ball	get ball	there ball	that box
want car	it bang	get Betty	there book	that Dennis
want do	it checker	get doll	there doggie	that doll
want get	it daddy		there doll	that Tommy
want glasses	it Dennis		there high[d]	that truck
want head	it doggie	see ball	there momma	
want high[a]	it doll	see doll	there record	here bed
want horsie	it fall	see record	there trunk	here checker
want jeep	it horsie	see Stevie		here doll
want more	it Kathy		there byebye car	here truck
want page	it Lucy	whoa cards[c]	there daddy truck	
want pon[b]	it record	whoa jeep	there momma truck	Bunny do
want purse	it shock			daddy do
want ride	it truck	more ball	beeppeep bang[e]	momma do
want up		more book	beeppeep car	(want do)
want byebye car				

Other Utterances

bunny do sleep	baby doll	find bear	eat breakfast
Lucy do fun	Betty pon	pon baby	two checker
want do pon[f]	byebye car	pon Betty	Betty byebye car
want drive car	Candy say	sleepy bed	Lucy shutup Lucy shutup Lucy

[a] "Put it up there."
[b] "Put on" or "up on" or both.
[c] "The cards are falling."
[d] "It's up there."
[e] "The car that goes 'beeppeep' is falling."
[f] "I want (you) to put (the jeep) on top."

at the marked point in *there* (—) *byebye car,* but never between *byebye* and *car.* Such marking of immediate constituents, however, has little relevance to the initial phase of development. Neither Gregory's speech nor Andrew's ever shows anything analogous to these elements.

Another feature of Steven's speech which is not present in either Gregory's or Andrew's at this stage is a generalized terminal vocative. No one listening to the play sessions has the least difficulty in distinguishing vocatives from other occurrences of proper names. Whether the intonational cues in Steven's speech alone would suffice to identify vocatives is not clear, since so many other cues are invariably present that it is difficult to find appropriate contrasts in the tape recordings. These terminal vocatives are omitted in Table 3. If one wishes to include them in Steven's grammar, one need only add a rule that, if "S" is an utterance, then "S, (proper name)" is also an utterance.

Table 3 indicates that Steven's word combinations have much the same structural features already described for Gregory and Andrew. Three-quarters of the combinations contain one or another of a small group of words (*want, get, it, there,* etc.) in utterance-initial position. For combinations contain *do* in final position. In a further four combinations a pivotal construction is an immediate constituent of a longer utterance (*bunny do sleep,* etc.). The remaining combinations are not classified.

There is substantial overlap between the sets of words that follow the various first-position pivots. Five of the words that follow *want,* eight that follow *it,* three that follow *see,* and eight that follow *there* occur after more than one pivot: essentially similar privileges of occurrence are therefore indicated for the first-position pivots. Two of the words that precede *do* also occur after first-position pivots. The formulae P_1X and XP_2 again summarize the pivotal constructions. Words occurring in the contexts P_1(—) and (—)*do* also occur as single-word utterances; there is again ground for identifying the X-class with the single-word utterances.

In Steven's corpus there is much more overlap among the sets of X-words that are found with each pivot than in Gregory's and Andrew's. No doubt this is because all Steven's utterances were recorded in special play sessions, so that there was greater constancy in the environmental stimuli eliciting Steven's utterances.

THE COMMON STRUCTURE OF THE THREE CORPORA.
The following structural properties appear to define the initial phase of development in these children.

(a)   There are two word-classes: pivots and X-words. The pivots are few in number; they tend to occur in several word combinations; and each is associated with a particular utterance position. Thus two subclasses are definable, P_1 associated with initial position, and P_2 with final position. The X-class is a large open class containing the child's entire vocabulary except for some of the pivots. X-words tend to recur in relatively few word combinations and do not appear to be tied to a particular utterance position; they occur alone or in the position complementary to that of the pivot word. One but only one of the children (Gregory) gives some evidence for a subdivision of the X-class.

(b)   Single-word utterances are X. Multiword utterances are either P_1X or XP_2, the former being much more frequent (for Gregory the formulae may be P_1X_1, X_2P_2).

The occasional utterances in the corpora that are more complex than the above (where a pivotal construction is an immediate constituent of a longer utterance) are taken to be early examples of constructions belonging to the next phase of development.

Structural formulae in linguistics can be construed in a weak or a strong sense. So far it has been asserted only that the sequences P_1X and XP_2 occur and are characteristic. Students of generative grammar, however, give a stronger interpretation to such formulae: the formula PX asserts that any P "can" occur with any X. To construct and test a generative grammar it is necessary to have information not only about grammatical utterances, but also about ungrammatical ones. Information of the latter sort is difficult enough to obtain with adult informants,[7] and seems clearly out of the question with children as young as these. Nevertheless, although it cannot be proved, it seems quite likely that the formulae P_1X and XP_2 are generative. The only alternative hypothesis is that, in the class of all grammatical sentences, some or all of the pivot words have unique sets of co-occurrents. By the fourth month both Gregory and Andrew had a recorded vocabulary of about 250 words, and internal evidence suggests that the true size may have been two or three times as large.[8] If each set of X-words that occur with a given pivot is a random sample from this class (as the generative interpretation of the formulae implies), very little overlap between any pair of such sets would be expected; even taking into account the fact that some X-words occur much more frequently than others and would, therefore, be more likely to appear in any set taken at random, the amount of overlap to be expected is limited, and, though difficult to estimate, seems unlikely to be greater than that actually found in the corpora. There is, therefore, no reason to think that any of the pivot words have cooccurrents which are unique in any special way (with the possible exception of *it* in Gregory's speech).

An objection which has been raised against the assumption that any pivot can occur with any X-word is that it puts into the children's mouths some implausible

---

[7] A. A. Hill, "Grammaticality," *Word* 17.1–10 (1961); H. Maclay and M. Sleator, "Responses to language: Judgments of grammaticalness," *IJAL* 26.275–82 (1960).

[8] By the end of the second month the recorded vocabulary was sufficiently large that the parents had difficulty in distinguishing which single-word utterances were new, and they recorded many fewer single-word utterances in the third and fourth months than in the second. However, during the first four months 150–200 words were recorded as having been uttered five times or more. There were probably many more less frequently occurring words which were not recorded. Even if the usual rank-frequency relation (Zipf's law, rf = K, in which the constant K approximates the total vocabulary, since it is the rank of the least frequently occurring word) fits the single-word utterances poorly, the total vocabulary must be very substantially greater than that recorded.

expressions which seem highly foreign to English. For example, the formulae would allow Gregory to generate *more hot, big dirty, allgone hot;* Andrew to say *see read, other fix, I shirt;* and Steven to say *that do, there up, high do.* This objection is sometimes based on the idea that the children's utterances are a recall, or delayed imitation, of things they have heard adults say. As against this, there are a number of expressions in the corpora which are sufficiently strange to render it most unlikely that the children had heard them e.g. *see cold, byebye dirty, allgone lettuce, no down, more high, want do pon, there high.* In one child, not reported here, *the* was an early pivot word, yielding such utterances as *the byebye, the up.* Moreover, several 'strange' combinations, similar or identical to utterances generated by the formulae, appear in the fifth and sixth months; examples are *more wet, allgone sticky* (Gregory, after washing his hands), *other fix* (= "fix the other one"), *more page* (= "don't stop reading"), *see stand up* (= "look at me standing up"), *this do* (= "do this"). Manifestly, the strangeness of an utterance is no criterion of its grammaticality at this age.

CONTINUITY WITH LATER DEVELOPMENT.

What is here called the first phase of development has been defined by a certain time period (the first four or five months), a low rate of increase in the number of word combinations, and the presence of a characteristic structural feature (the pivotal construction). In order to justify treating a continuous development as composed of phases described separately, it seems appropriate to add some general remarks about the nature of the next phase.[9]

No claim is made that any discontinuity exists between phases. The pivotaltype of construction continues long after the first five months, and new pivot words develop. However, several developments seem to occur more or less together around the fifth and sixth months. Forms in which pivotal constructions enter as immediate constituents have already been mentioned. The development that has most impressed the writer is the appearance of an increasing number of utterances in which an X-word (e.g. an English noun) occupies both utterance positions. Examples are *man car* ("a man is in the car"), *car bridge* ("the car is under the bridge"), *coffee daddy* ("coffee for daddy"). These are not pivotal constructions,[10] but seem rather to exemplify a primitive sentence form, in which both components can be expanded by a PX = X substitution rule, e.g., *man car* expanded to *other man#car, man#other car.* The large number of two-word utterances of this general type that appear around the sixth month give a random appearance to many word combinations in that phase of development. It may be this sentence form which has misled some observers into

---

[9] The next phase of development in these children will be fully discussed in a subsequent article. See also the longer discussions of children they have followed by Brown and Fraser, op.cit., and Miller and Ervin, op.cit.

[10] They may form constructional homonyms with pivotal constructions, e.g. *bàby cháir* ("little chair"; pivotal construction), usually without an intonation break, and *bàby # cháir* ("the baby is in the chair"). The two constructions, however, certainly cannot always be distinguished from their intonation alone (# is used here and in the text as a general juncture symbol).

suggesting that children's first word combinations are for the most part mere juxtapositions of words without syntactic constraints.[11]

The development of this sentence form may explain the very sharp increase around the fifth or sixth month in the number of different word combinations uttered. Since the X-class is very large, the addition of an XX construction (or of any construction admitting a large open class in both positions) to the existing PX and XP constructions would at once greatly increase the number of word combinations that the grammar is capable of generating. The statistical change is, therefore, explicable as a consequence of structural change.

SEQUENCE OF DEVELOPMENT

The order of appearance of the various word combinations shows a definite pattern. Gregory's third word combination was *see hat;* the next three were *see sock, see horsie,* and *see boy;* ten of his first 13 combinations contain *see* in first position. *Byebye plane,* the first word combination containing *byebye,* appeared in the third month; during the remainder of the month nine other combinations occurred containing *byebye* in first position. *Do it, push it,* and *close it* were all uttered at about the same time.

In the development of Gregory's language, it appears that from time to time a particular word is singled out, placed in a certain position, and combined with a number of other words in turn, often in quick succession. The words that are singled out in this way are of course the pivots. This sequence of development appears to be quite general. The majority of Steven's first word combinations contain *want* in first position. The same sequence occurs in Andrew's speech: *all* appeared in the first month, *other* did not appear until the third month and occurred in that month in five contexts; *no* and *there* appeared for the first time in the fourth month, both being quickly used in a number of different combinations. Less systematic observations on a number of other children suggest that this kind of development is quite typical of the initial stages of first-language learning (at least for the English language).

Throughout the first few months there is a large expansion of vocabulary. It seems clear that in this period the language expands rapidly in vocabulary by adding new members to the X-class, and that it develops structurally by singling out at intervals new pivot words.

Both functionally and developmentally, the distinction between open and closed word classes in the adult language (nouns, verbs, and adjectives vs. pronouns, prepositions, auxiliary verbs, etc.) seems quite parallel to that between X-words and pivots. The closed classes have relatively few members, and tend to serve in sentences as frames for the open-class words; historically their membership changes slowly. The

---

[11] Actually there are two parts to this assertion: (a) that the children learn the positions of certain words, and (b) that a sentence typically has just two positions—first and last. But (b) needs no discussion when utterances are just two words long. In experiments in children's learning of simple artificial languages, reported elsewhere (Braine, "On learning the grammatical order of words", *Psychological review,* in press) learning positions is explored when "position" in a sentence is defined by successive fractionations, i.e. when a sentence has just two positions, each of which may be occupied by a word or a phrase, and when each constituent phrase in turn may be divided into two positions.

pivots seem to play a similar role in utterances, also have few members, and add to their membership slowly.

WHAT IS LEARNED

It is suggested that a sufficient explanation of the structural features of the first phase is provided by the single assumption that the children have learned the positions of the pivot words, i.e. have learned that each of a small number of words "belongs" or "is right" in a particular one of two sentence positions.[11] While the evidence provided by the corpora might suffice without argument, it seems nevertheless desirable to make explicit the line of reasoning that leads to this inference.

In general, what a subject has learned is diagnosed from the generalizations that he makes. Thus, a naive rat, trained to jump for food towards an upright triangle in preference to a circle, will, when later confronted with a square and a circle, jump towards the square; but when the choices are an inverted triangle and a circle his jumps are randomly directed. The rat's generalizations provide information about what he must have learned in the original training: to jump towards something that an upright triangle shares with a square and does not share with an inverted triangle. Similarly, a child who has learned to indicate the past only by appending /id/, /d/, or /t/ to verbs would be expected to construct by generalization 'incorrect' forms like *singed* and *breaked*, and to inflect nonsense words used as verbs in response to questions in appropriately designed experiments, e.g. *This man is ricking. He did the same thing yesterday. Yesterday he (—).*[12]

What generalization phenomena would be expected to follow from the learning merely of the position of a word? The principal expectation is that the word would be used freely in the position involved, i.e. there should be no restriction on the words appearing in the complementary position. Thus, if *a* is a word whose position (first position, say) has been learned, then the frame *a* (—) should admit any word in the vocabulary. If this condition does not hold, i.e. if there is some set of words k_1, k_2, k_3, etc. which occur in the frame *a* (—) and another set l_1, l_2, l_3, etc., which cannot occur in this frame, then either the position of *a* has not been learned (in which case there is some other explanation for the occurrence of ak_1, ak_2, etc.[13]), or something more has been learned over and above the learning of the position of *a* (which accounts for the exclusion of al_1, al_2, etc.[14]).

While a word whose position is learned would be expected to occur in that position with some regularity, the consistency with which a word occurs in a position is not

---

[12] J. Berko, "The child's learning of English morphology," *Word* 14.150–77 (1958).

[13] For example, in the context (—) *boat*, Gregory places *byebye, pretty, nightnight*, and *big*. These are all pivots. Since the evidence indicates that not any word can precede *boat*, but only a small set, there is no basis for assuming that the position of *boat* has been learned. The occurrence of the specific utterances *byebye boat, pretty boat*, etc., can better be explained by assuming that the positions of *byebye, pretty*, etc. have been learned.

[14] For example, in the context (—) *it*, Gregory places *do, push, close, buzz, move*, and in the context P_1(—) he places such words as *boy, dirty, plane, hurt, mommy*, etc. If the occurrence of only verbs before *it* is not accidental, Gregory has not learned merely the position of *it*, but something more which limits its environment to English verbs.

by itself a useful criterion of whether its position has been learned. A word may occur consistently in a specific position without its position necessarily having been learned (e.g. *boat* in Gregory's corpus). Conversely, the fact that a word occurs in both positions is not necessarily a bar to the assumption that the child has learned that it is "right" in one of these positions, since a word may generalize freely in one position and occur only in specific contexts in the other position (e.g. *more* in Andrew's corpus seems to occur freely when in first position, but in second position occurs only in *no more*, i.e. following a pivot). The inference that the position of a word has been learned must be based primarily on the degree to which the word is free from limitation to specific contexts when it appears in a particular position.

It is clear from the earlier discussion of the grammatical structure that the pivots and only these tend to recur in particular positions without limitations on their context. Frames $P_1(—)$ and $(—)P_2$, which freely accept words in the vocabulary, are precisely the forms which would be expected if the children had learned the positions of a few words, and learned nothing else which would limit the occupancy of the complementary position.

CONCLUSION

The simplest account of the phenomena of the first phase of development seems to be as follows: out of the moderately large vocabulary at his disposal, the child learns, one at a time, that each of a small number of words belongs in a particular position in an utterance. He therefore places them there, and, since he has not learned anything else about what goeswhere in an utterance, the complementary position is taken by any single-word utterance in his vocabulary, the choice determined only by the physical and social stimuli that elicit the utterance. As a consequence of this learning, the word combinations that are uttered have a characteristic structure containing two parts of speech. One part of speech, here called pivot, comprises the small number of words whose position has been learned. The other, here called the X-class, is a part of speech mainly in a residual sense, and consists of the entire vocabulary, except for some of the pivots. During this first phase the language grows structurally by the formation of new pivot words, i.e. by the child's learning the position of new words. The language grows in vocabulary by adding the X-class.

A Cross-Sectional Study of the Acquisition of Grammatical Morphemes in Child Speech

Jill G. de Villiers and Peter A. de Villiers

Speech samples were taken from 21 children aged 16–40 months covering a wide range of mean utterance length. Presence or absence of 14 grammatical morphemes in linguistic and nonlinguistic obligatory contexts was scored. Order of acquisition of the morphemes was determined using two different criteria. The rank-orderings obtained correlated very highly with a previously determined order of acquisition for three children studied longitudinally. Age did not add to the predictiveness of mean length of utterance alone for grammatical development in terms of which morphemes were correctly used. The approximately invariant order of acquisition for the fourteen morphemes is discussed in terms of three possible determinants of this order. Frequency of use in parental speech showed no correlation with order of acquisition, but grammatical and semantic complexity both correlated highly and acquisition order.

INTRODUCTION

Brown (1973) describes the acquisition of 14 grammatical morphemes in the speech of three children, Adam, Eve, and Sarah, who were studied longitudinally. Speech samples were taken every 1 or 2 weeks from the time each child was about 2 years old, and these transcripts provided the data for the calculation of mean length of utterance (MLU) in terms of number of morphemes per utterance and for tracing the use of specific grammatical morphemes. The fourteen morphemes that Brown focuses on are the following: the present progressive inflection *-ing;* third person singular, both regular *-s* and irregular, e.g., *has;* past tenses, both regular *-d* and irregular, e.g., *went* or *fell;* the copula and auxiliary *be,* both contractible and uncontractible forms; the articles *a* and *the;* the prepositions *in* and *on;* and the regular plural and possessive inflections *-s.*

For each of these morphemes Brown defines obligatory contexts in terms of both linguistic constraints and the situation in which the utterance was made, i.e., in those contexts, for an adult, the morpheme would be obligatory in speech. Brown examined use of the morphemes in obligatory contexts as opposed to frequency of use in any construction since the latter depends largely on the topic of conversation in small

From *Journal of Psycholinguistic Research,* **2,** 3, 1973 Plenum Publishing Corporation, 1973. Reprinted by permission of Plenum Publishing Corporation.

This research was supported in part by PHS grant HD-02908 from the National Institute of Child Health and Development.

samples of child speech. Presence or absence of a morpheme in a context in which it is obligatory determines what the child *is able* to say as opposed to what the child *chooses* to say. Brown took as his criterion for acquisition of a morpheme its presence in 90% or more of such obligatory contexts in three successive speech samples from a particular child. The morphemes were then ranked in order of acquisition for each child and rank-order correlations (Spearman's rho) among the three orderings were calculated. Brown found a remarkable amount of invariance in the order of acquisition, since the rho values were as follows: for Adam and Sarah, + 0.88; for Adam and Eve, + 0.86; and for Eve and Sarah, + 0.87.

Unfortunately there are few comparable cross-sectional studies on the acquisition of these morphemes. Menyuk (1969), for example, does not consider all of these morphemes, and for those that she studied, she reports only the percentage of children at a given age who used a particular construction *at all*. This makes the data somewhat difficult to interpret as Cazden (1968) and Brown (in press) have shown that acquisition of most of the grammatical morphemes is a gradual process, the time from the first appearance of a morpheme to its consistent use in 90% of obligatory contexts spanning as long as a year.

If the order of morpheme acquisition is almost invariant, then taking a sample of speech from a child with a given MLU, one should be able to predict which morphemes will be present to criterion and which will not. In addition, it might be possible to predict the relative ordering of those morphemes still below criterion, if the growth curves of the morphemes are similar in shape.

The purpose of the present study is to provide cross-sectional data on the use of these fourteen morphemes in obligatory contexts in early child speech. Brown suggests that MLU and age taken together might be a better predictor of the acquisition of grammatical morphemes than either is alone, and cross-sectional data provide a clear test of this hypothesis.

METHOD

SUBJECTS

The subjects were 21 English-speaking children aged between 16 and 40 months who had participated in a previous study in which speech samples were taken from two 1½ hour play sessions.

PROCEDURE

The speech samples varied in size from 168 to 900 utterances with a mean of 360 utterances. The mean length of utterance was calculated for each child and the fourteen grammatical morphemes were scored as present or absent in obligatory contexts. To reduce variability, only transcripts providing five or more obligatory contexts for a given morpheme were used for that morpheme. For example, a speech sample that provided only one or two possible contexts for the plural inflection was not included in the analysis for plurals. Full details of obligatory contexts for each of the 14 morphemes are provided by Brown (in press), but the regular plural inflection -*s* serves as an illustration of these. A linguistic obligatory context for the plural might be a sentence including the words "two——" or "some——", or one in which the number of the subject constrained the number of the predicate, e.g., "They are ——." A nonlinguistic context might consist of the child's pointing to a group of identical objects, or requesting items that normally occur in the plural, such as socks. Occasionally children used an unmarked verb for which some inflection was clearly required, but unless it was clear from the context which morpheme had been omitted, these cases were discarded from the analysis.

RESULTS

Table 1 shows the percentages of obligatory contexts in which each morpheme was used by each child. The number of obligatory contexts for each morpheme was in general smaller in lower MLU samples because the constraints and variety of linguistic contexts that define obligation are themselves acquired over time.
We could not use Brown's criterion for acquisition of 90% presence in three successive speech samples since we only had one transcript of sufficient size for each child. The data were also too variable to modify the criterion for acquisition to 90% presence in three successive children ranked according to MLU. Therefore two different procedures for ordering the morphemes were used.

1. The morphemes were first ranked according to the lowest MLU sample at which each morpheme first occurred in 90% or more or the obligatory contexts. When more than one morpheme reached this criterion at the same MLU, the ranks were tied.
2. The second procedure used more of the data in that the percentages for each morpheme were summed across all the children and averaged, and then these mean percentages were ranked. This assumes that the morphemes have similar growth curves and maintain roughly the same relative ranking at each MLU value. Table 1 shows that some of the morphemes, in particular the articles, contractible and uncontractible copula, and the third person regular, do show gradual growth curves. Other morphemes have either very sparse data or reach criterion very early. Cazden (1968) has evidence that acquisition curves for the progressive, possessive, and plural inflections, and for the regular past and third person singular forms are also fairly similar and gradual for Sarah, while Brown (in press) shows similar curves for *in* and *on* for longitudinal data from Eve.

Table 2 shows the rank orderings of the 14 morphemes by the above two methods together with the average ranking for the three children studied by Brown. The rank-order correlations among the three orderings are as follows: Brown's data and method I, + 0.84; Brown's data and method II, + 0.78; method I and method II,

Table 1   Percentage of Obligatory Contexts for Each Morpheme in Which that Morpheme Was Correctly Used by Each Child[a]

Child	MLU	Age in Months	Size of Speech Sample	Present Progressive -ing	Preposition on	Plural -s	Preposition in	Past Irregular	Articles a and the	Possessive -s	3rd Person Irregular	Contractible Copula	Past Regular -ed	3rd Person Regular -s	Uncontractible Copula	Contractible Auxiliary	Uncontractible Auxiliary	Mean Percentage Across all Morphemes
Faryl	1.25	19	335	100		69.2			7.2	0		0						19.1
Zoe	1.31	16	908		92.8	91.6			2.8	0		3.5	44.4			0		41.9
Joshua	1.44	21	433		97.7	24.1	100		6.6					12.5				48.2
Jessica	1.58	19.5	297			84.0			2.0									17.2
Rachel	2.04	26	818	93.3	87.2	98.6	88.2	10.0	30.3			28.2		33.3	36.8	42.8		50.6
Hilary	2.08	26	290	58.3		33.3		100	46.5			55.8	0	0	33.3			46.2
Caleb	2.24	30	221	95.4	80.0	93.8	100		20.8			7.9	12.5	20.0				59.7
Chris	2.31	28	234	100	100	100	100	100	51.3			22.2		0	0			60.7
John	2.45	31	284		83.3	100			73.8			78.2		75.0	5.6			79.4
Karen	2.79	30	270		100	93.6	100		83.5			87.5		55.5	60.0		0	75.5
Mary	2.86	32	214		100	100	100		78.2			13.9			37.5			65.3
Andrew	2.87	28	254	100	100	93.5	100		64.6			80.8		14.3	16.6	53.3		81.2
Hannah	2.99	21	238	100	100	92.7	100		91.3			75.3		42.8		57.1		63.9
Eric	3.03	33	424	100	100	100	100	23.0	80.1	100	20.0	66.6			60.0			73.3
Amy	3.16	28.5	494	100	100	100	100	85.7	81.5		94.7	90.9	80.0	88.5		56.7	0	86.6
Danielle	3.68	30	564	91.7	100	80.0	95.4	93.3	83.2			45.3	88.8		43.9			65.6
Alexi	3.94	26	227		100	100	100		84.7	100		97.8						97.1
Elizabeth	4.10	33.5	200	85.7		92.3	100		82.9			71.4			87.5			88.5
George	4.23	29.5	444			96.6		48.3	98.6		87.5	94.9	100	94.3	84.7			89.4
Mindy	4.29	36	168	100		100	100	100	94.2			93.8	100	90.0	100			98.7
Michael	4.67	40	213			96.9	100		100			100	100	100	100	35.0	0	99.5
Mean percentage for each morpheme				87.5	95.7	87.6	98.9	70.0	60.2	50.0	67.4	55.7	60.8	44.7	51.2	35.0	0	

[a] The children are ordered according to MLU. Also shown are the age of each child, the number of utterances in the speech samples, and the mean percentages of morphemes correctly used by each child. The mean percentages of obligatory contexts in which a particular morpheme was used by all of the children is also given.

+ 0.87. The high correlation between the two ordering procedures suggests that at any given MLU the morphemes show a fairly similar ordering, as would be expected if the acquisition curves for the morphemes are similar not just for a single child, but for all the children taken together.

The children were ranked according to age, MLU, and the total percentage of the 14 grammatical morphemes that appeared in obligatory contexts in their speech. The rank-order correlation between age and MLU for the children in this study is + 0.76. The correlation between age and percentage of morphemes used is + 0.68, and that between MLU and morphemes is + 0.92. All the correlations reported are Spearman rank-order correlations corrected for ties. If age is partialled out as a variable in the correlation between MLU and morpheme percentages, using a Kendall partial-correlation procedure, the correlation is reduced by only a negligible amount to + 0.85.

DICUSSION

There is a high degree of correspondence between the orderings found in the present study and the ordering reported by Brown (in press). In fact, the correlations obtained between the two studies approach the magnitude of those found among the three children in Brown's longitudinal study. The major discrepancy between the present

Table 2   Order of Acquistion of the 14 Morphemes from Brown's Longitudinal Study, and in Terms of the Two Ordering Procedures Used in the Present Study

The 14 Grammatical Morphemes	Average Rank-Ordering for the Three Children Studied Longitudinally (Brown, in press)	Rank-Ordering for the Children in the the Present Study by Method I	by Method II
Present progressive	1	2	4
on	2.5	2	2
in	2.5	4	1
Plural	4	2	3
Past irregular	5	5	5
Possessive	6	7	11
Uncontractible copula	7	12	10
Articles	8	6	8
Past regular	9	10.5	7
3rd Person regular	10	10.5	12
3rd Person irregular	11	8.5	6
Uncontractible auxiliary	12	14	14
Contractible copula	13	8.5	9
Contractible auxiliary	14	13	13

data and those of Brown is the superiority of contractible over uncontractible forms of the copula and auxiliary *be*. This superiority was clear for 8 of the 12 children who had both types of context for the copula, with one tie. Brown found the reverse, and explains his results in terms of Labov's (1969) description of the grammar of non-standard Negro-English. The actual arguments are very complex, but the basic idea is that contractibles are more difficult to produce because an extra rule is required to contract them. Brown also argues that since uncontractibles constitute a separate syllable in speech, while contractibles do not, the former morpheme is more percepti-ble in the verbal input to the child and might therefore be learned first. On the other hand, it might be argued that if there is any limitation on the number of syllables per utterance in early child speech, the contractible might precede the uncontractible in production. The data from Brown are fairly sparse in the case of the auxiliaries, but in both studies the actual number of obligatory contexts produced for these construc-tions is much smaller than for the other morphemes and this alone might explain the discrepancy in the results. The number of phonological and grammatical forms of these morphemes of *be* is very great, and without a finer-grained analysis and a bigger speech sample, no firm conclusions can be drawn about the relative difficulty of the contractible and uncontractible forms.

It is apparent that MLU is a far better predictor of the acquisition of the 14 morphemes in the early stages of language development than is chronological age, which adds very little to the predictiveness of MLU alone. The high correlation between MLU and the overall percentage of the 14 morphemes that the children use correctly is not without significance, although MLU takes morphemes as its unit of measurement. There are many more grammatical morphemes in child speech which are not coded in this analysis. Furthermore, the children could string together content words with no extra function words at all but clearly they do not do so. Instead, as they produce longer sentences, children add the basic grammatical morphemes, and the order in which they add these morphemes to their speech shows a remarkable degree of invariance.

There are a number of possible determinants of the order of acquisition that we might consider. The first of these is *the frequency of these forms in the speech of the parents to the child*. In his longitudinal study Brown sampled not only from the speech of the three children, but also from the speech of the three pairs of parents to the children. He found a rather stable profile of frequencies for the morphemes in the parents' speech. However, there was a nonsignificant correlation between the rank ordering of frequency averaged across parental pairs and the mean order of mor-pheme acquisition of the children (rho $= + 0.26$). There was also no discernible relationship between individual differences in acquisition order for the children and differential frequencies of morpheme use across parents. If Brown's parental data are taken as representative of general parent-to-child speech, which is not too unwar-ranted an assumption in view of the stability of the frequencies across parents in his data, there are also nonsignificant correlations between frequency in parents' speech and the two orderings obtained in the present study. Rho values are $+0.35$ with method I ordering, and $+0.19$ with method II ordering. Thus no relation has been shown to exist between frequencies in parental speech and the child's order of acquisition of the morphemes.

The second possible determinant of order of acquisition is *grammatical complexity*. In view of the number of different grammars that have recently been proposed, one must of necessity choose one or more to represent the grammatical complexity of the morphemes. We have chosen to follow Brown in using the transformational grammar offered by Jacobs and Rosenbaum (1968). This allows a close comparison between our cross-sectional data and Brown's longitudinal data as related to grammatical complexity. Brown has also pointed out that the Jacobs and Rosenbaum transformational grammar is representative of many such generative grammars, and is fairly inclusive, offering treatments of 13 of the 14 morphemes. Furthermore, complexity orderings are not changed by every change in formal representation and are remarkably stable across a number of grammars.

Table 3 orders the morphemes according to transformational complexity in the simplest sense, i.e,. the number of transformations involved in the derivation of each morpheme in the Jacobs and Rosenbaum grammar. The possessive inflection is omitted because they do not provide a derivation for it.

The rank-order correlation between Brown's mean acquisition order and transformational complexity is + 0.80. Between complexity and the ordering by method I in this study the correlation is + 0.85, and between complexity and the method II ordering it is + 0.85. These correlations are all highly significant ($P < 0.01$). However, assessing the grammatical complexity of the morphemes simply in terms of the number of transformations in the derivation is a somewhat dubious procedure. It is not safe to assume that each transformation adds an equal amount of complexity since transformational rules may vary in internal complexity. Brown (in press) has suggested that *cumulative* complexity, i.e., the cumulative number of transformations, provides a better index of grammatical complexity. In these terms a construc-

Table 3   Ordering of 13 of the Morphemes in Terms of Grammatical Complexity Measured by the Number of Transformations in the Derivation of Each Morpheme

Morpheme	Transformations (Jacobs and Rosenbaum, 1968)	Complexity Ranking
Present progressive	Progressive affix T	3
in	Preposition segment T	3
on	Preposition segment T	3
Articles	Article T	3
Past irregular	Verbal agreement T	3
Past regular	Verbal agreement T, verb suffix T	7
Plural	Noun suffix T, article or nominal agreement T	7
3rd Person irregular	Aux agreement T, verbal agreement T	7
3rd Person regular	Aux agreement T, verbal agreement T, verb suffix T	10
Contractible copula		10
	Copula T, aux agreement T, aux incorporation T	
Uncontractible copula		10
Contractible auxiliary	Progressive affix T, progressive segment T,	12.5
Uncontractible auxiliary	Aux incorporation T, aux agreement T	12.5

Table 4   Predicted Order of Acquisition of Some Morphemes in Terms of Cumulative Grammatical Complexity

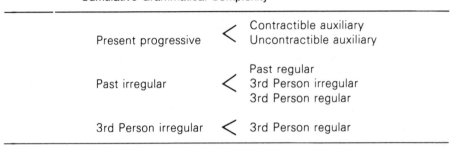

tion involving *x* + *y* transformations will be more complex than one involving only *x* or only *y*, and a construction involving *x* + *y* + *z* transformations will be more complex than all of these. Again, using the Jacobs and Rosenbaum grammar, cumulative transformational complexity gives rise to the partial ordering shown in Table 4.

This ordering predicts that the simple progressive should be acquired before the full progressive (aux + progressive) and this is confirmed by both our data and those of Brown. The predictions made by the partial ordering of the regular and irregular past and third person forms are also all confirmed by both orderings of the morphemes in this study. However, Brown points out two difficulties with the complexity ordering of the irregular and regular forms. First, Jacobs and Rosenbaum note that for irregular cases it would be necessary to "block" the operation of the verb suffix transformation. It is therefore questionable whether irregular forms should be considered simpler because the extra transformation for the regular form is explicitly blocked. Second, the wider variety of irregular allomorphs might be expected to contribute to the overall complexity of the irregular forms, but transformational complexity does not take this into account. Nevertheless, despite the above difficulties in determining grammatical complexity, be it in simple or cumulative terms, the high correlations obtained and the predicted orderings confirmed by our data suggest that transformational complexity may determine the order of acquisition of the morphemes.

A third possible determinant of acquisition order is *semantic complexity*. The task of ordering the morphemes in terms of semantic complexity is even more difficult than it was for grammatical complexity since there exists no systematic semantic analysis of all the morphemes. Brown (in press) considers many authors' characterizations of the major meanings of the 14 morphemes. He then attempts to determine for each morpheme which unitary meaning or meanings, out of the many that may be signalled by the morpheme in adult speech, were used by the children when that morpheme reached criterion, i.e., when the child first clearly controlled that meaning of the morpheme.

For example, Long (1961), Twaddell (1963), and Joos (1964) all recognize that the past tense in English signals two distinguishable meanings. One of these meanings is "earlierness," i.e. when the utterance refers to the occurrence of an event or state at some prior time, and the other meaning is the entertainment of some hypothetical possibility, e.g., "If I *were* in your place I *would* go." The past in the sense of earlierness can also be distinguished from the present perfect (*have* + *en*), which usually refers to earlier events but also implies current relevance. Of these various meanings of past forms in adult speech, only the meaning "earlierness" seems to be signaled in early child speech. The hypothetical and perfective uses appear only well into Stage V (MLU > 4.00 morphemes per utterance), when the simple past has been at criterion for some time.

In this way Brown isolates for each morpheme the major dimensions of meaning that occur in early child speech. These are shown in Table 5 ordered according to increasing number of such dimensions. The distinctions regular/irregular and contractible/uncontractible do not add dimensions of meaning and are therefore disregarded in this analysis. The first of each pair to reach criterion in the children's speech is considered since at this point the child first controls the semantic underlying these morphemes.

Brown notes that subcategorization is possible for some of the meanings, e.g., into alienable and inalienable possessive (Fillmore, 1968), but as no principle exists to enable one to decide how finely to subcategorize, he decides to consider only the major independent meanings. Some problems still remain in Brown's analysis, however. First, Brown points out that the children had other uses of *in* and *on* besides those implying containment and support. Both in Brown's study and in this study the children correctly used such phrases as "*in* a minute," "*on* TV," and "talk *on* the telephone." However, it can be argued that these are idiomatic and not semantically principled uses of *in* and *on*, and can therefore rightly be left out of the semantic analysis. These expressions are probably learned as routines by the child since they are not extended to new instances.

Second, there are probably two dimensions of meaning that are controlled by the child in early use of the articles. Brown considers in detail the dimension specific-

Table 5   Major Dimensions of Meaning of the Morphemes Found in Early Child Speech, Ordered According to Increasing Number of Unitary Meanings Expressed or Presupposed

Morpheme	Major Meanings	Complexity Ranking
Present progressive	Temporary duration	4
in	Containment	4
on	Support	4
Plural	Number	4
Past, irregular or regular	Earlierness	4
Possessive	Possession	4
Articles	Specific-nonspecific	4
3rd Person, irregular or regular	Number, earlierness	8.5
Copula, contractible or uncontractible	Number, earlierness	8.5
Auxiliary, contractible or uncontractible	Temporary duration, number, earlierness	10

Table 6   Predicted Order of Acquisition of Some Morphemes in Terms of Cumulative Semantic Complexity

Plural	3rd Person (irregular)	
		Auxiliary (contractible)
Past (irregular)	Copula (contractible)	

| | Present Progressive | < | Auxiliary (contractible) |

(Plural / Past (irregular) < 3rd Person (irregular) / Copula (contractible) < Auxiliary (contractible); Present Progressive < Auxiliary (contractible))

nonspecific, that determines which article, *a* or *the,* is to be used. He points out that in contexts in which it was possible to determine which of the articles was required, the children always used the correct one. Yet in both Brown's and the present study, the experimenters scored presence or absence of either article in obligatory contexts, and did not distinguish between the two articles. There is a more basic semantic dimension determining whether an article has to be used at all. This dimension seems to be "proper name" *versus* "common name" (or "an instance of the class of") in child speech, though there are many more subtle distinctions involved in adult use of the articles. The child might know that "Rover" is *a* or *the* dog, but would not call him "the Rover." Children therefore control both of these meanings when the articles reach criterion in their speech, and a second semantic dimension must be added to the articles in Table 5.

There is no general semantic theory that would enable us to determine the relative complexity of the independent unitary meanings shown in Table 5, but the ordering as it stands, plus the extra dimension for the articles, correlates highly with the order or acquisition of the morphemes. Corrected for the many ties, the rho values are + 0.86 with Brown's mean acquisition order, + 82 with method I ordering, and + 0.70 with method II ordering.

Once again it is safer to use a *cumulative* index of complexity (as defined earlier for transformational complexity) to partially order the morphemes. Cumulative semantic complexity gives rise to predictions for the acquisition order of five of the morphemes, as shown in Table 6. All of these predictions are confirmed by both acquisition orders in the present study.

In conclusion, both semantic and grammatical complexity to some extent predict the order of acquisition of the morphemes, but with the analyses of these variables currently available, it is impossible to separate out the relative contributions of each type of complexity since they make the same predictions. In fact, the order of acquisition may best be predicted by some combination of grammatical and semantic complexity, frequency, and perceptibility in speech. It is possible that no one factor can be considered of primary importance in determining the acquisition of the morphemes.

ACKNOWLEDGMENTS

We thank Professor Roger Brown for his encouragement and advice during this research and preparation of the manuscript.

REFERENCES

Brown, R. W. (1973). *A First Language: The Early Stages.* Harvard Univ. Press, Cambridge,
    Mass.
Cazden, C. B. (1968). The acquisition of noun and verb inflections. *Child Dev.* 39: 433–448.
Fillmore, C. J. (1968). The case for case. In Bach, E., and Harms, R. R. (eds.), *Universals in
    Linguistic Theory.* Holt, Rinehart and Winston, New York.
Jacobs, R. A., and Rosenbaum, P. S. (1968). *English Transformational Grammar.* Blaisdell,
    Waltham, Mass.
Joos, M. (1964). *The English Verb; Form and Meanings.* Univ. of Wisconsin Press, Madison.
Labov, W. (1969). Contraction, deletion and inherent variability of the English copula. *Language*
    45: 715–762.
Long, R. B. (1961). *The Sentence and Its Parts.* Univ. of Chicago Press, Chicago.
Menyuk, P. (1969). *Sentences Children Use.* The MIT Press, Cambridge, Mass.
Twaddell, W. F. (1963). *The English Verb Auxiliaries.* Brown Univ. Press, Providence, R.I.

Part 2
ORIGINS OF LANGUAGE FORM, CONTENT, AND USE IN INFANCY

The behaviors of infants relate in important ways to the later behaviors of children, and there has been considerable research attention given to describing infant behaviors and considering how infant behaviors are continuous with later language behaviors. In studies of infancy (see, for example, the recent survey in Cohen and Salapatek, 1975), both the questions that are asked and the results that are obtained usually bear on issues of basic, often innate, capacities, and the changes in capacities that result from the interaction of the child with the context. In many of these studies, information has been presented about development of those capacities of infants that are antecedents of or precursors to the form, content, and use of language. The readings presented here are a sampling of both the kinds of research currently being done with infants and the kinds of information about infants that relate to the eventual development of language.

The perception of the sounds of speech by two- to four-month-old infants was demonstrated in the study reported by *Eimas, Siqueland, Jusczyk, and Vigorito (1971)*. The acoustic parameters of the vocalizations made by infants in different contexts were described in the study by *Delack (1976)*. Both the studies by Eimas, et al. and by Delack present information about the antecedents of language form, and Delack's study goes somewhat further to implicate a possible relation between the form of infant vocalization and the factors that may influence how children learn to use vocalization. In the study by *Stern, Jaffe,*

Beebe, and Bennett (1975), the intricate dyadic exchanges between infants and their mothers that involve the monitoring of reciprocal gazing and vocalizing provide insight into the precursors of discourse in language use. Finally, the many studies in the literature that describe children's conceptual development—in particular the studies by Jean Piaget, his colleagues, and those influenced by him—provide a rich source of information about how infants come to have ideas about and to know about objects and events in the world. Such ideas eventually provide the content of language, when integrated with the capacities for language form and language use.

Speech Perception in Infants

Peter D. Eimas
Einar R. Siqueland
Peter Jusczyk
James Vigorito

Abstract. *Discrimination of synthetic speech sounds was studied in 1- and 4-month-old infants. The speech sounds varied along an acoustic dimension previously shown to cue phonemic distinctions among the voiced and voiceless stop consonants in adults. Discriminability was measured by an increase in conditioned response rate to a second speech sound after habituation to the first speech sound. Recovery from habituation was greater for a given acoustic difference when the two stimuli were from different adult phonemic categories than when they were from the same category. The discontinuity in discrimination at the region of the adult phonemic boundary was taken as evidence for categorical perception.*

In this study of speech perception, it was found that 1- and 4-month-old infants were able to discriminate the acoustic cue underlying the adult phonemic distinction between the voiced and voiceless stop consonants /b/ and /p/. Moreover, and more important, there was a tendency in these subjects toward categorical perception: discrimination of the same physical difference was reliably better across the adult phonemic boundary than within the adult phonemic category.

Earlier research using synthetic speech sounds with adult subjects uncovered a sufficient cue for the perceived distinction in English between the voiced and voiceless forms of the stop consonants, /b-p/, /d-t/, and /g-k/, occurring in absolute initial position (1). The cue, which is illustrated in the spectrograms displayed in Fig. 1, is the onset of the first formant relative to the second and third formants. It is possible to construct a series of stimuli that vary continuously in the relative onset time of the first formant, and to investigate listeners' ability to identify and discriminate these sound patterns. An investigation of this nature (2) revealed that the perception of this cue was very nearly categorical in the sense that listeners could discriminate continuous variations in the relative onset of the first formant very little better than they could identify the sound patterns absolutely. That is, listeners could readily discriminate

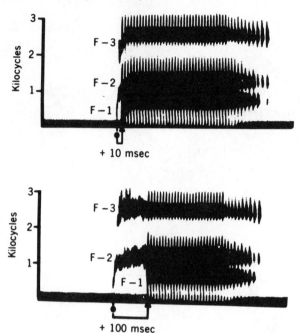

Figure 1. Spectrograms of synthetic speech showing two conditions of voice onset time (VOT): slight voicing lag in the upper figure and long voicing lag in the lower figure. The symbols *F-1, F-2,* and *F-3* represent the first three formants, that is, the relatively intense bands of energy in the speech spectrum. [Courtesy of L. Lisker and A. S. Abramson]

between the voiced and voiceless stop consonants, just as they would differentially label them, but they were virtually unable to hear intraphonemic differences, despite the fact that the acoustic variation was the same in both conditions. The most measurable indication of this categorical perception was the occurrence of a high peak of discriminability at the boundary between the voiced and voiceless stops, and a nearly chance level of discriminability among stimuli that represented acoustic variations of the same phoneme. Such categorical perception is not found with nonspeech sounds that vary continuously along physical continua such as frequency or intensity. Typically, listeners are able to discriminate many more stimuli than they are able to identify absolutely, and the discriminability functions do not normally show the same high peaks and low troughs found in the case of the voicing distinction (*3*). The strong and unusual tendency for the stop consonants to be perceived in a categorical manner has been assumed to be the result of the special processing to which sounds of speech are selected and thus to be characteristic of perception in the speech or linguistic mode (*4*).

Because the voicing dimension in the stop consonants is universal, or very nearly so, it may be thought to be reasonably close to the biological basis of speech and hence of special interest to students of language development. Though the distinctions made along the voicing dimension are not phonetically the same in all languages, it has been found in the cross-language research of Lisker and Abramson (5) that the usages are not arbitrary, but rather very much constrained. In studies of the production of the voicing distinction in 11 diverse languages, these investigators found that, with only minor exceptions, the various tokens fell at three values along a single continuum. The continuum, called voice onset time (VOT), is defined as the time between the release burst and the onset of laryngeal pulsing or voicing. Had the location of the phonetic distinctions been arbitrary, then different languages might well have divided the VOT continuum in many different ways, constrained only by the necessity to space the different modal values of VOT sufficiently far apart as to avoid confusion.

Not all languages studied make use of the three modal positions. English, for example, uses only two locations, a short lag in voicing and a relatively long lag in

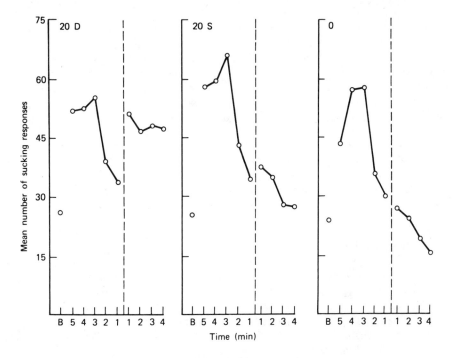

Figure 2.   Mean number of sucking responses for the 4-month-old infants, as a function of time and experimental condition. The dashed line indicates the occurrence of the stimulus shift, or in the case of the control group the time at which the shift would have occurred. The letter *B* stands for the baseline rate. Time is measured with reference to the moment of stimulus shift and indicates the 5 minutes prior to and the 4 minutes after shift.

voicing. Prevoicing or long voicing lead, found in Thai, for example, is omitted. Of interest, however, is the fact that all languages use the middle location, short voicing lag, which, given certain other necessary articulatory events, corresponds to the English voiced stop /b/, and one or both of the remaining modal values. The acoustic consequences for two modes of production are shown in Fig. 1; these correspond to short and long voicing lags, /b/ and /p/, respectively.

Given the strong evidence for universal—and presumably biologically determined —modes of production for the voicing distinction, we should suppose that there might exist complementary processes of perception (6). Hence, if we are to find evidence marking the beginnings of speech perception in a linguistic mode, it would appear reasonable to initiate our search with investigations of speech sounds differing along the voicing continuum. What was done experimentally, in essence, was to compare the discriminability of two synthetic speech sounds separated by a fixed difference in VOT under two conditions: in the first condition the two stimuli to be discriminated lay on opposite sides of the adult phonemic boundary, whereas in the second condition the two stimuli were from the same phonemic category.

The experimental methodology was a modification of the reinforcement procedure developed by Siqueland (7). After obtaining a baseline rate of high-amplitude, non-nutritive sucking for each infant, the presentation and intensity of an auditory stimulus was made contingent upon the infant's rate of high-amplitude sucking. The nipple on which the child sucked was connected to a positive pressure transducer that provided polygraphic recordings of all responses and a digital record of criterional high-amplitude sucking responses. Criterional responses activated a power supply that increased the intensity of the auditory feedback. A sucking rate of two responses per second maintained the stimulus at maximum intensity, about: 75 db (13 db over the background intensity of 62 db).

The presentation of an auditory stimulus in this manner typically results in an increase in the rate of sucking compared with the baseline rate. With continued presentation of the initial stimulus, a decrement in the response rate occurs, presumably as a consequence of the lessening of the reinforcing properties of the initial stimulus. When it was apparent that attenuation of the reinforcing properties of the initial stimulus had occurred, as indicated by a decrement in the conditioned sucking rate of at least 20 percent for two consecutive minutes compared with the immediately preceding minute, a second auditory stimulus was presented without interruption and again contingent upon sucking. The second stimulus was maintained for 4 minutes after which the experiment was terminated. Control subjects were treated in a similar manner, except that after the initial decrease in response rate, that is, after habituation, no change was made in the auditory stimulus. Either an increase in response rate associated with a change in stimulation or a decrease of smaller magnitude than that shown by the control subjects is taken as inferential evidence that the infants perceived the two stimuli as different.

The stimuli were synthetic speech sounds prepared by means of a parallel resonance synthesizer at the Haskins Laboratories by Lisker and Abramson. There were three variations of the bilabial voiced stop /b/ and three variations of its voiceless counterpart /p/. The variations between all stimuli were in VOT, which for the English stops /b/ and /p/ can be realized acoustically by varying the onset of the first formant relative to the second and third formants and by having the second and third formants excited by a noise source during the interval when the first formant is not present. Identification functions from adult listeners (8) have indicated that when the onset of the first formant leads or follows the onset of the second and third formants by less than 25 msec perception is almost invariably /b/. When voicing follows the release burst by more than 25 msec the perception is /p/. Actually the sounds are perceived as /ba/ or /pa/, since the patterns contain three steady-state formants appropriate for a vowel of the type /a/. The six stimuli had VOT values of −20, 0, +20, +40, +60, and +80 msec. The negative sign indicates that voicing occurs before the release burst. The subjects were 1- and 4-month-old infants, and within each age level half of the subjects were males and half were females.

The main experiment was begun after several preliminary studies established that both age groups were responsive to synthetic speech sounds as measured by a reliable increase in the rate of sucking with the response-contingent presentation of the first stimulus ($P < .01$). Furthermore, these studies showed that stimuli separated by differences in VOT of 100, 60, and 20 msec were discriminable when the stimuli were from different adult phonemic categories; that is, there was reliable recovery of the rate of sucking with a change in stimulation after habituation ($P < .05$). The finding that a VOT difference of 20 msec was discriminable permitted within-phonemic-category discriminations of VOT with relatively realistic variations of both phonemes.

In the main experiment, there were three variations in VOT differences at each of two age levels. In the first condition, 20D, the difference in VOT between the two stimuli to be discriminated was 20 msec and the two stimuli were from different adult phonemic categories. The two stimuli used in condition 20D had VOT values of +20 and +40 msec. In the second condition, 20S, the VOT difference was again 20 msec, but now the two stimuli were from the same phonemic category. In this condition the stimuli had VOT values of −20 and 0 msec or +60 and +80 msec. The third condition, 0, was a control condition in which each subject was randomly assigned one of the six stimuli and treated in the same manner as the experimental subjects, except that after habituation no change in stimulation was made. The control group served to counter any argument that the increment in response rate associated with a change in stimulation was artifactual in that the infants tended to respond in a cyclical manner. Eight infants from each age level were randomly assigned to conditions 20D and 20S, and ten infants from each age level were assigned to the control condition.

Figure 2 shows the minute-by-minute response rates for the 4-month-old subjects for each of the training conditions separately. The results for the younger infants show very nearly the identical overall pattern of results seen with the older infants. In all conditions at both age levels, there were reliable conditioning effects: the response rate in the third minute prior to the shift was significantly greater than the baseline rate of responding ($P < .01$). As was expected from the nature of the procedure, there were also reliable habituation effects for all subjects. The mean response rate for the final 2 minutes prior to shift was significantly lower than the response rate for the third minute before shift ($P < .01$). As is apparent from inspection of Fig. 1, the recovery data for the 4-month-old infants were differentiated by the nature of the shift. When the mean response rate during the 2 minutes after shift was compared with the response rate for the 2 minutes prior to shift, condition 20D showed a

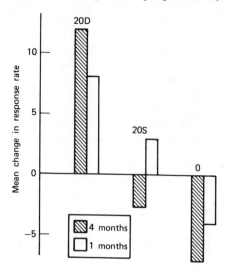

Figure 3. The mean change in response rate as a function of experimental treatments, shown separately for the 1- and 4-month-old infants. (See text for details.)

significant increment ($P < .05$), whereas condition 20S showed a nonsignificant decrement in responding ($P > .05$). In the control condition, there was a fairly substantial decrement in responding during the first 2 minutes of what corresponded to the shift period in the experimental conditions. However, the effect failed to reach the .05 level of significance, but there was a reliable decrement when the mean response rate for the entire 4 minutes after shift was compared with the initial 2 minutes of habituation ($P < .02$). The shift data for the younger infants were quite similar. The only appreciable difference was that in condition 20S there was a nonsignificant increment in the response rate during the first 2 minutes of shift.

In Fig. 3 the recovery data are summarized for both age groups. The mean change in response rate (that is, the mean response rate for the initial 2 minutes of shift minus the mean response rate during the final 2 minutes before shift) is displayed as a function of experimental treatments and age. Analyses of these data revealed that the magnitude of recovery for the 20D condition was reliably greater than that for the 20S condition ($P < .01$). In addition, the 20D condition showed a greater rate of responding than did the control condition ($P < .01$), while the difference between the 20S and control conditions failed to attain the .05 level of significance.

In summary, the results strongly indicate that infants as young as 1 month of age are not only responsive to speech sounds and able to make fine discriminations but are also perceiving speech sounds along the voicing continuum in a manner approximating categorical perception, the manner in which adults perceive these same sounds. Another way of stating this effect is that infants are able to sort acoustic variations of adult phonemes into categories with relatively limited exposure to speech, as well as with virtually no experience in producing these same sounds and certainly with little, if any, differential reinforcement for this form of behavior. The implication of these findings is that the means by which the categorical perception of speech, that is, perception in a linguistic mode, is accomplished may well be part of the biological makeup of the organism and, moreover, that these means must be operative at an unexpectedly early age.

REFERENCES AND NOTES

1. A. M. Liberman, P. C. Delattre, F. S. Cooper, *Language and Speech* 1, 153 (1958); A. M. Liberman, F. Ingemann, L. Lisker, P. C. Delatre, F. S. Cooper, *J. Acoust. Soc. Amer.* 31, 1490 (1959). It should be emphasized that the cues underlying the voicing distinction as discussed in the present report apply only to sound segments in absolute initial position.

2. A. M. Liberman, K. S. Harris, H. S. Hoffman, H. Lane, *J. Exp. Psychol.* 61, 370 (1961).

3. P. D. Eimas, *Language and Speech* 6, 206 (1963); G. A. Miller, *Psychol. Rev.* 63, 81 (1956); R. S. Woodworth and H. Schlosberg, *Experimental Psychology* (Holt, New York, 1954).

4. A. M. Liberman, F. S. Cooper, D. P. Shankweiler, M. Studdert-Kennedy, *Psychol. Rev.* 74, 431 (1967); M. Studdert-Kennedy, A. M. Liberman, K. S. Harris, F. S. Cooper, *ibid.* 77, 234 (1970); M. Studdert-Kennedy and D. Shankweiler, *J. Acoust. Soc. Amer.,* in press.

5. L. Lisker and A. S. Abramson, *Word* 20, 384 (1964).

6. P. Liberman,. *Linguistic Inquiry* 1, 307 (1970).

7. E. R. Siqueland, address presented before the 29th International Congress of Psychology, London, England (August 1969); —— and C. A. DeLucia, *Science* 165, 1144 (1969).

8. L. Lisker and A. S. Abramson, *Proc. Int. Congr. Phonet. Sci. 6th* (1970), p. 563.

9. Supported by grants HD 03386 and HD 04146 from the National Institute of Child Health and Human Development. P.J. and J.V. were supported by the NSF Undergraduate Participation Program (GY 5872). We thank Dr. F. S. Cooper for generously making available the facilities of the Haskins Laboratories. We also thank Drs. A. M. Liberman, I. G. Mattingly, A. S. Abramson, and L. Lisker for their critical comments. Portions of this study were presented before the Eastern Psychological Association, Atlantic City (April 1970).

Aspects of Infant Speech Development in the First Year of Life*

John B. Delack

INTRODUCTION

Despite a rather extensive literature on the subject, most research on the nature of infant speech can be characterized as impressionistically descriptive, or anecdotal, or speculative, or some combination thereof. Such studies have by and large ignored the structure, function and natural history of early vocal behavior, an empirically adequate specification of which is a necessary prerequisite to an understanding of the development of infant vocalizations and of their relationship to later linguistic usage. Likewise, reports have generally failed to recognize the dynamic interactions within the developing organism as a whole, eschewing discussion of concomitant neurophysiological maturation and cognitive growth. While detailed consideration falls beyond the scope of the present paper, some insight into the issues involved may be gained from recent treatises dealing with brain development (Jacobson, 1975), myelogenesis (Lecours, 1975) and the ontogeny of cerebral dominance (Zangwill, 1975). Problems relating to speech input and output requirements in acquisition have been treated by Mattingly (1973), and the interplay of physiological-cognitive factors with respect to early speech perception and production has been critically overviewed by Gilbert (1975). Suffice it to say that until experimental evidence can be adduced, interpreted and properly interwoven into a coherent description, definitive theories on the acquisition and development of speech and language must perforce remain only as desiderata.

In his comprehensive review of nonsegmental phonology in language acquisition, Crystal (1973b) points out that research in this area is meager and fragmented and documents the necessity for a careful account of such phenomena, particularly during the course of the first year of life. In spite of the difficulties inherent in data

Reprinted from The Canadian Journal of Linguistics/Le revue canadienne de linguistique N 21 (1976): 17-37, copyright by the Canadian Linguistic Association. Reprinted with permission.

*The research reported herein was supported in part by the Department of National Health and Welfare (Canada), under Federal Public Health Project No. 609-7-324 and Medical Research Council Grant No. MA-5369. The author would like to thank those who contributed most substantially to this project: Judith Davis for data collection and collation; Dale Stevenson for computer programming and graphic illustration; John Nicol for computer programming; Patricia Fowlow and Dale Stevenson for data analysis and interpretation; and, most importantly, the families involved in this study whose budding "child linguists" have tried to tell us something.

collection and analysis, and as the utility and necessity of such studies become better recognized and the experimental procedures by which "sense" may be gleaned from "nonsense" *qua* babbling are devised and refined, the reluctance of researchers to examine and account for developments in the important first year will diminish. As a contribution to this neglected field of study, the present report seeks to provide normative data on the nature of infant vocalizations in terms of specific acoustic parameters and to afford a glimpse at certain developmental aspects of vocal differentiation in infants through examination of their utterances in various environmental contexts. In this regard and prior to a discussion of the investigation and its results, it is germane to elaborate briefly on our approach and its underlying rationale.

Due to the myriad problems in the longitudinal specification of articulatory development, particularly involving the concomitant physiological maturation of the laryngeal and supralaryngeal vocal tracts, the need was manifested to study parameters of speech production more amenable to measurement. Based on the available evidence, an acoustic analytic and descriptive approach would appear to be the most appropriate method at the present time. Along these lines, the extant research on the nature and development of the infant cry is perhaps the most persuasive: Beyond their firmly buttressed descriptions of cry types, such studies document the existence of vocal differentiation ostensibly evoked by endogenous stimuli and becoming expressive of different internal states, such as hunger, pain and pleasure (cf. Wasz-Höckert et al., 1968), and support the morphological and functional relatedness of cry and non-cry vocalizations (Wolff, 1969). Instances of differential vocalization to objects and people have likewise been alluded to in the literature, but such comments have not been supported by systematic study (cf. Crystal, 1973a, 1973b; Lieberman, 1967). The most recent and impressive acoustic treatment of infant (crying, discomfort and vegetative) sounds, albeit on a sample of two female infants over the first eight weeks of life, may be found in Stark et al. (1975).

As noted above, it is of particular interest to have an empirically adequate characterization of infant speech and its development, preferably based on data obtained within a naturalistic setting. This latter condition would, of course, allow for the possibility of relating vocal behaviors to specific and noncontrived environmental interactions, which in turn would provide a means for a description of the ways in which such vocalizations may be differentially employed (instead of merely cataloging them as having been uttered *in vacuo*). Few investigations have examined infant vocal behavior in this light, despite the obvious significance of such relationships in the development of language and speech from a cognitive-communicative point of view. As a consequence, in addition to a developmental description of infant vocalizations in acoustic terms, we shall also be concerned with tracing the evolution of these utterances in the context of maternal vocalizations, as well as with respect to objects in the environment in an attempt to assay the ontogenesis of prosodic contrastivity during the first year of life. In so doing, we hope to be able to shed some light on "theoretical" controversies concerning the transition from babbling to speech, such as that which rages between proponents of an essential developmental continuity (empiricists or learning theorists, such as Skinner, 1957; Mowrer, 1952; Osgood, 1953; and Winitz, 1969) *versus* discontinuity (rationalists, nativists or maturationalists, such as Jakobson, 1968; Lenneberg, 1967; and McNeill, 1970); for an elaboration of these issues, cf. Delack (1974).

METHOD

The subjects selected for inclusion in this study were nineteen normal, healthy, full term and first-born infants (7 female, 12 male), all of whom were being raised in an exclusively monolingual English home environment, where all data were collected at biweekly intervals from one month to approximately one year of age. Extensive biographical information on the subjects and their families was collected over the course of the year, utilizing various psychological test instruments, questionnaires and diaries kept by the parents; for details of the data collection, including biographical information, cf. Delack (1974) and Fowlow (1975). Among other things, our subjects' families spanned the socioeconomic spectrum, with a middle-class mode, and while home environments varied, they remained stable and stimulating throughout the course of the study. Periodically, the infants' mental and motor capabilities were assessed by means of the *Bayley Scales of Infant Development* (Bayley, 1969); these assessments at three-month intervals indicated that our subjects developed normally. In this regard, our attempts to use the derivative scores as an alternative metric to chronological age by which to evaluate developmental trends have not as yet yielded viable results; i.e., using the gross scores as opposed to age did not significantly improve predictive power.

With respect to the vocalization data, in excess of 11,000 utterances were ultimately selected and examined for a full year on ten infants (4 female, 6 male) and for the first six months on the remaining subjects. These data constitute the spontaneous or reactive utterances of the infants under a variety of maximally normal home routines. The vocalizations selected for analytic purposes were those produced when the infants were completely alone (*S*), when "conversing" with the mother (*SM*) or with another adult (*SOP*), and when alone in the presence of various objects. These latter contexts were ultimately categorized according to the sensory modalities by which the objects would be primarily, or at least most likely, apprehended:

SV: Visual (mobiles, pictures, etc.),
SAV: Auditory + Visual (music boxes, radios, etc.),
STV: Tactile + Visual (stuffed toys, blankets, etc.), and
SATV: Auditory + Tactile + Visual (rattles, bells, keys, etc.).

These data were analyzed spectrographically with respect to the fundamental frequency (F_0) of the harmonic portions of the utterances, in terms of contour, duration and within-utterance range. The information thus obtained was then subjected to statistical analysis, in order to ascertain the trends of and the probable relationships among the established variables.

For the home recording sessions, Nagra IV–D tape recorders were utilized in conjunction with AKG D202E dynamic microphones and Ampex 434 low-noise audiotape recorded at 19.05 cm/s. For the spectrographic analysis, the recorded tapes were reproduced on an Ampex 440B tape deck and passed into a Kay Sonagraph, Model 7029A, with a frequency range of 80–8,000 Hz; in order to show up the harmonic structure of the vocalizations more clearly, only the 45–Hz narrow band pass filter was used. All tape recorders and reproducers were calibrated to give a flat response (± 2 dB) over a frequency range of 50 Hz–10 kHz. Measurement of fundamental frequency (based on the highest viable harmonic—generally the fifth) and duration on the spectrograms was carried out manually; F_0-contour and within-utterance range were calculated by a computer program specifically designed for the purpose. The IBM system 370 Model 168, primarily in conjunction with the OSIRIS–III statistical package, was utilized for the study. For complete details, cf. Fowlow (1975).

RESULTS AND DISCUSSION

Figures 1–4 graphically present our findings with respect to F_0, duration and range, as well as two indices based on these acoustic parameters, and are displayed according to the independent variables of age, context and subject. Solid lines represent the averaged data in terms of the given dimensions; dashed lines are curves predicted on the basis of an additive model utilizing a multiple classification analysis (= MCA; cf. Andrews et al., 1967), which demonstrates the main effects of a given predictor (or independent variable). The better the fit of the two curves, the more likely it is that the observable trends can be accounted for by the given predictor; where they evince

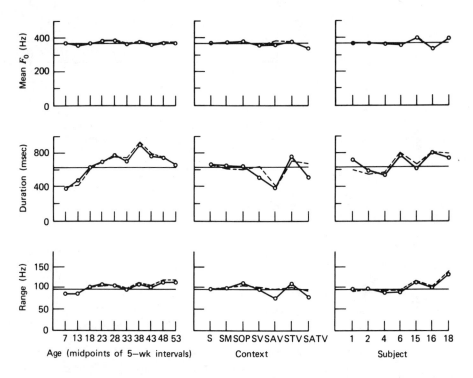

Figure 1. Females ($N = 7$): means of F_0, duration, and within-utterance range (4,540 vocalizations). Solid lines represent the averaged data: horizontal lines correspond to the overall means. dashed lines are predicted curves (MCA additive model)

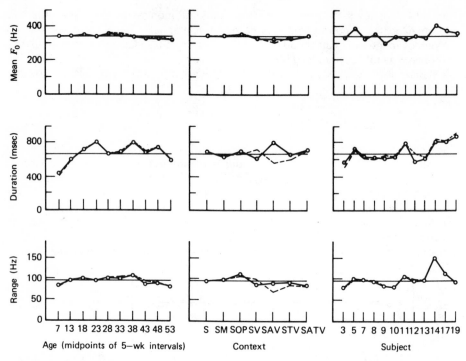

Figure 2. Males ($N = 12$): means of F_0, duration, and within-utterance range (6,828 vocalizations). Solid lines represent the averaged data, horizontal lines correspond to the overall means. Dashed lines are predicted curves (MCA additive model)

a less adequate fit, it is due in large measure to different trends with respect to either one or both of the other variables. Our confidence in the validity of the additive model is strengthened by the fact that subsets of the data in these dimensions follow the same trends, particularly with respect to the independent variables of age and subject.

As may be seen in Figures 1–3 (and in Tables 1–4 appended), the mean F_0 remains fairly stable over the first year, centering on 355 Hz. Females characteristically exhibit a higher F_0 (5–45 Hz) than males throughout this period, beginning at 365 Hz and ending with 370 Hz, peaking at approximately six months to 380 Hz. The males, on the other hand, begin at 350 Hz, dropping to 325 Hz by the end of the first year, again with a peak at 360 Hz at about six months. The disparity between males and females in trends of F_0 development may be attributable to variables not examined here, such as greater maternal restrictiveness *vis-à-vis* females (Lewis & Freedle, 1973), the disposition of mothers to respond imitatively to their female infants (Moss, 1967), and towards the end of the first year, the propensity of the infant for more effective "role-playing" or imitation of adult models (cf. Lieberman, 1967; Lewis, 1951; Piaget & Inhelder, 1966).

With respect to range and duration, sex differences will likewise be noted in Figures

1–3, albeit with rather large deviations about the means (given in the appended Tables). In general, there is a mean 50% increase in duration over the first year: For females, duration increases from 375 to 645 ms, with peaks of 775 ms at six months and 900 ms at nine months; for males, the increment is from 430 to 605 ms, with corresponding peaks at 805 ms and 815 ms, plus a lesser peak of 755 ms at eleven months. For both sexes, range increases by approximately 20%, from 80–85 Hz to 100–105 Hz at six months and continues to rise to 110 Hz for females, but drops back to 80 Hz for males by the first birthday.

Figure 4 summarizes the nonlinear relationship of range to duration over time, indicating their relative independence; however, it is not clear that the trend is strictly a function of age, as suggested by Figure 5. Another index of vocal development, arbitrarily specified as mean $F_0 \times$ Duration $\times$ Range, dramatically exhibits the peaking behavior seen in the individual graphs at 5–6 months and 9 months, the minor peak at 11 months becoming less evident. It is also apparent that duration is the feature which tends to show up developmental trends most saliently. Both range and duration are strongly constrained by contour, as suggested in Figure 5, which displays contours and their developmental status in three age categories; no radical

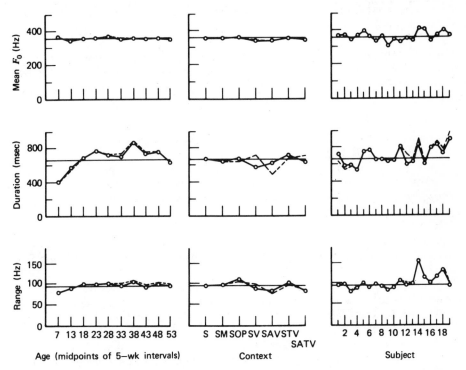

Figure 3. All subjects ($N = 19$): means of F_0, duration, and within-utterance range (11,368 vocalizations). Solid lines represent the averaged data; horizontal lines correspond to the overall means. Dashed lines are predicted curves (MCA additive model)

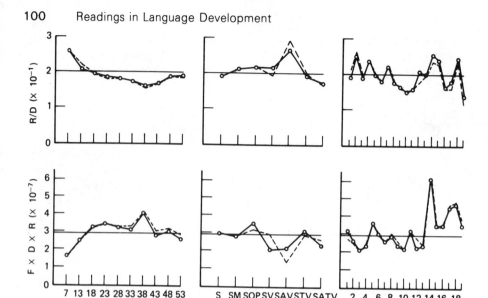

Figure 4. All subjects (*N* 19): means of range to duration and of mean F_0 × duration × range. Solid lines represent the averaged data; horizontal lines correspond to the overall means. dashed lines are predicted curves (MCA additive model)

developmental changes are to be noted, the trends' being a composite of those presented in Figures 1–3.

In the remaining graphs of Figures 1–4, distribution by subject of the various parameters and indices is presented, illustrating the intersubject variability. The contextual distributions show that females pattern somewhat differently from males for all three parameters in the object categories, which also evince a poor fit in terms of the MCA additive model; in addition to different trends with respect to age and subject, inapplicability of the additive model may be due to the arbitrary nature of the classifications, as well as to small numbers of observations (particularly in the *SAV* category).

The peaking behavior repeatedly observed in Figures 1–4 may be correlated with the advent of cortical control and organization of vocal output, as suggested by Bever (1961) and Tonkova-Yampol'skaya (1969). Further considerations may involve descent and growth of the larynx, as well as the concomitant readjustment of the supralaryngeal vocal tract and its growth (cf. Kirchner, 1970; Negus, 1930, 1949; Wind, 1970). In particular, there is an exponential growth of the vocal folds during the first six months, increasing in length from 3 mm at birth to a little over 5 mm, after which the developmental curve becomes rather flat and linear. By the age of nine months, the ratio of anteroposterior vocal fold length to the diameter of the lumen of the trachea, ca. 1:1.5, has reached the dimensions it will retain until puberty. While still in the process of maturation, the palatal arch has likewise assumed the vaulted proportions of the adult, rather than retaining the flat characteristics of the newborn. Prior to this point vocal tract mutability, with its consequences for vocal productions and feedback mechanisms, may effectively prevent the infant from adequately correlating auditory input and perceptual representations with vocal tract output. The

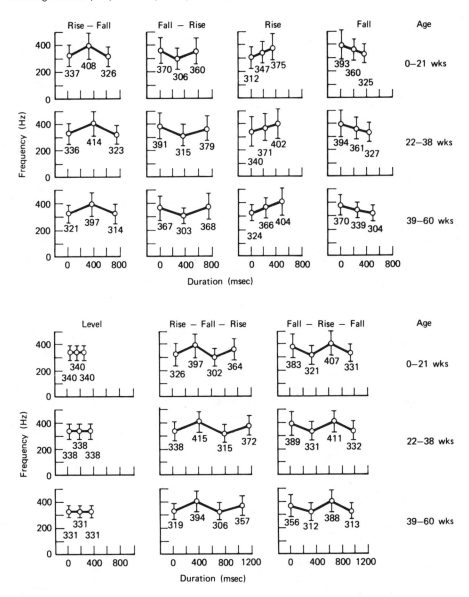

Figure 5.   Contours and their developmental status in three age categories for all subjects.

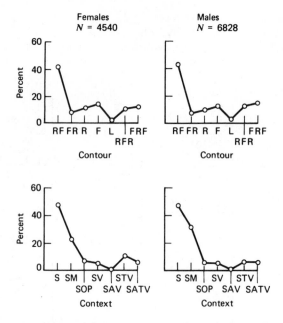

Figure 6. Percentage distribution of vocalizations by contour and context for females and
males.

relative constancy of vocal tract proportions by this time may well now achieve the degree of homeostasis necessary to render such difficulties, as discussed by Mattingly (1973), more amenable to specification and resolution, on the part of the infant. The sensory-motor aspects of early explorative mapping of the vocal tract and primitive syllabification have been experimentally examined by Zlatin (1975); such behaviors may form the rudimentary foundations for the knowledge and control of the tract, which in conjunction with the later relative stability of structural relationships may lead to similar structural uniformity in linguistic relationships. In this regard it can be noted that at this time the infant begins to concentrate on the segmental aspects of vocal production, in addition to the more precise imitation of adult speech (cf. Lewis, 1951; Piaget & Inhelder, 1966). Thus it would appear that the peaks observable in our data correspond to, or at least coincide with, several physiological and, as noted earlier, psychological milestones in the latter half of the first year of life.

Distributions of contours by age, context, sex and subject are appended in Tables 5 and 6. Figure 6 demonstrates the essentially identical distribution of contours for males and females: Not only is the rise-fall pattern predominant, but it also exhibits the most notable changes with respect to age (cf. Figure 7), increasing from 40% to 55% during the first year. The other contours do not appreciably alter their distributional configurations over time. A similar pattern exists in the percentage distribution of contexts, also present graphically in Figure 6: The primary difference between males and females involves the category *SM*, and to a lesser extent *STV*; this may be

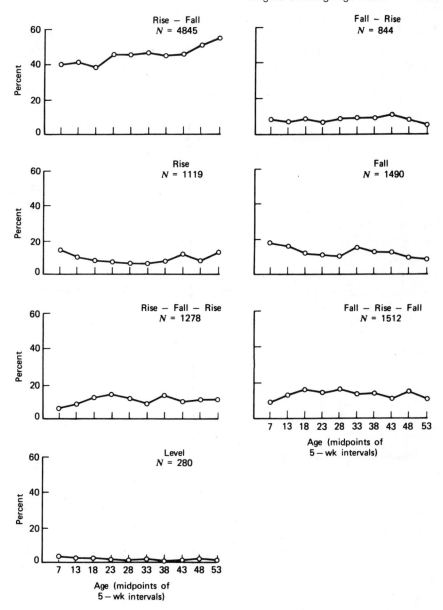

Figure 7.   Developmental trend of frequency of each contour for all subjects.

due to differential modes of maternal interaction *inter alia,* as noted earlier (cf. Lewis & Freedle, 1973; Moss, 1967). An intensive investigation of this aspect of our findings is currently in progress.

Figure 8 reveals the developmental findings in terms of contextual vocalizations.

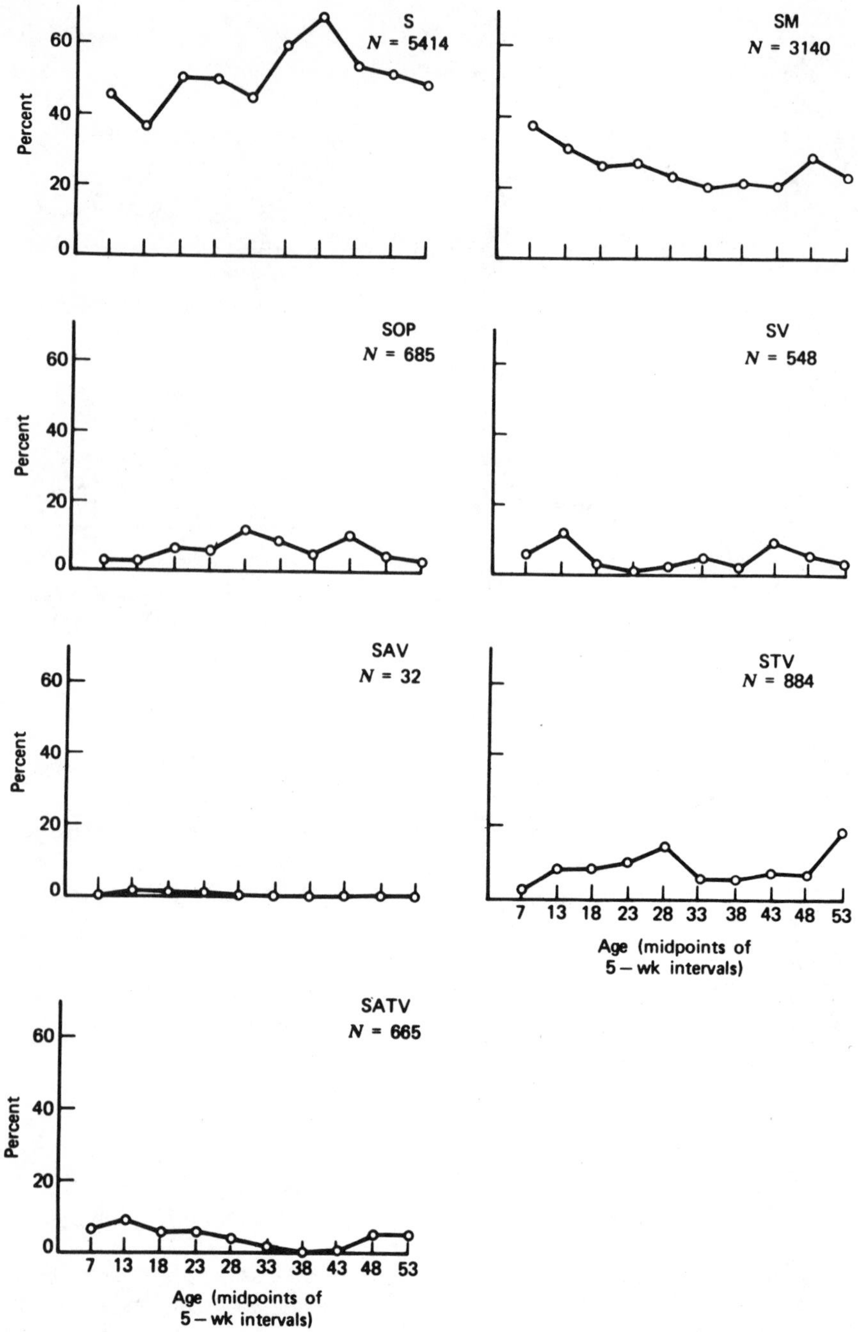

Figure 8.   Developmental trend of frequency of each context for all subjects.

Taken together, these distributional frequencies provide a measure of the infants' interests over the first year of life. The peaks found in the graphs may be due in part to our data collection procedures, which required sampling the occurrence of vocalizations rather than the lack of them during any given recording session. Such a qualification, however, does not necessarily impair the reliability or validity of our study; on the contrary, such observations reconfirm the significance of psychological and environmental variables within the framework of the infant's developmental schedule. As a result, the *S* category increases in frequency with age, with rather large excursions occurring at 4–5 months and again at nine months; during these periods the infants were more apt to vocalize when alone than otherwise. The *SM* category evinces a complementary decrease over time, with the largest percentage of vocalizations appearing at the beginning and end of the study; here, the subjects tended to spend more time with their mothers. The other person category, *SOP*, exhibits a rather random and hence unremarkable distribution, except to note that strangers were of salient interest to the infants around seven and ten months of age.

Turning to the object categories, the context *SV* peaks strongly between 3–4 months and again between 9–10 months. This is largely due in the first instance to life in the crib, where most of the collected utterances were directed to mobiles suspended from above; in the latter case, the high incidence is likely a reflection of the infant's interest in the surroundings, since many of the later sessions included sequences of the infant's gesturing or vocalizing at a distant object, whereupon the mother would respond by naming or describing the object. All such objects were included in the *SV* category because they were not noise-makers and the child generally did not have tactile access to them. The relative increase in frequency of the *STV* category from the outset to its peak at approximately six months, as well as a similarly high frequency of occurrence over the same period for the context *SATV*, can be attributed to the presence of toys in the circumscribed world of crib and playpen, where the infant spent much of the time. The *SAV* context played little role in this study, insofar as few exemplars of utterances in this category were elicited.

The distribution of contours by context is illustrated in Figure 9, which combines and reinterprets the data presented in Figure 6 (cf. also Table 5). While frequencies remain much the same across the contexts, detailed inspection of the distributions reveals differences sufficient to warrant a classification on the basis of contour expectancy. Statistical evaluation ($X^2 = 289.30$, df $= 36$, $p < .001$) yields a high probability of a real difference existing among the different distributions. These differences become more apparent when examined on the basis of their deviations from the mean (as in Figure 10), and more vividly so when such deviations are expressed as percentage deviations from the mean (as in Figure 11): Thus, each context may be described by a unique constellation of contours, insofar as they deviate uniquely from the mean; however, any predictive power so achieved is not great and should not be overrated, since some or all of it may be due to analytic artifacts. It is interesting to note that the distribution of contours in the *S* and *SM* categories are complementary when viewed on such an index, with contours which rise in their terminal portion being more frequent for *S* and less frequent for *SM*. By the same token, *STV* and *SATV* exhibit a similarly complementary patterning with respect to each other.

It should be remarked that although contours are construed here as complex composites of more basic features (i.e., variations of fundamental frequency in the temporal domain), they are not necessarily or uniquely determined by these; in fact, the converse could be true. In any event, the observed differences in contour distributions cannot be attributed solely to concomitant fluctuations in physical variables such as F_0, duration and range, since these may be constrained or governed by other factors (such as the state of the organism, including degree of wakefulness, concur-

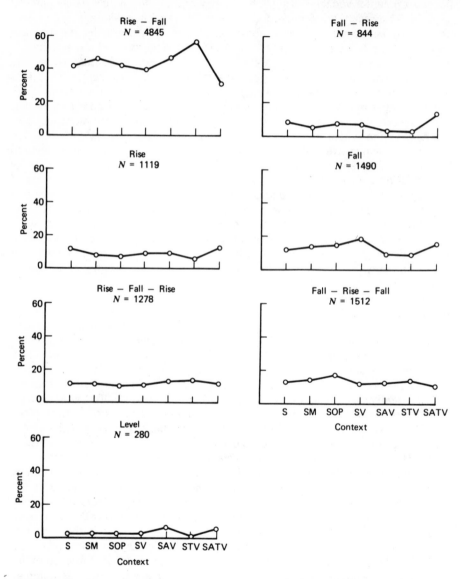

Figure 9.   Percentage distribution of contours by context for all subjects.

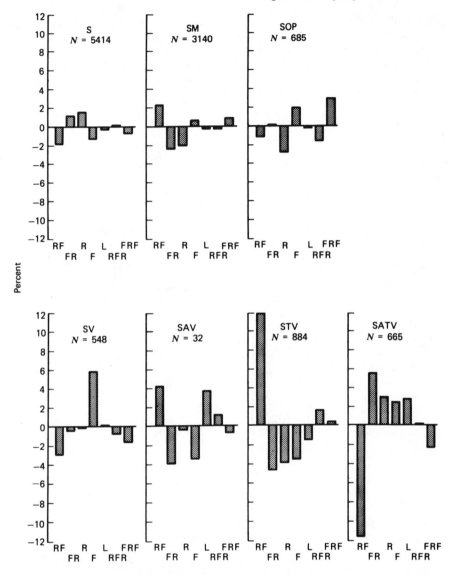

Figure 10. Contexts × contours: deviation from the mean of percentage distributions for all subjects.

rent motoric involvement, *inter alia*). Moreover, should the observed differences be more than artifactual, from either the cognitive psychological or physiological point of view, we do not know whether the infant is strategically manipulating contours, their associated features, or other variables which have not been examined. This aspect of our study can only afford a preliminary and intriguing glimpse at the ontogenesis of differential vocalization, whereby a productive experimental technique has been suggested which can now be refined to provide more definitive results together with meaningful interpretation.

In sum, we feel that, however qualified, the findings of our study document a very real, albeit circumscribed, capacity on the part of the infant for vocally differentiating environmental events, one of the basic components in the development of com-

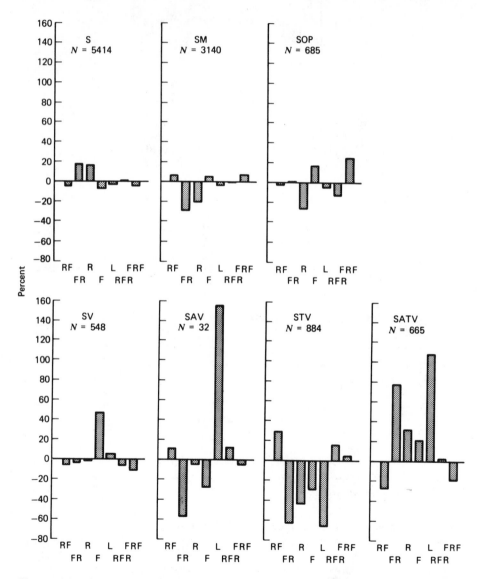

Figure 11.   Context × contours: percentage deviation from the mean of distributions for all subjects.

municative function. In general, we hold that there exists sufficient evidence (on the basis of this and correlative studies) to refute the parochial view that linguistic acquisition can only be discussed relevantly when the child's segmental phonetic repertoire begins to resemble that of the adult standard (cf. also Delack, 1974). In other words, we strongly support the hypothesis of continuity from babbling to speech (without subscribing to the equally untenable view that the infant enters this world as a *tabula rasa,* for which there exists no evidence). We are hopeful that our research will help to fill the *lacunae* of "ignorance about the fundamental development of prosodic contrastivity in children" (Crystal, 1973a: 33) during the all important first year of life and, more importantly, will ultimately provide a fund of information on infant vocalization, a proper description of which is necessary for the overall characterization of the development of communicative competence.

REFERENCES

Andrews, F. M., J. N. Morgan, & J. A. Sonquist. 1967. *Multiple Classification Analysis.* Ann Arbor, Michigan: University of Michigan Institute for Social Research.

Bayley, Nancy. 1969. *Bayley Scales of Infant Development.* New York: The Psychological Corporation.

Bever, Thomas G. 1961. Pre-linguistic behavior. Unpublished honors thesis, Harvard University. Cited in McNeill, 1970: 132-3.

Cohen, A., & S. G. Nooteboom (Eds.). 1975. *Structure and Process in Speech Perception.* Berlin: Springer-Verlag.

Crystal, David. 1973a. Linguistic mythology and the first year of life. *British Journal of Disorders of Communication* 8. 29–36.

Crystal, David. 1973b. Non-segmental phonology in language acquisition: a review of the issues. *Lingua* 32. 1–45.

Delack, John B. 1974. Prelinguistic infant vocalizations and the ontogenesis of sound-meaning correlations. *Bulletin d' Audiophonologie* 4. 479–99. [No. 6, Supplémentaire, Prélangage II: Prélangage de l'homme.]

Foss, B. M. (ed.). 1969. *Determinants of Infant Behavior IV.* London: Methuen.

Fowlow, Patricia J. 1975. The development of prosodic contrastivity during the first year of life. Unpublished M.Sc. thesis, University of British Columbia.

Gilbert, John H. V. 1975. Speech perception in children. In Cohen & Nooteboom, 1975: 312–35.

Jacobson, Marcus. 1975. Brain development in relation to language. In Lenneberg & Lenneberg, 1975: 105–19.

Jakobson, Roman. 1968. Child Language, Aphasia and Phonological Universals. The Hague: Mouton. [Janua Linguarum, Series Minor, 72].

Kirchner, John A. 1970. *Pressman and Kelemen's Physiology of the Larynx.* Rochester, Minnesota: American Academy of Ophthalmology and Otolaryngology.

Lecours, André Roch. 1975. Myelogenetic correlates of the development of speech and language. In Lenneberg & Lenneberg, 1975: 121–35.

Lenneberg, Eric H. 1967. Biological Foundations of Language. New York: Wiley & Sons.

Lenneberg, Eric H., & Elizabeth Lenneberg (Eds.). 1975. *Foundations of Language Development: A Multidisciplinary Approach,* Volume 1. New York: Academic Press.

Lewis, M. M. 1951. *Infant Speech: A Study in the Beginnings of Language.* London: Routledge & Kegan Paul, 1951[2].

Lewis, Michael, & Roy Freedle 1973. Mother-infant dyad: the cradle of meaning. In Pliner et al., 1973: 127–55.

Lieberman, Philip 1967. *Intonation, Perception, and Langauge.* Cambridge, Mass.: The M.I.T. Press.

McNeill, David. 1970. *The Acquisition of Language: The Study of Developmental Pycholinguistics.* New York: Harper & Row.

Mattingly, Ignatius G. 1973. Phonetic prerequisites for first-language acquisition. *Haskins Laboratories: Status Report on Speech Research* SR-34. 65–9.

Moss, Howard A. 1967. Sex, age, and state as determinants of mother-infant interaction. *Merrill-Palmer Quarterly* 13. 19–36.

Mowrer, O. Hobart. 1952. Speech development in the young child: I. the autism theory of speech development and some clinical application. *Journal of Speech and Hearing Disorders* 17. 263–8.

Negus, Victor E. 1930. *The Mechanism of the Larynx.* St. Louis: C. V. Mosby Co. 1949. *The Comparative Anatomy and Physiology of the Larynx.* New York: Hafner Publishing Co.

Osgood, Charles E. 1953. *Method and Theory in Experimental Psychology.* New York: Oxford University Press.

Pliner, P., L. Krames, & T. Alloway (Eds.). 1973. *Communication and Affect: Language and Thought.* New York: Academic Press.

Piaget, Jean, & Bärbel Inhelder. 1966. *La Psychologie de l'Enfant.* Paris: Presses Universitaires de France.

Skinner, B. F. 1957. *Verbal Behavior.* New York: Appleton-Century-Crofts.

Stark, Rachel E., Susan N. Rose, & Margaret Molagen. 1975. Features of infant sounds: the first eight weeks of life. *Journal of Child Language* 2. 205–21.

Tonkova-Yampol'skaya, R. V. 1969. Development of speech intonation in infants during the first two years of life. *Soviet Psychology* 7. 48–54.

Wasz-Höckert, O., J. Lind, V. Vuorenkoski, T. Partanen, & E. Valanne. 1968. *The Infant Cry: A Spectrographic and Auditory Analysis.* Lavenham: Spastics International Medical Publications/William Heinemann Medical Books.

Wind, J. 1970. *On the Phylogeny and the Ontogeny of the Human Larynx.* Groningen: Wolters-Noordhoff.

Winitz, Harris. 1969. *Articulatory Acquisition and Behavior.* New York: Appleton-Century-Crofts.

Wolff, Peter. 1969. The natural history of crying and other vocalizations in early infancy. In Foss, 1969: 81–109.

Zangwill, O. L. 1975. The ontogeny of cerebral dominance in man. In Lenneberg & Lenneberg, 1975: 137–47.

Zlatin, Marsha A. 1975. Explorative mapping of the vocal tract and primitive syllabification in infancy: the first six months. *Purdue University Contributed Papers—Speech, Hearing, Language* 5. 58–73.

Table 1   Fundamental Frequency
           (Mean/S.D. in Hz)

		Females	Males	Combined
Age (wks)	0–10	365/65	350/80	355/75
	11–15	350/55	345/80	345/75
	16–20	365/80	355/80	360/80
	21–25	380/65	340/65	355/65
	26–30	380/65	360/110	370/90
	31–35	360/65	350/80	350/75
	36–40	370/70	340/45	360/60
	41–45	355/60	330/70	340/70
	46–50	370/70	330/55	350/65
	51–60	370/60	325/60	345/65
Context	S	365/65	350/85	355/80
	S M	375/70	345/70	355/70
	S OP	380/70	355/90	370/85
	S V	350/55	330/40	340/50
	S AV	355/90	325/65	340/80
	S TV	375/65	330/50	355/65
	S ATV	335/60	345/80	340/75
Overall Mean		370/70	345/80	355/75

Table 2   Duration
           (Mean/S.D. in Milliseconds)

		Females	Males	Combined
Age (wks)	0–10	375/310	430/330	405/320
	11–15	480/380	610/425	575/415
	16–20	630/535	725/480	695/505
	21–25	695/620	805/560	760/590
	26–30	775/540	670/410	725/480
	31–35	705/505	690/470	700/485
	36–40	900/685	815/510	865/620
	41–45	760/520	695/465	725/490
	46–50	750/570	755/515	755/545
	51–60	645/450	605/375	625/415
Context	S	645/535	695/490	675/510
	S M	630/530	640/475	635/495
	S OP	620/470	705/490	665/485
	S V	485/435	615/420	565/430
	S AV	365/405	810/325	615/420
	S TV	740/660	660/380	705/560
	S ATV	485/435	730/520	625/500
Overall Mean		635/540	675/475	660/500

Table 3   Within-Utterance Range
             (Mean/S.D. in Hz)

		Females	Males	Combined
Age (wks)	0–10	80/75	85/70	85/75
	11–15	85/65	95/85	95/80
	16–20	100/80	100/80	100/80
	21–25	105/70	95/70	100/70
	26–30	105/70	100/85	100/80
	31–35	90/70	100/80	95/75
	36–40	105/80	105/60	105/70
	41–45	100/75	85/60	95/65
	46–50	110/85	90/55	100/70
	51–60	110/85	80/60	95/75
Context	S	95/75	95/80	95/80
	S M	100/75	100/70	100/75
	S OP	110/75	110/100	110/90
	S V	95/65	85/55	90/60
	S AV	75/60	90/85	80/75
	S TV	110/75	90/50	100/65
	S ATV	75/75	80/65	80/70
Overall Mean		95/75	95/75	95/75

Table 4   Summary Statistics by Subject
             (Mean/S.D.)

		Fundamental frequency (Hz)	Range (Hz)	Duration (msec)
Subject	101–F	365/80	95/80	705/570
	102–F	370/65	100/75	570/500
	103–M	340/65	85/65	580/435
	104–F	365/65	90/75	525/480
	105–M	395/105	100/90	740/520
	106–F	360/60	90/65	755/590
	107–M	330/50	100/60	645/500
	108–M	360/90	95/90	645/415
	109–M	305/75	85/80	630/480
	110–M	345/50	80/55	640/445
	111–M	325/65	110/65	795/450
	112–M	345/55	95/55	590/415
	113–M	335/50	100/55	630/410
	114–M	410/95	150/115	825/520
	115–F	405/75	115/90	595/470
	116–F	340/45	100/65	790/600
	117–M	370/70	115/95	825/615
	118–F	400/60	130/70	715/545
	201–M	365/40	95/55	890/555
Overall Mean		355/75	95/75	660/500

Table 5   Distribution (%) of Contours by Age, Context and Sex.

Contour:		R-F	F-R	Rise	Fall	Level	R-F-R	F-R-F
Age (wks)	N							
0–10	1518	40.0	7.9	14.6	17.9	3.9	7.1	8.6
11–15	2046	41.1	6.5	10.9	16.1	3.4	9.1	13.0
16–20	2498	38.3	8.3	9.2	12.2	2.6	13.4	16.1
21–25	2047	45.0	6.4	7.9	10.9	1.7	13.9	14.2
26–30	815	45.0	8.0	7.2	10.4	1.5	12.1	15.7
31–35	584	45.7	8.2	7.0	14.6	2.4	9.1	13.0
36–40	554	44.0	8.3	8.3	11.6	1.1	13.5	13.2
41–45	531	45.4	9.6	11.7	11.7	1.5	9.8	10.4
46–50	450	49.6	7.1	8.0	8.7	1.8	11.3	13.6
51–60	325	54.2	3.7	12.6	7.7	1.2	10.8	9.8
Context								
S	5414	41.0	8.8	11.6	12.2	2.4	11.3	12.7
S M	3140	45.2	5.3	7.9	13.8	2.4	11.1	14.3
S OP	685	41.6	7.4	7.2	15.2	2.3	9.8	16.5
S V	548	39.6	7.1	9.7	19.0	2.6	10.4	11.7
S AV	32	46.9	3.1	9.4	9.4	6.3	12.5	12.5
S TV	884	54.6	2.8	5.8	9.3	0.9	12.9	13.7
S ATV	665	30.8	13.1	12.9	15.6	5.3	11.4	10.8
Sex								
Female	4540	41.5	7.8	11.2	14.3	2.5	10.6	12.1
Male	6828	43.4	7.2	8.9	12.3	2.4	11.7	14.1
Total	11368	42.6	7.4	9.8	13.1	2.5	11.2	13.3

Table 6   Distribution (%) of Contours by Subject

Contour:	N	R-F	F-R	Rise	Fall	Level	R-F-R	F-R-F
Subject								
101–F	744	39.7	9.7	15.5	17.1	3.0	7.7	7.5
102–F	920	51.5	4.3	10.7	14.2	1.4	7.1	10.8
103–M	1249	32.7	12.2	10.6	18.6	2.8	11.4	11.7
104–F	1298	33.4	11.3	13.3	16.4	3.2	11.5	10.9
105–M	684	43.4	6.9	9.6	12.1	2.6	13.2	12.1
106–F	808	41.8	5.7	10.6	12.7	4.0	11.0	14.1
107–M	792	53.3	3.5	6.9	11.2	2.4	9.7	12.9
108–M	1053	30.3	11.1	17.7	12.5	5.6	11.4	11.4
109–M	661	50.7	5.1	12.9	12.3	2.4	9.4	7.3
110–M	415	41.4	8.9	8.9	11.1	1.2	11.1	17.3
111–M	730	59.3	3.3	1.6	7.7	0.5	12.2	15.3
112–M	255	57.3	3.9	2.4	7.8	1.2	13.7	13.7
113–M	271	43.2	4.1	4.4	8.1	1.1	14.0	25.1
114–M	219	47.0	1.8	0.9	11.4	—	12.3	26.5
115–F	238	44.5	4.6	7.1	11.8	0.4	14.3	17.2
116–F	208	35.1	9.1	6.3	9.6	1.4	21.6	16.8
117–M	269	48.0	5.2	3.3	11.9	1.5	12.6	17.5
118–F	324	50.6	5.6	2.5	8.6	—	13.3	19.4
201–M	230	34.8	5.7	3.0	9.6	0.4	15.7	30.9
Total	11368	42.6	7.4	9.8	13.1	2.5	11.2	13.3

Vocalizing In Unison And In Alternation: Two Modes Of Communication Within The Mother-Infant Dyad*

Daniel N. Stern, Joseph Jaffe, Beatrice Beebe, and Stephen L. Bennett

INTRODUCTION

Two laboratories studying dyadic communication have joined in an ongoing research project on the ontogeny of communication. One laboratory has engaged in the study of naturally occurring interactions between mothers and infants, particularly their "nonverbal" communication.[1-6] The other has focused on the rhythm of adult conversation.[7,8] Together, we are examining vocal and kinesic behaviors and their integration during the course of development. This paper presents a part of that ongoing study.

During the first half-year of life the infant communicates effectively through a variety of behaviors: head and body movement and tone, gaze, facial expressions, and vocalizations. By the age of three to four months, all of these behaviors can be integrated to form recognizable complex expressive acts. The distinction between vocal and other motor acts is less compelling at this point in development, and in fact, if made too sharply, may obscure a view of early vocalization. For instance, when watching a film of an infant, with the sound turned off, it is impossible to predict reliably when he is vocalizing. In social situations, there exists a wide range and variety of mouth behaviors, especially mouth-opening with head thrown up, which are extremely expressive and evocative.[4] These may or may not be accompanied by a vocalization. When a vocalization is added to the entire kinesic event, that event becomes importantly different. Nonetheless, infant vocalizations rarely occur (in a social situation) as an isolated motor act such as an adult can perform in speaking; rather, they occur as another element in the constellation of kinesic events that make up a communicative act. Furthermore, they occur within an interpersonal context in which the levels of arousal and affective tone are constantly changing. We thus have

From *Annals of the New York Academy of Sciences: Developmental Psycholinguistics and Communication Disorders,* **263,** 89–100, 1975. Reprinted by permission of the New York Academy of Sciences.

*This research was supported by The Grant Foundation and the New York State Department of Mental Hygiene.

examined mother and infant vocalization from the viewpoint that they are sound-producing kinesic events, as well as prelinguistic events which later transform into speech.

This paper was initially prompted by an unexpected finding. During play sessions, mothers and their three- to four-month-old infants vocalize simultaneously to a far greater extent than we had anticipated or than had been commented on in the literature. Early vocalizations appear to have at least one beginning within the mother-infant dyad as a *coaction system* in which each member is performing the same or similar behavior at the same time. This occurrence of behavioral coaction between mother and infant is common in kinesic communication and several examples were already familiar to us, in particular, mutual gaze and posture-sharing in the form of aligning the head in a parallel spatial plane. Both of these require simultaneous performance of the same behavior. Nevertheless, to the extent that we initially viewed early vocalization as "prespeech," we were unprepared for the considerable occurrence of simultaneous mother and infant vocalization. There were several reasons for this surprise. First, adult verbal conversations served as the model. In this situation maximum communication demands that speaker and listener exchange roles in an alternating fashion.[7,8] The difficulty of processing incoming information while simultaneously sending information requires this alternation. Second, it has been described that as early as the first few months of life, when babbling begins, mothers often create or shape an antiphonal or alternating pattern of vocalizations between themselves and their infants.[9] Similarly, we know that infant vocalizations can be conditioned, using the human voice or other social stimuli as reinforcers.[10–12] When the infant vocalization is viewed and treated as a response in the learning paradigm and the adult vocalization is used as the reinforcer, an alternating dialogic pattern will necessarily emerge. The alternating pattern may, in fact, be conditioned along with the vocalizations.

We present evidence that mothers and infants have two modes of vocalizing with each other that differ structurally and functionally: a coaction mode and an alternating mode. We suggest that coactional vocalizing is not simply an early developmental pattern that later transforms into the alternating pattern of conversational dialogue, but that it is also an enduring mode of human communication that shares much structurally and functionally with the kinesic systems of mutual gaze,[1,3] posture sharing,[13] and rhythm sharing.[14]

METHODOLOGY

SUBJECTS

Eight infants, consisting of four twin sets, were observed from their third to fourth month of life. Two monozygous and two dyzogous sets, five girls and three boys, were represented; individual differences or sex difference will not, however, be discussed. All infants had a normal developmental course. The mothers were primiparous, white, and middle socioeconomic class. For further details regarding the subjects, see Stern.[1]

DATA COLLECTION

The methods of data collection have previously been described.[1,6] The essential features involved repeated home visits, at least weekly for a month, during which an entire morning was set aside to videotape the naturally occurring, undirected mother-infant interactions as they normally unfolded: the recording on television tape of the gaze direction of each partner (i.e., whether they are gazing at the other's face), and the presence of vocalizations by mother and/or infant. Periods in which the infant was fussing and/or crying were excluded. This exclusion is very important in that mothers commonly vocalize simultaneously with the crying of their infants in order to soothe them. Also, although all infants were twins, only interactions between the mother and one infant were scored; i.e., all triadic interactions were excluded.

DATA SCORING OF DYADIC INTERACTIONS

Television tapes were replayed in the laboratory and viewed by four trained observers who operated a four-channel magnetic-tape event recorder. One observer scored whether the infant's gaze was "on" or "off" the mother's face, another simultaneously scored whether the mother's gaze was "on" or "off" the infant's face. Interrater agreement as to the presence of a gaze at the other's face was .96 and .93 as to its duration. The third and fourth observers separately scored the presence of maternal and infant vocalization, respectively. Interrater agreement as to the presence of a vocalization was .91, and .86 as to its duration. Accordingly, there are four separate behavioral variables: maternal gaze, infant gaze, maternal vocalization, and infant vocalization. Each of these four variables may occur separately or together in any combination. When each variable can either be "on" or "off," there exist 16 possible combinations of the four variables. Each separate combination is designated as a separate dyadic state. For the purposes of this paper we shall discuss only the two channels consisting of maternal and infant vocalization and the four dyadic states that result from their possible combinations: both silent, mother vocalizing while infant is silent, infant vocalizing while mother is silent, and both vocalizing. The magnetic tape with the channels scored is playing through a punch teletype machine which samples the magnetic tape every 0.1 seconds to determine which channels were "on" and accordingly, which of the possible dyadic states were present.

The punch tape is then fed into a PDP 12 computer programmed to print out how often each dyadic state occurred, its duration, and the percentage of time occupied by each state; in addition, a transition matrix is accumulated that shows the probability (in the next 0.1 second) of any dyadic state proceeding to any other dyadic state or remaining in the same state. When the computer print out is "retranslated," many simple questions can be asked, such as, "Are mother and infant vocalizations more or less likely than chance to occur simultaneously?"

An additional methodology was used to score and analyze portions of the data. This additional strategy was addressed to the question of whether incidences of co-occurring mother and infant vocalization might be related to the infant's level of affective arousal. For one infant only, the video recording of a play session was kinescoped and numbers were placed on each film frame. A frame-by-frame film analysis, without sound, was then performed.[15,6] All infant head, gaze, mouth, and, where possible, eye behaviors were scored on a time-flow record. The mother then looked at the film frame by frame, again without sound, and independently judged the infant's level of affectively positive arousal on a one to four scale. (For further details, see Beebe.[4]) The points in time at which the mother judged changes from one level to the next were then added to the time-flow record. Last, maternal and infant vocalization were then independently scored and superimposed on the time-flow record by frame number. By this procedure it is possible to correlate the different types of vocalizations (alternating, coactional, vocalizations occurring alone) with the maternal judgment of arousal level. The mother's judgments agreed (.85) with the independently arrived at experimental judgments of the infant's level of affectively positive arousal.

RESULTS

THE PREVALENCE OF A COACTION VOCALIZING PATTERN AND OF AN ALTERNATING VOCALIZING PATTERN

To determine whether a predominantly coactional or alternating dyadic vocalizing pattern was in operation, the odds ratio statistic was used[16] (see Figure 1). In an adult verbal conversation in which speaker and listener are exchanging roles, we would expect the greatest frequency to accumulate in cells "b" (when person A is speaking and B is silent) and "c" (where person B is speaking and A is silent). Much lower frequencies would be expected in cells "a" (during joint silence) and "d" (during interruptions where there is simultaneous speech). The odds ratio for such a conversation would be well below 1.0, and indeed, the analysis of 30 polite adult conversations revealed an odds ratio of 0.03.[17] If, on the other hand, persons A and B were engaged in choral speaking, the greatest frequencies would accumulate in cells "d" (when they were speaking together) and in cell "a" (when they were both silent). Lower frequencies would be expected in cells "b" and "c" (during short failures to start and stop speaking together). In such a coaction pattern the odds ratio would exceed 1.0. For analyzing the data, the formula shown in Figure 1 was altered to read

$$\text{O.R.} = \frac{(a+.5) \times (d+.5)}{(b+.5) \times (c+.5)}$$

to account for zero frequencies in one or more cells.

		Person A (Mother)	
		Silent	Vocal-izing
Person B (Infant)	Silent	a	b
	Vocal-izing	c	d

$$\text{Odds ratio} = \frac{a \times d}{b \times c}$$

Odds ratio < 1.0 indicates an alternating pattern
Odds ratio > 1.0 indicates a co-action pattern

Figure 1. Coaction versus alternating vocal dyadic patterns expressed in terms of the odds ratio statistic.

Table 1 shows the odds ratio and its level of significance as measured by a chi-

(O.R.)*

#	Twin Set 1				Twin Set 2				Twin Set 3				Twin Set 4			
	Twin N†	1A O.R.‡	Twin N	1B O.R.	Twin N	2A O.R.	Twin N	2B O.R.	Twin N	3A O.R.	Twin N	3B O.R.	Twin N	4A O.R.	Twin N	4B O.R.
1.	6679	2.48**	8683	1.61	1470	0.19	1098	1.05	4713	2.03*	980	0.68	2061	1.07	2295	1.41
2.	707	1.71***	1583	8.07*	2149	1.32	695	3.13*	732	0.29***	520	1.94	1424	1.86***	4382	0.77
3.	1917	4.65***	11284	3.62***	1006	1.27	854	2.42**	1717	5.75**	1122	1.80	2729	0.03	1451	1.14**
4.	3014	0.57			271	0.10	1926	0.50***	1911	1.02	805	1.59**	3330	0.78	4643	1.22**
5.	2493	1.26			608	0.85*	1102	4.55	2676	1.19	2538	19.45***	3593	0.81	6501	0.54
6.					3870	1.87			3317	0.28**	2487	0.27***	6646	1.15		
7.					713	0.35			3278	2.53	1077	0.03*				
8.					502	2.21**			1444	0.87	878	13.54				
9.					539	0.41			1314	1.08	1662	2.23				
10.					790	0.33			3078	1.18	3069	1.74				
11.					1905	1.27			2815	1.28	336	13.76*				
12.									4819	0.77	3133	0.62				
13.											502	0.32				
14.											964	2.13***				
15.											2716	0.50				
16.											2629	0.56				
17.											4313	42.85**				
Mean O.R. across all play sessions of each dyad		1.66***		3.32***		1.09		1.35*		1.32**		0.68**		0.96		1.11

*(*p<.05, **p<.01, ***p<.001).
†N = The number of observations taken at a rate of 10/second.
‡Mean O.R. across all sessions and all dyads = 1.20***

119

square test with a Yates correction[16] for each session of each infant-mother pair. In addition, the mean odds ratio for each infant-mother pair across all their play sessions, and the mean odds ratio across all pairs and all sessions are shown. This analysis revealed that of the 64 separate play sessions, forty showed an odds ratio greater than 1.0 (i.e., a coaction pattern), and fifteen of these reached significance. Twenty-four sessions showed an odds ratio of less than 1.0 (i.e., an alternating pattern), and eight of these reached significance.

When all sessions for each infant-mother pair were pooled, six pairs showed an overall coaction pattern (three reached significance), and two pairs showed an overall alternating pattern (one reached significance). When all sessions for all pairs were pooled the mean odds ratio was 1.20, indicating an overall coaction pattern significant at the .001 level.

It is interesting to note that twins 3A and 3B, who both showed significant patterns but in the opposite direction, are monozygous. This finding will be discussed below.

THE RELATIONSHIP BETWEEN THE DYADIC VOCALIZING PATTERN AND THE INFANT'S LEVEL OF AROUSAL

In order to test the clinical impression that coactional vocalizing occurs mainly during high levels of infant (and probably maternal) arousal, the frame-by-frame film analysis described above was performed. The five vocalizing categories were: infant vocalize alone; mother vocalize alone; infant vocalize in alternation; mother vocalize in alternation: coactional vocalizations. A vocalization was scored as alternating if it occurred within 1.0 second after the termination of a vocalization of the partner. If more than 1.0 second elapsed the vocalization was designated a vocalization alone.

Figure 2 shows the percentage of each type of vocalization that occurred at each level of affectively positive arousal. It can be seen that coactional vocalizations are heavily concentrated (60%) at the highest level of arousal, whereas alternating vocalizations of both mother (53%) and infant (54%) are more manifest at a midlevel of arousal.

THE RELATIVE CONTRIBUTION OF MOTHER AND INFANT TO THE FORMATION OF A COACTION PATTERN

The following four analyses (A–D) focus on the questions of how and who is mainly "responsible" for creating a coaction pattern.

Operationally, we have asked what the effect is of the presence of infant vocalization on the initiation and on the continuation, or termination, of maternal vocalizations, and vice versa, what the effect is of the presence of maternal vocalizations on the initiation and on the continuation of infant vocalizations.

A. *The Effect of the Presence of Infant Vocalization on the Initiation of Maternal Vocalization.* Table 2, Row 1, shows the difference, expressed as $\bar{D}$,[16] between the probability that the mother will initiate a vocalization when the infant is silent, compared to when he is vocalizing. The negative value of $\bar{D}$ in seven of eight dyads indicates that the mother is more likely to start vocalizing during an infant vocalization than when he is silent. This, of course, is contrary to the expected "rules" for adult conversational exchange.

Table 2   The Effect of Infant Vocalization on Maternal Vocalization, and the Effect of Maternal Vocalization on Infant Vocalization*

	D Value for Twin-Mother Dyad†							
	1A	1B	2A	2B	3A	3B	4A	4B
The Effect of infant vocalization on:								
The initiation of maternal vocalization‡	−.451	−1.393**	−.342	−.351	−.300	−.369*	−.220	+.096
The termination of maternal vocalization§	+.600*	+.525	+.562*	+.032	+.156	−.093	+.518*	+.003
The initiation of infant vocalization¶	−.617	−1.177***	+.152	−.357	−.261	+.021	−.467	−.116
The effect of maternal vocalization on:								
The termination of infant vocalization††	−.440	+.121	+.095	−.091	−.014	−.128	−.453	+.093

*(*p < .05, **p < .01, ***p < .001).
†The difference between the two probabilities is expressed as D̄ using a chi-square statistic to test the significance of the D̄.
‡p(Mother will initiate a vocalization when the infant is silent) minus the p (mother will initiate a vocalization when the infant is vocalizing).
§ p (Mother will terminate a vocalization when the infant is silent) minus the p (mother will terminate when the infant is vocalizing).
¶p(Infant will initiate a vocalization when the mother is silent) minus the p (infant will initiate a vocalization when the mother is vocalizing).
††p(Infant will terminate a vocalization when the mother is silent) minus the p (infant will terminate a vocalization when the mother is vocalizing).

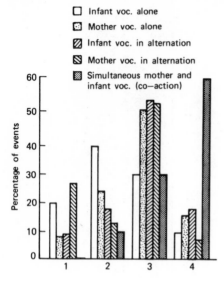

☐ Infant voc. alone
▣ Mother voc. alone
▨ Infant voc. in alternation
▧ Mother voc. in alternation
▦ Simultaneous mother and
   infant voc. (co—action)

Figure 2. The relative occurrence of different types of vocalizations at different levels of affectively positive arousal. (Infant vocalize alone, $N = 10$; mother vocalize alone, $N = 37$; infant vocalize in alternation, $N = 11$; mother vocalize in alternation, $N = 15$; coaction vocalizations, $N = 20$.)

B. *The Effect of the Presence of Infant Vocalization on the Termination of Maternal Vocalization.* Table 2, Row II, shows the difference between the probability that the mother will terminate a vocalization when the infant is silent compared to when he is vocalizing. The positive values of $\bar{D}$ in seven of eight dyads indicates that the mother is more likely to stop vocalizing during an infant silence than when he is vocalizing; i.e., she is more likely to continue vocalizing during his vocalization. Again, this is contrary to the expected adult conversational "rules."

C. *The Effect of the Presence of Maternal Vocalization on the Initiation of Infant Vocalization.* Table 2, Row III, shows the difference between the probability that the infant will initiate a vocalization when the mother is silent compared to when she is vocalizing. The negative values of $\bar{D}$ in six of eight dyads indicates that the infant tends to start vocalizing during a maternal vocalization.

D. *The Effect of the Presence of Maternal Vocalization on the Termination of Infant Vocalization.* Table 2, Row IV, shows the difference between the probability that the infant will terminate a vocalization when the mother is silent compared to when she is vocalizing. No clear trend is evident.

In summary, the mother is more likely to begin vocalizing when the infant is already vocalizing, and she tends to continue vocalizing while the infant is vocalizing. Both effects would tend to increase the likelihood of a coaction pattern. The infant, like the mother, tends to begin a vocalization while the mother is already vocalizing. This also would tend to produce a coaction pattern. However, the infant does not show a tendency to continue vocalizing during a maternal vocalization. This may be simply because his vocalizations are generally much shorter than hers. In any event, the "rules" of adult conversational dialogue are violated by both partners. The mother, however, appears to influence more strongly the production of the coaction pattern, just as it is found that she is more "responsible" for the production of the alternating pattern.

DISCUSSION

The data suggest that we are witnessing the parallel emergence of two separate modes of vocal communication, which differ structurally and functionally. From a larger biological perspective, it is not unusual for different species such as birds to develop both antiphonal and synchronous or coaction communication modes to serve different purposes.[18]

Both dyadic vocal patterns are demonstrable in the interactions of three-to-four-month-old infants and their mothers. The coaction pattern occurs almost twice as frequently as the alternating pattern, but all dyads appear capable of performing in both modes. The majority of individual sessions, however, are not patterned in either direction to an extent that reaches significance. This lack of pattern may prove to be a methodological artifact. Within any single play session the mother and infant may produce several short "runs" of alternating vocalizations, interspersed in the same session with several "runs" of coactional vocalizations. Several switches of pattern within a session may be common, depending on the interpersonal situation and the level of arousal. In fact, it is our clinical impression, although undocumented, that in any session both modes will be employed. However, since the analysis considers one play session as a single event, we can uncover only the predominant pattern for the entire session, thus making the majority of vocal interactions appear less patterned than they actually might be. In any event, at this stage of development most mother-infant dyads will manifest different patterns in different sessions, even though one of the patterns may be significantly more common throughout all their sessions.

At some point in the second year of life when verbal comprehension develops, we would expect the alternating pattern that facilitates this process to be not only well established but also the predominant one. Accordingly, we would expect a developmental shift in predominant pattern from coaction, seen at three to four months, to alternating, seen in adult dyads. (The Odds Ratio would be expected to reflect this shift by gradually falling below the critical value of 1.0 and decreasing further over time until it approximates the value of 0.03 seen in polite adult conversation.) We do not have the developmental data to document this probable course. However, the fact that the alternating pattern must emerge as the dominant one as verbal behavior is acquired does not necessarily argue that the coaction pattern is simply transformed under the influence of maternal shaping into an alternating one, and then disappears from use. The presence of both patterns at the very early developmental stage of three to four months, and the utilization of both patterns throughout life, as described below, suggests a parallel development for each.

A second reason to suggest that these two patterns emerge in parallel as functionally as well as structurally separate communication modes is that each is more likely to occur under different conditions of arousal and affect. Figure 2 indicates that the coaction pattern is mainly manifest during the highest levels of arousal, while the alternating pattern is more evident at midrange levels. It is a common experience that at high arousal levels at either the positive or negative end of the affective spectrum, mothers and infants will vocalize simultaneously. While the baby is fretting or crying, the mother most often will simultaneously say something like, "There, there," to sooth him. Similarly, at the far positive end, mothers and infants will laugh in unison. However, even short of this extreme, at moments when the infant (and almost invariably the mother, also) are at a high level of affectively positive arousal, they will vocalize together and appear to derive much enjoyment from it.

A probable explanation of the finding that twin 3A and mother show a predominantly coaction pattern while her monozygous sister, 3B, and mother show an alternating pattern relates to this issue of the influence of arousal level on vocal pattern. At each morning visit, this mother always awakened twin 3A first, fed her, and played with her. The mother then repeated this sequence with twin 3B. By the time mother got around to twin 3B, she was relatively "played out," and instead of pursuing the highly arousing, spontaneously playful behaviors she showed with twin 3A, she interacted with 3B at a relatively lower level of arousal and centered her play more around instructional behaviors. This clinical vignette supports our overall impression that during those parts of a play session when the mother is "teaching" her infant, an alternating pattern is mainly used. However, when the two start to really have fun together, they move into a coaction pattern. Given "identical" constitutions, it is striking that the mother can by three to four months so markedly influence in differential ways the vocal interactions she helps form with each twin. This is consistent with the finding that it is mainly the mothers' influence that determines the dyadic vocal pattern. A possible reason for the generally large amount of coactional vocalizing observed is that these mothers generally sought and achieved highly arousing interactions with their infants.

The existence of coactional vocalizing under conditions of high arousal is not unique to the mother-infant dyad but continues throughout life. It is instructive to consider occurrences of simultaneous vocalization among adults. As the interpersonal situation moves toward intense anger, sadness, joy, or expressions of love, the alternating dialogic pattern "breaks down" and coactional vocalizing again becomes a crucial communicative mode. Mutual declarations of love and vocalizations during love-making are an obvious example. In fact, an operatic love duet can be viewed as an excellent cultural representation of this phenomenon. Arguments provide another example. As an argument gets more "heated," interruptions (which are a form of coactional speaking) become more frequent and longer. At some point, the information in the verbalizations of the antagonists recedes in importance compared to the fight for the "floor"; i.e., the experience of being interrupted and talked at, while talking, becomes the primary communicative event, overshadowing whatever is being said.

Coactional vocalizing is a common occurrence among adults in a related human situation, namely, in defining group membership for a given purpose, or to state or establish group bonds. A variety of examples can serve: choral speaking, as in a pledge of allegiance; prayer, in recitative form; work songs or any group singing or chanting; political rallying behavior such as leader, "What do we want?", followers, "FREEDOM," etc.; peer group taunting of another child, "Sally is a yah-yah"; peer group celebrating a member during toasting behavior, "Here, here," etc. The joint vocalizations mentioned above usually carry a symbolic meaning that generally passes for their main purpose. However, they also appear to have a strong group-bonding effect, which, though less obvious, is often more important.

A football game provides several examples of how different subgroups can be defined by who vocalizes together; everyone in the stadium, players and audience, stand and sing together the national anthem. This defines the entire group participating in the sporting event. Then the cheer leaders for one side coordinate the coactional vocalization of one half of the stadium. This defines a rooting or fan group. Then the 36 players and several coaches of one team huddle before the start of the game, some rousing words are said, and the group breaks apart, making some vocalization together. This defines the entire working team. Then eleven members of the team go on the field, huddle to make a play, and break huddle, vocalizing together. This defines the playing unit. It is worth noting that each of these "units" is spatially defined, also. However, it is at moments of heightened arousal that they also "define" themselves by vocalizing together.

Many cross-cultural examples of collective simultaneous vocalizing to express group membership can be found in anthropological studies. Related but dispersed tribes gather together periodically to chant and move in unison as part of the ceremony that reestablishes group bonds.[14]

Byers describes an unusual form of joint vocalizing among the Yanamamo Indians in South America.[14] When two tribes that are potentially hostile come together for a feast, the two chiefs first engage in a ritual greeting ceremony consisting of what sounds like a "shouting match," during which both chiefs are simultaneously shouting at each other, each in synchrony with the other's vocalizations. This presumably serves an aggression-inhibiting function. Coberly[19] examined in ten cultures the process whereby Shamans "cure" a deviant member. In all cultures the Shamann collects a group of normals who are then made to chant, sing, clap, and/or move in unison. The deviant is then brought back into the group by his participating in the collective coactional activity.

In previous work we have found that the gaze behaviors of mother and infant form a "conversational" pattern that constitutes an early dialogic system.[1,3] This dialogic system is heavily coactional in that the response biases of both partners tend to create a preponderance of mutual gaze.[1] The present data indicates that the dyadic coactional vocalizing pattern conforms closely to the dyadic gazing pattern between mother and infant. Furthermore, coactional vocalizing occurs almost invariably during mutual gaze.[22] Accordingly, at given moments, the nature of the interpersonal interaction and its emotional tone are communicated by the mutual and simultaneous performance of both gaze and vocalization. These appear to be quite special moments for the dyad.

To the extent that vocalizing together, especially in conjunction with mutual gaze, is a form of establishing group membership or bonding, particularly under conditions of heightened arousal, the coactional vocalizations between mother and infant may fruitfully be considered an early attachment behavior that contributes to the formation of the mother-infant tie. Vocalizing in unison as a mutual experience of joy or excited delight in being with someone may be central to the creation of a positive experience of relatedness, and should, in this regard, be added to the growing list of human behaviors that bond a mother and infant together.[20,21]

We have provided evidence that two structurally different patterns of dyadic vocalizations exist between mother and infant by the time the infant is three to four months old. We suggest that both patterns develop as distinct modes serving separate communicative functions. The alternating mode transforms into the conversational dialogic pattern to function later in the exchange of symbolic information. The coaction mode transmits emotional communications expressive of the nature of the ongoing interpersonal relationship, as well as contributing to the formation of the relationship.

ACKNOWLEDGMENT

We gratefully wish to acknowledge the statistical advice given by Dr. Joseph L. Fleiss.

REFERENCES

1. Stern, D. N. 1974. Mother and infant at play: the dyadic interaction involving facial, vocal and gaze behaviors. In *The Effect of the Infant on its Caregiver.* Vol 1: 187–213. The Origin of Behavior Series. Lewis and L. Rosenblum, Eds. John Wiley & Sons Inc. New York, N.Y.
2. Stern, D. N. 1974. The goal and structure of mother-infant play. *J. Am. Acad. Child. Psychiat.* 13: 402–421.
3. Jaffe, J., D. N. Stern & J. C. Perry. 1973. "Conversational" coupling of gaze behavior in prelinguistic human development. *J. Psycholinguistic Res.* 2: 321–329.
4. Beebe, B. 1973. The ontogeny of positive affect in the third and fourth month of the life of one infant. Doctoral dissertation. Columbia University, New York, N.Y.
5. Bennett, S. L. 1971. Infant-caretaker interactions. *J. Am. Acad. Child Psychiat.* 10: 321–335.
6. Stern, D. N. 1971. A micro-analysis of mother-infant interaction. *J. Am. Acad. Child. Psychiat.* 10: 501–517.
7. Jaffe, J. & D. A. Norman. 1964. A simulation of the time patterns of dialogue. Scientific Report No. C5-4. Center for Cognitive Studies. Harvard University. Cambridge, Mass.
8. Jaffe, J. & S. Feldstein. 1970. *Rhythms of Dialogue.* Academic Press. New York, N.Y.
9. Bateson, M. C. Annals of the New York. Academy of Sciences: Developmental Psycholinguistics and Communication Disorders, **263**, 1975.
10. Rheingold, H. L., J. L. Gewitz & H. W. Ross. 1959. Social conditioning of vocalizations in the infant. *J. Comp. Physiol. Psychol.* 52: 68–73.
11. Weisberg, P. 1963. Social and nonsocial conditioning of infant vocalization. *Child Develop.* 34: 377–388.
12. Todd, G. A., A. Gibson & B. Palmer, 1968. Social reinforcement of infant babbling. *Child Develop.* 39: 591–596.
13. Scheflen, A. E. 1964. The significance of posture in communication systems. Psychiatry 27: 316–331.
14. Byers, P. 1975. Rhythms, information processing and human relations: toward a typology of communication. In *Perspectives in Ethology.* Vol. II. P. Klopfer and P. Bateson, Eds. Plenum Press. New York, N.Y.
15. Condon, W. S. & W. D. Ogston, 1966. Sound film analysis of normal and pathological behavior patterns. *J. Nerv. Ment. Dis.* 143: 338–347.
16. Fleiss, J. L. 1973. *Statistical methods for rates and proportions.* John Wiley & Sons Inc. New York, N.Y.
17. Jaffe, J. 1975. Unpublished.
18. Thorpe, W. H. 1961. *Bird Song: The Biology of Vocal Communication and Expression in Birds.* Cambridge University Press. Cambridge, Mass.

19. Coberly, L. 1973. An interactional analysis of ten curing ceremonies. M. A. Thesis. Columbia University. New York, N.Y.
20. Bowlby, J. 1969. *Attachment and Loss.* Vol. I Basic Books. New York, N.Y.
21. Ainsworth, M. D. S. 1969. Object relations, dependency and attachment. *Child Dev.* 40: 969–1025.
22. Stern, D. N. & J. Jaffe. In preparation.

Part 3
DEVELOPMENT OF LANGUAGE CONTENT/ FORM: VOCABULARY

The changing relations between the meaning or content of messages and the forms of messages is the main focus of *Language Development and Language Disorders*, and the readings in this section and the two sections that follow present several of the observational studies that were principal sources of the information that is presented in the text. With respect to the development of vocabulary in the second year, the selections from Leopold's 1939 diary study reproduced in Part I of these readings are particularly relevant. Many of Leopold's observations have been echoed again and again in more recent descriptions of the words that children learn. The paper by *Paul Guillaume* was first published in French in 1927, and the insights that Guillaume gleaned from his diary observations of his son's use of words in his second year were still relevant to research in the 1960s (see Bloom, 1973). *Hermina Sinclair (1970)* described the kinds of sensorimotor behaviors (in particular, play with objects) described by Jean Piaget in relation to children's single-words in the second year, and the selection that follows, from *Bloom (1973)*, presents a discussion of different kinds of words that children use in this same period. Together, these four readings document three basic conclusions about the single-word utterance period in child language. First, it is a period of continuous change, both in the kinds of words that are used and in the ways in which single words are used. Second, the words that children learn are intimately related to the ideas that they have about objects and events in the world. And, finally, the period in which children say only one word at a time is continuous with both the prior development of precursory behaviors in infancy and the subsequent appearance of combination of words; it is not a unitary "stage" in development.

First Stages of Sentence Formation in Children's Speech

Paul Guillaume

The history of different languages shows not only that words change their meanings but also that new grammatical devices evolve; this suggests that we could go back to a primitive state prior to grammar. In fact, though, a complete lack of morphological differentiation does not occur. When we see a new expression appear to fill a particular function, it is always at the expense of terms differentiated in another way. The language often contains an expression for that function already, so the new one supplants the old.

The facts that we cannot examine in the history of languages are available to us in the child. It is true that imitation of a language already formed is the principle of acquisition, but such assimilation cannot be entirely passive; it probably goes through a number of stages essential to the acquisition of any complex language. The same psychological mechanisms (for instance, the one which underlies analogical formations) probably play a part in languages being maintained and in their being acquired by individuals. Lastly, the problem of the development of the child's language is interesting in its own right, independently of any conclusions that could be drawn from primitive languages.

The procedure for this study is as objective as possible. It is a question of finding objective criteria for stages of language development, based both on understanding of the speech of others and on the child's spontaneous speech.

Comprehension will be defined by the child's reactions. Language is essentially a means for one man to act upon another; every expression has an imperative value; it is an invitation to react, to pay attention, or to recognize. Later on, when the aptitude for dialogue develops, it constitutes an invitation to respond with speech to the enquiries of the interlocutor. In assessing the replies, actions, or further speech, one has to take account of the material meaning of the words and of their functions (word order, inflections, particular grammatical devices). Difficulties arise from the inseparable nature of the form and content. The grammatical tools are bound to the meaningful words, and the sentence heard is part of an intuitive situation, so much so that the whole may accidentally provoke correct replies, without each speech

Les débuts de la phrase dans le langage de l'enfant. *Journal de Psychologie*, 1927, 24, 1–25. Translated from French by Eve V. Clark in C. Ferguson and D. Slobin (Eds.), *Studies of Child Language and Development*. Reprinted by permission of Presses Universitaires de France.

element having been understood in its own particular function. The points when the response is correct where the situation and the meaningful words alone are not adequate to prompt a correct response, and when new combinations of familiar words, conforming to the linguistic rules, are immediately given an interpretation, have to be noted.

One cannot extrapolate directly from language that is understood to spoken language. In order to explain the child's speech, it is not enough to allow for reversible associations which would be established between "ideas" and "words." The two functions are never that closely linked. The latter (words) lag behind the former. Those who more or less know a foreign language or dialect can often understand it but not speak it; one's native speech, likewise, in vocabulary and form, shows differences between speaking and understanding. This is because speech proceeds directly from imitation, while everything that is understood is not necessarily imitated. Speech is not only an invitation to act or to perceive; it also, under certain circumstances, invites repetition. The child repeats the word at the same time as he performs the action; the word is associated with games accompanied by words. The moment at which utterances become independent of the external verbal model must·be examined, not only because the utterance has been directly inspired by the situation but rather because the child has become capable of constructing a whole new utterance with familiar words according to the rules of the language.

Such distinctions are sometimes very minute; however, continuous observation of a few children who can be followed for several years and whose progress can be noted continually provides a certain safeguard. It is this method that we have followed, and supplemented, in some instances, by notes taken of the conversations of children between two and five years old in a kindergarten.

WORDS IN THE SPOKEN LANGUAGE AND IN THE WRITTEN LANGUAGE

It is a commonplace, nowadays, to say that in the child's speech the sentence—understood or uttered—is anterior to the words, or rather that there are neither real words nor real sentences. Later, an "awareness of words" will develop. But when? Certain facts lead us to believe that this occurs at a very late stage and does not appear until the start of scholastic education. Therein lies a misunderstanding about language which must first be cleared up.

The writing of half-literate people does not, it is said, show any awareness of individual words. I have collected a small set of letters documenting this. The letters represent different levels of education in the writers. In the letters there are three types of alternations made, all arising from the same cause: *segmentation, liaisons,* and *confusions of homonyms.*

In the liaisons, several words are treated as a single one: *aidi* (ai dit = I have said), *esque* (est-ce que = is it . . .), *cecerai* (ce serait = that would be), *semy* (s'est mis = placed himself), *set* (c'est = it is). In the segmentations, one word is split up: a *bitant* (habitant = inhabitant), *trou vais* (trouvais = found, 1 sg.), *tom bra* (tombera = will fall, 3 sg.), *a ses* (assez = enough), *sin cerre* (sincère = sincere), *en core* (encore = more, again), and so on. Sometimes the two occur together: *ja prend* (j'apprends = I am learning), *dé colle* (d'école = of school), and so on.

Liaisons and segmentations do not occur randomly; they often tend to wrongly isolate familiar words,[1] and above all, those words for which the writer knows the *graphic form*. He will write *sans* (= without, for *s'en* = of it, them), *sais* (= know, 1 sg., for *c'est* = it is), *long* (= long, for *l'on* = impersonal 3 per. pronoun). Segmentation lends itself better to these false perceptions; at least one of the isolated members is a small familiar word, article, pronoun, preposition, and so on. Examples: *de mande* (demande = ask, 3 sg.), *par le (parle = speak, 3 sg.), au temp* (autant = as much), *vous loire* (vouloir = to want), *et tant* (étant = being), *pret sans* (présent = present), *a vons* (avons = have, 1 pl.), *sous mis* (soumis = submitted, past part.). No doubt the preposition *sous* (= under) explains *sous mis;* the pronoun *vous* (= you) appears in *vous loire;* the adjective *pret* (= ready) provides the *t* of *pret sans;* the *p* of *au temp* (see above) comes from the word *temps* (= time, weather). If there is any doubt about the role of graphic memory in the segmentation of the sentence, we need only consider the very numerous examples in which letters or groups of letters visibly representing our pronouns, articles, or elided conjunctions are carefully separated from the rest of the word by an apostrophe. Note that such elements are seen as individual segments only in the written, not the spoken, forms. For example: *l'es* (les = pl. def. art.), *l'eur* (Leur = their), *l'ettre* (lettre = letter), *qu'and* (quand = when), *augu'un* (aucun = anyone), *qu'ar* (car = for), *l'orsque* (lorsque = since), *d'ont* (dont = whose), *d'éjà* (déjà = already), *m'a* (ma = my, fem. sg.), *c'est* (cette = this, fem. sg.), and so on.

This tendency is further demonstrated in the confusion of homonyms which is frequent even in the writing of those who do not use incorrect liaisons and segmentations. In the examples below, it can be seen that the word substituted retains its spelling; but one may write indifferently *ses* (= his), *ces* (= those), *est* (= is), *et* (= and); *non* (= no), *nom* (= name); *étais* (= was, 1 sg.), *été* (= been, past part., or = summer); *voie* (= way), *voix* (= voice); *prix* (= prize), *pris* (= taken, past, part., or prie = pray), *vent* (= wind), *vend* (= sell); *vie* (= life), *vit* (= saw, 3 sg.); *mes* (= my, pl.), *mais* (= but); *peu* (= little), *peut* (= can, 3 sg.); *ci* (= here), *si* (= if); *maire* (= mayor), *mère* (= mother); *paire* (= pair), *père* (= father); *crin* (= hair), *craint* (= fear, 3 sg.); *dont* (= whose), *donc* (= therefore), and so on.

In interpreting such facts as these, we must keep in mind that the people who write so badly do, however, speak their language fluently; their speech is not a simple mosaic of ready-made utterances applicable to each situation; they know how to *construct* sentences according to the rules of the language with the vocabulary at their disposal. The very way in which words are combined bears witness, in a sense, to their individuality and their differentiation. No one supposes that the person who writes *l'ettre* (for *lettre*) cannot say: *J'ai écrit une lettre* (= I have written a letter), *des Lettres* (= some letters), *J'ai envoyé ma lettre* (= I have sent my letter), *j'ai reçu votre lettre* (= I got your letter); *lettre* behaves as a single indivisible word in the spoken language (jusr like *car, déjà,* and so on; see above). If someone writes *sans* instead of *s'en,* that does not prevent him from saying *Je m'en vais* (= I am going away), *tu t'en vas* (= you are going away), *il s'en va* (= he is going away), and so on. Despite the arbitrary graphic liaisons and segmentations, the spoken sentence obeys rules

---

[1] See A. Lalande, La conscience des mots dans le langage, *Journal de Psychologie,* 1905 (January issue).

which provide it with well-defined points of articulation. The utterance is constructured from real elements which the speaker knows how to manipulate. Thus the grammatical differentiation of words does exist in a way in the spoken language even though the graphic forms of a substantive may be confused with those of a verb, that of a possessive pronoun with that of a demonstrative pronoun, that of a participle with that of an infinitive, and so on. The man who writes (without distinguishing them): *Il faut les donner* (infinitive) or *les donnais* (1 sg. imperfect) will say, correctly, *Il faut finir, il faut rendre* (infinitives); wherever the forms are differentiated by the sound, he knows perfectly well how to use the one and the other in any sentence construction.

The expression "awareness of words," therefore, has no exact descriptive value and can only give rise to misunderstandings. The individuality and differentiation of words depend on different layers of habits, and these terms take on a new meaning on each new occasion when one goes from the spoken to the written language, and from the latter to a logical and explicit grammatical analysis. In the educated adult, these functions have become closely welded; he passes easily from the one to the other. The written form becomes symbolic of the whole; however, it is superimposed fairly arbitrarily on the spoken form. It may be surprising that the graphic division of the sentence into words does not result from a simple graphic transposition of the words from the spoken sentence, the one being molded on the other or deduced from the other. But there is no perfect correspondence between the two systems of articulations in all their details (for example, the inflections of words could logically be separated from the stem). In fact, we have seen that the graphic segmentation above all reveals the influence of the written model rather than directly reflecting the organization imminent in discourse.

THE SENTENCE UNDERSTOOD, BUT UNDIFFERENTIATED

In order to give an account of the origin of the organization of discourse, we have to return to the first two years of childhood. Here we have a child of eight or nine months who already understands a series of sentences that signal familiar games: *Bats la mauvaise tête!* (= smack naughty head), to tap oneself on the head; *Envoie un baiser* (= blow a kiss), *Fais ami! ami!* (= make friends), to shake hands; *Danse l'espagnole! Danse la française!* (= dance the Spanish way! dance the French way!), indicating two poses with different hand positions; *Fais blablab* (= do blab), to make one's lips vibrate against a finger; and so on. Perhaps it is general form of the intonation pattern that is known rather than its elements. However, one could believe that all the sounds do not have the same value, that certain words stand out, that others are only subsidiary filling, embellishments, passing comments. One is never obliged to speak to a child with rigorously uniform and concise utterances. He hears variants, but also essential words bearing stress which are sometimes repeated. This does not hamper the child much, for he also begins to recognize the same sentences spoken by other people despite differences of voice pitch. It is quite possible, then, that certain words acquire a precocious individuality.

On the other hand, it is impossible to class these words into grammatical categories. This seems to be true even of the names of people (papa, mama, Marie, Suzanne). They are named at the time of certain actions; the names are imperatives, signals; one has to turn toward that person, look at him, smile at him, blow him a kiss, lean over to be picked up in his arms. There is no need to separate the name of the person and that of the action in this signal of complex experiences. The same goes for the personal name of the child. To ask at what point a child understands his name is to ask a strange question: one would have to describe in detail the succession of reactions which the name evokes. First, it is a commonplace summons: it is the attitude, the look of whoever says it that makes the child feel that it has something to do with him. It is a synonym of words like: *Attention!* (= here!), *Regarde par ici!* (= look over here!). It is the signal for interesting experiences, for an action in which he is to participate. It is an interjection, and imperative, as well as a name. The same reflections apply to the names of things: the attributes of the objects are inseparable from the actions related lo them which make them interesting.

What characterizes the period of the first sentences that are understood is the sporadic success of tests. If I say to P. (12.8),[2] "Donne à papa" (= give to papa), referring to a candy he has in his hand, he gives it to me. If I say to him, "Donne à maman" (= give to mama), he gives it to me again. I repeat my order. He puts it in his mouth. Thus there is nondifferentiation of or lack of attention to the special form of the utterance, a habit of guessing on the basis of the whole situation rather than according to an exact, analytic perception of the content of the sentence. The child replies randomly to every sort of question (Qui? = who, Quoi? = what, Comment? = how). He counts more on intuition than on language to make distinctions. He must be compared to the child who begins to read and continually tries to guess instead of carefully sounding out the word. When there are several ways of understanding something, there is always a special laziness over the least familiar methods. There is no doubt that at this stage, the least familiar thing is language. Even a correct understanding reveals more about the relations between each word and the intuitive situation than about the structure of the sentence. From 9.17 on, P. seemed to understand sentences like "Calinette à papa! Calinette à maman!" (= give papa a kiss, give mama a kiss): he put his hand on the cheek of the person named even if the latter made no gesture; but the sentence had to be repeated emphatically. The first time he was ready to perform, but hesitated over the person: it was at this point that I repeated "Á maman! Á maman!" (= to mama, to mama). This utterance was juxtaposed in some way to the first one rather than subordinated to it. The second part is interpreted by its occurrence in the concrete situation created by the first, and not by its function as a member of the sentence. According to a linguist who has thoroughly studied the origins of the sentence.[3] The words here are *predicates of the situation;* in reality, there are as many meaningful sentences as there are words. If the whole has a psychological unity, since it is a question of aspects of the same action, that unity is not yet that of a grammatical organism obeying the rules of a particular language; the whole has no more the structure of a French sentence than of a foreign sentence, of a sabir or of a creole, of a telegram or of an announcement. Even these comparisons are inadequate, because, for us, words are still separated into parts of speech; they appear as members of possible sentences; they are called complements

---

[2] The first number refers to the months, the second to the days of the child's age.
[3] Wegener, *Grundfragen des Sprachlebens,* 1885.

not only because of their material meaning but because of their ever-present formal value.

THE UNDIFFERENTIATED WORD SENTENCE

Spoken language confirms the absence of differentiation between words. We know that the child's imitation is a simplification. The same reasons that reduce a word to one syllable and even to one vowel underlie the condensation of our sentences to one word in the child (the easiest one to pronounce, the best known, the one that is stressed). A bit later on, the child adds to his utterances those sounds which correspond to the subordinate words. The progress which replaces *A plus* (= no more) with *Je n'en ai plus* (= I haven't any more) is of the same order as that which transforms *colat* into *chocolat* (= chocolate), and *ti* into *parti* (= gone). But alongside the phonetic aspect, there is both a semantic and a grammatical aspect: these are what we are interested in.

The first words are used in a variety of contexts which makes their definition difficult. *Papa* (P. at 12 months) is said in the presence of an object belonging to me, when the child picks up some paper, a card, my pen, when he goes into my empty study, when he wants to write, to come close to me, to see me, when he recognizes me after an absence. He says *maman* when he wants to suckle, to be picked up in someone's arms (even when addressing me), to attract the attention of his mother to an object he is displaying or to his physiological needs. *Nénin* is used to ask for the breast, but also to ask for a cookie. If one wanted to interpret this as a kind of verb meaning *Á manger* (= to eat), it would be difficult to explain his saying it when pointing to the red button of a garment, the point of a bare elbow, an eye in a portrait, the face of his mother in a photograph. *Tata* is said when he wants to sit on the pot or urinate, or when he has done so; when he sees a stain on the tablecloth, on an apron; when he puts a pencil, a copper ball, or piece of fruit, or a potato into his mouth; when he sees the dishwater, coffee grounds, someone he dislikes. *Blablab* means the action of vibrating one's lips against a finger, then the mouth, especially that of a child in a portrait, then every portrait, every drawing, the picture postcards that I sent when I was away, every manuscript or printed page, a paper or a book, but then it means the act of "reading" or the wish to read: almost all these meanings co-existed at age 11.15. For the same period, here is a list of words used in isolation; I have indicated the probable meanings, according to the context of use: these demonstrate the equivocal nature of the word, its fluctuations between a nominal and a verbal meaning. Almost all the words are related to familiar games: *Bo* (= brush or = to brush), *Ba* (= broom or = to sweep), *Pain* (= give bread or = eat bread,) *Bain* (= bath or to bathe), *Ke* (= key or = put the key in or take it out of the lock), *Papou* (= soup, = good soup, or = eat soup), *Papo* (= hat or = put on a hat), *Tit-tat* (= tic-toc, = watch, or = listen to a watch close to one's ear), *Mba* (= kiss), *Ba* (= box or = play with a box). One no more finds real adjectives than one does real substantives or verbs. The child repeats after us *Bon! Beau!* (= good! = pretty!) and ends up by saying them in the same situations. At first, these were exhortations or encouragements: "It's good" to make him eat up his soup; "It's pretty" to call his attention to something, and so on. *Bon* (= good) therefore also means *Eat!* or *the soup*. This is very true, for when he began spontaneously combining words much later he would ask for more soup, saying *Encore bon!* (= more good) and would refuse more saying: *Pas encore bon!* (= no more good).

We know that, according to Stern,[4] the development of the vocabulary has three stages: substance, action, quality or relation, in the sense that each phase sees a preponderant development of one category of words: substantives, verbs, adjectives, and prepositions. Thus, in the second phase, in one of the children studies by Stern, the number of verbs went from 4 to 21, while that of the nouns went from 23 to 73: the first class grows more quickly than the second. But what is the principle of the division into categories? Notice, first of all, that there is a residual category, that of the interjection, which, at the same time, grows from 17 to 28 words. Moreover, one glance at the contents of the groups shows that it is not a question of the categories to which the models imitated by the child would belong in our grammar. It is rather the value that the words take on in the child's language at that period. But the principle is a fine-drawn one and somewhat arbitrary in its application. Thus, for example: *ände* (Hände = hands) placed with the substantives, seemed only to be used at that period in relation to an action (being taken into one's arms). The distinction between interjections and verbs is undefinable: If *ei-schei* (ein, zwei = one, two, meaning "run") and *pieke-pieke* (a game) are verbs, why are *baba* (= to go for a walk), *Kikä* (= hide-and-seek), *tsch-tsch* (another game), *op! op!* (playing with a ball), *ei-ei* (game with a doll), *bitte bitte* (= please, please, to ask for something), *alle!* (= gone, finished) all interjections? From one count to another, interjections go into the category of verbs because their form rather than their meaning has changed, and the impression that one is left with of a rapid increase in the number of verbs is rather artificial. Stern himself noticed that the first meanings "show fluctuations which seem to defy all attempts at classification into ordinary categories" [p. 164]. He also says, "The distinction made above between interjections and substantives is only valid as far as external consideration of the grammatical form goes; from the psychological point of view, the separation has no basis. The verbal units of the child do not belong to any word class because they are not words but sentences." What then is external consideration of the grammatical form if not a consideration—a premature one—of what these words become later on? Grammatical categories cannot be defined save by functional facts; the relation between the word and the concrete situations, and the other words of the sentence. The examination of a child's vocabulary or of a collection of isolated word sentences never allows one to make these distinctions.

PSEUDOSENTENCES

When does the time come to begin calling a series of words uttered by the child a sentence? Two sets of facts have to be distinguished here: on the one hand, direct reproductions of ready-made sentences which cannot possibly be personal combinations of truly independent words: for example, *A pu* (il n'y en a plus = there isn't any more). *A bu* (ça brule = that's burning), *A peur* (j'ai peur = I'm frightened), *A ba* (a boire = to drink), *Ta y est* (ça y est = there you are), *Ptite pepée* (petite poupée = tiny dolly), *Donne à main* (donne la main = give [me] your hand), and so on; on the

---

[4] C. Stern and W. Stern, *Die Kindersprache*, 1907.

other hand, personal formations consisting of several word-sentences juxtaposed, the whole presenting no grammatical unity.

In practice, the two cases are fairly easy to distinguish; in the first, the intonation pattern is unbroken; in the second, the words are separated by pauses, and each word is stressed separately (we will separate the different elements by dashes corresponding to the naturally discontinuous nature of the utterance). Here are some examples of the second case. We suggested to the child that he feed from someone else; he replies *Apu-Maman!* (non, c'est maman que je veux = no, I want mama) (12.19). He insists on being allowed to suckle, then suddenly remembers that I oppose it (he was about to be weaned): *Nenin! Nenin! Papa?* (15.8). Seeing a baby cry, he asks for it to be given something to drink: *Nini peur bobo nénin* (regarde ce bébé! Il pleure! Il a mal! Il faut lui donner a boire = Look at the baby. He's crying. He's hurt. Give him something to drink) (17 months). Frightened when he sees that a gun is going to be fired, he says: *A peur A peur A pu Bobo* (J'ai peur, ne tire pas, ça fait mal = I'm frightened, don't fire, it hurts.) (15.8). Having had a fight with a little girl, he tells us: *A mord A peur Bobo Annette* (je l'ai mordue elle pleure, elle a mal, Jeannette = I bit her, she's crying, it's sore, Jeannette) (16.28).

Each vocal gesture spills out spontaneously from successive adaptations to a complex situation: let us not forget that it is always a question of mental interaction, whether the child wants to make the people around him intervene, interest them in what he feels, or whether they are seeking his confessions, his judgments, his explanations. Besides, each word is merely the incomplete echo of a sentence suggested to the child on another occasion in a similar situation. These groups of words must also be "translated" as a series of sentences. There is a rapprochement between the way the child expresses himself and the spontaneously used procedure to make him understand a sentence by breaking it up and by repeating it. Just as the child understands our sentences as a series of juxtaposed predicates of the concrete situation, so he speaks using word sentences which are directly linked to aspects of the situation. However, it is still too soon to look for grammatical links.

Lacking a grammar, do these series possess any syntax? Does the order of elements obey any rule? If there is one, it is quickly effaced by the extensive influence of imitation. But the problem is not very different from that of the syntax of groups formed by juxtaposition, no longer word sentences, but true short sentences. We can study it in either type of example. Theoretically, the order of the terms reflects the train of thought; it goes from the interesting, essential point to the secondary aspects. After the first word, the following ones emphasize, specify, explain, reply to unspoken questions. From this come the antitheses like the one in the example above (*A pu maman!* = no mama), or in the juxtaposition of three real sentences: *Nenin caca! Maman nenin! Papa bobo!* (je ne veux plus de ce sein—je veux celui de maman—mais papa gronderait = I don't want any more of this breast—I want mama's—but papa will complain) (15.24). The first part is a reaction to the suggestion made to him, the second indicates his personal wish, and then the thought of the consequence strikes him. Sometimes his thought leads from facts observed to a practical attitude, as when he threatens the doctor whom he blames for his mother's illness (20.4): *Docteur misère à maman caillou! baton!* (= Doctor—hurt mama—stone!—stick!). As in such sequences as: *Sou—sière* (sou—epicière = penny—grocer, that is, give me a penny so I can go to the store) (16.28); the second word is in apposition, explaining the main word. The same word may occur in different positions with different nuances of meaning: *Net—cop—Nini* (une amande—coupe-la—pour moi = an almond—cut it—for *me*) (18.2). *Nini—verre—à boire* (pour moi aussi!—dans un verre, comme les grandes personnes—à boire = for me too!—in a glass like the grown-ups—drink). In a story, the order of thought may be that of the events themselves, but it can also be the result of going from an interesting effect back to the cause. He tells of a small punishment: *Tape—bobo* (= smack—naughty) (13.27). On another occasion, he tells of falling down, saying, *Bobo—tête—coup* (= sore—head—hit) (18.18). In the first instance, it was a question of remembering something; in the second, it was a recent occurrence—he still feels the pain, while the accident itself is secondary. It is curious to see how the child interprets a complicated order that he is told to pass on: "Va dire à papa de venir chasser les mouches pour que tu puisses dormir, quand tu auras mangé à ta soupe" (= go tell papa to come and get rid of the flies so that you can sleep when you have finished your soup). The child translates: *Papa!—Soupe—Peït* [his name]—*Némir—Tape—Moute* (= papa—soup—Peït—sleep—smack—fly) (18.-27). Sometimes he retains the order of the events, sometimes he goes from the result to the cause. The child would never spontaneously try to express such a complicated sequence; however, he could produce a long chain of actions, each one being the cause of the next, if he had some personal aim. Thus L. (14.15) coming to look for her mother: *Maman, ici* (= mama, here. She pulls her over to an armchair), *Assis!* (assieds-toi = sit down), *Oper* (= pick me up), *Dédé* (= I want to sit in your lap), *À teter* (= let me suck). Each word is separated from the one following it by the action required of her mother. Concrete thought is foresighted and must go from the result to the means of achieving it in order to produce the actions in the desired order. Language, though, is still only a series of isolated reactions to aspects of the situation, insofar as the latter is changed by the performance of the actions. While concrete thought anticipates the future and can organize it, language remains a function of the present. There are no sentences, but an inorganic series of predicates of the situation.

THE FIRST SENTENCES—PEOPLE'S NAMES

Let us look for them first in comprehension of speech. At the beginning of his second year, the child appears to understand sentences like: "Brush papa . . . , mama . . . , Marie, . . . , your little brother (a doll)." A familiar game consisted of doing *coui-coui* (pinching one's nose), *dida-dida* (pulling one's ear), *bla-blab* (vibration produced by intermittently opening and shutting one's mouth with one's hand), and so on. These words are associated with the name of someone present (Do coui-coui to papa, to Mr. L., and so on), and the child plays the game. He adapts his action immediately to a series of people, and the new combination of words is understood straight away. A word like "papa" is here no longer a sentence but a member of a sentence. At first, such utterances had to be stressed word by word, so that the effect of the second is influenced by the intuitive situation already modified by the first one. No doubt progress consists of reducing the immediate effect of the first words perceived to an activity preparatory to the ultimate response, left in suspense until the completion of the sentence by the awaited "complements."

What are the first words affected by this progress? I have been struck by the role played by *people's names* in the sentences understood by children I have been able to observe. Their function in the sentence varies besides; they are subjects, direct or indirect complements, and so on. The word with which they are associated is still undifferentiated, signifying the total experience. At the same time, this seemed far less clear to me in the case of other combinations of familiar words. We have seen that P. (12.13) brushes the hair of one person or another when asked, and even does so to a doll (something he had not seen done). Then I said to him: "Brush the hat." (He knows the word "hat" in the sense that he knows how to find the object and put it on his head when asked, "Where is the hat? Put on your hat.") He does not understand the sentence. He lets go of the brush and picks up the hat, wants to put it on his head. If I repeat my order, he returns to the brush and wants to polish my shoes. Each of these two words tends to set off habitual reactions. The action proper is not performed. Notice that a construction of this type is always involved to some extent in the comprehension of sentences: if the child has never seen the prescribed action, the sentence he understands constrains his imagination to make the object appear in a new light whereby it can reasonably undergo the action expressed by the verb. If the action is one familiar to him, the form of the sentence suggests to him a function for the object which may not be the one he thinks of spontaneously. But, at the time of my observations, "hat" is not the name of an object. It suggests a certain experience with the hat, too specialized and too exact for it to be combined with his experience of the brush. On the other hand, at this same point, the names of *people* call forth a variety of actions without themselves specifying any one function: the child's thought is completed by the context. These are nouns that have really been differentiated.

The child's spontaneous speech confirms this development a little later on. He may still hesitate when the name is vocative. However, the link between the words becomes real when, instead of serving to attract someone's attention to some fact, the vocative becomes an invitation to participate in an action named by the other word, for example, in *Ici, Pepette* (= come here, Pepette) (L. 13.13). The relation is even closer in the following examples: *Adé papa, adé maman* (P. wants to put a die into his father's and mother's hands) (14.25); *A bo Baby* (= I brush Baby) (15.10); *Maman bobo* (= Mama sore; his mother has a sore on her lip) (15.17); *Ai a main a var* (= Mr. F., I want to hold his hand, see him) (the person named was not present); *Ahmed toutoute* (= Ahmed plays the trumpet); *Papa kir* (papa écrit = papa is writing) (16.24); *Sauveur caou* (Sauveur caillou = Saviour pebble; the Saviour, I'll throw him a pebble) (17.2). There are other examples cited above (*maman nénin, Papa bobo,* and so on.) The beginning of the eighteenth month definitely establishes this stage: this type of sentence becomes very frequent; at the same time, there is a tendency to reply to all sorts of questions, at random, with the name of a person. In the following month these combinations frequently expressed attribute or possession: *Taté papa* (café papa = coffee papa; must give coffee to papa); *A pour à Nini* (poudre à Nini = powder for Nini; put some powder on Nini); *Nini donner de l'eau* (= Nini give water); *Nini à bout* (Nini à bouche = in Nini's mouth); *Pantalon à papa, soupe à P.— Chocolat à bouche à papa* (= papa's trousers, P.'s soup—chocolate in papa's mouth) (19.22). His own name recurs continually in small sentences: *Chaise à P.* (= P.'s chair), *Donner à P.* (= give to P.), *P. travaille* (= P. is working), *P. veut les mettre* (= P. wants to do them), *P. il sait* (= P. he knows), *P. il fait* (= P. he does), *P. il pleure* (= P. he's crying), *P. est malade* (= P. is ill), *P. il veut* (= P. he wants it), *P. est la*

(= P. is there) (20 months). In his sister's speech, we find the same development of the sentence: *Viens ici, Foufou* (= come here, Foufou; the name is one used for her brother) (12.19), *Fait dédé* [dodo] *Foufou* (= is sleeping, Foufou), *Il a bobo, Foufou* (= he's hurt, Foufou) (14 months), *Foufou le néné* (F. est allé promener = F. has gone for a walk), *Foufou le pam* (F. est tombé = F. has fallen down), *Néné papa* (papa va promener = papa's going for a walk), *Le papo le papa* (le chapeau de papa = papa's hat), *Le bobo le maman* (maman a bobo = mama's hurt), *A bobo a maman Danane* (D. a bobo comme maman = D. is hurt like mama) (14.15). Notice that there are two names of people in the last sentence combined with a common attribute.[5]

In this type of sentence, the word associated with the person's name is difficult to characterize from the grammatical point of view. It is still undifferentiated, and—which comes down to the same thing—the function of the person's name remains indeterminate. If we wish to see one of the words as a verb, the proper name could sometimes be the subject (*Papa kir* = papa is writing), sometimes the complement (*Sauveur caou* = a pebble for Saviour). The idea of a verb is just as well conveyed by a substantive (*Adé papa* = die [dice] papa). When the name is the child's own, it can just as well be the subject as the direct or indirect object.

THE LANGUAGE OF "WANTING"

Besides personal names, another element in free combinations appears fairly precociously in sentences: this is the expression of wants, that is, the verbal expression of negative reactions (refusal of attentions, of objects, aversion to certain actions or treatments) and of positive reactions of wanting something (an object, an action, its continuation or renewal). These words fairly quickly come to represent attitudes with respect to a verbal suggestion—assent or dissent—to an awaited event—observation of the absence or presence of an object or fact. The language of "wanting" thus takes on an intellectual value.

The words are borrowed from a variety of categories in the imitated language, such as *A plus* (= I don't want any more, or = there isn't any more). *Pas, A pas, Non*[6] (= not, = no), to which must be added *Caca* (= dirty), an expression of aversion which is as expressive of wants as of emotion. The object of these negations goes at first unexpressed. They are word sentence, predicates of intuitive situations; but already the variety of unexpressed objects or facts to which these negations apply prepares for their appearance in two-word combinations at the next stage. In the combinations, the object of the negations does not yet have any definite grammatical form. *Pas momo* (= not sleep) (P. 14 months) can be interpreted either as "I don't want to sleep" or "I don't want the bed." Here are some other examples of these negations: *A pu papo* (= I don't want this hat) (P. 12.19), *A peu a pu* (= I don't want it to rain

---

[5] All the work on the first stages of sentence formation mentions a large number of combinations of people's names (or sometimes of individual personified objects) with another word. In the table where Stern listed the first sentences uttered by fourteen German, English, French and Polish children, we find no less than twenty-eight such out of a total of forty samples.

[6] We do not have any examples of *non* (= no) used in combinations. German children, though, often use *nein* (= no) instead of *nicht* (= not) in such cases.

any more) (P. 14 months), *Pas beau* (= not nice; referring to a dog), *Pas bon* (= not good; referring to an orange), (13.18), *Nénin caca* (= I don't want to suckle) (15.26).

From the twentieth month on, negation accompanies a large number of what might be called verbs: *A po pas* (je ne peux pas = I can't), *Sais pas* (= don't know) (20.4), *A pas vu* (= didn't see), *A trouve pas* (= don't find) (21.16). In another child's speech *A pas la mémé* (= not mama; refusing to let her brother climb on her mother's knee) (12.19). *A pas tété!* (= *ibidem*) (14 months).

We might be tempted to contrast affirmation with negation. But adherence to a desire or belief does not generally have to be expressed by a word; one simply obeys the suggestion. On the other hand, it is essential to defend oneself against someone else's wishes. *Oui* (= yes) does not appear in L.'s speech until 14 months (still very rare), nor in P.'s until 20 months. It remains an independent interjection. On the other hand, the child does have to demand the renewal or the continuation of certain actions; later on, the same words will be used to note the repetition of a fact or multiple examples of an object. *Encore* (= again, or = more) exists as a word sentence for P. at 14.3 (to ask again for a caress, a game to explain that he has not finished an action, to get some object back again: bread, cake, banana, and so on.) Sometimes he even uses it to ask for something for the first time. The diversity of complements soon gives rise to sentences expressing the complement: *Nénin encore* (= more good) (15.26). At 18.27, I notice that this word is the one that most frequently appears in his own two-word combinations with no pause between the words: *Encore bon* (= more food; asking for more soup), *Encore feuille* (= more leaf; pointing at leaves on a tree, one by one), *Encore des jujubes* (= more jujubes), *Encore une guenane* (= more pomegranate), and so on (20.17). The same evolution is found in utterances that are emotive rather than intellectual. They are first used absolutely in a variety of concrete cases, then later with complements expressed. Thus, P. says: *Peur* (= 'fraid) or *A peur* (= I'm afraid) when a strange woman picks him up (14.25), when in a dark room, when he is stung by an insect (14.30), when spoken to severely, when he hears a gunshot (15.5), when he is carried in a basket, when he nearly falls down (15.9), when he has been scolded, and so on. Later he says *A peur bebetes* (= 'fraid of bugs) in speaking of the ants he has just seen (they were not in sight at that instant). Similarly, *Bobo* (= sore, hurt), which expresses hurt and fear at the same time in a large variety of instances, comes to be used in a sentence: *A pour bobo* (= the powder hurts) (16.4).

Thus we have seen the distinction of two sorts of words as autonomous word sentences: on the one hand, people's names, and on the other, expressions of "wanting." These two now occur freely in combination with nouns that are undifferentiated in relation to a total experience. But these two word classes are like opposite poles in the language. People especially are the objects of individual concrete, stable perception and thought. They are also beings separate from the speaker, from his interests and his functions. They seem to exist "in and by themselves." Lastly, the words referring to them are easily detached from those referring to the experience as a whole, and become "names." on the other side, words expressing wants or desires are first of all *identical* to the speaker's feelings about his experiences; they are the verbal counterparts to his reactions, which are so little detached from him that they cannot at first be adequately characterized. The structure of the sentence expresses the dissociation of the primitive expression into one part that is represented or thought and into one part that is lived or acted.

THE NAME OF THE OBJECT

There is no great difference, particularly for the child, between things, animals, and people. He personifies and animates things; he goes easily from the combinations studied previously to sentences such as: *Sien, tape* (chien tape = dog, smack; that is, I smacked the dog) or L. (12.19) who watches water trickling from a gutter (which is generally called *dada*) and says: *Pipi dada* (= pee-pee gutter).

The names of things do not, strictly speaking, constitute a grammatical category: for us, the category of substantives has ended up including semantic equivalents of all words (names of qualities, actions, states, relations) and by finding the grammatical modes and constructions appropriate for each one. But the child's first substantives after the names of people are indeed names of *things* in a very narrow sense, as is shown in the vocabularies for the first half of the second year: they consist of the nouns for food, for objects connected with the games and needs of the child, above all manipulative objects, appropriate to his size and usage. We often notice very wide generic terms preceding specific names: for example, P. (13.27) uses *ato* (which seems to come from "marteau" = hammer) and until 14.22 uses it for the following: buttonhook, hand mirror, comb, handbag, a casserole, hairpin, wooden spade, key, gun, box, belt, wallet, ruler, puttees, bowl, safety pin, night light, coffee grinder, plate, and spoon. This master word never refers to people, animals, or food: it is equivalent to *machin* (= gadget) or *chose* (= thing).

It has often been said that there is a decisive point at which the child discovers "that everything has a name." Miss Sullivan, Helen Keller's teacher, has left us a dramatic account of this "discovery" (in a six-year-old child who develops suddenly), and psychologists have assumed that it also occurs, though much earlier, in the normal child. I have no idea where to situate this sudden revelation: the development of the names of things, in the period when this can be observed, proceeds at a steady pace. At 12.10, P. uses 6 names of objects; at 13.27, 11; at 14.3, 19; at 15.30, 26; at 16 months, 38; at 17.12, 53; at 18.6, 68; at 18.27, 79; at 19.22, 96; at 20.17, 118; at 21.15, 168 (this is counting the new words added to the existing ones without supplanting them). Questions about the names of things, whose appearance ought to coincide with the decisive moment, do not appear any more suddenly: *Ceca?* (qu'est-ce que c'est que cela = what is that) is repeated once in imitation at 16.28 and is at first rare; it is only at 22 months that it becomes a mania. It is not until the age of two years that the initially very rare inverse question appears: hearing someone say a new word, the child inquires about the object: *Que c'est ça 'a l'hopital'?* (= what is "at the hospital"). Is it not that the real series of analogical effects have been condensed into a sudden "discovery" generalization for the sake of a convenient explanation?

All these names appear at first as isolated word sentences. They are used to refer to diverse thought functions. Either they denote objects of some wish (the child demands them, announces that he wants to act upon them), or they serve for localization (the part of the body which hurts, the place he is going to), or else they designate the recognition of the object, they acknowledge its presence. The latter form seems to be important in building up the function of the noun. Generally, the object becomes independent of the action relating to it less easily than the person does. It appears in its relation to the "me," in the role which actual need or usage gives it. But later on, naming things becomes a great game for the child (for example, when he is shown pictures); this game is no longer subordinated to immediate use: it is the object and not its function which is foremost. It is recognized and named disinterestedly, ignoring all uses. The name tends, therefore, to take on a meaning independent of any action or relation in which the object would be the goal.

It is only in the sentence containing casual words that it truly gains this value. To avoid repetitions, the examples will be given with reference to the verbs, since their differentiation and that of the noun go hand in hand. The physiognomy, though, of the name is complete only when the distinction between individual and generic names has been made. This is not a primitive concept: it implies an opposition between the individual object and an ungiven whole to which it is compared. The young child lives too much in the present to be capable of this mental complexity. A group of functional facts allow us to follow this development. First, as a semantic index, notice the use of the same word for similar objects which are, however, too different to be confused: P. (13.27) uses *papo* for his hair, different women's hats, a military cap, and so on. The word *autre* (= other), understood at age 12.3, when it is applied to one of two objects forming a pair (breast, hand, foot, ear), is said, as a word sentence, to designate the other breast (14.24), the other slipper, the other ball (14.30), another identical cake (15.10), another variety of cake seen in the same box (15.12), another person (15.17), other lines (16.8), and so on. In a neighboring meaning, we see the word *encore* (= more) sometimes associated with the partitive *(des)*: *Encore une grenade, l'autre* (= another pomegranate, the other one), *Encore des jujubes* (= more candies) (20.17). The definite article becomes regular in the singular and plural at about 21.6. It had been preceded by the use of demonstratives: *celle-la* (= that one), *pas celle-là* (= not that one) and so on, applied to objects of the same type. The possessives *mon, ton* (= my, = your) appear at 21 months. In another child, I noted *mon* (= my, masc.), *le mien* (= mine, masc.), at 21 months, and *ton* (= your, masc.), *ta* (= your, fem.), *le tien* (= yours, masc.) at 23 months. The word *tous* (= all, masc. pl.) follows the enumeration of objects at 22.26. The indefinite pronoun *en* (object pron.) and article *un* (= a, an) at 23.10: *Tu en as?* (= have you got some), *Je voulais un petit oua-oua* (= I wanted a little doggie), *Je l'as un* (= I have it one) and finally the opposition between *même* (= same) and *autre* (= other) at 23.15. She asks of a character pictured several times in a book: *Que ce que c'est, l'autre? C'est le même* (= what is it, the other? It's the same). Therefore, the character of the common noun becomes clearer as the child masters various ways of expressing linguistically the notion of type.

THE VERB

The word sentences are often reproductions of our verbs. Here are some examples, in addition to those we have already cited: *Habir* (habiller = dress; ask to be dressed), *Por, Assis* (porter = carry; assis, asseoir = sit; asking to be carried or to be sat down), *Nener* (promener = walk, go for a walk), *Nemir* (dormir = sleep; "I want to sleep" or "I am sleeping"), *Our* (ouvrir = open; "I want to open it" or "open it for me"), *Lever* (= get up; asking to get out of bed), *Descendre* (= get down—from his chair), *Cour* (courir = run), *Tebe* (tomber = fall; expressing fear of falling), *Laver, Rézé* (= wash; arroser = water), *Monter* or *Monte* (monter = climb—on a chair, into bed, up a tree), *Donne, sonne* (sonner = ring; on hearing a bell), *Coule* (couler = flow; seeing water in a drain), *Grate, Travaille* (gratter = scrape; travailler = work; "I'm working"), *Jeter* (= throw; "I want to throw"), *Prendre* (= take, "I want to take, be taken"), *Boutonne, Pique* (= spotty; = bitten, by an insect; statement of fact), *Balance, Arrange* (balancer = swing; arranger = arrange; statements of fact), *Caché, Cassé* (= hidden; = broken; statement of fact), and so on. All these examples occur between 16.26 and 20.4. The model imitated is sometimes in the personal mode *(Habir, Por, Our, Cour* come from *habille, porte, ouvre, court)*, sometimes in the imperative or the infinitive *Assis, Nemir, Laver, Descendre)*. Occasionally two forms are found: *Our* (ouvre) and *Ouvrir* (infinitive), *Casse* and *Cassé* (past part.) or *Casser* (infinitive). However, it would be a big mistake to see in this the beginnings of verb conjugation. The child imitates a sentence he has heard: if he is on his chair and someone says to him: "Do you want to get down?" he will say *Descendre* (= get down) in such a context. (The frequency of the infinitive forms can be explained by the imitation of sentences introduced by *vouloir* = want to, *pouvoir* = be able to, *aller* = go, and so on. [these verbs are all followed by an infinitive construction in French] or by the prepositions *à, de pour,* also followed [in French] by an infinitive.) He says *Our* because he is imitating "Ouvre!" (= open!) or "Tu veux qu'on ouvre?" (= do you want it opened?). A little later on, in exactly the same circumstances, he will say *Ouvrir* because he is imitating "Tu veux ouvrir?" (= do you want to open it?), "Il fait ouvrir?" (= do you have to open it?)

To a certain extent, the form of the word is accidental. Naturally—it is the rule for all imitation—each new use tends to supplant the preceding one in evoking the verb form, which does not necessarily preserve the exact value that it had in its original use. Too much emphasis, therefore, should not be placed on these forms. The determination of person, tense, and mode are fortuitous; the child does not know how to use them to express the various nuances. But there is more to it: these forms are not even verbs, if what is called a verb is the word which in the total experience refers especially to aspect, action, or state; these forms still refer to the experience as a whole. The child will use a verb form and a nonverb form indifferently with *exactly the same meaning.* P. (18.2) says *Cour* or *Zouzoute* (courir = run; joujou = toy), *Nemir* or *Tasiet* (dormir = sleep; la sieste = rest), *Descendre* or *Par terre* (= get down; = on the ground), *À boire* or *De l'eau* (= drink; = water), *Tise* or *Dodo* (coucher = to sleep; = bed, sleep), *Por* or *A bas* (être porté = be carried; au bras = in arm(s)). Action is not truly isolated in language until both the agent and the object of the action have been differentiated.

However, before the sentence made up of several words appears, there is already a preparatory stage for the function of the verb when the word sentence is applied to different contexts whose common feature is essentially the action, while actors, objects, and situations vary. Every utterance has an individual origin; certain verbs are only used by the child, for a time, in connection with an undesignated person (himself), sometimes the subject, sometimes the direct or indirect object of the action. *Habir* (16.26) applies to *his* being dressed, *Némir* to *his* going to sleep, *Néné* to his going for a walk; *Lever* means "I want to get out of bed," *Descendre:* "I want to get down from my chair." Some pseudoverbs apply only to a particular object, for example: *Our* (ouvrir = open) to a door. But later on, the word becomes attached to the action: the subject, object, and context begin to vary. Thus, he says spontaneously: *Habir* (= dress) to suggest that I put on my slippers that he has brought me (the actual incorrectness of the expression [in French] indicates that it his personal generalization) (17.12). *Our* (= open) is applied not only to my door but to a piece of fruit, to a box, to a pea pod; one could claim that these too are imitations of the use of this word by other people, but that cannot be the case when he says *Our* (17.18) to ask for his shoes to be untied. *Tébé* is used when he is afraid of falling down, but also when I tip the chair I am sitting on. We have emphasized elsewhere[7] the roles of imitation and of assimilation of other people and of the child in the genesis of the verb.

Finally, the dissociation of the action, of the person, and of the object becomes evident in the language in the sentence of two or more words that contains a verb. The verb is combined with the name of a person, most often with that of the child himself. For example: *Donne à P.* (= give to P.), *P.* [veut, va] *les mettre* (= P. [wants to, is going to] put them), *P. il fait* (= P. he does), *P. il sait* (= P. he knows), *P. il peut pas* (= P. he can't), *P. il casse* (= P. he breaks) (20.4), *Monter à papa* (= climb up to papa) (20.11), *P. a mangé* (= P. has eaten) (20.17), *P. il pleure* (= P. he's crying), *P. est malade* (= P.'s ill), *P. a besoin* (= P. needs), *Papa fait la musique* (= papa is playing music), *P. a vu, a pas vu* (= P. has seen, hasn't seen), *Morte maman* (= mama is dead), *Morte Marie* (= Marie is dead) (21.6).

Even more often, the verb is associated with the name of a thing, for example: [Je] *tape les mouches* (= [I] swat [the] flies), [Je] *mange la soupe* (= [I] eat soup) (17.18), *Ote sie* (= take off shoe) (17.18), *Donne le contenu, donne la pelote* (= give the contents, = give the ball), [J'] *amasse de la terre* (= I'm piling up earth), *Fermée la fenêtre* (= shut, the window), *Cocottes mouillées, froid* (= birdies wet, cold), *Quitte la peau* (= take off the peel), *Donne la lettre* (= give the letter), *Donne de l'eau* (= give water), *Va chercher les chaussons* (= go and look for the shoes), *Fais voir la bande* (= show me the plaster), *Tourne la tête* (= turn your head), *Lève la tête* (= raise your head), *Cassées les jambes* (= broken, the legs), *Donne la main* (= give me your hand), *Partons à la maison* (= let's go back to the house) (20.4). Lastly, in the same period, we find a few combinations of three meaningful words, for example, *Donne chocolat a P.* (= give P. chocolate) (20.4). *Va chercher les chaussons a Papa* (= go and look for papa's shoes), *Donne la montre a P.* (= give P. the watch), *P.* [va] *chercher* [le] *Docteur* (= P. [is going to] look for [the] doctor) (21.16). At this stage, the personal construction of the verb with an object complement becomes so common that the child extends it to intransitive verbs: [Je] *travaille les cailloux* (= [I] am working the pebbles) (22 months). The anomaly of this utterance is a mark of his personal construction. He also speaks of *Taper les citrons* (= to hit the lemons, instead of "abattre les citrons" = knock down the lemons) (22 months). The two members of the sentence are both able to enter into combinations where each has its own function: the two have been differentiated.

The structure of the sentence is also defined by the word order. It is no longer a question of two or several word sentences juxtaposed, representing two instants of

---

[7] *L'imitation chez l'enfant.* Paris: Alcan, 1923, p. 155.

thought. The construction is required by the rules of the language; it no longer undergoes the capricious variations of the train of thought. Sometimes when the words come out in successive bursts, there is a tendency to reconstruct them afterwards in the normal order. One should not be deceived by some inversions. If P. says, *Fermée le fenêtre* (= shut the window), it is because he is imitating "elle est fermée, la fenêtre" (= it is shut, the window). If he says *Chercher Docteur* (= look for doctor), one has to understand "P. va chercher . . ." or " . . . veut chercher . . ." (= P. is going to look for . . . , or = wants to look for), and so on. The infinitives with an imperative meaning, preceding their complements, are elliptical reproductions of subordinate statements inttoduced by verbs like *vouloir* (= to want, wish) or by prepositions. The German child, under the same circumstances, will place the complement before the infinitive (*Flasche trinken* = drink water), and, for the same reasons, conforming to the rules of German, will also place the past participle at the end (Flasche trunken = water drunk), as well as the separable verb particles, frequently the only thing expressed (see Stern).

The development which separated a particular symbol for people from the undifferentiated word sentence has continued by isolating the symbol for objects. People and things correspond, in the total environment, to what is most distant from the subject, to what is most independent of his emotional and active life, although things are less likely than people to become autonomous beings and are rather more likely to be instruments of his needs and the passive objects of his actions. At the other pole of experience, the attitude of the subject, living rather than thinking, is isolated by the verbal aspect. The verb which in its turn becomes individualized, in a sense, prolongs the language of "wanting." The parallelism is clear if one considers the primitive forms. Whether the verbal forms from the word sentences or from the true sentences are taken into account, between the ages of 17 and 22 months in one of our children, about three quarters of the forms are imperative in meaning and only one quarter indicative. Words like *Encore* (= more) and *Donne* (= give) are scarcely separated by any nuance of meaning, and both take the same sort of complement. At the moment, the verb is above all an expression of "wanting" which tends to specify the modalities of the action required. Just as the terms of "wanting," positive or negative, become expressions of intellectual attitudes on the part of the subject with regard to the thought of others and of himself, so the verb rapidly comes to describe an action instead of requiring or announcing it: the indicative develops side by side with the imperative. Finally, to understand the evolution of expression of thought in a language like ours [French] consists of an arbitrary segmentation of experience as a whole, that is, both subjective and objective, in a way that corresponds to certain abstractions. The system, elaborated by the need to express more and more complex ideas by means of analogy which extends the categories, is difficult to assimilate in its present form. In order to master abstractions, one has to find images and symbols for them in something concrete. At the same time, a practical or emotional interest must correspond to this dissociation of reality. The human being, attitudes toward varied experiences, the objects and actions within experiences—these are the sum of the perspectives and interests of the child at the age which we have described. It is the expression of these aspects that he is assimilating into his language. This anthropocentricity is the key to the system of abstractions in the language, probably because therein lies its origin: the structure of the sentence and the functions of its members cease to seem artificial if one considers that language was first used to speak of man, and later of the whole of nature, in terms made for man.

The Transition from Sensory-Motor Behavior to Symbolic Activity

Hermina Sinclair

Preverbal, sensory-motor intelligence progresses to where the child needs some kind of representation for further cognitive progress and where his cognitive structures make such representation possible. Observational research shows that early symbolic behavior occurs only after objects have been endowed with certain physical and conventional properties and after certain kinds of creative organizational behavior have appeared. The beginnings of language can be studied as part of representational behaviour and may show such object- and subject-oriented duality in lexical and syntactic components.

Few human abilities are so general and at the same time so mysterious as our ability to speak and to understand language. Psycholinguistics is a fairly recent discipline, but well before the establishment of either psychology or linguistics as branches of scientific studies, man has meditated on this specifically human ability and its development, both ontogenetically and phylogenetically. Most linguists nowadays agree that all human languages are extremely complex systems, through which, by means of a small number of sounds (between 30 and 40) with distinctive characteristics, it is possible to formulate an unlimited number of different messages. Apart from a few clichés, most of what we say and hear is new, in the sense that we have never before said or heard the exact same sequence of words, but we have no difficulty in understanding or producing such novelties. Just how complicated, and at the same time how systematic, our languages are, has become clearer since the advent of transformational and generative grammar. But although great strides have been made (thanks to linguists like Harris and, particularly, Chomsky) in the formalization of the knowledge an accomplished speaker possesses (almost always only intuitively) of his language, the way in which an adult uses this knowledge and how the child acquires it remain an almost total mystery.

REFLECTIONS ON DEVELOPMENTS IN LINGUISTICS

The remarkable success of transformational grammar has had, in the Genevan view, two rather unfortunate consequences. In the first place, many psycholinguists have

From *Interchange*, **1**, 3, 1970, pp. 119–126. The Ontario Institute for Studies in Education, 1970. Reprinted by permission of the Ontario Institute for Studies in Education.

concluded that linguistic structures must be at least partly innate, since in their view no child would be able to construct an adequate grammar from the linguistic input he receives if he did not already possess a general idea of what grammar is. In the second place, transformational grammar has led many psycholinguists to the kind of studies of child language where linguistic competence is treated as an ability totally divorced from the rest of the child's capacites and, theoretically, to the wish to describe language acquisitions as an autonomous type of development, which, if it cannot be explained in and by itself, cannot be explained at all. The Genevan view, which is shared by a minority of students of child language—to name a few: Cohen (1969), Beilin & Spontak (1969), Francis (1969), Schlesinger (in press), and some collaborators of Brown—is, on the contrary, that language acquisition can be understood only by taking into account what is already known of cognitive development in particular and also of affective and social development. This view does not mean that everything about linguistic acquisition can be directly explained or at least interpreted by a cognitive developmental model, or that such a model can be directly applied to language acquisition. But it does mean that Genevan psycholinguists believe that the child's competence in producing and understanding speech proceeds basically according to the Piagetian model of cognitive development: through complex interaction between the individual's inner structures and pre-structures and the objects and people around him, by integration of the new into the old, and restructuration of the old into ever more general and higher-level mental constructs. However, as Brown (1969) has remarked, cognitive structures are *not* linguistic structures, or even sytactic structures, and we are still far from being able to spell out in linguistic terms how this development proceeds.

The achievements of generative transformational grammar have also had some fortunate consequences with regard to the study of language acquisition, in that the simplistic, associationist explanations have been shown to be totally inadequate, and that the accent has been put on the intensively constructive and creative activity of the child who is learning his mother tongue; several analyses of specific features of observational data have been published, e.g., Bellugi (1967).

Finally, though the new developments in linguistics may be just as far-reaching in phonology as in syntax, the studies of syntax emphasized the epistemological aspect, i.e., the implications for a theory of knowledge. As a result, interest in language studies shifted its emphasis, and almost all interesting studies of child language based either on experimental or observational data of recent years have been concerned with syntax. Since syntactic studies can hardly start before the child is at least capable of uttering two word-elements (to avoid the term "word" with its adult connotations) that have some kind of inferred link, a discontinuity has been introduced in language development whereby the single word-element phrases (holophrases) are regarded as two-element utterances of which one of the elements is implied, but not expressed, and no account is taken of all that goes on before (vocalizations, the building up of the sound-system of the mother tongue, the establishment of intonation and contour-patterns). This omission is regrettable for those psycholinguists who want to apply Piagetian theory to language acquisition, since this theory shows that all structures have to be understood in interactionist terms: i.e., not only through the modes of interaction between the subject and his environment (what he acts upon) but also through interaction between the underlying structure of his latest achievements and those that preceded them.

It is regrettable also from the traditional and common-sense point of view, which situates the mystery of language in the appearance of the "first word" (Stern, 1914; Vygotsky, 1962). Even more than the first tooth, the first steps, or the first smile, the first word has been seen as a milestone in the baby's development. This moment is when the baby really joins the human community; it is, or so it was thought, when his career as a rational being begins, whereas before he was more like a little animal. Curiously enough, this idea is sometimes found in very explicit terms amongst certain peoples; the Wishram of the northwest United States, for instance, believe that babies, coyotes, and dogs communicate with one another and that babies lose this capacity for inter-species communication as soon as they begin to speak their mother tongue.

It is, of course, only when intelligence was thought of as being verbal intelligence that "the mystery of the first word" could be linked to "the mystery of the beginnings of thought." In a sense, however, this question of the "first word" is the main topic of this article, but I shall try, first, to restate the problem in the light of Piaget's research in cognitive development and, secondly, to describe results of a current research project that throw some light on the question as it is reformulated.

A PIAGETIAN PERSPECTIVE ON SYMBOLIC DEVELOPMENT

A first point to make, which has been stressed in many of Piaget's and his collaborators' works, is the following: intellectual operations do not have their roots in language, but in the preverbal, sensory-motor period, where a system of abstract patterns (called "schemes") is formed that prefigures logical systems such as classes and relations as well as concepts of space, time, and causality. By the middle of the baby's second year, his behavior shows a certain coherence that makes it possible to infer underlying structures. He can set himself a short-term aim and go about reaching it in an ordered sequence of actions; he shows that he knows that he can go from one point to another and then retrace his steps to come back; he also knows that there are several ways of reaching the same place; he feels that certain things "belong together" and that certain actions have similar results. The bases for his later logical constructs as well as for his later knowledge of physics have been laid.

A second point is that, although all these things have been achieved without the help of language, thought cannot develop further without some kind of representation. But representation is not necessarily verbal representation. Language may be the most striking instance of what is called the symbolic function, but it is only one of its manifestations. Any behavior in which an object or event is represented by something else, by what is called a "signifier," is a manifestation of the symbolic function. During their second year, babies show many such behavior patterns: in make-believe play they may push a match-box along the table and make it collide with a salt cellar, representing the car that the day before crashed into the garage door. Or they may solve a practical problem that they could not have managed without some representation of the mechanics involved, however elementary. The following observation (Piaget, 1946) is a striking example of such behavior.

At the age of one year and four months, Lucienne (who already knows how to turn a box upside down so that its contents fall out and how to get something out of a box by putting a finger inside) is presented with a match-box into which she has seen her father put a watch-chain. The box is then shut, except for a slit 3 millimeters wide.

> Lucienne puts her finger into the slit, and gropes to reach the chain, but fails completely. A pause follows, during which Lucienne has a curious reaction which bears witness not only to the fact that she tries to think out the situation and to represent to herself through mental combination the actions to be performed, but also to the role played by imitation in the genesis of representation. Lucienne mimics the widening of the slit. She looks at it with great attention; then, several times in succession, she opens and shuts her mouth, at first slightly, then wider and wider. Due to inability to think out the situation in words or in clear mental images she uses a simple motor-indication as a signifier or symbol. (p.66)

Seen in this light, language is not an isolated phenomenon, which appears *ex nihilo* at a certain point in development, but is part of a more general function whose growing importance can either be observed (as in symbolic play and later in drawing) or be inferred from intelligent acts that could not take place without some kind of mental image. The first behaviors that cannot be explained without the supposition of a mental image seem to be imitative acts, especially in the case of imitations that do not take place while or immediately after a child perceives something—an object, a movement, a series of sounds—but after a certain lapse of time.

Céline at one year, four months, for example, has been on a regular visit to friends and has seen a butterfly batting its wings in the topmost corner of a windowpane. She has been looking at it intensively and flapping her arms—she imitates the butterfly's movement while she perceives it. A week later, on the next visit, she goes straight to the same window, looks up to the corner, and starts flapping her arms. A past event is being symbolized, some kind of mental image must be present. There remain, however, three differences between such symbolic acts and verbal behavior. First, although in every case we have to do with symbolizations of reality, using language adds another dimension, since words, unlike the gestures we have described, do not resemble reality in any clear way (apart from onomatopoeic expressions, which admittedly play a large part in the very first verbal productions). Second, unlike the objects that the child uses in his make-believe play as standing for something real (a matchbox for a car, a piece of paper for a plane) and that can be freely chosen by the child himself, words are conventional and their meaning is, to a certain extent at least, shared by all those who speak the same language. Third, although in his imitations and make-believe, the child can use a number of symbolizers that are loosely linked together in the general frame of play, words combine into sentences in no such haphazard way; their grammatical functions form a rule-governed system. Within the group of behaviors that attest the existence of the symbolic function, language has a special place. Nonetheless, from a theoretical as well as from an observational point of view, the link between the different types of symbolizing behaviors is strong and it does not seem that the mystery of the first word can be solved without taking into account all the different facets of the symbolic function in general. However, our knowledge of the way this general symbolizing ability is acquired is very scanty. Despite excellent studies on the development of drawing (Luquet, 1967), on the development of mental images as they can be explored through asking the child to make gestures, to choose between different representations, and to make drawings himself (Piaget & Inhelder, 1966), and on the development of play (Piaget, 1946), little has been done on the problem of how this general symbolizing capacity starts to evolve; all these studies concern periods where the symbolic function is already present in its basic forms.

PRELIMINARY RESULTS OF A LONGITUDINAL STUDY

Studies of later developmental stages have shown a direct dependence of the symbolic function on purely cognitive development. The problem that we felt had to be attacked concerns, in the first place, the question whether observational data can elucidate the way in which the symbolic function develops, and, second, whether such data can give us some idea of the link between symbolization and cognitive evolution (which, let us recall, has progressed a long way before any symbolic acts can be observed). With this aim in mind, our Parisian colleagues, Lézine and Stambak (two psychologists who specialize in studies of infant behavior), started a research project in 1968 for which they invited the collaboration of Inhelder and myself.

The study concerns the systematic observation of a group of infants from 12 to 26 months old, some of whom are being followed longitudinally. At the time of writing (January 1970), 136 infants had been observed in a Parisian nursery and 12 of them had been followed in monthly or fortnightly sessions. In these sessions, the children are seated for a quarter of an hour on the floor of a play-room in front of a collection of familiar objects and toys (a spoon, a plate, a sponge, a baby's bottle, a sheet of paper, a piece of cloth, a toy feather-duster, a toy broom, a mug, a hand-mirror, a doll, a baby-doll, a teddy bear, etc.). One of the experimenters attracts the child's attention to objects and then fades into the background, to intervene only if the child hurts himself or specifically asks for attention. From behind a one-way screen, several observers note down all the baby's activities, indicating the time-division by minutes. The analysis of this wealth of observational data is far from completed, even from the point of view to which we limit ourselves: the development of symbolic activity and its eventual link with cognitive stages. However, the results of a preliminary analysis seem to point the way toward at least a partially new approach to the problem and they may therefore have some heuristic value.

SOME CATEGORIES OF KNOWLEDGE AND ACTIVITY

Keeping in mind our double aim, we divided our data into three categories, which correspond to very general distinctions that play an important role in Piagetian theory.

1. In the first category we included all those activities that can be interpreted as concerning knowledge about the objects themselves (the discovery of

their properties: is this thing soft, smooth, heavy, pliable, does it make a noise, etc.).
2. In the second category we included those activities by which the infant introduces some organization into the objects (any spatial or functional arrangements: putting two or more objects together, one next to the other, one on top of another, one into another, etc.).
3. In the third category we included all those activities that can be interpreted as "acting as if" (using the sheet of paper as a blanket for the doll, for instance).

Each category included the entire age-range from 12 to 26 months, although it is only at the oldest level that it is possible to categorize the activities in a clear-cut way so that all observers agree. In the earlier stages, interpretation can be difficult, essentially because the behaviors have not yet become differentiated enough to be unequivocably classifiable in this manner. Before the general lines of development that seem to emerge from the data are described and specific examples given, it is necessary to explain the rationale behind the categorization of activities.

In his epistemological theory, Piaget makes a distinction between two different kinds of knowledge, one that derives from logico-mathematical experience, and the other that derives from experience with the actual physical reality. The first kind of knowledge is what has led man to construct mathematical and logical systems; the second kind has led him to construct physics. Logico-mathematical theory and the theory of physics are distinct in the history of science; they are also distinct in a developmental, psychological sense. They are, of course, similar in many ways; they are also interdependent in certain ways. Their common characteristic lies in the fact that in both types of knowledge the subject is acting on objects, modifying them in a meaningful manner and not simply copying reality; but the way in which knowledge is abstracted from the activity and the type of knowledge that is gained are different. Piaget often gives the following examples of child behavior to make the distinction clear; these examples stem from observational data and have also given rise to many of his well-known experiments. To quote (Piaget & Inhelder, 1969):

> In the case of logico-mathematical experience, the child acts on the objects, but the knowledge which he gains from the experience is not derived from these objects: it is derived from the action bearing on the objects, which is not the same thing at all. In order to find out that $3 + 2 = 2 + 3$, he needs to introduce a certain order into the objects he is handling (pebbles, marbles, etc.) putting down first three and then two or first two and then three. He needs to put these objects together in different ways. What he discovers is that the total remains the same whatever the order; in other words, that the product of the action of bringing together is independent of the action of ordering. If there is in fact (at this level) an experimental discovery, it is not relevant

to the properties of the objects. Here the discovery stems from the subjects actions and manipulations and this is why later, when these actions are interiorized into operations (interiorized reversible actions belonging to a structure), handling becomes superfluous and the subject can combine these operations by means of a purely deductive procedure and he knows that there is no risk of them being proved wrong by contradictory physical experiences. Thus the actual properties of the objects are not relevant to such logical mathematical discoveries. (p.124)

The only property of the objects themselves that is relevant in this case is the fact that objects like pebbles can be handled in this way; drops of water cannot. By contrast, it is just the properties of the objects themselves that are relevant when the child begins to discover regularities in the physical world: water flows, sand also, but in a different manner, balls roll and can be made to bounce; and so on. However, this distinction between two types of knowledge does not imply that some kind of physics experience exists in a pure form, without the subject introducing some kind of organization into the experiments he is performing. As we have said, in both cases the subject acts on objects, and the distinction bears on the way knowledge is gained and on the kind of knowledge that is gained.

THE BEHAVIOR PATTERNS OF THREE AGE GROUPS
Our subjects seem to exhibit behavior patterns that divide them into three different age-groups: roughly, from 12 months to 16 months, from 16 to 19 months, and from 19 to 26 months. Quantitatively speaking, this division can be justified by computing the number of different actions performed on the number of different objects per minute, and also by the choice of the objects handled. However, the analysis is not complete and for our present purpose it is more important to give typical examples for each age-group and for each category of behavior. Since the division into types of activity is much clearer in the eldest group, we start with the subjects between 19 and 26 months old. As far as possible, we give examples from the protocols of one child, Pierre, who has been followed longitudinally from 12 to 26 months.

1. 19 TO 26 MONTHS. Behavior category 1 (knowledge of the objects and their properties): The children of this group handle many of the objects in an "adultomorphic," conventional way; they already seem to have discovered objects' properties and normal usage. When they use one object to act upon another, both the choice of the instrument and of the object that is acted upon are adequate. For example, Pierre, at the age of 26 months, sweeps the floor with the broom, brushes his hair with the hairbrush, and dusts the book with a duster.
Behavior category 2 (knowledge obtained through the introduction of some kind of order into the objects): The children start to make certain arrangements, which seem to have some classificatory principle. For example,

in the session just mentioned, Pierre carefully puts the feather-duster next to the broom and spends some time aligning them properly.

Behavior category 3 (activities implying some kind of "make-believe"): At this level, several subcategories can be distinguished:

a. The children take the dolls or the teddy bear and treat them as if they were partners in a play-scene. For example, Pierre holds the hand-mirror in front of the doll's face, inclines it a little, puts the doll into the right position so that she can look at herself.

b. The children perform some activity that implies the symbolization of something absent. For example, Pierre pours water from the bottle (which is in reality empty) onto his neck, and then wipes his neck with his other hand.

c. The children act in such a way that a present object is symbolically substituted for an absent one. For example, Pierre puts the handle of the broom on the doll's mouth, holding the doll in a nursing position. His expression and movements indicate that the broom-handle represents a baby's bottle.

A general characteristic of this age-group is the appearance of organized series of activity, in which several actions follow one another inside a common framework. For example, Pierre takes the hairbrush and puts it to his hair; he begins to brush his fringe slowly, with his right hand; then he starts to brush the doll's hair. After a while, he takes the mirror, holds it in front of the doll's face, inclines it a little, and adjusts the position of the doll; then he brushes the doll's hair again and finally he brushes his own hair again.

2. 16 TO 19 MONTHS. The activities of this group are clearly at a less evolved level, but, on the other hand, they can still be divided into our behavior categories and they function as a preparation for the higher-level activities.

Behavior category 1: The children's activity is much more dispersed, and although the choice of the instrument is already adequate, the object that is being acted upon is chosen from a much wider range of possibilities. For example, Pierre, at the age of 19 months, dusts the doll's face with the feather-duster. He puts the spoon on the plate, then takes it off and tries to push it into the hairbrush. He brushes the baby's bottle with the hairbrush.

Behavior category 2: The children assemble certain objects, but it is difficult to distinguish spatial, categorical, and functional criteria in these arrangements. For example, Pierre puts the spoon in the mug, pushes it down with his left hand, takes the mirror into his right hand, tips the spoon out of the mug into the plate, takes it out again, puts it back into the mug, then puts it onto the plate, puts the hand-mirror into the mug, puts the spoon into the mug, and finally takes it out again and puts it back onto the plate.

There are moments when the spatio-temporal and causal aspects of their activities are clearer. For example, Pierre takes the spoon in his right hand and puts it on the floor. He then puts it upright and then flat on the floor and turns it around, then upright again, turns it in this position, puts it onto his right leg, then under his right leg, and then starts to tap on the floor with it.

Behavior category 3: At this age we can also distinguish several subcategories:

a. Make-believe activities involving the children's own body-attitudes. For example, Pierre rocks to and fro and pretends to fall asleep, he holds his head with his hand and closes his eyes. He stays in this position for a full two minutes, hunching up his shoulders higher and higher. When the observer moves toward him he opens his eyes and begins to laugh.

b. Make-believe activities involving the teddy bear or the doll. In this age-group also, the children quite often play with these toys. However, they do not seem to treat them in such a way that the toy bear or the doll is supposed to take part in the game; bear and doll are passive partners. For example, Pierre hugs the bear and gently pets the doll.

A general characteristic of this level is that sequences of activities that share a common context are much shorter and much less well integrated.

3. 12 TO 16 MONTHS. The activities of this group of subjects are much more dispersed. It seems as if for these children the sight or touch of the objects elicits certain action-patterns, any one of which can be applied to almost any object.

Behavior category 1: The children go in for a great number of what may be called instrumental activities, which help the discovery of object properties. For example, Pierre, at the age of 12 and 13 months, frequently uses two objects; he taps the mug with the broomhandle, he hits the plate with the feather-duster, he pushes the plate with the broom, he pushes the hairbrush energetically down onto the plate, and so on. Activities and objects used are changed in rapid succession. At this age, many activities concern only one object. For example, Pierre shakes the mug, he throws the plate, scratches the spoon, taps with the broom, etc.

Behavior category 2: Even at this age, the children assemble certain objects. However, it is impossible to distinguish spatial, categorical, or functional charactistics; these groupings could be interpreted in any way, but all observers have the impression that it would be quite unwarranted to assign any preliminary organizing aim to these assemblages. For example, Pierre puts one object into another, but this can just as much look like a functional grouping (e.g., spoon into mug) as like something completely haphazard (e.g., mirror into pot). He also puts one object next to another and one object on top of another.

Behavior category 3: No make-believe behavior can be distinguished in the activities
at this age-level.
Other behavior: By contrast, one other type of behavior is relatively frequent at this
age: activities that involve the child's own body. For example, Pierre
puts the bottle onto his leg, chews the broomhandle, takes objects into
his mouth; he also pulls his own hair, scratches his leg, folds and pulls
at his clothing. Oral activities, which are a frequent means of exploring
objects at an even earlier age, continue to be of importance at this
level.

IMPLICATIONS FOR THE DEVELOPMENT OF SYMBOLIC FUNCTION AND LANGUAGE ACQUISITION

Can the developmental sequence that we have briefly sketched throw any light on
the problem of the advent of the symbolic function and its eventual links with cognitive development during the sensory-motor period?

The first point to be made is that it seems that symbolic activity involving the use
of a signifier distinct from what is signified (for instance, the use of the broomhandle
"as if" it were a baby's bottle) does not start until knowledge of the objects and
organization of the subject's activities have progressed to a certain level. The first
symbolic substitutions appear when, on numerous occasions, the children show
behavior patterns that involve the conventional use of objects. These objects have
now been endowed with a number of properties, though certainly not yet in the adult
sense of the word. For instance, instead of saying that the child now knows that
something is soft, it might be better to say that he knows that it is "soft to the touch."
The properties are functional, but well established. From a common-sense point of
view, it seems indeed probable that objects have to be defined in a certain way before
they can represent something else or be represented by something else. As Furth has
remarked (1969, p.96) when a child uses a box as a bed in his play, "he knows what
a bed is and what a box is; precisely because of this double knowledge he can use
one as a symbol for the other." At the same time, the subject's action patterns have
undergone a development that is more difficult to define. It appears that they have
acquired a certain generality and abstraction that assure adequate adaptation to the
object to be handled, both in the case of instrumental activity and in that of spatial
and categorical organization. Second, several of these patterns are now coordinated,
i.e., adapted to one another; thirdly, they can now be arranged in a coherent succession within a general framework. All these factors mean that the underlying abstract
pattern (which Piaget calls a *schème*) becomes free of the material context. The
distinction between object and subject, necessary for the child to become a "knowing" rather than only an "acting" organism, has been established. Again, it seems
understandable that this development has to be achieved before any genuine symbolic activity can take place.

How does language acquisition fit into this developmental sequence that culmi-
nates in the start of symbolic activities? Our second set of observational data, on the

children's babbling and speech, has not yet been analyzed. The following few points are raised in a purely speculative manner.

Traditionally, it has been accepted that the very first stage in language acquisition is represented by utterances consisting of only one element; this element is not necessarily one "word" in adult language. *Atè* (corresponding to *par terre*—on the floor—said when something has fallen down) and *aplu* (corresponding to part of the sentence, *il n'y en a plus*—all gone) are typical examples. Without going into details, it can be maintained that present opinion has swung toward the idea that these holophrases are first instances of the topic-comment combination with the topic deleted. (Among French-language authors, Sêchehaye speaks of "principal-complément" as early as 1926.) Piaget (1946) calls these utterances "action-judgments" in contrast with the slightly later two-word utterances, which he names "observation-judgments." Though the exact nature of these very first verbal productions is not yet quite clear, especially if we want to know how they evolve from what went before and how they lead to what comes after, Piaget's expression seems to capture their character better than does any other. As he explains, these holophrases are translations of *schemes*, action patterns, which are themselves the first meanings. From this point of view, it would be preferable not to consider holophrases as topic-comment constructions with the topic deleted, but rather as a fusion between topic and comment. Action patterns themselves go through an undifferentiated stage and gradually become more differentiated; verbal patterns could well repeat this process. Again, from a common-sense point of view, can one really say that when a child says *atè* when a book falls off the table he comments ("it falls") on a topic ("the book")? Such expressions seem much nearer to an adult exclamation like "there!", which reflects a whole event without any analysis.

However, which ever way one looks at them, these first utterances still resemble personal symbols (for instance, the use of the broomhandle as if it were a baby's bottle) in their mobility and their rapidly changing content; but they are already conventional symbols, words, since they are taken over from adult language and since they share part of their adult meaning.

The mobile character of those first meanings is well illustrated by an example from Piaget's data (Piaget, 1946).

T. at 1;5 uses the term *aplu* to indicate a departure, then to indicate the throwing of an object onto the floor, then applied to an object that falls over (without disappearing), for instance, when he is playing with building blooks. A little later *aplu* means "remoteness" (anything out of reach) and then the game of handing over an object for somebody to throw it back to him. Finally, at 1;7 *aplu* takes on the meaning of "to start over again."

This mobility of meaning makes it very difficult for adult observers to notice these first "understandable" utterances; many may go unnoticed, particularly when the child does not articulate very clearly, as is frequently the case.

A slightly different category of holophrases consists of those that resemble denominations, some of which may be the result of direct training, but others occur spontaneously, such as "doggie," "pussy," or "car."

A second stage traditionally distinguished comprises two-word utterances—the beginning of grammar—although one may ask with Cohen (1969) if some of the holophrases are not a combination of a gesture (a nonverbal element of communication) and a word; for instance, when a child says "Mummy," pointing to his mother's coffee-cup, and then "Daddy," pointing to his father's cup. Such combinations can well be the precursors of the many utterances like "Mummy cup" (Mummy's cup). I should like to suggest that the topic-comment type (first fused, later differentiated) is linked to what we have called the organizing activity of the subject, whereas the denominational type relates to the object-knowledge aspect. Speculating even further, one can suppose that the early denominations constitute the beginnings of what later will be an organized lexicon and that early topic-comment utterances are the beginnings of what will develop into a rule-governed grammar. Just as with the object-knowledge and organizing activity of the subject, there is, of course, continuous interaction and interdependence. Word-meanings develop thanks to and together with grammatical structuration and vice versa.

Today, many papers on language acquisition seem to end with a question mark and the present paper is no exception. Only experimental data will really allow us to solve the mystery, but how should we go about obtaining them? Let us hope that observation and speculation may at least point the way.

REFERENCES

Beilin, H., & Spontak, G. Active-passive transformations and operational reversibility. Paper presented at meeting of S.R.C.D., Santa Monica, Calif., March 1969.

Bellugi, U. H. The acquisition of the system of negation in children's speech. Unpublished doctoral dissertation, Harvard University, 1967.

Brown, R. The first sentences of child and chimpanzee. Mimeographed paper, Harvard University, 1969.

Cohen, M. Sur l'étude du langage enfantin. *Enfance,* 1969, Mai-Sept., 231-272. (Reprint of *Enfance,* 1952, 5 (3).)

Francis, H. Structure in the speech of a 2½ year old. *British Journal of Educational Psychology,* 1969, 39, 291-301.

Furth, H. C. *Piaget and knowledge.* Englewood Cliffs, N.J.: Prentice-Hall, 1969.

Luquet, G. H. *Le dessin enfantin.* Neuchâtel: Delachaux et Niestlé, 1967.

Piaget, J. *La formation du symbole chez l'enfant.* Neuchâtel: Delachaux et Niestlé, 1946.

Piaget, J., & Inhelder, B. *L'image mentale chez l'enfant.* Paris: Presses Universitaires de France, 1966.

Piaget, J., & Inhelder, B. The gaps in empiricism. In A. Koestler (Ed.), *Beyond reductionalism.* New York: Hutchinson, 1969. Pp.118-148.

Schlesinger, I. M. Production of utterances and language acquisition. In D. I. Slobin (Ed.), *The ontogenesis of grammar.* New York: Academic Press, 1971.

Sêchehaye, A. *Essai sur la structure logique de la phrase.* Paris: Champion, 1926.

Stern, W. *Psychologie der frühen Kindheit.* Leipzig: Quelle und Meyer, 1914.

Vygotsky, L. S. *Thought and language.* Cambridge, Mass.: The MIT Press, 1962.

Developmental Change in the Use of Single-word Utterances
Lois Bloom

The use of single-word utterances is usually described as the first of the "developmental milestones" in language acquisition. But the essence of development is change and there has been an unfortunate tendency to overlook inherent variation in this period which might provide evidence of what children are learning in the course of this stage of development. It has generally been assumed in the literature that children simply accumulate a number of different words (that are most often noun forms in the adult model) until they begin to combine them into phrases. But what of the kinds of words that are used and the ways in which they are used in this period of time? It would be surprising if the only difference between the child of 12-13 months, the child of 15-16 months, and the child of 18-19 months was in the numbers of different words understood or used. Specifically, to look for the origins of grammar, one would like to be able to explain how the use of single words at one point in time is immediately antecedent to the use of syntax, whereas the use of single words at an earlier time is evidently not. The child of 13-14 months is usually not about to use syntax, whereas the child of 19-20 months frequently is.

THE DISTINCTION BETWEEN CLASSES OF SINGLE WORDS

The kinds of words that Allison used before she used syntax could be differentiated in at least two ways. To begin with, it was possible to study the distribution of different words in terms of relative frequency of occurrence and persistence of use. One could also describe the words in terms of their referential function—that is, their use in situations that had or did not have certain features in common.

THE FREQUENCY AND RELATIVE PERSISTENCE OF DIFFERENT WORDS

Allison's increasing use of new words in the period from 9 to 18 months did not result in a cumulative vocabulary or lexicon. That is, certain words were used for a time and then no longer used. One might expect that once a word is used by a child with some regularity in appropriate situations, then the word would continue to be used as

From L. Bloom, One Word at a Time, The Hague: Mouton, 1973, pp. 65-70. Reprinted by permission of Mouton Publishers, EDICOM Contracts & Subsidiary Rights, Holland.

similar situations recurred. This was not the case in the course of Allison's development.[1] By the age of 14 months, over 25 different words had been heard in Allison's
speech; however, within a one-week period there were never more than 10 to 12
different words occurring with regularity. The 25 different words she used from 9 to
14 months each occurred more than once, with consistent and recognizable form,
over a period of at least several days. However, many words dropped from use and
did not reappear until several or many months later. In some instances, the word
reappeared with different phonetic or lexical form. For example, the word for *flower*
at 14 months was [gájə]; at 18 months the word for *flower* reappeared as [fáwə]. The
word "dog" occurred from 12 to 13 months, and reappeared as "bowwow" at 19
months.[2] It was not possible, at the time, to discern any reason why such words
ceased to be used. For example, "dog" occurred originally when Allison (1) saw a dog
or different dogs, or (2) heard a dog bark, or (3) heard the clinking of a dog's identification tags. All of these experiences continued to occur. Allison both saw and heard
dogs; she simply did not say the word in the same situations.[3]

However, there was a small group of words that Allison continued to use persist-
ently and far more frequently than any other words in this same period of time from
9 to 17 or 18 months. This group of words included names of people—"Mama,"
"Dada," "Mimi," (her baby sitter) and "Baby" (both in reference to herself and to other
babies and to her dolls). All of these names of people has first occurred before 12
months. The remaining words that were used frequently and that persisted were
"there," "up," "uh oh," "no," "away," "gone," "stop," and "more." Table 1 presents
all of the words that occurred in the video tape sample of Allison's speech at age 16,

---

[1] Leopold reported a "mortality" for words in this same period of time in his daughter's
speech (Vol. 1, 159-160); Oscar Bloch also reported that words dropped out of use and
reappeared at a later time in the development of his three children ("Premiers stades du langage
de l'enfant," *Journal de Psychologie,* 1921); and Dorothea McCarthy referred to reports of both
cumulative and noncumulative vocabularies in early development ("Language development in
children," 1954, 526). The disuse of words after their initial appearance may explain why
growth of vocabulary before the last half of the second year is often described as slow. See,
for example, John Carroll. *Language and thought,* 1964, 32; Eric Lenneberg, *Biological foundations of language,* 1967, 131; and Dorothea McCarthy, "Language development in children,"
1954, 527.

[2] Bloch reported that such words that dropped out were different in form when they reappeared, reflecting the children's more recent phonological development ("Premiers stades du
langage de l'enfant." 1921).

[3] Allison did not spontaneously repeat the speech of others, that is, she did not imitate. She
did not attempt to imitate when asked to and she was not pressed to do so. It is worth
considering the possibility that children who do not appear to stop saying words after their initial
use—that is, children whose lexical acquisition is apparently 'cumulative' in the first half of the
single-word utterance period—are also children who spontaneously imitate or repeat utterances
that they hear. Their using a word with apparent persistence may simply reflect this propensity
to repeat a word heard in a previous utterance—with or without some intervening delay. That
is, they use the word because they have just heard it used in a particular context. Both Allison
and Hildegard Leopold did not spontaneously imitate, and both used words that did not persist
in active use. This connection between the tendency to imitate and the relative persistence of
different words is necessarily speculative but it is not unreasonable.

Table 1   Single-Word Utterances and their Frequency of Occurrence Allison at 16 months, 3 weeks

all gone, 1	there, 30
away, 9	turn, 1
baby, 19	uh, 2
car, 2	uh oh, 7
chair, 14	up, 27
cookie, 15	widə, 1
cow, 3	
Dada, 4	
dirty, 2	
down, 22	
girl, 3	
gone, 19	
here, 1	
horse, 1	Most Frequent: there, 30
Mama, 9	up, 27
mess, 2	more, 24
more, 24	down, 22
no, 21	no, 21
oh, 3	gone, 19
pig, 6	baby, 19
sit, 1	
stop, 1	

3 with the frequency of occurrence for each. The seven most frequent words (occurring at least 19 times) accounted for 65% of all single word utterances in the 40-minute sample.

Clearly, there was a small group of words that Allison used more frequently than other words. These words also tended to be used continually after their initial appearance. At the same time, there was a large number of different words that occurred relatively less frequently, with a tendency for some words to drop from use as other words came into use. The relative frequency and endurance of word-forms was less interesting, however, than how such words were used—in terms of aspects of the behavior and context in the speech events in which utterances occurred.

REFERENTIAL FUNCTION OF SINGLE-WORD UTTERANCES

It is commonplace to observe a child use the word "chair" in a context in which an object for sitting is the focus of the child's attention, "cookie" in a context in which a specific object for eating is the focus, and so on. A name of an object, such as "chair, makes nominal reference to a particicular object x, which is a member of a class of objects X_n that have certain configurational and functional attributes in common, and which distinguish them from classes of objects Y_n, Z_n, ... Although the child may use (or recognize) the word-form in reference to only a highly particular instance of the class X_n objects initially, he eventually extends the reference to different objects in different contexts. The basis for this generalization is usually easily recognized—features in common that can be seen, heard, or felt, and the common uses to which the objects can be put (like sitting and eating).

Certain other words in early lexicons do not make reference to classes of objects in the same way. The word "more" was first used by Allison when she was 16 months old and occurred in a situation in which she had frequently heard the word—during a meal, when offered a second portion of food, after she had already eaten a first portion. Two days after she had first used "more" to request the recurrence of food, she used the word to request her baby sitter to tickle her again, after having been tickled just previously. Subsequently, "more" also referred to another instance of an object in the presence of the original object; for example, Allison pointed to one shoe, commented "shoe," and then pointed to the second shoe and commented "more."

What are the features of context and behavior that would lead a child to extend the meaning of a word like "more" to refer to aspects of objects and events (like meat, tickling, and shoes) that, in themselves, differ from one another both perceptually and functionally? It is necessary for the child to perceive that such classes of objects or events as $X_n, Y_n, Z_n, \ldots$ have certain repeating behaviors in common—for example, they exist, cease to exist, and recur in his experience. The word-form "more" refers not to instances of phenomena $a_1, a_2, \ldots$ of a class of phenomena A_n. Rather, the instances $a_1, a_2, \ldots, a_n$ are a instances of $x_1, x_2, \ldots, X_n, Y_n, Z_n, \ldots$ objects and events. Thus, "more" is an inherently relational term—its meaning extends to and depends upon, in every instance, an aspect of behavior of some object or event in the environment. But the object or event has a status in the child's experience that is also independent of the "meaning" of "more."

Thus, the meaning of certain word-forms such as "more," "up," "no," "away" is inherently relational or transitive, which is essentially what Ingram attempted to account for in his description of the alternative uses of "up" by Leopold's daughter, Hildegard.[4] A word like "up" occurs in situations that vary with respect to different people as agents and different things as objects. But the meaning of "up" (or "more") does not depend on the agent-object relationship, as Ingram implied, but only on a specific aspect of their behavioral interaction, namely, the notion of 'upness' (or the notion of recurrence). Thus, it is also true that "up" refers to static conditions—for example, a book up on the shelf, where the agent does not matter at all. Another instance of a shoe, or "more shoe," does not necessarily involve an agent or anything else other than the prior or simultaneous occurrence of the same object or one very similar to it. The child comes to recognize recurrent phenomena—in certain instances the figurative and functional attributes of phenomena like chairs and shoes, in other instances behavioral or relational phenomena like the notions "upness," disappearance, or recurrence with respect to objects like chairs and shoes. Both kinds of phenomena come to be represented by the child as conceptual notions that can be conveniently coded by word-forms.

Thus, one way to differentiate among kinds of words in early pre-syntax lexicons has to do with referential function. When one considers the range of phenomena to

---

[4] David Ingram, "Transitivity in child language," 1971.

which a particular utterance by the child refers, it is possible to distinguish two kinds of word-forms: substantive forms which make reference to classes of objects and events that are discriminated on the basis of their perceptual features or attributes, and function or relational forms which make reference across such perceptually distinguished classes of objects and events.

REFERENCES

Bloch, Oscar, "Premiers stades du language de l'enfant", *Journal de Psychologie*, 1921, *18*, 693-712.

Carroll, John B., *Language and thought*, Englewood Cliffs, N.J.: Prentice-Hall, 1964.

Ingram, David, Transitivity in child language, *Language*, 1971, *47*, 888-910.

Lenneberg, Eric, *Biological foundations of language*, New York: John Wiley and Sons, 1967.

Leopold, Werner, *Speech development of a bilingual child*, Evanston, Illinois: Northwestern University Press, 1939-1949, 4 vols.

McCarthy, Dorothea, Language development in children. In Leonard Carmichael (Ed.), *Manual of child psychology*, New York: John Wiley and Sons, 1954.

Part 4
DEVELOPMENT OF LANGUAGE CONTENT/ FORM: VARIATION AND COMPLEXITY

The first two readings in this section deal with an important issue in the study of children's grammar—the relation between semantics and syntax. The paper by *Bloom, Miller, and Hood (1975)* describes the acquisition of action verbs in the period when mean length of utterance progresses from about 1.5 to about 3.0, and documents the variation in the language behavior of individual children that results from the intersection of different aspects of language learning. The conclusion that followed from that study was that language develops as children learn both the semantics and syntax of grammatical structure together. However, *Melissa Bowerman (1973)* reviewed the evidence of children's word combinations in several languages, and concluded that language learning is primarily semantic when children first learn to say sentences.

The nature of the linguistic categories that underlie the form and content of early sentences—whether they are predominantly semantic categories or more abstract categories of grammar (semantic-syntactic relationship)—is an issue that remains. It is not altogether clear how the issue will ultimately be resolved and even the boundaries that define the issue are vague. However, the consensus from a number of studies is that children learn the semantic relations between words as the content of their early sentences, and some syntactic means for representing the form of such sentences.

There has been a great deal of consistency among the children who have been described in different studies, particularly in the content of their early utterances. However, there has also been important variation in the form of children's language behaviors as well, and such intersubject variation is described in the discussion of the relative use of nouns and pronouns in early sentences (taken from the monograph by Lois Bloom, Patsy Lightbown, and Lois Hood, 1975). Different children appear to learn different aspects of the language system, with acquisition of alternative linguistic forms for encoding the same or similar content.

Another kind of variation, the intrasubject variation that characterizes the language behavior of individual children, was described in the study by *Bloom, Miller, and Hood (1975)*. Such variation was seen to occur, in particular, in connection with the increasing development of complexity in later language learning. There are several dimensions in the expanding complexity of children's language development, and these have been described in the literature in terms of how children learn different subsystems of grammar. Three grammatical subsystems that have received particular attention are the system of noun and verb inflection, the acquisition of negation, and the development of questions. The study by Jill de Villiers and Peter de Villiers that is reproduced in Part 1 of these readings is a report of the acquisition of grammatical morphemes; *Roger Brown's (1968)* study of the development of Wh- questions is an exploration of the several transitions that characterize the acquisition of the forms of children's questions.

Both the acquisition of nouns and pronouns (as described by Bloom, Lightbown, and Hood) and the acquisition of Wh- questions (as described by Brown) are basic for learning how to use language. That is, it is not enough to know only the alternative forms of nouns or pronouns, or the alternative forms of questions, it is also necessary to know when and in what circumstances to use a noun or a pronoun, and how and when to ask questions. Such aspects of language development have to do with the use of language, which will be taken up in Part Five.

Variation and Reduction as Aspects of Competence in Language Development

Lois Bloom, Peggy Miller, and Lois Hood

An explanation of what children know about language when they begin to use multiword utterances is a central concern in the study of child language. Two specific aspects of early sentences were investigated in this study: apparent constraint on length and the developmental interaction among grammatical complexity, lexical and discourse factors. In early child speech, first sentences are two words long, and sentences get longer as the child's acquisition of grammar increases. However, although utterance length is correlated with increased grammatical maturity up to a ceiling of about 4.0 morphemes, utterance length, per se, is not an index of the complexity of child sentences. Two-word utterances, for example, can represent a variety of relationships between constituents—compare "a book," "Daddy book," "new book," "read book," and "book table." It is reasonable that an explanation of why the child is limited to two or three words at a time, and how circumstances that influence sentence length and complexity change over time so that longer utterances occur, will contribute to an understanding of the linguistic system that children learn for coding information in multiword messages.

There are three main issues in the present study. The first has to do with the relative adequacy of different explanations of child language—pragmatic, semantic, action-based, or grammatical—in accounting for the variable length of child sentences. Braine (1974) and Schlesinger (1974) have explained early sentences in pragmatic terms; Bowerman (1973a), Greenfield, Smith, and Laufer (in press), Kates (1974), Park (1974), and Schlesinger (1971) have explained the structure of early sentences in semantic terms; Bruner (1974), Dore (1974), and McNeill (1974) have proposed that the child's sensorimotor (action) patterns prefigure and thus determine sentence patterns; and the proposals of Bloom (1970), Bowerman (1973b), and Brown (1973)

From *Minnesota Symposia on Child Psychology, Vol. 9*, pp. 3-55, ed. Anne D. Pick, University of Minnesota Press, 1975. Reprinted by permission of University of Minnesota Press.

NOTE: The research reported here was supported in part by Research Grant HD 03828 and Fellowship FI-MH-30,001 from the National Institutes of Health. We are grateful to Karin Lifter and Barbara Schecter for heroic assistance in processing the data, to Owen Whitby for advice with the statistical analyses, to Patsy Lightbown who shared in the genesis of the study and preparation of early drafts of the manuscript, and to William Labov, Margaret Lahey, and Cory Dude, who influenced the research reported here in various and important ways.

have centered on the nature of early rules of grammar. The thesis that will be presented here is an elaboration of the grammatical complexity hypothesis proposed originally in Bloom (1970): that utterance length is a function of development of the capacity for realizing the underlying grammatical complexity of sentences.

The second issue deals with the relative adequacy of different linguistic schemas that can represent grammar in child language. The specific questions are (a) whether there are constituents such as Subject, Verb, and Object in child language, and (b) if so, whether the representation of such constituents in a child language grammar is optional, indicating that constituents may or may not be basic to sentences (Brown, 1973), or obligatory, indicating that such constituents are basic to sentences, whether or not words that represent the constituents actually occur in particular sentences (Bloom, 1970). The evidence suggests that neither of the earlier formulations of optional or obligatory constituents was adequate. The model that will be presented here retains the concept of obligatory constituents, with the addition of probability factors that predict the frequency with which constituents are realized under different linguistic and nonlinguistic conditions. This variable rule model is within the paradigm for grammatical formulations proposed by Labov (1969) and by Cedergren and Sankoff (1974) for variation in adult language, and suggested by Brown (1973) for the development of grammatical morphemes.*

One consequence of Labov's variable rule model has been a reformulation of the competence/performance distinction. In the traditional view, competence consisted of a speaker's knowledge of language in the form of categorical rules for generating sentences. The actual production and comprehension of speech (performance) reflected competence interacting with, and distorted by, extralinguistic factors such as memory and attention limitations. In contrast, Labov's version of competence encompasses systematic variation among linguistic elements. He argues that a speaker's knowledge of language includes both categorical rules *and* variable rules which operate with particular probabilities in particular linguistic environments. Cedergren & Sankoff (1974) have pointed out that "the power of this [Labov's] approach lies in the uniquely well-defined and economical relationship which it posits between a

---

* The issue of writing formal rules has not been addressed in the present paper. The analysis of the child language data has been treated, thus far, apart from the problem of formalization for representing the information about child language. Labov's variable rules deal with constraints in the linguistic and nonlinguistic environments that favor or disfavor the application of certain syntactic and phonological rules. In our data, we have identified variation in the occurrence of major sentence constituents in child speech—a more radical variation than has been treated so far with the use of variable rules, although one that appears to be within the formal extension of variable rules that has been proposed by Cedergren and Sankoff (1974). In particular, in the application of probability theory to linguistics, Sankoff (see also, Suppes, 1970) has proposed that probability weightings of constituents in phrase structure rules is a realistic scheme for accounting for the actual production of sentences (W. Labov, personal communication). Such an application of probability theory is particularly attractive to the issue of the formalization of child language data; it allows for a rational explanation of the transitions between successive child grammars in terms of how the probabilities of rule application change over time and relate to different factors in the child's linguistic and nonlinguistic development.

probability distribution and a sample, or between a model and a simulation" (pp. 352–353).

The third issue, then, concerns which of the two notions of competence/performance best accounts for the variable length of child utterances. Bowerman (1973a) has suggested that the length of child utterances is constrained by performance factors, as traditionally defined. More specifically, Brown (1973) and Bowerman (1973a) have explained children's continued use of two-constituent sentences when they are able to produce three-constituent and four-constituent utterances as casualties of performance—in effect, linguistic mistakes.* Yet Bowerman expressed uncertainty about the status of performance constraints and decided that some constraints were important enough to be represented in grammatical rules, i.e., optional verb deletion transformations. Similarly, Brown proposed a categorical grammar in which subject and predicate constituents are represented as obligatory (p. 232), but elsewhere implied that constituents are optionally represented in competence (p. 238). It appears that attempts to apply the traditional competence/performance distinction have resulted in confusion about whether certain influences on child language reflect competence (and therefore should be represented by grammatical rules) or performance. The position taken here is that the length of child utterances is systematically related to both linguistic and nonlinguistic factors and that this covariation reflects linguistic competence.

Situational and intrapersonal performance factors that are nonsystematic, free variation, may well influence the length of child sentences. However, it is necessary to determine the extent to which variance in the length of utterances can be accounted for by systematic constraints on the child's knowledge of a linguistic code, before judging the free or residual variability of constituent relations. In the present observational study of children's language behavior, speech events were examined to determine the distribution of constituent relations, and how factors related to grammatical, lexical, and discourse development covaried with the occurrence of two-, three- and four-constituent relations as mean length of utterance increased from 1.0 to approximately 3.0 morphemes.

SUBJECTS AND PROCEDURES

The four subjects of the study—Eric, Gia, Kathryn, and Peter—are first-born children of college-educated parents, who lived in university communities in New York City. The longitudinal study began when the children were approximately 20 months old and continued until they were 36 months old. The observations of the present study were made when the children were, approximately, between 20 and 28 months old. Eric, Gia, and Kathryn were each visited in their homes every 6 weeks for approximately 8 hours, and Peter was visited every 3 weeks for approximately 5 hours. The

---

*."Constituent" refers to a major category term such as Subject, Verb, Object, or Place, and "constituent relation" refers to any relationships between two or among more than two constituents.

transcriptions of the children's language behavior, with description of interpersonal and situational context, provided the data for the present analysis.*

The first level of processing for the present study was to obtain the corpus of behavior for analysis. In an earlier study (Bloom, Lightbown, & Hood, 1975), approximately 25,000 utterances were processed in the period when mean length of utterance increased from 1.0 to about 2.5 morphemes. The results of that study included the sequence of development of the verb relations that were observed in multiword utterances. Two of these verb relations were the dynamic categories (involving movement) of Action and Locative Action. In Action events the movement affected an object in ways other than to change its location. In Locative Action events the goal of the movement was to change the location of an object. Utterances in these two categories formed the corpus for analysis in the present study, because (a) these were the semantic-syntactic categories that developed first and occurred most frequently for each child, and (b) the categories developed for each child with increasing complexity within and between constituents.

The procedure that was followed was to examine each of the transcriptions from the four children with mean length of utterance less than 3.0 morphemes to identify the speech events that included multiword utterances with Action and Locative Action constituent relations. Because the investigation concerned the relative frequency of different constituent relations, when more than one constituent relation was theoretically available, all imperatives (whether or not Agent was expressed) and all intransitive Action utterances were omitted from the analysis. Action intransitives exclude Objects, and imperatives can exclude Agents, so that each of these could not be compared with the relative occurrences of Agent-Verb and Verb-Object when the fuller Agent-Verb-Object constituent structure was theoretically possible.

The second level of processing consisted of successive hypothesis generating and hypothesis testing procedures to explore the developmental relation among utterances with two, three, and four constituents, to determine how grammatical, lexical, and discourse development interacted with utterance length. Each utterance was multiply coded to identify (a) the meaning relations between the words, (b) the addition of any grammatical marker or other complexity within or between constituents, (c) the lexical variability of verbs and the occurrence of nominal or pronominal forms, and (d) the relation to successive adult and self utterances.

RESULTS

Table 1 presents a description of each of the samples of language behavior from the four children and includes information about age, mean length of utterance, time, and numbers of utterances in each sample. The Roman numerals in the table (and in the text) were used only for convenience; they merely identify the successive samples from each child. Accordingly, Eric III, Gia III, and Kathryn III have in common the fact that the sample was the third in the longitudinal study of each. The Roman numerals

---

* The Eric, Gia, and Kathryn data were recorded and transcribed by L. Bloom: the data from Peter were recorded and transcribed by L. Hood and P. Lightbown. See Bloom (1970, pp. 234–239) and Bloom, Lightbown, and Hood (1975) for description of the procedures used in collecting and transcribing these observations.

Table 1   Summary Description of Speech Samples[a]

Child	Sample	Hours	Age	Mean Length of Utterance	Number of Syntactic Utterance Tokens
Eric	III	7.1	22,0	1.42	165
	IV	8.0	23,2	1.69	504
	V	8.0	25,1	2.63	1,056
	VI	8.0	26,3	2.84	1,575
Gia	II	6.7	20,2	1.34	341
	III	8.0	22,1	1.58	451
	IV	8.0	23,3	1.79	671
	V	7.5	25,2	2.30	1,071
	VI	6.0	27,1	2.75	1,286
Kathryn	I	5.5	21,0	1.37	284
	II	8.0	22,3	1.89	1,303
	III	9.0	24,2	2.83	2,385
	IV	7.8	26,1	3.30	1,655
Peter	IV	4.5	23,1	1.41	149
	V	3.0	23,2	1.33	258
	VI	4.5	24,1	1.75	420
	VII	4.5	25,0	2.39	643
	IX	4.5	26,1	2.62	793
Total					15,010

[a] Only spontaneous utterances were counted in the present study. See Bloom, Hood, and Lightbown (1974) for a comparison of spontaneous and imitative utterances.

that identify the Peter data are higher because samples were collected from Peter more frequently, with shorter intervals between each sample. The important variable that established comparability among the children was, by design, the range of mean length of utterance. It happened that the children were also similar in age during this period.

The results consist of (a) the sequential development of the categories Action and Locative Action, and the subcategories of Locative Action that were identified after further exploration of the meaning relations among constituents; (b) the relative distribution of constituent relations in sentences and the developmental change in the distribution of constituent relations, within each category and subcategory; and (c) the grammatical, lexical, and discourse factors that covaried with the distribution of constituent relations.

CATEGORIES OF VERB RELATIONS
The categories of Action and Locative Action identified in Bloom, Lightbown, and Hood (1975) were the following:*

1. ACTION. Utterances referred to movement by an agent that affected an object where the goal of the movement was not a change in the location of an object or person (see Locative Action). At least two of the three components of an action relation (Agent-Action-Object) had to be represented in the utterance in order for the utterance to be included within the category.

P:VII	(Peter trying to open box)	my open that
K:III	(Kathryn opening drawer)	open drawer
G:III	(Gia going to her bike,	Gia bike
	and then getting on)	Gia ride bike**
E:IV	(Eric has just reassembled train)	I made

2. LOCATIVE ACTION. Utterances in this category referred to movement where the goal of movement was a change in the location of a person or object.
In the present study, the following three Locative Action relationships were identified in the data according to whether the Agent of the Action was also the Object that was affected by the Action.

a. *AGENT-LOCATIVE ACTION.* Utterances in this category specified a movement by an agent that caused another object to change place, and the preverbal constituent, whether or not expressed, was the Agent.

E:V	(Eric puts discs on bed)	I put ə up here
G:IV	(Gia bringing lambs to toy bag;	Gia away ə lamb
	then drops them into bag)	
P:VII	(Peter holding recording tape)	put this down

b. *MOVER-LOCATIVE ACTION.* Utterances specified a movement in which the agent of the action was also the object that changed place, and the preverbal constituent, whether or not expressed, was the Mover.

K:IV	I sit down there
(then Kathryn sits on chair)	

---

* Only a few examples of the categories are given here; the appendix in Bloom, Lightbown, and Hood (1975) consists of an extensive sampling of all the categories of semantic-syntactic relations found in the time period reported in that study.

** Note that "Gia bike" might have alternative interpretations. In such cases, preceding and succeeding utterances were examined in an effort to determine the semantic-syntactic category to which the utterance would be assigned. If another utterance in the immediate context appeared to disambiguate the utterance in question, as in this instance, the utterance could be assigned to a semantic-syntactic category. If not, it was considered equivocal and was not included in subsequent analyses.

G:V (Gia stands up on large
         stuffed dog)   stand ə wow wow
E:III (Eric getting up from chair)   I get down

    c. PATIENT-LOCATIVE ACTION. Utterances in this category specified a movement
              by an agent that caused another object (patient) to change place, and
              the pre-verbal constituent, whether or not expressed, was the Patient.
              Patient-Locative Action utterances were semantically similar to Agent-
              Locative Action utterances, but formally similar to Mover-Locative Ac-
              tion utterances.

E:IV (fitting disc into block)   ə fits here
P:V (Peter putting tiny car under
         finger puppet's skirt)   goes on there
K:II (Kathryn pushing lamb through
          windows of doll house)   lamb go in there

    The distinction among Agent-, Patient-, and Mover-Locative Action utterances was
not imposed on the data at the outset but, rather, emerged during the course of the
analysis. The categories were distinguished further in that Agent-Locative Action
utterances shared one population of verbs, and Mover- and Patient-Locative Action
utterances shared a second population of verbs. As can be seen in Table 2, the two
populations of verbs overlapped only slightly.

Table 2   Rank Order of Most Frequent[a] Verbs in Three Locative Action
                    Categories
                    (Data Combined for All Children, All Samples)

Agent-Locative Action		Mover-Locative Action		Patient-Locative Action	
Verb	Frequency	Verb	Frequency	Verb	Frequency
put	287	go	132	go	285
take	48	sit	95	fit	65
away	26	go bye-bye	28	sit	34
turn	10	come	25	fall	30
out	9	get	18	bye-bye	11
get	7	fall	15	stand	6
fit	7	stand	11		
do	6	climb	9		
dump	6	jump	7		
sit	5	move	6		
		away	5		

[a] Includes verbs with frequencies of ⩾5.

Table 3   Proportional Distribution of Multiword Utterances in Action and Locative Action Categories

				Action		Agent		Locative Action Mover		Patient	
Child	Sample	MLU[a]	N	Prop.	Freq.	Prop.	Freq.	Prop.	Freq.	Prop.	Freq.
Eric	III	1.42	30	1.00	30	—	—	—	—	—	—
	IV	1.69	134	.65	87	.01	2	.02	3	.31	42
	V	2.63	310	.65	203	.15	46	.11	33	.09	28
	VI	2.84	606[b]	.65[b]	394[b]	.11	66	.08	51	.16	95
Peter	IV	1.41	56	1.00	56	—	—	—	—	—	—
	V	1.33	76	.88	67	.08	6	0	0	.04	3
	VI	1.75	111	.70	78	.15	17	.05	6	.09	10
	VII	2.39	172	.48	82	.27	47	.07	12	.18	31
	IX	2.62	200	.45	90	.28	55	.09	18	.19	37
Gia	II	1.34	39	.51	20	.36	14	.10	4	.03	1
	III	1.58	177	.81	144	.14	25	.01	2	.03	6
	IV	1.79	231	.65	151	.09	21	.13	30	.13	29
	V	2.30	392	.77	301	.06	22	.10	40	.07	29
	VI	2.75	489[b]	.72[b]	352	.12	58	.12	61	.04	18
Kathryn	I	1.32	80	.70	56	.05	4	.21	17	.04	3
	II	1.89	400	.73	291	.11	45	.04	16	.12	48
	III	2.83	684	.58	399	.22	148	.10	70	.10	67
	IV	3.30	619[c]	.58[c]	360[c]	.23	143	.14	87	.05	29

[a]Mean length of utterance (morphemes).
[b]Number of Action utterances estimated on the basis of average number at Times IV and V.
[c]Number of Action utterances estimated on the basis of average number at Times II and III.

SEQUENCE OF DEVELOPMENT

The proportion of utterances in each of the four categories (one Action and three Locative Action) is presented in Table 3. Action was always more frequent than Locative Action, and for Eric and Peter, Action appeared before Locative Action. There was intersubject variation within the subcategories of Locative Action: Gia and Peter learned Agent first, Eric learned Patient first, and Kathryn learned Mover first. As mean length of utterance approached 3.0, there was more consistency among the children: Agent-Locative Action was the most frequent for Gia, Kathryn, and Peter, and Patient-Locative Action was most frequent for Eric.

RELATIVE DISTRIBUTION OF CONSTITUENT RELATIONS

The relative frequency of two-, three- and four-constituent relations is presented in Tables 4 through 7 for the four children. As can be seen, the three- and four-constituent utterances increased, but the two-constituent utterances continued to occur. The frequencies of each of the individual constituents in each category were obtained and combined for the four children at four mean length of utterance levels in Figures 1 through 4. (See Table 8 for individual constituent data.) Verbs were the most frequently mentioned constituent in all categories. There was a strong tendency for the constituent that referred to the object affected by movement to be the second most frequent constituent (after verbs) in each category (Movers, Patients and Objects in Action, and Agent-Locative Action).

The notion of optionality (Braine, 1974; Brown, 1973) supplied the null hypothesis for testing the independence of the individual constituents in constituent relations. Two versions of the optionality model—one a homogeneous model and the other a heterogeneous model—were tested here in order to determine whether the obtained distribution was randomly generated. In both models the unconditional probabilities of individual constituents were combined to produce the conditional probability of the various constituent relations, given that the utterances contained at least two constituents.* The *homogeneous* random generation model assumed equal selection

---

* Single-word utterances cannot be assigned to semantic-syntactic categories because they are ambiguous with respect to potential constituent function. The problem of placing single-word utterances within a constituent structure was discussed at length in Bloom (1973, pp. 133–141), where it was pointed out that one cannot know if a child intends a linguistic function (such as "Agent" or "Mover" or "Possessor") when he says only a single word (such as "Mommy"). Interpretation of linguistic structure requires linguistic evidence (at least two constituents in relation to one another in an utterance) to disambiguate the child's intent, and rich interpretation of contextual evidence alone is insufficient. One can identify Action *events,* but different kinds of *linguistic* events can occur within Action events, as, for example, when the child eats another cookie and says either "more cookie" or "my cookie." Utterances that signaled such intentions, for example, as recurrence or possession alone, were not counted as *action* utterances in the present analysis (whether or not occurring in an action event) *unless* embedded in an Action Verb relation (e.g., "eat more cookie").

Table 4   Eric: Frequency Distribution of Constituent Relations in Action and Locative Action Categories[a]

Constituent Relations	Eric III (1.42)[b]		Eric IV (1.69)[b]		Eric V (2.63)[b]		Eric VI (2.84)[b]	
	Prop.[c]	Freq.[c]	Prop.[c]	Freq.[c]	Prop.[c]	Freq.[c]	Prop.[c]	Freq.[c]
Agent-Action-Object								
Agent-Verb	.03	1	.03	3	.12	25	—	—
Agent-Object	—	—	.01	1	0	1	—	—
Verb-Object	.65	20	.85	74	.46	93	—	—
Agent-Verb-Object	.33	10	.10	9	.41	84	—	—
Total Frequencies		31		87		203		
Agent-Locative Action-Object								
Agent-Verb	—	—	—	—	.17	8	.21	14
Agent-Object	—	—	—	—	—	—	—	—
Agent-Place	—	—	—	—	—	—	—	—
Verb-Object	—	—	—	1	.17	8	.27	18
Verb-Place	—	—	—	—	.17	8	.05	3
Object-Place	—	—	—	—	.07	3	.09	6
Agent-Verb-Object	—	—	—	—	.09	4	.21	14
Agent-Verb-Place	—	—	—	1	.24	11	.03	2
Agent-Object-Place	—	—	—	—	.02	1	—	—

	Freq.	Prop.	Freq.	Prop.	Freq.	Prop.
Verb-Object-Place	—	—	2	.04	2	.03
Agent-Verb-Object-Place	—	—	1	.02	7	.11
Total Frequencies	2		46		66	
Mover-Locative Action-Place						
Mover-Verb	2	—	25	.76	30	.59
Mover-Place	—	—	1	.03	—	—
Verb-Place	1	—	4	.12	2	.04
Mover-Verb-Place	—	—	3	.09	19	.37
Total Frequencies	3		33		51	
Mover (Patient)-Locative Action-Place						
Patient-Verb	23	.55	9	.32	38	.40
Patient-Place	8	.19	—	—	—	—
Verb-Place	8	.19	8	.29	23	.24
Patient-Verb-Place	3	.07	11	.39	34	.36
Total Frequencies	42		28		95	

[a] Intransitive verbs (that did not involve action on affected-Object) and imperatives (whether or not sentence-Subjects were expressed) were not counted.
[b] Mean length of utterance (morphemes).
[c] Prop. = proportion; Freq. = frequency of tokens.

179

Table 5   Gia: Frequency Distribution of Constituent Relations in Action and Locative Action Categories[a]

Constituent Relations	Gia II (1.34)[b]		Gia III (1.58)[b]		Gia IV (1.79)[b]		Gia V (2.30)[b]		Gia VI (2.75)[b]	
	Prop.[c]	Freq.[c]	Prop.[c]	Freq.[c]	Prop.[c]	Freq.[c]	Prop.[c]	Freq.[c]	Prop.[c]	Freq.[c]
Agent-Action-Object										
Agent-Verb	.15	3	.25	36	.17	26	.08	23	.09	5
Agent-Object	.15	3	.13	20	.15	23	.03	8	.02	1
Verb-Object	.65	13	.26	38	.37	56	.28	85	.02	1
Agent-Verb-Object	.05	1	.35	50	.30	46	.61	185	.22	13
Total Frequencies		20		144		151		301		
Agent-Locative Action-Object-Place										
Agent-Verb	—	—	.20	5	.14	3	.05	1	.10	6
Agent-Object	—	—	.04	1	—	—	—	—	—	—
Agent-Place	—	—	.12	3	—	—	—	—	—	—
Verb-Object	.93	13	.44	11	.33	7	.05	1	—	—
Verb-Place	.07	1	.12	3	—	—	—	—	—	—
Object-Place	—	—	.04	1	.29	6	.27	6	.28	16
Agent-Verb-Object	—	—	—	—	.19	4	.18	4	.12	7
Agent-Verb-Place	—	—	.04	1	.05	1	.18	4	—	—
Agent-Object-Place	—	—	—	—	—	—	—	—	—	—

	Freq.	Prop.	Freq.	Prop.	Freq.	Prop.	Freq.	Prop.	Freq.	Prop.
Verb-Object-Place	4	.07	3	.14	—	—	—	—	—	—
Agent-Verb-Object-Place	5	.09	3	.14	—	—	—	—	—	—
Total Frequencies	58		22		21		25		14	
Mover-Locative Action-Place										
Mover-Verb	26	.43	13	.33	13	.43	1	—	3	—
Mover-Place	—	—	—	—	1	.03	—	—	1	—
Verb-Place	6	.10	5	.13	8	.27	1	—	—	—
Mover-Verb-Place	29	.48	22	.55	8	.27	—	—	—	—
Total Frequencies	61		40		30		2		4	
Mover (Patient)-Locative Action-Place										
Patient-Verb	14	.78	4	.14	9	.31	5	.83	1	—
Patient-Place	—	—	6	.21	—	—	1	.17	—	—
Verb-Place	—	—	19	.66	5	.17	—	—	—	—
Patient-Verb-Place	4	.22	—	—	15	.52	—	—	—	—
Total Frequencies	18		29		29		6		1	

[a]Intransitive verbs (that did not involve action on affected-Object) and imperatives (whether or not sentence-Subjects were expressed) were not counted.

[b]Mean length of utterance (morphemes).

[c]Prop. = proportion; Freq. = frequency of tokens.

Table 6   Kathryn: Frequency Distribution of Constituent Relations in Action and Locative Action Categories[a]

Constituent Relations	Kathryn I (1.32)[b]		Kathryn II (1.89)[b]		Kathryn III (2.83)[b]		Kathryn IV (3.30)[b]	
	Prop.[c]	Freq.[c]	Prop.[c]	Freq.[c]	Prop.[c]	Freq.[c]	Prop.[c]	Freq.[c]
Agent-Action-Object								
Agent-Verb	.13	7	.10	30	.05	19		
Agent-Object	.18	10	.02	6	.01	3		
Verb-Object	.59	33	.54	156	.46	183		
Agent-Verb-Object	.11	6	.34	99	.48	194		
Total Frequencies		56		291		399		
Agent-Locative Action-Object-Place								
Agent-Verb	—	—	.04	2	.06	9	.03	5
Agent-Object	—	—	—	—	—	—	—	—
Agent-Place	—	—	.09	4	.01	1	—	—
Verb-Object	—	1	.29	13	.35	52	.21	30
Verb-Place	—	—	.13	6	.03	4	.03	5
Object-Place	—	3	.31	14	.01	1	.01	2
Agent-Verb-Object	—	—	.02	1	.32	48	.37	53
Agent-Verb-Place	—	—	.02	1	.05	7	.06	9
Agent-Object-Place	—	—	.02	1	.01	1	—	—
Verb-Object-Place	—	—	.04	2	.08	12	.14	20

	Prop.	Freq.	Prop.	Freq.	Prop.	Freq.	Prop.	Freq.
Agent-Verb-Object-Place	—		.02	1	.09	13	.13	19
Total Frequencies		4		45		148		143
Mover-Locative Action-Place								
Mover-Verb	.06	1	.50	8	.29	20	.31	27
Mover-Place	—	—	—	—	—	—	—	—
Verb-Place	.88	15	.19	3	.23	16	.24	21
Mover-Verb-Place	.06	1	.31	5	.49	34	.45	39
Total Frequencies		17		16		70		87
Mover (Patient)-Locative Action-Place								
Patient-Verb	—	3	.48	23	.43	29	.48	14
Patient-Place	—	—	—	—	—	—	—	—
Verb-Place	—	—	.25	12	.13	9	.28	8
Patient-Verb-Place	—	—	.27	13	.43	29	.24	7
Total Frequencies		3		48		67		29

[a] Intransitive verbs (that did not involve action on affected-Object) and imperatives (whether or not sentence-Subject were expressed) were not counted.

[b] Mean length of utterance (morphemes).

[c] Prop. = proportion; Freq. = frequency of tokens.

Table 7   Peter: Frequency Distribution of Constituent Relations in Action and Locative Action Categories[a]

Constituent Relations	Peter IV (1.41)[b]		Peter V (1.33)[b]		Peter VI (1.75)[b]		Peter VII (2.39)[b]		Peter IX (2.62)[b]	
	Prop.[c]	Freq.[c]	Prop.[c]	Freq.[c]	Prop.[c]	Freq.[c]	Prop.[c]	Freq.[c]	Prop.[c]	Freq.[c]
Agent-Action-Object										
Agent-Verb	—	—	—	—	.03	2	.22	18	.11	10
Agent-Object	—	—	—	—	.03	2	—	—	—	—
Verb-Object	.88	49	.96	64	.87	68	.60	49	.54	49
Agent-Verb-Object	.13	7	.04	3	.08	6	.18	15	.34	31
Total Frequencies		56		67		78		82		90
Agent-Locative Action-Object-Place										
Agent-Verb	—	—	.17	1	—	—	—	—	.13	7
Agent-Object	—	—	—	—	—	—	—	—	—	—
Agent-Place	—	—	—	—	—	—	—	—	—	—
Verb-Object	—	—	.33	2	.18	3	.25	12	.25	14
Verb-Place	—	—	.17	1	.24	4	.28	13	.20	11
Object-Place	—	—	.33	2	.50	7	.13	6	—	—
Agent-Verb-Object	—	—	—	—	—	—	.09	4	.15	8
Agent-Verb-Place	—	—	—	—	—	—	—	—	.07	4
Agent-Object-Place	—	—	—	—	—	—	—	—	—	—
Verb-Object-Place	—	—	—	—	.18	3	.23	11	.13	7
Agent-Verb-Object-Place	—	—	—	—	—	—	.02	1	.07	4

	Freq.	Prop.	Freq.	Prop.	Freq.	Prop.	Freq.	Prop.
Total Frequencies	6		17		47		55	
Mover-Locative Action-Place								
Mover-Verb	—	—	4	.67	10	.83	11	.61
Mover-Place	—	—	—	—	—	—	1	.06
Verb-Place	—	—	2	.33	2	.17	4	.22
Mover-Verb-Place	—	—	—	—	—	—	2	.11
Total Frequencies			6		12		18	
Mover (Patient)-Locative Action-Place								
Patient-Verb	—	—	2	.20	2	.06	2	.05
Patient-Place	—	—	—	—	—	—	—	—
Verb-Place	1	—	8	.80	23	.74	18	.49
Patient-Verb-Place	2	—	—	—	6	.19	17	.46
Total Frequencies	3		10		31		37	

[a]Intransitive verbs (that did not involve action on affected-Object) and imperatives (whether or not sentence-Subjects were expressed) were not counted.

[b]Mean length of utterance (morphemes).

[c]Prop. = proportion; Freq. = frequency of tokens.

Table 8   Individual Constituent Frequencies Presented as Proportion of Utterances in a Category Having the Constituent Expressed

Child	Sample	Action			Agent-Locative Action				Mover-Locative Action			Patient-Locative Action		
		Agent	Verb	Object	Agent	Verb	Object	Place	Mover	Verb	Place	Patient	Verb	Place
Eric	IV	.37(11)	1.00(31)	.97(30)	—	—	—	.57(26)	—	—	—	.81(34)	.81(34)	.45(19)
	V	.15(13)	.99(86)	.97(84)	.54(25)	.87(40)	.41(19)	.30(20)	.88(29)	.97(32)	.24(8)	.71(20)	1.00(28)	.68(19)
	VI	.54(110)	1.00(202)	.88(178)	.56(37)	.91(60)	.71(47)	.07(1)	.96(49)	1.00(51)	.41(21)	.76(72)	1.00(95)	.60(57)
Gia	II	—	—	—	(0)	1.00(14)	—	—	—	—	—	—	—	—
	III	.35(7)	.85(17)	.85(17)	.40(10)	.80(20)	.93(13)	.32(8)	.73(22)	.97(29)	.57(17)	1.00(6)	.83(5)	.17(1)
	IV	.74(106)	.86(124)	.75(108)	.38(8)	.71(15)	.52(13)	.33(7)	.88(35)	1.00(40)	.68(27)	.83(24)	1.00(29)	.69(20)
	V	.63(95)	.85(128)	.83(125)	.55(12)	.73(16)	.81(17)	.73(16)	.90(55)	1.00(61)	.57(35)	.79(23)	1.00(29)	.80(25)
	VI	.72(216)	.97(293)	.92(278)	.60(35)	.97(56)	.77(39)	.40(23)	.17(2)	1.00(17)	.94(16)	1.00(18)	1.00(18)	.22(4)
Kathryn	III	.41(23)	.82(46)	.88(49)	.22(10)	.58(26)	.71(32)	.64(29)	.81(13)	1.00(16)	.50(8)	.75(36)	1.00(48)	.52(25)
	IV	.46(135)	.98(285)	.90(261)	.53(79)	.98(145)	.86(127)	.26(39)	.77(54)	1.00(70)	.71(50)	.87(58)	1.00(67)	.57(38)
	V	.54(216)	.99(396)	.95(380)	.60(86)	.99(141)	.87(124)	.38(55)	.76(66)	1.00(87)	.69(60)	.72(21)	1.00(29)	.52(15)
Peter	IV	.13(7)	1.00(56)	1.00(56)	—	—	—	—	—	—	—	—	—	—
	V	.04(3)	1.00(67)	1.00(67)	.17(1)	.67(4)	.67(4)	.50(3)	—	—	—	—	—	—
	VI	.13(10)	.97(76)	.97(76)	(0)	.59(17)	.76(13)	.82(14)	.67(4)	1.00(6)	.33(2)	.20(2)	1.00(10)	.80(8)
	VII	.40(33)	1.00(82)	.78(64)	.11(5)	.87(41)	.72(34)	.66(31)	.83(10)	1.00(12)	.17(2)	.26(8)	1.00(31)	.94(29)
	IX	.46(41)	1.00(90)	.89(80)	.42(23)	1.00(55)	.60(33)	.47(26)	.78(14)	.94(17)	.39(7)	.51(19)	1.00(37)	.95(35)

186

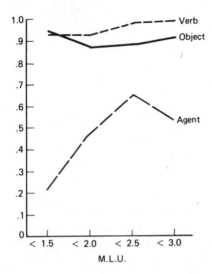

Figure 1.   Action: proportion of utterances that include the individual constituents, for all children combined at four M.L.U. points.

probabilities for each of the individual constituents. This probability was estimated by the method of maximum likelihood and was used to predict the distribution of constituent relations in Action, Mover-Locative Action, Patient-Locative Action, and Agent-Locative Action utterances. The observed distributions (Tables 4 through 7) were then tested statistically (by chi-square) for goodness of fit with the predicted distributions. The null hypothesis of no difference between the expected and observed distributions was rejected in 47 out of 48 testable trials, $p < .05$ in 9 trials, and $p < .001$ in 38 trials. This result could mean either that (a) the constituents were independently generated, but the selection probabilities were not equal, or (b) the constituents were not independently generated.

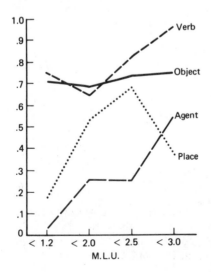

Figure 2.   Agent-Locative Action: proportion of utterances that include the individual constitutents, for all children combined at four M.L.U. points.

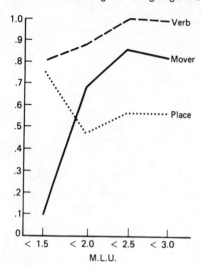

Figure 3. Mover-Locative Action: proportion of utterances that include the individual constituents, for all children combined at four M.L.U. points.

Homogeneous Model

Assuming equal probability of each constituent, in the three-term case, the three possible two-term constituent relations each had

$$p_2 = \frac{p^2 (1-p)}{[p^3 + 3 p^2 (1-p)]}$$

and the three-term constituent relation had

$$p_3 = \frac{p^3}{[p^3 + 3p^2 (1-p)]}$$

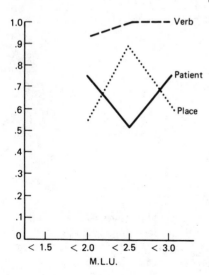

Figure 4. Patient-Locative Action: proportion of utterances that include the individual constituents, for all children combined at four M.L.U. points.

In the four-term case, the six possible two-term constituent relations each had

$$p_2 = \frac{p^2 (1-p)^2}{c}$$

the four possible three-term constituents relations each had

$$p_3 = \frac{p^3 (1-p)}{c}$$

and the one possible four-term constituent relation had

$$p_4 = \frac{p^4}{c}$$

where

$$c = p^4 + 4p^3 (1-p) + 6p^2 (1-p)^2$$

The *heterogeneous* random generation model was used to explore further these alternatives. This model assumed unequal selection probabilities for each of the individual constituents. Unfortunately, the model could not be applied to the Action, Mover-Locative Action, and Patient-Locative Action data since only four events were observable in each of these categories. For example, the observed events for Action utterances were: Agent-Verb, Verb-Object, Agent-Object, and Agent-Verb-Object. (The single constituent events of Agent, Verb, or Object could not be identified.) Because only four events were observable, there were too few degrees of freedom to permit the testing of the heterogeneous model. However, this model could be tested with the Agent-Locative Action data in which 11 events were observable. Accordingly, using the observed distribution, the individual constituent probabilities (Agent, Verb, Object, and Place) were estimated by the method of maximum likelihood and were used to predict the distribution of constituent relations.[*] Again, the observed distribution was tested against the predicted distribution, using the chi-square goodness of fit test. Of the 11 samples tested, six differences were significant with $p < .05$, and two approached significance with $p < .07$. It was concluded, therefore, that the individual constituents in Agent-Locative Action utterances were not independently selected.

Heterogeneous Model

Assuming unequal probabilities of each constituent:

$$p(n_1, n_2, n_3, n_4) = \frac{p_1^{n_1} q_1^{m_1} p_2^{n_2} q_2^{m_2} p_3^{n_3} q_3^{m_3} p_4^{n_4} q_4^{m_4}}{c}$$

where $n_i = 1$ if the ith component is present

0 if the ith component is absent,

$m_i = 1-n_i$

and c is the constant required to make the probabilities of the 11 observable cells sum to one, and may be computed as

$$c = 1-[p_1 q_2 q_3 q_4 + q_1 p_2 q_3 q_4 + q_1 q_2 p_3 q_4 + q_1 q_2 q_3 p_4 + q_1 q_2 q_3 q_4]$$

The null hypothesis of optional representation of each constituent—as tested by both the homogeneous and heterogeneous models—was rejected. Since the observed

---

[*] The computer program used to test the random generation model with four constituents was composed by Owen Whitby.

distribution was significantly different from the expected distributions, it was concluded that the variation among the constituent relations was systematic. The question then became one of accounting for the variation of the constituent relations, and attempting to determine why the two-constituent utterances continued to occur.

The two random generation models tested here fall within the paradigm for "probabilistic grammars" proposed by Suppes (1970). Suppes attempted to construct a probabilistic grammar for the noun phrases in a corpus of speech from a child, Adam, collected by Roger Brown and his associates at Harvard. Suppes suggested that only a probabilistic grammar could account for "the distribution of length of utterance, and the relatively sharp bounds on the complexity of utterances" in natural languages. The variable rules paradigm presented here goes beyond Suppes's analysis; it attempts to capture the relative effect of different aspects of a speech event in determining the probability with which individual constituents will co-occur.

GRAMMATICAL, LEXICAL, AND DISCOURSE COVARIATION WITH CONSTITUENT RELATIONS

The two-constituent relations that continued to occur could not have been intransitives in Action utterances (Agent-Verb) nor imperatives (Verb-Object) because these were not included in the analysis. The extent to which grammatical, lexical, and discourse factors in the child's competence could account for the variance in utterance length was explored before judging the extent to which the obtained distribution was owing to residual variability of the constituent relations (as suggested by Brown, 1973 and Bowerman, 1973a).

GRAMMATICAL VARIATION

There were two levels of analysis to determine the effect of added complexity on utterance length. In the first analysis, any addition to a constituent (inflections or modifications) or anything inserted between or after constituents (prepositions, adverbs, possessives, etc.) was counted as complexity added to the constituent structure. (See Table 9 for definitions of types of complexity.) If added complexity was more frequent in two-constituent utterances than in three-constituent utterances, there would be two equally plausible interpretations. The child could not add complexity to three or four constituents, or the child necessarily deleted one of the constituents with added complexity, because of (a) a *length* constraint—he could not *say* more than just three (or four) words (or morphemes), or (b) a *grammatical* constraint—he could not program the whole constituent structure when complexity intersected with any of the constituent relations.

In the first level of analysis, the frequency of any complexity was compared in two- and three-constituent relations. Complexity occurred more often with two constituents than with three constituents. The hypothesis that kinds of complexity were equally distributed among two- and three-constituent relations in the samples from the four children (for Action, Mover-Locative Action, and Patient-Locative Action) was tested by sign tests. In 15 out of 19 Action samples more Object or Other complexity occurred in two-constituent relations than in three-constituent relations. In 16 out of 23 Patient-Locative Action samples there was more Patient, Place, or Other complexity in two-constituent relations than in three-constituent relations. The probability of these results, using a one-tailed test, was less than .05 in both cases.

Table 9   Kinds of Complexity

Verb Complexity
1. All inflections for tense, for example, "ing," "-s", "ed"
2. The contracted copula
3. Modals, signaling intention most often, for example, "gonna," "want," "hafta," "lets," "lemme," and "shall"
4. Adverbs of   (a) manner, for example, "like this," "this way"
               (b) time, for example, "now," "right now"
               (c) recurrence, for example, "again"
5. Two-part verbs where the preposition did not signal direction of movement, for example, "put heater up," "turn light on"

Object, Place, Mover, and Agent Complexity
1. Inflection for plural
2. Definite article "the"
3. Demonstratives "this," "that," "these," "those"
4. Embedded relations (a) Possessor noun or pronoun
                     (b) Attributives, for example, "tiny," "red," "three"
                     (c) Recurrence ("more" or "another")

Other Complexity
1. Negation, for example, "I can't open it"
2. Place (when not a constituent of a locative verb, for example, "orange chair read a book")
3. Dative, for example, "Mommy give them milk and sugar"
4. Instrumental, for example, "Mommy lock ə keys"
5. Coordinate and subordinate relation with another clause, for example, "I want go door see my mommy."
6. Affirmative, for example, "alright," "okay"
7. Vocative, for example, "shall go in there Lois"
8. Introducers, for example, "and," "then"

Prepositions, counted as a separate complexity in locative relations, specified
1. Direction toward and away from place
2. Direction toward and away from speaker

In the Mover-Locative Action samples, Mover, Place, or Other complexity was equally distributed in two- and three-constituent relations. Similarly, verb complexity and prepositions were equally distributed between two- and three-constituent relations in all three categories.

The results for the individual children reached statistical significance (by chi-square) in only 5 of 12 trials for Kathryn and in only 5 of 16 trials for Gia (where a trial was defined as a possible comparison between two- and three-constituents, when at least five tokens of each constituent relation occurred, and at least three instances of complexity occurred) for Action utterances (Table 10). There were only occasional significant effects (by chi-square) for Peter and Eric in the Action category. In the

Locative Action category, the interactions could be statistically tested less often, and the significant effects were fewer. In the Agent-Locative Action subcategory, only the data from Kathryn resulted in more than occasional significant effects.

Verb complexity was observed more often when there was a pre-verbal constituent, so that Agent-Verb, Mover-Verb, and Patient-Verb utterances generally included more Verb complexity than did Verb-Object and Verb-Place utterances. Further, the form of the verbal complexity varied in relation to whether the pre-verbal constituent was Agent, Mover, or Patient. For example, third person singular -s occurred overwhelmingly with Patients; irregular (and then regular) past occurred with Agents and Movers, and, except for Kathryn, did not occur with Patients (see Bloom, Hood, & Miller, in preparation, for this analysis and discussion). Prepositions (in Locative Action categories) occurred more often when Place was mentioned. The other interactions in the data from Gia and Kathryn appeared to be as follows. In the Action utterances, Agents occurred less often with complex objects than with simple objects, and Objects occurred less often with complex verbs than with simple verbs. These results reached statistical significance in Kathryn II for Verb complexity and Kathryn III for Verb and Object complexity (chi-square, $p < .05$), and for Verb complexity in Gia III and IV (chi-square, $p < .001$).

The result of the first analysis of complexity was that when any morpheme added to a constituent relation was counted as complexity, two-constituent sentences could not be convincingly differentiated from three-constituent sentences, except for Kathryn and Gia, as indicated in Table 10. Two conclusions were possible given this result. The first conclusion was that there was no absolute limit on utterance length per se; the children did not use more two-constituent relations than three-constituent relations because it was difficult for them to say more than two words at a time. The second conclusion was that if there was a grammatical constraint, it was a more discriminating effect than could be observed by counting any and all additions to utterances as added complexity. The data were then examined at a second level of analysis, to determine whether particular kinds of additions within and between morphemes would differentiate between two- and three- constituent relations.

There were too few instances of complexity to permit separate statistical analysis of each sample from each child. Accordingly, data from the four children were combined. The five most frequent factors that intersected with Action constituent relations were (a) verb inflections, (b) two-part verbs, (c) definite articles and demonstratives, (d) embedded relations (possession, recurrence, and other attribution), and (e) plural -s. The data were analyzed for each of these factors separately, and the samples were combined according to these criteria: all samples were combined that contained two or more instances of a factor, with frequency of Subject-Verb-Object less than the frequency of Subject-Verb or Verb-Object. The data base was different for each of the five factors and for each of the categories. Grouping the samples in this manner for each of the five factors yielded a relatively large number of samples which met the criteria for verb inflections (10 Action samples from the four children). In contrast, only 7 (somewhat later) samples met the criteria for plural -s. Object complexity was an earlier development than was Verb complexity for Gia and Kathryn (who used nouns more than pronouns), and Verb complexity was an earlier development than was Object complexity for Peter and Eric (who used more pronouns than nouns). See Bloom, Lightbown, and Hood (1975) for a description of the nominal-pronominal development of the four children.

Table 10   Summary of Differences between Kinds of Complexity in Two- and Three-Term Action Constituent Relations

Sample	Agent-Verb/ Agent-Verb-Object Complexity			Verb-Object/ Agent-Verb-Object Complexity			Agent-Object/ Agent-Verb-Object Complexity		
	Object	Verb	Other	Object	Verb	Other	Object	Verb	Other
Eric									
III	—	np	np	nt	ns	nt	np	—	np
IV	—	np	np	nd	ns	ns	np	—	np
V	—	2 > 3**	ns	ns	ns	ns	np	—	np
Gia									
III	—	2 > 3**	nt	ns	ns	nt	ns	—	nt
IV	—	2 > 3**	nt	ns	nt	ns	3 > 2*	—	ns
V	—	ns	2 > 3**	2 > 3**	2 > 3**	ns	ns	—	ns
Kathryn									
I	—	nt	nt	ns	nt	nt	ns	—	nt
II	—	2 > 3**	2 > 3*	ns	2 > 3*	ns	np	—	np
III	—	2 > 3**	ns	2 > 3**	3 > 2*	ns	np	—	np
Peter									
IV	—	np	np	nt	nt	nt	np	—	np
V	—	np	np	np	np	np	np	—	np
VI	—	np	np	nt	ns	ns	np	—	np
VII	—	ns	nt	ns	ns	2 > 3*	np	—	np
IX	—	ns	2 > 3*	ns	ns	ns	np	—	np

nd = no difference.
np = not productive (<5 tokens in category).
ns = not significant.
nt = not testable (<3 instances of complexity).
> = direction of difference between number of constituents.
*significant at .05 level.
**significant at .01 level.

193

When the frequency of each of the factors was compared in two- and three-constituent Action relations, there was no significant difference (chi-square test) for verb inflections, the definite article and demonstratives, and plural -s. Each of these factors, then, did not increase the complexity of a sentence to differentiate between the number of constituents that could occur. The frequency of two-part verbs was significantly greater in two- than in three-constituent relations (chi-square $= 3.96$, $p < .05$), and the frequency of embedded relations was greater in two- than in three-constituent relations, but the difference was not significant (chi-square $= 2.58$, $p < .10$). This last result is more meaningful, however, when the frequency of each of the same relations (possession, recurrence, and other attribution) occurring alone is taken into account. For all of the children, when mean length of utterance reached 3.0, these relations were generally frequent, but were infrequently embedded in Action relations.

The categories with three-constituent relations were combined in order to compare other kinds of complexity (Action, Mover-Locative Action, and Patient-Locative Action). Negation was significantly more frequent in two- than in three-constituent relations (chi-square $= 12.28$, $p < .001$). However, there was no significant difference between two- and three-constituent relations with occurrence of the dative or clausal subordination and coordination.

Thus, the results of the two analyses of grammatical complexity revealed that different kinds of complexity had different effects on utterance length: verb inflections, prepositions, noun inflections, and determiners occurred as often with two- as with three-constituent relations; negation, two-part verbs, possession, recurrence, and other attribution occurred more often with two-constituent relations than with three-constituent relations.

LEXICAL VARIATION

VERBS.   There was greater Action and Locative Action verb variability (the ratio of number of different verbs to number of utterances) in two-constituent relations than in three-constituent relations, for all the children. All verbs were classified as old (having occurred in any previous sample) or new (having not occurred in a previous sample), and a comparison was made between the occurrence of new verbs in two- and three-constituent relations. The comparison was tested by sign test using the normal approximation to the binomial. The statistic for the distribution of new verbs was computed under the directional hypothesis that there would be more new verbs in two-constituent relations than in three-constituent relations against the null hypothesis that the verbs would be distributed equally. In 20 out of 31 samples there were more new verbs in two-constituent relations than in three-constituent relations. The probability of this result occurring by chance alone is .075. Thus, although more new verbs occurred in two-constituent relations than in three-constituent relations, the result was not statistically significant.

NOUNS.   The relative occurrence of nouns and pronouns was compared in two- and three-constituent relations. In an earlier study (Bloom, Lightbown, & Hood, 1975) noun/pronoun variation was found with a developmental shift from nouns to pronouns in the sentences of Gia and Kathryn, and a shift from pronouns to nouns in the sentences of Eric and Peter. In the present study, objects tended to be pronouns more frequently than nouns in three-constituent relations for all the children except Gia at Time IV. Gia at Time IV used pronouns more frequently in two-constituent relations (agents or objects) than in three-constituent relations. For Peter and Eric objects were nouns more frequently in Verb-Object than in Subject-Verb-Object. It appeared that nouns as objects represented a lexical constraint for Eric and Peter, and pronouns represented a lexical constraint for Gia at the time of the shift from nouns to pronouns (Time IV).

Further, when mean length of utterance was less than 2.0, Eric and Peter used a pronominal system for encoding Verb-Object and Agent-Verb-Object constructions. They did not produce Agent-Verb utterances until after they had begun to use noun forms as objects (when mean length of utterance exceeded 2.0). In contrast, Gia and Kathryn initially used a nominal system for encoding Verb-Object and Agent-Verb constructions. After they began using pronominal forms (mean length of utterance greater than 2.0), the proportion of Agent-Verb utterances decreased. Thus, for all four children, nominal objects and Agent-Verb constructions tended to covary. It was also possible that relative recency of nouns (old or new) was a factor that influenced the occurrence of two- and three-constituent relations, but the analysis of old and new nouns comparable to the verb analysis is not yet available.

DISCOURSE VARIATION

Patterns of discourse consisted of formal and semantic relations among successive child or child and adult utterances. Utterances that were successive shared the same topic (in the sense of "topic" discussed by Hymes, 1964), and were always semantically related to one another, and sometimes formally related as well. The most frequent kind of formal relationship was an expansion of the within clause structure in successive utterances; semantic relationship was a continuation of meaning (talking about the same topic) from one utterance to another, without maintaining the same structure. Some examples were:*

1. Formal expansions:

K:HI (Kathryn closing basket)   close it/I close it

G:IV (Lois is reading magazine to Gia) you read
      Lois: Read?

                                        read that magazine/you read that
                                        magazine

P:VII (Peter comes over to tape
      recorder to press button)   get ə button/I'm gonna get ə button

2. Semantic relations:

K:II (Mommy had been ironing)   Mommy iron shirt/fresh ə nice

P:IX (Peter's sister Jenny is in her
      cradle drinking her bottle)   Jenny she's drinking ə bottle
      Patsy: Is she?

                                         be quiet

---

*One subset of formal expansions is what Braine (1971) has called "replacement sequences."

E:V   (Eric makes toy dog and cat kiss)
      Lois: Who's kissing who?
      (Eric making them kiss again)   the dog's kissing cat
      Lois: Yes. That's right.

                              not crying

   Two- and three-constituent relations in Action utterances in the last two samples
from each child (Eric IV, V; Gia IV, V; Kathryn II, III; and Peter VII, IX) were compared
according to whether or not they occurred successively. The proportion of successive utterances (a) was similar in two- and three-constituent relations, (b) was always
high in both (at least .50, except for Subject-Verb-Object at Peter VII) and increased
developmentally for the four children (for example, at Peter IX, .71 of the Subject-
Verb-Object utterances were successive).
   Each successive utterance was considered in terms of its relation to a preceding
utterance and its relation to a subsequent utterance. The possible relations to a
preceding utterance were (a) first in sequence—that is, no preceding utterance, (b)
a formal expansion, (c) a semantic relation, and (d) other—including repetitions, re-
codings, etc. Relative to subsequent utterances, a particular successive utterance
could be (a) last in sequence—that is, no subsequent utterance, (b) formally expanded,
(c) semantically related, or (d) other.*
   It was possible to compare successive two- and three-constituent utterances on
these variables. Among the successive utterances, three-constituent relations were
more often formal expansions of a previous child utterance than were two-constituent relations. For the combined samples, this difference was significant (chi-square
$= 49.92, p < .001$) using the chi-square statistic for combining significance probabilities (Fisher, 1967). Semantic relations (not formally related) occurred less frequently
than formal expansion and occurred more often in two-constituent relations than in
three-constituent relations; but this difference was not significant ($p = .06$, by sign
test).
   More two-constituent relations than three-constituent relations in the eight samples were subsequently expanded and formally related to subsequent utterances, and
this difference was significant (chi-square $= 33.42, p < .025$), as tested by the chi-
square statistic for combining significance probabilities. Successive utterances that
were subsequently expanded included those that were the first utterance in a sequence. In seven of eight samples, more two-constituent relations than three-con-

---

*Most utterances were similar to example (a) below, in that the three-constituent utterance
was an expansion of a two-constituent utterance and, conversely, the two-constituent utterance
was expanded to a three-constituent utterance. However, there were utterances such as (b)
where the three-constituent utterance was not expanded from a two-constituent utterance and
(c) where the two-constituent utterance was not expanded to a three-constituent utterance.
(a)   G:IV   (Gia pulling out her tricycle)   ride like/Gia ride the bike
(b)   G:IV   man ride car
             Lois: Where is he?
             (Gia looking around for it)   man ride the car
(c)   G:IV   (Gia opens box of recording tape; open tape/
             trying to take tape out of box)   open tape stuck

stituent relations were first utterances. There were other kinds of relations represented among successive utterances, including repetition and recoding, but these were relatively infrequent and did not differentiate between two- and three-constituent relations.

GRAMMATICAL ELLIPSIS.   The final hypothesis that was tested in order to explain the variation in utterance length was the possibility that two-constituent relations could be attributed to grammatical ellipsis (described by Halliday & Hasan, in press, as "texting"); that is, the children could be taking into account prior linguistic reference by themselves and others, thereby eliminating redundant elements in their own speech. For example, "Mommy's going to the store. Daddy's going to the store." could be reduced in natural speech to "Mommy's going to the store. Daddy's going, too." Similarly, an answer to the question "Who's reading the book?" is "Mommy is reading the book," which could be reduced to "Mommy reading."

In order to explore the role of ellipsis, the relation between child utterances and preceding adult utterances was examined in all of the data (Action and Locative Action categories). All child utterances whether successive or nonsuccessive, were classified as contingent or noncontingent. A contingent utterance was formally or semantically related to the preceding adult utterance (see Bloom, Rocissano, & Hood, in preparation, for a more extended analysis of contingency in adult-child discourse). A necessary but not sufficient condition for ellipsis is that the elliptical utterance be contingent upon a previous utterance. If the proportion of contingency in two-constituent relations were greater than the proportion of contingency in three-constituent relations, then one might conclude that the children were using ellipsis in responding to adult speech. However, although the proportion of contingent utterances increased developmentally for the four children, the frequency of contingency was not different in two- and three-constituent relations.

Finally, contingent Action utterances in the last sample from each child were examined directly to determine (a) if the two-constituent utterance was elliptical, for example,

P:IX   Patsy: What are you looking for?
>   look for my pencil

and (b) if the three-constituent utterance occurred in an elliptical condition (that is, where the child utterance was at least partially redundant), for example,

P:IX   Lois: What are you gonna do?
>   I'm gonna fix it.

For Kathryn and Eric there were more three-constituent relations in elliptical conditions than there were two-constituent relation elliptical utterances, whereas for Peter and Gia the opposite was found. However, none of these differences were significant (by chi-square test). It was concluded that grammatical ellipsis, as it operates in adult speech, was not yet productive in the children's speech and could not be a factor accounting for the variable length of utterances. In contrast, the important conclusion that followed from the several analyses of discourse variation was that discourse, i.e., the preceding related utterances by the child or an adult, influenced the length of the children's utterances by providing memory support to facilitate the occurrence of three-constituent relations.

DISCUSSION

The major result of this study of grammatical complexity and constituent relations was the variable influence of grammatical, lexical, and discourse factors on increasing utterance length. No one factor emerged as clearly and consistently accounting for the variable occurrence of two-, three-, and four-constituent relations. Rather, each of the factors examined exerted an influence on some of the children some of the time; but none of the factors operated consistently for all of the children all of the time. Moreover, factors operated in both directions, to facilitate as well as to constrain sentences. At the conclusion of this study, there still remained the possibility that other, as yet unidentified, competence factors operated to affect utterance length in addition to those examined here and in addition to the nonsystematic effect of inherent variability.

There has been a proliferation of explanations of child language, and more theories than facts of child language have been reported. One reason for this has been that many of the findings reported in descriptions of child speech are relative and noncategorical; there are many exceptions from one study to another and within individual studies as well. It is becoming increasingly apparent that there are important differences as well as regularities among children learning the same and different languages. The interactions described here demonstrate the enormous complexity of the task of language acquisition, and cast immediate doubt on any simplistic explanations of child language that do not take such variation into account.

The model of child language that will be proposed here is a variation model, within the paradigm developed by Labov (1969), Cedergren and Sankoff (1974), Sankoff (1972), and Bailey (1973), and implicates, without actually specifying, the variable rules in children's knowledge that account for children's behavior. The major difficulty in specifying the form of such variable rules is the observation that there are conflicting influences on language behavior during development. On the one hand, there are influences, such as certain kinds of complexity and lexical novelty, that constrain utterance length and account, at least in part, for the occurrence of two-constituent utterances. At the same time, there are those developmental influences, such as lexical familiarity and the apparent aid to memory with successive discourse, that facilitate utterances and account for the occurrence of three- and four-constituent relations.

Before presenting the variation model, some of the alternative theories that have been proposed will be reviewed in light of evidence from the present study, and in relation to the original question of what children know about a linguistic system that enables them to code information in multiword messages. The three issues to be dealt with have to do with (a) the adequacy of pragmatic, semantic, action-based (sensorimotor), and grammatical theories of child language; (b) optional versus obligatory representation of major constituents in rules of grammar; and (c) the extent to which variation in child language is a reflection of underlying grammatical competence.

ALTERNATIVE EXPLANATIONS OF CHILD LANGUAGE

THE PRAGMATIC ARGUMENT.   Braine (1974) rejected the notion of reduction of a fuller underlying structure than is represented in child speech (Bloom, 1970), and proposed an alternative model to account for the disproportionate distribution of two- and three-word utterances. He suggested that the small number of three-word utterances in early speech reflects the probability with which two expansion rules may co-occur (such as the first rule that the sentence consists of a noun phrase and a verb phrase, and the second rule that the verb phrase includes a noun).

Unfortunately, this model is theoretically untestable. The events that must occur in Braine's model include the single constituents Subject, Verb, and Object, in addition to the combinations Subject-Verb, Verb-Object, Subject-Object, and Subject-Verb-Object. Braine's model predicts the occurrence of an Action utterance given an Action event and would thus have to include the probability of obtaining any utterance (whether an Action verb relation or not, e.g., "more cookie" or "my cookie"), as well as the probability of no utterance at all. The problems in identifying single constituents that have already been pointed out (footnote p. 177) are further compounded in Braine's model by the problem of identifying action events. Virtually all of the child's early utterances occur in dynamic (that is, action) events involving some kind of movement.

As an explanation of the probabilistic nature of the distribution of nouns and verbs in sentences, Braine proposed that the child's choice of words (or "lexical insertion") is "pragmatic, and not determined by syntactic or semantic structure"—a "process of construction by selecting a word that singles out something pragmatically salient" (1974, p. 455). The only direct evidence of such context saliency is the fact that such words and word combinations occur, and the resulting argument is unfortunately circular. Braine asserted that his formulation established continuity with the earlier single-word period since the same process of "lexical insertion" on the basis of "saliency" accounted also for "holophrasis." At the same time, however, Braine's formulation, and pragmatic explanations in general, establish a serious discontinuity with later development. Such claims fail to contribute to explanations either of (a) how the child eventually learns grammatical structure, or (b) the systematic (semantic-syntactic) regularities that are manifest among the earliest multiword utterances. However, the idea that the use of linguistic rules is probabilistically determined is important and is basic to the model proposed here.

Pragmatic explanations—that what the child mentions in sentences is determined by practical considerations in the situation—have been suggested by a number of investigators (for example, Brown, 1973; Park, 1974; Schlesinger, 1974). To a certain extent there is obvious truth in the claim; the words that the child learns, and the words that he uses, are the words that are practical and useful as well as meaningful for him. Pragmatics in philosophical theory is concerned with the origin, uses, and effects of signs (Morris, 1964). According to Rudolph Carnap, "the acceptance or rejection of abstract linguistic forms . . . will finally be decided by their efficiency as instruments, the ratio of the results achieved to the amount and complexity of the efforts required" (quoted in Morris, p. 46). Some pragmatic force no doubt does operate to determine the linguistic forms accepted or rejected by the child—motivating greater complexity in order to achieve greater results, while at the same time allowing less complex forms to be maintained when these require less effort to achieve the same results. But what is the operational explanation of "acceptance of a linguistic form" in development? One is still left with the problem of explaining what it means to accept (that is, to learn) the linguistic *forms* corresponding to pragmatically salient events.

Linguistic forms (words and structures with meaning relations) are not immediately and automatically given along with events; the linguistic forms that need to be learned necessarily transcend individual events. The child must learn words and how to combine words in consistent ways—regardless of the particular referents presented in all possible events. The child might use "read book" in one situation and then use "Mommy read book" in another because of a better result. But his use of "Mommy read book" is consistent with his use of "Daddy eat apple" and "Baby ride bike," and it is the essence of that regularity among many such utterances that must be explained.

It is apparent that saliency alone does not determine what children talk about when one considers the fact that child sentences represent only a limited set of the possible relations in events. For example, there are two notable omissions in the taxonomy of semantic-syntactic structures that have been identified in early child sentences—the dative (giving or showing something to someone) and the instrumental (using some means, such as forks, crayons, keys, etc., to achieve some end) (Brown, 1973). If what is talked about is what is salient for the child, it would follow that such relations are not expressed in action events because they are not salient. Such arguments simply use the result to explain the result; there is no independent verification of what constitutes saliency in events. The result is that children do not encode certain relations in early sentences, but the fact is that such relations are obviously salient in action events because the child performs or demands their occurrence. However pragmatic such aspects of events may be (when a child wants to draw, crayons are more salient than other objects) the children studied so far in this investigation and others use the corresponding linguistic forms only rarely (in this case the structural relation between such words as "crayon" or "fork" and Action verbs). The relative complexity of linguistic forms contributes to determining the kinds of information that children are able to represent in their messages (Bloom, Lightbown, & Hood, 1975; Slobin, 1971).

THE SEMANTIC ARGUMENT.   The notion of contextual salience—those aspects of events that happen to stand out and are most apparent and meaningful for the child —is necessarily related to the notion of cognitive salience: children notice and talk about those aspects of events that they already know or are learning about. Semantic explanations of child language have evolved from essentially this idea (e.g., Bowerman, 1973a; Brown, 1973; Kates, 1974; Schlesinger, 1974). Although there are different versions of the semantic explanation, the essential argument specifies what children are not doing as an apparently important part of specifying what they are doing: (a) children are learning semantic relations between words and word order rules to express semantic relations in sentences, and (b) children are not learning an abstract grammatical structure, that is, Subject-Predicate.

Kates (1974) was more explicit than Schlesinger (1974) in emphasizing how contextual saliency contributes to the child's "semanticity." She proposed that early two- and three-word sentences, as well as single-word utterances at an earlier time, derive from "focus-defined semantic categories," that depend upon the focusing experience of "some paradigm case," an initial event that focuses the child's attention on entities or relations between more than one entity. Such focus-defined categories are initially quite broad and only gradually are narrowed down, perhaps not until puberty, to adult (logic-defined) semantic roles such as Agent, Possessor, etc. Kates suggested that "syntactic patterns and some grammatical morphemes may simply be matched (associated) with certain [focus-defined] semantic categories and relations," and "once the form of the (predicative) sentence is acquired, and after the child is able to form logic-defined categories" he can use the form of the predicative sentence to express a propositional predication.

Kates's position is similar to the arguments presented by Bowerman (1973a) and Schlesinger (1971, 1974). The emphasis on semantics, that is, the emphasis on meaning relations as the basis for learning sentences, is well placed. However, grammatical morphemes and the rules of word order that encode information about objects and events are part of grammar, and grammar is both semantic and syntactic. The question at issue concerns the nature of the child's linguistic knowledge that underlies his ability to use syntactic patterns of word order with consistent semantic functions, that is, the form of predicative sentences. It should be obvious that whatever that linguistic knowledge is at age 2 years, it neither has the same form nor serves the same functions as the linguistic knowledge of the adult. However, the evidence indicates that the child's linguistic knowledge differs more in degree than in content from that of the adult. The question is, What does the child's knowledge of sentences consist of? The evidence from early sentences in the present study is relevant to evaluating the claim that semantic and not grammatical structure forms the basis for early sentences.

In the present study, there were two semantic contrasts represented in the relations of nouns to verbs. The first had to do with the force of the effect of an action on the different objects involved in the action, and the second was the distinction between animate and inanimate objects. With respect to the first semantic contrast, the relative frequency of Verb-Object in Action relations was matched by the relative frequency of Verb-Object in Agent-Locative Action, Mover-Verb in Mover-Locative Action and Patient-Verb in Patient-Locative Action. In addition, when the relative frequencies of the separate constituents in all the categories were compared, the result was that the Object, Mover, and Patient constituents occurred less frequently than Verbs but more frequently than the Agent and the Place constituents. This result —that the object affected by movement (whether an Object, Mover, or Patient) was mentioned more frequently regardless of the verb category—reflected an important semantic function and could be seen as support for the claim that sentence relations are semantic. However, although the semantic functions of Objects, Movers, and Patients were similar, they differed in their positions relative to verbs: Objects were post-verb constituents with Action and Agent-Locative Action verbs, and Movers and Patients were pre-verb constituents with Mover- and Patient-Locative Action verbs. Further, it could be argued that Patients in Patient-Locative Action utterances and Objects in Agent-Locative Action utterances had essentially the same semantic function: the child (or someone else) was the causative agent in both. Thus, when referring to the same event the children could (and often did) say "put lamb here" and "lamb go here," but they did not say *"go lamb here" or *"lamb put here."* It was not clear what the children's semantic understanding of "lamb go here" was, whether they distinguished *lamb moving* from *the lamb being moved*. However, even if the children had not yet sorted out the semantic relations, they were quite clear about the syntactic relations of such semantic functions: they consistently put the moving object (Patient or Mover) in pre-verb (Subject) position with certain verbs and in post-verb

---

* An asterisk next to an utterance means that it did not occur in the corpora.

(Object) position with other verbs. Although the children were learning semantic relations, the fact that words serving the same semantic function varied syntactically in relation to different classes of verbs, was evidence against the claim that sentence relations are only semantic relations.

The second semantic contrast, between animate and inanimate nouns, has been reported in the studies by Bloom (1970), Bowerman (1973a), Brown, Cazden, and Bellugi (1969) and de Villiers and de Villiers (1974). Sentence-subjects have been described as almost exclusively animate or pseudoanimate (e.g., bears and dolls); affected-objects in Action relations have been mostly inanimate. This result has been confirmed in the acquisition of German by Park (1974), leading to his claim that "animacy" is a strong semantic feature in early sentences with the resulting "rule" that animate objects are always mentioned first in sentences. However, in the present study, Patients were often inanimate (trucks, blocks, wheels, puzzle pieces, etc.) which was evidence that pre-verb constituents were not only semantically determined (on the basis of "animacy") but were also syntactically determined with respect to the functions of nouns in relation to different verbs, regardless of "animacy."

The reason why animate nouns predominate as Agents and Movers should be self-evident: actions and movements that affect objects are performed by persons or other animate beings. But, if it is self-evident why Agents and Movers in action events are animate, it is still necessary to explain why the animate-inanimate opposition is coded by word order with certain categories of verbs. There is a time, in the single-word-utterance period before syntax appears, when children do not differentiate between Agents and Objects in terms of the word order they use, and they are as likely to say "juice. Mommy." as "Mommy. juice." in successive single-word-utterances (Bloom, 1970, 1973; Smith, 1970). Learning syntax involves learning to make the animate-inanimate distinction a regularity through the use of word order relative to different verbs. Children learn the predicative function of different verbs which, if not the function of a *logical* predicate (in the sense of affirming or denying a property of or relation to a subject), is a *grammatical* predicate in the sense that it completes the meaning of the verb expressing an action by a subject or a state of a subject. If non–English-speaking children do not learn word order to signal the difference between functions of nouns relative to verbs, then they will learn whatever other linguistic devices are available to express such regularities.

Most investigators agree on the semantic relations expressed in early sentences and on the fact that there is a developmental progression in the acquisition of these relations. Part of the sequential aspect of acquisition is explainable on cognitive grounds—the fact, for example, that attribution develops after action verb relations appears to be owing to the earlier ability to discriminate among objects from different classes than to discriminate among members of the same class according to such parameters as relative size, color, etc. According to Bowerman (1973b), the fact that different semantic relations occur sequentially is evidence that children are learning separate semantic relations rather than a superordinate linguistic scheme or grammar. Different verbs mean different things, but there are also regularities among verbs that have different meanings, so that they form categories of superordinate meaning. Children learn such categories of verbs that share superordinate meaning (Action on affected-Object, for example) and that are also similar in structure (verbs taking Object as a complement, e.g., Action, verbs taking Place as a complement, e.g., Mover-Locative Action and Patient-Locative Action, and still other verbs that take both Object and Place to complete the verb meaning, e.g., Agent-Locative Action). The child does not need to express all possible verb relations from the beginning to demonstrate that he knows a structural regularity; rather, he makes an initial linguistic induction about structural regularity and continues to learn both the consistent and the variable uses of that regularity. That first linguistic induction is a powerful one, as the child's knowledge of relations among objects, his knowledge of words as referring to events, and his growing awareness of discriminable linguistic features (such as phoneme contrasts, word order, intonation, and stress) all come together for him in the insight that sentences are regularly occurring events with consistent relations between parts. However close the semantic regularities among sentences are to the conceptual regularities of experience, that insight is a *linguistic* insight about the structure of language. It is not an insight that functions as an abstract object for the child so that he can be aware of it or talk of it, nor is it the same as the adult intuitions about the nature or functions of sentences. But it is at once a part of what the child knows and a part of what adult language consists of.

THE SENSORIMOTOR ARGUMENT.   Attention to the semantics of child speech was followed almost immediately by a search for the origins of the child's knowledge of the meanings of words and led directly back to the developmental psychology of Jean Piaget (Bloom, 1970, 1973; Brown, 1973; McNeill, 1974; Nelson, 1974; Sinclair, 1970), and the philosophy of John Searle and John Austin (Bruner, 1974; Dore, 1973, 1974). The influence of Piaget is apparent in those explanations of child language that emphasize the importance of movement and action in determining which objects and events children first talk about. However, a much more explicit claim about the correspondence between actions and sentences was made by Bruner (1974) and by McNeill (1974). Both concluded that the pattern of child sentences is isomorphic with the pattern of child actions; Bruner specified that interaction between child and parent is a necessary condition for the relationship between sentences and actions to occur. McNeill suggested that the same sensorimotor action patterns that underlie child sentences underlie adult sentences as well through a process of "semiotic extension" (extension from the child to adult systems). Greenfield, Nelson, and Saltzman (1972) analyzed the intersection of components in children's actions with nesting cups and referred to such an analysis of actions that follow certain principles or rules of occurrence as a grammar of actions.

There is a correlation between the kinds of actions that children perform and some of the Action sentences that they learn to say, and adults do talk about actions. However, it is difficult to see how one can demonstrate anything more than a correspondence between regularities in action events, in that they involve a movement by an agent to affect an object, and regularities in the sentences children use to talk about action events, and in that they represent Agent, Action, and Object functions. Certainly, such a correspondence does not explain what the child's linguistic knowledge consists of, and the evidence in the present study can neither confirm nor deny the thesis that a grammar of language is a displaced grammar of actions. When a large enough sample of multiword utterances is examined, it is apparent that (a) events other than action and locative events are encoded (Bloom, Lightbown, & Hood, 1975) and (b) even within action events, reference is often made to one or another aspect of the event, without specifying an Action-Verb relation, for example, "that ə raisin" or "more raisin." The task remains to find what the alignment mechanism (for matching, mapping, or coding speech with action) might be. If word order in English is a direct print-out of the sequential components of an action event, as McNeill claimed, then one wonders why those same relationships are not expressed in the same way in all languages.

THE GRAMMATICAL ARGUMENT: REDUCTION

When mean length of utterance was less than 1.5, Kathryn and Gia could say "read book," "Mommy read," and "Mommy book"; but full Subject-Verb-Object strings, such as "Mommy read book," were rare. Similarly, at the same time, Kathryn could say "no read" and "no book," but *"Mommy no read" or *"no read book" did not occur.* There were two sources of evidence in those data for concluding that Action relations and negation were represented more fully in their underlying structure than in their surface structure: (a) the fact that the semantic interpretation of such utterances was, for example, *Mommy read book* or *Mommy no read book* and, more important, (b) the fact that among all the utterances in a particular sample all the possible partial relationships occurred—Subject-Verb, Verb-Object, Subject-Object. That is, from a large enough sample of the different constituent relations in her speech, one could infer that the child knew the fuller structural relationship Subject-Verb-Object. The explanation of these data in Bloom (1970) proposed that the child's knowledge of phrase structure operated only in conjunction with a reduction transformation that systematically deleted major constituents in actual sentences that occurred.

Several objections have since been raised against the reduction transformation indicating, at least in part, that the analysis and argument in Bloom (1970) were not sufficiently clear. One objection has been that the proposal of a fuller deep structure was the result of analyzing the child utterance in terms of the adult model and attributing to the child system what would be necessary for describing the utterance if an adult had said it (e.g., Bowerman, 1973a; Schaerlaekens, 1973). However, only evidence from actual child utterances was used to infer underlying structure. The effect of reduction was to delete constituents that were included in the child grammar because of their productivity in a large sample of utterances. Forms that did not occur at all or occurred only rarely in the child's speech could not be described as reduced, and many aspects of the adult model were entirely missing. For example, such forms as the auxiliary or possessive -s were not grammatically reduced or deleted in the child grammar; they simply were never there to begin with, so that reduction was not offered as an explanation of telegraphic speech, nor as an explanation of the nonoccurrence of aspects of adult speech. Further, the same analysis (fuller underlying structure and a reduction transformation) could not be applied to the data from Eric with similar mean length of utterance—even though the semantics of Eric's sentences were quite similar to the semantics of Gia's and Kathryn's—precisely because Eric did not represent all of the same separate constituent relations in his speech. Thus, child utterances were reduced with respect to their fuller underlying structure in the *child grammar* and not with respect to the structure of the adult model.

---

* Negation did not appear in Gia's speech until a later time (see Bloom, 1970).

Both Schlesinger (1971) and Bowerman (1973a) contested the claim in Bloom (1970) of a Subject-Predicate structure underlying child sentences and argued that such a claim would follow only from an analysis of child sentences that is based too closely on the adult model of grammar. Bowerman argued against the use of distributional evidence—the relative frequency of Verb-Object and Subject-Verb constituent relations—and this issue will be discussed below, in light of evidence from the present study. Bowerman (1973a) also pointed out that the syntactic tests of the reality of a Subject-Predicate distinction in the adult model (for example, that transformations such as the passive operate in the same way on constituents with different semantic functions) are not met in the evidence from child speech, since children do not use such transformations. But this argument turns on claims made for the adult grammar and could be faulted for the same reason that Bowerman presented the argument in the first place. The existence of a structure in child language needs to be justified by a test of the child speech data.

Part of the problem in making clear the rationale for the reduction transformation seems to have been that the model of grammar used in Bloom (1970) was the generative transformational grammar proposed originally by Chomsky (1957, 1965) for a fragment of adult English syntax. However, generative transformational grammar represents a theory of language, any language, including adult language but not excluding child language. The analysis in Bloom (1970) proceeded from the child speech data to generative transformational grammar as a theory of language for representing certain facts of child language. The use of the theoretical orientation to explain child language did not presume that whatever the theory represented in adult language would be found also in child language.

Brown (1973), Park (1974), and others criticized the reduction transformation because it appeared to be a linguistic rule that dropped out and so made the child grammar more complex in its earlier stages than in its later stages. However, rather than drop out, the process of reduction undergoes its own development and changes as the child grammar is progressively elaborated. Further, the fact of reduction is implicit in adult grammar and operates in conjunction with many derivational and transformational constraints. Thus, rather than being an expediency for explaining the interpretation of utterances, the reduction that occurs in the child grammar is a linguistic process that interacts with the integration and organization of categories and rule relations in the linguistic system. The fact that utterance length increases developmentally is an index of the development of such underlying processes as these in complex interaction with other processes such as memory organization and recall—none of which has been at all adequately described or explained (see Olson, 1973).

There is a difference between the reduction that is attributed to a limitation on linguistic programming span for sentences and two other kinds of linguistic omission or deletion. First, Brown and Fraser (1963) described early child sentences as "telegraphic"; children leave out the linking grammatical morphemes that adults would include if they produced the same sentences. For example, in the sentence "Mommy *is* driv*ing the* truck," the italicized forms would not occur in the corresponding child sentence. Second, there is the process of ellipsis that occurs with adult sentences to eliminate redundancy.

The operations of reduction and grammatical ellipsis are each the result, it is proposed, of underlying grammatical processes that account for sentences. In contrast, the notion of "telegraphic" speech is only a static description of the surface form of children's utterances when these are compared with adult sentences (Brown, 1973). The morphemes that are left out in child speech characterized as "telegraphic" are often those forms, such as verb inflections, that the child gives no evidence of having learned as yet. In contrast, the constituents deleted in the process of reduction and grammatical ellipsis are derived from complex structures that the child knows or is learning, according to other evidence from his behavior. Further, the analysis of discourse in the present study revealed that rules for grammatical ellipsis are learned by children only after they have learned the rules for generating the fuller, preelliptical forms.

The conditions for reduction were not spelled out in Bloom (1970) except to point to limitations in both lexical representation (the child did not know enough words or did not know enough about combining the words he was learning) and syntactic complexity (the child could not get all of the sentence together) as probable constraints on relating deep structures to surface structures. Bowerman (1973b) offered a version of the reduction transformation that specified obligatory constituents with optional deletion of verbs to account for the occurrence of Subject-Object strings. She emphasized that the constraint was not lexical, because the children she studied used what would be the appropriate verbs in other linguistic contexts. However, the evidence in the present study of the differential occurrence of old and new verbs (verb variability in two- and three-constituent relations) indicated that lexical constraint was indeed a factor. Knowing a lexical item involves more than being able to use that item in one or another context.

Brown (1973) offered a counterproposal for formally accounting for the same facts of limited utterance length, the distribution of partial constituent relations, and such discontinuous relations as Agent-Object (as in "Mommy sock"): that constituents are *optional* in their underlying representation rather than *obligatory* and then reduced. Brown did not spell out the conditions for exercising options in generating sentences. A serious objection to optionality, as Brown observed, is that it allows for the production of more complex utterances than occur, if all options are exercised. Further, it could imply that all constituents are equally likely to occur.

Cedergren and Sankoff have pointed out that:

> Whereas an obligatory rule operates on all input strings that satisfy its structural description, an optional rule may or may not apply to a satisfactory input string. In these terms, no accounting is or can be made of the fact that the option is subject to regular constraints revealed through patterns of covariation with elements of the linguistic environment and with non-language factors such as age, class, and social context. (1974, p. 333)

A third formulation then (after obligatory constituents with reduction and freely optional constituents) would specify the probability of deletion as determined by the conditioning factors under which it operates, in much the same way as the variable rules proposed by Labov (1969) accounted for contraction and deletion of the copula in English (see also Cedergren & Sankoff, 1974). In the present study comparisons were made of the linguistic conditions under which constituents were more or less likely to be represented in child speech. In this way, it was possible to specify the conditions under which a constituent did or did not occur (its variability or optionality) and the likelihood that it would occur in one or another linguistic context.

When the results of the examination of utterances in successive observations were compared for each of the children separately, there were: (a) a sequence in the development of Action and Locative Action categories, (b) a developmental increase in longer utterances while two-constituent utterances continued to occur, and (c) a consistent interaction among grammatical, lexical, and discourse variation with the occurrence of two-, three-, and four-constituent utterances. When the children were compared with one another with respect to their development in successive observations, there was: (a) some variation among the children in the development of the Action and Locative Action categories, (b) consistency among the children in the relative frequencies of different constituent relations, and (c) considerable variation among the children in the interaction among grammatical, lexical, and discourse factors with the number of constituents expressed.

In the original reduction argument, it was assumed that combining the partial constituent relations in producing the full constituent structure Subject-Verb-Object exceeded a complexity limit. The observation that the negation marker "no" occurred with a verb (e.g., "no sit"), or with a noun (e.g., "no chair"), but did not occur with both (e.g., "*no sit chair"), indicated that negation was an added complexity factor. The expectation in the present study was that any added complexity would be more likely to occur with two-constituent relations than with three-constituent relations. Negation and two-part verbs occurred significantly more often with two-constituent relations than with three-constituent relations, and there was a clear but nonsignificant trend in the same direction with embedded relations (object modification) in action events. Other additions within and between constituents occurred as often (proportionately) with three-constituent relations as with two-constituent relations. Although grammatical morphemes added "something more" to constituent relations and amounted to "cumulative grammatical complexity," as described by Brown (1973), grammatical morphemes did not represent added complexity in the same way that negation, two-part verbs, and embedded relations added complexity to sentences by constraining the realization of the full constituent structure. More important, however, other conditioning factors that were related to the lexicon and to discourse operated in conflicting directions to determine the likelihood that constituents would be represented in utterances.

Constituent relations were more or less likely to be deleted or, conversely, more or less likely to be represented or realized, according to certain lexical, complexity, and discourse factors that interacted with the constituent structure of sentences. The next step would be to specify (a) the interaction among the variation factors, and (b) the form of the constituent structure of sentences in an attempt to provide a variable rule model that includes the factors that accounted for the nonrandom distribution of two- and three-constituent relations in the children's early language.

THE GRAMMATICAL ARGUMENT: THE VARIATION MODEL

The model of variation in the children's sentences with mean length of utterance $>$ 1.0 and <3.0 morphemes included four factors: (a) a grammatical complexity factor

(C); (b) a lexical access factor (L); (c) a discourse interaction factor (D); and (d) a factor to account for the as yet unaccounted for variation, a residual variability (performance) factor (V).

Factor C was grammatical complexity that operated to constrain the constituent structure of sentences and consisted of another semantic-syntactic relation embedded or subordinated to the verb relation, including negation, possession, recurrence, and other attribution. The grammatical morphemes, that is, the verb auxiliaries, determiners, demonstratives, articles, and plural -s, represented a different level of complexity that did not interact to constrain constituent structure.

Factor L concerned the accessibility of words in the child's dictionary, in terms of a word's relative familiarity in (a) its reference function—access to the word in new situations—and (b) its syntactic function—access to the word in new linguistic contexts. Children learn words in their referential sense, with some representation of the constancy or regularity of figurative content, regardless of the particular situation to which the word may refer. But, children also learn words in their operative sense with potential variation in the meaning of a word as a function of its linguistic context.

Factor D was the effect of discourse—utterances from the child or another person —that complemented a particular utterance by the child. Factor V consisted, most generally, of whatever nonsystematic forces operated to influence the constituent structure of a sentence.

In the present study, the complexity, lexical, and discourse factors operated with different effects: either to facilitate or increase the probability of realizing one or another constituent relation, signified by an ↑ in the matrix below, or to constrain or reduce the probability of realizing one or another constituent relation, signified by an ↓ in the matrix below. Presumably, the V factor operated with two conflicting (↑ and ↓) effects as well, but since these were not directly observed in this study; their interaction could not be interpolated in the matrix below.

The matrix (Figure 5) presents the schematic interactions among three factors: complexity was a constraining factor (↓), discourse was a facilitating factor (↑), and lexical access was either a constraining (↓) or a facilitating (↑) factor. Presented in this way, it was possible to rank the cumulative effects of the factors in their interactions, according to the results of this study. Thus, the most constraining condition would be one without D↑ in which both L and C were ↓—the interaction between a new word (verb or noun) and complexity—with minimal support for the constituent structure, resulting in reduction (or nonrealization) of one or another constituent. The least constraining condition would be one without C↓ and with L↑ and D↑—familiar lexical

	L↓	L↑	D↑
C↓	1	2.5	4.5
L↓		2.5	4.5
L↑			6

Figure 5. Matrix of the interactions among complexity (C), lexical (L), and discourse (D) factors in the generation of sentences: 1 is the strongest constraint = reduction and 6 is maximum support = realization.

items and support from discourse—with resulting maximum support for realizing the full constituent structure.

Finally, the strength of each of these variables, and their effects, changed in the course of this study. But, although the inferred probability values of both $C\downarrow$ and $L\downarrow$ were developmentally attenuated in the time span of the present study, it is doubtful that they would ever disappear entirely. One would expect that $C\downarrow$ with the conditions $D\uparrow$ and $L\uparrow$ would not affect the constituent structure of sentences, but that $C\downarrow$ with the condition $L\downarrow$ without $D\uparrow$ would continue to constrain the structure in some way. The concept of reduction, then, is not an expedience for explaining semantic interpretation and partial constituent relations in child sentences. Rather, reduction is a grammatical process that changes, with respect to the conditioning factors under which it operates, in relation to other developments in the child's linguistic system. The reduction transformation (Bloom, 1970) was one linguistic scheme for representing these phenomena; the variation paradigm proposed here appears to offer a more informative scheme for representing the same phenomena.

CONSTITUENT STRUCTURE IN THE VARIATION MODEL

What are children learning when they learn to combine words to form sentences? The results of this investigation of Action and Locative Action sentences indicate that children are learning the constituent structure of sentences, with variable probabilities for realizing individual constituents. Verbs are central to the constituent structure: distributionally, they occur more frequently than other constituents; semantically, they specify the meaning relationship between the Subject and Complement forms; syntactically, they order Subject and Complement forms relative to each other. The occurrence of two nouns in an Agent-Object relationship was relatively rare; for only Kathryn and Gia did Agent-Object sentences account for more than .10 of the Action utterances. Such sentences were never productive for Eric and Peter. The frequency of Agent-Object sentences decreased substantially when mean length of utterance exceeded 2.0, and, with rare exceptions, they did not include any complexity. A lexical explanation of their occurrence seems most reasonable: the children did not know a particular verb or did not know enough about the syntactic function of a particular verb.

Further evidence of the importance of verbs to constituent structure was the fact that the partial constituent relations (for example, Agent-Verb and Verb-Object or Mover-Verb and Verb-Place) were integrally related to one another. Although such semantic-syntactic relations as possession, recurrence, and attribution seemed to be separate relations and probably were unrelated to one another, the relations of verbs to preceding and succeeding nouns (for example, Agent-Verb and Verb-Object) were not separate semantic-syntactic relations. The partial constituent relations were integrated into three- or four-constituent relations before mean length of utterance reached 2.0; and when Verb complexity and certain other kinds of complexity appeared, they were included in three-constituent relations as often as in two-constituent relations. In contrast, the other semantic-syntactic relations were embedded in verb relations only with difficulty, appearing more often in two-constituent relations than in three-constituent relations, but occurring most frequently in the data as separate sentences, even as mean length of utterance approached 3.0.

The constituent structure of Action and Locative Action verb relations included a pre-verb constituent with different semantic functions, that is, Agent, Mover, and Patient, and a post-verb constituent with different semantic functions, that is, Affected Object and/or Place, both in relation to different categories of verbs. The question of what the pre-verb Subject and post-verb Complement consist of has been raised often, particularly by those who have argued that children learn separate semantic relations rather than a superordinate grammatical relation such as Subject-Predicate. The evidence in the present study indicates that they are not separate concepts but, rather, are relations within a schema. Diagramatically, these schema relationships could be represented by a phrase structure tree diagram (keeping in mind that phrase structure trees are only hypotheses about mental grammar) as suggested by the evidence in the present study. This version of phrase structure represents the following information about the linguistic knowledge of the four children in this study learning English.

1. The constituent structure is a linguistic schema that entails relationships between Subject and Complement forms.
2. The meaning relationship between the Subject and Complement forms is mediated by the meaning of the verb.
3. The form of the verbal auxiliary (Verb complexity) is determined by the meaning relation between the Subject and the Verb.
4. The Subject-Verb-Complement constituents are obligatory in the linguistic schema, but the Complement can be variously represented as Affected-Object or Place or, as with Agent-Locative Action, both Object and Place.
5. The constituent structure can be complemented in a sentence by another linguistic schema, here represented only indefinitely by the dummy symbol Δ. This second linguistic schema can be an adverb, or recursive, that is, a second constituent structure that is subordinate or coordinate with the first. In any event, its occurrence in the sentence does not affect, that is, constrain, the constituent structure.
6. There is no longer reason to assume that Verb-Complement is a more unified grammatical relation than is Subject-Verb, on distributional grounds. In the present study, although Verb-Object was more frequent than Agent-Verb in Action utterances (as reported also by Brown, 1973), Mover-Verb and Patient-Verb were more frequent than Verb-Place. In addition to the distributional evidence, there was also the finding that the form and function of the verbal auxiliary was determined by whether the Subject functioned as Agent, Mover, or Patient: intention modals and progressive "-ing" occurred with Agents; third person singular occurred with Patients, etc.

Bowerman (1973a) cited the distributional evidence in her data as supporting a closer unity between Subject-Verb, than between Verb-Object, and suggested, on those grounds, that distributional evidence alone is insufficient to support a Subject-Predicate distinction. There is a strong tendency for intransitive Action verbs, and what might have been Mover-Verb or Patient-Verb utterances, to appear among the Subject-Verb utterances reported by Bowerman: .58 of the Subject-Verb utterances reported for two children from whom data were collected when mean length of utterance was less than 1.5 (our analysis of the first two samples from Kendall and the first sample from Seppo in appendixes in 1973b). Intransitive verbs would not be relevant to an analysis of the *relative* distribution of two-term Action relations, inasmuch as no apparent affected-object is involved and the two other possible two-term relations (Verb-Object and Subject-Object) were precluded from occurring. The difference between the children in Bowerman's study as compared with the children in the present study may have been a situational difference, in which events that happened to include either largely intransitive or transitive actions were tapped.

7. The negative marker and verbal auxiliary (Verb complexity) are distinct and separate from one another. Verb complexity was more likely to occur when the Subject was represented, and it occurred as often in three-constituent relations as in two-constituent relations. In contrast, negation rarely occurred when sentence Subjects were expressed and negation was represented significantly more often in two-constituent relations than in three-constituent relations.

8. Finally, the Subject constituent was always the least complex constituent in any of the categories. There was virtually no Agent or Mover complexity, and Patient complexity consisted of only occasional demonstrative pronouns.

The phrase structure tree in Figure 6 only describes the results of this study; it is not explanatory. It differs from the formulation in Bloom (1970) that described the data when mean length of utterance was less than 1.5 and before the distinction was made among the Patient, Mover and Agent-Locative Action relations. In terms of current linguistic theory, the syntax of the underlying constituent structure in Figure 6 is, perhaps, closer to the theory of McCawley (1970) than to that of Chomsky (1965). McCawley (1970) proposed that the verb in a sentence is determined by the Subject-Object relationship (and English is a "Verb-Subject-Object language"), which differs from the Subject-Predicate represented in a generative transformational grammar. Semantically, the constituent structure schema is consistent with the semantic analyses of Chafe (1970) and with the case distinctions proposed by Fillmore (1968) in that functions of nouns are specified in terms of their relations with verbs. The schema is inconsistent with Fillmore's proposals for grammar in that these meaning relations were defined contextually (rather than formally, according to prepositional markings on nouns). The functions of nouns and verbs in the two schemas are only superficially similar (both schemas refer to agents, objects, and locatives; but these functions are defined in altogether different terms).

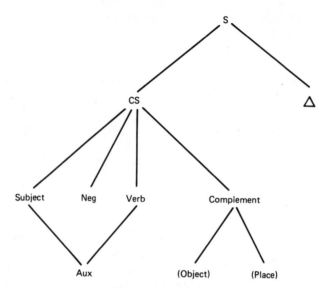

Figure 6. Diagram of the constituent structure (CS) of
sentences (S): Δ is another subordinate or coordinate
relation, e.g., an adverb or another constituent structure.

THE ROLE OF MEMORY. Two kinds of coding occur during the first two years:
conceptual coding for representing information about objects and events in the world
and linguistic coding for talking about, and understanding when others talk about,
objects and events in the world. This study has investigated schemas and processes
for linguistic coding, with the implicit assumption that linguistic schemas and processes represent (code, map, etc.) ideas (concepts, knowledge, etc.) about the world.
Linguistic competence entails the ability to access the linguistic code—to remember
the schema—relative to the child's attention to some element of experience. The
variable rules in the model of child grammar suggested here are, in some essential
sense, related to the development of memory processes.

Olson (1973) pointed out that increase in utterance length is not explained by
increase in immediate memory span; rather there is a simple correlation between
increasing utterance length and increasing memory span (that is, for digits, as classi-
cally measured) because both are the result of the development of some higher order
cognitive function: "the classical findings on memory span reflect the development
of the child's ability to handle verbal information rather than changes in memory or
information processing capacity *per se* . . . . Mean utterance length is not a performance restriction due to a simple memory-span limit [pp. 151 and 153]." These
remarks are addressed to the issue of short-term memory and its relation to utterance
length; the issue in the present study has to do with access to linguistic schemas in
long-term memory.

Olson (1973) pointed to another factor underlying the increase in mean length of
utterance: the use of "preprogrammed routines" or phrases which are actually a
"single label" rather than a programmed structural representation—what Leopold

(1949) and others have called "stereotype" phrases. Indeed, at Kathryn I, of the six Subject-Verb-Object Action sentences that were reported, only one included nominal Agent and Object ("man ride bus"). In contrast, the others included pro-forms (for example, "Mommy do it," "Baby do it," "I comb my pigtail") at the same time when there were no pronouns in any other utterances. Kathryn did not produce pronoun Objects or Agents in two-constituent relations until mean length of utterance approached 2.0 morphemes at Time II (see Bloom, Lightbown, & Hood, 1975 for the account of pronominal-nominal development). Thus, the fact that three-constituent relations were not proportionately less complex than two-constituent relations at Time I may have been due, in part, to the stereotyped nature of some of the longer utterances (see also, Clark, 1974).

Access to productive linguistic schemas—productive in the sense that such schemas derive from an underlying rule system—is a function of the relative strength of linguistic forms and structures in interaction with the elements of content that are coded. Such relative strength is determined by a number of factors, for example, recency of learning, frequency of application, lexical familiarity, etc. It is also clear that the child's use of a partial constituent relation can function as an assist, or memory prompt, for supporting the fuller constituent structure, as was apparent when such two-constituent relations and three-constituent relations occurred successively. It appears that the increase in utterance length reflects increased access to the fuller constituent structure that is represented in long-term memory—through lexical and discourse factors as well as other possible mnemonics that result from cognitive development.

Two current models of linguistic processing in adult studies may be relevant to the results of the study reported here. Thorndyke and Bower (1974) have presented data that describe how adults represent in long-term memory the meaning of sentences presented to them. They tested the two views that the propositional content of sentences can be represented according to (a) the semantic function of the noun in a sentence in relation to its verb, as represented in case grammar (Rumelhardt, Lindsay, & Norman, 1972) and (b) a model of parallel search through Subject, Verb, and Object constituents (Anderson & Bower, 1971). Although the data presented by Thorndyke and Bower (1974) favor the second of these alternatives, it is apparent that both views are somehow relevant to early child grammar and the results of this investigation. That is, the structure of sentences is mediated by the meaning of the verb, and the constituent verb relations appear to be schematized according to the relations among obligatory Subject-Verb-Complement constituents.

COMPETENCE AND PERFORMANCE.   Brown (1973) has suggested that children have grammatical knowledge of constituent structure but that they utilize this knowledge freely, thereby producing utterances of varying lengths. Not yet knowing the rules of discourse, children overgeneralize from the elliptical and truncated adult speech they hear and form the impression that it does not matter how much of a full sentence one says. The child may produce a full Agent-Verb-Object sentence, any single constituent, or any correctly ordered combination of two constituents. In terms of the competence/performance issue, Brown's account of the length of child sentences implies that the child's knowledge of language (competence) would enable him to produce full constituent utterances, but his inadequate knowledge of discourse (performance in Brown's terms) prevents him from doing so. The resulting child speech is characterized by an "oscillating, apparently lawless optionality [p. 241]."

Cedergren & Sankoff (1974) have criticized the notion of optionality for "fail[ing] to capture the nature of the systematic variation which exists even on the level of the grammar of a single individual" (p. 333). They argue that so-called "optional" possibilities are distributed in regular ways in the speech of individuals and speech communities, and that such regularities constitute linguistic competence. The results of the present study fit well into this conceptual framework. Contrary to Brown and others, the distribution of constituent relations in the children's speech was not random. For example, verbs were consistently the most frequently expressed constituent; the constituent that referred to the object affected by movement occurred second most frequently. Certain combinations such as Agent-Place rarely or never occurred. Moreover, the evidence was strong for concluding that children operate with some fairly well-defined notion of constituent structure but that knowledge is not categorical. Rather, particular linguistic and nonlinguistic factors have been shown to regularly vary with utterance length. Two-part verbs, embedded relations, negation, new verbs, and subsequently expanded child utterances all occurred more often with two-constituent utterances than with three-constituent utterances. It is hard to imagine how these results could be explained in terms of "lawless optionality." Instead, this systematic covariation reflects the child's underlying linguistic competence.

In conclusion, it is apparent that none of the existing explanations of early child sentences has been adequate, but neither have these attempts to explain children's linguistic knowledge been entirely wrong. Clearly, semantic considerations are integral to the schemas that children learn for representing information in messages. Pragmatic considerations enter into determining which linguistic forms are most useful to be learned. Action schemas function to provide the content for many of the child's sentences. However, the child comes to a linguistic induction about regularities in the relations between words that are, at once, both semantic and syntactic—having to do with the consistent ways in which words are ordered relative to one another in relation to some aspect of experience. That is the beginning of grammar; to what extent the child grammar can be captured by linguistic theories that are transformational or case-oriented is less important than the fact that certain regularities among sentences have been captured and represented by a linguistic schema—a schema that is less categorical than it is variable, but that is certainly systematic.

REFERENCES

Anderson, J. R., & Bower, G. H. On an associative trace for sentence memory. *Journal of Verbal Learning and Verbal Behavior,* 1971, 10, 673–680.

Bailey, C. J. Variation resulting from different rule orderings in English phonology. Unpublished manuscript, Georgetown University, 1973.

Bloom, L. *Language development: Form and function in emerging grammars.* Cambridge, Mass.: The M.I.T. Press, 1970.

———. *One word at a time: The use of single word utterances before syntax.* The Hague: Mouton, 1973.

——, Rocissano, L., & Hood, L. Adult-child discourse: Developmental interaction between information processing and linguistic knowledge. *Cognitive Psychology,* **8,** 1976.

——, Hood, L., & Lightbown, P. Imitation in language development: If, when and why. *Cognitive Psychology,* 1974, 6, 380–420.

——, Hood, L., & Miller, P. The development of grammatical morphemes in relation to the development of syntax. In preparation.

——, Lightbown, P., & Hood, L. Structure and variation in child language. *Monograph of the Society for Research in Child Development,* 1975.

Bowerman, M. *Early syntactic development: A cross-linguistic study with special reference to Finnish.* Cambridge: Cambridge University Press, 1973. (a)

——. Structural relationships in children's utterances: Syntactic or semantic? In T. Moore (Ed.), *Cognitive development and the acquisition of language.* New York: Academic Press, 1973. Pp. 197–213. (b)

Braine, M. D. S. Length constraints, reduction rules, and holophrastic processes in children's word combinations. *Journal of Verbal Learning and Verbal Behavior,* 1974, 13, 448–456.

Brown, R. *A first language, the early stages.* Cambridge, Mass.: Harvard University Press, 1973.

——, Cazden, C. B., & Bellugi, U. The child's grammar from I to III. In J. P. Hill (Ed.), *Minnesota Symposia on child psychology.* Vol. 2. Minneapolis: University of Minnesota Press, 1967.

——, & Fraser, C. The acquisition of syntax. In C. N. Cofer & B. Musgrave (Eds.), *Verbal behavior and verbal learning: Problems and processes.* New York: McGraw-Hill, 1963. Pp. 158–197.

Bruner, J. The ontogenesis of speech acts. Unpublished manuscript, Oxford University, 1974.

Cedergren, H., & Sankoff, G. Variable rules: Performance as a statistical reflection of competence. *Language,* 1974, 50, 333–355.

Chafe, W. L. *Meaning and the structure of language.* Chicago: The University of Chicago Press, 1970.

Chomsky, N. *Syntactic structures.* The Hague: Mouton, 1957.

——. *Aspects of the theory of syntax.* Cambridge, Mass.: The M.I.T. Press, 1965.

Clark, R. Performing without competence. *Journal of Child Language,* 1974, 1, 1–10.

de Villiers, J., & de Villiers, P. Competence and performance in child language: Are children really competent to judge? *Journal of Child Language,* 1974, 1, 11–22.

Dore, J. The development of speech acts. Unpublished doctoral dissertation, Baruch College, City University of New York, 1973.

——. Holophrases, speech acts and language universals. Unpublished manuscript, Baruch College, City University of New York, 1974.

Fillmore, C. The case for case. In E. Bach & R. Harms (Eds.), *Universals in linguistic theory.* New York: Holt, Rinehart and Winston, 1968.

Fisher, R. A. *Statistical methods for research workers.* New York: Hatner, 1967.

Greenfield, P., Nelson, K., & Saltzman, E. The development of rulebound strategies for manipulating seriated cups: A parallel between action and grammar. *Cognitive Psychology,* 1972, 3, 291–310.

——, Smith, J., & Laufer, B. Communication and the beginnings of language. New York: Academic Press. In preparation.

Halliday, M. A. K., & Hasan, R. Cohesion in English. London: Longman (English Language Series). In press.

Hymes, D. *Language in culture and society.* New York: Harper and Row, 1964.

Kates, C. A descriptive approach to linguistic meaning. Unpublished manuscript, 1974.

Labov, W. Contraction, deletion, and inherent variability of the English copula. *Language,* 1969, 45, 715–762.

Leopold, W. F. *Speech development of a bilingual child.* Evanston, Ill.: Northwestern University (4 volumes), 1949.

McCawley, J. D. English as a VSO language. *Language,* 1970, 46, 286–299.

McNeill, D. Semiotic extension. Paper presented at Loyola Symposium on Cognition, Chicago, Illinois, April, 1974.

Morris, C. *Signification and significance.* Cambridge, Mass.: The M.I.T. Press, 1964.

Nelson, K. Structure and strategy in learning to talk. *Monographs of the Society for Research in Child Development,* 1973, 38, Serial No. 149.

———. Concept, word, and sentence: Interrelations in acquisition and development. *Psychological Review,* 1974, 81, 267–285.

Olson, E. Developmental changes in memory and the acquisition of language. In T. Moore (Ed.), *Cognitive development and the acquisition of language.* New York: Academic Press, 1973. Pp. 145–157.

Park, T. Z. A study of German language development. Unpublished manuscript, Psychological Institute, Berne, Switzerland, 1974.

Rumelhardt, D. E., Lindsay, P. H., & Norman, D. A. A process model of long-term memory. In E. Tulving & W. Donaldson (Eds.), *Organization of memory.* New York: Academic Press, 1972.

Sankoff, G. A quantitative paradigm for the study of communicative competence. Prepared for the Conference on the Ethnography of Speaking, 1972.

Schaerlaekens, A. A generative transformational model for child language acquisition: A discussion of L. Bloom, Language development: Form and function in emerging grammars. *Cognition,* 1973, 2, 371–376.

Schlesinger, I. M. Learning grammar: From pivot to realization rule. In R. Huxley & E. Ingram (Eds.), *Language acquisition.* New York: Academic Press, 1971. Pp. 79–89.

———. Relational concepts underlying language. In R. Schiefelbusch & J. Lloyd (Eds.), *Language perspective—Acquisition, retardation, and intervention.* Baltimore, Md.: University Park Press, 1974.

Sinclair, H. The transition from sensory-motor behavior to symbolic activity. *Interchange,* 1970, 1, 119–126.

Slobin, D. I. Developmental psycholinguistics. In W. D. Dingwall (Ed.), *A survey of linguistic science.* College Park, Md.: University of Maryland, 1971.

Smith, C. An experimental approach to children's linguistic competence. In J. R. Hayes (Ed.), *Cognition and the development of language.* New York: Wiley, 1970.

Suppes, P. Probabilistic grammars for natural languages. *Synthese,* 1970, 22, 95–116.

Thorndyke, P. W., & Bower, G. H. Storage and retrieval processes in sentence memory. *Cognitive Psychology,* 1974, 6, 515–543.

Structural Relationships in Children's Utterances: Syntactic or Semantic?[1]

Melissa Bowerman[2]

Until recently, the investigation of children's knowledge of linguistic structure was based primarily upon analyses of the superficial form and arrangement of the words in their spontaneous utterances. In the last few years, however, there has been an increasing realization that we can discover much more about children's early linguistic competence if we take apparent meanings into account as well. It has been convincingly argued, especially by Bloom (1970), that children's utterances express a variety of structural relationships. Some of these relationships are not distinguishable purely on the basis of formal differences, however. As in the case of adult language, this gap between meaning and form can best be accounted for by postulating a distinction between deep and surface structure. The information which is necessary for assigning meanings to utterances is provided by the deep structure representations specified for them.

What is the nature of the deep structures of children's utterances? How should we characterize the structural relationships which children apparently intend? Attempting to answer these questions involves making judgments about what kinds of concepts and categories are functional in children's early linguistic competence, and perhaps also about what linguistic knowledge is innate as opposed to what must be learned.

The following discussion is divided in three parts. First some proposals which have been made concerning the structural relations of children's utterances are outlined. This is followed by an evaluation of certain aspects of these proposals, based primarily on data I have collected from two Finnish children. Seppo and Rina, and an American child, Kendall (Bowerman, 1973). Finally, I offer some suggestions and

From *Cognitive Development and the Acquisition of Language* Academic Press, Inc., 1973, pp. 197–213. Reprinted by permission of Academic Press, Inc.

[1] Portions of this paper appear in expanded form in Chapter 6 of the author's work *Early syntatic development: A cross-linguistic study with special reference to Finnish.* Cambridge University Press, 1973. They are used here by permission of the publisher.

[2] This reseach was supported in part by PHS Training Grant NS05362-10 from the National Institute of Neurological Diseases and Stroke to the Bureau of Child Research, University of Kansas.

supporting evidence for a plausible interpretation of the kinds of concepts underlying children's earliest constructions.

SOME EXISTING PROPOSALS ABOUT THE UNDERLYING NATURE OF CHILDREN'S UTTERANCES

One important issue on which researchers differ is whether the underlying structural relationships of children's utterances should be given a syntactic or a semantic characterization. McNeill (1966a, b, 1970a, b, 1971) has used transformational generative grammar as outlined by N. Chomsky (1965) to describe child speech. This entails postulating deep structures which are basically syntactic. The syntactic description of a sentence serves as input to the semantic interpretation of the sentence. The syntactic deep structures of a transformational grammar provide information about both the hierarchical organization of sentence constituents, or constituent structure, and the grammatical relations which hold between these constituents. Many linguists (e.g., N. Chomsky, 1965, pp. 71–72; Katz & Postal, 1964, p. 159) believe that certain grammatical relations are fundamental to the structure of sentences in all languages. These include the functions *subject of the sentence, predicate of the sentence, verb of the verb phrase,* and *direct object of the verb phrase.* McNeill proposes that the existence of language universals results from the inherent characteristics of the child's capacity to acquire language. He suggests, therefore, that knowledge of the basic grammatical relations is innate, and guides the child's understanding and production of utterances from the beginning of language development.

In a contrasting view of children's initial linguistic knowledge, Schlesinger (1971) has proposed that the components of the structural relationships expressed by children's utterances are semantic concepts like *agent, action, object,* and *location* rather than syntactic notions like *subject* and *predicate.* He notes that these concepts do not reflect specifically linguistic knowledge, but, rather, are determined by the more general innate cognitive capacity of the child. Children acquire language by learning realization rules which map underlying semantic intentions directly onto surface structures. Schlesinger's model of language acquisition, while explicitly a production model rather than a grammar, shares with the generative semantics accounts of grammar proposed by linguists such as Fillmore (1968) and McCawley (1968) the idea that semantic concepts are the primitive structural components of sentences. These are thought to be encoded by syntactic devices, rather than being themselves derived from the interpretation of more basic syntactic information.

In writing grammars for three American children early in their syntactic development, Bloom (1970) specified deep structures with the formal configurational properties which define the basic grammatical relations in a transformational grammar. Unlike McNeill, Bloom (1970, pp. 227–228) did not feel that knowledge of these relations is innate, but only that her subjects had learned some or all of the relations by the developmental points at which she placed her grammars. Elsewhere, Bloom (in press) has suggested that there is perhaps no important distinction between syntactic functions like subject of the predicate and object of the verb and semantic concepts like agent of the action and object of the action, since both are "necessarily linguistic categories, determined by formal criteria of arrangement and relationship."

She adds that the important distinction to be made is not among "domains of linguistic categories," but "between *linguistic* categories—categories that are dependent on formal specification of relationship— . . . and *cognitive* categories which may be experientially defined in quite another way."

The debate about the underlying structures of children's early utterances may be more than terminological, however. There may in fact be an important difference between interpreting a child's construction such as *man drive car* as *subject-verb-direct object* and as *agent-action-object acted upon*. Determining whether or not children's early linguistic competence includes a knowledge of syntactic relationships and the constituent structure they entail has some important consequences for a theory of language acquisition.

Before examining these consequences, let us consider briefly the difference between syntactic and semantic concepts. Syntactic concepts are more abstract than semantic ones. A verb may take several noun arguments, each performing a different semantic function such as *agent, object acted upon, location, instrument,* and so on. Deep structure syntactic functions are not always associated with particular semantic roles. Fillmore (1968), for example, has shown that the deep structure subjects of English sentences play such diverse semantic roles as agent (as in **John** *opened the door*), object involved (**the door** *opened*), instrument (**the key** *opened the door*), person affected (**John** *wants milk*), and location (**Chicago** *is windy*). Direct objects likewise do not have a constant semantic function. The subject and direct object for any particular verb, however, identify noun phrases in particular semantic roles. For example, the subject of the verb *eat* identifies the agent, while that of *want* identifies the person affected. Being able to implicitly identify the deep structure subject and direct object of a given sentence involves knowing which semantic roles function in these syntactic capacities for the particular verb involved. (See Brown, in press, for a further discussion of the differences between semantic and syntactic relationships.) What it means to understand an abstract syntactic function like *subject* is taken up in a later section.

Now let us return to the question of whether there is any essential difference between describing children's utterances in terms of syntactic relationships and in terms of semantic concepts. If we assume, with N. Chomsky, McNeill, Bloom, and many others, that adult competence includes knowledge of the basic grammatical relations, we must determine where this knowledge comes from. If we should find that knowledge of the basic grammatical relations is reflected in children's earliest utterances, it would at least be plausible to argue that this knowledge is not learned at all but rather constitutes part of children's basic capacity to acquire language. But if, in contrast, it turns out that these utterances are produced without a specific understanding of syntactic relationships but only with rules based upon semantic notions, we must then account for how the more abstract knowledge embodied in the basic grammatical relations is eventually attained. It is possible that achieving an understanding of the abstract, specifically linguistic relationships which hold between parts of sentences is an important part of the language acquisition process. If syntactic and semantic terms are not carefully distinguished and structural specifications like *subject-predicate* and *agent-action* are regarded as equivalent, we have no motivation to look for such a learning process.

EVALUATING PROPOSALS ABOUT CHILDREN'S DEEP STRUCTURES

How can we determine which interpretation of children's deep structures—the syntactic or the semantic—provides a closer approximation to the form of children's linguistic knowledge? Only by examining the data closely without preconceptions. A great advance in the study of child language was made in the early 1960s when several researchers (Braine, 1963; Brown & Fraser, 1963; Miller & Ervin, 1964) realized that children's word classes might not be the same as those of the adult language, and began to do distributional analyses of the words in children's constructions to see what classes in fact were functional. The same unbiased approach is needed now that we are looking at children's deep structures. We need to guard against assuming that children's deep structures have a certain form simply because an adequate description of the adult language must specify such a form for equivalent adult utterances. We may find that those structural phenomena of adult speech which motivate the postulation of syntactic concepts like subject and predicate are absent in child speech. In my view, the evidence available so far does not appear to be strong enough to justify crediting children in the initial stages of syntactic development with knowledge either of the basic grammatical relations or of the constituent structure upon which these depend.

CONSTITUENT STRUCTURE

Let us first examine constituent structure. In representing children's early utterances, McNeill, Bloom, and Schlesinger all provide an account of constituent structure in which three-term strings like *man drive car* and *mommy go store* are hierarchically organized along the traditional lines. The initial noun (N) constitutes one constituent, while the verb (V) plus the direct object or locative element constitute another. McNeill and Bloom, but not Schlesinger, consider the former the subject and the latter the predicate. According to McNeill (1971), this hierarchical organization results automatically from the child's application to sentences of his knowledge of the basic grammatical relations.

What is the justification for this analysis of the constituent structure of children's early three-term constructions? N. Chomsky (1965) notes that there are various ways to justify assigning constituent structure. One must show, for example, that "there are perceptual grounds for the analysis," or that the postulated intermediate phrases "must receive a semantic interpretation," or "are required for some grammatical rule," or "define a phonetic contour [p. 197, fn. 7]."

The few attempts to use strictly linguistic criteria to determine the constituent structure of children's early utterances have had inconclusive results. For example, Brown (unpublished materials) asked whether Adam, Eve, and Sarah, his three English-speaking subjects, regularly used the predicate verb phrase as an answer to *what are you doing?* or *what is it doing?* questions, as adult speakers do. He found that the children often did not respond to these questions at all and almost never answered them appropriately. The same is true of Kendall and of my two Finnish subjects. Brown also tried to determine whether in Adam's speech the privileges of occurrence of V + N were the same as those of V alone, which might have suggested that V + N should be considered as a single constituent. He found that the privileges of occurrence were the same, since both V and V + N could occur after initial nouns or pronouns. This finding does not constitute sound evidence for a verb phrase (VP) however, since N + V, or the subject plus the verb, also had the same privileges of occurrence as V alone: both could precede nouns or pro-locatives. Thus, on the basis of this test, either V + N *or* N + V could be considered a constituent substitutable for V alone. This was true not only in Adam's speech but also in that of my three subjects.

Other linguistic grounds which might be used to justify postulating a VP constituent in children's early utterances are also lacking. For example, children do not initially use phrases like "do (so)" which make reference to a preceding VP. In samples of speech from the earliest stages of word combining, one does not find sentences like *Daddy like cake. Mommy does too,* or *Johnny went home (and) so did Jimmy.*

In sum, no one has yet to my knowledge succeeded in demonstrating on purely linguistic grounds that the verb "belongs with" the direct object or the locative in child speech rather than, for example, with the subject—in other words, that verb plus direct object or locative is a constituent in a way in which subject plus verb is not. Arguments for a verb phrase constituent in children's utterances have been based on a weaker sort of evidence, evidence which bears only on the question of whether the verb plus the direct object or the locative element has a psychological unity for the child which the subject plus the verb lacks.

One such argument draws on the observation that verb–object strings are more frequent in early speech than subject–verb strings. This was true of Brown's subjects Adam, Eve, and Sarah and of Bloom's three subjects. McNeill (1970b) notes that the predominance of predicates without subjects over predicates with subjects in Adam's speech "would result if the sentences without subjects had existed in Adam's repertoire for some time [p. 1090]." McNeill (1966b, pp. 44–45) also suggests that children may initially practice subject noun phrases in isolation and only later realize that subjects and predicates can be brought together into one sentence.

According to this line of reasoning, which is based on the relative frequency of verb–object, subject–verb, and subject–verb–object strings in a speech sample, if some children from an early stage of development produced more subject–verb than

Table 1   Frequency of Production as a Clue to Constituent Structure: Number of Utterance Types of Subject-Verb, Verb-Object, and Subject-Verb-Object Strings in Samples of Spontaneous Speech[a]

	Kendall (English) MLU[b] 1.10	Kendall (English) MLU 1.48	Seppo (Finnish) MLU 1.42	Seppo (Finnish) MLU 1.81	Rina (Finnish) MLU 1.83
Subject-verb	19	31	25	64	21
Verb-Object	5	12	4	9	4
Subject-verb-object	—	7	7	8	19

[a] All samples contained a total of 713 utterance tokens (both constructions and single words) from consecutive tapes, except for the first from Kendall, which consisted of 136 construction tokens (102 types) noted by hand over a period of almost two full days.
[b] MLU: mean length of utterance (counted in morphemes), a measure of linguistic maturity.

verb–object strings, we might argue that for them, subject–verb had a psychological unity which verb–object lacked. Similarly, if even full subject–verb–object strings were more frequent than verb–object strings, perhaps subject–verb should be considered an initial unit to which object is added only later, just as McNeill suggests that verb–object is a unit to which subject is added later. These were, in fact, the distributional facts of the speech of my two Finnish subjects and my American subject. All of these children produced far more subject–verb than verb–object strings, and they produced either about equal numbers of verb–object and subject–verb–object strings, or more of the latter. Table 1 presents the relevant figures from samples of their spontaneous speech.

If we followed to its logical end the argument that constituent structure is revealed in the relative frequency with which these various strings are produced, we would have to conclude that for these children the hierarchical organization of sentence elements was not

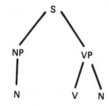

but rather

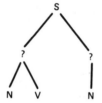

—in other words, that the subject plus the verb constituted one constituent and the direct object another. Such an organization would be a false step toward the adult understanding of constituent structure which we assume they will ultimately attain.

Another sort of argument that predicates have psychological unity is presented by Braine (1971b). Like McNeill, Braine has suggested that the first English sentences consist of a predicate with an optional subject. He finds evidence for this in children's "replacement sequences," a term he uses to describe sequences of utterances in which a short utterance is followed or preceded by a longer string which incorporates it and suggests what grammatical relations are intended by it. Braine found that these sequences tend to consist of an utterance without a subject followed by the same utterance with a subject. For example:

> chair . . . pussy cat chair
> want that . . . Andrew want that
> off . . . radio off
> fall . . . stick fall
> go nursery . . . Lucy go nursery
> build house . . . Cathy build house

Replacement sequences also occurred, although relatively infrequently, in the speech of the two Finnish children and of my American subject Kendall. Some of these did involve producing a predicate and then adding a subject. But many involved instead the operation of producing a subject first and then adding the predicate, or, even more interestingly, of producing the subject and the verb and then adding a direct object or a locative. The following are some examples:

> Seppo (translated):
> horsie . . . horsie . . . horsie sleeps
> chick . . . chick sings
> mother . . . mother opens
> daddy . . . daddy wash . . .
>   daddy . . . daddy already wash train
> this belongs . . . this belongs there
> Immi draws . . . Immi draws there
> man captain . . . comes . . . (to) take-care-of . . . man
>   captain comes . . . (to) take-care-of . . . bird . . . man captain
>   takes-care-of-bird.

> Kendall:
> 'lissa . . . 'lissa . . . 'lissa . . . 'lissa write
> Kendall . . . Kendall gone
> Kristin . . . Kristin sit chair
> Kendall innere . . . Kendall innere bed
> Kendall pick up (O + V) . . . Daddy pick up (S + V) . . . Kendall
> (O) . . .
>   Mommy pick up Kendall (S + V + O)

To summarize, arguments about constituent structure which are based upon the relative frequency of production of different types of strings or upon the characteristics of replacement sequences are not conclusive. Using these criteria on data from certain children leads to an analysis of constituent structure which specifies subject plus verb as one constituent and direct object or locative as another. It appears that frequency of production and the characteristics of replacement sequences may not be reliable clues to hierarchical organization. In short, we still do not know whether children produce their early subject–verb–object and subject–verb–locative constructions with the particular understanding of constituent structure which has been ascribed to them, or even with any concept of hierarchical organization at all.

THE GRAMMATICAL RELATION "SUBJECT OF"

What evidence is there that an understanding of the concept *subject of* is part of children's early competence? In transformational theory, the deep structure subject of a sentence is defined as the noun phrase immediately dominated by S. We have just seen that the analysis of constituent structure upon which this definition depends may not be applicable to children's utterances. If this is the case, then justification for crediting children with the concept *subject of* must come from elsewhere.

Why do we need the concept of deep structure subject for an adequate analysis of adult language? This is a difficult question. In my understanding, the answer might go something like this: In linguistic theory, the relationships which hold between underlying meanings and actual sentences are indicated by transformations. According to N. Chomsky's outline of grammar, the operations involved in transformations cannot be specified simply by reference to the semantic functions of words in sentences. For example, a rule for deriving passive sentences which specified that the word functioning as agent of the verb should become the object of the preposition *by* would be inadequate. Passives can also be created out of sentences in which there is no agent, like *your mother wants you* or *John sees Mary*. The constituent which becomes the object of *by* in passive sentences can only be defined in an abstract way, as a noun phrase with a certain syntactic function which we·call *subject*. The semantic function of this noun phrase is different for different subclasses of verbs. The need for the concept *deep structure subject* arises because there are transformations— including the one which derives passive sentences—which treat certain noun phrases as though they were identical for the purposes of a particular operation, even though they do not necessarily have identical semantic functions in their respective sentences. Such transformations can cause deep structure subjects to appear in a number of different positions and different syntactic roles in surface structure. But if a person's competence is such that he knows what the deep structure subject of a sentence is regardless of its position and syntactic function in surface structure, and if he knows what semantic role is associated with the grammatical function of subject for the particular verb involved, he will understand the sentence.

Fillmore (1968, p. 58) notes that some languages have been described as not having passives and others as able to express transitive sentences only passively. He argues that since these languages offer no choice of surface structure subject, the concept of subject is not applicable to them. To pursue this argument further, if a particular language lacked syntactic operations which treat a particular noun argument for each verb in the same way across a number of different verbs, and which could cause deep and surface structure subjects to differ, why would there be any need for the syntactic abstraction of *subject?*

The language of children appears initially to lack such operations. It has often been noted that children's early utterances can be generated almost entirely by the base component of a transformational grammar (Bowerman, 1973; Brown, Cazden, Bellugi, 1968, p. 40; McNeill, 1966b, p. 51). Virtually all constructions follow the simple active declarative pattern, although certain elements obligatory in adult speech are absent. Thus, no transformations need to be specified which require reference to a sentence constituent with the abstract syntactic function which defines subjects in adult speech. Deep structure and surface structure subjects are therefore always identical.

On what grounds can the abstraction of *subject* be made in the case of a language which lacks transformations requiring it? In simple active declarative sentences of adult English and Finnish, the particular noun argument of a verb which functions as deep structure subject (and therefore also as surface structure subject) governs person and number concord in the verb, is in the nominative case (pronouns only in English, nouns and pronouns both in Finnish), and has a characteristic position. In early child speech, subjects cannot be identified on the basis of either verbal concord or case, since verbs initially have an invariant form, personal pronouns are rare or absent, and (relevant only for the Finnish children) nouns in *all* syntactic roles are in the nominative, not just subjects.

This leaves only position as a basis for the abstraction of *subject*. The particular noun argument of the verb which functions as deep and surface structure subject in simple active declarative sentences typically occurs in preverbal position in both English and Finnish (other orders are possible as well in Finnish). This ordering is generally observed in children's early constructions. In studies of child speech, the noun which occurs in preverbal position is identified as the subject—provided that it would be considered the subject in adult speech too. But when the child produces constructions like *ball hit* and *apple eat*, we simply conclude that he has reversed the normal verb–object order. We do not consider the possibility that he might have mistakenly identified the wrong noun argument of a particular verb as subject, perhaps by analogy with sentences like *the toy broke, the door opened, the page ripped,* or *the ball dropped*. All of these sentences involve verbs which can take a noun which functions semantically as *object acted upon* as either subject or direct object, depending upon whether or not an agent is also expressed. The verbs *hit, eat,* and many others do not have this flexibility. It is conceivable that a child might at first not recognize this distinction between verb classes, and so would assume that all objects acted upon can be subjects in agentless sentences. In summary, then, we do not even make consistent use of position to help us identify subjects in children's utterances, even though it is the only criterion we have available. Instead, we simply rely on our knowledge of what the subject would be in equivalent adult utterances.

Occupation of identical position is in any event not a sufficient reason to assume identical syntactic function. For example, in the sentences *John eats cake* and *John goes home*, the nouns *cake* and *home* occur in the same position, but they do not perform the same syntactic function. Similarly, why should the first words in typical child utterances such as *John eat cake* and *John want cake* be considered to perform the same syntactic function when their semantic functions are different?

To summarize, the structural phenomena which require the concept of subject in adult speech are evidently missing in early child speech. To credit children with an understanding of the concept is an act of faith based only on our knowledge of the characteristics of adult language.

A SEMANTIC INTERPRETATION OF CHILDREN'S DEEP STRUCTURES

The purpose of the foregoing discussion has not been to demonstrate that children initially lack knowledge of the basic grammatical relations and of the constituent structure which they entail, but only to show that there is as yet no evidence in their spontaneous constructions that they have it. It is possible that children use this knowledge in their comprehension of adult sentences before their own productions begin to reflect it, but this has not been demonstrated.

Finding compelling support for either a syntactic or a semantic interpretation of the structural relations expressed in children's early utterances will probably require experimental study. Of particular interest will be information about the levels of abstraction at which children make generalizations to form novel constructions. However, nonsystematic evidence which suggests one interpretation or the other for particular children may be obtainable from samples of spontaneous speech. For example, if a child initially began to observe inflections or verbal concord only for agentive subjects, this would suggest that *agent* rather than *subject* was a functional concept for him. One bit of evidence of this sort comes from a Russian child, Zhenya (Gvozdev, 1961). Initially, Zhenya did not formally mark direct objects, but rather used the nominative form of the noun in all syntactic functions. When he began to acquire the accusative case, he used it only to mark those direct objects which designated the objects of action, particularly those occurring with verbs referring to the transfer or relocation of objects, such as *give, carry, put,* and *throw.* At this time, Zhenya rarely marked the direct objects of verbs like *read, draw,* and *make,* in which the relations between action and object are more complex. This pattern of marking indicates that at first Zhenya did not regard all direct objects as functionally equivalent, but only that subset of them which referred to objects acted upon in certain rather direct ways.[3]

Cross-linguistic comparisons of children's speech may also yield information about the concepts which are functional early in linguistic development. Striking similarities in the constructions of children learning unrelated languages provide some support for a semantic rather than a syntactic interpretation of the deep structures of early word combinations. The most common productive construction patterns across languages involve a fairly small set of relationships, which have been described in the literature in semantic terms such as *agent–action, action–object acted upon, object located–location, possessor–possessed,* and *demonstrator–demonstrated* (see Bowerman, 1973; Brown, in press; Slobin, 1970, for further discussion).

While these relationships can be given syntactic interpretations as well as semantic ones, the semantic descriptions often provide a more exact characterization than their syntactic counterparts. For example, the words in children's earliest utterances which appear to function syntactically as subjects or direct objects initially play a more restricted number of semantic roles than they do slightly later in development and in adulthood. Table 2 illustrates this observation. It lists the frequencies with which two- and three-term constructions expressing subject–verb–object relations in various semantic roles were produced in samples from my two Finnish subjects and one American subject, and from two Samoan children (Kernan, 1969). The samples are arranged by increasing MLU (mean length of utterance counted in morphemes, a measure of linguistic maturity). At the lower MLUs, there is a very strong tendency for sentence subjects to have an agentive relationship to the verb. Expressed in a different way, the verbs children initially use in subject–verb combinations are those which take agentive subjects—for example, *sleep, drive, eat, sit, sing, ride, go,* and *open.* Children's lexicons at first include only a handful of verbs which take persons affected or objects involved as subjects (e.g., *want, see, fall*), and these are often used without explicit subjects. In particular, states like *want* are rarely predicated of persons other than the child himself, so these verbs usually appear without subjects or at best are paired only with the child's name.

This suggests that children are initially not seeking the means of expressing the

---

[3] I am grateful to Dan I. Slobin for bringing this example to my attention.

Table 2 A Cross-linguistic Comparison of the Syntactic and Semantic Relationships Expressed in Early Subject-Verb-Object Constructions[a]

Syntactic relations	Semantic relations	Kendall (English) MLU 1.10	Seppo (Finnish) KLU 1.42	Kendall (English) MLU 1.48	Sipili (Samoan) MLU 1.52	Tofi (Samoan) MLU 1.60	Seppo (Finnish) MLU 1.81	Rina (Finnish) MLU 1.83
Subject-verb	agent-action	19	25	28	3	10	60	19
	person affected[b]-state	—	—	1	—	—	2	1
	object involved[c]-action	—	—	2	—	6	2	1
Verb-object	action-object acted upon	2	3	6	6	16	8	3
	action-object created[d]	—	1	1	—	—	1	1
	state-object[e]	1	—	1	—	—	—	—
	action-object	2	—	4	—	1	—	—
Subject-object	agent-object acted upon	1	3	—	—	—	2	3
	agent-object created	1	—	2	—	—	1	—
	agent-object	3	—	—	—	—	—	—
	noun-(has)-noun	2	—	2	—	—	—	—
Subject-verb-object	agent-action-object acted upon	—	7	7	—	1	8	9
	agent-action-object created	—	—	—	—	—	—	4
	agent-action-object	—	—	—	—	—	—	1
	person affected-action-object	—	—	—	—	—	—	4
	person affected-state-object	—	—	—	—	1	—	1

[a] Utterance types only (not tokens). All word orders of a given construction pattern are counted.
[b] Fillmore's Dative case, with verbs like *want, see, receive, be afraid*.
[c] Fillmore's Objective case, with verbs like *fall, break* (intransitive).
[d] Fillmore's Pactitive case, with verbs like *make, draw*.
[e] Object has been used as a neutral term to designate the direct objects of verbs like *want, look at, see, leave, find, read,* and *receive,* which are difficult to characterize semantically.

grammatical relation between subject and predicate but rather, more concretely, of expressing the interaction between an agent and the action he initiates. As MLU increases, more verbs which take nonagentive subjects come into use, and are increasingly frequently paired with noun or pronoun subjects referring to inanimate objects or to beings other than the child himself. Examples of such sentences are Seppo's *tower falls-over* and *mouse is–afraid*, Rina's *Rina receives cake*, and Tofi's *baby wants clothes*. It is difficult to decide whether the number of different semantic notions the child is working with has simply increased at this point or whether the more abstract and inclusive concept of *subject* has now become functional.

The case for a semantic interpretation of direct objects is less strong. In adult English and Finnish—I don't know about Samoan—direct objects can designate an object receiving the force of an action (*John hit* **the ball**), a person affected (*John murdered* **George**), or an object created (*John built* **a table**; *Rina draws* **a horse**). Direct objects play other semantic roles as well which are more difficult to characterize. I have grouped the direct objects of verbs like *want, look at, see, leave,* and *receive* together simply as *object* for lack of a better way to describe them. There is a tendency throughout the samples for direct objects to designate objects physically acted upon, but this is not so strong as the initial tendency for subjects to designate agents, nor is there the same sort of developmental trend towards diversification as there is for subjects.

These comparative data suggest that *subject* and possibly *direct object* are more powerful and abstract than the concepts which children use early in their linguistic development. The linguistic knowledge which underlies the earliest two- and three-word constructions may be no more complex than simple rules to order words which are understood as performing various semantic functions. In some constructions, a semantic relationship may be expressed simply by words occurring together without a characteristic ordering.

According to this view of language acquisition, children's initial efforts at word combination result from their discovery of ways to express various semantic relationships in the language they are learning. These semantic relationships are similar across languages because, as Schlesinger has proposed, they originate in the way human cognitive abilities process nonlinguistic experiences common to children everywhere. Children may be able to grasp the concept *initiator of an action* before the concept *person affected by a state or stimulus* becomes available to them. This would account for their early preference for verbs which name actions and require agents in the role of subject.

Of course, the semantic categories I have mentioned are not necessarily the particular ones children use. They are abstractions, although not at such a high level as syntactic concepts like *subject,* and perhaps children do not even make these abstractions. Possibly, for example, an individual rule is made for each verb specifying that the name for the one who initiates the particular action of the verb, such as eating or driving, precedes the name for the action. An abstraction could also be made at some intermediate level between the initiators of particular actions and the concept of agent.

When the deep structure relations expressed in children's early constructions are given a semantic interpretation, the question arises of how N. Chomsky's level of syntactic deep structure is acquired, if, in fact, it is acquired at all. Several investigators have argued that learning theories cannot account for the acquisition of information represented only in deep structure, since this is abstract and never directly exhibited in the speech to which the child is exposed (e.g., Bever, Fodor, & Weksel, 1965; McNeill, 1971). In particular, McNeill (1971) has argued that because the basic grammatical relations "can be consistently defined only in the deep structure of sentences, they are beyond the reach of any linguistic experiences a child may have [p. 23]."

Some researchers who advocate a semantic interpretation of children's early utterances, such as Schlesinger (1971) and Kernan (1970), resolve the problem of how children can learn something which is never directly represented in speech by arguing that they do not have to—that an abstract syntactic level of deep structure does not exist. Acquiring a language simply involves learning how to translate semantic intentions directly into surface structures.

Doing away entirely with syntatic deep structures need not be the inevitable outcome of a theory of language acquisition which holds that most aspects of linguistic structure are learned rather than innate. As Ervin-Tripp (1971) observes, "the weakest argument of all is the notion that if we cannot think of a way to teach something, it must not be learned or learnable [p. 190]." It seems plausible, both intuitively and on the basis of a certain amount of experimental evidence, that certain abstract representations of linguistic structure are included in a speaker's knowledge of his language, even though these may not correspond exactly to those outlined by Chomsky and may be at an intermediate level between a semantically described deep structure and the surface realization of sentences.

The argument that the basic grammatical relations are unlearnable simply because they are definable only in the abstract underlying representation of sentences is not very convincing. If we accept this, we must agree that all aspects of deep structure are unlearnable for the same reason. But many aspects of deep structure, as specified in transformational generative theory, are language-specific, such as the underlying order of constituents. If the deep structure representation of sentences is to be considered part of adult competence, we can only assume that these language-specific aspects of deep structure are learnable. To argue otherwise would be to support the untenable position that children are born with a bias toward acquiring the particular language they in fact learn. And if children command some process of learning powerful enough to make these abstractions purely on the basic of linguistic experience, why should the same process not also be able to deal with abstract concepts which are believed by some to be universal, such as the basic grammatical relations?

There is, in any event, some evidence that the basic grammatical relations themselves are not universal. As we noted, Fillmore (1968) observed that certain languages do not offer a choice of subjects and therefore appear to lack the process of subjectivalization. If, in fact, the subject–predicate division is language-specific, we must rule out the possibility that it constitutes part of children's innate knowledge.

It is possible that children can acquire an understanding of the basic grammatical relations through an increasing comprehension of the way various semantic relationships are formally dealt with in their language. The concept of *subject*, for example, might develop in the following way: the child initially formulates rules specifying that words designating initiators of actions precede words designating actions (or, alternatively, that the name of the one who initiates a particular action precedes the name of the action). As the child acquires verbs which take nonagentive noun arguments as subjects, he learns additional rules for the placement with respect to the verb of words performing such semantic functions as *person affected* and *instrument.* The concept of *subject* emerges when the child eventually realizes that nouns in various semantic roles are treated identically for different subclasses of verbs not only with respect to position but also with respect to transformational possibilities, and thus have an equivalence of function at a higher level of abstraction than the particular semantic functions they perform.

Parental speech may play an important role in the child's acquisition of abstract syntactic concepts. A study by Drach (1969) indicates that the sentences mothers direct to their children may be shorter, more grammatical, and syntactically simpler than those they address to other adults. Ervin-Tripp (1971) speculates that these speech modifications could make apparent "the phrases which comprise the basic units of language" and aid the child in recognizing constituent structure. A study of Pfuderer (1969) suggests that the syntactic complexity of mothers' utterances increases as their children mature. Such an increase in complexity could provide a sort of programmed text for introducing the child gradually to progressively more abstract and difficult syntactic relationships.

A mother may even unconsciously modify her speech in a way which facilitates the child's initial search for consistencies in the expression of semantic concepts and which perhaps even suggests to him which semantic concepts he should consider important. An analysis of a sample of 1000 utterances addressed to Seppo by his mother, taken from consecutive tapes, revealed that verbs which take agents in the role of subject occurred five and one half times as frequently as all verbs which take other semantic concepts as subjects combined (Bowerman, 1973). Unfortunately, control data are not available to indicate whether this emphasis was stronger in the mother's speech to Seppo than in her speech to adults. If it was, then it would seem that the agent–action relationship was especially heavily modeled in the input to Seppo, and other semantic versions of the subject–verb relationship which might initially have confused him were kept to a minimum.

SUMMARY

According to the view of language acquisition I have sketched, the linguistic knowledge which lies behind children's initial attempts at word combining may not and need not include information about the basic grammatical relations or the constituent structure they entail. There is, in any event, no compelling evidence as yet that it does. The characteristics of cross-linguistic data suggest the alternative view that children launch their syntactic careers by learning simple order rules for combining words which in their understanding perform semantic functions such as *agent, action,* and *object acted upon,* or perhaps other even less abstract semantic functions. Through additional linguistic experience a child may begin to recognize similarities in the way different semantic concepts are formally dealt with and to gradually reorganize his knowledge according to the more abstract grammatical relationships which are functional in the particular language he is learning.

REFERENCES

See Bibliography, p. 503 ff.

Pronominal-Nominal Variation in Child Language

Lois Bloom, Patsy Lightbown, and Lois Hood

Certain relational meanings in early sentences were defined in Bloom (1973) as *functional* relations: a constant form with specific meaning was combined with a number of different words, and the meaning of the constant form determined the meaning of the relation between the two words in combination. Brown (1973) has pointed out that such relations have the form $f(x)$ with a fixed value, f, combined with a variable (x) that can assume many values. Such relational forms make reference across classes of objects and events—that is, many different kinds of things exist, disappear, and recur. Children can talk about such behaviors with respect to many objects and events (such as cookies, airplanes, and tickling) that are themselves otherwise quite different from one another.

These functional relations were observed in the speech of all the children: for example, "no," "gone," or "no more" signaled negation (most often nonexistence), and "more" or "nother" signaled recurrence. Although the absolute frequencies in each of these categories tended to increase developmentally, their proportional frequencies decreased, leading to the conclusion that they were an earlier development than the verb categories for all of the children. Indeed, the functional relations were the most frequent in the earlier samples when syntax first emerged.

When mean length of utterance was less than 2.0, Eric and Peter continued the same kind of functional relations to encode particular functions in action, location, and possession relations: the pro-forms "I" or "my" as agent or mover, "it," "this one," or "that" as affected-object, "my" as possessor, and "here" or "there" as place. The structure that Peter and Eric learned, constant forms with constant functions, could be compared to a system of inflectional affixing or case marking which might be schematized as $Ax = X$, $Bx = X$, or $Ay = Y$, $By = Y$, where x and y are each constant relational forms that always mean the same thing relative to the different forms (A or B) with which they combine to create the relational meaning (X or Y). In this this way, Peter and Eric were able to talk about a great many objects in action and locative relations, and syntax did not depend on lexical learning for making particular reference to different objects. However, Peter and Eric knew the names of many objects and persons. They used these nominal forms in single-word utterances and in functional relations with such words as "no" and "more." There was also a certain amount of variation with the pronominal forms they learned to specify affect-

From "Structure and Variation in Child Language," *SRCD Monograph*, **40**, 2, 18–24, 1975. Reprinted by permission of the University of Chicago Press

ed-object and place relationships (e.g., "this one" and "it," and "here," "right here," "over there," "there," etc.) Thus, it was not the case that the pronominal forms with verbs were unanalyzed phrases learned by rote. Reference to place and affected-object occurred independently of verbs, and verbs also occurred independently as well as occasionally with noun forms.

The grammatical system that Peter and Eric learned consisted of relations between different verb forms and a number of constant functional forms such as "it," "there," and "my." Successive verb relations were learned by fitting new categories (such as locative action and then locative state) into the existing system of reference or grammar. However, whereas reference to affected-object (with "it," "this one," etc.) and place (with "here" or "there") included many different things and places, Eric and Peter referred only to themselves as agents and possessors (with "I" or "my") and did not also talk about other people as agents and possessors when MLU was less than 2.0 morphemes.

Within the same MLU period, Kathryn and Gia used the same kind of functional relations—constant forms in combination with many different forms—to represent the notions existence, nonexistence, and recurrence. However, Kathryn and Gia encoded other grammatical relations, with categories of nominal forms as *agent, affected object, place,* and *possessor* instead of a constant pronominal form for each grammatical relation. Thus, "Mommy," "Daddy," "Baby," "Kathryn," etc., formed a grammatical category *agent.* Such forms as "book," "cookie," "ball," "toy," "bag," etc., formed a grammatical category *affected-object;* such forms as "table," "floor," "outside," "bag" formed a grammatical category *place; affected-object* and *place* were not mutually exclusive. The fact that Kathryn and Gia developed action, locative-action, and possession relations at the same time was interpreted as evidence that they had learned the superordinate grammatical categories sentence-subject (including agents, actors, movers, and possessors), predicate-object (including objects of actions, locative actions, and possession), and predicate-complement (place), so that a number of semantic distinctions could be encoded within the same grammatical system that specified the relations among categories of nominal forms.

The relations between nominal categories in Kathryn's and Gia's speech could be schematized as $A + B = C/D$, where A and B were grammatical categories, and the relations between them, C or D, were superordinate category relationships with specific meaning, such as possession, action, or location. Kathryn and Gia learned an abstract grammatical structure here schematized as $A + B$, which could be used to represent several semantic distinctions, here schematized as C, D. The structure learned by Eric and Peter was different but equally abstract in that it was used to represent a number of semantic distinctions with each distinction dependent upon a linguistic operator or marker. The two systems of pronominal and nominal encoding are aspects of the adult model and, indeed, of language in general. All the children then were quite similar in their semantic knowledge, but there was variation among them in their knowledge of syntax—they were learning two different systems of semantic-syntactic structure that were virtually mutually exclusive in the beginning. There was an impressive consistency within each child and between Eric and Peter on the one hand and Kathryn and Gia on the other when MLU was less than 2.0.

The major development when MLU passed 2.0 was a shift in encoding and the integration of the two alternative systems of pronominal and nominal reference as

Table 1   Pronominal and Nominal Encoding of Sentence Constituents

Child Sample	MLU	Action								Locative Action					
		Possession-Possessor		Agent Actor		Affected-Object		Agent		Mover		Affected-Object		Place	
		Pro	Nom	Pro	Nom	Pro	Nom	Pro	Nom	Pro	Nom	Pro	Nom	Pro	Nom
Eric:															
II	1.19	—	—	—	1	4	2	—	—	—	—	—	—	—	—
III	1.42	2	1	7	1	14	4	—	—	2	2	—	2	1	3
IV	1.69	1	1	12	4	32ª	33ª	—	—	2	7	7	11	10	4
V	2.63	16	2	93	28	70ª	111ª	20	—	8	25	12	19	42	13
Gia:															
II	1.34	1	6	—	8	1	19	—	1	—	6	1	3	—	2
III	1.58	1	18	4	66	14	67	—	7	—	12	—	15	2	11
IV	1.79	7	33	7	106	17	120	—	5	1	31	1	16	15	27
V	2.30	61	30	163	48	79	193	8	4	22	22	8	18	24	44
Kathryn:															
I	1.32	2	13	4	19	4	44	—	1	4	1	2	2	—	9
II	1.89	32ª	34ª	9	99	41	81	2	12	6	28	22	25	35	37
III	2.83	104	38	123	92	128	212	21	17	15	28	55	49	56	58
Peter:															
III	1.37	2	3	—	—	5	2	—	—	—	—	1	3	3	1
IV	1.41	4	—	6	1	17	6	1	—	—	—	1	—	4	—
V	1.33	1	—	3	1	24	3	1	—	—	—	3	5	11	1
VI	1.75	12	—	8	—	23	13	—	—	2	1	7	10	18	4
VII	2.39	23	4	22	7	31ª	38ª	8	1	9	5	22ª	9ª	36ª	7ª

ªIncluded here are utterances with redundant coding, for example, "my Kathryn house" and "I fix it choochoo train."

233

presented in table 1 and figures 1 through 3. The figures represent proportional frequencies of *pronominal* encoding for agent and affected-object in action verb relations (figs. 2 and 3) for the four children, and possessor (fig. 4) for Kathryn and Gia.[6] The graphic representation of nominal encoding would, of course, be the mirror image of figures 2 through 4. As can be seen, even though the children started out (when mean length of utterance was approximately 1.3) with either one or the other linguistic system, there was a significant shift with development as both systems of reference were gradually integrated for all of the children. The occurrence of redundant coding (e.g., "fix it choo-choo train") occurred infrequently and only appeared in the data when MLU passed 2.0. Brown (1973) interpreted such utterances as a failure to analyze and segment the "it" from the verb form. However, in the present study, such utterances seemed to represent the children's attempt to learn the alternative forms of pronominal and nominal encoding in making the transition from one

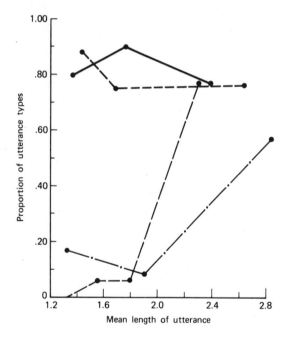

Figure 1. Pronominal encoding of agent and actor. The first data point for Peter represents the averaged data from Peter III, IV, and V, when MLU was virtually identical: – – – – – – – = Eric, ⸺ = Peter, ⸺ . ⸺ = Kathryn, — — — = Gia.

[6] Peter and Eric did not make the same transition for possession in this time period because possession was a later development for both.

form of reference to the other. Also, Gia often said one form and then the other, especially for agents, for example, "Gia lie down/I lie down." Such redundancy, although generally infrequent, occurred equally often in the speech of all of the children.

The same developmental trends were apparent in the pronominal-nominal interactions among constituents in locative-action relations. The data in table 1 confirm the distinction between action and locative-action verb relations for Peter and Eric: action relations took pronominal forms as affected-object, but in locative-action relations Peter and Eric used nominal forms as affected-object (with pronominal place). Further, agents (with affected-object) and actors (which were also in a sense the objects affected by the action) were productive in action relations (P IV and E III) before reference to agents (that moved another object) or movers (that were also the objects that moved) became productive in locative-action relations (P VII and E IV), apparently because action relations developed first.

Just before the pronominal-nominal shift there was a decrease in the proportional frequencies of utterances in the combined verb categories. This exception to the developmental increase in the proportional frequencies in the verb categories might have been the effect of the transition from one means of encoding to another.

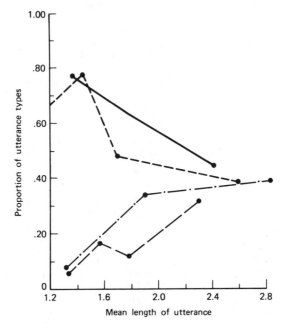

Figure 2. Pronominal encoding of affected-object. The first data point for Peter represents the averaged data from Peter III, IV, and V; when MLU was virtually identical: – – – – – – – = Eric, ———— = Peter, ——.—— = Kathryn, — — — = Gia.

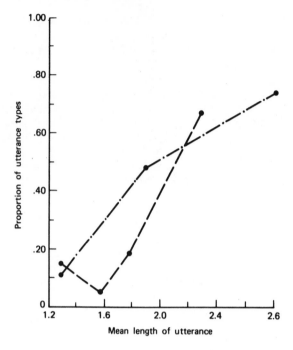

Figure 3. **Pronominal encoding of possessor:**
────── = Kathryn, ─ ─ ─ = Gia.

By the time MLU approached 2.5 morphemes, the variation among the children was greatly reduced. Kathryn and Gia had learned a primitive system of pronominal substitution for nominal categories, while Eric and Peter were learning categories of nominal forms to encode action, location, and possession. In terms of nominal and pronominal reference, the children were quite similar to one another when MLU approached 2.5 morphemes. *No matter how they started out, affected-object was most often nominal and agent was most often pronominal for all four children.* There was a crossover from predominantly pronominal to predominantly nominal encoding of affected object for Eric and Peter, and a crossover from predominantly nominal to predominantly pronominal encoding of agent for Kathryn and Gia.

The two different systems of semantic-syntactic structure when MLU was less than 2.0 morphemes could be compared with the traditional classification of language systems as synthetic-agglutinative or analytic-isolating. The system of pronominal reference that Peter and Eric learned for their early sentences could be described as "agglutinative," with a small number of constant morphemes (pronominal "it," "there," "my," etc.) added on to other morphemes to signal certain semantic distinctions (affected-object, location, possessor, etc.). In contrast, Gia and Kathryn learned a system whereby many different morphemes were combined with one another to signal the same semantic distinctions, and such morphemes were more isolatable and less dependent on one another. It is possible to conclude that the capacities for both pronominal and nominal encoding (or, put another way, for both agglutinative and isolating linguistic processes) exist among children, from the beginning of the use of syntax.

Other studies of child language may be interpreted as confirming the intersubject nominal-pronominal variation observed among the four children in this study. A fifth child, Allison, whose development was reported in Bloom (1973, pp. 233–257), used exclusively nominal forms in her early syntax, as can be seen in the data presented there. In other data from English-speaking children, reported by Huxley (1970) and Nelson (1973), there were children who appeared to use predominantly pronominal forms and other children who used nominal forms in their earliest syntactic utterances. Jn two unpublished studies by Lightbown (1973) and Vosniadou (1974), the speech of French- and Greek-speaking children was described, respectively, and the almost exclusive occurrence of either nominal or pronominal forms was observed in the early syntactic utterances of the different children. It appears that an individual child's first sentences are either nominal or pronominal, and the two systems of reference are not mutually substitutable in the beginning.

The variation among the children in the pronominal and nominal encoding of verb relations and possession can be attributed to the two strategies for syntactic encoding described in Bloom (1973). The first strategy is the linear combination of one word, having the same form and same meaning, with various other words, for example, "fix it," "eat it," "read it," etc., where "it" operates much like a formal marker. The second strategy is the hierarchical combination of categories of words, with a structural meaning that is essentially independent of the lexical meaning of each word separately. It seems that children can break into the adult linguistic code in one of (at least) two ways: with a system of formal markers, or with a system of rules for deriving grammatical categories. Both strategies would provide the child with a means for representing the same semantic information in his speech, with greater or lesser lexical specification, and both are aspects of the adult code. The choice of strategy (if there is a choice) as children begin to use syntax would appear to be the result of complex interactions between cognitive development and linguistic experience. Once a child has recognized the relations among objects and events that recur with different objects in different situations, he can begin to learn a system of syntactic coding that represents such information about events, in the speech that he hears and in his own speech. The aspects of the system that he learns will be determined at least in part by the kind of linguistic reference that he hears.

Parents may differ from one another in the relative extent to which they use pronominal or nominal forms in their speech to their children. Nominal forms may well predominate generally in speech to children for increased specificity or redundancy, for the sake of gaining attention, adding emphasis, or increasing clarity. The interaction in the present study was between investigator and child primarily, but in the mother-to-child speech that was recorded the four mothers did not differ from one another in the extent of pronominal reference.

The use of proforms in adult-to-adult speech is governed by a fairly explicit system of deictic reference (see, e.g., Fillmore 1971). Adults use proforms according to the information that speaker and listener share about events. If an object has already been named or otherwise pointed out in the situation, then the use of pronoun reference occurs with no loss of information because both speaker and listener know, for example, the particular object to which "it" refers, or the place to which "there" refers. Adults use proforms gesturally, when they also point out or otherwise indicate the object, action, or person of reference, and anaphorically, when the object, action, or person of reference has already been named by either speaker or listener in the situation. Whether one says "eat the spinach" or "eat it," or whether one says "the book is on the table" or "it's over there" depends upon what both the speaker and the hearer already know about the situation and about one another.

Children are exposed to systems of deictic reference, with shifting between nominal and pronominal forms, in both the adult-to-child speech that they hear and the adult-to-adult speech that they overhear. This intraspeaker variation that forms a part of adult competence and interacts with information about situational and interpersonal contingencies can be compared with the interspeaker variation among the children in their early use of pronominal or nominal reference. However, the use of proforms and substantive forms in the children's speech was not a system of shifting deictic reference; the children used either one or the other form of reference. The use of proforms by Peter and Eric was neither gesturally nor anaphorically conditioned, and when the pronominal-nominal shift for each of the children occurred it was not conditioned by such deictic constraints from the situation or awareness of the information shared with a listener.

Other kinds of evidence indicate that children who are less than 3 years old would not know such communication conventions for speaking and understanding that take into account the information that is shared between speaker and listener and that contributes to determining message form (e.g., Brown 1973; Flavell 1968; Glucksberg, Krauss, & Higgins 1975; Maratsos 1971). It appears then that children learn usage constraints on nominal and pronominal encoding *after* they acquire the formal linguistic means for shifting reference, which the children in this study began to acquire when MLU was approximately 2.5 morphemes and they were approximately 2 years old. How they proceeded to learn to take account of social, cognitive, and linguistic variables as the factors for shifting pronominal or nominal encoding, in their later development, remains to be determined.

REFERENCES

See Bibliography, p. 503 ff.

The Development of Wh Questions in Child Speech[1]

Roger Brown

The spontaneous speech of three preschool children is analyzed for evidence of the development of the kind of knowledge represented by current transformational treatments of Wh questions. The children are those participating in a longitudinal, naturalistic study of the development of grammar. The first Wh questions seem to be unanalyzed routines or constructions not involving transformations. As Wh questions become more complex and varied, several kinds of evidence of transformational knowledge emerge. All sorts of Wh questions are for a time produced in a form that adults do not model, but which is a hypothetical intermediate in the transformational analysis of adult forms. This child's form seems to involve a preposing operation but to omit a transposing operation. One sort of Wh question, the *Why* question, seems to be created by one child (Adam) as a direct transform of an antecedent declarative from the mother. In general, there is evidence that children in the preschool years do develop a grammatical structure underlying Wh questions that is much like the structure described in current transformational grammars. Because the abstract underlying structure is not strongly suggested by the surface form of Wh questions, it is difficult to see how it can be learned. However, there are recurrent discourse patterns, involving sentence and constituent exchanges, which are rich in structural information, and these may constitute the basis of a learning process.

A large part of the dialogue between a parent and a child at home consists of questions and answers, and very many questions are of the type that linguists call "Wh questions." Wh questions are those using an interrogative word from the set *Who, Whom, What, Where, When, Why,* and *How.* Contemporary generative grammars of English, designed to represent the grammatical competence of adult native speakers, all employ transformational rules in the derivation of Wh questions. The research to be described undertakes to determine whether or not there is evidence in the spontaneous speech of preschool children that such rules figure also in the child's competence. Some of the basic work on this problem has been done by my associate, Ursula Bellugi, and is reported by her elsewhere (1965).

From *Journal of Verbal Learning and Verbal Behavior,* **7,** pp. 279-290, 1968. Reprinted by permission of Academic Press, Inc.

[1] In somewhat different form, this paper was delivered as the Division 8 Presidential Address at the Seventy-Fourth Annual Convention of the American Psychological Association, New York, September 4, 1966. The research described was supported by Public Health Service Research Grant MH-7088 from the National Institute of Mental Health.

THE GRAMMAR OF WH QUESTIONS

Table 1(a) sets out some questions and answers in such a way as to expose the systematic relations existing among them. Consider first the two middle columns. Each question in "normal" form stands by the side of a semantically equivalent, but less frequent, "occasional" form in which the Wh word is in final position and is to be spoken with heavy stress and rising intonation. If someone said: "John will read the telephone book" one might respond "John will read *what?*" and this response is an occasional form. The occasional form for the subject nominal—the first entry—is unlike the others in the column in that the Wh word appears initially which is also the normal position.

The occasional forms (except the subject nominal) are all related to their normal counterparts by the same linguistic transformation. In describing the transformation let us take the occasional form as the base or starting point. The normal form can be created in two steps. The first, illustrated in Table 1(b), moves the Wh word from final position to initial position; we may call this "preposing." The second step, also in Table 1(b), interchanges the subject of the sentence and the auxiliary verb; we may call this "transposing." The two-step transformation will generate all the questions of the second column from their respective counterparts in the first column. It can be formulated more abstractly to work for all Wh questions, whatever the words involved.

Consider now the sentences of the last column which are examples of well-formed answers to the questions standing opposite them. The function relating the pairs of questions, the two middle columns, is easy to see because the members of a pair contain just the same words, and adjustments of order alone will create one member from the other. Question and answer, however, do not contain just the same words. They differ in the words that are italicized in each case and only in these words. The italicized words in the answers may be said to stand in place of the italicized Wh words. In the occasional questions the Wh word stands in the exact sentence locus of the italicized words in the answer. The normal questions, we know, shift the place of the Wh word. The material italicized in the answer is the material most directly responsive to the question. Indeed it is the only essential part of the answer. "What will John read?" "*The book.*" "When will John read?" "*This evening.*" In fact, each interrogative word is a kind of dummy element, an algebraic "x", standing in the place of a particular constituent of the sentence, the constituent identified in the left column of Table 1. The dummy word asks for specification of that constituent. It marks the spot where information is to be poured into the sentence, and the form of the dummy—whether *who, what, where, when,* or *why*—indicates the sort of information required.

Each answer in the rightmost column is simply one of a large number of possible answers. The particular answer does not stand in a one-to-one relation with the particular question, and so is not a simple transform of the question. Grammatically acceptable answers to the question: "What will John read?" are all noun phrases. Acceptable answers to the question: "Where will John read the book?" are all locative adverbials. In general, each kind of Wh question calls for an answer which is an instance of a particular major sentence constituent. These constituents also occur, of course, in sentences which are not responsive to questions.

Table 1 Systematic Relations Among Questions and Answers

Constituents to be Specified	Normal Questions	Occasional Questions[a]	Possible Answers
(a) Constituents, Questions, and Answers			
Subject nominal	"Who will read the book?"	"Who will read the book?"	"John will read the book."
Object nominal	"What will John read?"	"John will read what?"	"John will read the book."
Predicate nominal	"What is that?"	"That is what?"	"That is a book."
Predicate	"What will John do?"	"John will do what?"	"John will read the book."
Locative adverbial	"Where will John read?"	"John will read where?"	"John will read in the library."
Time adverbial	"When will John read?"	"John will read when?"	"John will read this evening."
Manner adverbial	"How will john read?"	"John will read how?"	"John will read slowly."
Explanation clause	"Why will John read?"	"John will read why?"	"John will read because he wants to."

(b) Generating Normal Questions from Occasional Questions

Base. "John will read what?"

Preposing. "What John will read?"

Transposing. "What will John read?"

---

[a]Indicates heavy stress and rising intonation.

A transformational grammar of adult English might represent the systematic relations of Table 1(a) in the following way.[2] Associated with each of the sentence constituents involved there is an abstract dummy element symbolized as "someone," "something," "somewhere," "sometime," etc. The derivation of a Wh question begins in the phrase structure with the selection of the abstract interrogative morpheme. Then, for the constituent which is to be specified in a well-formed answer, the dummy element is selected rather than some particular noun phrase, locative adverbial, time adverbial, or whatever. The base-structure derivation terminates in an underlying string which is just like the string underlying the occasional question, except that the dummy element stands where the interrogative words stand in the occasional questions of Table 1. The underlying strings are also like the full responsive sentences of Table 1, except that they contain the abstract interrogative morpheme and have dummy elements where the responsive sentences have specific instances of the critical constituents. To derive the normal questions from the underlying strings, two transformations are required: one that preposes the dummy element and a second that transposes the order of the subject noun phrase and the first member of the auxiliary. The interrogative words, *who, what, where,* etc. are supplied for both normal and occasional order questions by morphophonemic rules that replace the several dummy elements by the appropriate Wh words.

The question asked in this research is whether there is anything in the spontaneous speech of children which suggests that they learn psychological operations which might be represented by the rules described.

METHOD

SUBJECTS
The *S*s are three preschool children: Adam, Eve, and Sarah. The parents of Adam and Eve have college degrees; Sarah's parents have high-school degrees.

DATA
The research to be described here is carved out of a larger undertaking, a longitudinal naturalistic study of the development of English grammar. The principal data of the study are transcriptions of the child and his mother—occasionally also his father—in conversation at home. For each child we have at least 2 hrs of speech for every month, sometimes as much as 6 hrs.

The study does not cover the same chronological age range for the three children; it does cover the same range in terms of linguistic development. At the start of the study all three children were producing utterances whose average length in morphemes ranged between 1.5 and 2.0. The upper bound on utterance length for all the children was, at the starting point, 4 morphemes. We have used means and ranges of utterance length, simple statistics external to the children's grammar, to

---

[2] This description does not exactly reproduce any version (e.g., Katz and Postal, 1964; Klima, 1964) of the rules that might be used.

mark out an initial developmental period on which our analyses have thus far focused (see Fig. 1). The period begins with the line identified as Level I in Fig. 1 when the mean utterance length was 1.75 morphemes and the upper bound 4. It ends with the line identified as Level V when the mean was 4.0 and the upper bound 13. At the end of this developmental period Eve was only 28 months old, whereas Adam was 42 and Sarah 48. In terms of the utterance-length statistics the rate of the three children may be ordered as: Eve, Adam, Sarah. For this early period, utterance length is a fairly good index of general grammatical level, a much better index than age. Beyond Level V, utterance length is too variable to serve as an index of developmental level. The lines marked by Roman numerals in Fig. 1 fall at nearly equal intervals across the period. They mark five points for which we are writing full generative grammars. The Roman numerals will be useful to us as a term of reference for position within the period.

For the present research the following specific data were examined: all Wh questions from all three children in all transcriptions from Level I through Level V; all child answers to all Wh questions produced by parents in samples of 1400 utterances

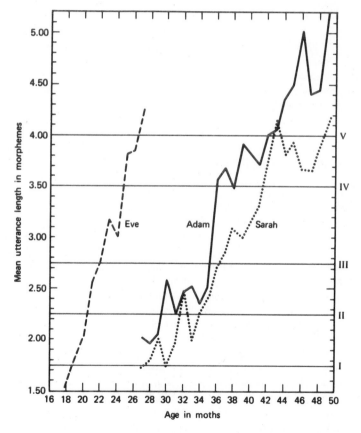

Figure 1. Mean utterance length and age in three children.

each, centering on Levels I, II, III, IV, and V; for Adam all answers to *Why* questions in all samples.

RESULTS

Because this is a naturalistic rather than an experimental study and because the analytic procedures are more linguistic than psychological, the report of results cannot follow the form usual in this journal. It has also been necessary to include in the "Results" section a considerable amount of discussion; the discussion is there to explain the relevance of the several analyses.

WH QUESTIONS BEFORE III

Prior to Level III there is no evidence that the rules we have described are functioning in the child's speech. It is not, however, the case that Wh questions are entirely absent from the child's speech in this period. For example, the predicate nominative question "What is that?" was produced very frequently. Since this question falls within the scope of the grammatical rules we have given, it is necessary to say why its production by the child should not be considered evidence of internal transformational processes.

To begin with, we do not assume that a child's utterance which is, from the adult point of view, a sentence with a certain kind of internal structure, must have that same structure for the child, nor even that it need be a construction for him. It should be remembered that by the time a child attains our Level I and begins to produce what look like short sentences he has already learned several hundred words. These words have no internal structure. They cannot be created by rules of construction. They must be learned as independent routines. Why should not the child, as he enters Level I, assume that language is always going to be this kind of a rote affair and learn a certain number of recurrent sentences as unanalyzed routines as, in effect, longer words?

It is a thing that can be done. At least it can be done by adults. Someone who likes vocal music and does not know any foreign languages may learn the titles or first lines of hundreds of arias and songs as routines. He controls what might be called Operatic Italian and Lieder Deutsch. He is prepared to say such things as "Di Quella Pira l'orrendo fuoco" or "Ging heut' morgen über's feld," and he has a rough idea of the circumstances in which each is appropriate; that is, they have semantic properties for him. But he is not prepared to sort out articles and prepositions or subjects and objects; not prepared to create closely related grammatical variants by changing number, gender, or tense and, therefore, not prepared to make analogical errors. His performance will be accurate, but limited and rigid. We find that the first appearances of a construction in child speech are often similarly accurate but rigid.

The grammatical analysis of any one utterance, the internal structure found in it, is not a function of that utterance alone, but also of the related utterances that are produced. The Prince of Denmark's name "Hamlet," for instance, is an unanalyzed word unless you happen to think of it in connection with *piglet*. Whereupon *Hamlet* cracks in the middle and one may be prepared to construct *hammish, ham-Latin,* and *ham-iron* by false analogy with *piggish, pig-Latin,* and *pig-iron.* It seems reasonable to suppose that given sentences in child speech may similarly yield up their internal structure progressively over time as they are related to an expanding set of other sentences. A child may have to reconstrue an utterance numerous times in the course of his development. It is quite possible that the kind of grammatical knowledge we have as adults, knowledge that relates each sentence to a vast network of other sentences, usually takes much longer to develop than the 3 or 4 yrs which have been claimed to be sufficient for the acquisition of basic grammar.

One sort of Wh question that our three children produced frequently before Level III was "What is that?" In fact, none of them said quite this. One could not hear any *is* in the question; it sounded like "What dat?" The little word *is* is a functor. Auxiliary verbs, prepositions, conjunctions, and inflections, the little words generally, are all functors and functors were mostly missing from utterances at Levels I and II; to be precise, they were missing from 78% of all the contexts requiring them. It is this omission of obligatory functors that we have in mind when we call the speech of this period "telegraphic" (Brown and Fraser, 1963).

The children said "What dat" hundreds of times in I and II; it was their most frequent question. This question was also produced hundreds of times by the mothers of the children though, of course, in a fuller form as "What is that?" or "What's that?" It was the most frequent question of both mothers and children. But there was a difference in the *closely related* questions produced by the two. Mothers produced, in good number, such variants as "What's this?", "What are those?", "Who is he?", "What is his name?", and "What do you think that is?" These were absent from the child's speech. It is the whole set of related forms and also the responses to them which motivate the transformational analysis we have given. For the simple routine "What dat?" no such analysis is needed.

For all of the Wh questions produced before Level III there are considerations which argue that the question was either a routine or a construction of some non-transformational type, but at Level III things changed. We began to find evidence that an underlying grammatical network was in process of creation. By the time the three children attained Level III they were producing numerous declaratives with noun-phrase subjects, main verbs, noun-phrase objects, and locative adverbials. By III also they were correctly answering questions calling for just these constituents about half the time. It seems then that the constituents were organized as such and that the children were able to take a Wh word supplied by a parent as the signal to supply an appropriate constituent member. We expected the next step to be the occasional question, since that question only requires that the dummy element (which becomes a Wh word) be selected from the constituent and supplied in place. In fact, that was not the next step—at least not the next step we could see, the next step in perform-ance. Occasional questions never became frequent for the children, and the first ones appeared somewhat later than III. This may be entirely a matter of grammatical performance, of what the children found "occasion" to say rather than of compe-tence or what they were able to say. As we shall see, the occasions on which these forms are used are special and may simply not have arisen for the child. The Wh questions produced at III were not occasional questions, but were rather a first derivative of such questions, a kind of invention that might develop if the grammatical rules we have described were in process of formation.

PRODUCTION OF A HYPOTHETICAL INTERMEDIATE

Table 2 reintroduces the original sets of grammatical Wh questions, but this time a third form stands between the two adult forms. From the point of view of adult grammar, this form is the actualization of a hypothetical intermediate string. It is the form that would result if morpho-phonemic rules were applied to the underlying string containing a dummy element after preposing, but in the absence of transposing. In short, Adam, Eve, and Sarah, produced a kind of Wh question which is neither the occasional nor the normal form, but an "ungrammatical" creation that lies midway between them.

The children produce two classes of question that might result from preposing without transposing. The first class may be called "Preposing Weak"; the thing that is weak is the evidence that questions of this class are produced by preposing. They are such questions as "What you want?" or "How you open it?" or "What his name?" These can be created, by preposing, from, respectively: "You want what"; "You open it how"; "His name what." However, they can all also be created by telegraphic reduction: "What you want" from "What do you want"; "How you open it" from "How will you open it"; "What his name" from "What is his name." So those of the child's questions which do not contain auxiliaries or the verb *be* or any inflection provide very weak evidence of preposing, and the majority of his questions must at first be of this type since auxiliaries and *be* and inflections are absent from all sentences.

The second class of questions may be called "Preposing Strong" because the questions in this class are strong evidence. There are actually two subvarieties. Suppose we have the questions "What he wants?" and "How he opened it?" The difference from the previous case is that the verbs are inflected. These sentences can be created, by preposing, from "He wants what" and "He opened it how," but there are no adult models from which they can be produced by telegraphic reduction. The

Table 2   The Child's Wh Question as a Hypothetical Intermediate in Adult Grammar

Occasional Questions	Child's Questions	Normal Questions
"Who will read the book?"	"Who will read the book?"	"Who will read the book?"
"John will read what?"	"What John will read?"	"What will John read?"
"That is what?"	"What that is?"	"What is that?"
"John will do what?"	"What John will do?"	"What will John do?"
"John will read where?"	"Where John will read?"	"Where will John read?"
"John will read when?"	[a]"When John will read?"	"When will John read?"
"John will read how?"	[a]"How John will read?"	"How will John read?"
"John will read why?"	[b]"Why John will read?"	"Why will John read?"

Prepose   Transpose

[a] These forms developed later than the others.
[b] This form developed at III for Adam but much later for the girls.

second subvariety of strong evidence consists of questions which include auxiliaries or the verb *be,* such questions as "What you will want?" and "Why you can't open it?" and "What his name is?" These also cannot be derived by reduction from adult models.

In all the samples from Level I to the beginning of Level III Adam produced only three of the Preposing Strong questions; in the samples from III through V he produced 145 of them. The Preposing Strong questions of the latter period include instances requesting specification of object nominals, predicates, locative adverbials, time adverbials, manner adverbials, and causal clauses. Preposing Weak questions began to appear prior to III; there were 60 of them in all, but they were limited to object nominals, predicates, and locative adverbials. From III through V there were more than 400 Preposing Weak questions, and they were of all the major Wh types.

The evidence from Eve and Sarah is less dramatic. Both produced large numbers of questions of the Preposing Weak variety from III through V. Of Preposing Strong questions, Eve produced only seven, and Sarah 18. The low frequency of these questions in Eve's speech is probably due to the fact that she usually omitted inflections and auxiliaries during the critical period and Preposing Strong questions require one or the other. By the time Eve was reliably producing inflections and auxiliaries, she had learned the adult form of the Wh question. In Sarah's case, on the other hand, there was a period in which Preposing Strong questions were produced in good number but it started later than III and lasted beyond V.

There is something more to the difference between Adam and the two girls. The difference in the frequency of Preposing Strong questions is an instance of a more general difference which was highly consistent from I to V. Adam produced ungrammatical forms (of the sort we call "errors of commission" to distinguish them from telegraphic reduction errors) at about four times the rate of either of the girls. From other data we have seen and from what parents tell us, children in general seem to vary greatly in the frequency with which they produce "commission errors"; probably this variation accounts for the fact that particular psychologists and linguists form unlike conceptions of language acquisition from informal observation of their own children. We do not know what causes the individual variation. In the case of the Wh questions, we have seen that when Eve and Sarah made errors they were the same kinds of errors that Adam made. And so it has been in general. For that reason we have assumed that the intellectual processes involved in learning grammar are common to the three children and simply more copiously "externalized" by Adam. We think of him as giving us a richer "print out." We turn now to some evidence of this kind; it was richly present in Adam's speech but not in the speech of Eve and Sarah.

A TRANSFORMATION ACROSS SPEAKERS

The derivation rules we have described for Wh questions presuppose the establishment of the major sentence constituents listed in the leftmost column of Table 1. The best evidence in the child's spontaneous speech that he has such constituents in his ability to make the right sorts of answers to the various Wh questions addressed to him, giving noun phrases in response to *Who* and *What* questions, locatives to *Where* questions, predicates to *What-do* questions, etc. In general, all three children did start giving well-formed answers of a given type before they themselves constructed Wh questions of the corresponding type. However, there was an exception.

In III, Adam began to produce *Why* questions in great quantity. Prior to III he had produced only five; from III through V he produced 269 of them. However in all the samples prior to III, though *Why* questions were quite often addressed to Adam, he produced exactly one response that could possibly be considered appropriate. In the other cases his responses were neither grammatically nor semantically well-formed; they were imitations of the last few words in the question or else quite irrelevant utterances. Eve and Sarah also responded inappropriately to *Why* questions prior to III, but they did not begin to produce *Why* questions at III. For the two girls, production waited upon appropriate response in the case of *Why* questions as in the case of other Wh questions; Adam alone broke the usual pattern.

It is not surprising that *Why* questions were not answered in a semantically sensible way in this early period—by any of the children. This is not surprising when you consider what is involved. A *Why* question such as "Why are the pencils in the refrigerator?" may be said to contain a presupposition; in this case it is the proposition: the pencils are in the refrigerator. This presupposition, as in the present case, often has a certain surprise value. What the *Why* question asks for, roughly speaking, is some salient premise out of a set of premises from which the presupposition can be deduced. In other words, the *Why* question asks a respondent to say something that will help to render logical, to account for or to explain, a rather surprising proposition. In the present instance, "Why are the pencils in the refrigerator?" one might answer "Because I wasn't thinking what I was doing" or, more mysteriously, "To keep them cold." Learning to answer *Why* questions means learning what explanation is.

Adam's *Why* questions beginning with III were "preposed" forms formally identical with his other Wh questions. We believe that these questions, in general, were derived by a single preposing transformation out of underlying strings with dummy elements, but Adam's *Why* questions could not have been derived in this way.[3] How then were they derived?

Much of the time Adam's *Why* questions were closely related to an immediately antecedent declarative from his mother. Table 3 contains a set of these. Some of the changes involved in moving from the sentences on the left to those on the right are not peculiar to *Why* questions. For instance, the telegraphic reduction process which eliminates *was, -ing,* and *a* from the antecedent declarative is general in child speech. Setting aside such nonspecific operations we may say that Adam's *Why* questions are a simple function of his mother's antecedent declaratives: the word *Why* is placed in front of the declarative.

In Table 3 we have also a set of questions with *Why-not* which also have apparent bases in the mother's speech. The transformation involved is a little more complicated than the previous one and not quite so rigid in form. Setting aside these details, what happens is that the words *Why not* are added in initial position to the mother's, usually negative, declarative. Sentences of the *Why-not* type lasted for just 6 weeks but were frequent in that period.

---

[3] Adult *why* questions cannot be derived in a way that is directly parallel to other Wh questions. We have not gone into the details because they do not alter the fact that Adam produced such questions when his responses gave no evidence that he could analyze them correctly with respect either to grammar or semantics.

Table 3   Why and Why not Questions from Adam III With Apparent Bases

Mother's Declaratives	Adam's Why Questions
"He was playing a little tune."	"Why he play little tune?"
"I see a seal."	"Why you see seal?"
"You bent that game."	"Why me bent that game?"
"Well, because she wanted to."	"Why she want to?"
"I think it's resting now."	"Why it's resting now?"

Mother's declaratives	Adam's Why not questions
"I guess I'm not looking in the right place."	"Why not you looking right place?"
"Because you weren't careful."	"Why not me careful?"
"I don't see any."	"Why not you see any?"
"You can't dance."	"Why not me can't dance?"
"You're going to have to buy another one and give it to Ursula because you're breaking that one."	"Why not me break that one?"

Where did Adam's *Why* and *Why not* transformations come from? Once in a long while his mother produced a *Why* question as a direct follow-up of a declarative repeating in her *Why* question the presupposition expressed in the declarative. Probably Adam was attempting to imitate this performance; but his imitation did not come out right. Suppose the antecedent declarative were "He can't dance." Mother would follow this with "Why can't he dance?" Adam's version, on the other hand, would be "Why he can't dance?" Mother not only preposes *Why;* she also transposes the subject and auxiliary. Adam only preposes. Probably he copied according to his present understanding—as children also do when they pretend to drive a car or read a newspaper. Perhaps his imitation took the form it did because that form was close to the general operation that Adam was using with his other Wh questions.

DISCUSSION

Let us entertain the possibility that the derivational rules we have described for Wh questions represent knowledge a child must have if he is to ask and answer the full range of such questions. The rules operate with sentence constituents like the noun phrase and locative adverbial. Therefore, the child must have a way of learning to organize together the diverse items that belong to each such constituent. The rules represent as semantically equivalent each occasional order question and its corresponding normal order question. Therefore, the child must have a way of discovering that these superficially unlike sentences have the same meaning. The derivational rules operate with abstract dummy elements that function as symbols for an unspecified instance of a constituent. Therefore, the child must be able to form from linguistic data of some sort the idea of an "unknown," an algebraic "x," that is of a given type.

The knowledge represented by transformational grammars is not, of course, explicitly taught by parents, but must somehow be derived by the child from linguistic data. To many students of child speech (e.g., McNeill, 1966) it seems that the linguistic data available to the child are so thin that we can only account for his knowledge by assuming that it is, in substantial degree, innate. It is possible, however, that the surface data seem as thin as they do because they are imagined in too static a form, as a set of still photos, unconnected model sentences. It may be as difficult to derive a grammar from unconnected sentences as it would be to derive the invariance of quantity and number from the simple look of liquids in containers and objects in space. The changes produced by pouring back and forth, by gathering together and spreading apart are the data that most strongly suggest the conservation of quantity and number. The changes produced in sentences as they move between persons in discourse may be the richest data for the discovery of grammar.

We can suggest the possibilities by describing the discourse patterns in which the occasional question occurs. The patterns appear in Table 4. The interaction role labeled "Other or Child" is at first played by others whom the child overhears. In the course of the period from I to V the child learns these roles himself and by the end of the period plays them to perfection. If we considered the child's performances in the several roles then we would have evidence of his control of the several kinds of knowledge represented by the derivational rules. If, however, we think of "Other" as in the role and the child as observer and overhearer of the interaction, then the patterns of Table 4 constitute instructional patterns from which grammatical knowledge might be extracted. Our discussion here concentrates on this second reading of Table 4.

The simplest pattern is the first. Mother sometimes finds an entire utterance unintelligible and responds by saying "What?" in a certain way. This "What?" is understood by the Other to be a directive to repeat—to say again What has just been said. The child knows his part in this game from the very start of our records. This first game has no clear instructional value in its own right, but it may be a necessary preliminary to the second game which does have such value. Sometimes the mother finds only a part of an utterance unintelligible and so she repeats what she has understood, replacing the constituent in which unintelligibility has occurred with the right kind of Wh word. Since the Wh word appears in the sentence position of the constituent, that is partially or wholly unintelligible, the result is an occasional question. The *occasion* is unintelligibility in a constituent; the question is a kind of probe. And the response is repetition of just the material displaced. In the simpler first game the response to the question is repetition of the total utterance.

What should exchanges of type II, produced by Other and overheard by the child, be able to teach the child? Fundamentally, the membership of the noun phrase (NP) constituent. Members are just those terms, of whatever shape and complexity, that can be supplanted by *what* in II. This function of tagging NP's is not served by II alone; it is potentially present also in the normal question-and-answer exchange that goes like this: "What do you want?" "I want milk." The important difference is that, in II, underlying relations are much more obvious: "I want milk." "You want what?" "Milk." The Wh word moves into the slot vacated by the particular NP and then the particular NP into the slot vacated by the Wh word. The tagging function implicit in II will work with simpler assumptions about the learning mechanisms than would be required for the normal exchange to work.

Table 4   Forms of Interaction Involving the Occasional Question

I. Say again		
(1) Other or child. "I want milk."	Mother. "What?"	Other or Child. "I want milk."
(2) Other or Child. "Put milk in glass."	Mother. "What?"	Other or Child. "Put milk in glass."
II. Say constituent again		
(1) Other or Child. "I want milk."	Mother. "You want whàt?"	Other or Child. "Milk."
(2) Other or Child. "Put milk in glass."	Mother. "Put milk whère?"	Other or Child. "In glass."
III. Constituent prompt		
(1) Mother. "What do you want?"	Other or Child. ———.	Mother. "You want whàt?"
(2) Mother. "Where will I put it?"	Other or Child. ———.	Mother. "Put it whère?"
IV. Supply antecedent		
(1) Other or Child. "I want it."	Mother. "You want whàt?"	Other or Child. "Milk."
(2) Other or Child. "Put milk there."	Mother. "Put the milk whère?"	Other or Child. "In cup."

The third pattern is initiated by the mother. She asks a question in the normal form, for example "What do you want?" and receives no answer. She then reformulates the question as "You want what?" She is, in effect, turning the question into a sentence-completion item and since mothers typically resort to this prompting form when the normal form has failed, they probably feel that it is easier to process. In our material the occasional form *was* more likely to elicit an appropriate answer than the normal. What should exchanges of type III be able to teach the child? Fundamentally, the equivalence of particular normal and occasional questions. Equivalents are just those questions that replace one another when no answer is forthcoming. Replacement in the absence of adequate response is a discourse relation that may serve generally to link superficially unlike sentences having the same base structure. We think of separable verbs, imperative forms, possessive forms, and others. In our materials it is common to find such a sequence as: "Adam, pick up your toys." "You pick up your toys."

The fourth pattern may be one that helps to create the idea of an abstract dummy element representing an unspecified constituent instance. One sort of word that resembles such an element is the so-called "pro-form," of which the "pro-noun" (e.g., *it*) is most familiar; but there are also pro-locatives (e.g., *here*), pro-verbs (e.g., *do*), pro-temporal adverbs (e.g., *then*), etc. In the fourth game, the mother has heard a sentence which includes a pro-form such as *it*, and she is uncertain of the referent or antecedent of the form. She thereupon repeats what she has understood and substitutes for the pro-form a Wh word. A Wh word standing in for a pro-form is not a request to repeat as it is in the second game. If it were, one would answer "You want what?" with "it." Instead the Wh form is understood to request specification of the antecedent and so the answer is "milk." What could this interaction teach the child who overhears it? It serves, in the first place, to define *it* into the noun phrase constituent since the pro-form can be supplanted by *what* as can all noun phrases. It further signals the special status of the pro-form within the NP since *what* does not elicit repetition, as it does when it replaces other NP's, but, rather, the provision of an earlier specific NP, the antecedent. The fourth pattern also shows that *it* is like *what* in that both can replace every sort of NP, but unlike *what* in that *it* does not request specification. These properties taken together came close to defining the dummy element utilized in the derivation of Wh questions.

A large amount of structural information is revealed with unusual clarity in the interactions of Table 4. The unusual clarity derives in considerable part from the use of the occasional question. This form is structurally intermediate between the normal question and its set of acceptable answers. It must be possible to discover the systematic relations between these extremes without the benefit of the middle term since many children who learn English do not have attentive mothers around to echo them and prompt them. However, it may be easier to discover the relation if the middle term is often heard. It may be accidental, but in our material the occasional form was used much more frequently by the mothers of the two children whose grammatical understanding developed more rapidly. In samples of 7000 utterances, Adam's mother produced occasional questions at the rate of 1 in 57 utterances; Eve's mother at the rate of 1 in 80; Sarah's mother at the rate of only 1 in 146.

What should cause a parent to use a great many "probes" and "prompts," which is what the occasional questions are? It might be a strong conviction that the child can understand what is said to him and a strong concern with understanding what he says. A parent less concerned to communicate and less optimistic about the possibilities may simply let the partially unintelligible sentence go by and may simply give up on unanswered questions. We have previously speculated (Brown and Bellugi, 1964) that this latter sort of parent will, when the child's speech is in the "telegraphic" stage, be less disposed to operate on his speech by the process called "expansion." In our materials, perhaps again accidentally (see Cazden, 1965), it was the mothers of the two more rapidly developing children who had the higher expansion rates. In any event, linguistic environments vary in structural richness and some dimensions of this variation may affect the quality and rapidity of the child's development.

In identifying discourse patterns that could serve to tag constituents, identify equivalents, and help to build dummy elements we have not, of course, given a complete empiricist account of the development of knowledge of the grammar of Wh questions. The problem remains, for example, of explaining how the child generalizes his lists of specifically tagged NP's and pairs of equivalent sentences into the full sets defined by the adult grammar. Innate knowledge may be involved here as elsewhere. However, our very limited exploration of interaction patterns and the information they might convey persuades us that the empiricist position has possibilities that have not yet been explored.

REFERENCES

Bellugi, U. The development of interrogrative structures in children's speech. In K. Riegel (Ed.), *The development of language functions.* Ann Arbor: Michigan Language Development Program, Report No. 8, 1965.

Brown, R., and Fraser, C. The acquisition of syntax. In C. N. Cofer and Barbara S. Musgrave (Eds.), *Verbal behavior and learning.* New York: McGraw-Hill, 1963.

Cazden, C. B. Environmental assistance to the child's acquisition of grammar. Unpublished doctoral dissertation, Harvard Univer., 1965.

Katz, J. J., and Postal, P. M. *An integrated theory of linguistic descriptions.* Cambridge, Mass.: The M.I.T. Press, 1964.

Klima, E. Negation in English. In J. A. Fodor and J. J. Katz (Eds.), *The structure of language: Readings in the philosophy of language.* Englewood Cliffs, N.J.: Prentice-Hall, 1964.

McNeill, D. Developmental psycholinguistics. In F. Smith and G. A. Miller (Eds.), *The genesis of language.* Cambridge, Mass.: The M.I.T. Press, 1966.

Part 5
DEVELOPMENT OF LANGUAGE USE/ CONTENT/ FORM

How language is used depends upon the needs that individuals have in relation to one another and in relation to the contexts in which speaking and hearing behaviors occur. *Michael Halliday (1974)* has focused upon the functions of language as the general basis for a theory of the nature of language and, in turn, as a particular perspective for the study of how children learn language.

Other research has been concerned more specifically with the ways in which children use alternative forms of language according to the requirements of the situation. One of the early studies that looked at alternation in language use was *Madorah Smith's (1934)* study of preschool children's questions, in which it was demonstrated that children speak differently to adults than to other children. *Catherine Garvey (1975)* looked at the different forms of speech that children use with one another and described the interactions between different forms of requests and responses. *David A. Warden (1976)* was concerned with children's ability to take into account information from the linguistic and nonlinguistic context in learning to use the alternative forms of pre-noun articles.

A Sociosemiotic Perspective on Language Development[1]

M. A. K. Halliday

1. This paper is an attempt to interpret the child's learning of his mother tongue as a sociosemiotic process. What is intended here by "sociosemiotic" will be largely left to emerge from the discussion; but in the most general terms it is meant to imply a synthesis of three modes of interpretation, that of language in the context of the social system, that of language as an aspect of a more general semiotic, and that of the social system itself as a semiotic system—modes of interpretation that are associated with Malinowski and Firth, with Jakobson, and with Lévi-Strauss, among others. The social system, in other words, is a system of meaning relations; and these are realized in many ways of which one, perhaps the principal one as far as the maintenance and transmission of the system is concerned, is through their encoding in language. The meaning potential of a language, its semantic system, is therefore seen as realizing a higher level system of relations, that of the social semiotic, in just the same way as it is itself realized in the lexicogrammatical and phonological systems.

A child who is learning his mother tongue is learning how to mean. As he builds up his own meaning potential in language, he is constructing for himself a social semiotic. Since language develops as the expression of the social semiotic it serves at the same time as the means of transmitting it, and also of constantly modifying and reshaping it, as the child takes over the culture, the received system of meanings in which he is learning to share.

How early does this process begin? Many studies of language development have begun at a point when the child's "mean length of utterance" exceeds one word; but this is already too late—the child may have a well-developed semantic system long before he begins to combine words, in fact long before he has any words at all, if by "words" we mean lexical elements taken over from the adult language. At the other end are references to a child having a communication system at the age of a few weeks or even days; no doubt he does communicate more or less from birth, but there are significant senses in which this communication differs from language, and it is

From *Bulletin of the School of Oriental & African Studies,* **37,** 1, 1974 Reprinted by permission of the school of Oriental and African Studies, University of London.

[1] This paper was written during my tenure of a fellowship at the Center for Advanced Study in the Behavioral Sciences, Stanford, California. I should like to express my gratitude to the Center for the opportunities thus afforded.

specifically language that we are concerned with here because it is language that enables him to construct a social semiotic. This does not mean that a child has no language until he has a linguistic system in the adult sense, but that there are certain features in respect of which we can say that, before a given stage, the child has not got language, and after this stage he has.

The material for the present discussion is taken from a fairly intensive study of the language development of one child, Nigel, from birth to two-and-a-half years. The early stages have been described to a certain degree of detail in two recent papers; [2] we shall not attempt here to recapitulate the description, but shall be concerned rather with its interpretation. However, the relevant facts concerning Nigel's language development will be presented and incorporated into the discussion.

With Nigel, the breakthrough into language occurred at the age of about nine months. At nine months old, he had a meaning system of five elements, of which two were vocalized and three realized as gestures. The two that were vocalized were

[ø] mid-low falling to low	"let's be together"
[ø] mid falling to low	"look (it's moving)"

The three realized gesturally were

grasping object firmly	"I want that"
touching object lightly [sic]	"I don't want that"
touching person or relevant object firmly	"do that (with it) again (e.g. make it jump up in the air)"

Here the child was on the threshold of language. Between nine and ten-and-a-half months, he developed a linguistic system. This system is set out in Fig. 1 (a). The gestures, incidentally, disappeared by the age of twelve months.

On what grounds are we calling this a "language"? It has no words and no structures. It is very clearly not a linguistic system in the adult sense, since it lacks the defining characteristic of such a system: it is not tri-stratal. An adult linguistic system has three strata, or levels: a semantics, a lexicogrammar (or "syntax"), and a phonology. This is what distinguishes it from all animal communication systems, which as far as we know are bi-stratal only. In similar fashion Nigel's system at this stage is bi-stratal; it has a semantics and a phonology, but nothing in between. Whether for this reason we should or should not use the terms "semantics" and "phonology" is not a major issue; let us say that the child has a bi-stratal proto-language consisting of meaning and sound, or a content and an expression. The elements of the system are signs in the sense of content-expression pairs.

---

[2] See M. A. K. Halliday, "Early language learning: a sociolinguistic approach," in William P. McCormack and Stephen Wurm (ed.), *Language as bisocial process: papers from the XIth International Congress of Anthropological and Ethnological Sciences, Chicago, 1973,* in press; and 'Learning how to mean', in Eric and Elizabeth Lenneberg (ed.), *Foundations of language development: a multidisciplinary approach,* UNESCO and International Brain Research Organization, in press. The figures in the present paper are reproduced from these two sources.

The reasons for regarding this as a form of language are twofold. In the first place, it has two positive features which can be used as criterial: systematicity, and functionality. There is a systematic relation between the content and the expression, and the content is interpretable in functional terms. In the second place, it shows continuity of development into the adult system. Of these it is the second point that is the more important, since it determines the relevance of the first; we know that these properties are important because they provide the essential links, the means whereby a child can grasp the nature of the adult language and interpret it as an extension of what he already has. The continuity of development, with many children (of whom Nigel was one), is not immediately apparent, if one is looking mainly at the outward manifestation of the system; but it is brought out by a consideration of the meanings, once we place these in something like the present sociosemiotic context.

2. In the language represented by Fig. 1, the expressions are clearly not, for the most part, imitations of words or any other elements of the adult language. They are the child's own invention. In general we cannot say where they come from; "ding-dong," "bow-wow," "yo-heave-ho", and other such classical sources are probably all represented somewhere. The point is simply that they are distinct from each other; although the IPA alphabet is not, at this stage, a relevant form of notation—what is needed is a prosodic or postural notation specially designed for developmental studies—it serves to suggest what was in fact the case, that there was surprisingly little neutralization of semantic contrasts by overlap in the expression.[3] It is likely that some children make more use of imitation in the expressions of their proto-language, using forms of words from the adult language; this is a source of difficulty for the investigator, since such forms are not at this stage being used as words (which would imply a lexicogrammatical stratum) but merely as expressions. A possible example of this is Nigel's [bø] "I want my toy bird"; the expression may be an imitation of the sound of the adult pronunciation of "bird" but it is not the word "bird"—there are no words at this stage. It does not matter, in fact, where the expressions come from; their function is to signal the meanings of the child's own system.

Where then do the meanings come from? These likewise are not imitations of meanings in the adult language. They are interpretable in functional terms. The content of the system is derived from what it is the child is making the system do for him. Hence in interpreting the content we need to start with some functional-semantic hypothesis, some notion of the developmentally significant functions that, on general sociocultural grounds (as well as from our knowledge of the nature of the adult language), we should expect to determine the content structure of the child's proto-language. For this purpose a simple framework was adopted of six basic functions: instrumental ("I want"), regulatory ("do as I tell you"), interactional ("me and you"), personal ("here I come"), heuristic ("tell me why"), and imaginative ("let's

---

[3] On questions of the transcription of child language, see the papers of the Child Language Project at Stanford University under the direction of Charles A. Ferguson; e.g. C. N. Bush, *On the use of the IPA in transcribing child language: a theoretical orientation and methodological approach*, Stanford University Committee on Linguistics, 1973. Up to the present this work relates to the mother tongue stage, beginning at what I have called Phase II, but the principles it embodies could be extended to apply to Phase I.

pretend").[4] The instrumental is language as a demand for goods and services, in the satisfaction of material needs; the regulatory is language used to control the behavior of those around, and adapt it to one's wishes. These are the more pragmatic functions. There is also a pragmatic element in the interactional, since it embodies the child's need for human contact; but here the meanings are the expression of the interaction itself, rather than of a demand for it. In its personal function, language is the expression of the child's own identity, his separateness from, and uniqueness with respect to, the environment of people and things; and this creates the context for the heuristic function, which is language in the exploration of the environment that is defined as the non-self. Finally language may function in the creation of an environment, an environment of the imagination that begins as pure sound and works its way up the linguistic system to become a "let's pretend" world of songs and rhymes and stories.

Meaning is meaning with respect to one or other of these functions. The meanings which a small child expresses in his proto-language may be glossed by locutions in the adult language such as "do that again" or "nice to see you, and shall we look at this together?"; but these—like the phonetic notations referred to above—are overly specific. We cannot adequately represent what the child means by wordings such as these, or even by semantic features drawn from the adult language. What is needed is, again, some sort of semantic representation that is analogously prosodic or postural. The content systems in Fig. 1 are an attempt to express the meanings in systemic terms, as sets of options deriving from the functions of the initial hypothesis. The assertion is that within each of these functions the child develops a small but open-ended, indefinitely expandable, range of alternatives, and that the total set of these sets of options constitutes his semantic system at the stage in question. The functions themselves are the prototypic social contexts of the child's existence, simple semiotic structures through which he relates to and becomes a part of the social system.

If they are viewed in this light it is easy to see that there is no place for anything like an "informative" function. The use of language in the sense of "I've got something to tell you," which tends to obsess adults, perhaps because they have learnt it with such difficulty, is irrelevant to a small child; it has no direct social meaning. It is also inaccessible to him, since it is wholly intrinsic to language; it is a function that derives from the nature of language itself. The other six are all extralinguistic; they arise, and can be realized, independently of language, though language immeasurably extends the meaning potential that is associated with them. Nigel began with four of them simultaneously, the instrumental, regulatory, interactional, and personal; after about four or five months he added the imaginative and, incipiently at least, the heuristic. Thus the functions that had been predicted were all clearly recognizable; but unlike what might have been expected, there was no clear developmental ordering among them such that the more pragmatically oriented functions developed before the others. Non-pragmatic elements were as prominent from the start; and this became very significant when the child moved on into the next phase.

----

[4] See M. A. K. Halliday, "Relevant models of language," *Educational Review (University of Birmingham)*, XXII, 1969; reprinted in *Explorations in the functions of language* (Explorations in Language Study), London, Edward Arnold, 1973.

Every element showing systematic sound-meaning correspondence, and interpretable in these functional terms (these two criteria in fact defined the same set), was entered in the system, provided it was observed operationally (in a context in which it was doing a job of meaning) with a certain minimum frequency. In practice throughout the six months or so of the "proto-language" phase, which we designate Phase I, all but two or three of the sounds provisionally interpreted as meaningful were observed with far more than minimal frequency, and, surprisingly perhaps, there was hardly any difficulty in identifying what was language and what was not. Practicing was excluded, on the grounds that the learning of a system is not a function of that system; Nigel did very little practicing as such, but made very extensive operational use of the resources he had. (It may be that practicing is never associated with the proto-language; Nigel provides no evidence either way, since he did not practice in Phase II either.) The system was reinterpreted and written up at intervals of six weeks, this being the interval which appeared to be optimal—neither so short that the account would be distorted by random non-occurrences nor so long that the system could not be seen in course of change. The correspondence with the child's age is as follows (NL-1 means "Nigel's Language 1" and so on):

NL-1	NL-2	NL-3	NL-4	NL-5
9–10½	10½–12	12–13½	13½–15	15–16½
NL-6	NL-7	NL-8	NL-9	NL-10
16½–18	18–19½	19½–21	21–22½	22½–24

There is a marked break between NL-5 and NL-6; NL-6 may be regarded as the beginning of what we are calling "Phase II." Much of the remaining discussion will center around an interpretation of what it is that is happening in Phase II; before coming on to this, however, I would like to insert a brief note about the concept of situation or social context.

3. A child is learning how to mean; but meaning takes place in an environment, not in solitude. What is the nature of the environment? On the one hand, it may be thought of as "what is going on at the time": the situation in which the language is actualized and comes to life. On the other hand, it may be conceived of as the social system, with the child himself in the middle of it.

Malinowski took account of both; he called the former the "context of situation" and the latter the "context of culture." Because of his interest in pragmatic speech, his characterization of the situation tended to be rather too concrete, a kind of scenario with props and stage directions; Firth replaced this with a more abstract account which allows us to interpret the situation as a generalized situation type, or social context. The situation is the environment of the text, of the meanings that are selected or "actualized" in a given instance. The culture is the environment of the system, of the total meaning potential. (Hence Firth did not develop Malinowski's context of culture; his focus of attention was not on the potential but on the typical actual.) So we can start from the concept of "situation" and define the context of culture as the set of possible situation types. This is equivalent to interpreting the social system as the total set of possible social contexts.

There is, however, another possible perspective, one that is complementary to this one. We can choose to define the situation by reference to the culture, instead of the other way round. We have defined the culture as a system of meanings, a semiotic system. A situation (always in the generalized sense of "situation type") is then a semiotic structure deriving from that system.

The various "ethnographies of speaking" that attempt to describe the relevant patterns of speech settings can be interpreted and evaluated in this light, as analyses of the semiotic structure of the situation, in its capacity as a determinant of the text.[5] The meaning potential that a child learns to express in the first phase serves him in functions which exist independently of language, as features of human life at all times and in all cultures. But, at the same time, and in the same process, he is constructing for himself a social semiotic, a model of the culture of which he is himself a member; and he is doing so out of the semiotic properties of situations, situations in which he is a participant or an observer. The understanding of this process constitutes what Berger refers to as the "microsociology of knowledge"— the social construction of reality from countless microsemiotic encounters.[6] Nigel at nine months has already embarked on this venture. His meaning potential develops as the representation of the social system and of his own place in it.

In this way a child, in the act of learning language, is also learning the culture through language. The semantic system which he is constructing becomes the primary mode of transmission of the culture. But we can also turn this point back on itself and ask the question, how has the place of language in the social system determined the nature and evolution of language? However remote this question may seem from current preoccupations—and it would not have been thought fanciful 100 years ago—it is one that we may well bear in mind while considering how, and more especially why, the child makes a transition from his own proto-language into the adult linguistic system.

4. Nigel continued to expand his Phase I language, extending the meaning potential within the four functions instrumental, regulatory, interactional, and personal, and later adding to these a small range of meanings in the other functions. The number of distinct meanings increased as follows.

NL-1	NL-2	NL-3	NL-4	NL-5
12	21	29	32	52

Fig. 1(*b*) represents the system at NL-5 (15–16½ months); the number of options under each heading is now

instrumental: 10   regulatory: 7   interactional: 15   personal: 16

the remaining four being "imaginative." Looking at the system with hindsight from the standpoint of its later development, we come to see that at least one of the

---

[5] For discussion of the situation as a semiotic structure cf. M. A. K. Halliday, "Talking one's way in: a sociolinguistic perspective on language and learning," in W. Bryan Dockrell (ed.), *Papers of the SSRC Seminar on Language and Learning, Edinburgh, 1973*, London, Heinemann, in press.

[6] See Peter L. Berger, "Marriage and the construction of reality," in Hans Peter Dreitzel (ed.), *Recent sociology, 2: patterns of communicative behavior*, New York, Macmillan, 1970; also Peter L. Berger and Thomas Luckmann, *The social construction of reality*, London, Allen Lane, the Penguin Press, 1967.

options should really have been interpreted as heuristic in function. By this time, however, the functional basis of the system is itself beginning to evolve into a new phase.

By NL-5, therefore, the system has expanded to something like four or five times its original measure of potential. Essentially, though, it is still a system of the same kind. The meanings continue to form a simple semantic taxonomy—with one small but extremely significant exception, which foreshadows things to come.

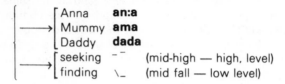

Here we have for the first time the intersection of two semantic systems, two simultaneous sets of options in free combination. Apart from this, Nigel can still only mean one thing at once.

Then, with quite dramatic suddenness, Nigel abandoned the glossogenic process. He stopped creating language for himself, and began to use the one he heard around him. This stage we shall refer to as Phase II. It corresponds to what is more usually regarded as the beginnings of language, because it is the point at which vocabulary (in the true sense, as distinct from imitations of word sounds) and structure start to appear; but from the present standpoint it is already transitional.

The changes that characterize Phase II can be summarized very briefly. Nigel learned grammar, and he learned dialogue. That is to say: (1) he replaced his own bi-stratal (content, expression) system by the adult tri-stratal system (content, form, expression, i.e., semantics, lexicogrammar, phonology); (2) he replaced his own one-way (monologue) system by the adult two-way system (dialogue). These processes began in NL-6 and were well established in NL-7 (18–19 months). They are the two critical steps into the adult linguistic system; we will explain and illustrate them in turn.

5. Lexicogrammar is, in folk-linguistic terminology, the level of "wording" in language that comes between meaning and sounding; it is grammar and vocabulary. Meanings are no longer output directly as sounds; they are first coded in lexicogrammatical forms and then recoded in sounds. The outward sign of a grammar is structures; that of a vocabulary is words, or lexical items. There is no very clear line between the meanings that are coded as grammatical structures and those that are coded as lexical items; the latter represent, as a rule, the more specific or more "delicate" options. By the end of NL-7 Nigel had a vocabulary probably amounting to some 200 words, together with the structures represented in the following examples: gɹì . . . gɪ̄ là *green . . . green light;* dã . . . da: dèbī *tiny toothpick;* ɔlow̄ tḭːkò: *hello teacosy;* gɪ̄: kà *green car.* All these appeared on the same day, which was the first day on which he had used any structures at all (on the criterion of intonation, i.e. composite forms on a single tone contour). These were followed next day by gɹːīːkà . . . blːu; kà . . . an̄ʰ *green car . . . blue car . . . another;* m̄ɔ: mì? *more meat;* m̄ɔ: mì? plī *more meat please;* t'u: bɔ̀ɔkɷ *two books;* and within a week by *green peg, more omelet, two* plus various items including *lorries, trains,* and *helicopters.* In

addition there were the following narratives, which form structures at the semantic level but not yet at the lexicogrammatical level.

ⁿdàⁿdā . . . pàɪ . . . [blowing]Φ ʷ . . . tɷya   *uncle . . . pipe . . . smoke . . . (like) train*

ʔɔʔ . . . tɹ̩l . . . tɛ̃əwè: . . . ōgɔ̀ . . . bābā   *broken . . . tree . . . take-away . . . all-gone . . . bye-bye*

bɪ̄kè . . . ōdlə . . . mɪ̃q . . . dàdà   *breakfast . . . oh-dear (I'm hungry) . . . milk . . . (and some for) daddy*

tʃɷ̀yā . . . là . . . gɪ̀ɪ   *train . . . light . . . green*

At this stage, the lexical items combine freely in semantic structures. They combine with partial freedom into grammatical structures; *more,* for example, combines freely with items of food, including countables such as *more cherries,* but it does not yet combine with *cars* or *trains.* The explanation of all this will appear below.

6. Dialogue is the taking on oneself, and assigning to others, of social roles of a special kind, namely those that are defined by language—the speech roles of ordering, questioning, responding, and the like. Nigel had launched into dialogue just four weeks before his first structures appeared; here are some early examples.

Nigel: ádᵛdà "What's that?." Mother: That's a plug. Nigel [imitating]: lɪkobā . . . . . ádᵛdà. Mother: That's a chain. Nigel: t̪ʉ̄t̪ʉ̄. Mother: No—not a train, a chain. Nigel [pointing to line drawn in side of bottle] ádᵛdà. Mother: That's a line. Nigel: ɹa: ɹa: ff [roaring, i.e. "a lion"].

Mother: Take the toothpaste to Daddy and go and get your bib. Nigel [doing so] dàd ā . . . nɪnɔnɪnɔ . . . t̪ʉ̄t̪ʉ̄ "Daddy . . . (give) noddy (toothpaste to him) . . . (get the bib with the) train (picture on it)."

Anna: We're going out for a walk, and we'll go and get some fish. Nigel [hopefully]: tɪkɷ "(And we'll get some) sticks." Anna: No, we're not getting any sticks today. Nigel [plaintively]: Lɔᵘ "(Aren't we going to lookfor) holes?" or "(What can I put in the) holes?."

Nigel [coming into study]: ɔ̄ɛ̃ɛ̄ɔ̄ bɷ̀uwɷ̀u "I want to (come and) draw (etymologically = "draw dogs") (with you)." Father: No, I'm working. Nigel: dādⁱkədà̀ "(You're) playing the tabla." Father: No I'm not playing dādɪkədà̀; I'm writing. Nigel: bɷ̀uwɷ̀u "(You're) drawing."

Mother [pointing]: Who's that? Nigel: n:ā "Anna." Mother [pointing to self]: And who's that? Nigel: m̄ā "Mummy." Mother [pointing to Nigel]: And who's that? Nigel: n̄ɪ̄ "Nigel."

Father: Where's my pudding? [Five minutes later it is brought in.] Nigel: dɛ̀ə "There."

If we analyze these specimens of dialogue in terms of Nigel's speech role potential, we find that he can:

1. respond to a WH- question (provided he knows that the answer is already known to the questioner);
2. respond to a command, acting it out and verbalizing as he does so;
3. respond to a statement, signalling attention and continuing the conversation;
4. respond to a response to something he himself has said; and
5. ask a WH- question (but only one, namely "What's that?").

Function	Content Systems		Articulation	Expression Tone	Gross
Instrumental →	demand, general		nā—	mid	give me that.
	demand, specific (toy bird)		bø	mid	give me my bird
Regulatory →	command, normal		e (mṇ)	mid	do that (again)
	command, intensified			wide: ff	do that right now!
Interactional →	initiation	normal (friendly)	ø: 'dø. 'dɔ	narrow mid	nice to see you (and shall we look at this together?)
		intensified (impatient)	ə̃n̄n̄e		nice to see you—at last!
	response		ɛ: ə	mid	yes, it's me
Personal →	participation →	interest — general	ø	low	that's interesting
		specific (movement)	'dɔ. bø: ø	low	look, it's moving (?a dog. birds)
	withdrawal →	pleasure — general	a	low	that's nice
		specific (taste)	n̄n̄	low	that tastes nice
			'g Iʌ	narrow low	I'm sleepy

Fig. 1(a) NL-1: Nigel at 9-10½ months.

Note: all above on falling tone: mid- midfall, narrow low- lowfall over narrow interval. etc.

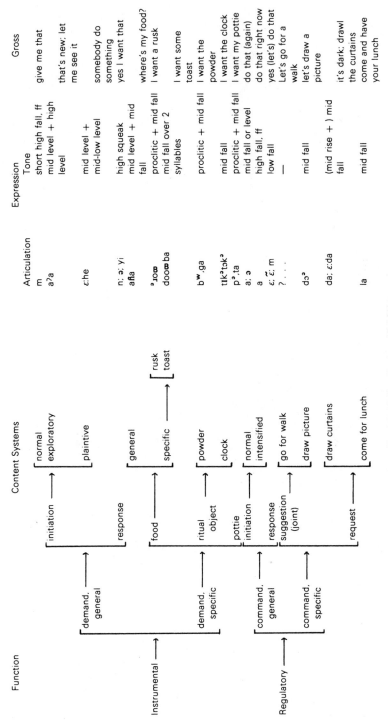

Fig. 1(b) NL-5: Nigel at 15-16½ months

265

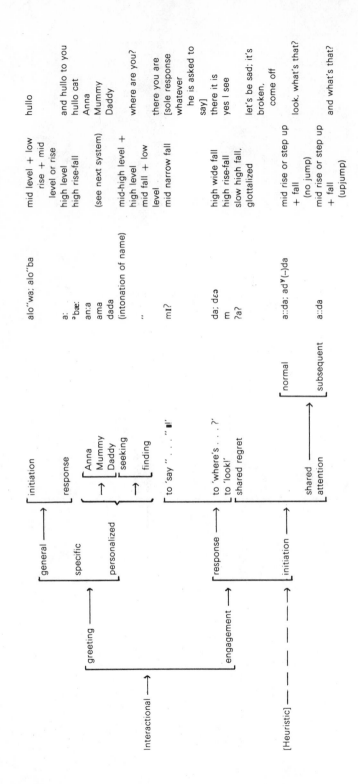

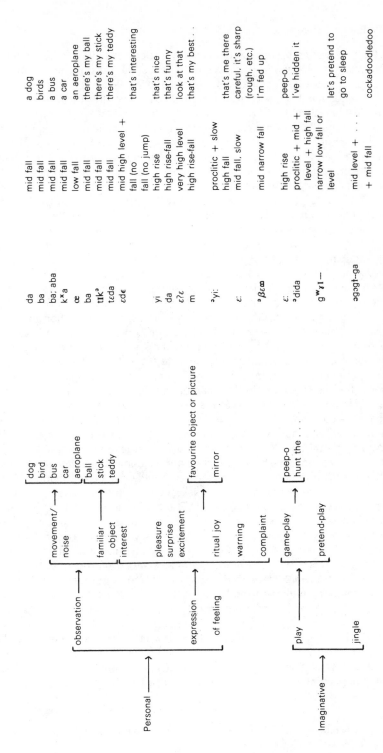

Fig. 1(b) NL-5: Nigel at 15-16½ months (continued)

267

This last is the only option he has for demanding a specifically linguistic response, and thus for initiating dialogue. It is important to stress that dialogue is interpreted as the exchange of speech roles; that is, it is language in functions that are created and defined by language itself, such as asking and answering questions. A response such as "Yes, do" to "Shall I . . . ?," or "Yes, I do" to "Do you want . . . ?," is not an instance of dialogue, since the responses are still extralinguistic in function; they express simple instrumental or regulatory meanings. Early in Phase I Nigel could already mean "yes" and "no" in such contexts, where they were fully interpretable in terms of his elementary functions; but he could not answer a yes/no question—because he could not use language to give information, to communicate experience to someone who had not shared that experience with him. It is for exactly the same reason that he cannot answer a WH- question unless he sees that the answer is available to the questioner also.

Communicating new information is a very sophisticated notion, since it is a function of language that is wholly brought about and defined by language itself. Hence it is conceptualizable only at a very late stage. Nigel did not grasp it until toward the end of Phase II, when he was completing the transition to the adult language system. When he did grasp it, he superimposed a further semantic distinction of his own, between imparting information that was new and verbalizing information that was already known and shared. Since at this time he controlled the grammatical system of declarative / interrogative, but not yet the semantic system of statement / yes/no question, he adapted the grammatical distinction to his own use; the verbalizing of shared information was realized by the declarative and the communicating of new information by the interrogative. So, for example, on being given a present by his uncle, he turned to his mother and said *Uncle gave you some marbles* (i.e., "you saw that Uncle gave me some marbles"; *you* = "me" regularly throughout this stage). He then ran out to show his father, who had not been present, and said *Daddy, did Uncle give you some marbles?* (i.e., "you didn't see, but Uncle gave me some marbles").

If utterances such as those we have illustrated are not communicating information, what are they doing? In the context of culture, of course, they are communicating information. As Mary Douglas puts it, "If we ask of any form of communication the simple question what is being communicated? The answer is: information from the social system. The exchanges which are being communicated constitute the social system."[7] This is exactly the social semiotic perspective which we are adopting here. But in the context of situation their function is not the communication of information to a hearer for whom it is new. Some of the utterances the child produces are clearly pragmatic in function: *"more meat"* means "I want some more meat." But others cannot be accounted for in this way, and we must look for some other interpretation. First, however, let us attempt an interpretation of the significance of the second phase in Nigel's language development. Why does the child abandon his own language-creating efforts in favor of the mother tongue? And, in particular, why does he take the specific steps of building in a grammar and learning dialogue?

7. The essential motivation behind both these moves can be seen in the inherent functional limitations of the child's Phase I system. It can no longer meet the require-

---

[7] Mary Douglas, "Do dogs laugh? A cross-cultural approach to body symbolism," *Journal of Psychosomatic Research*, xv, 1971, 389.

ments of his own social semiotic. Does this mean that it cannot express enough differentiation in meaning? In the long run, this is certainly true; but when Nigel moved into Phase II he was still very far from having exhausted the potential of his Phase I system—he could have added many more elements without undue strain on his own articulatory or his hearer's auditory resources. There is, however, a much more fundamental limitation on the proto-language, which is that it is impossible to mean more than one thing at once. This can be done only by the interpolation of a lexicogrammatical stratum. The reason for this is that, in order for different meanings to be mapped on to one another and output in the form of single, integrated structures, there has to be an intermediate level of coding in between the meanings and the sounds. This function is served by the lexicogrammar.

So for example when Nigel says [lɔ̌ᵘ], the meaning is already complex: something like "there are holes—and something must be done about them." His experience as an observer of holes is expressed in the articulation [lɔ̌ᵘ], and his personal stake in the matter, his own intrusion into the situation, is expressed by the rising tone and plaintive voice quality. This is possible only because he now has a coding level of grammar and lexis, a relational system lying not at the semantic or phonological interfaces but at the heart of language, a level of purely linguistic abstractions serving as an intermediary in what Lamb calls the "transduction" of meanings into sounds.[8] This system can accept meanings deriving from different functional origins and encode them into unified lexicogrammatical constructs, which are then output as "wordings"—patterns of ordering, word selections, intonation patterns, and the like.

The example we have just given shows this functional semantic mapping in its simplest form. The expression [lɔ̌ᵘ] represents a combination of the two most general functional components of meaning, the *ideational* (Bühler's "representational," Lyons's "cognitive," Hymes's "referential") and the *interpersonal* (Bühler's "conative" and "expressive," Lyons's "social," Hymes's "socioexpressive" or "stylistic").[9] The former is the observer function of language; it is the speaker reflecting on his environment. The latter is the intruder function of language; it is the speaker acting on his environment. It is a property of the adult language that it enables the speaker to do both these things at once—in fact it makes it impossible for him not to, though in infinitely varied and indirect ways toward which Nigel's utterance is no more than the first crude striving. But essentially this is what he is striving after: a plurifunctional system that enables him to mean more than one thing at once. It is for this that he needs a grammar.

By the same token, he needs a grammar in order to be able to engage in dialogue. Dialogue involves just this kind of functional mapping, of content elements on to

---

[8] Lamb no longer uses this term. But the view that we are adopting here of the levels, or "strata," of the linguistic system, and the relationship among them, is that of Lamb's stratification theory, which would provide a very plausible interpretation of the developmental processes involved. See, for example, Sydney Lamb's discussion in H. Parret, *Discussing language*, The Hague, Mouton, in press.

[9] Karl Bühler, *Sprachtheorie: die Darstellungsfunktion der Sprache*, Jena, Fischer, 1934; John Lyons, "Human language," in R. A. Hinde (ed.), *Non-verbal communication*, Cambridge, University Press, 1972; Dell H. Hymes, "Linguistic theory and the functions of speech," in *International days of sociolinguistics*, Rome, 1969.

situational elements; the same structure expresses both an ideational meaning, in terms of the speaker's experience, and an interpersonal meaning in terms of the speaker's adoption and assignment of speech roles. In the adult linguistic system, this requirement is embodied in the systems of transitivity and of mood. Transitivity expresses the speaker's experience of process in the external world, and mood expresses his structuring of the speech situation; as sets of options, the two are quite independent, but they combine to form integrated lexicogrammatical structures. Nigel is still far from having either a transitivity system or a mood system. But he is beginning to interact linguistically, and to build up a potential for dialogue.

Thus it is not the fact that his Phase I "proto-language" cannot be understood by other people that provides the impetus for the move into Phase II. There is no sign yet that he wants to interact verbally with people other than those in his immediate environment, who understand him perfectly well; but he does want to interact with them, and his proto-language does not allow for this. A simple exchange of verbal signals can, of course, be prolonged indefinitely in the proto-language, and often is; but it is impossible to engage in dynamic role play. The system cannot provide for the adoption, assignment, acceptance, and rejection of speech roles.

Here is one brief example showing the sort of multiple meaning and multiple role-playing that Nigel has mastered by the time he is well on into Phase II; it is taken from NL-9 (21–22½ months): Nigel [having fallen and hurt himself earlier in the day; feeling his forehead]: ád^{v}à "What' that?." Father: That's plaster, sticking plaster. Nigel: *Tell Mummy take it off* "(I'm going to) . . . " . . . [running to Mother] *Take it off* "take it off."

8. We can now interpret the strategy that Nigel adopted as the basis of Phase II. In § 4 above we cited the first instance of the breakdown of the simple semantic taxonomy that characterizes the Phase I language: the combination of naming a person (one person or another) and interacting with that person (in one way or another), e.g. [ǎn:ǎ] "Anna, where are you?." This is exactly the same phenomenon as was illustrated in the last section, where the meaning of [lɔ͜ᵘ] was "there are holes —and something must be done about them"; another early example was [k^{v}e:k^{v}], said on seeing a cake in the middle of the table and meaning "that's cake—and I want some!"

All these provide a preview of what is to come. If we look at the meanings of Nigel's Phase II utterances in functional terms, we find him apparently generalizing, out of the initial set of developmental functions which were recognizable in Phase I, two broad functional categories, or "macro-functions" as we might call them: one of them demanding a response, the other not. The response that is demanded is, at first, in terms of goods and services: "I want that," "do that again," and so on; increasingly, however, it becomes a demand for a verbal response, e.g., "what's that?" The other type of utterance, which demands no response, involves at first the observation, recall, or prediction of phenomena seen or heard: "I can see/hear," "I saw/heard," "I shall see/hear"; it then extends to narrative and descriptive contexts.

The first category clearly derives from the instrumental and regulatory systems of Phase I, and also in part the interactional; functionally we can label it pragmatic. The developmental history of the second category was much more difficult to follow; but it can be shown to derive, by an interesting and indirect route, from the interactional, in its non-pragmatic aspect, the personal, and the heuristic functions—the last of which we can see emerging in the later stages of Phase I when we look back at these from a Phase II vantage point. In brief, this appears to happen somewhat as follows. Nigel begins (NL-1–2) by using some external object, typically a picture, as a channel for interaction with others; cf. the gloss "nice to see you—and shall we look at this together?" (Fig. 1 (a)). He then (NL-3) separates the interactional from the personal element, the former developing into forms of greeting and the latter into "self" expressions of interest, pleasure, and the like. Then, as the split between the self and the environment becomes clearer, the interactional element reappears on a higher level, the attention being focused on an external object which the other person is required to name (NL-4-5): "Look at this—now you say its name" (Fig. 1 (b)). At first this is used only when the object is familiar—again, typically a picture—and the name already (receptively) known; it then splits into two meanings, one of which is a demand for a new name, one that is not known, the "what's that?" form illustrated earlier. The words that name objects are at the same time being learned productively, and are then used in the encoding of expressions of personal interest and involvement: "look, that's a . . . !" Thus out of a combination of the personal (self-oriented) and the heuristic (environment-oriented) functions of Phase I there arises a generalized non-pragmatic mode of meaning which is in contrast to the pragmatic mode identified above.

What is the function of such "non-pragmatic" utterances? Can we characterize their meaning in positive terms? Lewis already observed this distinction some 40 years ago; he uses the term "manipulative" for the pragmatic function, and labels the other "declarative."[10] This is adequate as a description, but does not really explain what these utterances mean. It seems, however, that their function is essentially a learning one. It arises, like the pragmatic function, by a process of generalization from the initial set of extrinsic functions of Phase I; and it is complementary to it, as reflection is to action. We can perhaps appropriately refer to it as the mathetic function; it is language enabling the child to learn about his social and material environment, serving him in the construction of reality. This function is realized, in the first instance, through the child's observing, recalling, and predicting the objects and events which impinge on his perceptions.

At the beginning of Phase II, all utterances are either one thing or the other: either pragmatic or mathetic. And when we look at the new lexical items coming into Nigel's system in NL-6-7, we find that the majority, probably more than three-quarters of them, come in in the context of the mathetic function, not the pragmatic. (Moreover, each word, and each structure, is at first specialized to one function only; they are not used in both.) This is partly explainable by reference to the greater situational dependence of the pragmatic mode; where the meaning is "I want. . . ," the speaker can often point to what it is he wants, so that Nigel continued to use the unmarked instrumental and regulatory options of Phase I well on into Phase II. But the observation also recalls Lévi-Strauss's remark that in all cultures "the universe is an object of thought at least as much as it is a means of satisfying needs."[11] We find this to be already a determining factor in the child's language development; language evolves

---

[10] See M. M. Lewis, *Infant speech: a study of the beginnings of language* (International Library of Psychology, Philosophy and Scientific Method), London, Routledge and Kegan Paul, 1936; second ed., enlarged, 1951.

[11] Claude Lévi-Strauss, *The savage mind*, London, Weidenfeld and Nicolson, 1966.

in the context of his thinking about the universe no less than in the context of his exploiting it.

9. It is largely thanks to Nigel himself that this aspect of his Phase II strategy, the contrast between a mathetic and a pragmatic mode, can be asserted with relative confidence. At a particular moment—the last week of NL-7, one week after the structural explosion discussed in § 5—he adopted a systematic distinction in intonation which he then kept up for some months. It was noticeable that, from that date on, every utterance had one tone contour, and that the tone was either clearly rising or clearly falling in every instance. The interpretation soon became apparent. All falling tone utterances were mathetic in function, and all rising tone utterances were pragmatic in function. Some examples from NL-7–8 follow.

Pragmatic

chuffa stúck "the train's stuck; help me get it out"
high wáll "let me jump off and you catch me"
háveit "I want that"
play ráo "let's play at lions"
squeeze órange "squeeze the orange"
bounce táble "I want to bounce the orange on the table, can I?"
water ón "I want the water turned on"
Anna help gréenpea "Anna help me to eat the green peas"
Dada come overthere nów "Daddy come over there now"
make cross tíckmatick . . . in Dada róom "I want to make a cross on the typewriter in Daddy's room"
chuffa under túnnel . . . getit fóryou "the train's in the tunnel; get it for me"
play rao bártok "I want to play at lions with me holding the sleeve of the Bartok record"

Mathetic

molasses nòse "I've got molasses on my nose"
red swèater "That's a red sweater"
chuffa stòp "the train's stopped"
loud Dvořak "that's a loud bit of the Dvořak record"
green stick find "the green stick's been found"
Dada black brùsh "that's Daddy's black brush"
man clean càr "the man was cleaning his car"
Anna make noise gràss "Anna made a noise with a piece of grass"
clever boy fix roof on lòrry "this clever boy fixed the roof on the lorry"
Dada come bàck . . . Dada come on fast chùffa "Daddy's come back; Daddy came on a fast train"
too dàrk . . . open cùrtain . . . lìght now "it was too dark; you've opened the curtains, and it's light now"

It may be pointed out that some of these utterances could be translated into either pragmatic or mathetic forms. But Nigel himself made the distinction clear. If the tone was rising, he was not satisfied until some response was forthcoming; whereas if the tone was falling, no response was expected. The following is a typical example showing both types of utterance, the one followed by the other: Dada got scrambled ègg . . . Mummy get for you scrambled égg "Daddy's got some scrambled egg; Mummy get some scrambled egg for me!"

Thus Nigel developed a clear functional strategy for Phase II, the phase that is transitional between his own proto-language and the language of the adult system. In what sense is it transitional? Here we come back once more to the sociosemiotic perspective. Phase II is defined as the period of mastering the adult language system; the end of Phase II is defined as the point when he has effectively mastered the system and can continue unhindered in his mastery of the language. It is unlikely that this point can be tied to any particular moment in time, but in Nigel's case it coincides roughly with the end of his second year, around NL-10 in the present study. The notion of transition, however, is perhaps more readily interpretable in functional terms. At the beginning of Phase II, it is "each utterance one function." This is what makes it possible for Nigel to put the intonation contrast to systematic use in the way he does (he cannot, of course, use it in the way English does, because the systems that are realized by intonation in English are as yet beyond his functional potential). Gradually in the course of Phase II he moves on, through a stage of "each utterance typically one principal function, the other subsidiary," to a final stage of "every utterance all functions." This is the pattern that is characteristic of the adult language.

How does this functional development take place? Not in the obvious way, which would be by some sort of transcategorization process in which sentence types were transferred out of one box into another. It happens through a reinterpretation of the concept of function on to a more abstract level, such that it becomes the organizing principle of the linguistic system itself. We could express this by saying that the "functions" of Phase I become "macro-functions" in Phase II and "meta-functions" in Phase III.

This, it seems, is the developmental source of the functional components of the adult linguistic system, the ideational and interpersonal referred to above. Whatever the specific use to which language is being put—and by the end of Phase II the child has indefinitely many (because they are indefinitely subclassifiable) uses of language —in all contexts the speaker has to be both observer and intruder at the same time. It is the pragmatic function that has provided the main context for the "intruder" systems of mood, modality, intensity, person, and the like, and the mathetic function that has provided the main context for the "observer" systems of transitivity, extent and location, quantifying and qualifying, and so on. But it is characteristic of the adult that, whatever the social context, the expression of his meanings in language involves both reflection on and interaction with the social system.

Hence in the course of Phase II the notion of "function" becomes totally distinct from that of "use." The adult has unlimited uses for language; but the typical adult utterance, whatever its use, has an ideational and an interpersonal component of meaning. At the same time, these "metafunctional" components of the adult language arise, however indirectly, out of the primary developmental functions of Phase I, where function was synonymous with use. The child's Phase I functional system, which is a system of the content in a "content, expression" language, evolves by generalization and abstraction into the adult's (Phase III) functional system, which is a system of the form in a "content, form, expression" language. It is in Phase II that the child makes the fundamental discovery that he can mean two things at once—he can both observe and interact with his environment at the same time; when he enters Phase III, all uses of language are mediated through this twofold meaning potential. The elementary functional contexts in which he first constructed his own proto-language are still there; they have evolved into the semiotic structures that we recognize as situations and settings of language use. What has changed is the meaning potential that he can deploy as an actor.

A schematic representation of the process of systemic-functional development as we have postulated it is given in Fig. 2.

10. It is not easy to say how much of Nigel's language learning strategies represents a general pattern, and how much is merely his own way through. Clearly the use of intonation to realize the pragmatic / mathetic distinction is an individual device; but the distinction itself may be a general feature—at least there seems nothing to suggest that it could not be. It is quite possible, on the other hand, that many children do not bother to create a Phase I language at all; almost certainly they do not display Nigel's dramatic shift from Phase I to Phase II. But one has to be careful here. It is clear that there is no single origin for the expressions of proto-language, and it could well be that some children already use imitations of adult sounds in this context; these would then appear to be words, although they would not in fact be functioning as items of vocabulary—there would still be no lexicogrammatical level in the system. Moreover many children use the holophrase as a transitional strategy, which makes the introduction of the lexicogrammar a much less sudden affair.

However that may be, the point to be emphasized here is that of continuity, not discontinuity. There is, with Nigel, a discontinuity in the expression, as well as, of course, the discontinuity that arises from the introduction of a third level of coding into the system. But there is no discontinuity in the content. The social functions that have determined the proto-language—satisfying immediate needs, controlling people's behavior, being "together," expressing the uniqueness of the self, exploring the world of the non-self, and creating a world in the imagination—all these evolve gradually and naturally into the social contexts and situation types that we characterize as semiotic structures; and the semantic systems, the meaning potential that derives from these functions, evolve likewise. The progressive approximation of the child's meanings to those of the adult, through interaction with and reinforcement by older speakers, begins before these meanings are (necessarily) realized through the words and structures of the adult language, and continues without interruption. Without this continuity the semantic system could not function effectively in the transmission of the social system from the adult to the child.

It is the essential continuity of the process of "learning how to mean," however early this process is considered to start, that we hope to bring out by adopting a sociosemiotic perspective. Our object of study here is still language; but it seems that additional light can be shed on language, especially where language development is concerned, if it is placed in the wider context of the social system considered as a system of meanings—hence the title of the present article. From another point of

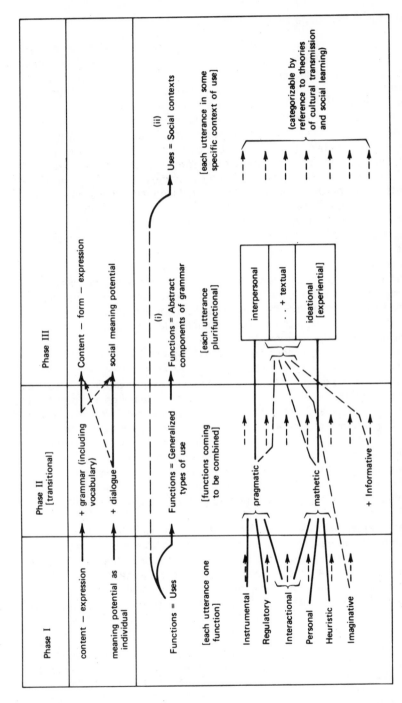

Figure 2. The original developmental functions evolve, at one level, via generalized categories of meaning into the abstract functional components of the linguistic system; and at another level, into the social contexts of linguistic interaction.

275

view, this is a means of bringing together the sociolinguistic and the semantic interpretations of language development, which at present remain rather unconnected.
In the sociolinguistic approach, learning the mother tongue is interpreted as the
progressive mastery of a "communicative competence," the use of language in
different social contexts.[12] But the notion of communicative competence, though
valuable as a temporary structure, a heuristic device for comparative developmental
and educational studies, does not relate to the nature of the linguistic system, or
explain how and why the child learns it. The semantic approach has focused mainly
on the child's learning of word meanings and other specific aspects of the ideational
component of the adult linguistic system.[13] But these studies do not in general relate
the system to its social contexts or to the functions that language serves in the young
child's life. Each of these fields of investigation constitutes, needless to say, an
essential element in the total picture. But they need to be brought together, through
some framework that does not separate the system from its use, or meaning from
social context.

We have been perhaps too readily persuaded to accept dichotomies of this kind,
with their implication that an interactional or "socio-" perspective is one in which the
focus is on behavior, performance, the use of the system "as opposed to" the system
itself. It is useful to be reminded that there are also sociological explanations, and that
an interpretation of language as interaction is complementary to, and no less explanatory than, a view of language as knowledge.

A child learns a symbolic behavior potential; this is what he "can mean" in terms
of a few elementary social functions. In the process he creates a language, a system
of meanings deriving from these functions, together with their realizations in sound.
The meanings are, in turn, the encoding of the higher-level meanings that constitute
the developing child's social system; first his own relationships with people and
objects, then the relationships among the people and objects themselves, then relationships among the symbols, and so on. In the process there comes a moment when
the child abandons the glossogenic trail—which we may speculate on as a model of
the evolutionary path of human language—and settles for the "mother tongue," the
language he hears from others. With this, given its potential for dialogue and for
multiple meaning, he can engage in an ongoing polyphonic interaction with those
around him.

Since the fact that language encodes the social system has in the long run determined the form of its internal organization, the child faces no sharp discontinuity at
this point; he is taking over a system that is a natural extension of that which he has
constructed for himself. His own functional semiotic now reappears at a more abstract level at the core of the adult language, in the ideational and interpersonal
components of the semantic system. All linguistic interaction comes to be mediated

---

[12] See, for example, Susan Ervin-Tripp, "Social dialects in developmental sociolinguistics,"
and Harry Osser, "Developmental studies of communicative competence," both in *Sociolinguistics; a crossdisciplinary perspective*, Washington, D.C., Center for Applied Linguistics, 1971.

[13] cf. Eve V. Clark, "What's in a word? On the child's acquisition of semantics in his first
language," in T. E. Moore (ed.), *Cognitive development and the acquisition of language*, New
York, Academic Press, in press.

through these two functions; and since they are not just aspects of the use of language, but are at the basis of the system itself, every actual instance of linguistic interaction has meaning not only in particular but also in general, as an expression of the social system and of the child's place in it—in other words, it is related to the context of culture as well as to the context of the situation. This explains how in the course of learning language a child is also all the time learning through language; how the microsemiotic exchanges of family and peer group life contain within themselves indices of the most pervasive semiotic patterns of the culture.

The Influence of Age, Sex, and Situation on the Frequency, Form, and Function of Questions Asked by Preschool Children

Madorah E. Smith

The purpose of this investigation was to study the influence of various factors on the questions of young children and the development of the interrogative sentence as used by them.

The material analyzed for this purpose consisted of 305 verbatim records of the conversation of 219 children ranging in age from eighteen to seventy-two months old, all from English-speaking homes, three-fourths of whom were in Iowa, 73 in Honolulu, 17 elsewhere. Two situations were studied; situation A when the child was alone with adults and situation C when he was engaged in free play with other children of preschool age. In neither situation was he addressed by the recorder, as his spontaneous conversation was desired. In situation C, 198 records were secured, and in situation A, 107. The records of boys and girls were almost equal, 153 being furnished by girls, 152 by boys. The average age in each situation was 43.6 months. (In age comparisons by full year two years equals eighteen months to twenty-nine months thirty days; by half-year two years equals twenty-one months to twenty-six months twenty-nine days, two-and-a-half years equals twenty-seven months to thirty-two months twenty-nine days.)

FREQUENCY OF QUESTIONS

Altogether 22,944 sentences were recorded of which 13 percent were questions making a total of 3095 questions asked by the children studied.

Sixteen percent of the sentences in situation A were questions and 12 percent of those in situation C; so that, although there were nearly twice as many records taken in the latter situation, the number of questions in each situation was approximately the same, being 1529 and 1566 respectively. The difference between these two percentages is 3.7 times its standard deviation. Twenty children were observed in both situations, the two records being taken on the same day or within a few days of each other. Fifteen of these children asked more questions in situation A, the average difference in percent of questions being 3.4 percent more in situation A for the 20 cases.

At every age level, whether the records are distributed on the full year or half-year

From *Child Development* 1933, 4, pp. 201-213. Reprinted by permission of the Society for Research in Child Development.

basis, the difference in percent of questions asked to all sentences used is in favor of situation A. Moreover, 22 percent of the records in situation C contained no questions while only 12 percent of those in situation A did not. The difference in this case is 2.4 times its standard deviation which means 992 chances in a thousand that this difference represents a true one.

One reason that more questions were asked in situation A than in situation C may be because young children prefer to ask questions of adults when possible. This is indicated by the fact that 28 percent of the 1032 questions found in the records made in situation C that indicated clearly throughout to whom the child addressed his questions, were directed to an adult present. This tendency was most marked in the case of the youngest children. Every question of the only child under twenty-two months who asked questions in situation C, was directed to one of the teachers in the nursery school. Fifty-six percent of the questions asked by all two-year-olds in situation C, 36 percent of those asked by three-year-olds, 28 percent of those by four-year-olds, 25 percent of those by five-year-olds and 17 percent of those by the older group were directed to an adult in spite of the fact that the child was actively playing in the midst of other children. The youngest children apparently didn't consider it possible that another child could help them out with the desired information, very seldom asking a question of any child. The older children would turn from their play with others to an adult present when bored by their companions: as when Betty aged three, after fruitless attempts at attracting attention by her stunts turns to ask the nurse in charge of her group, "You know our baby?"; or if their interest was aroused by an adult's actions as when Eugene aged four-and-a-half years noticing his parents leaving asks, "Where you all going, mother?"; or to seek permission as, "Could I hang it up?"; or to settle a dispute as when Kathleen aged four-and-a-half asks, "He spells t-e-a-t, teat. Two t's. Is that the way?" and Jackie aged four demands, "Can I use the hammer and not that big fat boy?"; or to seek an answer to a question their companions have failed to answer as when Hester, five-and-a-half years old inquires, "Miss V. where is Miss E.?" or for information that they assume their companions lack as when Eugene turns to the recorder to ask, "What makes ice cream?"

There was a difference of only 1 percent between the percentages of questions asked by boys and girls; the boys asking 1663 questions and the girls 1432. But at two years, the girls asked more questions. The difference is due mainly to the fact that more girls than boys use questions at this early age, the girls beginning to ask questions at an earlier age than do boys; for only 34 percent of the two-year-old boys asked any questions but 64 percent of the girls did. McCarthy's (3) figures show a similar difference, the percent of questions asked to sentences used being for her eighteen-months-old group,.4 for the boys and 4.7 for the girls and for the twenty-four-months-old group, 2.8 for the boys and 5.3 for the girls.

Comparing the sexes in the two situations, we find that there was no difference in the case of the boys as to the percent of children who asked questions, 80 percent of the boys using questions in each situation but there was a marked difference in the case of the girls. In situation A, 93 percent of the girls and in situation C, only 77 percent asked questions. This difference of 16 percent is 2.9 times its standard deviation giving 998 chances in a thousand that it is a true difference. However, when with adults, the boys who asked any questions used so many more in proportion than did the girls that the percent of questions asked to sentences used in situation

A was six more for the boys (19 percent) than for the girls (13 percent). The boys asked more questions in situation A but there was practically no difference in the two situations for the girls.

At each age level the proportion of questions to sentences increases up to the oldest age group studied in which case there is a drop (see Table 1). As there were so few cases in this group it would mean nothing, were it not that the same drop occurs in both situations, when the percentages are distributed by half-years, in another short series of records of bilingual children and at the corresponding mental age in situation C when percentages are calculated for each Mental Age. From each full-year age level from two to five years, the gain in percent of questions asked to all sentences used in the records is highly significant, the smallest difference, that between two and three years, being 3.1 times its standard deviation.

Further corroboration is found in the cases observed more than once. The 36 children from whom repeated records were taken showed the same tendency to ask more questions as they grew older up to four-and-a-half years after which there was no further gain.

From a mother's diary records of her 8 children which included random samplings of their conversation, all the sentences were taken and the percent of questions for each half-year calculated. Adding the repeated records for these children to the 36 in this study we find an irregularly increasing percentage of highest records occurring at each age up to four-and-a-half years where fifty-four percent of the records of the children for whom records were available at that age showed the highest percent of questions for each child occurred at four-and-a-half. At five years, only 38 percent, at five-and-a-half, 12 and at six years, 20 percent of the records were the highest for the particular child concerned.

This falling off might be due to lessened necessity to use questions as an attention-getting device as a greater variety of such devices are learned by children or as a result of their questions being ignored or answered unsatisfactorily or their learning other ways of satisfying their desire for knowledge.

Of the 305 records taken, 82 percent included questions. Most of those not containing questions were those recorded for the younger children. Only 49 percent of the two-year-olds asked questions; but 83 percent of the three-year-olds, 93 percent of the four-year-olds, 95 percent of the five-year-olds and 93 percent of the oldest group did. The difference between the first two percentages is significant being 4.4 times its standard deviation.

For 200 of the children, mental test records were available. Using only these records and distributing them according to mental age, the percent of questions asked increased quite regularly from 5 percent at two years to 17 percent at five years, falling to fourteen percent at six years of mental age, but arising again for the 14 children of seven and eight years mentally. The drop is found only in the case of records taken in situation C, but in situation A, the gain is but 1 percent from five to six.

FORM OF QUESTION

Interrogative words were used to introduce 1085 or 36 percent of the 3000 ques-

Table 1   Frequency of questions asked

	2 Years	3 Years	4 Years	5 Years	66-72 Mos.	All Ages
Number of children	65	75	75	75	15	305
Of boys	32	35	39	40	6	152
Of girls	33	40	36	35	9	153
In situation A	25	25	25	25	7	107
In situation C	40	50	50	50	8	198
Number of sentences						
used by all children	2,483	5,658	6,233	7,701	869	22,944
Boys	797	2,851	3,283	4,575	285	11,791
Girls	1,686	2,807	2,950	3,126	584	11,153
In situation A	968	2,881	2,356	2,914	334	9,453
In situation C	1,515	2,777	3,877	4,787	535	13,491
Number of questions						
asked by all children.	185	550	794	1,471	95	3,095
Boys	47	261	419	922	14	1,663
Girls	138	289	375	549	81	1,432
In situation A	88	279	352	774	36	1,529
In situation C	97	271	442	697	59	1,566
Percent questions of						
sentences for all children	8	10	13	19	11	13
Boys	6	9	13	20		14
Girls	8	10	13	17		13
In situation A	9	10	15	27	11	16
Boys	10	8	18	31		
Girls	9	11	13	20		
In situation C	6	10	12	15	11	12
Boys	3	10	11	13		
Girls	8	9	12	16		
Percentage of children asking						
questions all children	49	83	93	95	93	81
Boys	34	89	95	95	83	80
Girls	64	75	92	94	100	82
In situation A	60	96	96	100	86	88
In situation C	42	76	92	92	100	78
Percent of questions asked in situation C but directed to adults	56	36	28	25	17	28

Bilingual series

	2 Years	3 Years	4 Years	5 Years	66-72 Mos.	All Ages
Number of cases	5	15	9	10	6	46
Number of sentences	267	1,093	442	598	707	3,107
Number of questions	13	112	49	50	65	289
Percent of questions	5	11	11	8	9	9

Table 2   Form and function of questions asked

	Age in Years				In Situation		By		By All Children
	2	3	4	5	A	C	Boys	Girls	
Number of children	65	75	75	75	107	198	152	153	305
Number of questions	185	550	794	1,471	1,529	1,566	1,663	1,432	3,095
I. Causal questions, percent	3	4	7	10	11	5	10	4	8
II. Reality and history:									
Facts, time and invention, percent	6	10	16	16	17	12	16	13	14½
Place, percent	32	22	11	8	10	15	11	15	12½
III. Actions:									
Imperative, percent	2	9	11	10	6	14	10	10	10
What say, percent	8	7	6	4	4	7	6	5	5
Other acts, percent	18	27	31	35	34	28	29	33	31
IV. Name, percent	20	11	4	2	5	6	4	7	5
V. Classification and evaluation, percent	10	9	11	9	9	11	10	10	10

VI. Rules, percent	1	1	1	2	1	2	1	0	0
VII. Calculation, percent	2	1	4	1	4	4	2	0	0
Corroboration and approbation, percent	19	16	21	14	23	23	20	9	9
Interrogative words used									
What, percent	15	15	15	16	14	11	17	21	20
Where, percent	11	13	8	11	7	7	9	20	26
How, percent	6	4	8	3	9	9	4	1	1
Why, percent	4	2	5	2	5	6	3	1	1
Who, whose, which, percent	2	3	2	3	2	2	3	3	1
When, percent	0.6	0.8	0.4	0.6	0.5	0.8	0.6	0.2	0
What for, percent	1	1	1.5	1	1.6	2	1	1	0
All interrogative words, percent	40	40	40	39	41	37	38	46	49

Note: 2 questions, 1 of modality and 1 of logical reason not included in table.

283

tions asked by the children two to five years of age. Nineteen percent or 559 questions sought corroboration of the child's statement or approbation of his words or actions and were stated in such forms as: "She isn't making pie, is she?" (Girl of forty-one months) "Dat make O, don't it?" (Boy of forty-four months) "Isn't this a nice dress?" (Girl of sixty-three months). The remainder of the questions began with the copula, or an auxiliary verb, or some subordinate clause or were asked merely by inflection of voice. Examples are: "Do buttons go here?" (Girl of forty-eight months) "May I take the beanbag out?" (Girl of sixty-three months) "Is this the right way?" (Girl of sixty-three months) "If Mary dies, will that cotton go to heaven?" (Boy of forty-nine months) "Mama home?" (Girl of twenty-nine months).

The use of interrogative words decreased from 49 percent of all questions asked at two years to 37 percent at five years (see Table 2). This decrease in age is in line with Davis's (1) finding that adults used fewer interrogative words than did children. The difference in the use of such introductory words in questions in the two situations is negligible, only 2 percent; and the proportion of such words to questions was the same for both boys and girls.

Questions seeking corroboration or approbation were used with increasing frequency with growth in age, the proportion rising from 9 percent at two to 23 percent at five, the difference between these two proportions is more than 6 times its standard deviation and is highly significant. The difference in their use in the two situations is also significant; this type of question being used in 23 percent of the questions asked in situation A but in only 14 percent of those asked in situation C. The boys used this type in 21 percent of their questions, the girls in but 16 percent of theirs. The difference in this case is also significant being 3.5 times its standard deviation but the difference is not found at all ages for at two and five years the girls used more corroborative questions.

Of the particular interrogative word used *what,* occurring in 12 percent of all questions and *where,* which occurred in 11 percent of all, decreased in proportion with age quite regularly and significantly. *Who, whose* and *which,* which together introduced but 2 percent of all questions showed no correlation between frequency of use and age of child employing them. *How,* used in 6 percent of the questions, *when,* in 1 percent, and *why,* in 4 percent of all questions increased regularly with age, the difference from two to five years being more than three times its standard deviation in the case of *how* and *why.* Of these last three interrogative words, only *why* was used by the two-year-old group and that but twice and by the same child, a precocious girl of twenty-nine months with an I.Q. of 138.

FUNCTIONS OF QUESTIONS

For this analysis, Piaget's (4) classification was used with a few alterations; not subdividing causal questions so finely as, with our younger children, so few samples of this type were secured; and including under actions and intentions, two special groups. The first of these special groups was composed of those questions that asked for the repetition of another's remarks such as "What did you say?" or the more frequent though less courteous "Huh?" The second group consisted of those questions that partook of the nature of imperatives such as: "Don't take mine, will you?" (Girl of forty-one months) "Can we take this car?" (Boy of fifty-two months) "Will you hold this?" (Girl of forty-three months). Both of these special groups although somewhat different in type from other questions expect a response and even seek for information at times but their inclusion under separate headings makes it possible to consider the more purely interrogative sentences by themselves. (See Table 2.)

Piaget separates questions of cause introduced by *why* from such questions not so introduced. These two groups were approximately equal if all questions were considered but if the age groups are considered separately, the introductory word *why* was used less frequently in the causal questions from two to four years but more so at five years. Both types of causal questions numbered 236 altogether or 8 percent of all questions. In situation A, they composed 11 percent and in situation C but 5 percent of all questions asked. Boys at all ages asked more questions of this type than did girls, the percent of such questions being ten for the boys and four for the girls. Both the differences between sexes and between situations are significant, being in each case over 6 times their standard deviation. Piaget's case, a boy talking with an adult, used 18 percent of this type of question. Our five-year-old boys talking to adults used 16 percent. As Piaget's case was studied from six years three months to seven years one month, the somewhat larger percent is what would be expected on account of his greater age. Piaget's case asked more questions concerning natural phenomena and ours more about manufactured articles; a difference that is due to the tendency to confine questions to some extent to the immediate situation for his case was talking to his escort on walks outdoors and the majority of our records were taken indoors while the child was engaged with toys, puzzles, picturebooks, drawing and similar activities. The boys in Davis's (1) study also asked more causal questions.

The next large division of questions in Piaget's classification is that of Reality and History. The five categories under that head showed such marked differences in trend that they were studied separately. Questions of place comprising 13 percent of the total were usually introduced by the word *where* and were the most frequent of all at two years when they made up almost a third of the questions asked. They decreased rapidly in proportion to 8 percent at five. They were more frequent in situation C than in situation A and were used relatively more often by girls than by boys. Only one question of modality, "Was it real?" asked in situation A by a girl of forty-seven months was found in the entire series of questions. The proportion of questions of fact, time and invention, 14 percent of all, increase with age; the first type only to four years and the second type occurring for the first time at three years. They were found more frequently in the boys' records and were used relatively more often in situation A but the latter difference only is significant.

Examples of these types are: *Fact* "Did it freeze?" (Girl of forty-one months) "Is this their lunch?" (Girl of thirty-three months) *Time* "This is tomorrow, ain't it?" (Boy of forty-four months) "What time is it?" (Girl of fifty-six months) *Invention* "Is that un (a toy) squealing?" (Boy of forty-six months) "Spool, you are getting naked, aren't you?" (Girl of seventy-one months) *Place* "Where daddy?" (Girl of eighteen months) "Where you buy dat baby doll?" (Girl of thirty-one months).

Questions concerning human actions and intentions include the largest proportion of all questions, 46 percent. Those that were imperative in purpose but stated in the form of questions increase from 2 percent at two years to 11 at four years, falling to 10 at five. The increases from two to four or five years are significant, being in each case over six times the standard deviation. The requests for repetition of remarks however, fall regularly from 8 percent at two to 4 percent at five. Evidently as the child grows older, he understands better and does not need to have statements or questions repeated to him so often. These two forms are used more frequently in situation C and show no sex difference in frequency of use. The other questions of action or intention increase significantly in proportion from 18 percent at two years to 35 percent at five, and are used significantly more often by girls and in situation A. Examples are: " 'Ove Turley too?' " (Girl of twenty-seven months) "Will you buy medicine? Can you 'member?" (Boy of fifty-four months) "What are you writing?" (Boy of twenty-nine months) "Know Uncle Ed?" (Girl of thirty-nine months).

Piaget's fourth large category "Questions on rules" were used by only the four and five-year-olds. There were only 39 of them in all or about 1 percent of all questions. No sex difference was found but about three-fourths of these questions were asked in situation C. Examples are: "How do you spell Kathleen?" and "At Home, it would be all right, wouldn't it?"

The fifth big group of questions is that of classification comprising questions of name, logical reason and classification. Those questions asking simply for the name of an object or person composed one fifth of the questions asked by two-year-olds, ranking third in frequency at that age. The youngest child to ask any questions in situation C, a girl of nineteen months used this kind of question seven times in the course of an hour's observation, and only three other questions which were all questions seeking repetition of the answer to her questions. She was still using one-word sentences and her vocabulary was very limited so her question took the form of "Dat? Dat?" repeated until an answer was given as she pointed at the child or object of which she desired the name. Another girl in situation A, twenty-nine months old with a much larger vocabulary still used but one word "Tat?" when asking for names. Although this form of question was so frequent in this youngest group it comprised but 5 percent of all questions and occurred but one-tenth as frequently at five years as it had at two. Seven percent of the girls' questions and 4 percent of the boys' were of this type and it occurred slightly more often (one percent) in situation C than in situation A. Examples are: "What's in brush?" (Girl of forty-one months) "What's your name?" and "What's the name of this?" (Boy of fifty-four months).

There was only one question of logical reason in our series, nor did Piaget find it often; only 6 times in all the 750 questions asked by his case who was older than any of ours.

The questions of classification and evaluation remain the most nearly constant in proportion of any type. They compose 10 percent of the total number and vary no more than a minimum of 9 and a maximum of 11 percent at any age, in either situation or with either sex. Examples are: "What kind are these?" (Girl of thirty months) "That was joke, wasn't it?" (Boy of forty-three months) "Was the steamer also a boat?" (Boy of forty-two months) "Ain't it a shame for him to be a boy? . . . . With all them curls." (Boy of fifty-four months) "Aren't they funny men?" (Girl of forty months) "Isn't this a nice dress?" (Girl of sixty-three months).

The last category used is that of questions of calculation. There were 73 of these in our series. They were over 4 times as frequent in situation A and in boys' records as in situation C and in girls' records. They were found at only the upper age levels and twice as often at five as at four. Examples are: "How many have I got?" "How many minutes is ten o'clock?" and "If somebody gave Mary 2 apples and me 5, how many would that be?"

SITUATION

Whether the child was in situation A or C, his questions were in 94 percent of the cases concerned with some object, action or person either in the immediate situation or desired to be there by the child. Only 174 of the entire series of questions were not thus closely concerned with the child's immediate surroundings; and of these, there were but 52 which were not associated with some preceding conversation, action or the particular place where the child happened to be. Thus, Kathleen, forty-three months old asks, "I don't need to take a nap, do I?" She was eating her breakfast and after each other meal during the day, bed was in order. That this was her association is evident from her next remark, "When you've already been in bed, you don't need to take a nap." The questions apparently unconnected with the immediate surroundings included questions about time, as "What day's tomorrow?" (Bobby at forty-six months) people not present, as "Know Frank's sister?" (Doris at forty-one months) God, as "Who made God?" (John at four years) the knowledge of others as to the child's experiences as, "Know what my daddy told me?" (Carolyn at fifty months) connected with his romances as, "Don't you wish your knife would get up and butter your bread for you?" (Harry at five years) criticisms more wisely not expressed when the person criticized was present as when Margo (seventy months) waited until mother was safely out of the house before asking at a time when the question seemed quite irrelevant, "Don't you think mother looks silly in that new hat?"

CAUSAL QUESTIONS

Isaacs (2) gives an outline for the study of children's "why" questions applicable to those questions that are the same in nature as those introduced by "why" even if that word does not occur in the question. His outline would include some that Piaget classes under Actions and Intentions, which class he states might be subdivided into questions about the causes of actions and the other about the actions themselves. For an analysis of our questions according to Isaac's outline, we have added to our causal questions as treated above, others from the first subdivision of this third large group of Piaget's making a total of 300 causal questions. We also gathered for comparison 60 more causal questions taken from two other sources: a number of records of bilingual children which had been recorded exactly as those in our main series; and some diary records of her 8 children kept by the mother referred to above. (See table 3.)

Isaacs divides causal questions into 4 major groups. The first class is Affective and Expressional. It is similar to, though broader than Piaget's subhead of Contradictory. The child, helpless, surprised, vexed or in protest demands the reason for the interference with his purposes or expectations. These questions often consist of the single word "Why?" in response to a command. Thus Evelyn when she notices that daddy is leaving without her complains, "Why?" and Jackie refused permission to play outdoors in the rain protests, "Why?" Longer sentences of this type are: "Why don't you do it yourself?" (Girl of fifty-nine months, very much vexed) "Why don't you give me easy things?" (Boy of sixty-five months) "What's the matter with the old ball?" (Girl of fifty-four months thwarted in her attempt at securing the ball). The earliest age at which this type of questions was found in our records was twenty-nine months, when the four questions of this kind made up 57 percent of the total of 7 causal questions. Not one such question occurred in our special series before three years. This class of questions made up 15 percent of the main series and eighteen percent of the special series.

Issacs explains his second category of Epistemic questions as containing questions that occur when the child finds that his immediate experience turns into a sense of something wrong with knowledge and seeks the explanation. It may be because he finds a contradiction of anomaly and seeks its resolution as when five-year-old Marvin counting his beads inquires, "There's five there and I had five before, how comes that?" or five-year-old Ruth amazed at the information that God was not born exclaims, "How could he live?" The question may be asked in an attempt to learn the missing general rule for an unexpected or odd fact, as when Mary, at forty-two months asks concerning her shadow, "Why Mary walk on the floor?" Again noticing a difference or contrast, the child seeks the delimiting rule as when Paul, fifty-six months old demands "Why are they little girls? Why aren't they little boys?" Or the child does not understand some deviation from customary usage as when four-year-old John asks, "Why doesn't he spank him?" (since he is bad). Or he may be seeking the determining factor or law in the case as when Eugene at forty-six months asks concerning a firecracker, "How would it went bang?" and five-year-old Arthur inquires, "How do you set the clock?" or when five-year-old Bobby, not quite certain of the cause assumed says, "God makes it rain, doesn't He?" The question may be the result of a desire to discover what event determined a certain occurrence as when five-year-old Gloria asks, "What were you laughing about?" or Dicky, at forty-four months, solicitously inquires, "What made you sore, lady?"

The first 3 of the above subdivisions Issacs considers primary and the rest as derivative or causal and quasi-informational. This Epistemic group comprised 44 percent of the main series of causal questions and 33 percent of the special series. This type was much more used in situation A, where the proportion was 52 percent of all causal questions but the proportion of these questions in situation C was but 20 percent.

The third category is divided into Teleological and Motivational. The latter subdivision when introduced by *"Why"* corresponds to Piaget's class of Psychological

Table 3   "Why questions"

Asked at Year	Main Series					All Cases	In Situation			Special Series			
	2	3	4	5	6		A	C	3	4	5	6	All
Total number of questions	7	18	60	209	6	300	226	74	26	18	12	4	60
I. Affective and expressional, percent	57	22	8	13	83	15	12	23	31	17	8	75	18
II. Epistemic, percent	0	17	52	47	0	44	52	20	19	33	50		33
III. Teleological and motivational, percent	43	61	40	38	17	40	34	42	54	44	42	25	47
IV. Justificatory, percent				2		1	2			6			2
Word "why" used, percent	29	33	33	41	17	38							

Note: In the special series no two-year-olds asked questions.

Motivation; but, as he throws the corresponding questions when not introduced by *"why"* into the large group relating to Human Actions and Intentions, his rules of classification result in a smaller group. Questions under the first subhead, teleological, seek the purpose or function of an action or object as in Billy's question, asked at sixty-three months, "Why ambulance go?" and David's, asked at fifty-three months, "What are snakes good for?" and Paul's inquiry, made at fifty-six months, "These nails are just to nail it together, aren't they?" Teleological questions composed 9 percent of the main series and 7 of the special series.

Under the heading of Motivational questions which seek the motive or intention of another are included 31 percent of the main and 40 percent of the special series. This type was more common in situation C where forty-two percent of all questions were so classified as compared with 27 percent of those in situation A. Examples are, "Why don't you take your other overshoe off?" (Boy of forty-nine months) "Why do you want to see how good a bead-stringer I am?" (Boy of fifty-four months) "Why did you move your bench?" (Boy of five years) "Why she buy that baby doll?" (Girl of thirty-one months).

The last category of justificatory questions was very scantily represented. Only 4 questions of the main series and 1 in the special series were of this type and all of these were asked by five-year-olds. In this class of questions, the child demands the grounds for or reasons for rules, statements or beliefs. In Paul's question, "Why is this a puzzle?" he was seeking the reason for a statement just made to him.

SUMMARY

The most striking differences due to age found were:

1. The number and percentage of questions to total number of sentences increased with each half-year up to four years when both number and percent fall. The percentage of children asking questions was 49 at two years and increased each year until five when 95 percent of the children asked questions.

2. The same increase in percent of questions to total number of sentences used was found for mental ages from two to five years, a drop at six years mental age and a rise again at seven years.

3. The most frequent interrogative words used by the youngest children were *what* and *where. How, when* and *why* were not used at all at two years but increased in frequency at each age level studied while the what and where questions correspondingly decreased in relative frequency.

4. Almost half of the questions asked by two-year-olds were introduced by an interrogative word but only a third of the questions at five.

5. Questions that were most frequent at two years and decreased in relative frequency with age were, in order of frequency at two years:—those of place which inquired as to the whereabouts of persons or objects, and those asking for the names of persons or things.

6. Questions that increased significantly in proportion with age from two to five

years were questions of fact (e.g. Did it freeze?) time, invention, concerning number and calculation, concerning human intentions or actions (e.g. What are you doing?) and causal questions.

The most striking differences due to sex found were:

1. Girls asked more questions at two years.
2. Boys asked more causal questions and used *how* and *why* more than the girls did.
3. Girls asked more questions concerning social rules, the names of things and more questions of place.

The most striking differences due to situation found were:

1. Many more questions proportionately were asked in situation A than in situation C and there was a tendency especially among the younger children in situation C to direct many questions to adults.
2. Questions concerning human actions or intentions except when merely asking for repetition of question (What did you say?) or as a variation of the imperative were more frequent in situation A. So were questions of fact, time, invention, cause, calculation, and corroboration.
3. The most frequent questions asked in situation C were questions of place, name, classification, and the variation of imperative type.

Those differences favoring boys and situation A are for the most part in the same direction as those differences noted in the older children.

REFERENCES

(1) Davis, Edith A.: The form and function of children's questions. *Child Development,* 1932, **3,** 57-74.
(2) Issacs, Susan: *Intellectual growth in young children. With an appendix on children's "why"* questions by Nathan Issacs. New York. Harcourt, Brace and Company, 1930.
(3) McCarthy, Dorothea A.: *The language development of the preschool child.* Minneapolis. The University of Minnesota Press, 1929.
(4) Piaget, Jean: *The language and thought of the child.* New York. Harcourt, Brace and Company, 1926.
(5) Smith, Madorah E.: An investigation of the development of the sentence and the extent of vocabulary in young children. *University of Iowa Studies in Child Welfare.* 1926, **3,** No. 5.

Requests and Responses in Children's Speech*
Catherine Garvey

An investigation of children's ability to convey and respond to requests for action was based on the spontaneous speech of 36 dyads of nursery school children (3;6–5;7). Direct request forms (e.g. *Give me the hammer*) were frequent and the majority were acknowledged verbally. Examination of the contexts of direct requests indicated that speaker and addressee shared an understanding of the interpersonal meaning factors relevant to requesting. These meaning factors were invoked in justifying, refusing and in repeating or paraphrasing a request, and they also provided a basis for the communication of indirect requests. Examples of inferred requests are discussed, and a relationship between the structure of the speech act and conversational sequences is proposed.

INTRODUCTION

The purpose of this paper is to explore an aspect of communicative competence in young children. We know far more about the developmental course of syntax, of phonology, and of semantic systems than we do about the uses of speech to express, to inform, or to influence. How is the child able to request, to deny, to promise? One tradition of research has viewed the first stages of talking as the emergence of linguistic entities of one sort or another (Braine 1963, McNeill 1970). But utterances are, of course, simultaneously social acts. Some students of the ontogeny of language have suggested that the communicative functions of speech not only supply the principal motivating force for language acquisition (Luria & Yudovich 1968, Macnamara 1972), but also actually provide an abstract structure from which the elaboration of the linguistic code may proceed (Miller 1970). A progression from a prelinguistic stage of primitive speech acts to the establishment of conventionalized speech acts has been proposed by Dore (forth-coming). The latter (e.g. request) are linked, though not presumably in any simple one-to-one fashion, to the modality types (e.g. imperative), which are associated with the propositional content of a sentence (e.g. *You will close the door*). Before language appears, certain intrinsically social

From *Journal of Child Language,* **2,** 41–63, 1975. Reprinted by permission of Cambridge University Press.

[*] The research was supported by National Institutes of Mental Health Grant (1 RO1 MH 23883-01) and by National Science Foundation Grant (GS-31636). Thanks are due to Bernard Mohan for his valuable criticism of an earlier version of this paper. Requests for reprints may be sent to the author, Department of Psychology, The Johns Hopkins University, Baltimore, Maryland 21218.

gestures such as establishing a common focus of attention with another (showing) and offering something to another (sharing) are performed and can be reliably observed (Rheingold 1973). Some of these intentional acts acquire linguistic markers as the child begins to talk, as when pointing is accompanied by and often replaced by an existential predicate, e.g. *There (is a) duck.* Bruner (1975) offers examples of the way in which linguistic markers come to be paired with the act types that emerge from joint actions of child and caretaker.

From that point the rapid course of development is as complex and as difficult to attribute directly to imitation of external stimuli as is the development of the structure of the linguistic code. The child learns how to do things with words which he may have done earlier without words, such as to refuse or to offer. He will also learn to do some things that he has not done before as intentional public acts, such as making promises and qualifying them. He will further learn to use different utterance types to accomplish a given intent as, for example, when a child asks for a piece of cake by saying *Will you give me some cake?* or *I want some cake.* And he will learn rather complex verbal strategies to accomplish an intended outcome, such as preparing the conditions under which one act, a request for permission, will succeed when some other act has failed. Consider, for example, the following conversation between two four-year-olds.

A approaches a large toy car that *B* has just been sitting on:

A   *Pretend this was my car.*
B   No!
A   Pretend this was our car.
B   All right.
A   Can I drive your car?
B   Yes, okay. (Smiles and moves away from car)
A   (Turns wheel and makes driving noises)

A began by using a fairly common tactic among four-year-olds, requesting that *B* pretend that a desired state (*A*'s possession of the car) was actually in effect. When *B* refused, *A* modified the tactic, this time allowing hypothetical joint possession of the car. Finally *A* verbally granted total power over the car to *B*, and admitted her own submissive status by using a request for permission to drive *A*'s car. Skill in the use of verbal strategies by the time that speech is fluent but not mature implies a degree of competence in the pragmatic aspect of language which is as yet poorly understood.

The nature of this competence extends beyond knowledge of the syntactic and semantic structure of sentences. Cognitive operations of inference are required for the interpretation of another's non-direct verbal acts, and the child who employs such acts has encoded the verbal content in accord with some representation of the probable effects of alternative outcomes. The example suggests that the child is able to identify and select among some of the basic dimensions of socially constructed reality on which interpersonal perception of action and intent rest. Concepts of "belonging," of "want," "can," and "may," proposed by Heider (1958) as primes in our direct experiences of the social environment, are critical to the selection and interpretation of alternative verbal choices in social discourse. It appears that at the very time that features of the linguistic code are elaborated, the child's ability to encode and decode verbally formulated intentions in the service of purposive interaction has also increased.

The apparent paradox presented by the well-documented findings on the limited role of language in concept formation, problem-solving and the communication of objective information among preschool children and their reported facility with language in naturalistic settings has been pointed out by Blank (1974). It seems possible that research emphases on development of the linguistic code and on development of cognitive functions and intellectual operations have combined to obscure another, complementary aspect of development to which language both contributes and on which its growth depends. Further, the view that children's speech with peers is composed primarily of babbling and private or collective monologuing and that sustained, cohesive verbal exchanges are possible only when the conversation is guided or elicited by an adult (Piaget 1926) has discouraged systematic study of the form and content of children's spontaneous communication. Some recent evidence on the preschooler's skill in conveying and interpreting verbally encoded social meanings and at sustaining conversational interactions (Garvey & Hogan 1973) suggests that closer examination of these skills is justified.

A speech act approach provides a technique for joining linguistic means with classes of communicative intent, i.e. it treats utterance forms as realizations of purposive social gestures. Since we may view conversation as composed of orderly sequences of reciprocal gestures, the study of a speech act may shed some light on the two questions raised here. First, how does the child convey interpersonal meanings by speaking and interpret the intentions of others from their speech? Second, what are the bases for conversational sequencing, that is, how is connected discourse structured? To examine these questions and to show how they are indeed related, I will present an account of the communication of one speech-act type in the speech of nursery school children.

METHOD

SUBJECTS AND PROCEDURES

The subjects were 36 children from white, middle-class, predominantly professional families. There were 21 girls and 15 boys ranging in age from 3;6 to 5;7. Three children of the same age and from the same nursery school class were brought to the laboratory by their teacher. The three children were invited to draw straws to see who would get to play games with some little toys first and who could go to the playroom first. The child who drew the long straw was occupied with same–different discrimination tasks while the dyad went to explore the well-furnished playroom. The dyad was videotaped through one-way observation mirrors. After about 15 minutes the composition of the dyad was changed. In this way three dyads were formed from a triad and each child was observed in the playroom with two different partners. There were 12 dyads of younger children (3;6–4;4) and 24 dyads of older children (4; 7–5;7). Table 1 presents the age and sex composition of the dyads and the mean number of words per utterance of the members of the groups as an index of linguistic maturity.

Table I   Age, Sex and Mean Number of Words per Utterance of Members of Younger and Older Dyads

	Age (months)	Male	Female	Words per utterance
Younger group (N = 12)	Mean = 46.33 S.D. = 3.26 Range = 42–52	6	6	Mean = 4.76 S.D. = 1.13 Range = 3.14–7.4
Older group (N = 24)	Mean = 60 S.D. = 2.96 Range = 55–67	9	15	Mean = 6.18 S.D. = 1.56 Range = 3.7–10.1

Speech was transcribed and a narrative of the activities was prepared. The dyads produced on the average one utterance every 4.6 seconds. In the majority of dyads both children contributed a fairly equal amount of speech, and no child failed to supply at least one-third of the utterances produced by his dyad. Activities included individual and joint exploration of the room and toys, pretend play, and just conversing.

This corpus of peer interactions provided a sample of spontaneous speech free of immediate adult influence or facilitation. The toys and furnishings of the room elicited similar activities from most of the dyads. For example, a large wooden car with steering wheel and license plate placed in the room under a microphone was the center of action; driving it and organizing activities with it, such as going on a vacation, absorbed most dyads. Similarly, most children conducted conversations on the toy telephones and cooked a meal on the stove. Coordinating each other's actions in these various undertakings appeared to be an important motive for talking.

BACKGROUND OF THE ANALYSIS

There is a large family of social gestures whereby one person attempts to influence the behavior or attitude of another. This family, which we will call *interventions*, includes suggestions, invitations, prohibitions, requests for permission, and the request for action. The request for action (henceforth, *request*) was selected for study for three reasons. First, a successful request elicits an observable response on the part of the addressee. Second, several analyses of the request in adult speech are available. Third, requests implicate an interesting and important set of social meanings—that is, the desires or needs of one person are to be satisfied through or in conflict with the desires and needs of another person. Thus, requests may provide a means of studying the child's conceptions of some of the basic dimensions of interpersonal understanding.

The request is an illocutionary act whereby a speaker (S) conveys to an addressee (H) that S wishes H to perform an act (A). The theory of speech acts proposes that an utterance is composed of a proposition and a modality. Both elements are subject to the rules of the grammatical code of the language. For example, the utterance *Open the door* represents the proposition "H will open the door," and the modality "imperative," which deletes *you*, H and *will* and assigns appropriate intonation.

Simultaneously, the utterance conveys an illocutionary force, for in saying something a speaker also does something (Austin 1962); he performs an illocutionary act. The force of an illocutionary act can be indicated, in the simplest cases, by a performative verb, e.g. *I request that you open the door,* or by selection of a sentence type (modality) conventionally associated with the act; in the case of requests, this is the imperative, e.g. *Open the door!*

The force of an utterance does not derive solely from the modality or the proposition. An example will demonstrate that modality, proposition, and force are, to some extent, independent. The formula which represents a request is *request* (S, H (H will do A)). A speaker can convey a request by using a non-imperative utterance, e.g. *Would you mind opening the door?* But he can use an imperative utterance which rests on the propositional content "H will do A," and in doing so convey a warning rather than a request, e.g. a gunman might try to stop a hostage by pointing his gun and saying, *Take one step!*

The force of an utterance derives from a set of necessary and sufficient conditions relating on the one hand to the beliefs and attitudes of S and H and on the other hand to their mutual understanding of the use of linguistic devices for communication. If these conditions are met, then the illocutionary act is said to have been successfully and nondefectively performed. Conversely, the proposition that a speaker performed a given speech act entails that the conditions for that act were met (Searle 1969).

Given the formula for a request, which specifies the participant roles (S and H) and the propositional content ("Future Act of H"), the conditions which together underlie a sincere request are:

(a) S wants H to do A.
(b) S assumes H can do A.
(c) S assumes H is willing to do A.
(d) S assumes H will not do A in the absence of the request.

The essential condition that characterizes a request in a communication situation is that the utterance addressed by S to H "counts as an attempt to get H to do A" (Searle 1969: 66).

The fact that certain nonimperative utterances regularly convey the illocutionary force of a request has led to the proposal that "indirect requests" may rest on the sincerity conditions for the act, request. Gordon & Lakoff (1971) have suggested that, given these conditions, a speaker may convey a request by asserting the speaker-based condition, e.g.

(a) *I want you to open the door.*

or by questioning one of the hearer-based conditions, e.g.

(b) *Can you open the door?*
(c) *Would you be willing to open the door?*
(d) *Will you open the door?*

This proposal relates the sincerity conditions to many (though not all) of the linguistic variants by which adults can convey requests. We can thus ask: Do children's requests rest on such shared belief conditions and, if so, can children convey requests by asserting or questioning these conditions? In order to answer the question, we must show that the conditions operate in the children's spontaneous performance of requesting.

Other conditions which pertain to the successful performance of speech acts in general may have specific realizations in the act of requesting (Fillmore 1968, Labov 1970), but these conditions have not been formally related to linguistic variants. For example, a speech act must have a point; a request would be defective if the act which S asks H to perform had already been carried out. Also, the relative status of S and H must be appropriate to the speech act; a request might be defective if S asked H to perform an act which was clearly S's responsibility to carry out. Is there any evidence that children are aware of these more general conditions as they attempt to get another person to do something or respond to such an attempt?

In summary, if the sincerity conditions hold, the force of a request can be indicated by certain linguistic devices which specify the propositional content of a request. For the purposes of this investigation the devices are classified as follows:

Direct requests express the content, H will do A, directly, either in imperative utterances, e.g. *Open the door,* or with a performative marker, e.g. *I request that you open the door.*

Indirect requests (Type 1) embed the content, H will do A, into an utterance whose matrix clause references one of the four sincerity conditions given above.

Indirect requests (Type 2) embed the content, H will do A, into an utterance whose matrix clause does not reference one of the four sincerity conditions, at least in any obvious way. This type includes utterances which reference general conditions of participant status and/or some relevant property of the act such as its necessity, e.g. *You have to open the door.* Type 2 indirect requests also include utterances which embed the content, H will do A, into an imperative matrix clause. In this case, however, the imperative scope does not extend to the target act which S wishes H to perform, e.g. *See if you can open the door.*

Finally, adult conversation employs more devious means of getting an addressee to do something. S can indicate a desire for some state of affairs without actually saying that H is to bring about that state, e.g. *That door should be open,* or S can indicate a desire for something without specifying what H is to do, e.g. *I want some coffee,* or *Is there any coffee left?* If, in a given situation, these utterances actually "count as an attempt on the part of S to get H to do A," then S has left a considerable amount of the work to the addressee himself. In the first case H must infer that he is expected to open the door; in the second case H must not only infer that he is expected to do something but must also decide what the appropriate act will be. Such work is a normal part of cooperative conversation and is generally taken for granted by the participants in everyday interactions. One justification for calling such cases requests is that H may infer from them that the essential condition of requesting obtains, i.e. S wants H to perform A. We will call cases which fail to specify some feature of the proposition, H will do A, *inferred requests.* We can ask, then, whether inferred requests appear in this corpus of children's speech.

Requests achieve their *intended illocutionary effect* (IIE) if H is aware that S has made a request. If H complies with the request, then it is said to have achieved its *intended perlocutionary effect* (IPE). In this investigation, we must rely heavily on the achieved effects, as evidenced in H's behavior, to assess the children's competence in requesting.

Examination of the children's speech will proceed as follows. First, we will examine direct requests made by a child to his partner. Second, we will examine the context of these requests to determine whether the behaviors associated with requesting are sequenced in an orderly manner and are differentially distributed across members of the interaction. Third, we will look for meanings which recur in the contexts of direct requests. For example, does the children's behavior indicate that H's ability and willingness to perform A are factors in requesting or responding to requests? Fourth, we will use the structure and content of direct request contexts to identify indirect requests. Finally, we will briefly consider two examples of inferred requests.

DIRECT REQUESTS

Two judges inspected the corpus of speech for direct request forms. No instances of direct requests with performative verbs were found. All imperative utterances were subjected to the following test. Can the utterance be prefixed in its particular context with one of the performative tags *I request, I command, I order (you to)?* Interjudge agreement in applying this test was high (94%), and differences were resolved by discussion. The status or authority relationships that may distinguish request–order–command in adult speech were not clear-cut in this corpus and thus no further classification was attempted. Certain related types of interventions were excluded by the test formula. For example, proposals for joint action, which might be represented as *suggest/response* (S, H (S & H will do A)), specify that S will join H in doing A, e.g. *Let's play mothers and fathers.*

A total of 682 imperative utterances passed the test. Of these, almost one-sixth were excluded from further analysis as being ill-formed requests (i.e. S spoke to himself while carrying out the action himself or addressed the utterance to a toy), or as being poorly executed requests (i.e. H did not appear to hear S speak at all). The remaining utterances, the well-formed requests, totalled 565. Inspection of the consequences of these requests showed that 53% achieved their IPE, i.e. H complied with the request with or without comment. We considered that the IIE of a request was achieved if H indicated that he understood that a request had been made. Evidence included not only verbal compliance but objection, refusal or a conditional response contingent on the request. Of the 565 well-formed requests, 77% met with a verbal or nonverbal response which indicated that the request had achieved its IIE. The results are summarized for the younger and older dyads in Table 2.

The younger and older groups were similar in respect to number of requests and to the percentage of these achieving their intended effects, although the younger dyads did produce, on the average, somewhat more direct requests and more of these were well formed. Although no comparable data are available for adults, it appears that the children were reasonably successful in conveying direct requests. The prediction, "Ask and ye shall receive," holds true, however, only about 50% of the time.

Table 2   Direct Requests for Action and Their Effects

	Younger Dyads (N=12)	Older Dyads (N=24)
Total number direct request forms	270 (mpd=22.5)[a]	412 (mpd=17.1)
Total number well-formed direct requests	225 (mpd=18.7)	340 (mpd=14.2)
(a) % achieving IPE	54	52
(b) % achieving IIE	81	72

[a]mpd=mean per dyad.

STRUCTURE OF THE DIRECT REQUESTS

S often accompanied his request with a phrase or clause relating to the request, and H often did more than comply or refuse with a simple *No!* If S interpreted a response as noncompliant, he might repeat, paraphrase or reinforce the request with *Please*, or *Oh, come on.* In order to examine the clustering of behaviors around the request utterance we propose a structural unit, the *domain* of the request. The term domain refers to the scope of discourse within which the attention of the speaker and addressee is directed to the accomplishment of the request.

S and H are complementary roles in the sense that S initiates the request and H acknowledges it. As in many joint ventures, some of the work can be apportioned in different ways between the participants. For example, we might expect S to provide a well-specified and justifiable request. In fact, a child (or adult) S often fails to do this, so that H must ask for information before he can comply or refuse. If H does seek information, then S must respond to H by "repairing" the request in some way. Thus, the role structure of the request assigns different responsibilities to S and H but allows flexibility in coping with such contingencies as inadequate formulation of the request by S or failure to comply by H. The domain of the request thus represents the role structure of the request interaction and indicates the sequence of the complementary behaviors both under "normal" circumstances and in circumstances where difficulties arise. Fig. 1 presents the structural domain of the request.

S and H   (Ia)   Preparation of propositional content
S   (Ib)   Adjunct to request
S   II   Request
H and S   (III)   Clarification
H   IV   Acknowledgement of II

.   .   .   .

.   .   .   .

S   (V)   Acknowledgement of IV

Fig. 1. Structural domain of Request. (S = Speaker, H = Addressee. Optional elements enclosed in parentheses. Dotted lines indicate potential location of repeated request if IV is other than compliant acknowledgement.)

The obligatory components are S's request and H's acknowledgement, II and IV, respectively. With the acknowledgement H indicates awareness that S intended a request. Other components (Ia, Ib, III, V) are optional. We will briefly discuss the optional components of the domain.[1]

(Ia) PREPARATION OF THE PROPOSITIONAL CONTENT.   Before making a request S may try to make sure that the referring terms of the proposition are available to H. H would normally respond verbally if S asks a question, as in (1). If S makes a statement, H might simply redirect his attention, as in (2). In either case, S and H participate in this step.

(1) S (Ia)   *You see that hammer there?*
   H   *Yeah.*
   S II   *Hand it to me.*
(2) S (Ia)   *There's a fireman's hat.*
   H   (Turns to look)
   S II   *Try it on.*

Component (Ia) is generally composed of an act pair and, as such, can be analyzed as an independent exchange (a request for information and answer as in (1), or a comment and response as in (2)). In these discourses, however, (Ia) is subordinate to the request component, II.

(Ib) ADJUNCT TO THE REQUEST.   Of the direct requests, 111 were accompanied by a clause or phrase which was syntactically independent of the clause containing the imperative verb, or by a tag such as *All right?* or *Okay?* This material, the adjunct to the request, is produced by S and may either immediately precede or follow the request (with the exception of tags, which only follow requests).

(3) S (Ib)   *That's where the iron belongs.*
   S II   *Put it over there.*
(4) S II   *Roll this tape up for me.*
   S (Ib)   *I can't do it.*

(III) *Clarification.*   Following the request, H may ask a question about the utterance. The clarification component is composed of an act pair, a request for information from H and an answer from S. H may query the content of the request as in (5) or the force of the utterance as in (6). Often, however, the question simply indicates H's failure to hear what S has said.

---

[1] All classifications and categorizations are based on nonunique evidence, i.e. on responses which occurred in more than one dyad of children. This restriction was adopted to avoid importing idiosyncratic features into the analysis of the children's requests.

(5) S II *Hand me the truck.*
   H (III) *Which one?*
   S *The dump truck.*
(6) S II *Gimme the ladder.*
   H (III) *You want the ladder?*
   S *Yeah.*

The force of the request appears to hold throughout the clarification exchange; that is, component II does not need to be restated after (III) is completed.

The dotted lines in Fig. 1 represent the position in the domain in which component II, the request, can be repeated. Following a noncompliant acknowledgement or in the absence of an acknowledgement S may repeat or paraphrase his request. Repetition or paraphrase of the request is indicated by a subscript: II_r. Examples of repeated requests are given in the following sections.

(V) *Acknowledgement of the acknowledgement.*   If the request achieves its IPE, then S may mark the end of the domain by thanking H, e.g.

(7) S II *Tie that on for me, please.*
   H IV (Fastens tool belt on S)
   S (V) *Thanks.*

The domain of the request composed of the ordered optional and obligatory components suggests a basis for conversational sequencing: a minimal structure which can be optionally expended to "fore-arm" the request, to clarify a misunderstanding, or to cope with noncompliance. Investigation of other speech acts may reveal partial correspondence with this structure. For example, a request for information can be preceded by preparation of propositional content (Ia). Also, a clarification sequence (III) is itself an expandable component that can occur following other types of speech acts. In (8) a clarification component is repeated following an assertion:

(8) S *I'm going camping.* (Assertion)
   H *What?* (Request for clarification)
   S *I'm going camping.* (Response to request for clarification)
   H *Camping?* (Repeated request for clarification)
   S *Yeah* (Response to repeated request for clarification)
   H *Oh.* (Response to clarified assertion)

Within the corpus, performing a request appeared to entail the ability to apportion and sequence behaviors as indicated in this structural outline. Obviously, not all components were always present at one time, but sequences containing optional components in the order indicated were frequent. It seems reasonable to suggest that learning to produce discourse can be understood as learning to perform the component behaviors which contribute to the successful execution of speech acts, learning the relative order of these behaviors, and learning the appropriate distribution of roles which the alternating turns of the act domain require. The fact that the individual components themselves can be expanded or elaborated lends credibility to this type of structural analysis. This brief description of the structure of the request, however, is offered only as a preliminary step toward more detailed analysis of conversational sequencing. We will now turn to the content of the request domain.

CONTENT OF THE DIRECT REQUESTS

The structural domain of a request reflects a domain of relevance, a network of associated beliefs and motives. The set of jointly held assumptions which underlies the successful production and interpretation of the request also forms the basis for H's acknowledgement to that act and influences, as well, S's interpretation of H's behavior as responsive or nonresponsive. For example, if following a request H produces an utterance which does not reflect some member of that set of assumptions, his utterance will not be heard as an acknowledgement. S would assume that H has not heard his intended request or that he is wilfully ignoring it. It is true that we generally are able to classify types of responses to requests as refusal or compliance, but that classification rests on just those beliefs and motives which enable the request itself. By domain of relevance then, we mean to suggest that the performance of the request creates a field in which only a restricted set of beliefs are operative. (It is these which Searle (1969), Gordon & Lakoff (1971) and Labov (1970) have attempted to capture in the conditions postulated for requests and which we will explore in the children's speech.) Analysis of the content of requests should provide some evidence concerning this hypothesis. The strategy will be to examine the direct request domain (especially the adjuncts and acknowledgements) for indications of these critical beliefs, which we will call *meaning factors*.

ADJUNCTS *(Ib)*   Some evidence of the meaning factors constituting the domain of relevance of a request is provided in the adjuncts. In all, 111 requests were accompanied by adjuncts. The majority of these adjuncts offered a "reason" for making the request. Some of the reasons were objective, even logical. These referenced the antecedent or cause for the request, a relevant normative consideration, or a statement of the future goal which the request served. The following examples illustrate, but do not exhaust, the kinds of adjuncts displaying a relatively objective relation to the request (adjuncts are underlined).

(9) S requests H to stop leaning back on her:
    S II (Ib)   *Stop it.* <u>*You hurt my head.*</u> (Cause for the request)
(10) S requests H to take off the holster:
    S II (Ib)   *Get that off you.* <u>*You girls aren't men like that.*</u> (Normative
    consideration)
(11) S requests H to put curtain on:
    S (Ib) II   <u>*We have to get all bungled up.*</u> *Put it on your head.* (Future goal
    of request)

Other reasons provided in adjuncts were more subjective, i.e. they referenced the attitudes of the participants. Frequently the subjective reason expressed some need or desire on S's part, e.g.

(12) S, tugging, requests H to let go of table H holds:

      S II (Ib)   *Gimme, gimme that. I need that.*

S could also emphasize his own desire for the object or outcome that the successful request would produce, e.g.

(13) S requests H to come to back of car

      S II (Ib)   *Hey come here. I want to show you something.*

The expression *Okay?*, which accompanied many requests, was also classed as subjective. This adjunct queries the willingness of H to do A, e.g.

(14) S requests H to finish folding up measuring tape

      S II (Ib)   *Here, do that. Do the rest of that, okay?*

To summarize the above, three meaning factors recurring in adjuncts were tentatively identified:

(a)   S's reason for making the request. (Objective, $N = 34$)
(b)   S's desire or need for the outcome of A. (Subjective, $N = 9$)
(c)   H's willingness to do A. (Subjective, $N = 29$)

We will equate factor *(c)* with sincerity condition *(c)*: S assumes H is willing to do A.

ACKNOWLEDGEMENTS (IV).   If our hypothesis concerning the relevance structure of the request domain is correct, then acknowledgements should also reflect these meaning factors and perhaps introduce others associated with requesting. Verbal acknowledgement almost always accompanied compliant behavior, e.g. *Okay, All right.* However, H could go on to report on his accomplishment of A ($N = 11$), e.g.

(15) S II   *Just start the motor, okay?*

      H IV   *Okay.* (Makes motor noises) *It's started.*

Or, H could elaborate on the propositional content of the request ($N = 15$), e.g.

(16) S II   *Call up a good guy.*

      H IV   *I will. I'll call a doctor.* (Lifting receiver)

The responses *I will, I'll call,* confirm the analysis of the propositional content as Future Act of H. Also, the responses illustrated above indicate S and H's understanding that H was, before the request, not in the process of doing A or had not intended to do A. Thus, we will equate this meaning factor with sincerity condition *(d)*: S assumes H would not do A in the absence of the request.

On the basis of S's behavior following the acknowledgement, we distinguish two kinds of noncompliant acknowledgements: temporizing responses and out-right refusals. S regularly reacted differently to these two types: in the first case he waited and in the second case he repeated the request or terminated the episode.

(17) illustrates a temporizing acknowledgement. H implied that he would comply but postponed compliance. S appeared to recognize that his request had been ac-

knowledged and not refused, and was, therefore, still in force. He waited for the promised performance.

(17) S requests H to get on car.
    S II *Come on, get on.*
    H IV *As soon as I finish putting out this roaring fire.* (Plays fireman)
    S (Waits)
    H IV (Comes to car)

In other cases S seemed to recognize that the request had not and probably would not succeed. Presumably he interpreted the acknowledgement as a refusal, for he repeated the request in identical or varied form or attempted to strengthen it. In (18) an outright refusal elicited a repeated request which was also refused, though a reason was added to the refusal.

(18) S II *Gimme that ladder.*
    H IV *No.*

   . . . .
    S II$_r$ *Yes.*
    H IV$_r$ *No, I got it.*

To return to the bases for noncompliance acknowledgements, a query on H's part concerning the reason for the request was not generally perceived as an outright refusal, but rather as a temporizing acknowledgement.

(19) *H queries reason for request.* ($N = 5$)
    S requests H to come in behind the couch:
    S II *Get in here.*
    H IV *How come?*

Acknowledgements which were taken as outright refusals did not necessarily include a morphological or semantic negative. They did consistently invoke certain other considerations. (20)–(25) show the bases for outright refusals, i.e. the statement of any of the following considerations counted as a refusal.

(20) *H is unable to do A.* ($N = 6$)
    S requests H to roll up measuring tape:
    S II *Here, do that. Do the rest of that, okay?*
    H IV *I can't.*
    (S continues to fold the tape himself)

(21) *H is not willing to do A.* ($N = 4$)
    S requests H to play tug-of-war with the table:
    S II *Get the table.*
    H IV *No, I don't want to do that.*

   . . . .
    S II$_r$ *Yeah, please.*

(22) *H does not need or want the outcome of A. (N = 6)*

    S requests H to wait while he brings snake to car:

    S II *Wait for the snake to come.*

    H IV *I don't need the snake.*

    (S takes snake over to the mirror, abandoning request)

(23) *H is not obliged to do A. (N = 4)*

    S requests H to hand over ladder:

    S II *Mary, gimme that ladder.*

    H IV *I don't have to.*

    (S repeats request by paraphrasing it)

(24) *H has a prior or conflicting right to some resource. (N = 8)*

    S requests H to get off the wooden car:

    S II *Get off my fire engine.*

    H IV *I'm on it.*

(25) H is not the appropriate person to do A. *(N = 5)*

    S requests H to put on a dress-up hat:

    S II *You put this on.*

    H IV *No, you.*

The acknowledgements support the evidence from adjuncts that S and H believe that S has a reason for making the request, for H may query that reason. Also, the factor of H's willingness is confirmed: negation of willingness on H's part constitutes a refusal. As with adjuncts, *need* and *want* are closely associated, and H's statement, *I don't need* (outcome of A) counted as a refusal.

H made no explicit mention in the acknowledgements that he knew that S wanted him to do A. (Direct reference to this factor does occur in adult speech, e.g. *You really want me to do that?*) But H's behavior showed his awareness of S's desire. For example, in requesting that H hand over a tool, S said *Gimme it.* H replied *You can have this* (offering a toy other than the one requested). Such a substitution, which certainly acknowledges the request, was generally perceived as a refusal. It does represent an attempt to satisfy S, even though H is not willing to comply with S's specific request. These substitutions are interpreted as direct evidence of H's awareness of sincerity condition (*a*): the fact that S wants H to do A.

H's ability to do A appeared as a relevant factor in the request domain. Stating that H was unable to do A counted as a refusal. That S accepted this response as reasonable grounds for relinquishing the request supports the claim that, in requesting, S had assumed the operation of sincerity condition (*b*): H is able to do A. In no instance did S repeat a request which met with the acknowledgement *I can't.*

Other factors expressed in noncompliant acknowledgements were not such effective deterrents as *I can't.* S often repeated the request if the perceived refusal referenced H's obligation to do A, e.g. *I don't have to;* his prior rights, e.g. *I'm on it;* or his role as appropriate recipient of the request, e.g. *You do it* With very few exceptions all nonunique acknowledgements to the direct requests in this corpus have now been accounted for.

The importance of "reasons" to the request domain deserves further comment. Not only is S expected by H to have a valid reason for making his request, but it may be argued that H is expected by S to have a valid reason for noncompliance. A simple *No!* encouraged repetition of the request. The various factors referenced by H in refusing can be viewed as subcategories of reasons since these were often volunteered following an unequivocal *No!*, e.g. (18). Further, S could question H's failure to respond. This suggests that an understanding existed that, in general, H would have a reason for failing to acknowledge a request. (26) supports this inference:

(26) S rings the telephone repeatedly—H does not respond:

    S *Why don't you answer me?*
    H *I don't know.*
    S *Well, ANSWER me.*
    H *Hello.* (Picking up telephone receiver)

Although further evidence is needed on the way a reason factor operates in the request, we have seen that reasons are invoked by S (in adjuncts) and by H (in acknowledgements). S and H assume that S has a reason for making the request, that in the absence of a reason for not complying, H will comply, and that if H does not do so, a reason for his dereliction is available.

In summary, adjuncts and acknowledgements shared two meaning factors, one relating to a belief on S and H's part that the request was motivated by a reason, and the other relating to an assumption that H was willing to do A. Acknowledgements explicit introduced additional factors relevant to the request domain. S was able to interpret utterances expressing these additional factors as acknowledgements, even though they indicated noncompliance. We can now modify the tentative list of factors, add these further factors, and indicate which were interpreted as reflecting awareness of the sincerity conditions of requests.

(a) The request and response are reasonable.
(b) S (wanting the outcome of A) wants H to do A. (Sincerity condition *(a)*)
(c) H is willing to do A. (Sincerity condition *(c)*)
(d) H is able to do A. (Sincerity condition *(b)*)
(e) H is obligated to do A.
(f) H is an appropriate recipient of the request.
(g) H has rights which may conflict with the performance of A.
(h) Before the request H did not intend to do A. (Sincerity condition *(d)*)

These meaning factors constitute the domain of relevance of a direct request. They appear to be shared by S and H and provide not only a basis for understanding utterances as requests but for interpreting utterances as responses to requests. We can now inquire whether the expression of any of the factors can count as an indirect request in the children's interactions.

INDIRECT REQUESTS

Eight meaning factors were shown to recur in the domain of direct requests for action.[1] If young children are able to use or interpret utterances other than those of imperative form as requests, that is, to produce and respond to indirect requests, then we might expect that the factors underlying direct requests also provide the basis for the indirect requests.

Two judges identified 75 episodes (18 from younger dyads, 57 from the older) in which H appeared to interpret what S said as a request, i.e. H acknowledged (by complying or by challenging on the basis of one of the factors relevant to direct requests) an utterance whose propositional content included "Future Act of H." Thus, only episodes in which an IIE appropriate to a request occurred could be included in this count. (Inferred requests, which fail to specify H or A in the propositional content, were, of course, excluded.) Working backwards from the acknowledgements of these tentatively identified requests, a limited number of types of utterances were found to be interpreted as requests. We will begin with Type 1 indirect requests, i.e. requests in which the propositional content "H will do A" is embedded in a matrix clause which references one of the four sincerity conditions.

INDIRECT REQUESTS (TYPE 1)

Examples are presented below, cross-referenced when appropriate to the meaning factors (a)–(h) identified in examination of the direct requests. The number of times each utterance type occurred is also noted.

(27) S asks *if H is able to* take the doll in the car: (Factor *(d)*, N = 7)

    S II *Father, can you take the baby?*

    H IV (Reaches out for the doll)

(28) S asks *if H wants to* get on the car: (Factor *(c)*, N = 26)

    S II *Wanta get on my new car? Wanta get on my new car? Want to?*

    H IV *Oh, I'm coming.* (Closes lunch box and climbs on car without great enthusiasm)

---

[1] We assume that a different inventory of factors must constitute a different speech act. For example, another act type which has "Future Act of H" as propositional content differs from Request on specific factors. According to Searle (1969: 66–7) Advise includes the factors that S believes that A will benefit H and H believes that A will benefit H. However, a factor attributed to Request, i.e. that S wants H to do A, is either absent from or relatively unimportant to Advise.

(29) S asks if H will put hammer into tool belt: (Factor *(h)*, *N* = 15)

    S II *Will you put this hammer in for me?* (Hands H hammer)

    H IV (Puts hammer in tool belt)

    S (V) *Thank you, I'll take it now.* (Retrieves tool belt)

The instances of indirect requests conveyed by *Will you . . . ?* may be related to the acknowledgements to direct requests of the form *I will.* More formal versions of these utterances also occurred, though only among the older dyads. Four cases employing *Would you . . . (do A)?* were acknowledged as requests. In addition to these, there were four other instances of polite versions which were excluded from the 75 acknowledged requests. In these four episodes the child spoke to a toy or to an imaginary person by telephone; two employed *Would you . . . ?* and two *Could you . . . ?* Six of the eight polite request forms occurred in role enactment and were delivered in an exaggeratedly adult manner.

In these Type 1 indirect requests, the propositional content, H will do A, was embedded in a matrix clause which reflected meaning factors corresponding to the sincerity conditions. S could convey a request by asking if H is able to do A; if H is willing to do A; and if H will do A. The expression of Factor *(b)*, which corresponds to sincerity condition *(a)* (S wants H to do A), was not observed to function as an indirect request.

INDIRECT REQUESTS (TYPE 2)

Of the remaining factors which were shown to be relevant to direct requests, expressions of the reason factor *(a)* and of the factor of H's obligation *(e)* were accepted as indirect requests. Thus, the following Type 2 indirect requests were observed.

(30) S asks *if H has a reason for not* tickling him: (Factor *(a)*, *N* = 9)

    S II *Why don't you tickle me*

    H IV *Okay.* (Does)

The mechanism by which such an utterance can count as a request is that S notes that H is not doing A, and then asks whether H has a reason for not doing it. Justification of the potential of this locution to count as a request was provided by episodes in which *Why don't you (do A)?* was paraphrased as a direct request, e.g.

(31) S requests H to put on a feather hat:

    S II *Why don't you try this on, okay?*

    H (III) *What?*

    S *Try this on.*

    H IV (Puts on hat)

In all indirect requests discussed thus far the propositional content of the request was embedded in interrogative matrix clauses. Only one declarative utterance type appeared to function as an indirect request, and five of the six tokens were produced by younger dyads. S could convey a request by asserting that H was obliged to do A. Such requests employed the matrix clauses, *You have to . . ., You gotta . . .,* and *You better (do A).* This type reflects meaning factor *(e)*, e.g.

(32) S says that *H has has* make a phone call: (Factor *(e)*, $N = 6$)

    S II   *You have to call.*

    H IV   *Okay.* (Picks up phone and makes ringing noise)

One Type 2 indirect request employed an imperative matrix clause, *Don't forget*. . . . Three of the four acknowledged instances of this request were produced by older dyads, e.g.

(33) S requests that *H not forget to* smoke an Indian pipe: ($N = 4$)

    S II   *Don't forget to smoke your pipe. It's night time.*

    H IV   (Takes up pipe and play-smokes it)

The mechanism by which such an utterance can count as a request is that S makes the assumption that H is going to do A and then requests that H not forget to carry out this intention. This type of strategy might be interpreted as violating the sincerity condition, "S assumes that H will not do A in the absence of the request."

In summary, of the 75 episodes which were originally identified, 67 were accepted as indirect requests and the criterion that H acknowledged S's request that H perform A. The rejected instances failed on the criterion of nonuniqueness. The younger dyads produced 15 of these 67 indirect requests, and the older dyads 52. Of the 67 indirect requests, 75% achieved their IPE. Table 3 summarizes the analysis of the 67 Type 1 and 2 indirect requests.

Table 3 indicates that younger dyads employed fewer indirect requests than older dyads, although their production of direct requests (as shown in Table 2) slightly exceeded that of the older dyads. Type 1 indirect requests ($N = 48$) essentially conform to the sincerity condition analysis proposed for adult speech (although speaker-based assertions such as *I want you to do A* were not observed). Type 2 indirect requests ($N = 19$) do not conform to the sincerity condition analysis but do reflect meaning factors relevant to the domain of requests. We need further instances of this type to analyse the more complex strategies they represent.

The basis for the analysis of indirect requests was the recurrence of a set of meaning factors identified in the domains of direct requests. Adjuncts, acknowledgements, clarifications and repeated requests also occurred with indirect requests and reflected the same set of meaning factors.

We have offered evidence that children's requests and responses to the requests are based on shared awareness of a set of specific interpersonal meanings. Expression of certain of these meanings (those reflecting the set of sincerity conditions postulated for adult requests) can function as Type 1 indirect requests. The children also seem to be aware of other meanings relevant to requesting and can use them to convey Type 2 indirect requests.

INFERRED REQUESTS

In all requests considered thus far, the propositional content, "H will do A," was specified. Can H acknowledge as a request an utterance which does not specify H will do A? That is, do inferred requests occur in this corpus? Two types of episodes

Table 3.   Type 1 and Type 2 Indirect Requests and Meaning Factors
             Underlying Them

	Younger Dyads (N = 12)	Older Dyads (N = 24)
Type I		
Factor (d) (H's ability)	1	6
Factor (c) (H's willingness)	4	22
Factor (h) (H had not intended to do A)	2	13
Type 2		
Factor (a) (Reason)	2	7
Factor (e) (H's obligation)	5	1
Factor (?) Don't forget to	1	3
Total indirect requests	15	52

suggest that a cooperative H can correctly infer that S has issued a request in this way.

In one type the utterance expresses S's need or desire for some object. The same type of utterance which was observed as adjunct (expressing S's desire) to a direct request can also stand alone as an inferred request. In (34) such a request followed immediately after a direct request.

(34) S and H are writing letters; S first asks H to give her the paper:
    S II *Hey. Now give me that.*
    H IV (Throws paper to S)

    . . . .
    S II *I need that pencil.*
    H IV *Here.* (Tosses the pencil to S)

In (35) H is distributing toys to herself and to S:

(35) S II *A purse. I want a purse.*
     H IV *I'm sorry. Wait.* (Hands one to S)

Both *I want . . .* and *I need . . .* (a thing) can be interpreted as a request that H give a thing to S. These requests (*N* = 7) reflect Factor *(b)*. They leave H the task of inferring that he is expected to perform a suitable action.

A large number of episodes in the corpus involved the use of a "pretend" strategy. Although these have not yet been fully analyzed, some "pretend" utterances function as inferred requests. In (36) S's utterance was interpreted by H as a request that H let go of a stuffed fish that S wanted, and H did leave the fish with S. At the pretend level, H refused to grant ownership of the fish to S. But at the level of the inferred request H complied, i.e. H let go of the fish.

(36) S II   *Pretend fishy was mine.*

    H IV   *Okay.* (Walks off) *But he's really mine.*

If similar pretend episodes can be correctly classified as inferred requests, they represent a sophisticated strategy for attempting to get H to do A.

SUMMARY AND DISCUSSION

Play sessions of 36 dyads of preschool children provided a corpus of spontaneous speech for an investigation of children's ability to convey and respond to verbal requests for action. A direct request was defined as an imperative utterance which could be prefixed in its specific context with a performative tag, e.g. [I request you to] *Leave it alone!* The contexts of direct requests showed a patterning of behaviors which was described as the structural domain of the request. The structural domain represents ordered obligatory and optional components of the request as apportioned to roles of Speaker and Addressee. Within this domain, eight meaning factors were invoked by both S and H. Four of these factors reflected the sincerity conditions which have been proposed for adult requests, and the remaining four reflected more general conditions relevant not only to requesting but to other speech acts as well.

Indirect requests were identified on the basis of H's behavior following an utterance which reflected the propositional content "H will do A." S could convey a request by querying one of the hearer-based sincerity conditions or, less frequently, by a query, assertion or order based on one of the more general meaning factors. Direct and indirect requests and their responses provide support for the hypothesis that children are aware of the interpersonal meanings on which the Request speech act is based. Two examples of inferred requests were presented. Such requests do not specify all elements of the propositional content so that their successful performance depends, in part, on H's ability to infer some element of the content.

Younger dyads and older dyads produced about the same number of direct requests, and both groups were equally successful in achieving the intended effects by means of direct requests. Far fewer indirect requests were observed, and the older dyads produced on the average twice as many successful indirect requests as the younger dyads. Since the meaning factors relevant to requests were also expressed by the younger dyads (in adjuncts, acknowledgements, and repeated requests) we cannot conclude that this difference indicates inadequate conceptualization of the belief conditions on requests on the part of the younger children.

It was assumed that the children's level of linguistic competence was such that alternative utterance forms were available to them, i.e. that they could say what they meant. But it was clear that they could also mean something other than what they said, i.e. they could convey a request or a refusal indirectly. This ability was attributed to the children's mutual understanding of the meanings which constitute the request.

For children of the age range that was observed, the request for action rests on a set of meaning factors which are relatively specific, which may be expressed in variant utterance forms, and which are available to the child in either the discourse role of requester or of recipient of the request. It would be difficult to defend the view that the request forms had been learned solely as utterance types and that the meaning factors were not actually a part of the children's social and linguistic competence. If this were so, it would be impossible to explain how the numerous and superficially variable forms of H's utterances could be interpreted by S as refusals, as temporizing acknowledgements, or as nonresponsive to S's request, and it would be impossible to explain how S was able to paraphrase a request.

One might argue that S did not really react to H's acknowledgements but only to the fact that the act referenced in the proposition had or had not been accomplished. Perhaps S used situational information rather than the shared meaning factors encoded in the acknowledgements to decide whether his request should be repeated, whether he should just wait or perhaps abandon the request. Undoubtedly S did make use of nonverbal indications of H's intent to comply or not, just as H must have attended to nonverbal cues of the sincerity or appropriateness of S's request.

The interpersonal meanings do, indeed, rest on the participants' perceptions of what are, essentially, nonlinguistic conditions. They are products of S and H's interpretation of each other's situated behavior and represent an aspect of social competence. But we have also shown that S and H share an understanding of how these beliefs and attitudes may be encoded in their language. For example, S's differential responding to H's verbal postponements and verbal refusals, and his failure to repeat requests after H stated his inability to comply, indicate that the *verbal* formulations of the acknowledgements influenced S's subsequent behavior. Thus the request, as speech act, reflects an intersection of social and linguistic competence.

Although a request may be acknowledged by a nonverbal gesture, most requests in this corpus elicited a verbal response as well. Many requests initiated or were embedded in longer sequences of contingent utterances and served as the nucleus, or "target illocutionary act" (Mohan, forthcoming), of a verbal interaction. Analysis of these episodes suggests a relationship between a speech act and units of connected discourse. Although the relationship is undoubtedly a complex one, it must rest, in part, on two aspects of the speech act: its role structure and its meaning structure.

The role structure assigns reciprocal responsibilities to the participants. S is responsible for producing an intelligible, reasonable, appropriate, and effective request, while H must offer an intelligible, reasonable, appropriate, and effective acknowledgement, regardless of whether he wishes to comply or not. The meaning structure of the request provides the bases on which S and H can mutually interpret and evaluate each other's performance as meeting or failing to meet these responsibilities. A conversation results from their attempts to carry out their respective roles under the difficulties that befall speech acts in actual use.

Research on the use of language and on children's spontaneous speech and social behavior is still in the preoperational stage. The analyses proposed here are, of course, subject to refinement, addition or outright correction. The study will have accomplished its objective if it provides an impetus for further investigation of an important but relatively unexplored aspect of social development.

REFERENCES

Austin, J. L. (1962). *How to do things with words.* New York: O.U.P.
Blank, M. (1974). Cognitive functions of language in the preschool years. *DevPsych* **10.** 229–45.

Braine, M. D. S. (1963). On learning the grammatical order of words. *PsychRev* **70**. 323–48.
Bruner, J. (1975). The ontogenesis of speech acts. *FChL* **2**. 1–19.
Dore, J. (forthcoming). *The development of speech acts*. The Hague: Mouton.
Fillmore, C. J. (1968). Verbs of judging: an exercise in semantic description. In C. J. Fillmore
        & D. T. Langendoen (eds), *Studies in linguistic semantics*. New York: Holt,
        Rinehart & Winston.
Garvey, C. & Hogan, R. (1973). Social speech and social interaction: egocentrism revisited. *ChD*
        44. 562–68.
Gordon, D. & Lakoff, G. (1971). Conversational postulates. *Papers from the Seventh Regional
        Meeting of the Chicago Linguistic Society*. 63–84.
Heider, F. (1958). *Psychology of interpersonal relations*. New York: Wiley.
Labov, W. (1970). The study of language in its social context. *SG* **23**. 30–87.
Luria, A. R. & Yudovich, F. (1968). *Speech and the development of mental processes in the
        child*. London: Staples Press.
Macnamara, J. (1972). Cognitive basis of language learning in infants. *PsychRev* **79**. 1–13.
McNeill, D. (1970). *The acquisition of language*. New York: Harper & Row.
Miller, G. (1970). Four philosophical problems of psycholinguistics. *PhilosSci* **37**. 183–99.
Mohan, B. (forthcoming). Do sequencing rules exist? *Semiotica*.
Piaget, J. (1926). *The language and thought of the child*. New York: Harcourt, Brace & World.
Rheingold, H. L. (1973). Sharing at an early age. Presidential address presented to the American
        Psychological Association Meeting, Montreal.
Searle, J. (1969). *Speech acts: an essay in the philosophy of language*. London: C.U.P.

The Influence of Context on Children's Use of Identifying Expressions and References

David A. Warden

Three experiments are reported, each examining young children's ability to use the indefinite article to introduce a new referent to a context of discourse, and the definite article to refer to an already-introduced referent. The context of the speaker's referring expressions is varied in terms of the nature of, and the listener's knowledge of, the referents. The results indicate that children under five years fail to take account of their audience's knowledge of a referent—their referring expressions are predominantly definite. Between five and nine years, children inconsistently introduce referents with indefinite expressions. It is argued that mastery of the introductory function of *a* requires decentration on the part of the speaker.

In any study of children's language, it is necessary to examine not only the syntactic and semantic aspects of sentence structure, but also the relationship between a verbal utterance and its nonverbal context. It is obvious, for example, that nonlinguistic variables such as the speaker's intention and the listener's expectation exercise considerable constraints on successful communication. These contextual variables are particularly relevant when one examines the use of referential language. From a psychological point of view, referring is analogous to pointing, insofar as the referential capacity of language enables a speaker to point to an item verbally by means of a *referring expression*, e.g. "That man . . . "; once an item has been picked out in this way, a speaker may comment upon it by using a *predicative expression*, e.g. " . . . bought my car."

Many writers (e.g. Gruber, 1967; Bloom, 1970) have noted that very young children, under 30 months, seldom use referring expressions, particularly when the referent is manifest; rather their utterances are predominantly predicative. Moreover, when a child begins to refer, his referring expressions often fail to identify his referents for a listener; for example, children use pronouns such as *he* and *it* in a notoriously careless manner.

In order to produce an appropriate referring expression, which a listener will understand, a speaker must select his expression from a number of alternatives so that it is appropriate to the context of the discourse. He must decide, for example, whether

From *British Journal of Psychology*, **67**, 1976, 101–112. Reprinted by permission of Cambridge University Press.

his referent is something that requires introduction and explanation, or whether it may be assumed to constitute common knowledge between himself and his audience. His choice of referring expression will also be influenced by his intention; for example, he may wish to emphasize his referent (*this* book), or indicate to whom it belongs (*my* hat), or he may merely wish to name the referent (*a* pterodactyl). A child must therefore master not only the variety of resources for making a reference in English, but also the cognitive factors that determine which referring expression is appropriate in a particular context. The experiments reported here represent an attempt to study one aspect of children's use of referring expressions, namely their use of the definite and the indefinite article.

It has been traditionally supposed that the articles *the* and *a* represent the conceptual opposition between definiteness and indefiniteness. However, this contrast forms only part of their function, and a fuller linguistic analysis reveals several semantic uses and interpretations (e.g. Christophersen, 1939; Strang, 1962; Warden, 1974). For example, the indefinite article may be used not only in an indefinite sense ("I need a hammer"), but also in a nominative sense ("That is a hammer") and an identifying sense ("There is a hammer in that drawer"). In the first case, the reference is to any member of the class of hammers; in the second case, a particular item is described as being one member of the class of hammers; and in the third case, a particular hammer is being introduced to a context of discourse for the first time. Although the nominative and identifying uses of *a* are similar, in that both are concerned with the marking of unity rather than the marking of indefiniteness (Perlmutter, 1970), naming an item and identifying it remain distinctly different operations. For example, in the nominative sentence "That is a hammer," the indefinite noun phrase does not identify anything—the referent has already been identified and is now referred to by the expression "That"; whereas in the sentence "There is a hammer in that drawer," the indefinite noun phrase identifies a particular item. Furthermore, the nominative sense of *a* is not affected by the contextual factors which constrain the use of the identifying sense of the article; a speaker need not take account of his listener's prior knowledge of a referent when he is naming it; whereas this is precisely what he must do if he wishes to refer to it. When a speaker wishes to refer to a previously unidentified referent, he must first introduce it to the discourse by using an indefinite noun phrase, or identifying expression (Vendler, 1967); once an item has been identified in this way, it may be referred to with a definite noun phrase. It is with this complementary use of the articles that the following experiments are concerned, and the terms *identifying expression* and *reference* will henceforth be used to indicate these respective uses of indefinite and definite noun phrases. The first experiment also compares children's ability to use *a* nominatively and in identifying expressions.

The age range of the children in these studies was partially dictated by the feasibility of conducting controlled experiments with very young children. Naturalistic evidence (e.g. Bloom, 1970; Brown, 1973) suggests that function words such as the articles appear in children's spontaneous speech around three years of age. In an earlier study (Warden, 1974), an attempt was made to elicit referential speech from children between three and five years old, in a controlled experimental setting. However, it was clear that relatively few children below four years were capable of directing their use of language to such nonegocentric goals as describing events to an audience. In the first two experiments reported, therefore, four-year-old children were used as subjects.

EXPERIMENT I

The aims of the first experiment were threefold. First, the experiment was designed to discover whether young children are sensitive to the identifying function of the indefinite article, and to the anaphoric function of the definite article, namely, referring back to a previously identified item. Do young children identify specific referents with an indefinite noun phrase, or is the process of "pointing" too intrinsically definite for them to realize the need for an indefinite expresseion? Second, it was necessary to establish that adults, whose language is the model toward which the child is developing, do, in fact, make appropriate use of identifying expressions and definite references. And third, children's ability to use the indefinite article nominatively and in identifying expressions was compared. Naturalistic evidence (e.g. Bloom, 1970) suggests that children first begin to use the indefinite article when they are naming an item. It is predicted, therefore, that children will master the nominative use of *a* before they use this morpheme appropriately in identifying expressions.

METHOD
Twenty children, between the ages of 4 years 3 months and 4 years 9 months, and 20 adults, average age 20 years, acted as subjects. Only native speakers of English were used.

A farmyard scene was arranged on a table, using the following sets of identical model animals: three horses, four cows, four pigs, four hens, four ducks and four sheep. A portable tape-recorder was concealed under the table to record the subjects' verbalizations.

Each subject was presented with four tasks. Two of these tasks (the description tasks) required him to describe an action involving two model animals, manipulated by the experimenter, in which one animal knocked the other animal down: the other two tasks (the naming tasks) required the subjects to name a previously unidentified animal indicated by the experimenter. The order of presentation of these four tasks was counterbalanced using a simple ABBA design, with one half of the subjects receiving a description task first (Group 1), and the other subjects (Group 2) receiving a naming task first. As the purpose of the experiment was to discover whether the subjects could use identifying expressions appropriately in the description tasks, a stratagem was necessary to ensure that such expressions were required in the experimental context. When presenting these tasks to the children, therefore, the experimenter blindfolded himself and manipulated the animals from memory. The children were instructed as follows: "I'm going to make some of the animals move about and do things, and I want you to tell me what's happening. I'm going to put this mask on, so I won't see anything, and I won't know what animals are moving or what they are doing. I want you to tell me." It was hoped that this strategy would also induce the children to describe the events fully, and not merely point to the referents. The blindfold was not used with adult subjects, who were merely asked to describe the events, but to imagine an audience who could not see them. In the naming tasks, the experimenter picked up an animal and asked "What's that?"

To perform appropriately on the four tasks, the subjects should use the indefinite article in all their referring expressions. In the naming tasks, they should respond to the question "What's that?" with a reply of the form "*a +noun*"; and in the description tasks, their responses to the instruction "Tell me what's happening" should be of the form "A + noun is ———ing a + noun" (e.g. "a cow is chasing a duck").

RESULTS

The subjects' referring expressions were scored as either definite or indefinite: definite noun phrases usually contained the definite article, although the demonstrative article *that* was used occasionally, and the pronoun *he* appeared three times in the children's descriptions: indefinite noun phrases contained the indefinite article, although the numeral *one* was sometimes used in the description tasks. The proportional use of indefinite expressions by adults and children in the two tasks is shown in Tables 1 and 2. In both these tables, Group 1 subjects received a description task first, and Group 2 subjects received a naming task first.

Clearly, there was no age difference in the use of articles in the naming tasks; both adults and children consistently used the indefinite article (see Table 1). Comparing the children's use of the indefinite article in the naming and description tasks, the prediction that children would master the nominative use of *a* before its use in identifying expressions would seem to be borne out: using the Wilcoxon matched-pairs signed-ranks test, it was found that the children used the indefinite article significantly more often in the naming tasks than in the description tasks ($n = 18$; $T = 0$; $P < 0.005$, one-tailed). Their descriptions were marked by the use of inappropriate definite references. The adults, as predicted, used identifying expressions more often than the children (see Table 2). By scoring the number of identifying expressions used by each subject, and applying a Kendall's S test for a condition of one dichotomy, this age difference proved to be significant ($S = 240$; $P < 0.001$, one-tailed).

One unpredicted result may best be described as a "task order effect." Apparently, the order of presentation of the four tasks affected the use of identifying expressions. Group 2 subjects, who received a naming task first, were more likely to use an

Table 1   Proportional Use of the Indefinite Article in Naming Tasks

	Group 1	Group 2
Adults	1.00	1.00
Children	1.00	1.00

Table 2   Proportional Use of Identifying Expressions in Description Tasks

	Group 1	Group 2
Adults	0.50	0.80
Children	0.12	0.30

identifying expression in the description tasks than Group 1 subjects, who began with a description task (see Table 2). Although this group difference was not significant, the fact that it was apparent in the descriptions of both the adults and the children suggests that it was not just a chance result. It would appear that the act of naming created a set for the indefinite article, thereby increasing the likelihood of an identifying expression in subsequent discourse.

Finally, we had expected the adults to use identifying expressions consistently in the description tasks. The fact that they did not do so suggests that the contextual conditions under which a speaker realizes the need for an identifying expression were not met in this experiment. A speaker need not identify an item verbally if his audience can see it; he may refer to it immediately. In this case, although every effort was made to impress on them that they were to describe the events to an audience who could not see the referents, the adults may have assumed that the referents were already identified, that they were talking to the experimenter, who was moving the animals anyway. The children, too, may have assumed that the experimenter, even blindfolded, somehow shared their view of the events. If so, this assumption could have affected their use of the articles, although children's use of referential language may be less sensitive to such contextual factors. The following experiment was intended to obviate this weakness of design.

EXPERIMENT II

The main aim of this experiment was to discover the extent to which adults and four-year-old children take account of the social context when they are constructing a referring expression. A definite reference to a previously unidentified item is acceptable if the speaker and his audience are looking at the referent together; but when a speaker mentions a previously unidentified item which his audience cannot see, he must use an identifying expression. It is predicted that adults are sensitive to the social context and will vary their use of identifying expressions and definite references appropriately.

In the previous experiment, the children's referring expressions were marked by an absence of identifying expressions and an inappropriate use of definite references. We now wish to discover whether or not children's referring expressions are sensitive to changes in the social context. In other words, did the results of Experiment I reflect the children's assumption that, in that context, the referents were already identified, or do children consistently fail to use identifying expressions, regardless of context?

This experiment also examined the hypothesis that a previously unidentified referent is more likely to be referred to if it is isolated rather than if it is a member of a group. It is suggested that the group situation is more likely to emphasize the need for an identifying expression when talking about one member of that group.

METHOD

Thirty-two adults and thirty-two children, all native speakers of English, comprised the two experimental groups. The children were in the age range 4.0–4.8; the adults were again students, average age 20.

The experimental stimuli were sixteen line drawings of animals, drawn in black ink on white cards. Each drawing depicted a scene in which one animal chased another animal across the picture. Four different pairs of animals were used: a cat chasing a mouse; a horse chasing a cow; a duck chasing a sheep; and a dog chasing a hen. Each of these animal pairs appeared on four drawings, each time in a different setting. For example, there were four drawings in which a cat chased a mouse; in one of these drawings, three cats were sitting in the background of the picture; in another, three mice were shown in the background; while in a third, three mice and three cats were shown sitting in the background; only in the fourth drawing were the cat (agent) and mouse (object) the only animals present.

The sixteen drawings were divided into four groups of four such that each animal pair appeared once in each group. Also, each group contained one drawing depicting each of the four settings. For example, the four drawings in one group were:

1. A cat chases a mouse.
2. A horse chases a cow (with three cows in the background).
3. A dog chases a hen (with three dogs in the background).
4. A duck chases a sheep (with three ducks and three sheep in the background).

In addition to these 16 drawings, one further picture was used as a trial card. This card showed four foxes all chasing four rabbits.

Each subject received one group of drawings, presented one at a time. One half of the subjects (16 adults and 16 children) looked at the drawings with the experimenter (the Social condition), and the other subjects looked at the drawings by themselves (the Isolated condition). The presentation of the four groups of drawings was counterbalanced over subjects, as was the order of presentation of the drawings within each group.

The trial card was shown first, and each subject was asked to describe what was happening in the picture. During this trial, the subject and the experimenter looked at the drawing together.

RESULTS

Referring expressions were classified as either definite, indefinite or undetermined. Definite noun phrases usually contained the definite article, although the children also used the demonstrative articles *that* and *these*, and the pronouns *him, it, they* and *them*. Indefinite noun phrases included the determiners *a, one* and *another*. Although undetermined referring expressions are usually classified as indefinite, the frequency of occurrence of such expressions, e.g. *"Cat* is chasing *mouse,"* made it necessary to include a separate "undetermined" category. Tables 3–5 show the mean frequencies of each of these three categories of referring expressions, as they were used by adults and children in both experimental conditions. The data in these tables are not, of course, independent: each subject contributed eight referring expressions, and so the scores in any one cell sum to eight over the three tables.

The adults used fewer definite and more indefinite referring expressions than the children, in both experimental conditions (see Tables 3 and 4). Scoring each subject for the number of definite and the number of indefinite referring expressions he produced, and applying Kendall's S test for a condition of one dichotomy, four comparisons were made. The adults and children in the Isolated condition were

Table 3   Mean Number of Definite Referring Expressions

	Isolated Condition	Social Condition
Adults	2.1	3.4
Children	4.4	5.0

Table 4   Mean Number of Indefinite Referring Expressions

	Isolated Condition	Social Condition
Adults	3.3	3.4
Children	2.1	2.1

Table 5   Mean Number of Undetermined Referring Expressions

	Isolated Condition	Social Condition
Adults	2.6	1.2
Children	1.5	0.9

compared for their use of definite referring expressions and indefinite referring expressions, and similar comparisons were made for the two groups in the Social condition. Only one of these group comparisons yielded a significant result: in the Isolated condition, the adults produced significantly fewer definite references than the children ($S = 123$; $P = 0.007$, one-tailed). The absence of a group difference in the use of definite references in the Social condition does accord with our hypotheses. The adults used definite references considerably, though not significantly, more often in the Social condition than in the Isolated condition (Kendall's $S_c = 57.7$; $P = 0.108$, one-tailed); whereas the children produced approximately the same frequency of definite references in both conditions (Kendall's $S_c = 6.7$; $P = 0.45$, one-tailed). In other words, the adults responded to variation in the social context more than the children did, at least as far as their use of definite references was concerned. However, the different experimental contexts did not influence the frequency of identifying expressions produced by either group. This was surprising in the case of the adults, who were expected to produce such expressions more frequently in the Isolated condition than in the Social condition. Concomitant with the relatively low frequency of indefinite articles produced by adults in the Isolated condition (see Table 4) was a surprisingly high frequency of undetermined referring expressions produced by the same group (See Table 5). These undetermined expressions were invariably subject noun phrases, and the omitted determiner was therefore the first word in the sentence.

There was no significant difference between conditions in the children's use of either definite or indefinite referring expressions. However, one difference did emerge from their descriptions: a significantly higher frequency of context-bound, deictic (i.e. pointing) words occurred in the Social condition. Such words as *that, him, it, they,* which were classified as definite referring expressions, were used sixteen times by children in the Social condition, and only three times by children in the Isolated condition. The adults did not use context-bound referring expressions in either condition. Scoring each child for the number of such expressions that he used, and applying Kendall's S test for a condition of one dichotomy, this condition difference was significant ($S_c = 96$; $P = 0.028$, two-tailed). As there were no other reliable differences in the children's descriptions, the scores in the two conditions were combined, and a Wilcoxon matched-pairs signed-ranks test showed that children used definite referring expressions significantly more often than indefinite referring expressions overall ($n = 27$; $T = 69.05$; $P < 0.002$, one-tailed).

It was suggested that definite references might be more likely to occur if the referent was isolated, as the presence of other group members might emphasize the need for an identifying expression. The results disprove this hypothesis; neither the adults nor the children discriminated reliably between isolated and nonisolated referents in their use of definite and indefinite referring expressions.

Finally, the adults were expected to use some definite references in the Social condition, and this they did. But they also used definite references in the Isolated condition, when they were expected to use only identifying expressions. Once again, the adults seem to have made certain presuppositions regarding their audience's knowledge of the referents, presuppositions which the experimental task was designed to eliminate. In order to discover whether children can use identifying expressions appropriately, it is necessary to design a task in which adults consistently use identifying expressions. In an attempt to achieve this, the experimenter took no part in the communication process in the next experiment; experimental subjects acted as speaker and listener.

EXPERIMENT III

This experiment was designed to eliminate such contextual variables as "shared perception" and "prior knowledge" from the referential context. Each subject was presented with a cartoon story which he was required to tell to another subject who could not see the drawings. By using a story-telling situation, it was hoped to remove the repetitive element which was present in Experiment II, and which may have induced a stereotyped, and unnatural, use of referring expressions. It was also decided to study a wider age range of children, and examine developmental changes in the use of definite and indefinite referring expressions. It was predicted that, as a child gets older, he will use progressively fewer inappropriate definite references to introduce a new referent.

METHOD
Four groups of children, in the age ranges 3.0–3.11, 5.0–5.11, 7.0–7.11, 9.0–9.11

respectively, and one group of adults, average age 20 years, acted as subjects in the experiment. There were 16 subjects in the three-year-old group, 20 subjects in each of the five-, seven- and nine-year-old groups, and 10 subjects in the adult group.

Two cartoon stories, drawn in black pencil on white cards, were used. Each story comprised three sequential events, and each event was drawn on a separate card. The two stories were matched in referential content: each contained three animate referents and one inanimate referent; each referent appeared in at lease one picture, and at least two referents reappeared in a second picture. It was intended that each subject would mention four referents once, and at least two referents a second time, in the course of telling the story. The two stories may be described as follows:

Story A: A dog is chasing a hen (picture 1). A cow stops the dog, and the hen is hiding behind the cow (picture 2). The hen has laid an egg (picture 3).

Story B: A cat is walking under a tree, and a bird is sitting in the tree (picture 1). A dog chases the cat up the tree (picture 2). The bird is flying away (picture 3).

The subjects were tested in pairs, with the subjects in each pair being selected from the same age group. Subjects were seated at opposite ends of a table, and a screen was placed between them to prevent the listener from seeing the cartoons, and to emphasize to the speaker (story-teller) that his audience was ignorant of the content of his story. The two subjects took turns as speaker and listener; one subject told one of the cartoons to his partner, and then the roles were reversed, and the other subject told the second story. The order of presentation of the two stories were alternated. The three cards of each story were placed, face down in the correct order, in front of the storyteller, who was instructed to turn them over and tell the story to his partner. The listener was instructed to attend carefully to the story, and try to remember it, because he was going to be asked to repeat it afterwards. Although listeners were asked to repeat the stories they heard, in order to maintain face validity, the purpose of this instruction was to emphasize to both subjects, and in particular to the speaker, that they were to tell the stories to each other. The subjects' stories were tape-recorded for subsequent transcription.

RESULTS

Almost every subject mentioned the four referents in his story once, and at least two of the referents a second time. The subjects' referring expressions were scored as definite or indefinite, and as a first or a second mention of the referent. Most definite and indefinite expressions contained the definite and the indefinite articles respectively; undetermined noun phrases were scored as indefinite, and context-bound references (e.g. *he, it*) were scored as definite.

There was no reliable difference in the pattern of responses to stories A and B, and the scores from these stories were combined. These scores, expressed as percentages of the total number of referring expressions produced, are shown in Table 6. Table 6 shows that, for example, when the nine-year-olds mentioned a referent for the first time, 82 percent of their referring expressions were indefinite; this percentage represents 66 out of a total of 80 referring expressions produced by that group (20 subjects x 4 referents).

Two results stand out in Table 6. First, the adults always used identifying expressions and references appropriately. Second, there were very few age differences in the type of referring expressions used to mention a referent for the second time;

Table 6   Definite and Indefinite Referring Expressions in the Story-Telling Task

Subject Group	First Mention		Second Mention	
	Definite Expression	Indefinite Expression	Definite Expression	Indefinite Expression
Adults	—	100	100	—
Nine-year-olds	18	82	100	—
Seven-year-olds	39	61	100	—
Five-year-olds	38	62	90	10
Three-year-olds	54	46	92	8

almost all subjects, from three years upwards, used a definite reference. It was when a referent was being mentioned for the first time that subjects' referring expressions differed, and consequently statistical analysis is directed to these differences.

BETWEEN GROUP DIFFERENCES.   Each subject was scored for the number of indefinite referring expressions he used to introduce a referent. A Kruskal–Wallis one-way analysis of variance revealed significant differences between subjects on this measure ($H = 48.9; P = 0.001$). The Mann–Whitney U test was applied to each adjacent pair of subject groups in order to identify the source of this significant difference; in fact, every group difference except that between the five- and the seven-year-olds was significant in the expected direction. Adults used more indefinite expressions than nine-year-olds ($U = 45; P < 0.01$); nine-year-olds used more than seven-year-olds ($U = 111; P < 0.01$); seven-year-olds used more than three-year-olds ($U = 119; P < 0.025$); and five-year-olds used more than three-year-olds ($U = 106; P < 0.01$).

WITHIN GROUP DIFFERENCES.   The sign test and the Wilcoxon matched-pairs signed-ranks test were used to compare the frequency with which definite and indefinite referring expressions were used by the subjects in each group to introduce a referent. The three-year-olds were the only group to use more definite than indefinite referring expressions at first mention, but this difference was not significant. All the other groups made greater use of indefinite expressions. This difference was significant for the adults ($n = 10; P < 0.001$, one-tailed) and the nine-year-olds ($n = 18; P < 0.0001$, two-tailed), but it was not significant in the seven- or the five-year groups.

A number of qualitative aspects of the children's stories are noteworthy. Table 6 shows that the three- and five-year-olds used a fairly high proportion of indefinite expressions at first mention. However, 70 percent of the three-year-olds' indefinite expressions and 45 percent of those produced by the five-year-olds occurred in nominative sentences, e.g. "It's a cat," and do not therefore constitute identifying expressions, because naming an item presupposes its identification. Another point of interest lies in children's inconsistent use of the articles, particularly in the five- and seven-year groups. Several children appeared to understand the rule which requires a referent to be identified with an indefinite expression, and introduced a referent in this manner; but they then immediately introduced another referent with a definite reference, e.g. "A cat jumped up a tree and the dog came along." Furthermore, in the same age groups, namely five and seven years, several children made spontaneous self-corrections in their use of articles; each correction was of the same type, namely, the child would introduce a referent with a definite reference, hesitate, and then repeat his referring expression using the indefinite article. It was also observed that one highly sophisticated three-year-old used identifying expressions and references appropriately throughout his story.

GENERAL DISCUSSION

The adults only used the articles consistently correctly in Experiment III and therefore it may be inferred that certain contextual assumptions did affect their referring expressions in Experiments I and II. As these factors may also have affected the children's referring expressions, the results of Experiment III should offer the best indication of children's referential ability. In fact, these results generally supported the results of the previous experiments; younger children used significantly more inappropriate definite references than older children. What conclusions can therefore be drawn from these experiments, regarding young children's ability to use the articles appropriately? In the first place, children master the nominative use of *a* before its use in identifying expressions. When they named an item, four-year-old children used an indefinite expression (Experiment I), but when they placed a referent in a particular context, by describing an event, they revealed a significant tendency to use a definite reference (Experiments I and II). The children seemed to be operating with an article usage rule stating that referents are specified by virtue of their participation in an event, for example, "The cow is running"—Which cow?—"The one that is running." Young children fail to take account of the social context of their reference, or of their audience's knowledge of the referent, when they construct a referring expression. They fail to recognize the need for an indefinite expression when introducing a referent for the first time in a discourse; consequently, they also fail to recognize the constraints on the use of the definite article, namely that its use indicates an already-identified referent.

The most obvious explanation for a child's failure to identify referents is that he is unable to adopt his audience's point of view. From his own egocentric viewpoint, a referent is specified as soon as he (the speaker) is familiar with it; he fails to realize that his audience will only become familiar with his referent after he has identified it for them verbally. And the results of Experiment III suggest that a child reaches nine years of age before he reliably identifies his referents for an audience. However, if children's failure to identify referents is attributed to their egocentricity, why did nearly every child from four years upwards produce at least some identifying expressions? Were they only partially egocentric? Furthermore, why did the children who used context-bound referring expressions in Experiment II only do so in appropriate contexts, namely, when their audience could see the referents? It may be argued that five-year-old children can be nonegocentric in their use of referring expressions, for example, when using demonstratives; but that they are still grappling with the implications of nonegocentricity for the use of the articles. It seems likely that children's difficulty with the articles stems from the dual function of the indefinite article, namely, to indicate either an indefinite referent or a specific, but previously unidentified, referent. In the former case, a speaker need only consult his own knowledge of a referent, whereas in the latter case he must take account of his listener's knowledge. Children may be forced to rely on the definite article until they have mastered the identifying function of the indefinite article; and this mastery will depend on an awareness of their audience's point of view. The fact that most children sometimes used the indefinite article in their descriptions may indicate their partial awareness of the need to identify referents. However, it should be emphasized that many of the indefinite expressions produced by the three- and five-year-olds in Experiment III occurred in nominative sentences, and cannot be taken as evidence of the ability to identify referents.

Maratsos (1974) has produced experimental evidence to suggest that, by four years of age, children understand the difference between a definite and an indefinite referring expression, and will use these expressions appropriately. However, Maratsos' experimental studies only cover a limited area of referential speech. Most of his evidence is based on question and answer sessions in which he told children a story, and then asked a *wh* question, to which the children were supposed to give an answer of the form "the + noun" or "a + noun." The stories and questions were constructed to test three types of referring expressions: Task 1—a referent is identified in the story (an X), and the child should therefore answer with an anaphoric definite reference (the X); Task 2—a group of items are mentioned in the story (Xs), and the child's answer is required to identify one of them (an X); Task 3—an indefinite, nonidentifying expression is used in the story (an X), and the child should repeat this indefinite use of *a* in his answer (an X). Despite the ingenuity of this study, it is open to a number of criticisms. Task 1, testing children's ability to use anaphoric references, does not distinguish between children who refer because the referent has already been identified, and children who always refer, regardless of whether their referent has been identified. Task 2, testing children's use of identifying expressions, fails to distinguish between children who are using identifying expressions, and those who are merely naming. More generally, it may be argued that a speaker's ability to use the articles appropriately can be revealed most clearly when he is allowed to provide the verbal context for his referring expressions, rather than being constrained to respond to a verbal context imposed on him by an experimenter, as in Maratsos' studies. It seems quite possible that, by asking his subjects for a name in response to a question, Maratsos may have biased their responses in favor of the nominative indefinite article. Although it is not being suggested that the verbal context is the only contextual influence on referring expressions, nor that descriptive language represents all linguistic behavior, the descriptive tasks employed in the present study would seem to be more generally representative of the referential use of language.

In conclusion, the experimental results reported above revealed some surprising contextual effects on the use of articles. In Experiment I, the task-order effect suggested that a subject's perception of the task and the function of his utterance may influence his decision to use a definite or an indefinite referring expression. Another odd result was the adults' failure to determine some of their referents in Experiment II, particularly in the Isolated condition. Perhaps this result may be explained as the poor enunciation of a relatively unimportant function word at the start of a sentence, but why then was there a difference between the conditions? And why did this effect not appear to the same extent in children's descriptions? It can only be suggested that some as yet unknown contextual factor, such as whether the listener is patently looking at the referent, or attending to the speaker, may be relevent here. It is of interest that children were less affected by these factors than adults. Clearly, referring expressions are influenced by context, both verbal and nonverbal. With this in mind, this exploration of children's use of the articles in referring expressions remains incomplete. In each of the above experiments, similar contexts were used; the referents were always in front of the speaker, and he was in face-to-face contact with his audience. The physical presence of both referents and audience may have encouraged the use of definite references, particularly by young children. It may be that young children would use identifying expressions more readily in contexts where either the referents are absent (e.g. recounting of a prior event) or the audience is absent (e.g. a telephone conversation). It also seems important to discover when children realize the dual function of the indefinite article, and whether the "indefinite" sense of the article is mastered first.

This paper is based on a thesis submitted by the author in accordance with the regulations governing the award of the degree of Doctor of Philosophy in Psychology at University College London. The author acknowledges with thanks the invaluable advice provided by Dr. P. N. Johnson-Laird during the course of this work.

REFERENCES

Bloom, L. (1970). *Language Development: Form and Function in Emerging Grammars*. Cambridge, Mass.: The M.I.T. Press.
Brown, R. (1973). *A First Language: the Early Stages*. Harvard University Press.
Christophersen, P. (1939). *The Articles: a Study of Their Theory and Use in English*. London: Oxford University Press.
Gruber, J. S. (1967). Topicalization in child language. *Found. Lang.* **3**, 37–65.
Maratsos, M. P. (1974). Preschool children's use of definite and indefinite articles. *Child Dev.* **45**, 446–455.
Perlmutter, D. M. (1970). On the article in English. In M. Bierwisch & K. E. Heidolph (eds.), *Progress in Linguistics*. The Hague: Mouton.
Strang, B. M. H. (1962). *Modern English Structure*. London: Arnold.
Vendler, Z. (1967). Singular term. In Z. Vendler (ed.), *Linguistics in Philosophy*. Ithaca, N.Y.: Cornell University Press.
Warden, D. A. (1974). An experimental investigation into the child's developing use of definite and indefinite referential speech. (Unpublished Ph.D. thesis, University of London.)

Part 6
DEVELOPMENTAL INTERACTION BETWEEN UNDERSTANDING AND SPEAKING

Studies of children's speaking have generally been observational studies—where the investigator observes children in naturalistic situations, usually at home, and describes the child's spontaneous behaviors. In contrast, most studies of children's understanding have been experimental studies—in which different linguistic and nonlinguistic variables in the situation are changed or manipulated so as to observe what children understand of one or another linguistic form when they are asked to respond in different circumstances. Most experimental studies, such as many of those included in earlier sections of this book, have focused on a particular aspect of language (such as pre-noun articles or different verbs).

The studies that are reproduced in this section were concerned with comprehension more generally in relation to the production abilities of children in the early stages of the development of grammar. In the study by *Robin Chapman and Jon Miller (1975)*, children were asked to manipulate objects to demonstrate that they understood the order relations between subject-verb-object words, and the spontaneous speech of the same children was examined to determine how often they preserved subject-verb-object order in the sentences that they produced. In the study by *Elizabeth Shipley, Carlota Smith and Lila Gleitman (1969)*, children at different levels of language development were presented with commands that were varied with respect to completeness (single-words and telegraphic and well-formed commands) to test their comprehension. The study by

327

Jill de Villiers and Peter de Villiers (1974) that is reproduced here was designed to sort out the different capacities that appear to underlie different kinds of language behaviors—capacities for comprehension, production, and grammatical judgment.

Word Order in Early Two and Three Word Utterances: Does Production Precede Comprehension?

Robin S. Chapman, and Jon F. Miller

Comprehension and production of subject-object order in semantically reversible sentences with animate or inanimate subject and object was studied in an object-manipulation paradigm. Three groups of five children each, average mean utterance length 1.8, 2.4, and 2.9 morphemes, respectively, participated. Children preserved subject-object order with respect to the verb significantly more often than they used ordering information to determine the event to be demonstrated; that is, grammatical production preceded comprehension. Comprehension of the subset of the sentences with animate subject and inanimate object was near 100%, however, suggesting the presence of semantic strategies for subject-object comprehension.

Recent syntactic analyses of the early two- and three-word utterances of normal English-speaking children have led investigators to infer an underlying subject-verb-object structure for a majority of the sentences (Bloom, 1970). That is, a syntactic basis is postulated for word ordering in early two- and three-word utterances. Add to this postulate another, derived from the work of Fraser, Bellugi, and Brown (1963), that comprehension of syntactic structure precedes production of those structures. The QED of this syllogism is that children whose productions give evidence of an underlying subject-verb-object basis should be able, at the same or an earlier time, to comprehend sentences in which word order is the only signal to deep structure subject and object relationships. For instance, the child should be able to act out or identify the picture for each of the two sentences, "The boy is pushing the girl" and "The girl is pushing the boy," if his utterances offer evidence of subject-verb-object structure.

There is some reason to believe, however, that the foregoing conclusion is incorrect. Fraser et al. (1963), Carrow (1968), and Owings (1972) all report failures to comprehend subject-object relations in the active voice among children aged three years one month to five years, although Bever (1970) has reported that children between two and three years old respond 95% correctly to an unspecified reversible

From *Journal of Speech and Hearing Research,* **18**, 355–371, 1975. Reprinted by permission of the American Speech and Hearing Association.

test sentence. Children from ages three to five years are usually well beyond the early two- and three-word utterance stages in which Bloom (1970) has identified subject-verb-object structures. De Villiers and de Villiers (1972) report that judgment of correct word order by children is a difficult task not mastered till poststage V (MLU = 4.0). Further, examinations of the scoring procedures used in the 1963 study, one of the few to study both processes in the same children, have cast doubt on the premise that comprehension precedes production at all (Fernald, 1972; Baird, 1972) when guessing rate is controlled by more appropriate scoring procedures.

The existence of a strict developmental ordering for comprehension and production of syntactic form has also been questioned on theoretical grounds. Bloom (1973) has argued that attributing comprehension of structural relations to children in the one-word stage of production is inappropriate. Huttenlocher (1974) has recently gathered longitudinal data that may be interpreted as supporting this view. Bloom (1973, 1974) has further raised the question of whether comprehension of linguistic form always takes precedence over production in the multiword utterances of children. She analyzes comprehension and production as mutually dependent but different underlying processes and cites the importance and availability of nonlinguistic context as an additional cue to the semantic relations coded by sentence structure.

There is documentation that children may comprehend sentences through the use of superficial linguistic characteristics (for example, noun-verb-noun sequences [Bever, 1970], order of mention of sentences [Clark, 1971; Epstein, 1972], probable semantic relationships among the words [Bever, 1970; Slobin, 1966], or facts about the immediate nonlinguistic context [Huttenlocher, Eisenberg, and Strauss, 1968; Huttenlocher and Strauss, 1968; Huttenlocher and Weiner, 1971]). But we have tended to assume that these strategies were overlaid on a basic capacity to understand sentences on the basis of linguistic form alone (Bever, 1970). It is possible, however, that such strategies may constitute the only means by which children can comprehend sentences at the early stages of linguistic development.

Bloom's arguments, the confirmation of comprehension strategies based on context, the reevaluation of work directly comparing syntactic comprehension and production, and the discrepancies between recent independent studies of developmental milestones in comprehension and production have converged to lead us to examine the prediction that syntactic production will actually precede comprehension based on syntactic structure alone. Specifically, we predict that the appropriate subject-verb-object ordering will appear in the child's utterances earlier than the time when sentence word order alone is used by the child as a cue to deep structure subject and object status. This hypothesis is not as surprising as it seems when one remembers Bloom's (1974), Bever's (1970), and Huttenlocher's (1974) arguments that multiple cues for comprehension exist, word order being only one of the possible sentential and referential cues. (See Chapman [1974] for a discussion of the various forms of hypotheses relating comprehension and production.) The very young child ordinarily has the support of the referent situation for comprehension and may seldom need to rely on word order alone in the natural language situation. The present study is a test of his ability to do so in a comprehension task, compared to his ability to encode subject and object in appropriate order in a production task.

METHOD

SUBJECTS AND GROUPS

Three groups of five subjects each participated in the study. The children were drawn from middle- to upper-middle-class homes in terms of their parents' educational and occupational level. The sex, age, and mean length of utterance (MLU) in morphemes of each child are indicated in Table 1.

MLU was the basis for grouping. Children of Group I correspond roughly to Stage I (MLU = 1.75) children in Brown, Cazden, and Bellugi's terms (1969); those of Group II to Stage II children (MLU = 2.25); and those of Group III to Stage III (MLU = 2.75). No child was excluded from the study who met the MLU criterion for a group.

SPEECH SAMPLE

The spontaneous verbal interaction of mother, child, and experimenter was tape recorded during an hour visit by the experimenter, yielding 50 to 150 child utter-

Table 1   Description of Subjects

Subject Identifier	Mean Length of Utterance	Age	Sex
Group I			
C	1.89	2;1	M
K	2.01	2;2	F
H	1.70	2;1	F
R	1.53	1;8	M
L	1.76	2;2	F
Mean	1.78	2;0	—
Group II			
A	2.56	1;11	F
J	2.33	2;1	F
K	2.20	1;11	M
M	2.39	1;8	F
R	2.40	2;0	F
Mean	2.38	1;11	—
Group III			
B	2.92	2;5	F
S	2.84	2;7	F
C	2.84	2;4	F
K	2.97	2;4	F
A	3.11	2;8	F
Mean	2.94	2;6	—

ances for MLU computation. Utterances were transcribed in standard orthography unless the transcriber was uncertain of the appropriate interpretation, in which case the International Phonetic Alphabet was used. Mean utterance length was computed following Brown's (1973, p. 54) procedure with the following additions:

1. If nonnegated versions of the contracted auxiliaries, for example, *can't, don't,* or *won't,* appeared in the speech sample, the negated versions were counted as two morphemes rather than one.
2. If sentences were conjoined by *and,* each sentence (plus its preceding *and*) was treated as a separate utterance for purposes of the count.
3. If the child produced a long string of conjoined words or phrases based on, for example, objects in the room, the string was omitted from the count.
4. Utterances that were imitations or partial imitations of preceding adult speech were marked. If the number of such imitations was greater than 20% of the child's utterances, MLU was computed only for spontaneous utterances. Only one subject in this study produced enough imitations for this procedure to be invoked.

SENTENCES
The 24 sentences used in the comprehension and production tasks are presented in Table 2. Twelve of the sentences were exact reversals of the other 12 with respect to subject and object. They were constructed from the use of three familiar animate nouns (*boy, girl,* and *dog*), three inanimate nouns (*car, truck,* and *boat*), and transitive verbs (*hit, chase, bump, push, pull,* and *carry*). The verbs would permit either animate or inanimate subject and object. The Wepman and Hass (1969) list for five year olds was scanned for the highest frequency verbs bearing the desired selection restrictions. Only *chase* did not appear in the list. *Leave* was originally selected instead of *carry* but proved confusing to children in pretesting. The first four verbs listed have also been used in one or more of the major sentence comprehension studies (the ICP test of Fraser et al. 1963; Slobin, 1966; Carrow, 1968; Owings, 1972). Present progressive tense was chosen as that most appropriate for describing an ongoing event. Evidence also indicates earlier (Stage III, MLU = 2.75) productive marking of the present progressive (Brown et al., 1969) than of the third person singular present in child utterances.

STIMULUS OBJECTS
Six toys were used in the comprehension and production tasks: a plain wooden car, a dump truck, a sailboat, flexible boy and girl dolls, and a plastic dog.

COMPREHENSION TASK
The six toys were arranged in front of the child and a sentence presented. The child's task was to pick out the two relevant toys and demonstrate the sentence (for example,

Table 2. Sentences Used in Conjunction and Production Tasks

Subject, Object	Original Sentences	Subject, Object	Reversed Versions
+Animate +Animate	The boy is hitting the girl. The girl is carrying the dog. The dog is chasing the boy.	+Animate +Animate	The girl is hitting the boy. The dog is carrying the girl. The boy is chasing the dog.
+Animate −Animate	The dog is chasing the car. The boy is carrying the truck. The girl is pulling the boat.	−Animate +Animate	The car is chasing the dog. The truck is carrying the boy. The boat is pulling the girl.
−Animate +Animate	The boat is hitting the girl. The truck is bumping the dog. The car is pushing the boy.	+Animate −Animate	The girl is hitting the boat. The dog is bumping the truck. The boy is pushing the car.
−Animate −Animate	The truck is pulling the boat. The boat is bumping the car. The car is pushing the truck.	−Animate −Animate	The boat is pulling the truck. The car is bumping the boat. The truck is pushing the car.

333

boy hitting girl). Verbal instructions given to the child were "Do what I say," together with an initial set of practice sentences with feedback to insure that the task was understood. If the child failed to pick out the two toys for the practice of experimental sentences (usually through inattention to task or perseveration on previous sentence), the experimenter handed them to him and repeated the sentence.

PRODUCTION TASK
The child watched the experimenter perform an action with two of the six toys and was asked to describe the action in a sentence through one of the following instructions, whichever proved most effective: "What's happening?" "What's going on?" "What am I doing?" The task was preceded by sample sentences in which the experimenter modeled the child's response, if necessary. If the child became inattentive, the experimenter demonstrated the action and then allowed the child to demonstrate it while producing a description.

PRETESTING
To insure that each child knew the lexical items used in constructing the sentences, each item was pretested for both comprehension and production. The first test session began with the pretest, in which the child was asked to point to each toy as it was named. He was then asked to name each toy as the experimenter pointed to it. The actions exemplified by each of the six verbs were then labeled and demonstrated to the child. For instance, the experimenter would say *hitting* while demonstrating *boy hitting girl*. The child was then asked to demonstrate and produce each of the six verbs following their production and demonstration by the experimenter. All children were successful in these pretest tasks.

COMPREHENSION SCORING
Responses to the comprehension task were scored for comprehension of the subject-object relation specifically. A response was scored as correct if the action was appropriately demonstrated with the appropriate subject-object assignments; as wrong if the action was appropriately demonstrated with subject and object reversed; as no response; or as undecidable if the child's attention to word order could not be assessed from the response (for example, *boy hitting girl* demonstrated by crashing the two together simultaneously, or the wrong action modeled, or wrong toys chosen). Infrequently, a child picked only one wrong toy from the same semantic feature set as the target (such as *truck* for *car*) and the response was accepted for further scoring. If an unscorable response was retested, the outcome of the second test was that used in categorizing the response.

Thus the responses scored were either demonstrations of the subject-verb-object sentence (right) or demonstrations of its reversed form object-verb-subject (wrong). Guessing rate for a scorable response, given that the child did not attend to word order as a cue to subject and object status, would then be 50%.

PRODUCTION SCORING
Responses to the production task were scored specifically for the appropriate ordering of subject and object with respect to the verb. The categories used were correct,

including subject-verb-object, subject-verb, verb-object, or subject-object sentences (synonym substitutions were accepted); wrong, including object-verb-subject, verb-subject, object-verb, or object-subject sentences; no response; or undecidable, including all responses on which subject-object ordering could not be determined (for example, verb only). The guessing rate for correctly ordering subject, object, or both subject and object with respect to the verb in a scorable response would again be 50% following these scoring procedures.

PROCEDURES

Two testing sessions and an optional third one were held with each child following the speech sample session. Twelve comprehension sentences were presented to each child during the first session, after completion of pretesting. These were either the 12 original sentences of Table 2 or their reversed versions, randomly determined. The set of 12 sentences was independently randomized for each subject. If the child did not respond, responded in an undecidable fashion, or was uncooperative during the major portion of a comprehension test session, the unscorable sentences were retested in the following session (this occurred infrequently).

The production task, using the second set of sentences, followed the comprehension task in the first session. The remaining 12 sentences were demonstrated by the experimenter in an independent random order for each child. If the child did not respond to sentences, or if he responded with undecidable productions during the major portion of a production session, the unscorable sentences were repeated at the end of the next session or in a third session (this occurred for most children).

The procedure of the second session was identical to that of the first, except that the sets of 12 sentences used with each task were exchanged. A third session was held if unscorable sentences from the second session tasks needed to be retested. All sessions were tape recorded and notes made of the child's productions and sentence demonstrations.

RESULTS AND DISCUSSION

COMPREHENSION VS PRODUCTION

For each child on each task a percent correct score was computed by dividing the number of right responses by the number of scorable responses (right plus wrong). The actual numbers of scorable instances are tallied in Table 3. Percent correct scores are given in Table 4. For each group, a one-tailed correlated t test, $df = 4$, was run on the percent correct scores. The difference between production and comprehension was significant for every group; t test values were 3.77 ($p < 0.01$), 2.26 ($p < 0.05$), and 3.83 ($p < 0.01$) for Groups I, II, and III, respectively. No arcsine transformation was applied to the percentage data, since F_{max} tests showed no violation of the homogeneity of variance assumption.

For each group, those instances in which a child gave a scorable response to a sentence on both the comprehension and production task were tallied according to the correctness of each response. Percent correct for each task for this subset of the

Table 3   Distribution of Scorable Responses (24 possible)

Tasks	Subject Identifer					Percent Scorable Response (Σ Scorable Rs/120) $\times$ 100
Group I	C	K	H	R	L	—
Comprehension	24	18	17	15	18	76.7
Production	16	11	17	7	13	53.3
Group II	A	J	K	M	R	—
Comprehension	8	14	21	21	20	70.0
Production	3	3	14	10	10	33.3
Group III	B	S	C	K	A	—
Comprehension	19	21	20	23	19	85.0
Production	6	20	11	13	13	52.5

data is displayed in Table 5, where the total number of responses represented is 55, 37, and 60 for Groups I, II, and III, respectively.

The pattern of performance in each group is clear: correct word order for subject and object is observed significantly more often in speaking than in serving as a cue to subject and object in the comprehension task. To couch this finding in the language of earlier studies, production precedes comprehension in grammatical acquisition for subject-object structure.

Table 4   Percent Correct (100 X right/(right + wrong) scores

Tasks	Subject Identifier					Mean Percent Correct Score
Group I	C	K	H	R	L	—
Comprehension	54.2	72.2	64.7	80.0	61.1	66.4
Production	81.2	72.7	94.1	100.0	92.3	88.1
Group II	A	J	K	M	R	—
Comprehension	62.5	78.6	61.9	61.9	75.0	68.0
Production	100.0	100.0	57.0	100.0	80.0	87.4
Group III	B	S	C	K	A	—
Comprehension	73.7	57.1	65.0	87.0	78.9	72.3
Production	83.3	85.0	81.8	100.0	84.6	86.9

Table 5   Percent Correct on Each Task for Sentence Subset with No Unscorable Responses

Task	Group I	Group II	Group III
Comprehension	40	76	70
Production	60	81	88

SCORING ASSUMPTIONS

Certain aspects of the scoring procedure deserve further scrutiny because of their importance for the interpretation of this and other studies. Note first that had these data been scored solely on the basis of number right (the procedure of earlier studies) then we would have inappropriately concluded that comprehension preceded production. This paradox arises because the observed probability of a missing, undecidable, or irrelevant response is much greater in the production task than in the comprehension task. This phenomenon occurs both in the object manipulation paradigm and in the picture tasks used in the imitation-comprehension-production task replications; the relevant data for the present study were summarized in Table 3.

The substance of the methodological criticisms raised by Baird (1972) and Fernald (1972) is that the number right scoring procedure is invalid when guessing rates are not identical; new scoring procedures and task paradigms must be characterized by (1) equivalent guessing rates in the two tasks and (2) a scoring procedure specific to the syntactic structure under investigation. These conditions are met by the scoring procedures of the present study if one accepts the assumption that the exclusion of unscorable responses does not differentially bias the probability estimate obtained from the scorable responses.

An alternate way to deal with unscorable responses would be to adopt Fernald's (1972) treatment, in which 50% correct–50% incorrect designations are randomly assigned to unscorable responses. This treatment of unscorable data is tantamount to assuming that the subject is guessing and, therefore, not able to attend to order on any of the unscorable items. When the number of unscorable responses becomes large, as it does in production tasks with very young children, the effect is to reduce (or increase) toward 0.50 the probability of a correct response as computed from scorable instances. In the case of the hypothesis tested here, Fernald's correction would lead to the mean estimated percent correct scores shown in Table 6. The correction attenuates the task effect to nonsignificance in all three groups.

We believe the Fernald correction to be a reasonable and conservative choice when missing or unscorable data are infrequent in comparison to scorable data. (Note that the correction is conservative only with respect to our hypothesis that production precedes comprehension.) When the proportion of unscorable responses is large, as it is here, however, we believe that the correction may seriously distort the inferences drawn from the data. In support of this view is our observation that most children spent much time off task, often earning an unscorable response simply through responding to distracting stimuli, rather than through inability to respond to the sentence.

Table 6   Estimated Percent Correct When Unscorable Responses are Treated as Guesses. Means of Individual Scores Were Computed According to the Formula

$$\frac{R + \frac{1}{2}\ (\text{no response} + \text{undecidable})}{24} \times 100.$$

Task	Group I	Group II	Group III
Comprehension	61.6	62.5	69.2
Production	70.0	61.7	69.5

A more direct test of the correctness of the guessing assumption can be obtained from the production task by comparing children's unconditional probabilities of responding correctly or incorrectly to the conditional probabilities of either response on retest, given that the first response had been unscorable. This computation is made possible by our procedures of routinely retesting children on unscorable production responses. The unconditional and conditional probabilities are displayed in Table 7 for both correct and incorrect production responses. Correlated t tests for each group ($df = 3$ or 4 as noted) reveal that conditional and unconditional probabilities of being right do not differ significantly for any of the groups, nor do the conditional and unconditional probabilities for being wrong. The conditional probabilities of being right or wrong on retest of unscorable items, however, differ significantly in two of the three groups by two-tailed correlated t test (Group I, $t = -3.507$, $df = 3$, $p < 0.05$; Group II, $t = -4.503$, $df = 4$, $p < 0.05$; Group III, $t = -2.200$, $df = 3$, NS). These findings contradict the assumption underlying the Fernald correction and support the assumption made here that unscorable responses do not signal an internal knowledge state of the organism any different from that signaled by the scorable responses.

There is another assumption underlying our treatment of the data, namely, the assumption that the original sentence or demonstration and its reversed counterpart are equally often scorable.[1] To examine whether this was indeed the case in our data we computed for each group the proportion of scorable responses for a sentence or demonstration pair given to the original member of the pair as listed in Table 2. We then averaged these proportions (which should each be near 0.50) and computed the standard deviation for the 12 sentence pairs group by group. For comprehension, Groups I through III, means (and SDs) are as follows: 0.49 (0.072); 0.51 (0.060); 0.44 (0.069). For production, the source of many more unscorable responses, means (and SDs) are as follows: 0.48 (0.204), n = 11; 0.74 (0.237), n = 10; 0.50 (0.259). Scorability, then, is primarily a property of sentence pairs rather than individual sentences. The controlling contrasts are maintained even though some responses are unscorable.

---

[1] E. Martin, personal communication.

Table 7   Probability of Giving a Correct or Incorrect Production Response
Unconditionally on First Test or Conditionally on Second Test, Given that First
Response was Unscorable

Score	Subject Identifier					Mean of Individual Probability Scores
Group I	C	K°	H	R	L	
Probability of right response on first testing	0.375	—	0.458	0.042	0.250	0.281
Probability of right response on retest of unscorable sentences	0.333	—	0.454	0.261	0.333	0.345
Probability of wrong response on first testing	0.000	—	0.042	0.000	0.000	0.011
Probability of wrong response on retest of unscorable sentences	0.250	—	0.000	0.000	0.056	0.077
Group II	A	J	K	M	R	
Probability of right response on first testing	0.083	0.166	0.125	0.166	0.166	0.141
Probability of right response on retest of unscorable sentences	0.056	0.158	0.294	0.300	0.333	0.228
Probability of wrong response on first testing	0.000	0.000	0.166	0.000	0.042	0.042
Probability of wrong response on retest of unscorable sentences	0.000	0.000	0.118	0.000	0.083	0.040
Group III	B	S	C	K	A°	
Probability of right response on first testing	0.083	0.667	0.125	0.458	—	0.333
Probability of right response on retest of unscorable sentences	0.150	0.250	0.428	0.400	—	0.307
Probability of wrong response on first testing	0.000	0.083	0.042	0.000	—	0.031
Probability of wrong response on retest of unscorable sentences	0.050	0.250	0.071	0.000	—	0.093

°No retest data available on subject.

COMPREHENSION OF SENTENCE SUBSETS

Percent correct scores were computed for each subset of six sentences as defined by animacy of subject and object. These are summarized by group in Table 8. Unscorable responses were distributed approximately equally among the four sentence sets. Performance is consistently near 100% for that subset of sentences possessing an animate or human subject and an inanimate object. For the shorter MLU groups, performance on the reversals of those sentences (inanimate subject, animate object) is below chance, indicating that the children were demonstrating the reverse word ordering for the majority of these sentences. Performance on other sentences (animate subject and object or inanimate subject and object) is intermediate. Relative size and color of objects were confounded with animacy in the present study; the animate objects were somewhat smaller and more colorful than the plain wooden vehicles. Thus size and color constitute alternative explanations to animacy for the observed variation.

PRODUCTION OF SENTENCE SUBSETS

Percent correct scores for each subset of six demonstrations were also computed for the production task. These are summarized by demonstration set and group in Table 9. The actual number of wrong responses recorded for each group was eight, with approximately equal distribution across the four demonstration subsets; thus some of the variability in Table 9 reflects differences in number of scorable responses given to different subsets. The distribution of scorable responses among demonstration subsets for each group is summarized in Table 10. When Table 9 is compared to Table 8, it is evident that percent correct scores in production are high across all subsets and are clearly not patterned in the same fashion as comprehension scores, albeit at ceiling levels. Comparison of Table 10 with Table 8 indicates that the patterning of scorable responses given to each demonstration subset is also substantially different from percent correct scores in comprehension, with the possible exception of Group II. The strategies underlying correct encoding of an event, then, would appear to differ in kind from the strategies underlying demonstrated comprehension of a sentence. This conclusion offers additional empirical support to Bloom's (1974) closely reasoned comparison of the two processes.

A second set of analyses of the production data was undertaken in response to Bloom's (1974) query as to whether correct productions might not reveal the effects of an animate-inanimate sentence strategy simply through the encoding, or failure to

Table 8   Comprehension of Sentence Subsets: Mean Percent Correct by Group

Subject-Object		Group I	Group II	Group III	Mean
+Animate	+Animate	76.2	71.4	52.0	66.5
+Animate	−Animate	95.7	90.0	95.8	93.8
−Animate	+Animate	36.4	40.9	73.0	50.1
−Animate	−Animate	53.8	71.4	70.3	65.2

Table 9   Production of Sentence Subsets: Mean Percent Correct by Group

Subject-Object		Group I	Group II	Group III	Mean
+Animate	+Animate	80.0	88.9	82.3	83.7
+Animate	−Animate	89.5	81.8	87.5	86.3
−Animate	+Animate	85.7	87.5	94.7	89.3
−Animate	−Animate	90.5	75.0	81.8	82.4

encode, of subject (depending on animacy) and object (depending on animacy). That is, children might selectively include the subject only when it was animate or the object only when it was inanimate. We first examined the distribution of utterance types in each group for utterances scored correct. Table 11 presents this information. It can be seen that the majority of correct responses were of the form verb-object, a finding we are hesitant to interpret as evidence for the psychological primacy of the predicate because the eliciting question was often a "what-doing" one. A two-word encoding across the subject-predicate boundary (subject-object), however, was markedly infrequent in these data.

We then examined the distribution of utterance types for each demonstration subset. In Table 12 we have summarized the percent of time that a correct response to a demonstration subset mentioned the subject, and the percent of time that it mentioned the object. Inspection of Table 12 reveals a tendency to encode objects as a function of animacy only for Group II, and this tendency is the opposite of the encoding strategy to be predicted on the basis of the comprehension data. The children in Groups I and III usually encode the object, regardless of animacy. The subject of the sentence also appears to be encoded regardless of animacy, but less frequently than the object; encoding takes place less than half the time. Again, we conclude that the child's encoding strategies bear no obvious direct relation to his decoding strategies in early stages of language acquisition.

COMPREHENSION AND PRODUCTION STRATEGIES

We have concluded from the findings that the competence to be attributed to the child on the basis of comprehension is less advanced and different from the compe-

Table 10   Percent of Scorable Responses Given to Each Sentence Subset by Group

Subject-Object		Group I	Group II	Group III	Mean
+Animate	+Animate	15.6	20.4	27.0	21.0
+Animate	−Animate	29.7	45.8	25.4	33.6
−Animate	+Animate	21.9	18.8	30.2	23.6
−Animate	−Animate	32.8	36.4	17.5	28.9

Table 11   Percent of Each Type of Correct Production Response by Group

Utterance Type	Group I	Group II	Group III	Mean
Subject-Verb-Object	21.4	11.1	34.6	22.4
Subject-Verb	12.5	19.4	7.3	13.1
Subject-Object	5.4	5.6	1.8	4.3
Verb-Object	60.7	63.9	56.4	60.3

tency to be attributed on the basis of production for the ordering of subject and object. Two important problems follow from this conclusion. First, what factors within the sentence serve to enhance or depress comprehension performance in the absence of additional context? This is the information necessary to test proposed strategies of sentence comprehension and proposed developmental orderings of those strategies.

One such proposal consistent with the findings is that linguistically less-advanced children decode subject-object relations in sentences lacking referential support on the basis of a lexical semantic strategy; the animate noun is assigned subject status and the inanimate noun, object status. A second proposal could be stated as: assign agent status to the animate noun and object-of-action status to the inanimate noun. It is probable that many of the sentences the young child hears are of the form animate subject–inanimate object, or more specifically, agent-action-object of action, rendering either strategy a plausible one to adopt. (Slobin, 1970; Bowerman, 1973; and Brown et al., 1969 report that the subjects and objects of two-word sentences produced by children in the recent cross-cultural and longitudinal studies are overwhelmingly of this form.) Such a strategy might or might not be overridden by immediate context allowing the child to assign subject and object status to nouns directly on the basis of event properties (for example, first to move) rather than lexical ones.

A second problem raised by the study is to account for good production performance and what we will presume to be good comprehension performance within the referent situation, as opposed to the relatively poor performance in comprehension of sentences alone. The examination of patterns of performance on sentence subsets in comprehension and production shows that the strategies for comprehending,

Table 12   Production of Sentence Subsets: Percent of Correct Responses Including Subject and Object by Group

Subject	Object	Group I Subject	Object	Group II Subject	Object	Group III Subject	Object	Mean Subject	Object
+Animate	+Animate	37.5	100.0	37.5	100.0	64.3	85.6	46.4	95.2
+Animate	−Animate	58.8	82.3	33.3	77.8	33.3	88.8	41.8	83.0
−Animate	+Animate	50.0	83.3	14.3	100.0	55.6	100.0	40.0	94.4
−Animate	−Animate	15.8	87.5	50.0	58.3	28.6	100.0	31.5	81.9

lacking context, appear to be different from the strategies for producing sentences, given context. The fact that comprehension within the situation may depend on a whole set of cues that are made unavailable in controlled comprehension testing, however, means that we have little systematic evidence at present on how comprehension may be accomplished within context.

One attractive account of comprehension of a sentence spoken within the referent situation is accomplished by the following algorithm: (1) match the nouns and verb of the sentence with their contextual referents and (2) infer the relations among the lexical items on the basis of the events witnessed. This would require only lexical comprehension, rather than syntactic comprehension. Smith (1970) and Bowerman (1973) have raised similar speculations about early comprehension strategies within a referential setting. Bowerman, in particular, has suggested that the acquisition of semantic concepts similar to Fillmore's (1971) case category concepts (for example, agent, instrument) is developmentally ordered in both comprehension and production and must be acquired prior to any syntactic generalization such as subject of sentence.

There is some evidence supporting this proposed algorithm for comprehension in context. Shipley, Smith, and Gleitman (1969) report that children in the one-word stage respond relevantly more frequently when single words are presented than when those words are embedded in nonsense or meaningful context. Wetstone and Friedlander (1973) have recently reported that children in the one- and two-word stages of production respond as correctly or relevantly to questions and commands with distorted word order as to those with normal word order, responding to both at above-chance levels. Huttenlocher (1974) is exploring the adequacy of the proposed algorithm in her longitudinal study of comprehension.

The corresponding algorithm for production would lead the child to (1) identify these lexical items corresponding to the salient elements of the referent situation (for example, agent, action) and (2) apply an ordering rule for the lexical items on the basis of their conceptual status (for example, agent-first). Even in this formulation, of course, the child's production strategy results in a word-ordering rule. There remains the puzzle, then, of why the child appears unable to take the product of such a procedure, a sentence, and reverse his rule by inferring the relations among referent objects from the word order information. It is just this irreversible aspect of thought, however, that has been said to characterize the general intellectual functioning of the preoperational child of approximately two to seven years old (Piaget, 1950). We may argue, then, that the failure to use word cues in comprehension when word order is observed by the child in production is simply one instance of the preschooler's many failures to reverse processes that he can carry out in one direction. In this view, comprehension and production processes would not necessarily share the same linguistic competence until the child had attained a concrete operational stage (at approximately age seven) in which the potential reversibility of the processes in each mode should make a common basis of linguistic knowledge available in both modes. This particular prediction we plan to investigate in further work.

Two important studies of comprehension of word order, which were unavailable to us during our work, have appeared since the completion of this study. De Villiers and de Villiers (1973) have reported that seven children in early Stage I (MLU 1.00 to 1.50) similarly failed to attend to word order when acting out sentences, showing frequent reversals or acting themselves as agent upon a single object. The sentences were of the form "Make the horse kiss the cow." Both sentence nouns were either animate or inanimate. For children in the MLU ranges corresponding to the present study, however, the de Villiers report somewhat higher proportions correct (75 to 81%) and fewer reversals than those found here in the comprehension task. The source of these differences is unclear, although different sentence structures, objects, or subject selection factors are candidates. On tests of reversible passive sentences, children failed to show the pattern of errors indicative of a word-order strategy until early Stage IV (MLU 3.00 to 3.50), when they also averaged 85% correct on actives for the first time. If one believes that attention to word order should emerge both as a pattern of correct responses on reversible active sentences and as a pattern of incorrect responses on reversible passives, then the de Villiers' study and the present one are consistent in placing the acquisition of that word-order strategy post-Stage III.

Strohner and Nelson (1974), in a second study of sentence comprehension published after the completion of the present one, report that older two and three year olds show a word-order strategy in acting out reversible actives part of the time (80% correct) but switch to a most probable event interpretation if the sentence permits it (for example, "The mouse chases the bear" is interpreted as "The bear chases the mouse"), particularly when pictures make the two alternative events clear. Not until five years of age, in the Strohner and Nelson study, do children act out probable and improbable active sentences with equal and accurate facility.

These studies, together with the present one, support the view that the young English-speaking child's use of word-order information as a cue to subject and object status is limited and acquired late in contrast to his observance of subject-object word order in his speech. Whether semantic or probable event strategies such as those previously discussed must be invoked to account for discrepancies in comprehension and production only of the subject-object relation of the earliest sentences, or constitute the more correct account for a large body of developmental data now viewed as evidence for syntactic acquisition, is an issue whose decade has come among developmental psycholinguists. We currently believe not only that early language learning is semantic but also that control of the syntactic device of word order in production will precede the comprehension of senterces on the basis of word order alone. The explanation of this developmental sequence will be found, we think, in the natural language learning situation's differential demands for attention to word order in production versus comprehension, rather than in any necessary ordering of the two events.

ACKNOWLEDGMENT

This study was supported by Project Grant 130596 to the senior author from the Graduate School of the University of Wisconsin. An earlier version of the paper was presented to the Fifth Annual Child Language Research Forum, Stanford University, April 7, 1973. We thank the participants in that forum; Lois Bloom, Eve Clark, and Ed Martin; our colleagues attending the Professional Seminar, Department of Communicative Disorders, University of Wisconsin; the members of the Wednesday Psycholinguistics Seminar, University of Michigan at Ann Arbor; and our research assistant Diane Gallagher for their constructive comments and questions about the study. Their contributions, of course, should not be construed as an endorsement of the authors' conclusions. Reprint requests should be addressed to Robin S. Chapman, University of Wisconsin, Department of Communicative Disorders, 1975 Willow Drive, Madison, Wisconsin 53706.

REFERENCES

Baird, R., On the role of change in imitation-comprehension-production test results. *J. verb. Learn. verb. Behav.,* **11,** 474–477 (1972).

Bever, T. G., The cognitive basis for linguistic structures. In J. Hayes (Ed.), *Cognition and the Development of Language.* New York: Wiley (1970).

Bloom, L., *Language Development: Form and Function in Emerging Grammars.* Cambridge: MIT Press (1970).

Bloom, L., *One Word at a Time: The Use of Single Word Utterances Before Syntax.* Hague: Mouton (1973).

Bloom, L., Talking, understanding, and thinking. In R. L. Schiefelbusch, and L. L. Lloyd, (Eds.), *Language Perspectives: Acquisition, Retardation, and Intervention.* Baltimore, Md.: University Park Press (1974).

Bowerman, M. F., Structural relationships in children's utterances: Syntactic or semantic? In T. E. Moore (Ed.), *Cognitive Development and the Acquisition of Language.* New York: Academic (1973).

Brown, R., Cazden, C., and Bellugi, U., The child's grammar from **I** to **III.** In J. P. Hill (Ed.), *Minnesota Symposia on Child Psychology, Vol. 2.* Minneapolis: Univ. of Minnesota Press, 28–73 (1969).

Carrow, M., The development of auditory comprehension of language structure in children. *J. Speech Hearing Dis.,* 33, 105–108 (1968).

Chapman, R. S., Discussion summary of Area IV: The developmental relationship between receptive and expressive language. In R. L. Schiefelbusch and L. L. Lloyd, (Eds.), *Language Perspectives: Acquisition, Retardation, and Intervention.* Baltimore, Md.: University Park Press (1974).

Clark, E. V., On the acquisition of the meaning of "before" and "after." *J. verb. Learn. verb. Behav.,* **10,** 266–275 (1971).

de Villiers, J., and de Villiers, P., Development of the use of word order in comprehension. *J. psychol. Res.,* **2,** 331–341 (1973)

de Villiers, P. A., and de Villiers, J. G., Early judgments of semantic and syntactic acceptability by children. *J. psychol. Res.,* **1,** 299–310 (1972).

Epstein, H. L., The child's understanding of causal connectives. Doctoral dissertation, Univ. of Wisconsin (1972).

Fernald, C., Control of grammar in imitation, comprehension and production: Problems of replication. *J. verb. Learn. verb. Behav.,* **11,** 606–613 (1972).

Fillmore, C. J., Some problems for case grammar. In R. J. O'Brien (Ed.), *Report of the Twenty-Second Annual Round Table Meeting on Linguistics and Language Studies.* Washington, D.C.: Georgetown Univ. Press, 35–56 (1971).

Fraser, C., Bellugi, U., and Brown, R., Control of grammar in imitation, production, and comprehension. *J. verb. Learn. verb. Behav.,* **2,** 121–135 (1963).

Huttenlocher, J., The origins of language comprehension. In R. L. Solso (Ed.), *Theories in Cognitive Psychology.* Potomac, Md.: Lawrence Earlbaum (1974).

Huttenlocher, J., Eisenberg, K., and Strauss, S., Comprehension: Relation between perceived actor and logical subject. *J. verb. Learn. verb. Behav.,* **7,** 527–530 (1968).

Huttenlocher, J., and Strauss, S., Comprehension and a statement's relation to the situation it describes. *J. verb. Learn. verb. Behav.*, **7**, 300–304 (1968).

Huttenlocher, J., and Weiner, S., Comprehension of instructions in varying contexts. *Cog. Psych.*, **2**, 369–385 (1971).

Owings, N., Internal reliability and item analysis of the Miller-Yoder Test of Grammatical Comprehension. Master's thesis, Univ. of Wisconsin (1972).

Piaget, J., *The Psychology of Intelligence.* London: Routledge and Kegan Paul (1950).

Shipley, E., Smith, C., and Gleitman, L., A study in the acquisition of language: Free responses to commands. *Language*, **45**, 322–342 (1969).

Slobin, D., Grammatical transformations and sentence comprehension in childhood and adulthood. *J. verb. Learn. verb. Behav.*, **5**, 219–227 (1966).

Slobin, D., Universals of grammatical development in children. In G. B. Flores d'Arcais and W. J. M. Levelt (Eds.), *Advances in Psycholinguistics.* New York: American Elsevier, 174–186 (1970).

Smith, C., An experimental approach to children's linguistic competence. In J. Hayes (Ed.), *Cognition and the Development of Language,* New York: Wiley 109–136 (1970).

Strohner, H., and Nelson, K., The young child's development of sentence comprehension: Influence of event probability, nonverbal context, syntactic form, and strategies. *Child Develpm.*, **45**, 567–576 (1974).

Wepman, J., and Hass, W., *A Spoken Word Count.* Chicago: Language Research (1969).

Wetstone, H., and Friedlander, B., The effect of word order on young children's responses to simple questions and commands. *Child Develpm.*, **44**, 734–740 (1973).

A Study in the Acquisition of Language: Free Responses to Commands

Elizabeth F. Shipley, Carlota S. Smith, and Lila R. Gleitman

This study reports an experiment concerning the spontaneous responses of young children to commands differing in structural format and semantic content. The results indicate that syntactic comprehension exceeds production in 'telegraphic' speakers. Based on these results, conjectures are offered about the techniques which a child might use in coping with his linguistic environment.

Empirical investigation of the development of language has usually focused on the child as a speaker, and primarily on his spontaneous verbalizations. From this work, a picture of the successive stages of speech of the English-speaking child begins to emerge. The recent studies of Braine 1963, Miller & Ervin 1964, Brown & Fraser 1964, and Weir 1962 describe the period in which the child begins to put two or three words together under a unified intonation contour that sounds to experimenters (and mothers) like a rudimentary sentence. Roger Brown has coined the term "telegraphese" to describe this kind of speech, for the child's utterances contain precisely those items we would want to keep if we were paying by the word.

The psychologists who have chronicled the development of language to this point have attempted to provide a description of the child's organization of linguistic material by inference from these spontaneous telegraphic utterances. For example, these psychologists reason that even at this very primitive stage of speech, the child's utterances seem to be internally structured. The words in the child's utterances are not haphazardly ordered. Words differ in their positional privileges; i.e., the child who says *ball throw* does not, in general, alternatively say *throw ball*. Thus, from the evidence of spontaneous speech alone, psychologists infer that there are already classes of words at this stage, though these classes may differ from those of the mature speaker.

It seems clear, however, that the study of spontaneous speech does not provide a sufficient basis for understanding what the child "knows" about language at various stages of development. There is ample evidence, from three decades of failure by the Bloomfieldian linguists, that a study of spontaneous speech, however objective and comprehensive, forms a poor basis even for the study of adult language. Chomsky

---

From *Language*, **45,** 2, Linguistic Society of America, 1969. Reprinted by permission of the Linguistic Society of America.

1964 has pointed out that the use of this dubious basis for studying children's language multiplies these difficulties by a rather large factor. Therefore, a study of children's verbalizations may not provide the kinds of information needed in developing a theoretical description of the course and process of language acquisition. Linguistic inquiry has succeeded only when, abandoning the attempt to collect and codify natural speech, it began to ask about the individual's organization of language —what has come to be called his "linguistic competence."

Do the primitive utterances of young children reflect an incomplete knowledge of the language, a "telegraphic competence"? Certainly, when the adult's tongue slips, we do not thereupon question his knowledge of English. Perhaps the childishness of children's speech is similarly the effect of performance difficulties—e.g., poor articulatory control, distractibility, limited memory-span—distinguishable in principle from deficits in linguistic organization. The child may be linguistically sophisticated in a way that he is unable to display in actual performance.

In the work we will describe here we have tried to discover whether the child's spontaneous utterances can be taken as direct indications of his linguistic competence; or whether, as is the case for adults, spontaneous speech is a limited and biased source of information. Like the psychologists cited earlier, we are studying the child at the stage in which he speaks telegraphic English, roughly the period between 15 and 30 months of age. By studying the appropriateness of children's reactions to various syntactic and semantic structures, we hope to begin to extricate the question of competence in the child from his performance in speech.

The distinction between performance and competence in the child is a critical one for understanding how language emerges in the individual. Chomsky 1965 and others (e.g., Lenneberg 1967, McNeill 1966) have taken a strong nativistic stand on this issue: language is assumed to emerge as a function of neurophysiological maturation, and aspects of underlying linguistic structure are taken to be inherent in cognitive organization. In support of this view, linguists have argued that the onset of language is regular and tied to other aspects of maturation—that it appears more or less independently of practice, in spite of environmental and physical handicaps, and has a critical period. Chomsky 1959 has shown that the acquisition of language cannot be acounted for in the terms of Skinnerian learning theory. Particularly, transformational linguists have asserted that the speech of adults is so chaotic (interlaced with errors, interruptions, changes of direction, etc.) as to make learning by inductive generalization virtually impossible: the learner's data simply will not support the kinds of inductions he is called upon to make. Thus the Chomskyan linguists take the position that the child comes equipped with very specific principles concerning the nature of syntactic structure—from which, given a corpus of natural speech, he can deduce the details of the language he happens to be exposed to.

Most developmental psychologists studying language acquisition suppose, on the contrary, that the child is endowed with more general organizational and procedural abilities (by no means specific to language) that enable him to form inductive generalizations from regularities that exist in the speech he hears (see particularly Braine, MS). They suggest certain features in the child's language environment that might, for example, give hints as to how to form lexical classes: differential stress (adjectives are spoken more loudly than articles); positional restrictions (nouns often appear in last position in an utterance, while articles and adjectives rarely do); and semantic consistencies (a noun is very often the name of a person, place or thing, while a verb is often an action). Thus these psychologists suggest that the child might be more successful than linguists have been in abstracting the structure of language from a consideration of regularities in the stream of speech.

In the empirical work reported here, we try to ask about the child's underlying knowledge when his spontaneous speech is at various stages of 'telegraphese'. Specifically, we ask whether the child notices semantic and syntactic anomalies that would suggest a level of knowledge not reflected in his speech. Further, we try to approach the question of the ways children process novel material: What does the child do when he hears speech that is not meaningful to him, or that is structurally anomalous? To investigate these matters, we study the child's responses to speech that is systematically varied. We cannot ask for overt judgments of acceptability, meaningfulness, or grammaticalness, as is frequently (and fruitfully) done in the study of adult linguistic organization. Instead we must infer the child's organization of what he hears from other behavior, from the APPROPRIATENESS of his responses to various verbal stimuli. In this experiment the verbal stimuli are commands and the appropriate response is, of course, obedience. In this indirect way we try to ask our subjects, as linguists do: 'Is the following a grammatical sentence in your dialect?'

PLAN OF THE EXPERIMENT

The plan of the experiment was to give to very young children a number of commands, varied systematically in syntax and content, to see if they might not react in visibly different ways to the constructional types. Different responses to stimuli whose semantic content was identical, but whose syntactic structure differed, might be taken as an indication that the child found one of these sequences in some way bizarre or illegitimate. Similarly, sentences with apparently normal structure which contained some meaningless (nonsense-word) material might elicit some special sorts of response.

Our technique was simply to deliver the various utterance types to the child under apparently normal circumstances, and to gauge his responses. This technique has obvious analogies to the linguist's elicitation procedures in which he merely asks "Would you say this?" or "Is this sentence acceptable to you?" On the other hand, there are obvious and inescapable differences, for here we are implicitly asking: "Would you expect me to say this?" or "Is this sentence acceptable from me to you?"

Given that this approach to discovering the child's linguistic competence is a plausible one, there are, nonetheless, enormous difficulties in collecting data of these kinds from young children, partly because of the nature of the subjects themselves, partly because of the lack of available techniques for sensible childwatching. We believe we have had some success in these ventures, but not without much time and some pain. It seems appropriate, both because of the difficulties and the final fruitfulness of the techniques we used, to present the method and procedure of these experiments in somewhat greater detail than usual.

SUBJECTS

The subjects were eleven children, seven boys and four girls, ranging in age from 18 to 33 months. All came from middle-class professional or academic families. All children exhibited some instances of telegraphese in their natural speech. Subjects were ranked by their "verbal maturity" from a sample of their natural speech, median utterance length being the index selected (the rationale for this choice is given in full in the Appendix).[1] The ranking derived from this index conformed to our subjective impressions of how well these children spoke English. On the basis of median utterance length, as well as from other indices such as the use of function words, inflectional endings, intelligibility etc., it was clear that the subjects fell into two groups. The telegraphic group (seven subjects) spoke classical telegraphese: their median utterance length ranged from 1.4 to 1.85 words. It is this group whose responses are of greatest relevance to the experiment, these being the speakers who themselves produce the kinds of utterances used as stimuli. A second group consisted of four holophrastic speakers whose ability to combine words at all was in question. Although there were instances of two-word utterances in these children's speech, these were so rare as to suggest that they may represent merely benefit-of-the-doubt decisions by the transcriber. Median utterance length for these children ranged from 1.06 to 1.16 words. In discussing the results, we will distinguish the telegraphic from the holophrastic group because behavior across the groups in response to the stimuli was quite different, while behavior within the groups was orderly.[2]

STIMULI

In pre-experimental sessions with each child, six toys were selected that he could name. For each of these toys a different command (imperative sentence) was constructed with a different verb. Whenever appropriate for the toys, three referentially specific verbs such as *throw* (for *ball*), *blow* (for *horn*), and *bang* (for *drum*), and three vague verbs such as *find* or *show* or *give* were used. A set of stimuli was constructed with eight utterance types that varied along two dimensions: the syntactic form of the utterance, and the familiarity of the words in the utterance. Each toy name appeared in a command of each utterance type. The utterance types constructed for each subject were as given below.

STIMULUS CATEGORIES: ALL-ENGLISH FORMS

(a)   The well-formed command (**VFN**). A well-formed or "grammatical" command consists of a monosyllabic verb, two "function-words" (a preposition or pronoun, followed by *the*), and the noun toy-name; for example

Throw me the ball!
V   F   N

---

[1] Of course we never know, for any child, or any single utterance, exactly how many "words" have occurred within the sentence. *All gone* may be two words, or it may be a holophrase. However, the large and consistent differences among children make it possible to distinguish the groups in a natural and consistent fashion.

[2] Data for two children whose speech was more advanced are excluded from the results reported here, since they are obviously inappropriate subjects for a study of primitive speakers. We have included data for these subjects, however, in the study of natural speech reported in the appendix. One other child of the minimum age was dropped after several sessions because he gave neither verbal nor behavioral responses to any of the stimuli. Three of the children had participated for several sessions in pilot studies, but at least six months elapsed between participation in the pilot studies and the main experiment. There was no sign that participation in the pilot study led to differences in performance in the main experiment.

(b) The telegraphic command (VN). A telegraphed command approximates some of the spontaneous speech of our subjects by eliminating the function words. It thus consists of a verb followed by a noun; e.g.

Throw ball!
V   N

(c) The lengthened telegraphic command (LVN). This format increases the length of the telegraphed command to at least the length of the well-formed command by preceding the former with *please*, and the child's name; e.g.

Please, Johnnie, throw ball!
L   V   N

(d) The isolated noun command (N). This format again reproduces utterance types noted in the subjects' natural speech. It consists merely of the toy-name itself; e.g.

Ball!
N

PARTIAL-NONSENSE FORMS.   For the following stimulus-types, we replace either the verb or the function words (or both) with nonsense forms of identical syllable count. Each nonsense form reflects English phonological rules, and follows the word-stress pattern of the English it replaces. The nonsense forms are indicated by upper-case letters (X, Z).

(a) Well-formed command with nonsense function words (vZN). The function words are replaced by a bisyllabic nonsense word stressed on its first syllable; e.g.

Throw ronta ball!
V   Z   N

(b) Well-formed command with nonsense verb (XFN). The verb is replaced by a nonsense monosyllable; e.g.

Gor me the ball!
X   F   N

(c) Well-formed command with nonsense function words and nonsense verb (XZN). Here both function words and verb are replaced by the same nonsense material developed for (a) and (b) above; e.g.

Gor ronta ball!
X   Z   N

(d) Telegraphic command with nonsense verb (XN). The verb of the telegraphed command is replaced by the nonsense verb; e.g.

Gor ball!
X   N

A list of 48 stimuli was constructed for each child. (Recall that since the toys may differ for the different children, the nouns and verbs also differ. The nonsense words differ as well, for we had to avoid inconvenient morphophonemic effects that might interfere with intelligibility). Toy-names (nouns) were randomized in blocks of six, utterance-types in blocks of eight.

PROCEDURE

We had hoped to pre-record the stimuli and present them on tape, so as to achieve a greater degree of control over delivery. However, pilot work showed that the children rarely responded to the recorded stimuli (though they were beguiled by the machine itself). Stimuli therefore were presented live. Since the mother was obviously the most familiar source of speech to the child, she presented the stimuli. Mothers were pretrained in the child's absence until their delivery of the various stimulus-types was judged to be natural and consistent.

It was our intention that all stimuli be delivered with mild imperative intonation. We cannot really know, however, precisely how well this intention can be implemented with the syntactic and morphological deformations introduced. Clearly there are gross intonational differences between, e.g., the well-formed command and the lengthened telegraphic command, if both are pronounced "normally." Later we will describe some partial evaluation techniques for the effects of delivery of the various stimulus types.

The experimenter spent one or two preliminary sessions with each subject in his home, and at this time selected the experimental toys and learned the child's name for each. Tape recordings of these sessions also provided the samples of natural speech. Experimental sessions were also conducted in the child's home.

Since these children were too young for a highly structured choice situation, a free-response technique was developed. Three adults were present: the mother, the experimenter, and an additional observer. They engaged in normal conversation with one another and with the child as well if he was interested. All toys except those used in the experiment were removed from the room. The experimental toys were placed on the floor two to three feet apart, within a triangle formed by the three adults. On occasion the mother delivered a stimulus. The child had no set task that he knew of to perform, other than what the stimulus prompted him to do.

The child's behavior after each stimulus was delivered was recorded in various ways. All experimental sessions were recorded on tape, and the experimenter and the observer made independent written records of each trial. These records included reports of objects looked at, touched, and played with, as well as verbalizations within the 90-second interval after the stimulus. Similar information was also solicited from the mother after the two independent records were completed. The experimenter further recorded the time of occurrence of the child's responses (looked, pointed, ran, picked up, etc.) by tapping on the recorder microphone, and kept a written record of the sequence of movements represented by the taps.

Appropriate opportunities for presenting a stimulus arose from three to twelve times during each 40- to 60-minute session. We made every effort to ensure that the child noticed the stimuli; they were not presented while he was engrossed or while he was holding one of the toys. Before giving a stimulus, the mother addressed the child by name. If she thought he responded to his name she then gave the stimulus immediately; if she judged he did not attend to his name, she said something irrelevant and waited for another opportunity. At least three minutes elapsed between stimuli, usually much longer.

After a stimulus was presented, the adults did not initiate conversation for 90 seconds, although they responded to overtures from the child as they normally would. This condition was imposed so that secondary responses, elicited by the mother's further encouraging remarks and actions, would not contaminate response to the linguistic stimulus.

We had planned to replicate the experiment (reversing the order of the list of stimuli) with all subjects. However, scheduling problems or sickness prevented this with three subjects.

RESPONSE CLASSIFICATION

A simplified description of the child's behavior following each stimulus presentation was derived (1) from the written reports of the experimenter and the observer, along with the supplementary comments from the mother, and (2) from the tape recordings of the experimental sessions.[3] We selected behavior criteria which seemed to offer intuitively plausible evidence of how the child regarded the various stimulus types. We found it possible to make a reliable classification of the child's behavior into a limited number of categories.

On most trials the child said or did something; but occasionally he was inert. Further, some of his behavior was judged to be unrelated to· the stimulus—e.g., looking at or playing with objects not mentioned in the stimulus, talking about the tape recorder or the experimenter, etc. All behavior not obviously related to the stimulus is omitted from this analysis. The response categories which we derived are given below.

RESPONSE CATEGORIES: ACTION RESPONSES

(a)   TOUCH. Sometimes the children did what the command implied: they came into physical contact with the toy named in the command. Any behavior that involved such contact with the toy we called "touch," and we took this behavior as an indication that the child had accepted the utterance as a "good" command and was making the natural response; i.e. he was obeying.[4]

---

[3] If the adults disagreed about the occurrence of a particular response (e.g., the experimenter said the subject touched the toy, but the observer said the subject did not), then the response was not counted. However, if one adult made a report that was not made by the others (but was not contested), then the report was accepted and the response included for analysis. This decision was made because uncontested solitary reports were expected: occasionally only one adult could see the child.

To test the legitimacy of this decision, we compared trials where the experimenter's report of the subject's behavior was unsupported, but uncontested by either of the other adults, with trials where the experimenter and the observer reported the same behavior. There was no sign of a bias in the experimenter's unsupported reports (e.g., there was no tendency for the experimenter to report more or less looking at the toy for stimuli which contained nonsense).

[4] It might be argued that merely touching the toy ought to be distinguished from action that indicates that the verb, too, was understood. For example, if the stimulus is *Blow on the horn!*,

(b)   LOOK. Often the child looked at the toy named in the stimulus, without touching it. With the three adults in their strategic positions around the room, it was possible to score this response with fair certainty, though obviously with less reliability than for the gross activity implied by "touch," or for verbal responses which we could re-observe by listening to tapes of the experimental sessions.

VERBAL RESPONSES.   We could readily distinguish two kinds of verbal response that seemed related to the experimental procedure. Of course the children said other things (just as they did other things) that were irrelevant to the experiment.

(a)   REPLY. Occasionally, the child said something that might be taken as a sensible reply or a query about the stimulus. For example, in response to *Give me the truck*, the child might say *Mommy get it* or *Whereza truck?* Sometimes the sensibleness of the reply was in question: in response to the same command, the child might say *Red truck*. We called all these responses "reply," because we could not legitimately distinguish among them.

(b)   REPETITION. We distinguish between replies and repetitions of the commands. A verbal response is scored as a repetition in case the subject repeats all or part of the command in the word order given in the stimulus, and without adding any new material. No attempt is made to guess the intent of the child; some "repetitions" may be questions, others comments, but all are scored the same. Cues to intent, such as question intonation, could not be scored reliably.

THE RELEVANT RESPONSE.   It is useful both conceptually and statistically to have a "cover" response category for all responses that indicate that the child was aware of the stimulus. When we say the child has made a relevant response, he has either touched or looked at the toy, or repeated or replied to the command. The "relevant response" thus indicates that the child heard at least the noun in the stimulus.

EVALUATION OF DELIVERY.

It is possible that a child responds to differences in the mother's delivery of the stimuli, rather than to differences in the stimuli themselves. Given that the mother believes some stimuli are odd, she may communicate this belief to the child. However, there is internal evidence that makes it most unlikely that the children were

---

one might distinguish between blowing on it and throwing it. However, many of the stimuli lack a verb, so this distinction is not appropriate. It will be shown that this further distinction is in any case quite irrelevant to the responses of these subjects: the appropriate action is independent of the presence of a verb.

discriminating certain cues from the mother rather than differences in the stimuli: Since the mothers could not know the appropriate response patterns for the various groups (they were in fact unaware of the existence of two groups), one must suppose that whatever cues they might give the child would be the same, or only haphazardly different, for all children. Thus, for example, suppose that mothers deliver structurally anomalous stimuli in such a way as to indicate to the child that the utterances are indeed bizarre; this would not lead to the consistent group differences we find.

Nevertheless, we conducted a further test for biases in delivery. Blind judgments of the mother's delivery of the noun portion of the stimulus were made for selected stimuli for two subjects. For Carl, vfn and Xfn were used; for Helen, Lvn and vn. These pairs of utterance types were selected because the material adjacent to the noun is the same in each pair. These subjects were selected because they exhibited large differences in frequency of touch-responses for the two utterance types. The appropriate portion of each stimulus, the toy-name, was clipped, and a tape was constructed of the mother uttering the toy-name only. Two judges were told that subjects obeyed on one-half the trials, as indeed they did. They then listened to the tape of toy-names and decided independently for each noun whether or not they thought the child obeyed the command that contained that noun. The results are unambiguous. The judges' predictions of what the child actually did were no better than chance.

RESULTS AND DISCUSSION

EFFECTS OF SYNTACTIC STRUCTURE

The relation between the verbal sophistication of the subjects and their tendency to obey commands delivered in various structural formats is shown in Table 1. For the group of telegraphic speakers the effect is uniform: each of these seven children obeys well-formed commands more frequently than he obeys either two-word or one-word commands. (Each of these comparisons is significant at the.016 level by a binomial test, two-tailed.) For the holophrastic group, there is an opposing trend: those children who do not yet combine words consistently, if at all, tend as a group to obey the child-form commands more frequently than they obey the well-formed commands.

If we restrict our analysis to trials on which we are sure the child attended to the stimulus (i.e., where he made a relevant response), we find no overlap between the two groups of children: all holophrastic speakers obey more often with single word commands than with well-formed commands, and all telegraphic speakers obey more often with well-formed commands than with single word commands. (This finding is significant at the.01 level by a chi-square test.) The results for vn are similar but less sharp.[5]

---

[5] Similar results, although in general less strong, are obtained from the other measures of comprehension we used: All the children whose speech was telegraphic also replied more often to vfn than to vn, and five of these seven replied more often to vfn than to n. The results for the reply category were not clear-cut for the holophrastic group, who in general replied less often (Table 2). Moreover, latency reflects the structure of the command in a similar way. Five of the seven telegraphic children obeyed more quickly after vfn than after n or vn, while only one of the four holophrastic children obeyed more quickly after vfn than after n or vn.

Table 1   Obedience and Verbal Maturity
The percent of trials with a touch for well-formed stimuli (VFn) and childforms (N and vn).Within the groups the subjects are ranked on the basis of their spontaneous speech.

| Subject | Syntactic Structure | | |
| | Adult-Form | Child-Form | |
	vfn	vn	n
Telegraphic Group			
Carl	58	33	33
Dottie	36	27	15
Eric	38	28	25
Fran	64	54	21
Gregory	57	25	37
Helen	62	38	33
Ira	54	33	50
Group Average	53	34	31
Holophrastic Group			
Jeremy	0	33	16
Karen	83	75	80
Linus	42	16	46
Mike	16	50	33
Group Average	35	44	44

Figure 1 summarizes the results. The effectiveness of child-forms (N and VN) in eliciting obedience is compared to the effectiveness of well-formed commands (VFN). Individual differences in responsiveness (the tendency to respond on every trial), which are considerable, have been eliminated by presenting the data as ratios.[6] Clearly the two groups are affected differently by syntactic structure.

These data suggest that well-formed commands are more effective than child-forms in eliciting obedience for the children whose speech is clearly telegraphic. Thus any characterization of these children's linguistic knowledge by an examination of their speech alone clearly fails to account for the fact that they discriminate more speech forms than they use. That children distinguish between utterance types that they use and other utterance types is perhaps not surprising. What is surprising is that just those utterance types they themselves did not use were more effective as commands: the telegraphic children responded most readily to the well-formed sentences.

The data for children below this telegraphic level of natural speech suggest a natural progression. Those who appear to be at the single-word, or holophrastic,

[6] Over-all responsiveness seems largely to be a personality variable rather than a linguistic variable; there was complete overlap of the groups. Over-all responsiveness (percent of all trials with a touch) among these subjects ranged from 11% (Dottie) to 72% (Karen).

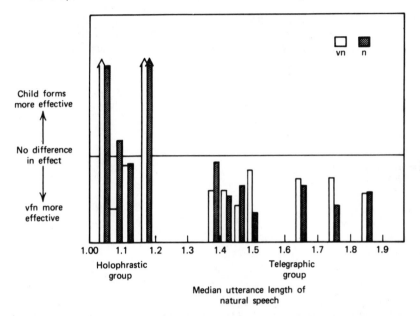

Figure 1. Syntactic structure and obedience at different levels of verbal maturity. The relative effectiveness of the two child-forms of commands (vn and n) compared to well-formed commands (vfn) for each child. The height of the bar represents the percent of child-form commands which elicited a touch, divided by the percent of vfn commands which elicited a touch. The data for the individual subjects are ordered from Carl on the extreme right to Mike on the extreme left.

stage in production prefer to respond to speech at or just above their own productive limit (the vn and n commands).

These results imply that linguistic competence will be underestimated, perhaps with bias, when inferred simply from spontaneous speech—a result necessarily anticipated by those who take an innatist view of the emergence of language. Of course, the fact that comprehension precedes production, in this sense, poses no particular difficulty for a learning-theoretic view. Some support for the view that language is learned may come from the finding that the effectiveness of well-formed commands increases with verbal maturity, implying that there may well be stages of competence which developmentally precede the ability to reflect them in speech. The suggestion in our data that child-forms are more effective commands for the less verbally mature points to an intermediate stage on the way to the competence of the adult speaker.

It is possible to argue that the difference between the child's responses to child-forms and adult-forms is accounted for if we suppose he merely discriminates the gross foreshortening of the child-form stimuli. Length (in words or syllables) and well-formedness are confounded in Table 1 and Figure 1. It will be recalled that we developed a lengthened form of the telegraphic command (i.e., a long but not well-formed command) to test this possibility. Table 2 summarizes the effects of syntactic structure for the two groups of subjects, and shows that the lengthened telegraphic

Table 2   The Effects of Syntactic Structure on the Occurrence of Various
Response-Types for Telegraphic and Holophrastic Speakers
Cell entries represent the percent of trials on which each
response-type was observed, averaged over subjects.

Response-Type	Adult-Form	Syntactic Structure		
		Child-Form		
	vfn	vn	n	Lvn
Touch				
Telegraphic group	53	34	31	32
Holophrastic group	35	44	44	37
Reply				
Telegraphic group	38	28	39	32
Holophrastic group	34	21	19	15
Repetition				
Telegraphic group	5	16	16	10
Holophrastic group	17	15	13	19

sentence (Lvn) is no more liable to lead to obedience (touch) than the child-form commands, n and vn. Does this result conclusively counter the objection that a discrimination of sheer length is all we have shown? The answer is of course subject to the reservations expressed earlier; there are consistent intonational differences between the well-formed sentence and the lengthened telegraphic sentence.

Further examination of Table 2 shows that one of the responses, repetition, does not show the same pattern. If anything, repetitions are rarer with well-formed commands for the telegraphic group. The data here are too sparse to support conclusive interpretation, but they are consistent with the conjecture that children repeat what is to them anomalous: repetitions of well-formed sentences are relatively frequent for the holophrastic group, while repetitions of child-forms are more frequent for the telegraphic group. We reserve further discussion of the function of repetition until we discuss the effects of semantic anomaly.

EFFECTS OF SEMANTIC PROPERTIES OF THE STIMULI

It will be recalled that approximately half the stimuli contain some nonsense material, in addition to the toy-name. We were interested in asking how the child responded to commands whose semantic properties were not transparent. Notice that this stimulus-situation is probably quite unlike that faced by college sophomores when they perform a task involving nonsense words: the college sophomore is in a position, as an expert at English, to decide that the unknown material is indeed meaningless. For the 18-month old child, many English words are novel, and therefore no rational child of that age should conclude that there is anything inherently peculiar about these unfamiliar stimuli.

Some major effects of semantic anomaly are the same for all subjects, regardless of their differing verbal sophistication (Table 3). This is not surprising, since the nonsense words were no more well-known to one group than to another; but, as we have shown, the various structural types were better known to the more advanced subjects. We can therefore discuss over-all effects of semantic anomaly for all subjects before turning to a discussion of those effects as related to verbal maturity.

RESPONSES INDICATING COMPREHENSION OF THE NOUN.   All subjects save one gave a relevant response less often when the stimulus contained nonsense. (This finding is significant at the.012 level by the binomial test, two-tailed.) Figure 2 presents for each subject individually the effectiveness of the nonsense-containing commands, relative to the effectiveness of the commands without nonsense, in eliciting a touch. It is apparent here that the two groups are similar.

At first glance, it might seem that the subject inclines to do nothing with nonsense-containing stimuli because there is no intelligible command for him to obey. But this explanation cannot account for the results: there is as much intelligible material in the stimulus *Dog!* as there is in the stimulus *Gor ronta dog!*; yet the subjects did make

Table 3   The Effect of Nonsense on the Occurrence of Various Response-Types for Telegrahic and Holophrastic Speakers. Child-forms of commands. (n, vn, Lvn compared to Xn) and adult-forms (vfn compared to Xfn, vZx, XZn) are considered separately. Cell entries are the percent of trials on which a given response-type was observed averaged over subjects. Significance levels are based on t-tests in which the data for the two groups were combined.

| | Command Type | | | |
| Response-Type | Child-Form | | Adult-Form | |
	All-English	Nonsense-Containing	All-English	Nonsense-Containing
Touch				
Telegraphic group	32	22	52	33
Holophrastic group	42	22	35	34
Significance level	p <.01		p <.01	
Reply				
Telegraphic group	32	20	38	32
Holophrastic group	18	10	34	18
Significance level	p <.05		p <.05	
Relevant Response				
Telegraphic Group	66	55	74	62
Holophrastic group	71	64	74	57
Significance level	Not sig.		p <.05	

a relevant response to the former more often than to the latter. Relevant responses occurred on 67% of the trials with N, but on only 55% of the trials with XZN (averaged over subjects).

Nonsense at the beginning of the stimulus (XFN, XZN, and XN) interfered with a relevant response (Table 4). Note, though, that all such stimuli lack a verb. Perhaps initial nonsense interfered most tellingly with a relevant response because much semantic information (*Throw. . .*) was lost; but if the second item was nonsense, very little semantic information (. . . *me the* . . .) was missing. This supposition loses plausibility when we note that the verbless but nonsenseless *Ball!* elicited the relevant response more often than did stimuli with a nonsense verb (Table 4). The conjecture is further weakened when the effect of the verb on the subject's behavior is examined: if the verb was present, was the subject more likely to do what it implied? The data are clear here: given that the child touched the toy at all, a verb-related action was less likely when the verb was there than when it was not! With a verb in the stimulus, verb-related action occurred on 61% of the trials; without a verb, verb-related action occurred on 70% of the trials: a ball is to throw. A child told to *Horn!* blew on the horn more often, if anything, than when told *Blow the on horn!*, provided he came in contact with the toy at all. Thus absence of the verb is a poor explanation for why initial nonsense (and deletion of the verb) reduced the likelihood of a relevant response.

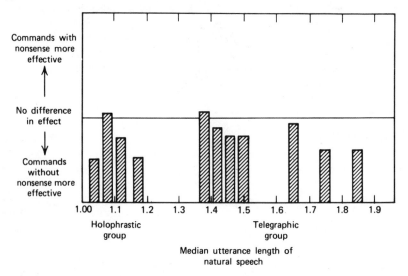

Figure 2.   The effect of nonsense on obedience at different levels of verbal maturity. The relative effectiveness of commands with nonsense (XN, vZN, XFN and XZN) compared to commands without nonsense (N, vN, LvN and vFN) for each child. The height of the bar represents the percent of commands with nonsense which elicited a touch, divided by the percent of commands without nonsense which elicited a touch. The data for the individual subjects are ordered from Carl on the extreme right to Mike on the extreme left.

Table 4   The Effect of the Presence of an English Verb and of the Presence of Nonsense on the Occurrence of a Relevant Response
Cell entries are the percent of trials on which a relevant response was observed averaged over all subjects.

Semantic Properties of the Stimulus	Stimuli with an English Verb	Stimuli without an English Verb
All-English stimuli	vn, Lvn, vfn 70	n 67
Stimuli containing nonsense	vZn 65	Xfn, XZn, Xn 58

The problem with nonsense-containing stimuli was obviously not that something was missing, but that something was there, something that was unintelligible and that somehow gave the subject pause. We suggest that unknown material may have "turned the child off"—or perhaps, failed to turn him on. We cannot, from what we have done, say why: perhaps he was distracted by trying to understand the nonsense; perhaps he found complicated talk onerous, or assumed it was not addressed to him. In any case, if the subject "tuned out" before before the stimulus ended, he could not hear the noun, he would be unaware of the stimulus toy, and thus he could not (except by chance) make any relevant response.

It might be suggested that if the child listens primarily when he recognizes the beginning of the utterance, thus biasedly reducing his linguistic input, he will create for himself a simplified and less chaotic corpus with which to form those 'inductive generalizations' that learning theorists rely on to explain his acquisition of the language.

REPETITION.   Although all responses related to comprehension of the noun in the stimulus decreased when the stimulus contained nonsense (Table 3), there was one response that nonsense did not depress: namely, repetition. Repetitions occurred on more trials with nonsense than trials without nonsense (see Table 5). As shown in Table 2, repetition was also more likely to occur with structures anomalous to the child.

The relative effectiveness of nonsense in eliciting repetitions increased with verbal maturity, as shown in Figure 3 and Table 5. The telegraphic group repeated more often with nonsense stimuli than with no-nonsense stimuli. For the holophrastic group this difference was smaller with child-forms and was in the opposite direction for well-formed commands: there was a clear decrease in repetition when nonsense was introduced. In contrast, it should be noted that the tendency of children to repeat verbal material in ordinary circumstances DECREASES with growing maturity (see, e.g., Brown & Bellugi 1964); similarly, the over-all tendency to repeat decreases as a function of maturity in our subjects for 'normal' speech (i.e. for well-formed, all-

Table 5   The Effect of Nonsense on the Occurrence of a Repetition for
            Telegraphic and Holophrastic Speakers
            Child-forms of commands (n, vn, Lvn compared to Xn) and
            adult-forms (vfn compared to Xfn, vZn, XZn) are considered
            separately. Cell entries are the per cent of trials on which a repetition
            was observed averaged over subjects.

	Command Type			
	Child-Form		Adult-Form	
	All-English	Nonsense-Containing	All-English	Nonsense-containing
Telegraphic group	15	24	5	15
Holophrastic group	16	18	17	12

English commands). Only when the stimulus contained nonsense did our more mature
subjects repeat as frequently as the less mature subjects.[7]

What is the function of repetition for these children? Since, for the telegraphic
speakers, repetition was increased when the difficulty of the linguistic stimulus was
increased, we can conjecture that repetitions play some role in language development: what is not already familiar is practiced. Moreover, when the child repeats, he
is more likely to obey (this is true for all subjects). Even though the nonsense material
reduced obedience over-all, there was a greater tendency to obey on those trials
where a repetition occurred. Thus the practice may have assisted in comprehension.

There is a close analog to this finding in the Russian work on inner speech. Sokolov
(as reported in Slobin 1966) measured covert verbalizations (muscular activity in the
articulatory system), which are presumably repetitions of the input, for adults reading
and listening to their native language and a foreign language. Covert verbalizations
are much more frequent for the foreign language; and the more difficult the foreign
language, the more frequent they are. For our subjects, it was also the "foreign"
speech which led to greater repetition. Both anomalous words and anomalous constructions led the child to repeat.

But why should semantic anomalies be relatively more effective in prompting the
more verbally mature child to repeat, as compared to the less mature? We suspect
that the semantically anomalous stimuli were so far beyond the immature children's
comprehension as to preclude so organized a response. Children seem to repeat what

---

[7] In pilot work (six months prior to their participation in the experiment) Gregory and Helen
were given some commands which contained nonsense and some which did not. No-nonsense
commands were more effective (relative to nonsense commands) in eliciting repetitions when
these children were in the pilot study than they were six months later. With increasing age, and
presumably increasing verbal maturity, both children showed the same change in the effects of
nonsense which appears when we examine different children at different levels of verbal
maturity. Thus we have some longitudinal validation of our findings.

is just a little bit beyond them, and this would appear to be a rather efficient way of increasing knowledge at an orderly rate. This notion is consistent with the finding that the more mature children are, as a group, more likely to repeat the nonsense in the nonsense stimuli than are the less mature children. The material that is repeated may be determined by what puzzles the child, but it must be sufficiently available to allow repetition.

SUMMARY AND CONCLUSIONS

We have raised the question of whether a description of linguistic development may be derived from an examination of the child's natural speech. Our data show that children make discriminations that are not reflected in their speech. Children whose speech is telegraphic readily obey well-formed commands, and less readily obey telegraphic commands. Thus a description of the child's spontaneous utterances does not do justice to his linguistic organization. In some fairly clear sense, comprehension seems to precede the production of well-formed sentences.

But this is not the puzzle in our findings; no doubt, production involves some skills in addition to those required in comprehension, a fact chronicled again and again in the literature on learning and perception. What is truly surprising is that those utterances which a description of natural speech would specify as typical for the child are

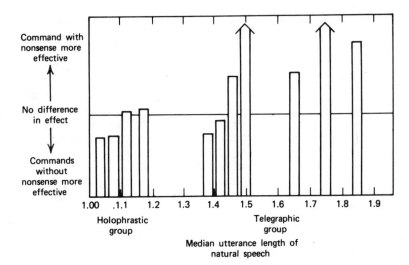

Figure 3. The effect of nonsense on repeating at different levels of verbal maturity. The relative effectiveness of commands with nonsense (XN, VZN, XFN and XZN) compared to commands without nonsense (N, VN, LVN and VFN) for each child. The height of the bar represents the percent of commands with nonsense which elicited a repetition, divided by the percent of commands without nonsense which elicited a repetition. The data for the individual subjects are ordered from Carl on the extreme right to Mike on the extreme left.

just those utterances which are less effective to him as commands. Could he understand what he himself says less well than he understands what others say? Presumably not, but he seems to understand that there is something more natural—at least for the adult—in what the adult says. The well-formed utterances which the child never uses are nonetheless the more effective and compelling commands. This it seems necessary to posit some knowledge in the child about the structure of adult-forms, knowledge that will make the adult-form a "better command" than the child-form for the child. A description of natural speech leaves this implicit system entirely out of account. Therefore, in no sense can recent descriptions of children's speech—no matter how closely the format of these descriptions conforms to transformational accounts—be taken as grammars of child language.[8]

We have shown so far that the child is more "competent" with language than his early speech would by itself imply. But to what extent is he competent from the beginning? i.e., in what sense may his knowledge of language be taken as the product of unlearned cognitive functions? Our data suggest that competence, as well as performance, seems to change and grow. Not only speech, but the perception of what is well-formed, changes with increasing verbal maturity: the immature group prefers to respond to child-forms, while the telegraphic group prefers to respond to adult-forms. Such facts can of course be encompassed either within maturational or learning-theoretic approaches equally well, at least at the present state of our knowledge. The nativist position is not sufficiently articulated to allow predictions about the kinds of speech and perceptual organization that ought to show up relatively early in development. For the present, at least, the predictions concerning the course and process of acquisition are not obviously different for nativists and empiricists; indeed, the nativist, just like the empiricist, suggests that the child constructs limited interim grammars (see, e.g., Chomsky 1965) on his way to linguistic competence.

The argument for innate linguistic competence is made on the basis of quite different kinds of observation; no one expects the child to be born speaking English, or to speak it at all without a good deal of exposure to the speech of others. The question is: how much of what is learned can be accounted for by inherent regularities in the input itself (i.e. in heard speech), and how much must be accounted for by granting the learner dispositions to deal with the input in specific ways? Chomsky has argued with much justice that a comparison between a haphazard sample of speech and the grammar itself (presumably the way language is ultimately organized in the mind) leaves little doubt that the task in inferring the latter from the former is difficult to the point of improbability. On such grounds, it is argued that the child must bring a great deal of apparatus into the learning situation. Nor would psychologists in general disagree with this estimate; but there is some question whether what the child brings to the situation is knowledge about language, or certain general methods for organizing various kinds of sensory input.

Our data allow some tentative speculations on these matters. Our subjects' responses to novelty, both syntactic and semantic, suggest some general techniques

---

[8] We are making the usual assumption of linguists that the same grammar is relevant both to comprehension and production of speech. While such an assumption seems clearly parsimonious when mature speakers are considered, it is perhaps less compelling as applied to children.

through which they may approach the buzzing confusion of the ambient linguistic environment. If, for example, the child does not 'tune in' to excessively complex or unfamiliar speech, this selective listening may provide him with a tractable corpus. Such filtering need imply very little in the way of prior linguistic knowledge. Long sentences, sentences that begin in an unfamiliar way, can perhaps be ignored. There is little doubt, in addition, that the mother does some filtering of her own; lexically and constructively complex requests are unlikely to lead to any overt response from the child, and mothers surely know this. Convenience dictates that we provide children with a simplified linguistic situation. To this extent the child's effective linguistic environment is not the total, indefinitely variable, corpus of adult speech, nor a haphazard sample of that total. Thus the child need not begin his grammar construction with unselected data.

In the same vein, the child appears to use repetition as another method for approaching the linguistic environment selectively. He repeats what is just a bit beyond him in natural speech, what is just a little bit odd. We need not assume that the child is 'trying to learn' when he makes this selection; how could he know what to pick out to try to learn unless he knew it all in advance? Whatever the child's intent or capacity, he is apparently unable to repeat long complicated material that is far beyond his comprehension. Thus what can be chosen for repetition—for recontemplation or rehearsal—is also highly selected. In short, we suspect that the child comes equipped with a set of capacities, and also incapacities, which assure that he will respond selectively to the linguistic environment. It seems to us premature to speculate about the specificity of such predispositions to language.

In sum, we have tried to create a situation in which the child could display his current linguistic knowledge, even if he could not do so by producing well-formed sentences. The results suggest that the child makes distinctions not evident in speech at some stages, and that these distinctions vary with linguistic maturity. Further, the child seems to have ways of biasing his linguistic input so that the flow of new information can be controlled.

There is general agreement among psychologists and linguists that the differences between spontaneous speech and knowledge in young children may be very extreme. Psychologists studying natural speech have worried about this problem, not only because the impression one gets of children's language from children's speech may be an underestimate, but because it may be biased in unknown directions. We believe our experimental technique is a step forward in this connection. Perhaps more important, we are convinced that there must be techniques for systematic observation. Otherwise, little that is substantive can be added to or subtracted from the linguist's philosophical assertion that linguistic competence is innate.

APPENDIX: NATURAL SPEECH

For each child, 100 intelligible utterances were transcribed from tape recordings of preliminary sessions. Exact immediate repetitions of his own utterances by the child were not counted, and are excluded from the analysis. A single transcriber worked with the natural speech samples of all thirteen subjects and provided the data used in this analysis. Thus, if any transcriber bias exists, it enters into the data of all subjects equally. In an attempt to evaluate the reliability of the transcriptions, the transcriber made a second transcription some months later of the tape of Linus' utterances. This child was selected because of the low intelligibility of his speech. Although the specific utterances judged intelligible differed markedly in the two transcriptions, the percent of intelligible utterances is remarkably similar (67% and 70%), as is the median utterance length (1.09 and 1.12).

The transcriber was instructed to be generous in counting words: if there was a suggestion of two words, two words were counted even if they were elided; e.g., *wanna* in *wanna drink* would be scored as two words. The transcriber was instructed to err on the side of omission with respect to grammatical features such as suffixes in the child's speech. Features were transcribed as present in an utterance only if clearly heard.

We next examined utterance length, intelligibility, and the frequency of certain grammatical features in a search for a realistic measure of verbal maturity.

UTTERANCE LENGTH.

Characterization of natural speech in terms of utterance length involved several decisions. First, there is the question of which utterances should be included. (Note that we have omitted all immediate repetitions of the child's own utterance.) Some investigators (e.g., Brown & Fraser) have omitted all single word utterances; since these are often answers to questions, their frequency may reflect the frequency of questions addressed to the child rather than the child's tendency to use one-word utterances in preference to more complicated ones. We chose to include single-word utterances because the experimenter seldom directed questions to the child in these sessions; instead, she played with toys, and the child's speech was ordinarily comment about or participation in the play.

A second problem is the measure used to characterize utterance length. The mode did not discriminate among our subjects, so median utterance length was selected as the measure. Median utterance lengths for the thirteen children are shown in Table 6. It can be seen that, on the basis of this measure, the subjects fell naturally into three groups. Two children formed a group of mature speakers, and utterances of three or more words were as common in the speech of these children as shorter utterances. Further, many of their utterances were well-formed sentences. Seven children formed a group of intermediate or telegraphic speakers, whose speech tended to be fairly evenly divided between single-word utterances and longer utterances. The four children in the group of least-mature speakers had few if any utterances longer than one word. Those few utterances counted as containing more than a single word may represent the transcriber's benefit-of-the-doubt decisions. Thus we have called these children holophrastic speakers.

INTELLIGIBILITY.

An index of intelligibility was obtained by counting the number of consecutive utterances examined in order to find 100 completely intelligible ones. We see in Table 7 that the children varied greatly in this respect and that there was overlap among the three groups established on the basis of median utterance length.

Intelligibility enters in two ways into a consideration of verbal maturity. First, since adult speakers are more intelligible than children, intelligibility might be considered an independent index of verbal maturity in our sample of subjects. Second, it may be more difficult to detect the presence of grammatical features in the less intelligible children, and we may therefore systematically underestimate their linguistic sophistication. The positive correlations of intelligibility (Table 8) with the various grammatical features (see below) support both these possibilities. On the one hand, intelligibility correlates significantly with the presence of verbs; since it is relatively easy to hear verbs, this does suggest that intelligibility might be a separate measure for these subjects. However, intelligibility correlates most highly with those features which are hard to hear (noun and verb suffixes). When we instructed the transcriber to beware of attributing a grammatical feature unless it was clearly heard, we guaranteed that children who were hard to understand would also be low in the incidence of various grammatical features. If we remove the effects of intelligibility statistically, we may have a purer picture of what features go together in children's speech than if we are at the mercy of the transcriber's ear for subtle cues to sophisticated speech.

GRAMMATICAL FEATURES
We examined the children's speech for the presence of certain grammatical features: verbs, verb auxiliaries, verb suffixes, noun suffixes, articles, pronouns, and transformational constants. For each child we determined the number of utterances in the speech sample which contained an instance of a grammatical feature. Transformational constants were found in the speech of only two children (Andy and Billy, the most advanced speakers on most counts), and are not considered further. For each

Table 6   Median Length of Utterances in Natural Speech Sample

Subject's Age in Months	Subject	Median Length
Mature Group		
30	Andy	3.50
33	Billy	2.50
Telegraphic Group		
23	Carl	1.85
19	Dottie	1.75
25	Eric	1.65
29	Fran	1.48
28	Gregory	1.43
21	Helen	1.41
32	Ira	1.40
Holophrastic Group		
24	Jeremy	1.16
20	Karen	1.10
24	Linus	1.09
18	Mike	1.06

Table 7   Grammatical Features and Intelligibility
The rank of each subject is based on the frequency of occurrence of the grammatical feature in a sample of natural speech. (The rank of 1 indicates the subject with the most instances of the feature). High intelligibility is indicated by a low number (e.g. a rank of 1.5). Dashes indicate no instances were found.

Subjects	Intelligibility	Verbs	Verb Aux.	Pronouns	Verb Suffix	Noun Suffix	Articles
Mature Group							
Andy	4.5	1	1	1	1	3	5
Billy	1.5	2	2	2	2	4	2.5
Telegraphic Group							
Carl	9	5	3	3	—	—	7.5
Dottie	1.5	8	—	10	5	2	1
Eric	8	7	4	5	3	—	—
Fran	3	9	—	4	4	1	4
Gregory	4.5	4	5	8	6	6.5	9
Helen	7	3	—	7	—	—	7.5
Ira	10.5	6	—	6	7	—	6
Holophrastic Group							
Jeremy	10.5	12	—	11	8	5	2.5
Karen	12	11	—	—	—	—	—
Linus	6	10	—	—	—	6.5	—
Mike	13	13	—	9	—	—	—

grammatical feature, the children were ranked on the basis of the frequency of the feature in the speech sample; the rankings are given in Table 7. It seems clear that the children fall into the same three groups on the basis of the frequency of the various grammatical features as they do on the basis of median utterance length.

This tendency for the various grammatical features to appear together in the children's speech can be expressed by correlations between rankings on the different features. Table 8 shows such correlations: note that all are positive. To evaluate the effect of intelligibility as an artifactual basis for the obtained positive inter-correlations of the grammatical features, partial correlations were performed holding intelligibility constant. Although the correlations among the grammatical features are reduced when intelligibility is held constant, all correlations remain positive and five remain significant. Thus intelligibility is not the sole basis for the positive intercorrelations.

The inter-correlations among the grammatical features are suggestive. There appear (Table 8) to be two important groups of features or factors: (a) verbs, verb auxiliaries, and pronouns; and (b) noun suffixes and articles. Although the correlations are relatively high (and are significant) for features in the same feature-group, they are near zero for features in different groups. Verb suffix, the sixth feature, correlates fairly highly with all other grammatical features. When intelligibility is statistically held

Table 8   Inter-correlations of Natural Speech Measures and the Correlation of
Each Measure with Age
(Kendall Rank Order Correlation Coefficient)
All correlations are positive; correlations larger than .41 are significant
at the .05 level or better.

	Age	Intell.	Verbs	Verb Aux.	Pro-nouns	Verb Suffix	Noun Suffix	Articles
Median Length	.38	.56	.59	.71	.66	.65	.39	.38
Age		.39	.41	.38	.45	.55	.24	.30
Intelligibility			.47	.31	.29	.53	.62	.50
Verbs				.62	.54	.38	.13	.22
Verb Auxiliaries					.68	.51	.11	.08
Pronouns						.54	.13	.30
Verb Suffix							.58	.42
Noun Suffix								.55

constant, the significant correlations among factors in the first group, and also those between the factors in the first group and the verb suffixes, are still significant. Thus the first factor, perhaps a verb-phrase factor, is in no sense an artifact of intelligibility, as the latter factor may be.

The inter-correlations of the grammatical features suggest that, for some children, the noun-phrase may develop first: children who use articles also tend to inflect nouns. For other children the verb-phrase appears to develop first: the use of verbs and verb auxiliaries (obviously) go together. The correlation of pronouns with these verb features suggests that pronouns may be used in place of more complex noun phrases by children who have elaborated the verb phrase.

There is a suggestion of a sex difference in natural speech. Males tend to use more verb-phrase features: the five children who use verb auxiliaries are male. Females tend to use noun-phrase features, especially articles; three of four females, compared to four of nine males, use articles. Perhaps the apparently greater proficiency of males in the verb aspect of language is related to their greater motor activity.

SELECTION OF THE MEASURE OF VERBAL MATURITY.

Given the various analyses of the natural speech samples, how are we to decide on a measure of the sophistication of the speech of these children? There is obviously no principled answer to this question, for in general we cannot decide what features of speech are somehow more important in deciding which child's speech is more adult-like. For this latter reason, we could not combine the various indices (thus equating their importance) to derive a composite ranking of the subjects. As a compromise solution, we chose median utterance length as the index on various grounds.

It is clear that utterance length is a better index than age, since for each grammatical feature the correlation with utterance length is higher than the correlation with age (Table 8). We reject intelligibility as the index, since it is at least in part the effect of a motor skill which may be independent of other linguistic knowledge. We reject the grammatical features as our index for two partially related reasons: we cannot combine these features to derive a single index, for we do not know whether they are equally important; and we cannot choose any one of them because of the obtained variation in the order in which these features emerge in speech. These decisions leave only the index of utterance length.

The relatively high correlation of both grammatical features and intelligibility with utterance length suggests that these indices at least in part are measuring the same thing. Moreover, agreement between two transcriptions—even for the least intelligible of the subjects—suggests that the utterance-length index is a reliable one.

REFERENCES

Bellugi, Ursula, and Roger Brown (eds.) 1964. The acquisition of language. (Monographs of the Society for Research in Child Development, 29.) Chicago: University of Chicago Press.

Braine, Martin D. S. 1963. The ontogeny of English phrase structure: the first phase. Lg. 39.1–13.

——.MS. The acquisition of language in infant and child. To appear in The learning of language, ed. by Carroll Reed. Champaign, Ill.: National Council of Teachers of English.

Brown, Roger, and Ursula Bellugi. 1964. Three processes in the child's acquisition of syntax. Harvard Educational Review 34.133–51.

Brown, Roger, and Colin Fraser. 1964. The acquisition of syntax. Bellugi & Brown 1964:- 43–79.

Chomsky, Noam. 1959. Review of Verbal behavior, by B. F. Skinner. Lg. 35.26–58.

——. 1964. Formal discussion. Bellugi & Brown 1964:35–9.

——. 1965. Aspects of the theory of syntax. Cambridge, Mass. :MIT Press.

Lenneberg, Eric. 1967. Biological foundations of language. New York: Wiley.

McNeill, David. 1966. Developmental psycholinguistics. The genesis of language, ed. by Frank Smith and George A. Miller, 15–84. Cambridge, Mass.: MIT Press.

Miller, Wick, and Susan Ervin. 1964. The development of grammar in child language: Bellugi & Brown 1964:9–34.

Slobin, Dan I. 1966. Soviet psycholinguistics. Present-day Russian psychology: a symposium by seven authors, ed. by Neil O'Connor, 109–51. Oxford: Pergamon Press.

Weir, Ruth. 1962. Language in the crib. The Hague: Mouton.

Competence and Performance in Child Language: Are Children Really Competent to Judge?

Jill G. de Villiers and Peter A. de Villiers

The notion of competence as it applies to child language is critically assessed in the light of evidence collected from a number of linguistic performances which share the same word-order rule. These performances—production, comprehension, judgment and correction—parallel Moravcsik's (1969) formulation of Chomsky's criteria for tacit knowledge of a rule, i.e. competence. It was found that these criteria are not all satisfied until the child is four or five years old, as the performances appear at very different points in time. Alternative criteria for tacit knowledge are suggested, with specific models of each performance replacing a general model of competence for early child speech.

> It seems clear that the description which is of the greatest psychological relevance is the account of competence, not that of performance, both in the case of arithmetic and the case of language . . . Obviously one can find out about competence only by studying performance, but this study must be carried out in devious and clever ways, if any serious result is to be obtained. (Chomsky 1964: 36)

The distinction between the competence and performance of a speaker/hearer has loomed large in recent philosophical, linguistic, and psychological studies of language. In the opening pages of his *Aspects of the theory of syntax*, Chomsky formulates the following distinction: "We thus make a fundamental distinction between *competence* (the speaker/hearer's knowledge of his language) and *performance* (the actual use of language in concrete situations)." Competence is the knowledge of an ideal speaker/hearer, "in a completely homogeneous speech-community, who knows its language perfectly and is unaffected by such grammatically irrelevant conditions as memory limitations, distractions, shift of attention and interest, and errors (random or characteristic) in applying his knowledge of the language in actual performance" (1965: 3–4).

Many developmental psycholinguists have taken the quote from Chomsky about the psychological importance of competence at face value and have set out to

From *Journal of Child Language,—,* 11–22, 1973. Reprinted by permission of Cambridge University Press.

discover the formal grammatical rules that might describe the young child's speech at different stages of linguistic development. They have tried to write a grammar for the child's speech as one might try to write a grammar for an unknown adult language, in the hope that this might characterize the competence of the child, i.e. his knowledge of the language, as it begins to approximate the language of the adult. Typical of such approaches are the studies of the spontaneous speech of American children by Miller & Ervin (1964), Bloom (1970), and Brown and his co-workers (Brown, Fraser & Bellugi 1964; Brown, Cazden & Bellugi 1968). McNeill has gone so far as to assume that a transformational grammar (Chomsky 1965) is the psychologically correct description of the knowledge of the adult and states that "language acquisition consists of learning transformations" (1970: 72).

There are two main problems with these attempts to write a grammar for the child. First of all, there is the problem of when to include a rule in the grammar. Is mere presence of a construction or grammatical inflection in the speech of the child sufficient evidence to attribute to him the grammatical rules which are thought to govern the adult's use of that construction or inflection? Menyuk (1969) takes the first appearance of a morpheme in the speech of a child as evidence for the existence in the child's grammar of the rules governing that morpheme. However, Brown (1973), Cazden (1968) and de Villiers & de Villiers (1973) have pointed out that it may take more than a year from the first appearance of a morpheme in its obligatory contexts in a child's speech to its consistent use by the child in 90 percent of such contexts. They can find no evidence that the rules are used systematically in some contexts but not in others. For long periods of time, identical sentence contexts are produced within a few minutes of each other, but one may contain the obligatory morpheme while the other does not. From a descriptive viewpoint these rules would appear to be probabilistic for a considerable period of time in child speech (Brown 1973). If we ascribe probabilistic rules to the child we must look for the variables which determine these variations in performance. It is possible that the use of a rule is conditional upon certain other parameters such as length of sentence or importance of communication, but these parameters have not yet been spelled out.

Secondly, most of these descriptions of the competence of the child have relied heavily on an analysis of a corpus of child speech. Yet Chomsky (1964) has argued that a corpus of speech is almost useless in determining the true grammar of the child. His rejection of the corpus as sufficient stems from the inadequacies of this approach in traditional linguistics. He argues that the rules of grammar, i.e. competence, are manifested in the speaker's performance, but additional nongrammatical factors such as memory limitations and random errors distort the picture, making it difficult to write a grammar from spontaneous speech alone. Since competence underlies several different performances, namely production, comprehension and the speaker's responses to deviant material, evidence should be collected from all of them. Then performance errors show up as inconsistencies in the overall description of the underlying rules of grammar. For example, a memory limitation in speech may not operate in comprehension, or a person who makes errors in speaking may recognize them as errors in judging such sentences.

Recently Moravcsik (1969) set forth the criteria used by Chomsky in attributing tacit or unconscious knowledge of a rule (i.e. competence) to a speaker/hearer. (i) The rule in question will fit the relevant aspects of conduct. (ii) The rule provides a reliable basis for predicting the agent's future conduct. (iii) The agent must have beliefs with regard to what does and does not constitute a violation of the rule. The approach of writing grammars from a corpus of child speech concentrates on criterion (i); generative linguists have taken (iii) as the primary data for the writing of grammars for adults. This paper will ask whether such tacit knowledge of a linguistic rule can be ascribed to young children. It will describe a series of studies investigating the development of certain linguistic performances which can be described by the same grammatical rule, namely subject-verb-object word order in English. Word order is frequently used in English to signal the underlying semantic relations in the sentence. It has been proposed that as soon as children begin combining words, they are sensitive to the constraints of word order. Thus Slobin has suggested (1973: 197) that "It seems that a basic expectation which the child brings to the task of grammatical development is that the order of the elements in an utterance can be related to the underlying semantic relations."

PRODUCTION

The child first begins combining words around the age of eighteen months. Brown *et al.* (1968) have called this early language development Stage I, in which the child's mean length of utterance (MLU) is between 1.00 and 2.00 morphemes per utterance. At this stage, the child produces only a few of the total possible combinations of single words in his vocabulary (McNeill 1970, Brown 1973). These combinations coincide closely with those used by adults to signal underlying semantic relations such as agent–action–object, possessor–possessed, object–location, etc. Since the child produces that word order appropriate to the adult's interpretation of the child's semantic intent, this has been taken as evidence that the child is using word order to distinguish meanings (Schlesinger 1971, Brown 1973) or grammatical relations (Bloom 1970, McNeill 1970).

Word order is typically reported as more consistent for children learning languages with fixed word order such as English as opposed to languages with relatively more freedom in this respect such as Finnish (Bowerman 1970) or German (Brown 1973). Burling (1959) and Braine (1970) do give examples of more frequent deviant word order in the speech of two English-speaking children, but most studies report extremely few deviations from appropriate word order in English (Bloom 1970, Brown 1973, de Villiers & de Villiers, in press).

However, a close look at the words which a child produces in agent versus object position suggests that they may conform to semantic rather than syntactic roles. McNeill (1970) maintains that the child from the first knows the grammatical relations of subject and object. However, Bowerman (1970) and Brown (1973) find most of the linguistic evidence for these categories to be lacking from Stage I speech. They therefore conclude that the categorization of the child's early utterances in terms of subject and object distinctions is too general. Schlesinger (1971) suggests that the child may better be described as maintaining agent–action–object word order rather than subject–verb–object order. The underlying semantic relations are thus marked by word order in Stage I. However, it is also the case that agents are generally animate things, objects inanimate (Bowerman 1970). So for example, the child produces *Mommy sandwich, Bambi go, pick glove* (Brown 1973). We looked at instances of agent–action–object, agent–action, action–object and agent–object in the spontaneous speech of eight children in early Stage I (MLU 1.00–1.50). 87 percent of these utterances conformed to the limitation animate agent/inanimate object. A further 8 percent used normally animate names for toys as objects of an action, and it is possible that the child did not regard these toys as themselves animate. Hence at this stage of child speech a word's position in a simple declarative sentence may be determined by very general semantic properties of its referent, such as "animate," and not by its syntactic (e.g. subject) or semantic (e.g. agent) relations to other words.

To some extent each of these categories, subject, agent, or animate, can be imposed on the data. Nevertheless, it is unwarranted to simply impose the categories that are necessary for the description of adult speech without evidence that these are functional for the child. The crucial evidence to decide between agent versus animate categories is the appropriate use by the child of reversible sentences, e.g. *Mommy kiss baby*, but the child does not produce these in Stage I.

COMPREHENSION

The experimental study of comprehension has the advantage that the experimenter has some control over the possible alternatives available to the child. Sentences in which only word order is used to signal underlying semantic and syntactic relations can be presented to the child, who might never produce such a critical set in his own speech. Hence, there has been a great deal of interest in the child's comprehension of reversible active and passive sentences, that is, sentences with no semantic constraints on which noun could be the agent of the action.

Fraser, Bellugi & Brown (1963) first looked at the child's ability to point to the picture portraying for example: *The dog bites the cat* versus *The cat bites the dog*. Lovell & Dixon (1965) tested twenty children on this same procedure. Their subjects averaged thirty months old and could pick out the correct picture on 60 percent of the trials. Another procedure is simply to ask the child to act out a reversible sentence. Ostensibly he has two alternative interpretations of the sentence; in practice, he can do almost anything. Bever, Mehler & Valian (in press) considered only those trials on which the children either acted out the sentence correctly or reversed its meaning. They found that children aged two to three years old could correctly interpret reversible actives on 95 percent of those trials. If all of the trials are considered, including those on which the children made "other responses," their children in fact acted out the sentences correctly on about 70 percent of all trials. It is not clear how many of these children were in Stage I since no other measure of linguistic development was taken.

We (de Villiers & de Villiers, in press) used a similar technique to that of Bever et al., in addition to which we took mean length of utterance as a measure of the child's linguistic development. We found that children in early Stage I (MLU 1.00–1.50) were unable to make use of word order to comprehend the reversible active sentences. They showed no preference between use of either noun as agent when presented with a sentence such as *Make . . . the truck push the car*. Again the children were not limited by the alternative interpretations that we thought possible. A frequent response was for the child to push the truck and the car. If word order is completely flexible for these children, this third semantic interpretation, i.e. with the verb processed first as in the imperative form, is as likely as the other two. In fact the three agents are all equally probable in the performance of the children in early Stage I. Only those children in late Stage I (MLU 1.50–2.00) or with a still higher MLU could correctly act out reversible actives. At this point only is there evidence that the child is using word order information in the absence of semantic limitations to understand the sentence.

In view of the frequent claim that comprehension precedes production (Fraser et al. 1963, McNeill 1970) it is worth considering why comprehension apparently lags behind production of correct word order. First, in the comprehension task we used three-term sentences, and these are extremely rare in the speech of early Stage I (three out of 1,600 utterances by children in our study). By the time the child is in late Stage I he is able to comprehend the reversible actives and is also at this point producing a much larger proportion of three-term utterances. Furthermore, in the spontaneous speech of these children such reversible sentences are virtually never produced; there are semantic limitations governing which nouns can be agents. In our comprehension task, the only cue to meaning was word order. It is not normally the case that there are less contextual constraints on comprehension than there are on production. The child is usually provided with many environmental and interpersonal cues to aid comprehension, e.g. intonation patterns, gestures and limitations on possible actions. As an illustration, if a child is playing with a baby doll and the experimenter hands him a doll's bottle with the instruction "Make the baby drink the milk," the sentence is practically redundant. To the extent that there are different degrees of semantic constraint operating in comprehension and production it will prove difficult to conclude which precedes the other.

It is, therefore, very possible that in both production and comprehension a semantic heuristic precedes a grammatical rule; that syntactic roles are slowly differentiated from an initially semantic rule.

Overgeneralization has been taken as strong evidence for the knowledge of a rule by the child (McNeill 1970), e.g. the overgeneralization of the regular past -*ed* ending (Ervin 1964). In the case of the word order rule, it is instructive to compare the child's comprehension of reversible active and passive sentences. At a certain point in development (3; 6–4; 6 years in Bever et al.'s study; MLU 3.00–3.50 in de Villiers & de Villiers, in press), children treat the first noun of the reversible passive sentences as the agent and hence systematically reverse their meaning. Bever (1970) has suggested that these children are overgeneralizing the word order rule of the more frequent active sentences. However, it is not apparent why the children do not treat the passives in this manner as soon as they accurately comprehend the active sentences. Instead, children at an earlier stage of MLU (1.50–3.00) who perform very accurately on reversible actives show no preference between the nouns in choosing the agent of the reversible passive sentences. It would appear that a considerable amount of overlearning of the rule is necessary before it is overgeneralized.

JUDGMENT AND CORRECTION

Gleitman, Gleitman & Shipley (1972) suggest that children as young as two years show the "germ of the ability" to contemplate the rules of their own language, and that this could constitute the primary data for determining the linguistic knowledge of the child as for the adult. Previous attempts to elicit judgments of the "silliness" of sentences (Brown et al. 1964) had seemed doomed to failure, but Gleitman et al. made ingenious use of role-playing to convey the difficult instructions to the child. The child received simple imperatives that were either well formed (e.g. *Bring me the ball*) or of deviant word order (e.g. *Ball me the bring*) and was asked to judge them as "good" or "silly" in the context of a game with his mother. He was required to repeat sentences that were "good" and "fix up" those that he considered "silly." Their three subjects, aged about thirty months, could discriminate between well formed and deviant sentences in this way, though they accepted over 50 percent of the wrong-word sentences as "good." Gleitman et al. conclude that the children were sensitive to the word order rule.

It was the way the children "fixed up" the silly sentences that engaged our attention. Of the few corrections made, the majority were semantic changes. A few corrections changed both semantics and word order (e.g. *Box the open* to *Get in the box*), while only three of the nineteen corrections obtained changed word order alone. Since one cannot tell from the judgment alone how the child is interpreting the sentence, nor on what grounds he may be judging it to be "silly," these corrections become crucial data.

We (de Villiers & de Villiers 1972) used a modification of Gleitman et al.'s procedure with several children whose linguistic ability was measured in terms of MLU. The child played a game with two puppets in which he helped to teach one puppet who "said things all the wrong way round" how to talk properly. The puppet spoke correct (e.g. *Pat the dog*) or reversed (e.g. *Cake the eat*) word order imperatives which the child had to judge as "right" or "wrong" (to avoid the semantic connotations of "silly"). We also asked him to tell us the "right way to say it," rather than to "fix it up," and thus hoped to maximize the possibility that the child would respond to word order rather than semantics. In a second session the same game was played but with semantically anomalous imperatives (e.g. *Drink the chair*) instead of reversed–word–order imperatives.

This study involved only eight children, but the following developmental sequence was suggested when the children were ordered in terms of MLU:

(1) The least advanced children accepted the wrong-word-order sentences as often as the correct imperatives, and furthermore, appeared to be extracting the underlying proposition since they often acted it out (e.g. *Teeth your brush*—the child made teeth-brushing motions). These same children could, however, quite accurately distinguish the semantically anomalous sentences, though they could not offer corrections.

(2) Children slightly more advanced than them could selectively reject the wrong-word-order imperatives, but not correct them. These children could, however, offer corrections for the semantically anomalous sentences, which they accurately judged as wrong.

(3) More advanced children could selectively reject and "correct" the reversed-word-order imperatives, but the corrections seemed guided by semantic considerations rather than just word order, as with the children in Gleitman et al.'s study (e.g. *House a build* to *Live in a house*).

(4)   Only the most advanced children gave word order corrections to the reversed-word-order imperatives.

Only when the child offers a correction can we distinguish between two important possible interpretations of Moravcsik's third criterion for tacit knowledge (Grandy 1973):

(a)   The child knows that a sentence violates the rules, whatever they are; and

(b)   The child knows that a sentence violates a particular rule.

Most of the children in the present study and both of the children who offered corrections in the Gleitman et al. study clearly knew that there was something wrong with the reversed-word-order imperatives, but when required to correct what was wrong, they focused on the semantics of the sentence. These same children at the end of the game produced "wrong" sentences for us to judge, which were semantically anomalous, even though they had only received reversed-word-order imperatives to judge. At this stage one cannot conclude that the child knows which particular rule is violated, even tacitly, if it is not guiding his corrections. Gleitman et al. (1972) are assuming too much in suggesting that such a child is contemplating the grammatical structure of his language.

Since corrections are so important for determining the possible basis for the child's judgments, we have recently completed a study which investigated more fully the development of the ability to correct reversed word order. The subjects were twelve four-year-old children and the same puppet technique was used to elicit judgments. All of the children were significantly better than chance at calling the reversed-word-order imperatives "wrong" and saying that the correct imperatives were "right." Table I shows the complete data from this study. The rank order correlation between the accuracy of their judgments and their ability to give a direct word order correction was +0.76 (Spearman's rho). Three of the children who were over 80 percent accurate in their judgments were still making more semantic corrections than word order corrections.

All of the children in this study were in Brown's Stage V (MLU > 4.0). Since MLU is relatively insensitive to differences in linguistic development after this point (Brown 1973), the children's ability to act out reversible passive sentences was used as an index of their development. The rank order correlation between the percentage of direct word order corrections given by the child and the number of reversible passive sentences which he correctly acted out was +0.77. This high correlation is of some interest since comprehension of reversible passive sentences requires manipulation of the word order, for the agent is the last word in the sentence. A similar task faces the child when he is asked to correct the word order of a simple reversed imperative.

DISCUSSION

We have considered the development of a number of different performances each concerned with the same syntactic rule in English. This approach was suggested by Chomsky (1964) as a method for approaching a true characterization of the linguistic

Table 1   The Accuracy of Judgments of Correct and Deviant Word Order
Imperatives and Type of Correction for Twelve Four-year-Old Children,
Together with Their performance on Reversible Passive Sentences.
The Children Are Ordered According to Percentage of Word Order
Corrections

	Accuracy of Judgments (%)	Corrections(%)			Passives	
		Word Order Correction	Semantic Correction	Failed to Correct	Correct	Reversed
Patrick	100.0	100.0	0.0	0.0	5	1
Christopher	95.0	100.0	0.0	0.0	4	2
Rachel	100.0	90.0	10.0	0.0	6	0
Nina	95.0	88.9	11.1	0.0	3	3
Michelle	85.7	88.9	11.1	0.0	5	1
Elizabeth	100.0	66.7	33.3	0.0	2	4
John	100.0	55.5	33.3	22.2	4	2
Rafico	81.8	54.5	9.1	45.4	0	6
Lory	94.7	50.0	40.0	10.0	2	4
Monte	80.9	22.2	55.5	33.3	0	6
Zachary	80.9	9.1	63.6	27.3	2	4
Tracy	80.0	0.0	62.5	37.5	1	5

competence of the child. However, Chomsky's original optimistic hope of finding
"across the board" advances in the use of syntactic rules is not borne out by the data,
as these performances are acquired at very different times in linguistic development
(see Table 2).

According to Moravcsik's (1969) criteria, we cannot attribute tacit knowledge of
the subject–verb–object word order rule until the child can recognize violations of
that rule and show by his corrections that the basis for his judgment is word order.
If we take judgment as a necessary criterion for knowledge we must conclude that
this rule is not part of the child's competence until he is four or five years old. But
for as long as a year before this, he has been able to act out sentences in which the
only cue to meaning is word order, to say nothing of producing sentences in accordance with this rule.

How then shall we characterize the child's use of word order? We could deny that
he knows that grammatical rule, and specify instead the various semantic or perceptual heuristics he could be using instead. However, for some tasks, particularly the
comprehension of reversible active sentences, the subject–verb–object rule may be
the best description. How else could the child correctly act out these sentences if
word order is the only cue to meaning?

Perhaps we should admit different criteria for the attribution of tacit knowledge of
a rule. Fodor (1968) suggested that the rules of language are psychologically real if

Table 2   A Summary of the Developmental Sequence for Each of the Four Performances, with Respect to MLU

MLU	Stage	Production	Comprehension	Judgment	Correction
1.0-1.5	Early stage I	Correct use of word order in active sentences with semantic constraints	Random performance on acting out reversible active sentences. Good comprehension if strong semantic constraints		
1.5-2.0	Late stage I	Many more three-term (agent-action-object sentences produced. Reversible actives rarely produced	Good comprehension of reversible actives, i.e. use of word order information alone		
2.0-2.5	Stage II				
2.5-3.0	Stage III			Unable to judge reversed word order as 'wrong'	
3.0-3.5	Early stage IV		Systematic reversal of reversible passives. i.e. over-generalization of active word order	Can judge semantic anomaly but not reversed word order as 'wrong'	No corrections
3.5-4.0	Late stage IV				Corrections of semantic anomaly only
4.0-4.5	Early stage V			Accurate judgments of both semantic anomaly and reversed word order	Semantic corrections for 'wrong' word order sentences
	Later development		Correct comprehension of reversible passives		Direct word order corrections

379

they are needed as part of an "optimal simulation" of a speaker/hearer's perform-ance. "Optimal" need not mean idealized, most logically consistent, or simplest, but rather an optimal simulation should be that which best mirrors the actual performance of the child, with all its systematic errors and limitations on the application of rules. It need not be a general model for the child's grammatical knowledge; we are not committed to the notion of a single rule being manifest in different linguistic perform-ances.

Then an important question to be addressed in the area of child language develop-ment is why certain semantic and perceptual (Bever 1970) heuristics are adopted, and how they finally give rise to the syntactic rules which older children are known to use (Gleitman et al. 1972). More specifically, one might ask what factors or pressures lead to the acquisition of a rule for one particular performance before other performances which require that same rule, and at what stage there is transfer of new rules across performance boundaries, as there might be for the adult.

Fodor (1972) suggests it is not useful to set up a general characterization of the mode of thought or cognitive structure of the child; that cognitive development might best be described as a gradual broadening of "quite specific computational abilities" which are limited at first to a small range of tasks. We could not agree more with this suggestion; however, we find the description even more appealing when it is applied to language development itself.*

REFERENCES

Bever, T. G. (1970). The cognitive basis for linguistic structures. In J. R. Hayes (ed.), *Cognition and the development of language*. New York: Wiley.

Bever, T. G., Mehler, J. H. & Valian, V. V. (in press). Linguistic capacity of very young children. In T. G. Bever & W. Weksel (eds), *The acquisition of structure*. New York: Holt, Rinehart & Winston.

Bloom, L. (1970). *Language development: form and function in emerging grammars*. Cambridge, Mass.: M.I.T.

Bowerman, M. F. (1970). Learning to talk: a cross-linguistic study of early syntactic develop-ment, with special reference to Finnish. Doctoral dissertation, Harvard Univer-sity. (Published as *Early syntactic development: a cross-linguistic study with special reference to Finnish*. London: C.U.P., 1973.)

Braine, M. (1970). The acquisition of language in infant and child. In C. Reed (ed.), *The learning of language: essays in honor of David Russell*. New York: Appleton-Century-Crofts.

Brown, R. W. (1973). *A first language: the early stages*. Cambridge, Mass.: Harvard University Press.

Brown, R. W., Cazden, C. & Bellugi, U. (1968). The child's grammar from I to III.In J. P. Hill (ed.), *Minnesota symposium on child psychology*. Minneapolis: University of Min-nesota Press.

Brown, R. W., Fraser, C. & Bellugi, U. (1964). Explorations in grammar evaluation. In U. Bellugi & R. W. Brown (eds), *The acquisition of language*. Monogr. Soc. Res. Child Devel. 29.

---

*Preparation of this paper was supported by NSF grant GS 3791 x to Professor Roger Brown.

Burling, R. (1959). Language development of a Garo and English-speaking child. *Word* **15**. 45–68.

Cazden, C. (1968). The acquisition of noun and verb inflections. *ChD* **39**. 433–48.

Chomsky, N. A. (1964). Discussion of paper by Miller & Ervin. In U. Bellugi & R. W. Brown (eds), *The acquisition of language*. Monogr. Soc. Res. Child Devel. 29.

———(1965). *Aspects of the theory of syntax*. Cambridge, Mass.: M.I.T.

de Villiers, P. A. & de Villiers, J. G. (1972). Early judgments of semantic and syntactic acceptability by children. *JpsychRes* **1**. 299–310.

de Villiers, J. G. & de Villiers, P. A. (1973). A cross-sectional study of the acquisition of grammatical morphemes. *JpsychRes* **2**. 267–78.

———(in press). Development of the use of word order in comprehension. *JpsychRes*

Ervin, S. (1964). Imitation and structural change in children's language. In E. H. Lennenberg (ed.), *New directions in the study of language*. Cambridge, Mass.: M.I.T.

Fodor, J. A. (1968). The appeal to tacit knowledge in psychological explanation. *JPhilos* **65**. 627–40.

———(1972). Some reflections on L. S. Vygotsky's *Thought and Language*. *Cognition* **1**. 83–97.

Fraser, C., Bellugi, U. & Brown, R. W. (1963). Control of grammar in imitation, comprehension and production. *JVLVB* **2**. 122–35.

Gleitman, L. R., Gleitman, H. & Shipley, E. F. (1972). The emergence of the child as grammarian. *Cognition* **1**. 137–64.

Grandy, R. E. (1973). Grammatical knowledge and states of mind. *Behaviroism* **1**. 16–23.

Lovell, K. & Dixon, E. M. (1965). The growth and control of grammars in imitation, comprehension and production. *JChPsycholPsychiat.* **5**. 1–9.

McNeill, D. (1970). *The acquisition of language*. New York and London: Harper & Row.

Menyuk, P. (1969). *Sentences children use*. Cambridge, Mass.: M.I.T.

Miller, W. & Ervin, S. (1964). The development of grammar in child language. In U. Bellugi & R. W. Brown (eds), *The acquisition of language*. Monogr. Soc. Res. Child Devel. 29.

Moravcsik, J. M. E. (1969). Competence, creativity and innateness. *Philosophical Forum* **1**. 407–37.

Schlesinger, I. M. (1971). Production of utterance and language acquisition. In D. I. Slobin (ed.), *The ontogenesis of grammar: a theoretical symposium*. New York: Academic Press.

Slobin, D. I. (1973). Cognitive prerequisites for the development of grammar. In C. A. Ferguson & D. I. Slobin (eds), *Studies of child language development*. New York: Holt, Rinehard & Winston.

Part 7

PROCESSES IN LEARNING LANGUAGE FORM

Learning language form is the result of contact between linguistic and nonlinguistic categories. The first two readings in this section consider that either linguistic categories *(Brown, 1968)* or nonlinguistic categories *(MacNamara, 1972)* are necessarily primary for language learning. It is more likely, however, that something like both processes that are argued separately by Brown and Mac-Namara, actually operate at the same time—that linguistic and nonlinguistic categories are mutually influential on one another in the course of their acquisition. The papers by *Dan Slobin (1973)* and *Eve Clark (1973)* can be interpreted as exploring the possible strategies that children use in making the contact between linguistic and nonlinguistic categories. Slobin's concern is primarily with learning grammar; Clark is concerned with the acquisition of the meanings of particular relational words.

The fact that children tend to repeat what they hear has often been pointed to as a basic process in learning language form. The paper by *Lois Bloom, Lois Hood, and Patsy Lightbown (1974)* explored the role of imitation in the lexical and grammatical learning of children who had just begun to combine words for their earliest sentences. Finally, the paper by *Catherine Snow (1972)* represents the burgeoning literature in the 1970s that has described the linguistic environment of children learning language. The speech of caretakers has been described in order to explore how the input that children receive is responsive to the needs that children have for learning the forms of language.

The Original Word Game
Roger Brown

In the Original Word Game one learns to speak a language. There must always be someone who knows the language (the tutor) and someone who is learning (the player). The movements of the game are, in outline form, as follows. The tutor speaks the language in accordance with the semantic and grammatical custom in his community. The player observes the performance of the tutor and learns to recognize equivalent utterances. The player forms hypotheses about the nonlinguistic categories eliciting particular utterances. In forming the categories of speech and the nonlinguistic categories that govern speech the player is seldom able to control the selection of instances. These are presented to him, sometimes in a random manner, sometimes in a systematic order determined by parent, teacher, or informant. The player is, therefore, concerned with reception strategies. He tests his hypotheses about the nonlinguistic categories by attempting to produce the utterance in appropriate circumstances. The tutor compares the player's utterances with his own anticipations of such utterances and, in this way, checks the goodness of fit of the player's concepts with his own. He improves the fit by correction. In simple concrete terms the tutor says "dog" whenever a dog appears. The player notes the equivalence of these utterances, forms a hypothesis about the nonlinguistic category that elicits this kind of utterance, and then tries naming a few dogs himself.

All of us have been players of the Original Word Game, as children, as students, or as anthropological linguists. The player with the greatest handicap is the child. He must learn the motor skill of producing linguistic utterances and must also learn to categorize both speech and nonlinguistic reality in conformity with the habits of the tutor. These part processes are the rudiments of the game. They can be picked up one at a time or all three can develop together. For the child this process of first-language learning is also the process of cognitive socialization. The categories of the parental tutors are, in large measure, the categories of the culture.

THE MOTOR SKILL

Speech as a response is an operant rather than a respondent. We cannot elicit utterances from a child but must wait for them to be emitted. For some reason

Appendix in J. Bruner, J. Goodnow, and G. Austin, *A Study in Thinking*, John Wiley & Sons, 1956. Reprinted with permission.

children vocalize very frequently and this vocalization moves in the direction of the speech patterns of the family. This drift in the direction of language may be produced by selective reinforcement coming from adults. They will favor a vocalization to the degree that it approximates a recognizable speech pattern. Mowrer (1950), in his efforts to train birds to talk, found that it was necessary to nurture the bird while speaking to it. Under these circumstances, Mowrer reasons, the speech of the trainer becomes a secondary reinforcer. When the bird in isolation produces sounds it will be rewarded by those that most resemble human speech and this generalized secondary reinforcement will increase the probability of humanlike sounds until they dominate the bird's song. In similar fashion we may suppose the child's babbling will change in the direction of speech. Finally, control of speech is probably gained through some sort of imitation—both the matched dependent and copying behavior described by Miller and Dollard (1941). The contention of Miller and Dollard that imitation is a learned technique is supported by the many studies of speech acquisition which report that true imitation does not occur until the eighth month or later. It is not clear that even all of these mechanisms are adequate to explain the motor control of speech. Of one thing, however, we may be certain. The player of the game can practice speech sounds and the tutor can selectively reinforce without worrying about the patterning of the sound. Thus a child may practice saying "dog" as a response to the utterance of this word by his tutor rather than as a response to instances of the category. Or he may say it in response to one member of the category, never learning to identify new instances. Motor control is, then, just one of the rudiments of the game.

THE PERCEPTION OF SPEECH

Dorothea McCarthy (1946) in her review of the literature on acquisition of language by children concludes that speech comprehension precedes the ability to produce speech. The evidence for comprehension is usually the child's ability to designate some object or objects in response to a command. In most cases it seems not to have involved the identification of new instances and, on that account, we should hesitate to credit the child with the concept in question. The ability to respond to a command such as "Show me your book" by pointing to a particular book is not sufficient evidence that the child knows the meanings of these terms. The ability does, however, have important implications. It tells us little about speech comprehension but much about speech categorization. If the child can respond appropriately to a variety of commands then he must have learned to recognize certain utterances as equivalent and others as distinctive. He has made a beginning with the problem of perceiving speech as it is perceived by his community.

Even on this very simple level we are likely to make erroneous conclusions unless controlled observations are made. Meumann (as reported in Lewis, 1936) found that his child could respond to the question *"Wo ist das Fenster?"* by pointing to the object in question. He was tempted to conclude that the child understood the question but decided to follow it with *"Où est la fenêtre?"* To his amazement the child responded as before and did so again when asked "Where is the window?" It would have been unreasonable to conclude that the child was trilingual. In answer to a fourth question, *"Wo ist die Tür?"* the child again indicated the window. Evidently he had not been responding to phonemic patterns at all but to the interrogative pitch contour which was common to the four questions. Many observations suggest that children do not at first categorize speech in terms of the finicking phonemic contrasts the community insists upon but are at first disposed to attend to the pitch contours, the loudness patterns, and the emotional qualities of vocalization. Had Meumann instituted discrimination training the child would have revised his categories. When his response to *"Wo ist das Fenster?"* was reinforced and his response to *"Wo ist die Tür?"* not reinforced he would have re-examined these equivalent stimuli and eventually discovered at least one of their differences.

There are indications that considerable time is required for the speech categories to be apprehended in their full complexity. Joos (1948) estimates that this learning is not complete before puberty. Goldstein (1948) reports that aphasic patients sometimes retain the ability to understand the speech of the members of their immediate family though the speech of strangers, especially those with regional dialects or accents, is unintelligible. We have little information on the evolving perceptual categories of speech though it is clear that such information is of great importance to the psychology of language.

The infant can learn to categorize speech by learning to pattern his pointing responses to such commands as "Show me your nose; show me your eyes; show me your toes," etc. In this case the perception of speech is an isolated rudiment of the game. It can be combined with learning motor control in the process of copying speech. The player attempts to approximate the speech of his tutor. His efforts are approved or corrected and in that process he learns to recognize the equivalence or nonequivalence of the sounds his tutor produces and the sounds he produces. Even this complex process is not the complete word game. It leaves out the most critical aspect: the categorization of the nonlinguistic world, the formation of the concepts that pattern speech.

THE CATEGORIZATION OF THE NONLINGUISTIC WORLD

We might learn to categorize the nonlinguistic world by testing hypotheses formed from sensory contact with that world. Presumably there are sensory attributes which have a kind of prepotency for the child. He might begin by categorizing in terms of these attributes. Perhaps he treats all shiny coins as equivalent and distinct from the array of dull coins. He reveals this concept to his tutor by giving some equivalent response to the shiny range and another response to the dull range. This response could be verbal or nonverbal. He might call one group dimes and the other pennies, or he might kiss the one group and throw the others away. His tutor could then correct this categorization and eventually the child would learn the proper designation for each kind of coin. Clearly this process would be an immensely complicated one. Nonlinguistic reality is categorized in terms of an enormously varied population of attributes. There is an economy available to us here in the fact that speech can provide a first-level categorization of all social reality in terms of a smaller number of attributes.

The experimenter in a concept-attainment study uses the responses of his subject to infer the concepts of that subject. An array of stimuli given an equivalent response is categorized together. Suppose, for a moment, that a child who is playing the game uses the responses of his tutors as a guide to equivalence and difference in nonlinguistic reality. He could have a cue to what is edible and what is inedible by noting what is eaten and what is not eaten. Mother might be distinguished from father by the fact that his uncle kisses the one and shakes the hand of the other. The categories "bed," "chair," and "floor" could be distinguished by noting which entities are lain upon, sat upon, and stood upon. In each realm of experience we have a different set of response categories giving evidence of concepts. Using the nonlinguistic responses of others as a guide to the categories of reality we should have to learn a set of response equivalents very nearly as complex as the stimulus equivalents in the world. This point is difficult to see because we are so familiar with such response categories as sitting, standing, or kissing. The point may be clearer if we imagine a community in which kin of one sort elicit a nod of the head in their direction while kin of another sort elicit a nod in the direction of the dwelling of the wife's family. We could not discover these kinship categories until we learned to classify properly the two kinds of nod and this might take considerable learning.

In a particular case the player might notice a response on the part of his tutor—a movement of head, of eyes, and hands. His problem is to discover the defining attributes of this response so that he can identify a recurrence and use this functional equivalence as an attribute of the governing nonlinguistic concept. The difficulty is that he does not have proper knowledge of the list of attributes of nonlinguistic discriminating responses. He is not in the position of the subjects of Bruner, Goodnow, and Austin who are told beforehand that attributes consist of the number, shape, and color of certain figures. The player has the problem of attribute analysis. He can scarcely use the wholist or focussing strategy since this would require him to hold all attributes of the first instance in mind and the attributes are not yet identified. He is more likely to use a part-scanning strategy, betting on one feature of the response and probably forced to revise his hypothesis a good many times.

With regard to linguistic responses the player is in a more favorable position. From a relatively small number of experiences of speech categories it is possible to discover all the defining attributes of any future utterances—the phonemes of the language. It is, furthermore, possible to learn that any semantic utterance will be a conjunctive category defined by phonemes in a particular sequence. Once the speech system has been grasped, then, there really is no problem of category attainment so far as linguistic utterances are concerned. A subject in the experiments reported by Bruner, Goodnow, and Austin knows in advance that there are three values for each of four attributes that may help to define the category in question. The subject does not, of course, know which of the attribute values present in an initial positive instance are defining of the category to be attained. To find that out is the experimental task. The player of the Original Word Game who hears /kæt/ knows that these three phonemes, in the sequence given, define the speech category. He has only to remember the response in these terms to recognize new instances. The player is not, of course, in this position when he first hears speech. The point is that his experience in forming the first speech categories can bring him great secondary benefits. Incidental learning of the structure of speech can teach him to perceive new utterances in proper categorial fashion. The study of nonlinguistic responses cannot yield such benefits since these responses do not constitute a system. It has been suggested to me by M. Wallach that a partiality for linguistic cues in the formation of concepts is itself a kind of strategy, a content selection strategy, since this partiality can maximize information, decrease cognitive strain, and regulate risk.

The Game is not complete when the player is able to categorize the speech of his tutor. He must discover the stimulus attributes governing the tutor's verbal behavior. The child's parent will not always be nearby to tell him what is "hot." He must learn to recognize hot things by their stimulus attributes.

Once we have learned what is distinctive and what is equivalent in a man's speech we have a key to his thought and to the culture he represents. Consider the categories "ball" and "strike" in baseball. These are extremely complex categories. In terms of stimulus attributes there is little likelihood that we would think of grouping together a pitch over the plate at the proper height, a swing that misses, and a hit that falls foul, yet all these are strikes. In terms of nonlinguistic response it might take some time for us to notice that the batter manifests some degree of chagrin after any one of these or that when three of these occur he leaves the plate and returns to the dugout. The response equivalences here are rather complicated. Walking forward in the right direction means four balls have occurred. Walking in the same direction with one's team means that enough strikes have accumulated to send them into the field. Consider how the umpire makes concept formation easier. He denotes each entity as a "Strike!" or a "Ball!" The shout locates the entity in space and time. It says, "Look here and now." The phonemic equivalence of his many shouts of "Strike" and their class difference from the cries of "Ball" tell us what entities go together and which are distinct. In speech we have a small number of highly available attributes providing a first approximation to all concepts. We have a common currency of cognition.

The utterance attribute will orient the player toward contemporaneous stimuli and will tell him when the important nonlinguistic stimuli recur. Even with these aids the categorization of nonlinguistic reality is a formidable problem. In the beginning there is no listing of attributes and no possibility of holding in mind the total nonlinguistic circumstances accompanying a given utterance and, therefore, no possibility of using a wholist reception strategy. With experience certain attributes, favored in the culture, will be noticed and can serve as a basis for first hypotheses. Because of its systematic character language can again be helpful. If, for instance, the parts of speech have a reliable semantic, then knowledge of the part of speech membership of an utterance could guide the player in his selection of attributes. If nouns usually name persons or places then a nominal utterance (recognized as such from its speech context or its phonemic structure) would suggest which kinds of nonlinguistic attributes were likely to be significant. Once a first language is learned it will strongly affect our attempts at translating a new language. If we hear a brief continuous utterance from a native who holds a coconut in his hand we will identify the utterance as a word and guess that it means coconut or hand or holding since these are nonlinguistic categories coded by words in our native speech. For many closely related languages one or another of these few hypotheses is likely to be correct. If the new language is a polysynthetic tongue in which the category "man-grasps-food-in-right-hand" can be expressed in a word we might guess wrongly for a very long time. Our conception of the kind of category that can elicit a word would lead us astray.

No brief treatment can do more than suggest the ways in which linguistic utterances are able to facilitate the acquisition of the concepts that one must possess to participate in a culture. Changing word order in English so as to reverse subject-object relations has a consistent meaning and so directs us to the nonlinguistic changes that may be expected to accompany this juggling of linguistic sequences. Appending "-ed" to an utterance identifies it as a verb in the past tense and, to one familiar with English, this is sufficient information to suggest the changes that have occurred in the nonlinguistic category eliciting the uninflected verb. In general, the systematic phonology and grammar of speech reduce the number of hypotheses about the nonlinguistic category to a relatively probable few.

In any case, however, the player must test his hypotheses. The beauty of the Game is that the player can now produce utterances as responses. The tutor can use the phonemic structure of the language to infer the categories of the player and can cause revision of these categories by correcting the player's usage of terms. The small boy who generalizes incorrectly from his father's naming behavior and calls any animal that goes on all fours a "dog" will be corrected until he learns to identify new instances correctly. To play this second part of the Game it is necessary to be able to produce approximations of speech sounds. Still, a parental tutor may allow considerable latitude here, tolerating "bow wow" until the child has grasped the category and then concentrating on changing the label to "dog." Both aspects may be worked on at once with the tutor correcting both usage and pronunciation. This Game may be played concurrently with many other activities. The child and his father can play as they walk along the street, father naming, child trying, father correcting. Concepts can be learned without direct contact with ultimate attributes that may have serious consequences. The child may be told by his father when it is "safe" to cross the street. After a while the child will tell when *he* thinks it "safe" and the father will correct his usage. When the child can pattern the word "safe" as the father patterns it in his mind the father will attribute to him the concept in question. He may then allow the child to cross streets alone. The whole process of trial and correction can be accomplished using the name as a surrogate for action that would have brought the child into perilous contact with the ultimate attributes of the traffic itself. The laboratory concept-attainment experiment is likely to differ from the usual situation in that the ultimate attributes of the concept will be the experimenter's verbal behavior. A subject learns the concept so that he can anticipate whether the experimenter will identify cards as instances of the concept. There is no purpose beyond this in the learning. In the child's learning, parental speech is not usually the ultimate attribute. Beyond this there will usually be physical or social attributes of the greatest importance.

BIBLIOGRAPHY

Bruner, J. S., Goodnow, J.J., and Austin, G. A.: 1956. *A Study of Thinking.* New York: Wiley.

Goldstein, K.: 1948. *Language and Language Disturbances.* New York: Grune & Stratton.

Joos, M.: 1948. *Acoustic Phonetics.* Baltimore: Linguistic Society of America

Lewis, M.M.: 1936. *Infant Speech.* London: Kegan Paul.

McCarthy, D.: 1946. "Language Development in Children." In L. Carmichael (Ed.), *Manual of Child Psychology.* (1st ed.) New York: Wiley. Pp. 476–581.

Miller, N.E. and Dollard, J.: 1941. *Social Learning and Imitation.* New Haven; Yale Univ. Press.

Mowrer, O. H.: 1950. *Learning Theory and Personality Dynamics.* New York: Ronald Press.

Cognitive Basis Of Language Learning In Infants

John MacNamara[1]

The main point of the paper is that infants learn their language by first determining, independent of language, the meaning which a speaker intends to convey to them, and by then working out the relationship between the meaning and the expression they heard. The assumptions on which the thesis rests are discussed, the main one being that a speaker's linguistic system and his intentions are distinguishable. Evidence in support of the thesis itself is adduced at three levels: lexicon, syntax, and phonology. An attempt is made to describe the strategies, nonlinguistic as well as linguistic, by which children use meaning to decipher language.

The thesis of this paper is that infants learn their language by first determining, independent of language, the meaning which a speaker intends to convey to them, and by then working out the relationship between the meaning and the language. To put it another way, the infant uses meaning as a clue to language, rather than language as a clue to meaning. This thesis is a strong form of the theory that meaning plays an important part in language learning. Its most respectable antecedent is Brown's (1958) "original word game." I would like, however, to make use of recent developments in linguistics and psycholinguistics in developing the theory, and I would also like to present a theory which, unlike earlier ones, integrates vocabulary, syntax, and phonology.

The theory relates mainly to the beginning of language learning. Obviously once he has made some progress in language, a child can use language to develop his thinking. I am not, therefore, casting doubt on the belief that our thinking is enriched or brought into focus by language. Further, I am prescinding from the more general question of the extent to which our thinking is conditioned by the linguistic environ-

From *Psychological Review*, **79**, 1, 1–13, January 1972. Copyright 1972 by the American Psychological Association. Reprinted by permission.

[1] Many of the ideas in this paper come from discussion with Nancy Katz of the McGill psychology department whose doctoral work is in this area. I am particularly grateful to her. I also owe much to Dick Tucker, Rose-Marie Weber, Charles Taylor, Roy Wright, Harry Bracken, Michael Corballis, all of whom either were or are my colleagues at McGill, and to Gillian and David Sankoff of the University of Montreal.

Requests for reprints should be sent to John MacNamara, Department of Psychology, McGill University, Montreal, Canada.

ment in which we live, and from problems relating to advanced levels of language, in particular certain aspects of poetic expression.

The approach to language learning which I am proposing had for some time been neglected in linguistics and in psycholinguistics. Part of the reason for this was the uneasiness with which behaviorism handled semantics. Even more important, however, was the impact of structuralism in linguistics which, following a suggestion of Bloomfield's (1933), sought to settle all grammatical questions without appeal to meaning. The advent of transformational grammar, in many respects so critical of linguistic structuralism, did nothing to change this situation. Indeed, in *Syntactic Structures,* Chomsky (1957, Ch. 9) went a little further than Bloomfield and seriously questioned the view that meaning could be an aid to the discovery of grammar. The paucity of references to meaning in the literature on child language during the 10 years that follow the appearance of *Syntactic Structures* is scarcely a coincidence (for overviews see McNeill, 1966a, 1966b). In the late 1960s, however, grammarians came to rely more on semantics than before. Chomsky (1968) uses semantics to counter several arguments against the grammar which he had proposed; the arguments against him came from a group of transformational grammarians, such as Lakoff (1968), Lakoff and Ross (1967), Fillmore (1968), and McCawley (1968), who largely abolished the distinction between grammar and syntax. This turn of events, whatever the ultimate fate of the contending grammars with which it is associated, has engendered a readiness to seek a basis for language learning in infants among nonlinguistic cognitive principles. Perhaps the earliest and so far the most important study of child language in the new key is Bloom (1970). (A general swing in this direction can be seen in several books and articles, e.g., Brown, 1970; Ervin-Tripp, 1970; Kernan, 1969; McNeill, 1970; Slobin, 1971.)

While most of what has appeared on child language has focused on the production of speech, I would like to focus on the comprehension of speech. Some recent papers have indeed studied comprehension (Clark, 1971; Chomsky, 1969; Donaldson & Balfour, 1968). These, however, deal with children well beyond the initial stages of language learning. I know of only a very few papers which deal with the ability of two-year-old infants to comprehend speech (Shipley, Smith, & Gleitman, 1969; Smith, 1970). I would like to get behind these fine studies and to draw attention to the cognitive strategies which an infant brings to the task of comprehending speech. Apart from some very general remarks on such strategies (see, e.g., Chomsky, 1965, pp. 31 ff.; Fodor, 1966), the topic has been quite neglected. It is, however, a topic which is basic to the whole examination of language learning and, moreover, one which, as I hope to show, permits us several possibilities for empirical research. But first, some remarks on meaning.

I will use *meaning* to refer to those intentions which a speaker wishes to express in language, and following the lead of Frege (1952), I will regard sentences as names for the intentions which they express. Meanings can be assertions, negations, commands, and questions; they may include a reference to the speaker's physical environment, to his feelings (of pain, pleasure, uneasiness, etc.), and to his ideas or concepts. They may also include his attitudes of belief or doubt toward his assertions. In other words, meaning refers to all that a person can express or designate by means of a linguistic code. The code on the other hand consists of a set of formatives and syntactic devices whose main function is to relate meaning to the phonological system of the language.

I prefer to leave the problem of meaning at that, simply because I do not believe that we are able to define it more precisely without losing it. Perhaps the clearest attempts of behaviorists to treat meanings as mediating responses are those of Osgood (1963) and Mowrer (1960). With Fodor (1965), however, I regard all such attempts as unfortunate and misguided. Equally unfortunate and misguided, in my opinion, are the attempts of positivists such as Carnap (1956) and Quine (1960, 1961) to eliminate as far as possible talk about meaning and to replace it with talk of things present to the senses. All such attempts seem to me to purchase clarity by impoverishing human intelligence and by ignoring the dynamism of the act of understanding. Further than this, there is no need to go for the purposes of the present paper.

In stressing the distinction of meaning and linguistic code, I do not wish to imply a functional separation of thought and language. This would end up in what Quine (1960, p. 206) calls the "fallacy of subtraction," that is, the fallacy that meaning is what is left over when language has been filtered out. The fallacy can be avoided if with Saussure (1959, pp. 111 ff.) we regard an utterance as the embodiment of thought in language. Saussure points out that without thought, language is useless, and he also claims that thought without language is nebulous. While not going so far as to say that without language all thought is nebulous, I find Saussure's general thesis reasonable. Meaning and the linguistic code are best treated as though they were elements of a compound, much in the way that oxygen and hydrogen are the separate elements which combine to form molecules of water. That is, the two are not usually experienced separately, though they are distinguishable.

The thesis that infants use meaning as a clue to the linguistic code rests on the assumption that in the period when infants begin to learn language, their thought is more developed than their language. Support for this assumption is to be found in the work of Vygotsky (1962), Piaget (1963), and Sinclair-de-Zwart (1969), who adduce evidence that the development of thought is at first independent of language. They emphasize that at about the age of one, when an infant begins to understand language, he has already made many observations on the world about him, on himself, and on his own activities: he has succeeded in classifying many things and has seen the relationship between, for example, his own activities and the movement of various objects.

The thesis also has the support of the findings on cognition and affect in the deaf (for an overview see Vernon, 1971). Though there are difficulties in the interpretation of this work, it seems reasonably clear that persons who are severely retarded in language development nevertheless reveal all the essentials of human thought processes and human affect. It follows that thought and affect are distinguishable from language and that they can develop without benefit of language. It also follows that initially they can develop, independent of language, and outpace the growth of language in normal children.

EVIDENCE FROM VOCABULARY

At first sight it might appear that to learn the vocabulary of his language is the simplest linguistic task which confronts the infant. It might appear that all he has to do is to relate objects in the external world with their names. However, this illusion of simplicity soon disappears when we reflect on the vocabulary itself. Not only are there numerous names and descriptive terms which can be applied to a single object, but it soon transpires that descriptive terms refer to objects only through the speaker's complicated network of concepts (see Odgen & Richards, 1938). But how is the infant to match words and concepts?

In *Word and Object,* Quine (1960) argues convincingly, it seems to me, that no empirical test or set of tests could ever convince a reasonable but sceptical linguist that what appeared to be equivalent terms in two languages were in fact equivalent in meaning. The example he gives is of a linguist in a strange country who hears what seems to be the word for a rabbit. How is he to know whether the word might not mean "fur" or "head" or "animal" or "rabbitlike shape" or indefinitely many other things? Since, however, linguists make such decisions all the time and since it would be obtuse to deny that they are highly successful, it follows that they do not behave like Quine's sceptical linguist. They must rely on cognitive strategies which they bring with them to the task of describing a language.

Quine's arguments can be applied (though my use of them would not have his support) with few changes to the infant in the process of learning vocabulary. Like the adult linguist, the child's success depends on a set of cognitive strategies which function as shortcuts in the task of relating symbols to a speaker's intentions. That there must be such a set is evident from the fact that neither in the linguistic code nor in the physical environment are there sufficient constraints to explain how an infant could have even the most superficial success. For example, children do not form bizarre concepts to include foot and floor and exclude all else. There are quite marked constraints on what will be grouped together in a concept. Unfortunately the study of these cognitive constraints, which at the perceptual level interested the Gestalt psychologists, has been largely neglected, so most of what can be said about them is of a very tentative nature.[2]

It is obvious that an infant has the capacity to distinguish from the rest of the physical environment an object which his mother draws to his attention and names. It seems clear too that in such circumstances he adopts the strategy of taking the word he hears as a name for the object as a whole rather than as a subset of its properties, or for its position, or weight, or worth, or anything else. The same strategy would serve equally well in the numerous cases where something happens which draws an infant's and other people's attention to a particular object and they use the occasion to mention the object's name. Indeed the literature records several errors which, on the reasonable assumption that adults are good at guessing what children mean, show that the child is using just such a strategy (e.g., Blount, 1969, p. 62). An

---

[2] In addition to the Gestalt work on perception, which is surely related to concept formation, there is the extensive work of the ethologists on innate release mechanisms in lower animals and the part played in such mechanisms by selective attention to certain aspects or events of the environment (see Miller, Galanter, & Pribram, 1960, Ch. 5). The impact of the ethological work is to increase the credibility of a theory which incorporates restraints on perceptual attention and on concept formation in humans.

example is to be found in Hoffman (1968) who recounts that at the age of 17 months, one infant whom she was studying used to refer to the kitchen stove as *hot.* The likely explanation is that her mother told the infant not to touch the stove saying *"it's hot,"* and the infant took *hot* to be the object's name. The theory thus exemplified fits in with some facts. Children learn names for colors, shapes, and sizes only after they have learned names for many objects. That is, names for entities are learned before names for certain attributes.

However, names for at least some of the various states, conditions, and activities of entities come very early. *Daddy* can be *gone, sitting down,* or *clipping the hedge.* A *toy* can be *broken.* One can *open* a *book* or *close* it. It is not that a state like *sitting down* is more clearly delineated than a color like *red;* the referents for each category show enormous variability. But the categories differ in at least one important and highly relevant respect. States and activities such as those just mentioned are not permanent attributes of entities, whereas colors and shapes usually are. If there is a differential set in small children to attend to varying states and activities rather than unvarying attributes, we need look no further for an explanation for the order in which the corresponding terms are learned.

A further hypothesis is that the child will not learn the name for states or activities until he has firmly grasped the name for at least some entities which exemplify such states and activities. Thus the order of learning would be as follows: names for entities, names for their variable states and actions, and names for more permanent attributes such as color. Perhaps the best research strategy would be first to test this hypothesis on clear-cut examples of each class. If the results are favorable, an argument based on construct validity would subsequently enable us to determine whether a particular doubtful term referred to a variable state or to a permanent quality in the child's world. The age at which the child learns the term would be the clue.

Some of the earliest words an infant learns to understand are proper names which single out the named object's individuality, for example, the names of his brothers and sisters and the name of the family dog. Other names are shared by many objects and connote what these objects hold in common. There are syntactic consequences attached to the distinction; one cannot speak of *a Fido,* but one can speak of *a dog.* Yet it seems unlikely that the young infant can use such evidence to distinguish between the two types of names. On the other hand, it is not at all improbable that he should assume that certain objects such as spoons have only common names, while other objects such as dogs and people should have proper names.[3] He may at first treat common and proper names when referring to the same objects—*Fido is a dog*—as optional proper names. If so, he will learn to differentiate when he discovers that only the family dog is called *Fido,* whereas all dogs are called *dog.*

Initial investigation suggests that infants treat higher order common names as collective nouns.[4] For example a two-year-old child will treat "toys" as a collective noun which refers to a group of objects. Thus, while allowing that a particular object is a *truck* or a *train,* he will deny that it is a *toy.* On the other hand, he knows well

---

[3] Indeed some preliminary observations made by Nancy Katz of small babies support the idea that they do make this discrimination.

[4] The work referred to in this paragraph is being done by Nancy Katz.

what is meant by his *toys*. Moreover his response—that the *truck* is not a *toy*—does not seem to depend on what the surrounding objects are. It is the same whether or not the truck is surrounded by other toys or by objects which are clearly not toys, like spoons and cups. Thus it seems as if, for the child, *toy* is not a hierarchical term which contains *trucks* as a subcategory. It remains to be seen how children get themselves out of this situation, but presumably it is by a process similar to that which enables them to distinguish between proper and common nouns.

The pronouns, too, might appear impossibly difficult if we did not presuppose on the child's part the ability to guess their semantic force. How else could he learn to say *I* when he is addressed as *you?* Indeed autistic children usually fail to make this reversal.

So far we have dealt with some of the aspects of learning words which have referents in the concrete world of the environment, but there are also words which seem to refer primarily to cognitive operators and only secondarily to physical objects. Some such words, for example, *and, or,* and *true,* are acquired very early. Slobin and Welsh (in press) record a 27-month-old child's correct and spontaneous use of *and*. Brown, Fraser, and Bellugi (1964) record *all* and *more* as well as *some* for a 24-month-old boy. Even if some of the instances when such words are used are of doubtful validity, others seem genuine enough. It is inconceivable that the hearing of a logical term should generate for the first time the appropriate logical operator in a child's mind. Indeed the only possibility of his learning such a word would seem to be if he experienced the need for it in his own thinking and looked for it in the linguistic usage about him.

EVIDENCE FROM SYNTAX

One might imagine that an infant who addresses himself to the task of learning syntax would to begin with adopt a simple hypothesis. He might, for example, suppose that a single semantic relationship would always be expressed by means of a single syntactic device or structure. Conversely, he might adopt the hypothesis that any change in syntactic structure signaled a change in semantic structure. However, such strategies would probably be less of a help than a hindrance. Consider 1 and 2 in each of which the same message is expressed by two different surface structures:

1. a. Give the book to me.
   b. Give me the book.
2. a. My hair is black.
   b. I have black hair.

Consider, too, 3 in which there is even a change in the syntactic category to which *kiss* belongs without any change in meaning:

3. a. Give me a kiss.
   b. Kiss me.

On the other hand, 4 shows that a single syntactic device can signal several different semantic structures:

4. a.   In a minute (time "when").
   b.   In a minute (time "how long").
   c.   In a box.
   d.   In a temper.

The task of the child is to detect the structures of syntax and relate them to semantic structures. The preceding examples show that the two are related in a rather flexible manner. The consistencies and regularities of syntax are to some extent independent of those of semantics. How, then, does the infant manage to relate the two? In keeping with the main lines of this paper, my answer will be that he uses independently attained meaning to discover at least certain syntactic structures that are of basic importance.

While I imagine that this position has the intuitive support of many students of child language, it runs counter to the assumption once widespread among linguists that syntax can be, even must be, described without recourse to meaning. Though few linguists would subscribe to this assumption today, the matter is so basic to the present discussion that it merits more than a cursory dismissal. Consider 5:

5. a.   The boy struck the girl.
   b.   The girl struck the boy.

How is the infant to know that these two sentences are not stylistic variants like 1a and 1b, or like 2a and 2b? There is in fact no way to decide the matter unless one has independent access to the meaning, probably through observing what is happening at the time sentences such as 5a and 5b are uttered. This is to say that without recourse to meaning, one could not discover so basic a syntactic device as the use of word order in English to express the subject-predicate relationship. The decision to treat 1a and 1b as stylistic variants must depend on the child's appreciation that while books can be given to people, people cannot be given to books. Thus the child must use his nonlinguistic knowledge to arrive at the notions of direct and indirect object and at the alternative ways of signaling them in English.

Before going on to speculate about how a child might use meaning to unravel syntactic puzzles, there are two qualifications to be made. First, not all syntactic puzzles must be or can be solved by semantic means. For example, gender in Indo-European languages does not correlate with any nonlinguistic classification of objects. Further, the rule that determines the number of the verb in English on the basis of the number of the surface subject is surely a purely syntactic one. Thus, though 6a and 6b mean roughly the same thing, the number of the verb is different in the two sentences:

6. a.   The boys strike the girl.
   b.   The girl is struck by the boys.

It is quite apparent then, that the child must have great skill in detecting the syntactic regularities of his language whether or not they can be tied in some way to meaning. Something of the French child's skill in relating word endings to gender can be seen in Tucker (1967).

The second qualification relates to the difference between *discovering* the syntactic devices of a language and *stating* them. A syntactic device which could not have been discovered without the aid of meaning might nevertheless be stated without any reference to meaning. To illustrate, a person who was intent on distinguishing Fords from Chevrolets might begin by reading the tradenames which appear somewhere on every car. After a time, however, he might come to rely on the shapes of fenders, rear windows, etc. There would even be a certain advantage in switching from tradename to distinctive features, since the latter can be recognized at a greater distance. Similarly in the realm of language. For example, it is altogether improbable that a child could discover the difference between transitive and intransitive active verbs without the aid of meaning. The presence or absence of following noun phrases is not an adequate criterion, as the examples of 7 shows:

7. a. John drove.
   b. John drove a car.
   c. John drove home.
   d. I walked.
   e. I walked home.

The child must appreciate at some cognitive level that the action of driving has an effect on "car" but not on "home," and that the action of walking does not have an effect on "home."

The grammarian, on the other hand, might distinguish the two sorts of verbs by whether or not they have passives. Actually, this test is inadequate (see Lyons, 1968, Ch. 8), but it will serve as an illustration. Let us now suppose that a list of verbs which have no passive forms has somehow been formed. It follows that one can tell whether or not a verb is intransitive by whether or not it appears on the list. There is no need to refer to meaning. The fact, then, that children need meaning to establish the two classes of verbs and to decide which class a particular verb belongs to does not preclude the possibility or usefulness of formal tests which make no reference to meaning.

But to return to the main line of the discussion, how does the infant use meaning as a clue to certain syntactic devices? The most likely avenue to explore here is the prior learning of vocabulary, principally nouns, verbs, and adjectives. It seems natural to suggest that children initially take the main lexical items in the sentences they hear, determine referents for these items, and then use their knowledge of the referents to decide what the semantic structures intended by the speaker must be. This is in fact the strategy implicit in my treatment of examples 1 to 7. Once the children have determined the semantic structures, their final task is to note the syntactic devices, such as word order, prepositions, number affixes, etc., which correlate with the semantic structures. Such a strategy will yield most of the main syntactic devices in the language.

It is important to note, however, that the establishment of different semantic relationships among the formatives of a sentence does not immediately establish different syntactic relationships. For example, the relationship between *boy* and *ball* in 8a is quite different from the relationship between them in 8b:

8. a. The boy kicked the ball.
   b. The boy liked the ball.

Yet in each, *ball* can be taken as the grammatical object of the verb. On the other hand, the relationship between *I* and *home* in 9a is different both syntactically and semantically from the relationship between them in 9b:

9. a. I like home.
   b. I walk home.

The fact that *home* is not the direct object of *walk* in 9b is indicated by the fact that most nouns which follow *walk* are preceded by *to* or *toward:* one *walks to town, to the table, toward the door.* Perhaps the child notes this fact and combines it with the semantic information to arrive at the conclusion that the syntax of sentences such as 9b is different from that of sentences like 9a. This is of course highly speculative, but two general conclusions seem warranted: (*a*) the child cannot discover many syntactic structures without the aid of meaning, and (*b*) the child is prodigiously skilled at noting the regularities in the language which he hears.

The hypothesis that prior knowledge of vocabulary items and their referents is basic to the learning of syntax suggests that we return for a moment to some of the ideas discussed in the section on vocabulary. There it was noted that children at one stage take a word like *toys* as a collective noun rather than as a higher order noun with subcategories, *truck* and *doll.* It follows that *toys* should always be plural for the child at that stage, and that while he will understand 10a he will either not understand 10b or treat it as equivalent to 10a:

10. a. Those are your toys.
    b. That is your toy.
    c. A truck is a toy.

It follows further that he will not understand sentences like 10c in which the same referent is placed in two classes at once. Some of these matters are testable, but to go further at the present time would be to court disaster.

So far in this section, we have been concerned with declarative sentences, but there are of course many other forms of speech act such as questions and commands. How the child learns to categorize speech acts correctly is almost a complete mystery, except that his doing so also presupposes an ability to determine the nature of the act independent of its syntactic form. In this connection, two observations will have to suffice. Lieberman (1967, pp. 44 ff.) cites evidence for the existence of an innate tendency in babies to react positively to friendly tones of voice and negatively to angry ones. Perhaps repeated commands tend to assume an angry tone, and so an angry tone might come to be taken by the child as an indication that he is either to do something or stop doing it. Later in the same book (p. 132), Lieberman examines 14 languages and finds that in 12 of them, questions can be signaled by means of rising pitch. While rising pitch is not then a universal marker of questions, it seems to have very wide currency as such. Could it be that children tend naturally to take rising pitch as a marker that a question is being asked?

But apart from such suprasegmentals, it seems clear that there must be a set of universal signs, of face, physical gesture, and bodily movement which the child interprets correctly and thus among other things comes to distinguish among speech acts. The evidence for such a set is growing (see Vernon, 1971), but as yet little is understood about how they relate to the learning of language. This is surely an important area of research. In the meantime we will have to content ourselves with the observation that the different forms of speech act probably correspond to deeply rooted mental attitudes of asserting, seeking for information, wishing to have others perform certain acts, etc. Indeed, such attitudes must be either innate or develop almost without benefit of learning. Endowed with such a set of attitudes, the child will be on the lookout for means of expressing them, nonverbal as well as verbal, and in this way come to discriminate the forms of different speech acts.

These suggestions of how an infant might use independently attained meaning to discover syntax are of course tentative. Yet they have the general support of several of the findings about the *production* of speech. For example, the suggestion that prior knowledge of vocabulary is vital to the learning of syntax fits well with the initial stages of speech production. First come single words that, as Bloom (1970), McNeill (1970), and several others have pointed out, infants employ to express a variety of semantic structures. Thus the single word milk can express: "This is milk," "Is this milk?," "I want milk," "I want more milk," etc. This indicates a heavy reliance on vocabulary items without supporting syntax. Moreover, when the child comes to combine words into two-word sentences, he continues to omit many of the syntactic features which adults include, such as plural and possessive markers, tense markers, auxiliaries, articles, etc. Yet Bloom (1970) has argued very forcibly that he does so for lack of syntactic processing space rather than for lack of semantic sophistication, and she was the support of many scholars in the area (see, e.g., Brown, 1970; McNeill, 1970; Schlesinger, 1971).

The point is equally clear when we consider children's attempts to repeat adult sentences. Brown and Bellugi (1964) and Brown and Fraser (1964), for example, pointed out that when required to repeat sentences, small children fasten onto meaning, drop the function words such as prepositions, and convey the substance of the message by means of the principal words. Slobin (1971) examines the data from several studies of child language in many countries and many different languages, and claims that such "telegraphese" is one of the universals of language learning.

In this connection it is also interesting to note the several suggestions in the literature that parents pay little attention to their small children's grammar, and only correct them on points of fact and discipline (see Bellugi-Klima, cited in Cazden, 1969). This observation, which is repeated in Gleason (1967), in Brown, Cazden, and Bellugi (1969), and in Brown and Hanlon (1970), implies that children learn grammar incidentally while parents attempt to put their thoughts and behavior right. However, too much must not be made of this point since children can learn from their parents remarks only if they can understand them, which probably implies after the very earliest stages, some knowledge of adult syntax. Indeed Shipley et al. (1969) found that small children made good use of adult syntactic devices in understanding adult sentences even if the children did not employ such devices in their own speech.

There is one further support in the literature for the thesis that in language learning the thrust to learn syntax comes mainly from meaning. It is the observation that children acquire first those grammatical devices which have a clear semantic force, such as numerous uses of tense and number markers, and only later acquired those which, like gender, have not (see Slobin, 1966). Indeed Slobin (1971) erects this into a tentative universal:

> Rules related to semantically defined classes take precedence over rules relating to formally defined classes.

I only know of one argument against the general thesis of this section. In an otherwise stimulating paper, Bever (1970, pp. 305–306) argued against the primacy of semantics in language learning. He presented sentences such as 11a and 11b to small children of varying ages:

11. a.   The mother pats the dog.
    b.   The dog pats the mother.

He required them to act out the meanings of the sentences with toys and found that relative to their performance on sentences like 11a, two-year-olds performed better than older children on sentences like 11b. That is, the two-year-olds seemed to be less upset by the improbability of the second type of sentence. Bever argues:

> The implication of this is to invalidate any theory of early language development that assumes that the young child depends on contextual knowledge of the world to tell him what sentences mean independent of their structure [p. 306].

This is a perplexing interpretation, seeing that in fact the younger children had interpreted the improbable sentences correctly more often than one might have expected. After all they were doing just what they were told. Besides, in absolute terms, the older children gave more correct responses to the improbable sentences. Indeed all sorts of explanations for the results other than the one given by the author come readily to mind.

EVIDENCE FROM PHONOLOGY

The relationship between speech sounds and meaning is quite as loose as that between syntactic structures and meaning. A single speech sound either on its own or in combination with others frequently signals many different meanings, while just as frequently a variety of speech sounds signal a single meaning. Examples of the first sort of complexity are well known and beloved by punsters. There is *meat* and *meet,* or *watch* in the sense of "look at" and *watch* in the sense of "time piece." The other type of complexity is less well known and is worth spending some time on.

Phonological theory distinguishes between two major sorts of variation in the speech sounds of a language, one which is accompanied by variation in meaning and one which is not. Languages vary considerably, however, in their rules for assigning a particular variation to one category rather than another, and so the infant has to *learn* which is which. Examples of variation in sounds which are not accompanied by variation in meaning are many of the regional variations in the pronunciation of English or even the peculiarities of individual speakers. An example of a variation in sound which in English conveys a difference in meaning is that between *ship* and *sheep*. The interest of this example is that Spanish speakers have great difficulty in noticing the change because in Spanish it is of no importance.

I will give one further example to underscore the complexities in phonology which an infant may encounter and the need for access to meaning in order to master them. In modern Irish, the initial consonant of the word *bád* (boat) is modified after the definite article as indicated in 12:

12. Case   Normal script   First consonant
    Nom.   *An bád*   [b]
    Gen.   *An bháid*   [v]
    Dat.   *An mbád*   [m]

What is noteworthy is that elsewhere in Irish, initial [m] and [b] for example, are contrasted as can be seen from the pair, *moladh* (praise) and *boladh* (smell). However, after the article in the dative case the initial [b] of *boladh* is replaced by [m] so that it sounds identical with *moladh*. We have, then a variation in sound which is sometimes accompanied by a variation in meaning and sometimes not.

In all, we have discussed three types of phonological variation, one accompanied by change of meaning, one not accompanied by change of meaning, and one which is sometimes accompanied by change in meaning and sometimes not. We began this section with changes in meaning without any change in sound. How is the infant to find his way through this many branched puzzle?

The answer must be that the infant is able to relate sound and meaning because he is able to tell what the speaker is speaking about independent of the speaker's language. This follows naturally from the evidence presented. The infant cannot use the sound system of a language to get at the meaning until he has learned the system. There seems to be little in the sound system itself which could direct the child in the choice of which sound differences to attend to and which to ignore. However, if he can determine the meaning and has sufficiently acute powers of auditory discrimination to begin with,[5] the infant can use meaning as the key to the sound system and thus arrive at the most elementary building blocks of his language.

---

[5] There is now some evidence that infants are born with very fine powers of discrimination for speech sounds, and that learning for them consists mainly in ignoring differences in sound. The relevant material is well reviewed in Kaplan and Kaplan (in press).

Roger Brown (1958, pp. 213 ff.) describes a highly relevant experiment in his chapter on the original word game. He showed chips of different colors to native English speakers; each color was "named" with a nonsense syllable. Certain syllables differed only in vowel length which is not phonemic in English. The subjects were asked to group the chips in accordance with their names. Brown found that length of vowel was ignored if the corresponding chips differed little in color, but if the difference in color was marked, then different groups of chips were formed to correspond to the long and short vowels. In other words, subjects used the physical properties of the objects named as clues to the phonological units employed in naming them. Though his subjects were adults, the conclusion can be extended to infants without undue hesitation.

The claim that the infant uses meaning as the key to phonology needs to be filled out with details of how he does so, but unfortunately we know very little of the process. My remarks here are intended mainly as suggestions for further investigation. Let us begin by returning to the Irish example. Clearly the infant must use the fact that the referent is constant to arrive at the appreciation that [bád], [váid], and [mád] are all different realizations of the same phonological entity. In other words there are three different surface realizations of the same underlying morphophonemic form. Similarly, he must use the fact that *moladh* and *boladh* refer to different things (at least in equivalent environments) to avoid the mistake of treating these two words as different realizations on the same morphological entity. But while such a strategy works well for the examples I gave, how is the infant to avoid applying the constancy-of-referent strategy indiscriminately with disastrous phonological consequences? For example, *Fido* and *dog* might well be used to refer to a single animal, but to treat them as different surface realizations of the same phonological deep structure would be fatal. *Little* and *small* have more or less the same meaning, but they are phonologically quite distinct. The solution is that the various realizations of the Irish word *bád* are instances of a very general and simple phonological regularity. The rule for the dative (somewhat simplified), for example, is to voice the initial consonant if it is unvoiced and if it is voiced to replace it with the homorganic nasal (i.e., the nasal most closely related from an articulatory point of view). Part of the child's capacity to learn a language is his ability to detect such phonological regularities. Meaning alone cannot reveal them, though it probably directs the child to look for them. There are no phonological regularities relating *Fido* and *dog* or *little* and *small*. In the absence of such regularities the infant does not attempt to relate them phonologically despite the correspondences in meaning.

To learn a language involves relating a system of intentions to a phonological system. To know the one is not *ipso facto* to know the other. Indeed the two are often related only through a complex system of syntax. I have had to have recourse to the syntactic system more than once in the foregoing discussion. For example, the phonological modifications of initial consonants in Irish are a function of syntactic rules which presumably must be learned together with the phonological modifications themselves. The combination of phonology and syntax are also presumably involved in the explanation of how the infant manages to distinguish such homonyms as *meat* and *meet*, and such nonhomonyms as *moladh* and *boladh*. This is hardly surprising in view of the fact that phonology and syntax are theoretical distinctions which are employed in the description of what is experientially a unit, the speech act.

To explain the learning of phonology by means of syntax is not, however, to abandon the main thesis of this paper. In the previous section I argued that the learning of most basic syntactic relationships is possible only with the aid of meaning.

CONCLUDING REMARKS

I have treated of the learning of vocabulary, syntax, and phonology in separate sections, but the three could not be kept apart. It was necessary to base the learning of syntax in large part on knowledge of vocabulary, and it was necessary to base the learning of phonology in some part on knowledge of syntax. At this point it might be as well to correct the impression that infants use meaning to learn vocabulary, vocabulary to learn syntax, and syntax to learn phonology. It was not my intention to propose anything so neat. It is evident that some syntactic learning cannot be based on a knowledge of the referents of the lexical items employed. Similarly, phonology cannot be entirely dependent on prior knowledge of syntax. To argue that it was would be to argue in a circle, because without some independent grasp of phonology one could not perceive either words or syntactic devices. One cannot at once make the perception of vocabulary and syntax dependent on knowledge of phonology and make knowledge of phonology dependent on knowledge of vocabulary and syntax. The way out of this circle is to recognize that the interdependencies are only partial, though it is important to appreciate that at present they are quite obscure.

I have continually insisted on the child's possessing nonlinguistic cognitive processes before he learns their linguistic signal. By this I do not intend to endow the infant at birth with a complete ready-made set of cognitive structures. I accept Piaget's thesis that children gradually develop many of the cognitive structures, which they employ in association with language. Neither do I suggest that the child has a complete set of cognitive structures at the moment when he begins to learn language. All that is needed for my position is that the development of those basic cognitive structures to which I referred should precede the development of the corresponding linguistic structures. Since the acquisition of linguistic structures is spread over a long period, there is no reason that the acquisition of the corresponding nonlinguistic ones should not also extend well into the period of language learning.

I have repeatedly compared the infant to a linguist engaged in describing a language which to him is new. This seems a fair comparison provided the limp is recognized. Clearly, the infant does not produce explicit rules whereas the linguist does. The linguist aims to make explicit the native speaker's latent knowledge. Otherwise the tasks of infant and linguist are similar. Hockett (1961) points out that in fact no linguist has ever succeeded in deciphering a language without making use of meaning. He instances the Rosetta Stone which carried the same message in three languages, Greek, Demotic, and Hieroglyphic Egyptian. Because they knew Greek, Young and Champollion succeeded in deciphering the other two languages which no one at the time was able to read or understand. Similarly, Old Irish was deciphered by a Bavarian scholar named Johanne Kasper Zeuss. He worked on seven Latin manuscripts which carried glosses in Old Irish explaining the text. His great work, *Grammatica Celtica*, appeared in Latin in 1853, the first grammar of Old Irish.

It is not too fanciful to think of the infant as treating the sentences he hears as glosses on the events that occur about him. The grammar he writes is not in Latin or in any other language, but in some neurological code of which as yet not a single letter has been deciphered.

REFERENCES

Bever, T. G. The cognitive basis for linguistic structures. In J. R. Hayes (Ed.), *Cognition and language learning*. New York: Wiley, 1970.

Bloom, L. *Language development: Form and function in emerging grammars*. Cambridge, Mass: The M. I. T. Press, 1970.

Bloomfield, L. *Language*. New York: Holt, Rinehart & Winston, 1933.

Blount, B. G. *Acquisition of language by Luo children*. Berkeley: Language Behavior Research Laboratory, University of California, 1969.

Brown, R. *Words and things*. New York: Free Press, 1958.

Brown, R. *Stage 1. Semantic and grammatical relations*. Cambridge, Mass.: Harvard University, Department of Psychology, 1970. (Mimeo)

Brown, R., & Bellugi, U. Three processes in the child's acquisition of syntax. *Harvard Educational Review*, 1964, **34**, 133–151.

Brown, R., Cazden, C. B., & Bellugi, U. The child's grammar from I to III. In J. P. Hill (Ed.), *1967 Minnesota symposium on child psychology*. Minneapolis: University of Minnesota Press, 1969.

Brown, R., & Fraser, C. The acquisition of syntax. In U. Bellugi & R. Brown (Eds.). The acquisition of language. *Monographs of the Society for Research in Child Development*, 1964, **29**, 43–79.

Brown, R., & Hanlon, C. Derivational complexity and order of acquisition in child speech. In J. R. Hayes (Ed.), *Cognition and the development of language*. New York: Wiley, 1970.

Carnap, R. *Meaning and necessity*. (2nd ed.) Chicago: University of Chicago Press, 1956.

Cazden, C. B. The psychology of language. In L. E. Travis (Ed.), *Handbook of speech, hearing and language disorders*. (Rev. ed.) New York: Appleton-Century-Crofts, 1969.

Chomsky, C. *The acquisition of syntax in children 5 to 10*. (Res. Mono. No. 57) Cambridge, Mass.: The M. I. T. Press, 1969.

Chomsky, N. *Syntactic structures*. The Hague: Mouton, 1957.

Chomsky, N. *Aspects of the theory of syntax*. Cambridge, Mass.: The M. I. T. Press, 1965.

Chomsky, N. *Deep structure, surface structure, and semantic interpretation*. Bloomington: Indiana University, Linguistics Circle, 1968. (Mimeo)

Clark, E. V. On the acquisition of the meaning of *before* and *after*. *Journal of Verbal Learning and Verbal Behavior*, 1971, **10**, 266–275.

Cromer, R. F. "Children are nice to understand": Surface structure, clues for the recovery of a deep structure. *British Journal of Psychology*, 1970, **61**, 397–408.

Donaldson, H., & Balfour, G. Less is more: A study of language comprehension in children. *British Journal of Psychology*, 1968, **59**, 461–471.

Ervin-Tripp, S. Structure and process in language acquisition. In, *Report of the twenty-first annual round table meeting on linguistics and language studies*. Washington, D. C.: Georgetown University Press, 1970.

Fillmore, C. J. The case for case. In E. Bach & R. T. Harms (Eds.), *Universals in linguistic theory*. New York: Holt, Rinehart & Winston, 1968.

Fodor, J. A. Could meaning be an r_m? *Journal of Verbal Learning and Verbal Behavior*, 1965, **4**, 73–81.

Fodor, J. A. How to learn to talk: Some simple ways. In F. Smith & G. A. Miller (Eds.), *The genesis of language*. Cambridge, Mass.: The M. I. T. Press, 1966.

Frege, G. *Philosophical writings.* (Ed. by Peter Geech & Max Black) Oxford: Basil Blackwell, 1952.

Gleason, J. B. Do children imitate? Paper presented at the international conference on oral education of the deaf, Lexington School for the Deaf. New York, June 1967.

Hockett, C. F. Linguistic elements and their relations. *Language,* 1961, **37,** 29–53.

Hoffman, M. Child language. Unpublished master's thesis, McGill University, Department of Psychology, 1968.

Kaplan, E. L., & Kaplan, G. A. Is there any such thing as a pre-linguistic child? In J. E. Lot (Ed.), *Human development and cognitive processes.* New York: Holt, Rinehart & Winston, in press.

Kernan, K. T. The acquisition of language by Samoan children. Unpublished doctoral dissertation, University of California, Berkeley, Department of Anthropology, 1969.

Lakoff, G. Instrumental adverbs and the concept of deep structure. *Foundations of Language,* 1968, **4,** 4–29.

Lakoff, G., & Ross, J. R. *Is deep structure necessary?* Cambridge, Mass.: Author, 1967.

Lieberman, P. *Intonation, perception and language.* Cambridge, Mass: The M. I. T. Press, 1967.

Lyons, J. *Introduction to theoretical linguistics.* Cambridge: Cambridge University Press, 1968.

McCawley, J. D. The role of semantics in a grammar. In E. Bach & R. T. Harms (Eds.), *Universals in linguistic theory.* New York: Holt, Rinehart & Winston, 1968.

McNeill, D. Developmental psycholinguistics. In F. Smith & G. A. Miller (Eds.), *The genesis of language.* Cambridge, Mass.: The M. I. T. Press, 1966. (a)

McNeill, D. The creation of language by children. In J. Lyons & R. J. Wales (Eds.), *Psycholinguistics papers: The proceedings of the 1966 Edinburgh Conference.* Edinburgh: Edinburgh University Press, 1966. (b)

McNeill, D. *The acquisition of language: The study of developmental psycholinguistics.* New York: Harper & Row, 1970.

Miller, G. A., Galanter, E., & Pribram, K. H. *Plans and the structure of behavior.* New York: Holt, Rinehart & Winston, 1960.

Mowrer, O. H. *Learning theory and the symbolic process.* New York: Wiley, 1960.

Ogden, C. K., & Richards, I. A. *The meaning of meaning.* New York: Harcourt, Brace & World, 1938.

Osgood, C. E. *Psycholinguistics.* In S. Koch (Ed.), *Psychology: A study of a science.* Vol. 6. New York: McGraw-Hill, 1963.

Piaget, J. Le langage et les opérations intellectuelles. In, *Problèmes de psycho-linguistique.* (Symposium de l'association de psychologie scientifique de langue française.). Paris: Presses Universitaires de France, 1963, 51–72.

Quine, W. V. *Word and object.* New York: Wiley, 1960.

Quine, W. V. *From a logical point of view.* Cambridge, Mass.: Harvard University Press, 1961.

Saussure, F. de. *Course in general linguistics.* New York: McGraw-Hill, 1959.

Schlesinger, I. M. Production of utterances and language acquisition. In D. Slobin (Ed.), *The ontogenesis of grammar.* New York: Academic Press, 1971.

Shipley, E. F., Smith, C. S., & Gleitman, L. R. A study of the acquisition of language: Free responses to commands. *Language,* 1969, **45,** 322–342.

Sinclair-de-Zwart, H. Developmental psycholinguistics. In D. Elkind & J. H. Flavell (Eds.), *Studies in cognitive development: Essays in honor of Jean Piaget.* New York: Oxford University Press, 1969.

Slobin, D. I. Acquisition of Russian as a native language. In F. Smith & G. A. Miller (Eds.), *The genesis of language.* Cambridge, Mass.: The M. I. T. Press, 1966.

Slobin, D. I. Universals of grammatical development in children. In G. B. Flores d'Arcais & W. J. M. Levelt (Eds.), *Advances in psycholinguistics.* Amsterdam: North Holland, 1971.

Slobin, D. I., & Welsh, C. A. Elicited imitation as a research tool in developmental psycholinguistics. In C. A. Ferguson & D. I. Slobin (Eds.), *Readings on child language acquisition.* New York: Holt, Rinehart & Winston, 1972.

Smith, C. An experimental approach to children's linguistic competence. In J. R. Hayes (Ed.), *Cognition and the development of language.* New York: Wiley, 1970.

Tucker, G. R. French speaker's skill with grammatical gender. Unpublished doctoral dissertation, McGill University, Department of Psychology, 1967.

Vernon, M. Language development's relationship to cognition, affectivity and intelligence. Paper presented at the meeting of the Canadian Psychological Institute, St. John's Newfoundland, June 1971.

Vygotsky, L. S. *Thought and language.* Cambridge, Mass.: The M. I. T. Press, 1962.

Cognitive Prerequisites for the Development of Grammar[1]

Dan I. Slobin

A METHOD FOR REVEALING LANGUAGE ACQUISITION STRATEGIES

Given the primacy of cognitive development in setting the pace for the development of linguistic intentions, it follows that many linguistic forms cannot appear in the

From the revised version of "Developmental psycholinguistics," in *A survey of linguistic science,* edited and copyright by William Orr Dingwall. College Park: University of Maryland/Linguistics Program, pp. 298–400. Reprinted by permission of William Orr Dingwall.

[1] The growth of the ideas set forth in this paper has been greatly stimulated by discussion with many students and colleagues. It is a pleasure to acknowledge some of them here: H. David Argoff, Melissa F. Bowerman, Ursula Bellugi, Thomas G. Bever, Roger Brown, L. Dezső, Susan Ervin-Tripp, John Gumperz, Paul Kay, Jonas Langer, David McNeill, Melanie Mikeš, Lubisa Radulović, Grace Wales Shugar, Peyton Todd, Plemenka Vlahović. Part of the work reflected here has been supported by the Language-Behavior Research Laboratory of the University of California at Berkeley, which is supported by PHS Research Grant No. 1 RO1 MH 18188-02 from the National Institute of Mental Health. This support is gratefully acknowledged. This paper was originally presented at the Fifth Meeting of the Southeastern Conference on Linguistics (SECOL V), University of Maryland, May 9, 1971. My thanks to the organizer of that meeting, William Orr Dingwall, for allowing me to reprint this paper here.

child's speech until he is capable of grasping their meaning. If the stages of cognitive development are universal—as I would like to believe—then a very strong developmental psycholinguistic universal can be set forward: *The rate and order of development of the semantic notions expressed by language are fairly constant across languages, regardless of the formal means of expression employed.* (Note that this proposition applies to semantic *intentions,* rather than the formal marking of intentions. Thus, for example, Brown's children would be credited with the four verb meanings, in this sense of intention, at the stage when all of their verbs were in the root, uninflected form.)

If this universal is true, and if communicative intentions can be reliably assessed from a combination of contextual and partial linguistic cues, then we have a powerful research tool for probing the information processing devices used and developed by children to understand speech and to construct grammars. What is needed is a taxonomy and coding scheme for pre-linguistic intentions. We are beginning to develop such a system at Berkeley, in the hope that it will be possible to establish a stable and universal sequence of pre-linguistic communicative intentions.[2] If this is the case, then one can measure the lag between the appearance of a communicative intention and the mastery of the conventional linguistic form which the child's native language offers for the realization of that intention. (See footnote 6 for a criterion of mastery.) The lag between the first attempts to express a meaning and the acquisition of the relevant linguistic forms should vary from language to language, determined by the psycholinguistic complexity of the formal means used by a particular language to express the intention under consideration. With sufficient information on the sorts of formal devices which appear difficult to learn, we will be in a position to make a much clearer formulation of the capacities and strategies involved in language acquisition. It is necessary to compare formal devices used to express the same semantic intentions in order to insure that the children studied are at roughly the same level of cognitive development, and that the devices are used for similar purposes.

A TEST CASE: DEVELOPMENT OF LOCATIVE EXPRESSIONS

In effect, this research tactic attempts to separate the bilingual child into two monolingual children who are following the same sequence of communicative intentions. A useful test case of the proposed method, therefore, begins with a re-examination of locative development in the Hungarian-Serbo-Croatian bilingual girls mentioned above. Our procedure will be to compare development of the formal means of locative expression in several languages; to propose a developmental universal based on inductive generalization of these finding; and to propose a psycholinguistic operating principle which may be a partial determinant of the general finding. The locative example will clarify the procedure.

---

[2] The current version of our analysis is based on an enrichment of Fillmore's "case grammar" (1968). A similar approach is currently being followed by Martin Braine at Santa Barbara (personal communication). Francesco Antinucci and Dominico Parisi, at the Istituto di Psicologia in Rome, are developing what promises to be an extremely valuable model on the basis of generative semantics.

You will recall that the development of Hungarian locative inflections was in advance of Serbo-Croatian locative prepositions. Why should the Hungarian locative expressions be easier for the child to acquire? In order to attempt an answer, it will be necessary to look briefly at the grammatical devices for locative expression in the two languages. Hungarian has an abundance of nominal inflections which express combinations of position and direction. For example, with the word *hajó* "boat," there are forms such as *hajóban* "located in the boat," *hajóból* "moving out from inside of the boat," *hajótól* "moving away from next to the boat," and so on. The inflections are all monosyllables, and systematically encode position, motion toward a position, and motion away from a position. They apply to all nouns (there is no grammatical gender in Hungarian). Serbo-Croatian, like English, has a number of prepositions which encode locations: the equivalents of "in," "on," "from," and so on. And, like English, some of these prepositions encode direction (as English "to" and "from"), while some do not distinguish between direction and position (compare: "Put it *in* the box" and "It is *in* the box"). In addition, unlike English, Serbo-Croatian encodes the distinction between position and direction by means of noun inflections. The accusative is used when an ambiguous preposition like *u* "in" is used directionally, and the locative case is used when such a preposition is used positionally (e.g., *kuća* "house," *u kuću* "into the house," *u kući* "located in the house"). The situation is even more complex in Serbo-Croatian, because of a variety of semi-arbitrary pairings of preposition with case. For example, *blizu* "near," *do* "as far as," and *iz* "from/from out of" must take genitive nouns; *k* "toward" takes the dative; *pri* "at/near" takes the locative; etc. In both Serbo-Croatian and English, position vs. direction is sometimes uniquely signalled by one preposition or compound preposition (such as "toward," "out of," and so on), and sometimes one preposition fails to distinguish between the two senses (as "in" and "on"). Serbo-Croatian is more complex, however, in that every preposition governs a noun inflection. Sometimes this inflection is meaningful, distinguishing position from direction, and sometimes it is redundant. Furthermore, the particular phonological realization of a given inflection is determined by the gender and by the final sound of each particular noun.

Why, then, is the Hungarian locative acquired before the Serbo-Croatian locative in bilingual children? In the most general terms, it seems obvious that the Hungarian means of locative expression is simpler: the locative marker is always at the end of the noun only, always unambiguously and consistently indicates both position and direction to or from. The example demonstrates—at the very least—that a system which can be described by a small set of consistent and regular rules is easier to learn than one less consistent and regular—even by children under the age of two. But we can go beyond impressionistic statements such as these. The value of such cross-linguistic examples—I have proposed—is to teach us something about the ways in which children process speech.

The Hungarian locative is expressed by noun *suffixes*. This fact may facilitate acquisition, in that the end of a word seems to be perceptually salient. Little children will often imitate only the last part of a word, saying, for example, *raff* for *giraffe* in English, *sáyim* for *mixnasáyim* in Hebrew (Bar-Adon, 1971), *hibb* for *ᶜam-yḥíbb* in Arabic (Omar, 1970), etc. Unstressed initial syllables, prefixes, and prepositions are very frequently omitted in child speech, as virtually all observers have noted. Furthermore, evidence from Czech, where all words receive initial stress, suggests that the ends of words are perceptually salient even if unstressed. Pačesová (1968), reporting on a detailed longitudinal study of a Czech boy, presents numerous examples of omission of initial stressed syllables in Czech child speech. She notes that if "stress were to be the relevant factor in the abbreviating operation, the syllabic prepositions, being stressed in Czech, should have been early in appearance and, as for shortening, they should have been preserved, which is certainly not the case" (p. 205).

Another argument for perceptual salience of word endings comes from studies in acoustic phonetics. A paper by Kim Oller (1971) has brought to my attention the fact that phoneticians have noted the existence of final-syllable lengthening in many languages (e.g., Russian [Zlatoustova, 1954]; Swedish [Lindblom, 1968]; English, Spanish, German, French [Delattre, 1966]). Oller (p. 13) entertains a suggestion of Ernest Haden (1962) "that final-syllable lengthening cues listeners to the fact that a linguistic unit has terminated." Thus there is additional support for the argument that word endings attract the child's attention.

In regard to our bilingual example, this suggestion of differential perceptual salience could be checked carefully by having children imitate Hungarian and Serbo-Croatian sentences and note what is omitted. This check remains to be carried out, but other evidence supports the suggestion that part of the difference in ease of acquisition has to do with the pre- or post-nominal location of locative markers in the two languages. The prepositions are missing from the earliest stages of Serbo-Croatian monolingual child speech, and inflections begin to emerge before prepositions (Mikès, 1967; Mikeš and Vlahović, 1966; Pavlovitch, 1920). Inflections are word-final, and would be more perceptually salient on the above interpretation. The best support for this suggestion is the finding that Serbo-Croatian children begin to express the difference between position and direction by adding noun inflections rather than prepositions.

Additional evidence comes from cross-linguistic comparison. Russian, which is extremely similar to Serbo-Croatian, demonstrates the same pattern of prepositional and inflectional acquisition described above (Gvozdev, 1949). The first locatives are noun-noun combinations, as in the example given earlier of "pot stove." At the next level, the first inflections emerge, and the child distinguishes between position and direction by contrasting the locative case with the dative and accusative cases. At this stage the child is expressing the locative notions "in" and "into," "on" and "onto," and "toward," using inflections and no prepositions. Later, when prepositions emerge, it is first just *these* prepositions which are used—performing the same functions as the earlier prepositionless utterances. Several months later a flood of prepositions comes—the equivalents of "under," "behind," "through," "along," and so on.

Rūķe-Draviņa (1959, 1963) presents the same picture in Latvian, with early inflectional marking of "in," "on," and "from," and later emergence of prepositions. She notes that: "Endings, as case markers, generally occur earlier than the corresponding prepositions" (1963, p. 141); and that prepositions are learned gradually, with difficulty, and are often omitted even after they emerge in Latvian child speech.

In English, too, prepositions tend to be omitted in early child speech, but the English-speaking child has no inflections available to use in the place of prepositions. When prepositions do emerge in English, the first ones are "on" and "in" (Brown, in press, chap. II), followed almost immediately by a large number of other prepositions

(Brown, unpublished data). It is as if the child had to develop to the point where he could attend to prepositions; he then uses them first for well-practiced locative notions, and quickly develops the means for expressing a wide range of such notions.

The suggestion of perceptual salience can be approached obliquely in English. Well before the acquisition of prepositions, English-speaking children are using locative verb particles like "on," "off," "down," and so on. These tend to occur toward the ends of utterances in adult speech addressed to the child: "Put the shirt on," "Take your shoes off," and so on. Some of these particles are frequently present as one-word utterances (Braine, 1963; Leopold, 1939; Miller and Ervin, 1964). The same is true of analogous German verbal particles, such as *ab, an, auf, mit,* and so on (Leopold, 1939; Park, 1970). By contrast, Slavic verbal particles of this sort are prefixed to the verb (the equivalents of "down-fall," "off-take," etc.). Grace Shugar (1971), in longitudinal studies of Polish child speech, reports that locative verbal prefixes of this sort emerge at the same time as prepositions in Polish—that is, relatively later then they do in English. For example, *od* "off of/away from" emerges simultaneously as a verb prefix (e.g., *odjechałt* "rode away," *odpadł* "fell down") and as a preposition (e.g., *od mamy* "away from mama"). Since the Polish locative particles are placed before the verb, they are probably at the same level of perceptual saliency as prepositions.

Thus the argument is that if a language expresses locative notions by means of inflections and post-verbal particles (and, by extension, postpositions), acquisition of the verbal expression of locative notions will be facilitated. This can now be checked by comparison with other languages of this sort. Preliminary data on the acquisition of Turkish (my data), Finnish (Argoff, forthcoming), and Korean (Park, 1969)—all similar to Hungarian in this respect—suggest that this is the case. The argument can now be re-phrased, by inductive generalization, as a suggested universal of grammatical development:

UNIVERSAL: Post-verbal and post-nominal locative markers are acquired earlier than pre-verbal and pre-nominal locative markers.[3]

---

[3] The notion of "earlier" is crucial to the understanding of such proposed developmental universals. There are two operational criteria of "earlier": (1) If both means of expression are available in a given language, one will appear in development at a younger age than the other. This can be ascertained in either longitudinal or cross-sectional studies. If A and B are linguistic devices taken to be ordered in psycholinguistic complexity, one would expect to find a given child using either A or both A and B, but not B alone. (2) If only one means of expression is available in a given language, the relevant variable is the time from first reliable *unmarked* intention to express the notion encoded by the linguistic form and the first reliable and appropriate use of that form. Only longitudinal study is applicable in this case. Brown (in press) has proposed a useful criterion of reliable and appropriate mastery of a linguistic form. He suggests that one examine the contexts in a corpus of child speech in which a given grammatical form is obligatory, and set an acquisition criterion in terms of "output-where-required." He has found it useful to define mastery of grammatical morphemes as appropriate production in 90% of obligatory contexts. For purposes of cross-linguistic test of a universal, one would measure the lag between the intention to express the content encoded by A and B and the mastery of A or B in terms of Brown's 90% criterion. The lag between emergence of communicative intent and

This developmental universal is undoubtedly not limited to the expression of locatives. In fact, it seems to reflect a general early tendency on the part of the child to attend to the ends of words when scanning linguistic input in a search for cues to meaning. This is a sort of general heuristic or *operating principle* which the child brings to bear on the task of organizing and storing language. Phrased roughly, one can say that the following is one of the basic "self-instructions" for language acquisition:

OPERATING PRINCIPLE A: Pay attention to the ends of words.

We have seen this operating principle reflected in data on word imitation and in the acquisition of locative expressions. It is also evident in the acquisition of other inflectional systems. For example, accusative and dative inflections are very early acquisitions in inflected languages like Russian, Polish, Serbo-Croatian, Latvian, Finnish, Hungarian, and Turkish—where they are realized as noun suffixes. But these inflections are relatively late in the acquisition of German (Stern and Stern, 1907), where they are realized as forms of prenominal articles. English articles are also lacking at early stages of development. It is not the semantic nature of articles which accounts for the omissions in German and English, because the Bulgarian article, which is a noun suffix, appears early in child speech (Gheorgov, 1908). Apparently Operating Principle A is at work here as well, making it relatively difficult for the child to detect German inflections. The principle also accounts for the finding (Grégoire, 1937) that the first negative element in early French speech is *pas*—the final member of the separated pair *ne . . . pas.*

All of these findings taken together suggest a general developmental universal, based on the supposition that Operating Principle A is one of the first operating principles employed in the ontogenesis of grammar:

UNIVERSAL A1:   For any given semantic notion, grammatical realizations in the form of suffixes or postpositions will be acquired earlier than realizations in the form of prefixes or prepositions.[4]

---

the acquisition of A should be shorter than the lag between the emergence of intent and the acquisition of B.

[4] Greenberg (1957) presents a closely related argument in terms of the psycholinguistic bases of linguistic change. He explores Sapir's observation, corroborated by his own experience, "that prefixing is far less frequent than suffixing in the languages of the world" (p. 89). Greenberg adduces a number of possible psychological causes for a regular historical development away from prefixes to suffixes and finally to isolating linguistic systems. Greenberg examines this phenomenon as an example of the role of psychological factors in language change. The suggestions made here about attention to suffixes in child language development provide an important link to his chain of reasoning. (Of course, additional sorts of psycholinguistic factors will have to be introduced to account for development of an isolating language into either a prefixing or a suffixing one. In consonance with the present argument, however, Greenberg notes that the latter course of historical development is more frequent [p. 93].)

In order for this universal to be manifested, a number of language-definitional universals must be taken for granted (e.g. that there are words, that the meaningful unit is smaller than the word, that sounds can express grammatical relations as well as make reference, and so on). In addition, the emergence of inflections requires at least one other basic operating principle:

OPERATING PRINCIPLE B: The phonological forms of words can be systematically modified.

Numerous observers have reported a period of playful modification of words which precedes the emergence of inflections. Werner and Kaplan, reviewing the European diary literature, note (1963, p. 155):

> there are some indications reported in the literature which suggest that long before the child grasps the role of form-changes as grammatical devices, he grasps the fact that forms of vocables may be modified to express some qualification of, or affective reaction to an event.

They cite many examples of playful reduplication, suffixing, and so forth. In languages which provide inflectional diminutive or affectionate forms, such inflections are among the first to emerge. Shugar (1971), for example, cites early Polish diminutives for names (e.g., *tatunia* [= *tata* "father"] and *mamunia* [= *mama*]) and for other words (e.g., *śliweczka* [= *śliwka* "plum"] and *jabłuszka* [= *jabłko* "apple"]). Pa̧nesová (1968, p. 216) gives remarkable examples from the early speech of a Czech boy who inserted extra syllables into adjectives in order to intensify their meanings. For example, the child had the following series for the adjective *veliky* "big": [velikej]—[velika:nskej]—[velikana:nskej]—[velikanana:nskej]; and *malý* "little" was changed to: [mali:]—[maliŋki:]—[malineŋki:]—[malilineŋki:]—[malulilineŋki:].

  Children frequently experiment with the forms of words before they discover the meanings of particular formal changes. For example, Rūķe-Draviņa (1959) gives numerous examples of the early noncomprehending use of linguistic forms in Latvian:

> The inflections -a/-e (nominative) and -u/-i (accusative) are used in free variation as alternative pronunciations of nouns at age 1;6, not being differentiated for the two case meanings until 1;8.
>   The plural ending is occasionally attached to nouns referring to singular objects before the acquisition of the pluralization rule.
>   Masculine and feminine adjectives are first used indiscriminately, ignoring the gender of the associated noun.

In all of these Latvian examples the form in adult speech is salient (according to Operating Principle A) and is fairly regular. A similar example is the English plural, which sometimes appears in early child speech as an alternative pronunciation of nouns.[5]

Operating Principles A and B present part of an explanation for the relative ease of acquisition of Hungarian locative inflections: the inflections are presumably perceptually salient, and the child is presumably prepared to manipulate the forms of word endings in his production. These principles both relate to ongoing speech processing—the deployment of attention in speech perception and the production of grammatical markers in speaking, although they also have implications for the kinds of linguistic rules which will be formed. Another set of determinants of ease of acquisition has to do more directly with rule organization factors—both simplicity and consistency of rules from a formal point of view, and semantic consistency. In the Hungarian system the locative marker is directly bound to the noun, while in the Serbo-Croatian system it is divided between a pre-nominal preposition and an inflection. In addition, the choice of formal markers for locative expression is semantically consistent and non-arbitrary in Hungarian, but is much less principled and orderly in Serbo-Croatian. A full answer to the question posed in our test case, therefore, will require operating principles for rule formation as well as for language processing. Principles of this sort will be advanced later in the paper, in connection with broader ranges of data. (See Operating Principles D and G, below.) The test case has played its role in demonstrating the types of cognitive prerequisites to grammatical development which can be revealed by the method outlined above.

Broadly speaking, there are three classes of such prerequisites: (1) those related to the underlying semantics of utterances, (2) those related to the perception and production of speech under short-term constraints, and (3) those related to the organization and storage of linguistic rules.[6] The first class of prerequisites falls within the

---

[5] It should be noted that there are considerable individual differences between children in their propensity to play with form when not expressing meaning. For example, of the two girls studied by Roger Brown, Eve had a period of free variation of singular and plural forms, whereas Sarah did not use the plural inflection until she could use it correctly. The problem of individual differences between children in their approaches to language acquisition has not been addressed frequently in developmental psycholinguistics, but is obviously of great importance—especially in light of the typically small samples required by longitudinal research methods. Wick Miller (1964a) has made a valuable observation in this regard:

> There are individual differences in grammatical development . . . some children are more prone to invent their own grammatical patterns, patterns that have no relationship to adult patterns. The early grammatical rules for some are limited and quite regular, and for other children they are more variable and more difficult to define. Some children are quite willing to speak at almost any time, whether or not they have the appropriate grammatical structures at hand to express their thoughts, whereas others are more reserved in this regard, and will avoid talking at all, or will use a clumsy circumlocution . . . . I am inclined to think that the variations that are closely tied to formal features of language reflect innate individual differences.

[6] Cf. the distinction made by Braine (1971) in his recently-proposed "discovery-procedures"

domain of the general psychology of cognitive development; the remaining prerequisities must be elaborated by developmental psycholinguistics. These are essentially *language processing variables* which can be conceptualized in terms of *operating principles* such as those proposed above. A number of such operating principles, and the predicted developmental universals which flow from them, will be proposed in the last section of this paper. Such operating principles guide the child in developing strategies for the production and interpretation of speech and for the construction of linguistic rule systems. The operating principles function within a framework of constraints on linguistic performance. These constraints must be considered before enumerating specific operating principles in more detail.

CONSTRAINTS ON LINGUISTIC PERFORMANCE

By and large, the language processing variables to be discussed below are determined by the fact that human language is produced and received in rapid temporal sequence. That is to say, because we communicate through the rapidly fading, temporally ordered auditory modality, we must have strategies for quickly programming and deciphering messages. The sorts of processing variables considered here are therefore closely linked to general perceptual and performance-programming principles. Some of them may well be special biological adaptations for language processing, or may have evolved in connection with language—but the issue of evolutionary origin need not be decided here.[7]

The constraints on linguistic performance are both short-term and long-term. The short-term have to do with the ongoing use of speech, and the long-term with the storage and organization of the linguistic system. Child and adult alike must operate under pressures of fading signal and fading auditory image; child and adult alike must have ready access to stored linguistic rules in programming and interpreting utterances. Although short-term sentence processing span increases with age, similar performance constraints are present in childhood and adulthood. Bever (1970a,b) has proposed that certain linguistic structures are not found in human language because they cannot be processed perceptually; it is likewise true that certain linguistic structures are not found in child language because they exceed the child's processing span. Because this span increases with age, it is evident that many universals

---

model of language acquisition between (1) concept learning, (2) the scanner, and (3) the memory component. The operating principles proposed here are aimed at specifying some of the properties to which the scanner is sensitive and some of the organizational features of the memory. In addition, Braine's model posits a preferential order or hierarchy among the properties noticed by the scanner. The property hierarchy (cf. Chomsky's "simplicity metric") for a given language would result from the application of the operating principles (e.g., the suggested preference for word-final markers), as well as a possible preferential order of application of some operating principles.

[7] It may well be that human skills associated with auditory pattern perception, production and perception of rapid temporally-ordered auditory sequences, and so forth, originally evolved to subserve the function of linguistic communication. Once evolved, however, such skills can be applied to a broader range of functions. For example, music may owe its existence to skills originally evolved for linguistic purposes.

of linguistic development are based on increasing temporal scope of processing operations. This is, of course, true of speech production as well as speech perception.

Processing span at first is quite literally limited to the number of terms which can occur in an utterance. Almost all investigators report a two-word (or two-morpheme) stage of development. During this period the child can typically express such relations as agent-verb, verb-object, and agent-object, but cannot unite all three terms into a single utterance. The advance from two-word to three-word utterances involves filling in a three-term sequence with fragments which earlier occurred as two-word utterances (cf. Brown, in press, Chap. I; Bowerman, 1970). That is, with maturation, the child reaches the point at which all of the sub-parts of an agent-verb-object sentence can be spoken in a single utterance. Adjective-noun combinations, which also occur earlier as two-word utterances, can be combined into three-word sentences as well, but this requires deletion of one of the other terms—generally the subject—producing verb-object strings with a nounphrase in object position. Thus the child can say, for example, "Mama drink coffee" and "Drink hot coffee," but not "Mama drink hot coffee."

At this early stage, then, output length limitations are quite severe—literally limited to words rather than to structures or to linguistic operations. Such limitations do not occur in adult speech, and this aspect of development seems purely to be based on maturation of a very simple sort of short-term processing capacity. At somewhat later stages, however, one finds the same sorts of processing limitations as in adult linguistic performance—but down to child scale. For example, both adults and children have difficulty dealing with material interposed between related parts of a sentence (cf. Operating Principle D, below). The only important age difference is in terms of how much material can be interposed without losing track of one's place in a sentence. For example, children may have difficulty in dealing with a doubly modified object noun between verb and particle—as in "He called the little old lady up"—whereas adults may tolerate a longer intetvening string. But for both children and adults short-term limitations constrain the amount of material which can be interpolated before production or interpretation of utterances breaks down. In similar fashion, children are limited in the number of grammatical operations which can be performed in an utterance (Bellugi, 1968), but this limitation does not differ in kind from limitations on adult linguistic performance.

I am proposing, therefore, that the short-term limitations under which children operate—beyond the very early limitations on absolute sentence length—are universal human limitations on sentences processing, and that they are based on general perceptual and information-processing principles. The nature of their development can be revealed by the general psychology of perceptual development.

Constraints on production and comprehension are intimately related—especially in child speech, where the forms the child uses in his own speech must be those he has been able to perceive in the speech of others. Thus the operating principles proposed below relate closely both to comprehension strategies (cf. Bever's "perceptual mapping rules") and to the sorts of linguistic rules originally preferred by the child. To a great extent, the form of linguistic rules is determined by the short-term processing limitations, because the rules refer to a system which is represented in the auditory-acoustic modality, and because they must be called into play during rapid speech processing. In fact, at the beginning levels, it could be that there is little difference between short-term processing strategies and linguistic rules. That is to say, the child's knowledge of language—beyond the definitional knowledge proposed at the outset—is represented chiefly by the techniques he uses to interpret and produce sentences.[8]

SUGGESTED UNIVERSALS IN THE ONTOGENESIS OF GRAMMAR

In the remainder of the paper I propose some very specific language processing strategies. The approach is to define a set of presumably universal operating principles which every child brings to bear on the problem of language acquisition. From these operating principles, a number of more specific strategies can be derived, finally resulting in language-specific strategies for the acquisition of aspects of a given native language. Although the operating principles and universals have been arrived at through the same procedures spelled out in the locative test case reviewed above, the format in the following section is more terse, working down from broad operating principles to suggested developmental universals, summarizing data which support those universals (marked by § in the text below). The universals are hopefully phrased in such a way that they can be supported, modified, or abandoned in the light of future research.

WORD ORDER

One of the earliest and most pervasive operating principles has to do with attention to order of elements in an utterance. It seems that a basic expectation which the child brings to the task of grammatical development is that the order of elements in an utterance can be related to underlying semantic relations.

OPERATING PRINCIPLE C: Pay attention to the order of words and morphemes.

UNIVERSAL C1:   The standard order of functor morphemes in the input language is preserved in child speech.

§ No observers report deviant orders of bound morphemes. Burling (1959) found that post-verbal and post-nominal morpheme order was always correct in Garo, where long strings of ordered affixes occur. The same is true of Turkish, Finnish, and Hungarian child speech. The elements of the English auxiliary phrase always occur in their proper order (e.g., "has not been reading," "will not be able to come," etc.).

UNIVERSAL C2:   Word order in child speech reflects word order in the input language.

---

[8] Beyond these language-specific constraints, however, many linguistic universals are undoubtedly shaped by general constraints on the kinds of rules which the human mind can function with. I suspect that if other complex domains were formally described to the extent that language has been so described we would find similar constraints on the abstract structure of rules.

The phrasing of this universal is purposely vague, because the data are, as yet, imprecise. Earlier, limited data had suggested that children would adhere to fixed word order regardless of the degree of freedom of word order in the input language (Slobin, 1968). More recent data (Bowerman, 1970) indicate considerable individual differences between children in this regard.

§ Word order in child speech is typically reported as more consistent in languages with fixed word order (e.g., English, Samoan) as opposed to languages with relatively more freedom in this regard (e.g., German, Slavic languages, Finnish, Turkish). (But see Burling [1959] and Braine [1971] for examples of deviant word order in English child speech.)

§ American children tend to retain word order in sentence imitation (Brown and Fraser, 1963; Fraser, Bellugi, and Brown, 1963), whereas Polish children (Shugar, 1971) and Russian children (Dingwall and Tuniks, in press) frequently change word order in imitating sentences.

§ A Finnish child studied by Bowerman (1970) seemed to have acquired the dominant word orders of adult Finnish by the time his mean utterances length was 1.42 morphemes. Bowerman presents the following figures on the frequency of occurrence of various orders of subject, verb, and object in the speech of the child and his mother (figures represent numbers of utterances in recorded natural conversation):

	Child	Mother
SV	44	47
VS	4	5
VO	4	16
V	1	3
SVO	7	32
OSV	1	0
OVS	0	1
VSO	0	1
SOV	1	1

UNIVERSAL C3:   Sentences deviating from standard word order will be interpreted at early stages of development as if they were examples of standard word order.

§ Fraser, Bellugi, and Brown (1963) found that English-speaking pre-schoolers would interpret passive sentences as if the order of elements were subject-verb-object. For example, "The girl is pushed by the boy" is matched with a picture of a girl pushing a boy. In other words, children's interpretations conform to the order principle, bur reverse meaning. Bever (1970a, p. 298) has proposed as a general strategy of English sentence interpretation: "Any *Noun-Verb-Noun* (NVN) sequence within a potential internal unit in the surface structure corresponds to *actor-action-object.*" He presents extensive data in support of this strategy. McNeill (1970, p. 124) proposes a similar strategy.

§ Conjoined sentences referring to two temporally ordered events are first given the interpretation that order of mention matches order of occurrence, even if the conjunction indicates otherwise (E. V. Clark, 1971; Cromer, 1968; Hatch, 1969). (E.g., it is relatively more difficult for children to understand sentences of the form "Event 2 *after* Event 1" and "*Before* Event 2, Event 1" than sentences of the form "Event 1 *before* Event 2" and "*After* Event 1, Event 2.")

§ Universal C3 is apparently applicable even in inflected languages, which allow more flexibility of word order than English. Roeper (1973) investigated German children's attention to word order and inflection. The standard word order for German imperatives is verb-indirect object-direct object (V-IO-DO), with inflected articles indicating the roles of IO and DO. The inflections make it possible for adults to vary the order of the two nouns without losing sense or grammaticality. When offered V-DO-IO sentences for imitation, some children tended to switch articles, placing the dative article on the first noun and the accusative on the second. That is, children showed their command of the inflections *and* their reliance on word order: they interpreted the first noun after the verb as the indirect object, and inflected the article preceding that noun accordingly. Similarly, in a comprehension task, Roeper found that V-DO-IO sentences were frequently comprehended as if they were V-IO-DO. Thus in both imitation and comprehension many children tended to rely on word order over inflections as a guide to grammatical relations.[9]

§ C. Chomsky (1968) and Cromer (1970) have demonstrated that children have difficulty in correctly interpreting sentences of the type "John is easy to see," where the surface subject corresponds to the object in deep structure. Children as old as six interpret the first noun in such sentences as subject.

SURFACE PRESERVATION OF UNDERLYING STRUCTURE
Psycholinguistic research suggests another sort of operating principle which is tied to the fact that speech is produced and processed sequentially in a rapidly fading modality. In its most general form, this principle states that interruption or rearrangement of linguistic units places a strain on sentence processing—both in production and reception. In other words, there is a pressure to preserve the internal or underlying structure of linguistic units in their surface manifestations. A number of strategies can be related to this principle—both strategies for speech perception and strategies for the formation and use of rules of production.

OPERATING PRINCIPLE D: Avoid interruption or rearrangement of linguistic units.

---

[9] The operation of language processing variables can also be discerned in the process of language change (cf. Bever and Langendoen, 1971). For example, inflections are replaced by word order in the development of pidgin forms of a language, thus suggesting that order is a more basic device than inflections. It is also probably the case that all languages make use of word order as a basic linguistic means of signalling underlying relations, while the use of inflections is not universal.

UNIVERSAL D1:   Structures requiring permutation of elements will first appear in non-permuted form.

§ English yes-no questions first appear in non-inverted form (e.g., "I can go?"); inversion of subject and auxiliary is also absent in the first forms of wh-questions (e.g., "Where I can go?") (Brown, Cazden, and Bellugi, 1969; Klima and Bellugi, 1966).

§ The first relative clauses in English appear in sentence-final position without inversion (e.g., "I know what is that") (Menyuk, 1969).

UNIVERSAL D2:   Whenever possible, discontinuous morphemes will be reduced to, or replaced by continuous morphemes.

§ Slavic case inflections are first used to express the contrast between position and direction, in the absence of prepositions—i.e., the locative notion is, at first, not marked on both sides of the noun (as discussed above).

§ The first form of the English progressive is the verbal inflection -*ing* with no pre-verbal auxiliary (Brown, in press, Chap. II; and many others).

§ The first form of French negation is *pas*, the final part of the discontinuous morpheme, *ne . . . pas* (Grégoire, 1937).

§. The discontinuous Arabic negative /*ma-* . . . *š*/ is acquired later than the prefixed negative /*miš*/ by Egyptian children, although both are equally frequent. Children under 3;6 have a general negation rule of /*miš*/ + *S*, even when incorrect by adult standards (e.g., /*huwa miš rāh*/ instead of /*huwa ma-rāh-š*/ 'he not went'). Above 3;6, the discontinuous /*ma-* . . . *š*/ is never substituted for /*miš*/ but the opposite substitution does occur (Omar, 1970).

UNIVERSAL D3:   There is a tendency to preserve the structure of the sentence as a closed entity, reflected in a development from sentence-external placement of various linguistic forms to their movement within the sentence.

§ Early negative forms in English are attached to primitive sentences ("No do this"), later moving within the sentence ("I no do this" and, with auxiliary modal development, "I can't do this") (Bellugi, 1967; Klima and Bellugi, 1966; Menyuk, 1969; Snyder, 1914).[10]

§ Finnish yes-no questions require attachment of a question particle to the word questioned, and movement of that word to the front of the sentence. Acquisition of this form of question is exceptionally late in Finnish children (Argoff, forthcoming;

---

[10] But Shugar (1971) reports early sentence-internal placement of a negative particle in Polish, and proposes: "It would seem that relative freedom of word position in sentences as well as experience with diminutive infixes might facilitate such re-arrangements within linguistic units like sentences in the Polish language."

Bowerman, 1970). An earlier form of yes-no question in Finnish child speech consists of a sentence-final interrogative particle (S + *vai* or S+*yoko*) (Argoff, forthcoming).

§ Sentence-final relative clauses ("I met a man who was sick") are earlier to develop than embedded relative clauses ("The man who was sick went home") (Brogan, 1968; Menyuk, 1969; Slobin and Welsh, 1973).

UNIVERSAL D4:   The greater the separation between related parts of a sentence, the 'greater the tendency that the sentence will not be adequately processed (in imitation, comprehension, or production).[11]

§ Brogan (1968), in analyzing unpublished imitation data gathered by Carolyn Wardrip, found that sentences (1) and (2) were easy for preschoolers to imitate, while (3) posed considerable difficulty:
  (1) He knows how to read because he goes to school.
  (2) I saw the man who fell down.
  (3) The man that fell down ran away.

Note that sentence length and number of embedded sentences do not account for these findings. What is difficult is not embedding, but *self*-embedding, as exemplified in (3). Similar findings are reported by Menyuk (1969); Slobin and Welsh (1973), and Smith (1970).

CLEAR MARKING OF UNDERLYING RELATIONS
Children scan adult sentences for cues to meaning, and are aided by overt morphological markers which are regular and perceptually salient. Such markers probably play a similar role in production, helping the child keep track of where he is in the transition from thought to utterance. With maturation and psycholinguistic development, the child develops an increasing ability to derive deep structure from minimal cues. Bever (1970a, p. 350) has set forth "a view of sentence complexity according to which the more internal structure material that is implicit in the external structure, the harder the sentence, since the child must contribute more information to the sentence himself."

Children apparently prefer that grammatical functors be not only present wherever possible, but also that they be clearly marked acoustically. In fact, functors may be more clearly marked acoustically in child speech than in adult speech. Levina has noted that for Russian children

clarity and accuracy of pronunciation appear first of all

---

[11] This is, in fact, not a developmental universal, but a statement of a general psycholinguistic performance constraint. As pointed out above, the only age difference is in severity of the constraint. Watt has phrased this universal in terms of a "theory of cumulative assignments" (1970, p. 151): ". . . psycholinguistic parsing complexity increases with the amount of deep structure whose correct assignment is postponed; with the length of sentence over which the postponement must be carried; and with the complexity of misassignments whose rescission returns the processor to an earlier point in the sentence."

in the inflections. At the same time the word stem continues to sound inarticulate . . . . The work carried out
by the child in connection with rudimentary distinctions
of grammatical meanings . . . facilitates more articulate
perception of the acoustic composition of words at this
stage (quoted by Leont'yev, 1965, p. 101).

Rūķe-Draviņa (1963) notes that in Latvian child speech newly acquired conjunctions and other connecting words are stressed, even if unstressed in adult speech.

OPERATING PRINCIPLE E: Underlying semantic relations should be marked overtly and clearly.

UNIVERSAL E1:   A child will begin to mark a semantic notion earlier if its morpho-logical realization is more salient perceptually (ceteris paribus).

§ The notions of "more salient perceptually" and *"ceteris paribus,"* of course, are in need of more precise definition. Operating Principle A and the discussion of locative expressions offer some support for Universal E1. (Cf. early acquisition of the Hungarian locative inflections, the Bulgarian suffixed article *-at/-ta/-to,* etc.).

§ The Hungarian-Serbo-Croatian bilingual children acquired the Serbo-Croatian accusative inflection *-u* earlier than the corresponding Hungarian inflection *-t,* using it on words of both languages.

§ The development of the passive is late in Indo-European languages, where it typically requires several morphological changes, as well as a change in word order in many languages. By contrast, the Arabic passive is learned early by Egyptian children (Omar, 1970), where it is formed by a prefixed */it-/* on the past tense of the verb, with obligatory agent deletion and preposing of underlying patient. Although several factors are at play in this comparison, the marking of the passive by a single clear prefix is probably one of the reasons for its early acquisition in Arabic.

§ The following finding, reported by Shugar (1971) for Polish child language devel-opment, suggests a role for perceptual salience in inflectional development: "The following oppositions emerged: singular vs. plural in nouns, verbs, and pronouns; first vs. second person singular in verb endings; nominative vs. accusative case for femi-nine nouns; masculine vs. feminine gender both in pronouns and verb-endings. Most of the above differentiations seem to rest upon a new phonological acquisition: an acoustically clear differentiation of /a/ and /e/."

UNIVERSAL E2:   There is a preference not to mark a semantic category by Ø ("zero morpheme"). If a category is sometimes marked by Ø and sometimes by some overt phonological form, the latter will, at some stage, also replace the Ø.[12]

---

[12] It may be necessary to draw a distinction here between marked and unmarked categories

§ The Russian noun singular accusative is marked by Ø for masculine nonhuman and neuter nouns. Such nouns are first marked with the acoustically salient feminine accusative -*u* by Russian children (Gvozdev, 1949; Pavlova, 1924; Slobin, 1966, 1968; Zakharova, 1958). The very same is true of Serbo-Craotian language development (Mikeš and Vlahović, 1966; Pavlovitch, 1920).

§ Gvozdev's (1949) Russian child used the masculine and feminine -*ov* for all plural genitive nouns, replacing the feminine plural genitive Ø.

§ Arabic nouns are given in the singular (Ø) with numerals over 10; but Egyptian children tend to use plural noun forms with all numerals (Omar, 1970).

UNIVERSAL E3:   If there are homonymous forms in an inflectional system, those forms will tend not to be the earliest inflections acquired by the child; i.e. the child tends to select phonologically unique forms, when available, as the first realization of inflections.

§ The first noun instrumental inflection used by Russian children is the masculine and neuter -*om,* rather than the more frequent feminine -*oy* (Gvozdev, 1949; Pavlova, 1924; Slobin, 1966; 1968; Zakharova, 1958). The suffix -*om* has only one homonym (masculine and neuter locative adjective inflection), while -*oy* represents five homonymous inflections (singular adjective inflections for masculine nominative and feminine genitive, dative, instrumental, and prepositional cases).

UNIVERSAL E4:   When a child first controls a full form of a linguistic entity which can undergo contraction or deletion, contractions or deletions of such entities tend to be absent.

§ Bellugi (1967) has noted the clear enunciation of "I will"—even in imitations of sentences containing "I'll"—at a developmental stage at which special attention is paid to the auxiliary system.

§ Slobin and Welsh (1973), in a longitudinal study of elicited imitation, found numerous examples in which their subject supplied elements in her imitation which had been optionally deleted in the model sentence (e.g., Model: "I see the man the boy hit." Child: "I see a man who a boy hit.")

UNIVERSAL E5:   It is easier to understand a complex sentence in which optionally deletable material appears in its full form.

§ This statement is a version of Bever's suggestion that "the child . . . has some difficulty with constructions that depend on active reconstruction of deleted internal

---

(Greenberg, 1966). Children do not insist on an inflectional marker for the nominative case in the Slavic languages, although such overgeneralization is technically possible. Little English-speaking children are content to leave the third person verb singular uninflected (a category which is generally unmarked in the world's languages), while they overgeneralize the plural (e.g., "sheeps") and the past tense (e.g., "cutted") to all possible cases.

structure" (1970a, p. 351). Psycholinguistic research on adults, such as that carried out by Fodor, Garrett, and Bever (1968), has shown that multiply self-embedded clauses are very difficult for adults to understand (e.g., "The pen the author the editor liked used was new"). There are, presumably, too many interruptions to keep track of. Such sentences can be made significantly easier for adults to understand if each embedded clause is marked by a relative pronoun (e.g., "The pen which the author whom the editor liked used was new") (Fodor and Garrett, 1967; Hakes and Cairns, 1970). The notion here is that one scans a sentence perceptually, searching for cues to underlying meaning, and that the relative pronoun facilitates a particular strategy for interpreting multiply embedded sentences—namely, that in a sequence of *noun- relative pronoun-noun-transitive verb*, the first noun is object and the second subject of the following verb.

Children, of course, cannot understand multiply self-embedded sentences, but they can begin to understand sentences with one embedded clause. For example, Charles Welsh and I found that a two-year-old girl could imitate many sentences with embed- ded clauses marked by relative pronouns, and that her imitations showed that she understood the appropriate underlying relations (e.g., Model: "The man who I saw yesterday got wet." Child: "I saw the man and he got wet."). Note that her imitation has preserved meaning, showing that she was able to decode the structure, but that she has avoided interruptions in her version. She gives back the full forms of the two underlying sentences, supplying the deleted repetition of the subject: "I saw the man" and "He got wet." [13] (This is further evidence for Operating Principle D.) At this stage of development, the child is unable to interpret sentences from which the relative pronoun has been deleted (e.g., Model: "The boy the book hit was crying." Child: "boy the book was crying"). These structures were clearly beyond her compe- tence at this level, and were treated as word lists. (Cf. the example given above under Universal E4, drawn from a later stage in the development of the same child. In that example the deleted relative pronoun is supplied by the child in her imitation, indicat- ing her ability to interpret the deletion, along with the need to mark the relative clause overtly with the pronoun in her own production.) (Slobin and Welsh, 1973).

§ Olds (1968) found that boys aged seven, nine, and eleven responded more quickly to instructions in which a relative pronoun was present (e.g. "The piece that your opponent moved may be moved two spaces") than to the corresponding shorter sentences from which the pronoun had been deleted (e.g. "The piece your opponent moved may be moved two spaces").

§ C. Chomsky (1969) and Olds (1968) found that children were less likely to misinterpret the verbs "ask" and "tell" when a pronoun indicated the underlying subject of an embedded sentence. For example, (1) and (2) were more difficult to interpret than (3) and (4):

(1) Ask Laura what to feed the doll.
(2) Tell Laura what to feed the doll.

---

[13] Note that this example also shows that the perception rules are not identical to the production rules. That is, the child can retrieve meaning from structures which she cannot yet produce.

(3) Ask Laura what you should feed the doll.
(4) Tell Laura what she should feed the doll.

OVERREGULARIZATION

Perhaps the most widely noted aspect of child speech has been children's tendency to overregularize or overgeneralize. Virtually every observer has noted some examples of analogical formations, overextension of regular principles, etc., and a comprehensive list of examples cannot be attempted here. Rules applicable to larger classes are developed before rules relating to their subdivisions. There is a tendency to apply a linguistic rule to all relevant cases. In short:

OPERATING PRINCIPLE F: Avoid exceptions.

UNIVERSAL F1: The following stages of linguistic marking of a semantic notion are typically observed: (1) no marking, (2) appropriate marking in limited cases. (3) overgeneralization of marking (often accompanied by redundant marking), (4) full adult system.

§ A classic example is the development of the English past tense, as represented by the following schematic sequence of stages of strong and weak forms in past tense contexts: (1) break, drop; (2) broke, drop; (3) breaked, dropped; (4) breakted, dropted; (5) broke, dropped (Slobin, 1971a).

§ Stage (3) can consist of substages of successive overgeneralizations, in which one form drives out another (cf. the discussion of "inflectional imperialism" in Slobin, 1968). For example, Russian children first use the masculine and neuter -om inflection for all singular noun instrumentals; then replace this with the feminine -oy; and only later sort out the two inflections (Zakharova, 1958). Simiarly, Russian children first use the feminine past tense for all verbs, regardless of the gender of subject noun; then use only the masculine for all verbs; followed by a period of mixed usage and eventual separate marking of verb past tense to agree with gender of subject noun (Popova, 1958).

§ The Arabic plural has a number of irregularities and inconsistencies, as described earlier in this paper (a large number of irregular forms; a separate dual; singular nouns with numerals over 10; separate forms for "counted" vs. "collected" senses of given nouns). The regular feminine plural suffix is widely overgeneralized, and "was strongly preferred for pluralizing nonsense nouns by children of all ages" (Omar, 1970, p. 375).

UNIVERSAL F2: Rules applicable to larger classes are developed before rules relating to their subdivisions, and general rules are learned before rules for special cases.

§ Gvozdev's (1949) Russian child did not distinguish between mass and count nouns, requiring that every noun have a singular and a plural form. Thus he pluralized mass nouns (*bumagi* "papers"), counted mass nouns (*odna sakhara* "one sugar"), and invented singulars for plural nouns which have no singular forms in Russian (e.g., *lyut* as the singular for the collective noun *lyudi* "people"). Similar phenomena have been frequently reported for English-speaking children.

§ Masculine animate nouns take a special accusative inflection in Russian. Subdivision of the noun class into the categories of animate and inanimate masculine for purposes of accusative inflection is typically late in Russian children, who prefer to use a single accusative form for all nouns (Gvozdev, 1949; Solov'yeva, 1960).

§ C. Chomsky (1969) found late acquisition of the special rules involved in the use of the verbs "promise" and "ask" in English. "Promise" is a special case in that it violates the "Minimal Distance Principle" (Rosenbaum, 1967) generally used to decide on the subject of an infinitival complement verb; e.g., in (1) the subject of the complement verb is "Bill," but in (2), where "promise" appears, the subject is "John."
(1) John wanted Bill to leave.
(2) John promised Bill to leave.

"Promise" *consistently* violates the Minimal Distance Principle, while "ask" is *inconsistent*—cf. (3), where "Bill" is the subject of the verb in the complement, and (4), where "John" is the subject:
(3) John asked Bill to leave.
(4) John asked Bill what to do.

While "promise" is consistently exceptional, "ask" is inconsistent. Chomsky found that full comprehension of "promise" came at an earlier age than full comprehension of "ask," suggesting that it is easier to learn a consistent exception than an inconsistent exception.

SEMANTIC MOTIVATION FOR GRAMMAR
The overgeneralizations engendered by Operating Principle F are always constrained within semantic limits. The child applies an appropriate inflection or function word within a grammatical class, failing to observe a detailed subdivision of that class, but errors in choice of functor are always within the given functor class. There are numerous examples in the cross-linguistic data of the principle that rules relating to semantically defined classes take precedence over rules relating to formally defined classes, and that purely arbitrary rules are exceptionally difficult to master (see footnote 4). Simply stated:

OPERATING PRINCIPLE G: The use of grammatical markers should make semantic sense.

UNIVERSAL G1:   When selection of an appropriate inflection among a group of inflections performing the same semantic function is determined by arbitrary formal criteria (e.g. phonological shape of stem, number of syllables in stem, arbitrary gender of stem), the child initially tends to use a single form in all environments, ignoring formal selection restrictions.

§ The examples cited under Universals E2 and F1 also support Universal G1. For example, a common error in both Russian and Serbo-Croatian child speech is to use the frequent and perceptually salient feminine accusative -*u* on masculine and neuter nouns as well as feminine nouns. But, when it is used, the -*u* inflection is added only to nouns, and not to other parts of speech, and only to indicate the direct object of action or the goal of directed movement. Thus the proper inflection is picked to express semantic intention (accusative inflection), though the child does not yet follow the subselections within that class on the basis of gender and phonology. For each particular grammatical case category, the Slavic child apparently selects one salient case ending to express the semantic of that case in connection with all nouns. The underlying grammatical rule, therefore, is semantically appropriate, but only formally deficient.

§ In languages requiring agreement between adjective and noun, case and number agreement is acquired before gender agreement. In Russian, for example, the child uses a single adjective inflection for each case and number combination, but does not make gender distinctions (e.g., one singular nominative for all genders, one plural nominative, etc.) (Gvozdev, 1949).

§ Mikeš and Vlahović (1966) report for Serbo-Croatian that case distinctions and the singular-plural contrast are acquired before gender distinctions (both selection of gender-conditioned noun inflection and agreement between noun and modifier in gender). They note that children stop themselves before expressing proper gender much more frequently than for other grammatical decisions.

UNIVERSAL G2:   Errors in choice of functor are always within the given functor class and subcategory.

§ Gvozdev (1949) points out that although there are many confusions as to the proper suffix to employ within a given Russian case category, the child never uses one case instead of another. For example, although the Russian child uses an instrumental noun inflection which fails to agree with the noun in gender, he does not express the notion of the instrumental case by means of a dative inflection, a verb tense inflection, etc.

§ English-speaking children at first fail to appropriately subdivide prepositions according to their detailed semantic functions, but do not confuse prepositions with conjunctions or other parts of speech, and so forth. Miller and Ervin note, in summarizing their longitudinal study: "The children seldom used a suffix or function word with the wrong lexical class." (1964, p. 26).

UNIVERSAL G3:   Semantically consistent grammatical rules are acquired early and without significant error.

§ A Samoan child studied by Kernan (1969) had learned to appropriately use the articles *le* + comon noun and '*o* + proper noun/pronoun at the two-word stage. Thus a choice of articles based on a clear semantic feature—[+ human]—was acquired at a very early stage of development.

§ Roger Brown (in press, Chap. II) has found that the English progressive is the only inflection which never overgeneralizes in American child speech. That is, children never add the progressive to "state" verbs, saying things like "wanting," "liking," "needing," "knowing," "seeing," or "hearing"; but they freely use the progressive with a large number of "process" verbs. Brown argues that there is a clear semantic distinction between verbs which take the progressive inflection and those which do not. Those not allowing the progressive all indicate involuntary *states,* while those allowing the progressive indicate *processes* which can be voluntary when predicated of people. This is the only subclassification of English words, for inflectional purposes, which is semantically principled. There is no principled basis for remembering, for example, that some verbs form irregular past tenses, or that some nouns have irregular plurals. These lists must be learned by rote, and the result is that such forms are overregularized in child speech. It is easier to apply a rule uniformly than to block it for unprincipled reasons, and so, long after they show their knowledge that one cannot say "I am knowing," children persist in saying things like "I knowed" and "two sheeps."

CONCLUSION

What has been sketched out on the preceding pages is only an outline of what some day may evolve into a model of the order of acquisition of linguistic structures. It has several major components, all of which must be elaborated. The first component, I have argued, is the development of semantic intentions, stemming from general cognitive development. The child, equipped with an inherent definition of the general structure and function of language, goes about finding means for the expression of those intentions by actively attempting to understand speech. That is to say, he must have preliminary internal structures for the assimilation of both linguistic and non-linguistic input. He scans linguistic input to discover meaning, guided by certain ideas about language, by general cognitive-perceptual strategies, and by processing limitations imposed by the constraints of operative memory. As in all of cognitive development, this acquisition process involves the assimilation of information to existing structures, and the accomodation of those structures to new input. The speech perception strategies engender the formation of rules for speech production. Inner linguistic structures change with age as computation and storage space increase, as increasing understanding of linguistic intentions leads the child into realms of new formal complexity, and as internal structures are interrelated and re-organized in accordance with general principles of cognitive organization. All of these factors are cognitive prerequisites for the development of grammar. While we can disagree about the extent to which this process of developing grammars requires a richly detailed innate language faculty, there can be no doubt that the process requires a richly structured and active child mind.

REFERENCES

Argoff, H. D., Forthcoming doctoral dissertation on the acquisition of Finnish. Univer. Calif., Berkeley.

Bar-Adon, A., Primary syntactic structures in Hebrew child language. In A. Bar-Adon and W. F. Leopold (eds.), *Child language: A book of readings.* Englewood Cliffs, N.J.: Prentice-Hall, 1971, Pp. 433–472.

Bellugi, U., The acquisition of negation. Unpubl. doct. dissert., Harvard Univ., 1967.

Bellugi, U., Linguistic mechanisms underlying child speech. In H. Zale (ed.), *Proceedings of the Conference on Language and Language Behavior.* New York: Appleton-Century-Crofts, 1968.

Bever, T. G., The cognitive basis for linguistic structures. In J. R. Hayes (ed.), *Cognition and the development of language.* New York: Wiley, 1970. Pp. 279–362. (a)

Bever, T. G., The influence of speech performance on linguistic structure. In G. B. Flores d'Arcais and W. J. M. Levelt (eds.), *Advances in psycholinguistics.* Amsterdam: North-Holland, 1970. Pp. 4–30. (b)

Bever, T. G., and D. T. Langendoen, A dynamic model of the evolution of language. *Ling. Inquiry,* 1971, **4**, 433–464.

Bowerman, M. F., Learning to talk: A cross-linguistic study of early syntactic development, with special reference to Finnish. Unpubl. doct. dissert., Harvard Univer., 1970. [Cambridge Univer. Press, 1973.]

Braine, M. D. S., The ontogeny of English phrase structure: The first phase. *Language,* 1963, **39**, 1–13.

Braine, M. D. S., On two types of models of the internalization of grammars. In D. I. Slobin (ed.), *The ontogenesis of grammar: A theoretical symposium.* New York: Academic Press, 1971. Pp. 153–186.

Brogan, P. A., The nesting constraint in child language. Unpubl. paper in series "Language, Society, and the Child," Language-Behavior Res. Lab., Univer. Calif., Berkeley, 1968.

Brown, R., *A first language.* Cambridge, Mass.: Harvard Univer. Press, 1973. (Chap. I: Semantic and grammatical relations; Chap. II: Grammatical morphemes and the modulation of meaning.)

Brown, R., C. Cazden, and U. Bellugi. The child's grammar from I to III. In J. P. Hill (ed.), *Minnesota Symposia on Child Psychology,* Vol. 2. Minneapolis: Univer. Minn. Press, 1969. Pp. 28–73.

Brown, R., and C. Fraser. The acquisition of syntax. In C. N. Cofer and B. S. Musgrave (eds.), *Verbal behavior and learning: Problems and processes.* New York: McGraw-Hill, 1963. Pp. 158–197. [Also in U. Bellugi and R. Brown (eds.), The acquisition of language. *Monogr. Soc. Res. Child Developm.,* 1964, **29** (1), 43–79.]

Burling, R., Language development of a Garo- and English-speaking child. *Word,* 1959, **15**, 45–68.

Chomsky, C., *The acquisition of syntax in children from 5 to 10.* Cambridge, Mass.: The M.I.T. Press, 1968.

Clark, E. V., On the acquisition of the meaning of *before* and *after. J. verb. Learn. verb. Behav.,* 1971, **10**, 266–275.

Cromer, R. F., The development of temporal reference during the acquisition of language. Unpubl. doct. dissert., Harvard Univer., 1968.

Cromer, R. F., "Children are nice to understand": Surface structure clues for the recovery of a deep structure. *Brit. J. Psychol.,* 1970, **61**, 397–408.

Delattre, P., A comparison of syllable length conditioning among languages. *Int. Rev. appl. Ling.,* 1966, **4**, 183–198.

Dingwall, W. O., and G. Tuniks, Government and concord in Russian: A study in developmental psycholinguistics. In B. Kachru, R. B. Lees, Y. Malkiel, and S. Saporta (eds.), *Papers in linguistics in honor of Henry and Renée Kahane.* Urbana: Univer. Ill. Press, in press.

Fillmore, C. J., The case for case. In E. Bach and R. T. Harms (eds.), *Universals in linguistic theory.* New York: Holt, Rinehart and Winston, 1968. Pp. 1–90.

Fodor, J. A., and M. Garrett, Some syntactical determinants of sentential complexity. *Percept. & Psychophys.,* 1967, **2**, 289–296.

Fodor, J. A., M. Garrett, and T. G. Bever, Some syntactic determinants of sentential complexity, II: Verb structure. *Percept. & Psychophys.,* 1968, **3**, 453–461.

Fraser, C., U. Bellugi, and R. Brown, Control of grammar in imitation, comprehension, and production. *J. verb. Learn. verb. Behav.,* 1963, **2**, 121–135.

Gheorgov, I. A., *Ein Beitrag zur grammatischen Entwicklung der Kindersprache.* Leipzig: Engelmann, 1908. [Also in *Arch. ges. Psychol.,* 1908, **11**, 242–432.]

Grégoire, A., *L'apprentissage du langage.* Vol. 1, *Les deux premières années.* Vol. 2, *La troisième année et les années suivantes.* Paris: Droz, 1937; Paris/Liège: Droz, 1947.

Greenberg, J. H., Order of affixing: A study in general linguistics. In J. H. Greenberg, *Essays in linguistics.* Chicago: Univer. Chicago Press, 1957. Pp. 86–94.

Greenberg, J. H., Language universals. In T. A. Sebeok (ed.), *Current trends in linguistics,* Vol. 3. The Hague: Mouton, 1966, Pp. 61–112. [Also published separately by Mouton: Series Minor, Nr. LIX, 1966.]

Gvozdev, A. N., *Formirovaniye u rebenka grammaticheskogo stroya russkogo yazyka,* 2 parts. Moscow: Akad. Pedag. Nauk RSFSR, 1949. [Reprinted in A. N. Gvozdev, *Voprosy izucheniya detskoy rechi.* Moscow: Akad. Pedag. Nauk RSFSR, 1961. Pp. 149–467.]

Haden, E. F., Accent expiratoire. *Studies in Ling.,* 1962, **16**·(1), 23–39.

Hakes, D. T., and H. S. Cairns, Sentence comprehension and relative pronouns. *Percept. & Psychophys.,* 1970, **8**, 5–8.

Hatch, E., Four experimental studies in syntax of young children. Tech. Rept. 11, Southwest Regional Lab. for Educational Res. & Developm., Inglewood, Calif., 1969.

Kernan, K., The acquisition of language by Samoan children. Unpubl. doct. dissert., Univer. Calif., Berkeley, 1969. [Working Paper No. 21 (1969), Language-Behavior Res. Lab., Univer. Calif., Berkeley.]

Klima, E. S., and U. Bellugi, Syntactic regularities in the speech of children. In J. Lyons and R. J. Wales (eds.), *Psycholinguistics papers.* Edinburgh: Edinburgh Univer. Press, 1966. Pp. 183–208.

Leont'yev, A. A., *Slovo v rechevoy deyatel'nosti.* Moscow: Nauka, 1965.

Leopold, W. F., *Speech development of a bilingual child: A linguist's record.* Vol. 1, *Vocabulary growth in the first two years.* Vol. 2, *Sound-learning in the first two years.* Vol. 3, *Grammar and general problems in the first two years.* Vol. 4, *Diary from age 2.* Evanston, Ill.: Northwestern Univer. Press, 1939, 1947, 1949a, 1949b.

Lindblom, B., Temporal organization of syllable production. *Speech Transmission Lab. Quart. Progress & Status Rept.* (Stockholm, Royal Inst. Technol.), 1968, **2** (3), 1–5.

McNeill, D., *The acquisition of language: The study of developmental psycholinguistics.* New York: Harper & Row, 1970. [Coincides in large part with chapter of same title in P. H. Mussen (ed.), *Carmichael's manual of child psychology,* 3d. ed., Vol. 1. New York: Wiley, 1970, Pp. 1061–1161.]

Menyuk, P., *Sentences children use.* Cambridge, Mass.: The M.I.T. Press, 1969.

Mikes, M., Acquisition des catégoires grammaticales dans le langage de l'enfant. *Enfance,* 1967, **20**, 289–298.

Mikeš, M., and P. Vlahović, Razvoj gramatičkih kategorija u dečjem govoru. *Prilozi proučavanju jezika, II.* Novi Sad, Yugoslavia, 1966.

Miller, W. R., and S. M. Ervin, The development of grammar in child language. In U. Bellugi and R. Brown (eds.), The acquisition of language. *Monogr. Soc. Res. Child Developm.,* 1964, **29** (1), 9–33.

Olds, H. F., An experimental study of syntactical factors influencing children's comprehension of certain complex relationships. Rept. No. 4, Harvard Center for Res. & Develop. on Educational Differences, 1968.

Oller, D. K., The effect of position-in-utterance and word length on speech segment duration. Unpubl. paper, Depts. of Psychol. and Ling., Univer. Texas, 1971.

Omar, M. K., The acquisition of Egyptian Arabic as a native language. Unpubl. doct. dissert., Georgetown Univer., 1970. [To be published by Mouton.]

Pačesová, J., The development of vocabulary in the child. Brno: Univer. J. E. Purkyne, 1968.

Park, Tschang-Zin, Language acquisition in a Korean child. Working Paper, Psychologisches Institut, Univer. Münster, Germany, 1969.

Park, Tschang-Zin, The acquisition of German syntax. Working Paper, Psychologisches Institut, Univer. Münster, Germany, 1970.

Pavlova, A. D., Dnevnik materi. Moscow, 1924.

Pavlovitch, M., Le langage enfantin: Acquisition du serbe et du français par un enfant serbe. Paris: Champion, 1920.

Popova, M. I., Grammaticheskiye elementy yazyka v rechi detey preddoshkol'nogo vozrasta. Vopr. psikhol., 1958, 4 (3), 106–117. [English translation: Grammatical elements of language in the speech of pre-preschool children.

Roeper, T., Theoretical implications of word order, topicalization, and inflections in German language acquisition. In C. Ferguson and D. Slobin (Eds.), Studies of child language development. New York: Holt, Rinehart and Winston, 1973. Pp. 541–554.

Rūķe-Draviņa, V., Zur Entstehung der Flexion in der Kindersprache: Ein Beitrag auf der Grundlage des lettischen Sprachmaterials. Internatl. J. Slavic Ling. & Poetics, 1959, 1/2 201–222. [English translation: On the emergence of inflection in child language: A contribution based on Latvian speech data.

Rūķe-Draviņa, V., Zur Sprachentwicklung bei Kleinkindern: Beitrag auf der Grundlage lettischen Sprachmaterials. 1. Syntax. Lund: Slaviska Ínnstitutionen vid Lunds Universitet, 1963.

Shugar, G. W., Personal communication re study of Polish acqusition, January 31, 1971.

Slobin, D. I., Abstracts of Soviet studies of child language. In F. Smith and G. A. Miller (eds.), The genesis of language: A psycholinguistic approach. Cambridge, Mass.: The M.I.T. Press, 1966. Pp. 361–386.

Slobin, D. I., Early grammatical development in several languages, with special attention to Soviet research. Working Paper No. 11, Language-Behavior Res. Lab., Univer. Calif., Berkeley, 1968.

Slobin, D. I., and C. A. Welsh, Elicited imitation as a research tool in developmental psycholinguistics. In C. Ferguson and D. Slobin (Eds.), Studies of child language development. New York: Holt, Rinehart and Winston, 1973. Pp. 485–497.

Smith, C. S., An experimental approach to children's linguistic competence. In J. R. Hayes (ed.), Cognition and the development of languages. New York: Wiley, 1970. Pp. 109–135.

Synder, A. D., Notes on the talk of a two-and-a-half-year-old boy. Pedag. Seminary, 1914, 21, 412–424.

Solov'yeva, O. I., Metodika razvitiye rechi i obucheniya rodnomu yazyku v detskom sadu. Moscow: Uchpedgiz, 1960.

Stern, C., and W. Stern, Die Kindersprache: Eine psychologische and sprachtheoretische Untersuchung. Leipzig: Barth, 1907. (4th, rev. ed., 1928).

Watt, W. C., On two hypotheses concerning psycholinguistics. In J. R. Hayes (ed.), Cognition and the development of language. New York: Wiley, 1970. Pp. 137–220.

Werner, H., and B. Kaplan, Symbol formation. New York: Wiley, 1963.

Zakharova, A. V., Usvoyeniye doshkol'nikami padezhnykh form. *Dolk. Akad. Pedag. Nauk RSFSR,* 1958, **2** (3), 81–84. [English translation: Acquisition of forms of grammatical case by preschool children.]

Zlatoustova, L. V., [Duration of vowel and consonant sounds of the Russian language.] *Uch. zap. Kazan'skogo Gos. Univer. im. V. I. Ul'yanova-Lenina,* 1954, **114** (6), 99–123. [Cited in Oller, 1971. See L. V. Zlatoustova, *Foneticheskaya struktura slova v potoke rechi.* Kazan', 1962.]

Nonlinguistic Strategies and the Acquisition of Word Meanings*

Eve V. Clark

The present study proposes that children's apparent comprehension of certain words is at first dependent on a combination of their linguistic hypotheses about a word's meaning and certain nonlinguistic strategies. Children aged 1;6-5;0 were given instructions requiring comprehension of the locative terms *in, on* and *under.* The results showed that children go through three stages: At first, they consistently use certain nonlinguistic strategies that can be characterized by two ordered rules; next, they apply these rules to only one or two of the locative instructions; and finally, they exhibit full semantic knowledge of the three word meanings. Because of these nonlinguistic strategies, the younger children always appear to understand *in* correctly, sometimes appear to understand *on* and never understand under. It is argued, nevertheless, that these nonlinguistic strategies determine the order of acquisition of the three locative terms.

Recent work on the acquisition of word meanings suggests that children begin by using certain nonlinguistic strategies based on their perceptual knowledge. Indeed, they have obvious recourse to perceptual information in the numerous overextensions that have been observed during the first year or so of language use (between about 1;0 and 2;6). For example, the earliest meaning ascribed to a word like *apple* is often something like "[SMALL X] & [ROUND X]." The child's interpretations of these percept-based features, size and shape, are then used criterially in applying the word *apple* to other objects such as door-knobs, rubber balls, round light switches and paperweights. These overextensions, characteristically based on features of shape, size, movement, sound, texture and taste, are well documented in diary studies of the acquisition of a large number of different languages (E. Clark, 1973b).

These overextensions might be best explained as the outcome of the young child's hypotheses about word meaning. His hypotheses would seem to take the general

From *Cognition,* **2,** 161–182, 1973. Reprinted by permission of Edicom, N.V.

*This research was supported in part by the National Science Foundation, GS-30040. Deborah Rosenblatt assisted in running the first two experiments, and Carol B. Farwell helped with Experiment 3. I am grateful to the staff of Bing Nursery School, the Stanford Child Care Center and the parents of the children for all their cooperation. I would like to thank Herbert H. Clark for making detailed comments on the manuscript at various stages, and lastly I wish to acknowledge an anonymous reviewer whose remarks substantially improved this paper.

Requests for reprints should be sent to the author at Committee on Linguistics, Stanford University, Stanford, California 94305, U.S.A.

form of "A word refers to some identifiable [perceptual] attribute of the object pointed to." Thus, the child is relying on the perceptual knowledge that he already has of the things around him when he begins to form hypotheses about the meanings of new words. These linguistic hypotheses then lead him to act on the assumption that the feature or attribute he has picked out *is* what that particular word designates. Therefore, any other object that matches those features can be "named" by the same word (E. Clark, 1974). It is therefore the child's interpretations of his percepts, his knowledge about the properties of objects, that provide a basis for some linguistic hypothesis for assigning meaning to "new" words.

Children, however, also show certain biases in their treatment of the world around them that bear no direct relation to their linguistic hypotheses. For example, if a young child is shown a piece of chocolate and a pebble and is allowed to choose one, he will probably always choose the chocolate. This choice would then be independent of the meanings of words used in the instructions to choose; his choice is the outcome of a nonlinguistic strategy. This form of behavior is traditionally referred to as a preference or a response bias and may be present in the child (or the adult) for a variety of reasons. If the child relies consistently on such preferences, though, it is important to identify them. This is because they could make it appear that the child had understood something when, in fact, his response was simply due to a nonlinguistic strategy. This question is a particularly important one where children's comprehension of word meanings is concerned. The child might appear to have grasped the adult meaning of some complex word when he was actually only responding on the basis of a nonlinguistic strategy.

There are therefore two ways of looking at many comprehension studies. First of all, the child's responses, including his errors, could be treated as if they were the outcome of his linguistic hypotheses about the meanings of particular words. Secondly, the child's responses could be regarded as the outcome of some nonlinguistic strategy. However, these two approaches are often impossible to separate. For example, there have been several studies of the relational terms *more* and *less* in which children appeared to interpret the word *less* as if it meant *more*. For instance, whenever children were asked to choose from two trees either the one with *more* apples or the one with *less*, they always chose the one with the greater number (Donaldson and Balfour, 1968; Donaldson and Wales, 1970; Palermo, 1973). There are two possible explanations that might be offered for these data, explanations that have not been clearly distinguished in the discussions of what *less* actually means to the child. The first explanation assumes that the child is relying on his linguistic hypothesis about the meanings of *more* and *less*, namely that both words refer to amount or quantity [+ Amount], and to the positive pole, i.e., the greater of two or more amounts [+ Polar]. This is the correct meaning for *more*, but not for *less*. This analysis will be called the full semantics hypothesis.

An alternative explanation for the same data makes a weaker assumption about the child's meanings for the two words. Instead of assuming that *more* and *less* are synonymous, both with the meaning of *more*, one could suppose that both word meanings are actually incomplete and that the child's responses are based on the partial meaning that he has for both *more* and *less*, in combination with certain nonlinguistic strategies. Thus, the child might know only that both *more* and *less* refer to amount [+ Amount]. This tends to be supported by the children who, when asked to show which tree had more apples on it, replied *Both of them, That one does an' that one, Both the trees, They two ones, Each tree,* and so on. Other children, asked to make the amount *less* on one tree (the one with more) objected: *But it is less on that tree* (Donaldson and Wales, 1970, p. 248). In addition to this partial semantic knowledge, the child at this stage would be assumed to have a nonlinguistic strategy of usually choosing the greater of two or more amounts or the more extended object on a dimension such as length or height. H. Clark (1970) appealed implicitly to such a notion in suggesting that the first stage in the acquisition of *more* and *less* involves only a nominal sense of the words, i.e., both words refer only to amount, and that one had to assume that the best exemplars of amount for the young child are those objects with greater amount. This assumption has since been tested experimentally by Klatzky, Clark and Macken (1973). They showed that children found it significantly easier to learn the meanings of nonsense syllables that referred to relatively greater extent along several dimensions than to learn their polar opposites. Thus, in the case of *more* and *less*, the child would know that both words meant [+ Amount], but would not yet have learnt the feature [+ Polar]. It only appears that he has [+ Polar as well as [+ Amount] because of the strategy of choosing the greater amount. This explanation, based on the combination of partial semantic knowledge and a nonlinguistic strategy, will be called the partial semantics hypothesis.

The full semantics hypothesis and the partial semantics hypothesis should be distinguishable if one could find a situation in which the child treated WORD$_1$ as if it meant the same as WORD$_2$ in some contexts, while at the same time treating WORD$_1$ as if it meant WORD$_3$ in another set of contexts. One would thus be able to demonstrate that the two incompatible senses consistently given to WORD$_1$ were not random but, in fact, could be ascribed to the child's use of certain nonlinguistic strategies. This has not actually been shown in the case of *more* and *less*, although it has been shown, in effect, by the overextended uses of early words like *apple* (E. Clark, 1973b). If the child's responses to any particular words can be shown to be the outcome of a little semantic knowledge (if that) combined with certain nonlinguistic strategies, then it would be clear that the full semantics hypothesis would make too strong a claim about the extent of the child's semantic knowledge. The partial semantic hypothesis, in contrast, is concerned with precisely that interaction, the way in which the child relies on nonlinguistic strategies prior to, and during, the acquisition of word meanings. These two hypotheses are not true or false in general, but they may be contrasted for any particular word or set of words.

In the present paper, I shall present some comprehension studies of locative prepositions in an attempt to explore one set of strategies and their relationship to the young child's semantic knowledge. During the acquisition of the terms *in, on* and *under,* children appear to treat the word *under* as if it means *in* in some contexts, but as if it means *on* in others. This suggests that this is a case where the partial semantics hypothesis, with its nonlinguistic strategies, might provide a better account of the data than an explanation based on the full semantics hypothesis.

EXPERIMENT 1

METHOD
Each child was asked to follow instructions containing the words *in, on* and *under* in contexts that allowed both correct and incorrect responses. The instructions were of the form *Put the x in [on, under] the y,* where *x* was one of eight small toy animals, and *y* one of six reference point objects (henceforth RPs). The child's task was to correctly locate one object, *x,* with respect to the RP,*y*.[1] The six RPs, shown in Figure 1, were chosen because each allowed two of the three spatial relations being named in the instructions. Thus, the box on its side and the tunnel each allowed an object to be placed either *in* or *on* the RP. The dump truck and the crib each allowed either *in* or *under,* and the table and the bridge each allowed either *on* or *under.*

There were 24 instructions in all, with eight for each of the three prepositions *in, on* and *under.* Each preposition occurred twice with each of the four RPs that allowed the relation, e.g., *in* occurred twice each with the box, the tunnel, the truck and the crib. The names of the eight animals each occurred three times in all, once each with each preposition. The instructions were divided into two identical blocks of 12, and the order of instructions within each block was randomized separately for each subject.

The subjects were 70 children (31 male and 39 female) taking part in a larger study of the acquisition of spatial terms in English. All the children were native speakers of English and had no contact with other languages in the home. The older children

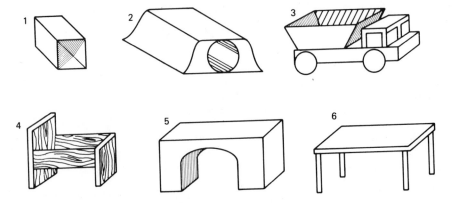

Figure 1.   *The reference point objects (RPs) used in Experiment 1: Items 1 and 2 allow the relations IN and ON; items 3 and 4 allow the relations IN and UNDER; items 5 and 6 allow the relations ON and UNDER*

---

[1] The children in these experiments always picked up *x,* rather than *y,* and then placed it in relation to *y.* Thus, the RPs were always treated as reference points. Other research has shown that young children find it impossible to place B when told "A is on top of B"; they can always do the task, though, if told to place A (Bem, 1970; Huttenlocher, Eisenberg and Strauss, 1968; Huttenlocher and Strauss, 1968).

(2;6-5;0) were attending Bing Nursery School, Stanford; the younger ones (1;6-2;5) were contacted through Bing Nursery School and the Stanford Child Care Center. The children were divided into seven age-groups at six-monthly intervals, with ten children in each group: I. 1;6-1;11 (mean age 1;9); II. 2;0-2;5 (mean 2;3); III. 2;6-2;11 (mean 2;9); IV. 3;0-3;5 (mean 3;3); V. 3;6-3;11 (mean 3;9); VI. 4;0-4;5 (mean 4;2); VII. 4;6-4;11 (mean 4;8).

Each subject was interviewed separately in a small experimental room at the nursery school. (Five subjects from Group II were seen under comparable circumstances at the child care center.) The children in the two youngest groups (aged 1;6-2;5) generally had one parent present throughout, seated slightly behind the child and out of his line of sight. The parent made no comments during the experimental trials. Each child was first asked to name each of the RPs and the animals. The child's own names for the objects were used throughout the session wherever these differed from the ones originally assigned. Then the experimenter gave the child the two blocks of 12 instructions each. Some of the younger subjects had a short break between the two blocks; all completed the task, with no responses omitted, in a single session that lasted between ten and 20 minutes.

RESULTS

The data will be analyzed first in terms of how the children carried out the instructions they were given where a correct response is a response that appears to reflect adult-like knowledge of the word meaning in question. Following this, the kind of errors made will be used as the basis for analyzing the data in terms of possible non-linguistic strategies where a 'correct' response is defined as consistent, predictable use of a particular strategy.

For the first analysis, the percentage of correct responses to each instruction is shown for all seven age groups in Table 1. Because of the low error rate and absence of any significant differences between age groups for subjects over 3;0 years (Groups IV-VII), an analysis of variance was performed only on the data from the three youngest groups. These three groups differed from each other significantly overall, $F(2,27)$

Table 1   Percentage of Correct Responses to Instructions with in, on and under by Age Group[a]

Instruction	I	II	III	Age group IV	V	VI	VII
IN	94	98	96	100	100	100	100
ON	61	72	80	96	94	100	100
UNDER	4	57	98	89	100	100	100
Mean:	53	76	91	95	98	100	100

[a] Each percentage based on 80 data points.

$= 6.00, p < 0.001$. The interaction between age groups and instructions, $F(4,54) = 12.66, p < 0.001$, showed that the three kinds of instructions improved differentially with age (see Table 1).

The three instructions, *in, on* and *under*, also differed significantly overall, $F(2,54) = 30.45, p < 0.001$. Within Group I (1;6-1;11), instructions containing *in* produced significantly more correct responses than those containing *on*, $t(54) = 3.50, p < 0.005$, and instructions containing *on* produced significantly more correct responses than *under*, $t(54) = 5.93, p < 0.001$. Within Group II (2;0-2;5), *in* was still significantly better than *on*, $t(54) = 2.43, p < 0.025$, and then *under*, $t(54) = 4.04, p < 0.001$. But the difference between *on* and *under* was no longer significant. Within Group III (2;6-2;11), there were no significant differences between the three instructions.

A further analysis was carried out to see if the RPs had any effect on the responses given. For each instruction, there were two pairs of RPs that differed in their properties. For example, with *in*, one pair of RPs allowed *on* as the alternative relation (box, tunnel) and the other allowed *under* as the alternative relation (truck, crib). For the *in* instructions as a whole, those used with the truck and the crib were significantly easier than those with the box and the tunnel, $t(54) = 2.19, p < 0.05$. The *on* instructions were also easier where the alternative relation was *under* (bridge, table) rather than *in* (box, tunnel), $t(54) = 9.29, p < 0.001$. For the *under* instructions, there were slightly fewer errors with the bridge and the table than with the truck and the crib (44% versus 50%), but this difference was not significant. These data are shown in Table 2. A correct response therefore seems to depend in part on the particular properties of the RP.

The errors made reveal a very consistent pattern. If the RP was a container of any kind (i.e., box, tunnel, truck, crib), the younger children tended to act as though all the instructions contained *in*. Whenever the RP was not a container but had a supporting

Table 2   Percentage of Correct Responses to Each Instruction for Each RP by Age Group[a]

	Instruction								
	In			On			Under		
Age group:	I	II	III	I	II	III	I	II	III
RP:									
box	80	100	85	50	50	75	—	—	—
tunnel	95	90	100	15	50	60	—	—	—
truck	100	100	100	—	—	—	0	55	100
crib	100	100	100	—	—	—	0	45	100
bridge	—	—	—	80	95	90	10	70	90
table	—	—	—	100	95	95	5	60	100

[a.] Each percentage based on 20 data points.

surface (i.e., bridge, table), these children tended to treat all the instructions as though they contained *on.* The error data can therefore be characterized as below, where correct responses are shown in (a) and errors in (b) for each type of RP:

(1) RP allowing *in* or *under*   (a) instruction *in* elicits "in"
   [truck, crib]   (b) instruction *under* elicits "in"
(2) RP allowing *in* or *on*   (a) instruction *in* elicits "in"
   [box, tunnel]   (b) instruction *on* elicits "in"
(3) RP allowing *on* or *under*   (a) instruction *on* elicits "on"
   [bridge, table]   (b) instruction *under* elicits "on"

Thus, *in* appears nearly always to be interpreted correctly, and *on* is also interpreted correctly unless the RP is a container. *Under* is never correct because the options are always either "in" or "on." While this pattern of error could simply reflect the order of acquisition of the three prepositions, according to some measure of complexity, it could also be the result of applying two simple, ordered rules based on the child's non-linguistic knowledge of the usual or expected spatial relationship between *x* and the RP:

Rule 1: If the RP is a container, *x* is inside it
Rule 2: If the RP has a horizontal surface, *x* is on it

These two rules are strictly ordered in the sense that Rule 1 is always applied. In the event that it fails, Rule 2 is applied next. The use of Rule 1 predicts the error of *on* going to "in," and of *under* going to "in," while Rule 2 predicts the error of *under* going to "on." The use of two such ordered rules accounts for 92% of the errors made by the youngest group (1;6-1;11) and for 91% of the errors made by Group II. The error rate for Group III is less than 10% overall, but the two rules still account for 71% of these errors.

The data presented in Table 1 above were scored with the assumption that the child had some linguistic hypotheses about, and even adult-like knowledge of, the meanings of *in, on* and *under.* Thus, a response appropriate to the instruction was assumed to indicate knowledge of the word meaning. This knowledge will be referred to as the adult schema. The percentage of responses accounted for by such semantic knowledge is shown by the mean correct for each age group. In the youngest group, the adult schema accounts for only 53% of the responses given. Since each RP offers a choice of two locative relations, e.g., *in* and *on* with the box, there is a 50% probability that the child could pick the "semantically correct" relation by chance. Thus, the data from Group I appear to indicate almost total absence of adult-like semantic knowledge. In contrast, if the child does know the meanings of all three prepositions, the adult schema should account for 100% of the responses given, as indeed it does for the older groups shown in Table 1. The means in Table 1 indicate, therefore, that the percentage of responses accounted for by the adult schema (semantic knowledge) increases with age from a chance 50% to 100% of the responses given.

However, the responses scored as errors according to the adult schema criteria suggest that the child actually begins by using non-linguistic strategies like Rules 1 and 2, and only relinquishes these strategies when he learns what the words *in, on* and *under* mean. Responses based on the use of the two ordered rules (1 and 2) will be called the child schema. The percentage of data accounted for in each age group by use of the child schema is shown in Table 3. In the case of *in,* the use of Rule 1 cannot be distinguished from use of semantic knowledge (the adult schema). With *on,* however, the use of the child schema can be differentiated from that of the adult schema in those instances where *on* contrasts with *in,* i.e., with the box and the tunnel. This is because Rule 1 will always apply in these instances, giving the response "in," until the adult schema takes over and Rule 1 ceases to be applied. Where *on* contrasts with *under,* there is again no way to distinguish between use of Rule 2 in the child schema and semantic knowledge in the adult schema. Thus, the appearance of the adult schema with *on* will signal a drop to 50% of the *on* responses accounted for by the child schema. In the case of *under,* the child schema should account for all the responses until the child learns what *under* means. Once the adult schema takes over, the child schema will be unable to account for any of the responses to *under* (see Table 3). The mean percentage of responses accounted for overall by the child schema in each age group should therefore decrease from 100% at the earliest stage (Group I and younger) to 50% as the child acquires the meanings of *in, on* and *under.* The means of the data accounted for by the child schema appear in Table 3. The decrease between Groups II and III, down to 54%, coincides with a large increase in the data accounted for by the adult schema, up to 91% (Table 1). There is therefore a cross-over between the child schema and the adult schema in terms of the amount of data accounted for at different stages.

It is evident, therefore, that the data presented in Table 1 for Groups I and II are *not* a direct reflection of how well children of this age "understand" the spatial prepositions *in, on* and *under.* Instead, they appear to reflect the children's use of prior nonlinguistic strategies (the child schema) that are used in the virtual absence of comprehension.

EXPERIMENT 2

The next experiment was designed to provide independent evidence for the nonlinguistic strategies that seemed to be being used by the younger children in Experiment

Table 3   Percentage of Responses Accounted for by Use of Ordered Rules 1 and 2 by Instruction and Age Group[a]

Instruction	Age group						
	I	II	III	IV	V	VI	VII
IN	94	95	96	100	100	100	100
ON	79	72	62	54	54	50	50
UNDER	96	43	3	11	0	0	0
Mean:	89	69	54	55	51	50	50

[a] Each percentage based on 80 data points

1. If these particular strategies—the child schema—are in fact independent of the linguistic input using locative words (the instructions containing *in, on* and *under*), they should also appear in situations where the young child hears no locative words in the task. It is necessary to show that these nonlinguistic strategies are really present in the child because there is practically no data available on the kinds of nonlinguistic strategies that the young child might have in his repertoire to rely on prior to, and during, the process of acquiring language.

Children were therefore asked to copy a configuration of *x* and *y* modelled by the experimenter, a procedure adapted from Laurendeau and Pinard (1970). It was hypothesized that if a young child was using a nonlinguistic strategy such as that described as the child schema, he should "correctly" copy any configuration that conformed to Rules 1 and 2. However, those configurations not conforming to the child schema should produce predictable errors in the form of a relationship that does conform to the two rules.

METHOD
Both the experimenter and the child, seated side by side, began with one each of a pair of RPs in front of them on the table. The experimenter modelled a configuration by placing *x* in a particular spatial relationship to his own RP, then handed the child an identical *x* and asked him to do the same or to make it like the experimenter's. The child received no other verbal instructions and the spatial relationship was never named. Each child was presented with ten different configurations (shown in Table 4) of an RP together with a small animal, *x*. The experimenter's and the child's RP and *x* were always identical. Six of the ten configurations in Table 4 conformed to the rules given in the child schema, and four did not. If the children used Rules 1 and 2, then they should make errors on the four starred items.

The subjects were the 20 children from Groups I and II of Experiment 1. The second experiment was run within three weeks of the first, and, as in the first, one parent generally accompanied the younger children into the experimental room. Each child received the set of ten configurations in a different random order and took between five and ten minutes to complete the task of copying.

RESULTS
Fifteen of the 20 subjects in this experiment made a total of 40 errors. Of these, 38 were predicted errors, occurring on items 3, 5, 8 and 10 (starred in Table 4), and only two were not predicted. Since six of the ten items in Table 4 conformed to the child schema, and only four did not, the *a priori* probability of making a predicted error was lower than that of making an unpredicted error. Yet 13 of the 15 subjects making an error made only predicted errors, while the remaining two subjects, with one unpredicted error each, made more predicted than unpredicted errors ($p < 0.001$, by Sign Test). Overall, the percentages of errors accounted for by the four starred items in Table 4 was 93% for Group I (because of the two unpredicted errors), and 100% for Group II. In other words, whenever the experimenter's configuration was one that could be achieved simply through use of the child schema (ordered Rules 1 and 2), the child made no errors. Nonetheless, it is clear that the task, on the whole, was treated as a copying task because reliance on the child schema alone would have

442   Readings in Language Development

Table 4   Configurations Used in Experiment 2

Configuration	Applicable Strategy[a]
1. *x* on upside-down glass	Rule 2
2. *x* in upright glass	Rule 1
3. *x* beside upright glass, with no contact	*Rule 1
4. *x* on block	Rule 2
5. *x* beside block, with no contact	*Rule 2
6. *x* on bridge	Rule 2
7. *x* under bridge	Rule 1[b]
8. *x* beside bridge, with no contact	*Rule 2[c]
9. *x* in crib	Rule 1
10. *x* under crib	*Rule 1

[a] Prediction of which rule will be applied in making response; starred items are predicted to produce errors because of the use of either Rule 1 or Rule 2 where neither actually should be applied.

[b] This is assuming that the bridge space may be treated as a container since there is contact and an enclosure-like space involved. It is possible that this should also apply in the case of item 8.

[c] This prediction is based on the fact that the bridge has a surface and no real container-space. However, it is possible that Rule 1 may apply here, as with item 7.

produced a total of 80 errors on the four starred items. The actual error total therefore represents an error rate of 48%, not one of 100%.

The predicted errors on the four items not conforming to the rules are shown in Table 5. In general, the particular errors made can be attributed to the use of Rules 1 and 2. Rule 1 would account for the errors in (i) and (iv) in Table 5, while Rule 2 would account for those in (ii) and (iiia). However, eight of the children making an error on Item 8 [shown in (iii) of Table 5] placed *x* underneath the bridge rather than on it. One possible explanation for this is that the children were treating the hollow rounded space below the lower surface of the bridge *as a container* (see Figure 1). If this were the case, the errors in (iiib) could be attributed to use of Rule 1. This proposal is backed to some extent by several children in Group II who spontanously described placements under the bridge as "in here." However, there were no errors of this kind on item 6 (Table 4) where the model configuration has *x* on the bridge. Nor were there any responses of this kind from the two younger groups in Experiment 1.

There were only two unpredicted errors, made by two subjects in the youngest group. Both errors occurred on item 1 (*x* on upside-down glass), and both consisted of the child's turning up the glass and placing *x* inside it. One of the children also turned up the experimenter's glass and did the same thing with it. A similar manipulation of the experimenter's RP also occurred with item 3 where four children who made the predicted error of placing *x* in the glass then proceeded to "correct" the experimenter's configuration also. Again, these four children all came from the youngest group (1;6-1;11). The manipulation of the glass so its opening was upwards, i.e., in the normal orientation for a glass, is similar to the manipulation of the box on its side by several of the younger children in Experiment 1; it, too, was consistently turned so that its opening was upwards. This suggests that young children may have certain expectations about the proper orientation of objects based on their experience of what the usual orientation is. This point will be taken up further in the final discussion. Lastly, among the responses that were counted as correct copies of the configurations in items 3, 5 and 8, there were a number that maintained the spatial relation between x and the RP in all respects save one: x was juxtaposed to the RP so that there was contact between them. This occurred five times with item 3 (x placed against the side of the glass), eight times with item 5 (x placed against the side of the block), and ten times with item 8 (x placed against the side of the bridge). Juxtaposition with contact, therefore, also seemed to play a role in making locative placements. This use of juxtaposition suggests that contact may be necessary for the child to attribute a relation in space to the pair formed by x and the RP.

The results of Experiment 2, therefore, provide strong independent evidence for the presence of the nonlinguistic strategies—the child schema—that appeared to be being used in Experiment 1. Young children rely on the same nonlinguistic strategies in a copying task as they do in a comprehension task using the words *in, on* and *under.*

EXPERIMENT 3

Semantic knowledge (the adult schema) and nonlinguistic strategies (the child schema) may coincide in the kind of response given by the child. In the case of the word *in,* it may be impossible to find out which basis the young child is relying on for his response. However, both *on* and *under* in Experiment 1 allowed some separation of the child schema and adult schema (Tables 1 and 3). The present experiment uses a somewhat different technique from that of Experiment 1 in order to look at the

Table 5   Errors Made on Critical Configurations in Experiment 2

	Item	Experimenter's model	Subject's erroneous copy	Number of Instances
(i)	3	x beside upright glass with no contact	x inside glass	14
(ii)	5	x beside block with no contact	x on block	7
(iii)	8	x beside bridge with no contact	(a) x on bridge (b) x under bridge	2 8
(iv)	10	x under crib	x in crib	7

transition from use of the child schema to use of the adult schema with different materials. In a pilot study, children were asked to manipulate an RP so that it would conform to the instruction given. For example, if the RP was an upright glass but the instruction contained the word *on,* the child was to turn the glass upside-down so as to be able to place *x* on a surface. This task proved to be very difficult, even for considerably older children, so a different technique was devised in which the child had to choose one from a pair of RPs in placing *x.*

METHOD

Each child was presented with a pair of RPs, identical in all respects save orientation: One had its opening upwards, and the other its opening face down on the table. With them, the child was given an instruction of the form *Put the x in [on, under] a y.* The pairs of RPs used were two opaque plastic tubs 3.7 cm high and 6.2 cm in diameter, two transparent plastic glasses 7.4 cm high and 6.2 cm in diameter at the rim, and two opaque plastic boxes 7.4 cm on a side, with no lids. The objects to be placed were six toys small enough to fit inside the RPs. The RPs were always presented in pairs, with left-right positions counterbalanced with opening-up versus opening-down orientations. Each of the three prepositions, *in, on* and *under,* was used six times, twice each with each pair of RPs, for a total of 18 instructions. The instructions were presented in two identical blocks of nine each; within each block the instructions were randomized separately for each subject.

The subjects were 20 children (6 male and 14 female) in two age groups, corresponding as nearly as possible to Groups II and III from Experiment 1:

A.   1;10–2;2 (mean age 2;1)
B.   2;6–3;1 (mean age 2;10)

All the children were native speakers of English and had no exposure to any other languages in the home.

Each child was interviewed separately at Bing Nursery School as in the previous experiments. The child was told he was to choose the correct RP of the two in front of him after he heard each instruction. He was also told he could move the RPs if he wanted to and was shown various manipulations by the experimenter. If the child completed the first block of instructions with no sign of fatigue, he was given the second immediately. Otherwise, he received the second block the following day. (Only three children from Group A required two visits.) The task as a whole took between 10 tnd 15 minutes to complete.

RESULTS

The percentage of correct responses according to the adult schema for each of the three instructions is shown in Table 6. The older group, B, made significantly more correct responses overall than the younger group, $F(1,18) = 10.19, p < 0.001$. There was also a significant difference between the three instructions, $F(2,36) = 10.08,$ $p < 0.001$; those instructions containing *in* elicited significantly more correct responses than either *on* [$t(36) = 2.92, p < 0.01$] or *under* [$t(36) = 4.41, p < 0.01$]. The difference between *on* and *under* failed to reach significance. When the two groups are considered separately, the younger children, Group A, produced significantly more correct responses to *in* than to *on* [t (36)= 2.75, $p < 0.01$] or than to *under* [t (36)= 4.02, $p < 0.01$]. *On*, though, did not differ significantly from *under* [t (36)= 1.27]. The older group, B, showed no significant differences among the three instructions. These results are directly comparable to those for Groups II and III in Experiment 1 (see Table 1).[2]

Errors in this analysis consisted of choosing the (upright) container RP with *on* or *under*, or of choosing the uppermost surface of the upside-down RP with *in* or *under*. Because of the nature of the RPs,[3] *under* was necessarily more difficult in this experiment for the younger children because a correct response always involved some manipulation. Whichever RP was chosen had to be tilted or lifted up in order to place *x* underneath. In other words, with manipulation, either RP could be correct; without manipulation, both were wrong. There was a significant decrease in the number of errors from Group A to Group B with both *on* [t (36)= 2.99, $p < 0.01$] and *under* [t (36)= 3.59, $p < 0.01$]. This decrease shows that the child must have gained some semantic knowledge about the three instructions. Notice that the adult schema only accounts for 51% of the data overall in Group A, but in Group B, it accounts for 80% (Table 6).

Table 7 presents the data scored according to use of the non-linguistic strategies, represented by ordered Rules 1 and 2 of the child schema. In the case of *in*, the child schema accounts for the same amount of data as the adult schema. It is never

Table 6   Percentage of Correct Responses by Instruction with Choice of an Appropriate and Inappropriate RP for Each Age Group (Adult Schema)[a]

Group	Mean Age	In	On	Under[b]	Mean
A	2:1	87	43	23	51
B	2:10	100	77	63	80

[a] Each percentage based on 60 data points.
[b] Either RP was an inappropriate choice for under unless the child manipulated it so as to insert *x* underneath, in which case either RP was appropriate.

[2] The subjects in Group A were also run on Experiment 1 to make quite sure they were comparable to the original subjects from Groups II and III in Experiment 1.

[3] A protracted attempt was made to find pairs of RPs that could be inverted that would allow *on/under* and *in/under* as well as *in/on* as possible relations, without any direct manipulation being necessary. Since we were unable to find any suitable objects, the present RPs were chosen as a compromise.

Readings in Language Development

Table 7   Percentage of Responses Accounted for in Experiment 3 by the Child
              Schema
              (Ordered Rules 1 and 2)[a]

| | | Instruction | | | |
Group	Mean Age	In	On	Under	Mean
A	2;1	87	57	48	64
B	2;10	100	23	17	47

[a] Each percentage based on 60 data points.

possible, therefore, in this type of experiment to separate the responses due to the
child schema from those due to the adult schema for instructions with *in*. The data
elicited by *on*, in contrast, can be differentially accounted for by use of the child
schema versus the adult schema. Since the child is always presented with two RPs,
one with opening up and one with supporting surface up, the situation is unlike that
of Experiment 1. Here the child has to choose between two RPs. Therefore, if he is
using the child schema, he should always chose the RP with its opening up, i.e., the
container, since Rules 1 and 2 are strictly ordered. As a result, the child schema
should account for 100% of the responses to begin with and later decrease to 0%.
However, many of the children in Group A had evidently already learnt something
about the meaning of *on* (the adult schema) because the child schema only accounts
for 57% of the data. For Group B, this percentage has decreased still further to 23%
(Table 7). The same form of argument holds in the case of *under*. Use of the child
schema with pairs of RPs should again account for 100% of the data initially, with
the percentage decreasing to zero as the child acquires the meaning of the word. For
Group A, the child schema accounted for 48% of the data on *under*, while for Group
B, it accounted for only 17%. Overall, the child schema accounts for slightly more
data than the adult schema for Group A (64% versus 51%), but by Group B, the child
schema accounts for considerably less than the adult schema (47% versus 80%) (see
Tables 6 and 7). By the time children know the meanings of all three words perfectly,
the maximum amount of data that the child schema could account for with these
materials would be 33%; this is because the child and adult schemas cannot be
separated in the responses for *in*, although they can be completely separated for both
on and *under*. These data provide still further support for the existence of the nonlinguistic strategies embodied in Rules 1 and 2. The results also provide additional
evidence that the transition from use of the child schema to use of the adult schema
is fairly near completion for all three locative terms, *in, on* and *under*, at age 2;6 to
3;0.

DISCUSSION

The children in these three experiments appeared to rely heavily on certain nonlinguistic strategies prior to, and during, the acquisition of the locatives *in, on* and *under*.
The children can best be viewed as progressing through three stages: A stage where

they rely on nonlinguistic strategies plus partial semantic knowledge of the words; a transition stage; and a stage where they rely on full semantic knowledge of the words.

According to this view, the children at the first stage (Group I in Experiment 1) do not understand *in, on* and *under* at all, except perhaps that they are locative. Instead, they base their responses to *in, on* and *under* on a nonlinguistic strategy characterized by two ordered rules:

Rule 1: If the RP is a container, *x* is inside it
Rule 2: If the RP has a supporting surface, *x* is on it

So when presented with RPs that are containers, the children always treat *in* as if they understood it correctly, but they treat *on* and *under* as if they meant the same as *in*. When presented with RPs that have supporting surfaces but are not containers, the children always treat *on* as if they understood it correctly but treat *under* as if it meant the same as *on*. Thus, the children at this stage appear to use *in* correctly all the time, *on* correctly some of the time and *under* correctly none of the time, even though they understand all three words identically. The children do, however, appear to know at least that *in, on* and *under* refer to spatial location [+ Locative], rather than to some other relation. All the children in Experiments 1 and 3, even the youngest, consistently constructed locative relations, placing *x* at least in contact with the RP, *y*. None of the children, for example, treated the relation as an agentive one and made *x* push *y*, or move *y* in any way. These children apply the same two rules in copying tasks in which no locative terms are mentioned at all. The data from Experiment 2, then, constitute independent evidence for the existence of the nonlinguistic strategies proposed to account for the data from Experiments 1 and 3.

The children in the transition stage to full semantic knowledge (Groups II and III in Experiment 1 and Groups A and B in Experiment 3) show partial, but not complete, competence with the adult meanings of *in, on* and *under*. In the present data, the children gave semantically appropriate responses to most of the *on* instructions and up to half of the *under* instructions. Just as for the children at stage one, these children were always correct for *in* instructions, but it is not possible to separate responses to *in* that were based on Rule 1 from those that were based on semantic knowledge. However, there is some other evidence that suggests that these children may already know the full meaning of *in* by this stage. Brown and his colleagues have observed that when children begin to produce their first two prepositions, *in* and *on*, they always appear to use the two terms correctly (Brown, 1973; Brown, Cazden and Bellugi, 1969). These two prepositions are the first to be used spontaneously and first appear sometime after the age of 2;0. In the present study also, several of the older children spontaneously used the preposition *in* to describe (correctly) some of the placements in containers in the copying task (Group II from Experiment 2).

These data, and in particular the data on *under*, therefore, support the partial semantics hypothesis over the full semantics hypothesis for the child's earliest responses to *in, on* and *under*. At first, the young child does not know anything about the meaning of these words, except, perhaps, that they refer to location. The child's responses are the result of his dependence on certain nonlinguistic strategies—Rules 1 and 2—which operate both in comprehension tasks (Experiments 1 and 3) and in tasks involving no locative instructions (Experiment 2). So when the child treats *on* as if it meant *in*, he is doing so not because he thinks *on* means [+ Locative] and

[+ Containment], but because he thinks *on* means [+ Locative] and because he is using a nonlinguistic strategy in conjunction with this partial meaning.

Instead of assuming that the younger children know that *in, on* and *under* refer to location, though, one could suppose that they do not pay any attention to the instructions. This would still be fully consistent with the use of nonlinguistic strategies. If the child did not pay attention *and* did not have any nonlinguistic strategies to fall back on, he should respond randomly, or even not respond at all. However, the data showed that the children were all responding in a very consistent manner even if they were not attending to the instructions. The main difficulties with this approach are that one still has to explain why children should apparently begin to attend after age 2;0, and why they consistently treated the relation between *x* and *y* as a locative one.

The nonlinguistic strategies themselves would presumably have to be derived from the child's conceptual knowledge about the objects and events around him. This general knowledge is based on his interpretations of his percepts. While the particular strategies examined in the present study appear to depend on his knowledge of containers and supporting surfaces, the children also appeared to make use of their knowledge about the usual or canonical orientations of some objects (H. Clark, 1973). For example, many of the younger children manipulated the box so its opening faced upwards (Experiment 1); they often righted the upside-down glass in Experiment 2, and three children subsequently righted the experimenter's as well; and they showed a general preference for putting objects *in* the crib rather than under it. (A few of the children in Group III explicitly objected to the *under* instruction although they then carried it out correctly.) Although there was not a sufficient range of RPs in these experiments to assess the extent to which the young child might depend on such knowledge, other investigators have also found some evidence of reliance on the usual or canonical orientations of objects. For example, Ghent (1960) found that three-year-olds had significantly greater difficulty in recognizing pictures of realistic objects when the pictures were rotated 90° left of right, or 180° from their normal upright position. The younger the children, the more dependent they were on the expected or familiar orientation for recognition. This dependence was no longer noticeable by age 5;0.

If reliance on such nonlinguistic strategies is widespread during the acquisition of language, then it is possible that they play an important role in determining the order of acquisition of certain linguistic distinctions. Slobin (1971) proposed that the main determinant of order of acquisition for linguistic (semantic) distinctions was their relative cognitive complexity, but it is not obvious how to measure the cognitive complexity of different linguistic forms. The child's reliance on nonlinguistic strategies, though, suggests one possible approach. These nonlinguistic strategies may provide the basis for the child's *linguistic hypotheses* about the meanings of words. If so, it becomes very important whether or not the responses based on strategies coincide with those based on semantic knowledge. One could argue that, wherever such responses coincide, the child actually has very little to learn, but that where they do not coincide, he has much more to learn before he will acquire that meaning. The distance between the two types of response could be treated as a measure of the cognitive complexity of the semantic distinctions involved in the meanings of the words in question. For example, *in* should be cognitively simpler than either *on* or *under* because it requires minimal adjustment of the child's hypothesis about its meaning, where this hypothesis is derived from the nonlinguistic strategy, namely, in this instance, Rule 1.[4] *On* should be more complex because the child has to learn first that only the second of the two ordered rules coincides with the meaning of the word. *Under* should be more complex still because neither Rule 1 nor Rule 2 will produce any responses that coincide with the actual meaning of the word. This approach would argue that the order of acquisition of these three locatives should be *in* first, then *on,* and lastly *under.*

The data from the present study are all quite consistent with this proposed order of acquisition, but it is difficult to tell whether *in, on* and *under* are actually acquired in that order. This is because the present experiments do not fully separate the responses based on a nonlinguistic strategy from those based on semantic knowledge for the words *in* and *on.* Theoretically, it is possible to separate these two accounts for the responses. For example, the young child could be shown an RP that had a supporting surface but was not a container and asked to put *x* in the RP. If the child balked at such an instruction, he could be credited with the knowledge that *in* means containment, and not support. Indeed, this technique was tried in a pilot study, but even many of the older children were unwilling not to comply, and they always tried to place *x* somewhere, even when they showed full semantic knowledge in a task like Experiment 3. Such judgments of inappropriateness are extremely hard to elicit from children under age 3;0.[5]

It has been argued that children begin with nonlinguistic strategies and then use these as the basis for their first linguistic hypotheses; because of this, certain meanings can be regarded as cognitively simpler than others. This approach could also be taken to a number of other studies of comprehension. In the acquisition of *more* and *less,* for instance, one could argue that it is a nonlinguistic strategy ("Pick the greater amount") that provides the basis for the child's linguistic hypothesis about the feature [+ Polar]. The positive term, *more,* should be cognitively simpler than *less* because responses based on the strategy coincide with the real meaning of *more.* The same argument could be made with respect to the positive members of all the dimensional adjective pairs, e.g., *big, tall, long, wide,* etc. The strategy of choosing the object with the greater extent or amount coincides with the meanings of the positive terms (Donaldson and Wales, 1970; Klatzky, Clark and Macken, 1973).

There are also other phenomena that may be explained by the child's use of nonlinguistic strategies, but it is difficult to know if this explanation is the right one. For example, Bever (1970a, 1970b) found that very young children appeared to interpret reversible passives such as *The cat was chased by the dog* as if they were actives, i.e., *The cat chased the dog* (*cf.* also Slobin, 1966). Bever argued that both children and adults use a parsing "strategy" of identifying noun-verb-noun sequences and then assigning to those elements the semantic roles of actor-action-object in that order. The question that remains is where the order implicit in the underlying semantic relations comes from. It could be derived from the child's nonlinguistic knowledge: The nonlinguistic strategy in this instance would be based on the child's knowledge that certain objects (people?) could do some action, and this action resulted in a

---

[4] The use of *in* where there are no obvious containers will eventually lead to some readjustment here also, e.g., *The man in the photograph, The ball in the middle.*

[5] It is possible that a technique such as that used by Donaldson and Lloyd (1974) might prove more viable for this type of experiment.

change in a further class of objects at a subsequent time. On the other hand, it could be argued that the child has generalized the actor-action-object pattern from the typical use of active sentences in English. At this point, it is impossible to tell which of these two accounts is the more viable.

A similar argument could be put forward to account for the child's reliance on order of mention in reconstructing the actual order in which a sequence of events occurred. When young children are asked to act out the events described in a sentence like *The boy jumped the fence after he patted the dog*, they consistently treat the first clause as a description of the first event, and the second clause as a description of the second event (E. Clark, 1971; Ferreiro, 1971). Young children also tend to describe a series of events in time in the order in which they happened (E. Clark, 1973a). The child could have an *a priori* nonlinguistic strategy of acting out and talking about events in the order in which he remembers them, with the assumption that they occurred in that order. This nonlinguistic strategy then leads the child to make the linguistic hypothesis that the order of mention always reflects actual order. Alternatively, of course, children may have realized that adults normally talk about events in the order in which they occur, and it is this that accounts for their initial order of mention strategy.

To sum up, the present study has shown that in their attempt to comprehend *in, on* and *under*, young children rely on a combination of linguistic hypotheses about the word meanings and certain nonlinguistic strategies. Furthermore, it has been argued that these nonlinguistic strategies probably form the basis for their hypotheses about the meanings of new words. Thus, the degree of coincidence between responses based on a nonlinguistic strategy and responses based on semantic knowledge may determine the relative cognitive complexity of different linguistic forms and hence determine their order of acquisition.

REFERENCES

Bem, S. L. (1970) The role of comprehension in children's problem-solving. *Dev. Psychol.,* 2, 351–358.

Bever, T. G. (1970a) The cognitive basis for linguistic structures. In J. R. Hayes (Ed.) *Cognition and the development of language.* New York, Wiley, Pp. 279–352.

——(1970b) The integrated study of language behavior. In J. Morton (Ed.) *Biological and social factors in psycholinguistics.* Urbana, Ill., University of Illinois Press. Pp. 158–209.

Brown, R. (1973) *A first language: The early stages.* Cambridge, Mass., Harvard University Press.

Brown, R., Cazden, C. B. and Bellugi, U. (1969) The child's grammar from I to III. In J. P. Hill (Ed.) *Minnesota symposium on child psychology,* Vol. 2. Minneapolis, Minn., University of Minnesota Press. Pp. 28–73.

Clark, E. V. (1971) On the acquisition of the meaning of *before* and *after. J. verb. Learn. verb. Beh.,* 10, 266–275.

——(1973a) How children describe time and order. In C. A. Ferguson and D. I. Slobin (Eds.) *Studies of child language development.* New York, Holt, Rinehart & Winston. Pp. 585–606.

——(1973b) What's in a word? On the child's acquisition of semantics in his first language.

In T. E. Moore (Ed.) *Cognitive development and the acquisition of language.* New York, Academic Press. Pp. 65–110.

——(1974) Some aspects of the conceptual basis for the first language acquisition. In R. L. Schiefelbusch and L. L. Lloyd (Eds.) *Language perspectives—Acquisition, retardation and intervention.* Baltimore, Md., University Park Press.

Clark, H. H. (1970) The primitive nature of children's relational concepts. In J. R. Hayes (Ed.) *Cognition and the development language.* New York, Wiley. Pp. 269–278.

——(1973) Space, time semantics and the child. In T. E. Moore (Ed.) *Cognitive development and the acquisition of language.* New York, Academic Press. Pp. 28–63.

Donaldson, M. and Balfour, G. (1968) Less is more: A study of language comprehension in children. *Brit. J. Psychol.,* 59, 461–472.

——and Lloyd, P. (1974) Sentences and situations: Children's judgments of match and mismatch. In *Proceedings of symposium on current problems in psycholinguistics.* Paris, CNRS.

——and Wales, R. J. (1970) On the acquisition of some relational terms. In J. R. Hayes (Ed.) *Cognition and the development of language.* New York, Wiley. Pp. 235–268.

Ferreiro, E. (1971) *Les relations temporelles dans le langage de l'enfant.* Genève, Droz.

Ghent, L. (1960) Recognition by children of realistic figures in various orientations. *Can. J. Psychol.,* 14, 249–256.

Huttenlocher, J., Eisenberg, K., and Strauss, S. (1968) Comprehension: Relation between perceived actor and logical subject. *J. verb. Learn. verb. Beh.,* 7, 527–530.

——and Strauss, S. (1968) Comprehension and a statement's relation to the situation it describes. *J. verb. Learn. verb. Beh.,* 7, 300–304.

Klatzky, R. L., Clark, E. V. and Macken, M. (1973) Asymmetries in the acquisiton of polar adjectives: Linguistic or conceptual? *J. exp. child Psychol.* 16, 32–46.

Laurendeau, M. and Pinard, A. (1970) *The development of the concept of space in the child.* New York, International Universities Press.

Palermo, D. S. (1973) More about *less:* A study of language comprehension. *J. verb. Learn. verb. Beh.,* 12, 211–221.

Slobin, D. I. (1966) Grammatical transformations and sentence comprehension in childhood and adulthood. *J. verb. Learn. verb. Beh.,* 5, 219–227.

——(1971) Developmental psycholinguistics. In W. O. Dingwall (Ed.) *A survey of linguistic science.* Linguistics Program, University of Maryland. Pp. 298–400. [Reprinted (1973) as 'Cognitive pre-requisites for the development of grammar'. In C. A. Ferguson and D. I. Slobin (Eds.) *Studies of child language development.* New York, Holt, Rinehart & Winston. Pp. 175–208.]

Imitation in Language Development: If, When, and Why[1]

Lois Bloom, Lois Hood, and Patsy Lightbown

In order to explore the function of imitation for first language learning, imitative and spontaneous utterances were compared in the naturalistic speech of six children in the course of their development from single-word utterances (when mean length of utterance was essentially 1.0) to the emergence of grammar (when mean length of utterance approached 2.0). The relative extent of imitation, and lexical and grammatical variation in imitative and spontaneous speech were determined. There were intersubject differences in the extent of imitation, but each child was consistent in the tendency to imitate or not to imitate across time. For those children who imitated, there were both lexical and grammatical differences in imitative and spontaneous speech, and a developmental shift from imitative to spontaneous use of particular words and semantic-syntactic relations between words. The results are discussed as evidence of an active processing of model utterances relative to the contexts in which they occur for information for language learning.

When a child says something in response to what someone else says, he can either repeat what he hears or say something that is more or less related to it. The two possibilities, to imitate or not to imitate, are represented in the following speech events from two different children:[2]

Cognitive Psychology, **6**, 380–420, Academic Press, Inc., 1974. Reprinted by permission of Academic Press, Inc.

[1] This study was supported by Research Grant HD 03828 from the National Institute of Child Health and Development, and Fellowship F1-MH-30,001 from the National Institute of Mental Health, United States Public Health Service, to Lois Bloom. We thank Margaret Lahey for many comments and many questions; Ruth Gold, Owen Whitby, Donald Hood, and Lynn Streeter for valuable counsel given on statistical matters, and Thomas Lightbown for drafting the figures. We have benefited from presenting portions of this study to Colloquia at the Universities of Illinois, Michigan, and Pennsylvania, and the Psycholinguistics Circle of New York. Requests for reprints should be sent to Lois Bloom, Teachers College, Box 5, 525 W. 120th St., N. Y., N.Y. 10027.

[2] Utterances on the right were spoken by the child. Material in parentheses on the left describes the situational context, and utterances from the adults are presented on the left without parentheses. Roman numerals after a child's name refer to a particular speech sample; that is (1) occurred in the first sample from Peter, Time I, (2) occurred in the second sample from

(1) Peter I: age 21 months, 1 week; MLU: 1.04

    (Peter opening cover of tape recorder)   open/open/open

    Did you open it?

    (Peter watching the tape recorder)   open it

    Did you open the tape recorder?

    (Peter still watching the tape recorder)   tape recorder

(2) Allison II: age 19 months, 2 weeks; MLU: 1.02 (Allison jumped up, almost hitting her head on overhead microphone; the microphones in the studio had been placed and adjusted by the cameraman before video filming began; Allison touches the microphone, turns to Mommy)   man

    Man. That's the microphone. That's the microphone.

    (Allison pointing to another microphone on lavaliere around Mommy's neck)   Mommy

    Yeah, Mommy has a microphone.

    (Allison looks at overhead microphone)

    That's another microphone.

    (Allison still looking at overhead microphone)   man

In the two situations, "tape recorder" and "microphone" were relatively unfamiliar. Peter had not seen tape recorders before; Allison had not seen a microphone since the first video session three months earlier. Peter repeated the word he did not know, whereas Allison named something that was associated with the word she did not know. Both children were processing information about language. In order to determine whether or not imitation is important for processing speech relative to the events to which it refers, it is necessary to determine the extent to which children imitate the speech they hear, when imitation occurs if it occurs, and why it occurs. This study described the extent to which imitation occurred in the speech of six children and explored the function of imitation for lexical and grammatical learning in their early language development.

There has always been considerable disagreement about the importance of imitation for language development. One prevailing assumption has been that a child needs to repeat the speech that he hears in order to learn it. For example, according to Jespersen, "one thing which plays a great role in children's acquisiton of language, and especially in their early attempts to form sentences, is Echoism: the fact that children echo what is said to them" (1922, p. 135). Kirkpatrick (1909) and others believed that children are virtually compelled to imitate and that they imitate not only what they themselves have seen or done previously, but also totally novel behavior. Bloch (1921), Guillaume (1926), Lewis (1951), and others described a critical stage of imitation that comes between the stage of comprehension and the beginning of

---

Allison, Time II. MLU (mean length of utterance) was computed for morphemes in the first 100 utterances; neither immediate self-repetitions nor imitative utterances were counted. See, however, the further discussion of different MLU computations and values in the section on semantic-syntactic structure.

speech. However, Fraser, Bellugi, & Brown (1963) concluded from an experimental study of elicited imitation that imitation preceded comprehension in development, and there were early observers, for example, Meumann (1903) and Thorndike (1913), who discounted the importance of imitation for language development altogether.

The behaviorist view of language learning would expect new behaviors to be imitated before they can be incorprrated into an individual's repertoire of behaviors; for example, Mowrer (1960), Jenkins and Palermo (1964), and Staats (1971). In 1941, Jakobson (1968 translation) pointed out the contradiction between behaviorist views of language learning that emphasized the importance of imitation on the one hand and the notion of creativity in rationalist accounts of the nature of language on the other. The contradiction was elaborated by Chomsky (1959) and in recent debates about theories of language development (see, for example, the papers and discussions in Bellugi & Brown, 1964; Smith & Miller, 1966; Dixon & Horton, 1968; and Slobin, 1971). It has been argued that if the child's task is to discover the rules of grammar that make it possible to speak and understand sentences never spoken or heard before, then imitating a sample of utterances would not be very helpful. In the theory of generative grammar (Chomsky, 1957 and 1965), underlying sentence structures and not actual utterances themselves are the relevant data, and underlying structure cannot be imitated (see, for example, Slobin, 1968, and McNeill, 1970).

Apparently, only two studies have actually compared children's imitative and spontaneous utterances. Ervin-Tripp (1964) compared the word order of imitative and spontaneous utterances in the speech of five children; Kemp and Dale (1973) compared grammatical features in the imitative and spontaneous utterances of 30 children. Both of these studies concluded that imitative speech was not "grammatically progressive," that is, that neither word order nor grammatical features were more advanced in imitative than in spontaneous utterances. However, other impressions have been contradictory. Bloom (1968), Slobin (1968), and Brown (reported in Slobin, 1968) commented that something more than casual observation of children's speech has suggested that imitative utterances were different and somewhat beyond the grammatical level represented in spontaneous utterances. Shipley, Smith, and Gleitman (1969) reported that children who were just beginning to use multiword utterances were more likely to repeat a command that contained a nonsense word (for example "throw *ronta* ball") than a command with only real words—which led them to conclude that imitation might be a factor in lexical learning.

To the extent that a child must hear a lexical item before he can use it, one might consider that much of a child's speech is imitative. Leopold (1949, Vol. 3), Piaget (1962), and Sinclair (1971) have taken just such a broad view of imitation in development—that as a child incorporates experience in cognitive memory, virtually all of his own behavior imitates a model that, if not actually present in the context, would be represented mentally. However, if all behavior in the young child is imitative, then the task of explaining behavior remains, and imitation loses considerable force as a process that might contribute to development. In order to explore the function of imitation as a process in language development, it was necessary to define imitation in a way that made it possible to examine the developmental relationship between behaviors that were and were not imitative.

PROCEDURES

For the purpose of this study, only behavior that followed from an actual model was considered imitative. An utterance was *imitative* (a) if it occurred in a natural situation (that is, without the child being asked or prompted to imitate); (b) if it repeated all or part of a preceding model utterance from someone else; (c) if it did not add to or change the model other than to reduce it by leaving something out; and (d) if no more than five utterances (from the child or others) intervened after the model. The arbitrary limit of five utterances was chosen as intuitively reasonable for establishing an imitative utterance as one that occurred in the context of the model. All other utterances were considered *spontaneous.*[3]

The study focused on the period of language development in which children progress from using only one word at a time (when mean length of utterance is essentially 1.0) to the emergence of grammar and the use of structured speech (when mean length of utterance approaches 2.0).

Data were obtained from six children in this developmental period from single words to syntax: Eric, Gia, Jane, Kathryn, and Peter were each visited in their homes periodically, and their speech was audio recorded using the procedures described in Bloom (1970, pp. 234–239). The children interacted primarily with an investigator; their parents were present and interacted with them only part of the time. The speech samples from Eric, Gia, Jane, and Kathryn were collected and transcribed by L. Bloom. The speech samples from Peter were collected and transcribed by L. Hood and P. Lightbown, who took turns at playing with Peter and taking notes about the situational context and behavior. The interactions with the sixth child, Allison (L. Bloom's daughter), were video recorded in the audiovisual studio at Teachers College, Columbia University, using the procedures for recording and transcribing described in Bloom (1973, pp. 138–141). The speech samples that were obtained from the six children are described in Table 1 in terms of length of sessions, age, mean length of utterance (MLU), and numbers of utterances. In Table 1 and throughout this report the term *type* refers to a particular utterance, and the term *token* refers to an occurrence of an utterance type. Thus, the utterance "read that book" was one type that, occurring four times in a sample, had four tokens. As a multiword utterance, "read that book" is also a syntactic utterance type. As can be seen, the data for analysis consisted of more than 17,000 utterances from the six children in the period from MLU of 1.0 to MLU of approximately 2.0, and age 18 months to 25 months. All of the children were first-born, and their parents were college educated.[4]

---

[3] Slobin (1968) suggested that the most important function of imitation for language acquisition might be the opportunity for a child to imitate adult expansions of his own utterances. Such utterances, which represented less than.01 of the data examined by Slobin, were not distinguished from other imitative utterances in the present study. When a child's utterance was expanded or repeated by an adult and the child subsequently repeated his own initial utterance (either *unchanged* or *reduced*), the second utterance was also considered spontaneous.

[4] This investigation is one part of the longitudinal study of the language development of four of these children (Eric, Gia, Kathryn, and Peter) from the ages of 19 to 36 months. The decision to study imitation was made after the data were collected for the larger study, so that the data presented here were not collected for the specific purpose of the study of imitation.

Table 1   Summary Description of Speech Samples

Child	Time	Sample Specifications			Number of Utterances			
		Length (Hours)	Age (Months, weeks)	Mean Length of Utterance	Total Types	Total Syntactic Types	Average Types per Hour	Total Tokens
Allison	I	0.75	16, 3	1.06	49	11	70	283
	II	0.75	19, 2	1.02	67	4	77	321
	III	0.75	20, 3	1.13	118	19	157	379
	IV	0.75	22, 0	1.73	168	94	224	271
Eric	I	4	19, 1	1.10	96	23	24	296
	II	6	20, 2	1.19	179	72	30	615
	III	6.7	22, 0	1.42	363	176	52	1043
	IV	3	23, 2	1.69	311	185	104	629
Gia	I	6.7	19, 2	1.12	246	83	37	1045
	II	3.3	20, 2	1.34	282	149	85	933
	III	5	22, 1	1.58	310	197	65	804
	IV	2.1	23, 3	1.79	300	194	143	601
Jane	I	5	18, 2	1.29	350	82	70	1144
	II	2.5	20, 0	1.27	239	111	96	438
Kathryn	I	5	21, 0	1.32	432	226	86	917
	II	1.7	22, 3	1.89	443	303	260	697
	III	1.7	24, 2	2.83	474	427	279	642
Peter	I	3	21, 1	1.04	171	21	59	610
	II	3.5	21, 3½	1.09	136	12	39	418
	III	4.5	22, 2	1.37	302	119	65	1052
	IV	4.5	23, 1	1.41	363	165	82	1166
	V	3	23, 2½	1.33	255	129	83	583
	VI	4.5	24, 1	1.75	594	424	133	1364
	VII	4.5	25, 0	2.39	685	551	152	1195

Three separate analyses were performed. First, the extent and consistence of imitation were determined for each child in terms of the proportion of utterance types that were imitated in each session. Second, the imitative and spontaneous occurrences of lexical item tokens were observed within each session and across successive sessions. Third, all multiword utterances were examined for regularities in form and meaning in order to determine categories of semantic–syntactic structure. Imitative and spontaneous utterance types in each category were then compared within each session and across successive sessions. The procedures and results for each of these analyses will be presented before discussing the results as they relate to the function of imitation for language development.

THE EXTENT AND CONSISTENCY OF IMITATION

The first concern was to determine whether or not the children imitated the speech that they heard and the extent to which an individual child's tendency to imitate was consistent across time. Following this, imitative and nonimitative utterances were compared for each child in order to determine if there were lexical and structural differences between the two kinds of utterances.

Every utterance in each speech sample was coded as spontaneous or imitative according to the working definitions given earlier. Table 2 presents the proportion of utterance types that occurred only spontaneously, only imitatively, or both spontaneously and imitatively.[5] It is immediately apparent that there were differences in the extent to which the children imitated. The proportion of imitation in Allison's speech was never more than .06, whereas the proportion of imitation in Peter's speech was always at least .27. For most of the children,[6] the relative tendency to imitate that was observed in the first speech sample continued until MLU reached 2.0 morphemes. Only Kathryn showed an appreciable change over time. Because the difference between Time I and Time II was so great, Kathryn's speech at Time III was analyzed even though MLU was 2.83 and thus beyond the limits of the study. The lower proportion of imitation at Time II continued at Time III; .09 of the different utterances at Time III were imitative.

There were marked differences then in the extent to which the different children imitated, but each child was impressively consistent in the tendency to imitate across time, as can be seen in Fig. 1. According to these results, imitation is not required behavior for learning to talk; two of the children progressed from single-word utterances to MLU of 2.0 without imitating the speech that they heard. It appears that part of the confusion in the early literature about the relative importance of imitation for language development may be attributed to the fact that different observers were watching different children, who did or did not imitate.

It might be hypothesized that the nonimitating children were indeed imitating but their imitation was somehow "delayed." To explore this possibility, the latency of

---

[5] Utterance *types* (each different utterance counted as a type) rather than utterance *tokens* (the number of occurrences of a type) were used for computing these proportions inasmuch as the focus of the study was on the relation of imitation to the development of linguistic representation. Differences in form and change in form were more relevant for evaluating language learning than overall use or frequency of forms. Computation using item frequency (tokens rather than types) would have resulted in a smaller proportion of imitation in the speech of all of the children since different spontaneous utterances usually occurred more frequently than different imitative utterances.

[6] Jane's family moved away following the second recording session, and there is no information about her language development after that time.

Table 2   Proportion of Utterance Types that Were Only Spontaneous, Only Imitative, or Both Spontaneous and Imitative

Child	Time	All Utterances			Only Syntactic Utterances		
		Sp	Im	Sp+Im	Sp	Im	Sp+Im
Allison	I	.85	.04	.11	.91	.09	—
	II	.88	.06	.06	1.00	—	—
	III	.92	.04	.04	.95	—	.05
	IV	.94	.04	.02	.98	.11	.01
Eric	I	.71	.17	.12	.69	.22	.09
	II	.73	.15	.12	.76	.18	.06
	III	.73	.17	.10	.76	.21	.03
	IV	.76	.17	.07	.78	.16	.06
Gia	I	.69	.14	.17	.86	.13	.01
	II	.87	.07	.06	.94	.05	.01
	III	.88	.06	.06	.92	.06	.02
	IV	.96	.04	—	.97	.03	—
Jane	I	.38	.42	.20	.47	.49	.04
	II	.60	.32	.08	.57	.41	.02
Kathryn	I	.53	.36	.11	.64	.34	.02
	II	.86	.11	.03	.88	.11	.01
Peter	I	.30	.42	.28	.34	.57	.09
	II	.48	.31	.21	.59	.33	.08
	III	.58	.27	.15	.68	.28	.04
	IV	.54	.34	.12	.57	.36	.07
	V	.55	.27	.07	.66	.30	.04
	VI	.58	.34	.08	.57	.38	.05

imitation, in terms of the number of utterances that intervened between the model and its reproduction, was determined for each of the speech samples. The occurrence of imitative utterances was compared in two different conditions: immediate imitation, with no intervening utterance, and nonimmediate imitation that occurred with at least one but not more than five intervening utterances.

The number of imitative utterance types with token frequency of immediate imitation greater than token frequency of nonimmediate imitation was compared with the number of imitative utterances with nonimmediate frequency greater than immediate frequency. Table 3 presents the results of a sign test of the hypothesis that immediate and nonimmediate imitations were equally likely to occur. In the first entry in Table 3, for example, for Eric at Time I, there were 27 imitative utterance types; two of

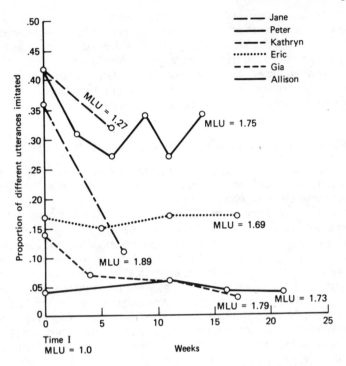

Figure 1. Relative extent of imitation. The proportion of different utterances imitated by each child at each Time.

these had equal numbers of immediate and nonimmediate tokens and were not included in the analysis. Three of the remaining 25 had frequency of nonimmediate imitation greater than frequency of immediate imitation, and 22 had frequency of immediate imitation greater than frequency of nonimmediate imitation. The probability of this result given the hypothesis of no difference between immediate and nonimmediate imitation was less than .001. As can be seen in Table 3, there was a significant difference between immediate and nonimmediate imitation ($p < .005$) for the imitating children (Eric, Jane, Peter, and Kathryn at Time I) whose overall proportion of imitation exceeded .15, and for Gia at Time I when the proportion of imitation was .14. Thus, if these children imitated, they tended to do so immediately, with no utterances intervening between an imitative utterance and its model.

However, for the nonimitating children, for whom the overall proportion of imitation was less than .15 (Kathryn at Time II, Allison, and Gia), the difference between immediate and nonimmediate imitation was not significant (except for Gia at Time I). Thus, there was some evidence that the nonimitating children might actually have been imitating a model that was further removed than the original five-utterance limit that had been established in defining imitation for this study. In order to test this, the spontaneous utterances from Allison and Gia were classified again after extending to ten the number of utterances that could intervene between the model and its "imitation." In the four samples of Allison's speech, there were only four imitations of a model that occurred with at least five and no more than ten intervening utterances; in 5.6 hr of Gia's speech (the middle third of each sample), there were 10 such utterances. If so few imitative utterances occurred within a ten-utterance boundary, there was no reason to expect that there would be imitative utterances beyond that limit. Indeed, it might well be questioned whether such utterances were even imitative at all, or whether they might have occurred in any event.

COMPARISON OF IMITATIVE AND SPONTANEOUS SPEECH

After it was established that the extent of imitation varied from child to child but remained consistent for each child, it was necessary to determine how imitation functioned for those children who imitated.

There was a clear division between the utterance types which a child imitated and those which he produced spontaneously, as can be seen in Table 2. Any utternace type which had at least one spontaneous and one imitative token is included in the Sp+Im column. The number of utterances with both spontaneous and imitative tokens was relatively small for all the children and tended to decrease as MLU increased. When only the syntactic utterances were taken into account, there was an even stronger separation of spontaneous and imitative utterances. Furthermore, many of the utterances represented in the Sp+Im column were high-frequency utterances with many spontaneous tokens and only two or three imitative tokens. For example, at Peter IV, the utterance "in there" occurred 15 times spontaneously and one time imitatively.

LEXICAL ITEMS
One function of imitation that has often been suggested is that imitation helps children learn new words.

DIFFERENT POPULATIONS OF WORDS.   In order to test whether there were two different populations of words in the children's speech at each Time, the following procedure was used. The proportion, p, of lexical item tokens which were imitative was calculated for each speech sample, both for single-word utterances and words used syntactically. The entries for words used syntactically were found by separating each syntactic utterance into its "word parts" and counting each word separately. For example, the utterance "need another one" was counted as one occurrence each of "need," "another," and "one." The frequency of imitative versus spontaneous tokens of each word which occurred three or more times within a speech sample was compared with the distribution expected on the basis of the binomial expansion using the value of p for that speech sample. If the two-tailed probability of obtaining the observed split between imitative and spontaneous tokens was less than .05, that word was considered to have an extreme split between imitative and spontaneous use. After the number of words with extreme splits was found, a binomial test with $p = .05$ was applied to ascertain the likelihood of this number of extreme splits occuring in each sample. For example, for Peter at Time I, of 59 single-word utterances that occurred at least three times, 16 of them split in an extreme way between

Table 3   Comparison of Immediate and Nonimmediate Imitation

Child	Time	Number of Utterances		Proba-bility (less than)
		Freq. of Nonimm. Greater Than Freq. of Imm.	Freq. of Imm. Greater Than Freq. of Nonimm.	
Eric	I	3	22	.01
	II	11	30	.01
	III	30	56	.01
	IV	22	46	.01
Jane	I	8	212	.01
	II	15	71	.01
Peter	I	15	98	.01
	II	19	52	.01
	III	40	79	.01
	IV	37	118	.01
	V	21	67	.01
	VI	39	200	.01
Kathryn	I	35	122	.01
	II	35	26	.90
Gia	I	22	47	.01
	II	18	20	.44
	III	26	12	.99
	IV	4	9	.14
Allison	I	4	2	.89
	II	3	3	.66
	III	6	5	.73
	IV	5	3	.85

their spontaneous and imitative frequencies; the probability of observing this many extreme splits was $<.001$. Thus, it was concluded that for this sample there were two populations of single-word utterances, those used spontaneously and those used imitatively.[7]

Table 4 presents the number of words with extreme splits, the total number of words in the analysis (words that occurred three times or more), and the binomial probability of observing a ratio of words with extreme splits to total number of words at least

---

[7] This test was devised by Ruth Gold.

Table 4   Summary of Statistics Used to Test for Two Populations of Words,
               Imitative and Spontaneous

Child	Time	Single-word utterances			Words Used Syntactically		
		No. of Words with Extreme Splits	No. of Words in Analysis	Proba-bility (less than)	No. of Words with Extreme Splits	No. of Words in Analysis	Proba-bility (less than)
Eric	I	1	29	.77	0	4	.83
	II	8	44	.01	0	14	.49
	III	5	67	.24	7	37	.01
	IV	3	37	.28	2	49	.71
Peter	I	16	59	.01	0	3	.86
	II	3	44	.38	3	7	.01
	III	23	79	.01	6	31	.01
	IV	14	89	.01	8	52	.01
	V	4	34	.09	7	40	.01
	VI	4	49	.23	36	113	.01
Jane	I	18	101	.01	4	14	.01
	II	5	24	.01	2	34	.51
Kathryn	I	7	64	.05	9	69	.05

this extreme for those Times when the overall proportion of imitation of different utterances was greater than .15.[8] As can be seen, for all the samples except Eric at Times I and IV, the results were significant for single-word utterances and/or words used syntactically. It is clear that there was a strong tendency for the children to use certain words only spontaneously and certain other words only imitatively. However, there appeared to be different explanations for the split between imitative and spontaneous occurrence for single-word utterances and words used syntactically.

Single-word utterances. The results for single-word utterances were less than convincing at first glance. The number of words that split in an extreme way in their imitative and spontaneous frequencies was not significant for Peter at Times II, V, and VI, nor for Eric at Times I, III, and IV. However, as can be seen in Table 4, for the three samples from Peter that were not significant, the number of words that occurred

---

[8] In those samples where the proportion of imitation of different utterances was less than .15 (see Table 2), there were too few imitative occurrences of different words and so the test could not be applied.

three or more times so that they could be counted in the analysis was smaller than in those samples where the results were significant.

Inspection of the data from another perspective—the number of utterances, regardless of how often they occurred, that split with either no spontaneous and only imitative, or only spontaneous and no imitative occurrence, in the same samples—revealed that Eric and Peter used most words only spontaneously or only imitatively. The proportions of utterances with such splits, even though not extreme enough to be significant, was at least .75 (and in 4 of the 6 samples at least .85). Thus, it appeared that even in these samples from Peter and Eric, there were indeed two populations of words. A possible explanation of why these samples had so few words with extreme splits was that Peter and Eric simply did not talk very much in these samples, and thus words were not likely to occur frequently, either spontaneously, imitatively, or both (see Table 1). Thus, the test of significance applied to lexical items was just not sensitive enough for data where the sample of speech was relatively small. The test depended on words occurring with high frequency. When there were enough words occurring often enough, the test of significance impressively supported the observation that single-word utterances tended to be imitative *or* spontaneous.

Words used syntactically. The results for words used syntactically were significant for 8 out of the 13 speech samples. The fact that the words the children used spontaneously in syntactic constructions tended to be different from the words used imitatively in syntactic constructions could have two explanations. On the one hand, the differences might be evidence for differentiation of lexical items as was apparent in the analysis of single-word utterances. On the other hand, when imitating words in a syntactic construction, the children might in fact have been imitating an aspect of the syntax rather than the particular lexical item that was included in the construction. The two kinds of imitation, lexical and grammatical, could not be separated in any analysis that looked at each speech sample separately. For this reason, the samples from Eric and Peter were analyzed in terms of change over time.

PROGRESSION FROM IMITATIVE TO SPONTANEOUS USE. If imitation leads to the learning of particular lexical items, then one could expect that those words that were imitative at an early Time, if repeated at successive Times, would gradually come to be used spontaneously. The hypothesis that a significant proportion of words would progress from mostly imitative occurrence to mostly spontaneous occurrence in the period of study was tested in the following way. For those children whose overall proportion of imitation was above .15 for more than two sessions, a Spearman rank-order correlation was found for each word that (a) occurred in at least two sessions, (b) was imitated at least once and spontaneous at least once, and (c) showed *some* change across time, either from imitative to spontaneous or spontaneous to imitative.

Spearman rank-order correlations were found between session ranks and observed ranks of the ratio of imitative occurrences to total number of occurrences. This procedure was applied separately to single-word utterances and words used syntactically. The number of sessions varied from 2 to 6 for Peter and 2 to 4 for Eric, according to the number of sessions in which a given word occurred, and the session ranks changed accordingly. If a word occurred in all 6 sessions from Peter, the ranking of sessions was 1, 2, 3, 4, 5, 6; if a word occurred in only 4 of the sessions from Peter, the sessions in which the word occurred were ranked 1, 2, 3, 4. If the ratio of imitative occurrences to total number of occurrences was the same for more than one session, the average of the ranks was used. For example, for the word "off," the ratios of imitative tokens to total number of tokens were 1/1 at Time I, 1/2 at II, 0/4 at III, and 0/3 at IV, for Times I–V from Eric. The session ranking (Times I–IV) was 1, 2, 3, 4, and the observed ratio ranking was 1, 2, 3.5, 3.5, with a resulting rho of .50. For the word "foot," the imitative to total ratios were 0/1 at Time I and 1/6 at Time III, with no occurrences at Times II and IV. The session ranking was 1,2 and the observed ranking was 2,1, with a resulting rho of −1.00. A t test was performed on the Spearman rank-order correlations with the null hypothesis that the mean correlation equals zero.

For Peter, there was a significant trend for imitative occurrence of single words to decrease over Time. The mean correlation (rho=323) was significantly different from zero (t(132) = 5.14, p < .001). This was not the case for words used syntactically (rho = .04, t(102) = .5012). For Eric, the reverse was true. For words used syntactically, the mean correlation (rho = .255) was significantly different from zero (t(51) = 2.329, p < .05), while for single-word utterances it was not (rho = .047 t(57) = .429). Thus, there was a progression across time as imitation of a particular lexical item decreased while the spontaneous use of that item increased, for single-word utterances in Peter's speech, and for multiword utterances in Eric's speech. These differences between Peter and Eric were consistent with the differences found between them in the semantic-syntactic functions of imitation in multiword utterances which will be discussed subsequently.

In sum, imitation played a role in the acquisition of new lexical items for the children in this study whose overall imitation was greater than .15. To the extent that spontaneous use was an index of knowing a word, it could be concluded that the children imitated words that they did not yet know. At any particular time, the children did not imitate words they used spontaneously and did not use spontaneously the words they imitated. Further, there was a clear trend for individual words that were originally imitative to become predominantly spontaneous at later times.

SEMANTIC-SYNTACTIC STRUCTURE

Classifying multiword utterances according to the relations between words resulted in a taxonomy of semantic–syntatic categories that allowed several comparisons to be made. Within one sample of speech from an individual child, both the relative occurrence of the different relations and different utterance forms could be compared in imitative and spontaneous speech. It was then possible to compare successive samples of speech from the same child to determine the developmental interaction between imitative and spontaneous speech. In this way it was possible to evaluate the role of imitation for semantic learning (between categories) and syntactic learning (within categories), and to demonstrate that imitation did indeed function in the acquisition of grammar for those children who imitated.

The semantic–syntactic categories were identified by observing the relationship between an utterance and aspects of the child's behavior and the context in which the utterance occurred. Although one cannot know the full scope of semantic intention for any particular utterance, that is, precisely what a child means by what he says, there was relatively little difficulty in knowing what the children were talking about. Virtually all of the utterances occurred in relation to what the children (and the adults) could see, or in relation to what the children had just done, were doing, or were about to do. The semantic–syntactic categories were dependent on (a) the child's utterance occurring in direct reference to the event that was encoded in the utterance and (b) the inclusion of at least two words in the utterance with an identifiable relationship between them. Adult interpretations were very much context- and utterance-bound, so that the categories of semantic–syntactic relations were directly derived from the child speech event data rather than being a predetermined system of analysis.

Four of the categories represented verb relations (whether or not an actual verb was one of the words) that were identified in terms of (a) whether or not movement accompanied an utterance and (b) the goal of movement, when movement occurred. These criteria were contextual and distinguished between action and state relations and between locative and nonlocative actions and states. Of all the relations in the children's speech that expressed action, the overwhelming majority of them entailed action on an affected object or the goal of a change in location. Such verbs as "get up" and "fall down," which are intransitive in the adult model, were productive as locative action verbs in the present study; such intransitive verbs as "turn around" and "dance," which were categorized as Actions (without Affected-Object), did not occur productively (with productivity defined as five different utterances at a particular Time).

For several of the verbs in each of these categories, one could argue for a different classification based on adult introspective evidence. The verb "get" was an example of the dilemma that sometimes arose in distinguishing between action and locative–action events. One could argue that "get" involves movement that changes the location of an object. However, the child's goal in "getting" appeared to be more the act of obtaining than a change in location of the object, and utterances such as "get it" and "get cookie" were classified as *Action-on-Affected-Object*.

The following definitions were used for categorizing the relations between words in multiword utterances:[9]

1. ACTION-ON-AFFECTED-OBJECT.   Utterances made reference to movements that affected an object in some way other than with the goal of changing its location. Actions entailed an agent-of-action, although not always specified, that performed the action to affect an object. Action relations included "eat cookie," "make ə bridge," "push ə button," etc.
2. PLACE- AND OBJECT-OF-LOCATIVE-ACTION.   Utterances made reference to movements that had the goal of affecting an object by changing its location in space. Place, although not always specified, was always entailed in a locative relation. Locative actions involved an agent-of-locative-action that performed the movement, if the locative action affected an object. When the same referent was both agent and affect-

---

[9] A more explicit account of categories with verb relations and their development in the speech of five of the children is presented in Bloom, Lightbown, and Hood (1975).

ed-object (person), the agent-affected-object function was specified as mover. That is, a mover both performed the movement and changed location (for example, "Patsy" in "Patsy sit down"). Locative-action relations included "put on there," "sit chair," "on tape," etc.

3. STATE-LOCATION-OF-OBJECT. Utterances made reference to the location of an object in events in which there was no movement that caused the object to change location. Locative-state relations included "sit chair," "baby lie down," etc. (without movement).

4. STATE AND STATE-AND-CAUSATIVE-OBJECT. Utterances specified an internal state that was transitory in events in which an object caused the internal state specified by the verb. States always entailed a person-affected, for example "(person-affected) want (causative-object)." However, in this study, person-affected was rarely specified except by /ə/, the apparent precursor of "I." Other *State* utterances specified a transitory state of an animate object that did not entail a causative object, for example, "Baby tire(d)" or "Nancy crying." Utterances that referred to an inherent state (nontransitory) of an inanimate object, for example, "Balloon broke," were classed among the Attributives.

5. ATTRIBUTION. Utterances made reference to properties of objects with respect to (a) an inherent *state* of the object, for example, "broke" and "sharp"; (b) a *specification* of an object that could distinguish it from others in its class, for example, "red," "big," and "bread" in "bread book"; and (c) *quantity* of objects (usually "two"). Attributive state forms were often derived from verb forms in the adult language. In actuality, it appeared that all of the adjectives were used by the children in an absolute sense, to indicate an inherent property of an object, rather than in a comparative sense, to indicate the relative dimension of the property according to some standard.

6. POSSESSION. Utterances made reference to objects within the domains of different persons. A class of words (such as "Mommy," "Daddy," "Baby") could mean the same thing (Possessor) in relation to a class of different words (such as "sweater," "shoe," "record") that meant something else (Object-Possessed) or, alternatively, Object-Possessed could be specified in relation to a constant pro-form such as "my."

7. EXISTENCE. Utterances made reference only to the fact of an object in the environment as the child either looked at it, pointed to it, touched it, or picked it up. This class of utterances has been called "Ostention" by Braine (1971) and Schlesinger (1971) and "Nomination" by Brown (1970). *Existence* was signaled by /ə/ (as an apparent article) or variants of the demonstrative form "this," "that," "thats," etc.

8. NOTICE. Utterances called attention to the existence of an object and included a notice verb such as "see," or "look," or the form 'Hi' as in "Hi spoon."

9. NONEXISTENCE.   Utterances made reference to the disappearance of an object or the nonexistence of the object in a context in which its existence might somehow be expected, and included such terms as "no," "all gone," "no more," "away." Other functions of negation (for example, *Rejection* and *Denial*) were not productive in syntactic utterances in the period studied here.

10. RECURRENCE.   Utterances made reference to the reappearance of an object, or another instance of an object or event with or without the original instance of the object still present, with the forms "more" or "another."

It is important to point out that certain categories which one might expect to be represented did not occur in the data. Most notably, comparative constructions (with "more-less" or "same-different"), indirect object (*"give Mommy"), the conditional (*"cold coat"), identity (*"Mommy lady"), the instrumental (*"eat fork") were virtually nonexistent. Whatever the children were able to understand of the relations among objects and events in the world around them (their cognitive development), they coded only a restricted set of such relations in the speech that they used. Moreover, not all of the categories were represented to the same extent in the speech of the different children (for example, there was no instance of attribution in Allison's speech and few possessives in Eric's speech until Time IV). Although there were differences in relative extent, there were not any different categories represented. (See Bloom, Lightbown, & Hood, 1974 ms., and Brown, 1973.) There were anomalous, ambiguous, or otherwise uninterpretable utterances in each sample. However, the proportion of different utterances accounted for in the analysis of the semantic-syntactic relations between words that follows was at least .90 for all of the samples except Peter at Time VII (.89) and Eric at Time IV (.82).

The relative occurrence of spontaneous and imitative utterances in each of the categories will be reported: (a) for categories in which there were at least five utterance types at a particular Time, and (b) for those Times in which the proportion of different imitative utterances exceeded .15 of the total number of different utterances: Peter, Times I–VII; Kathryn, Time I; Jane, Times I and II; and Eric, Times I–IV. The criterion of an overall proportion of imitation of .15 was used because there were too few different imitative utterances below that level to allow a meaningful comparison between imitative and spontaneous speech to be made. Utterance types that had both spontaneous and imitative tokens were not included in this analysis; they represented less than .10 of all of the syntactic utterance types from all of the children, and they did not include any new categories.

The evidence of the interaction between imitative and spontaneous speech for semantic–syntactic learning will be presented as frequency data: the number of imitative and spontaneous multiword utterance types within each category of semantic-syntactic relationship. In all of the samples, there were several Noncontrastive categories in which there was either no difference in the form of imitative and spontaneous speech, or there were virtually no imitations. For other categories it was possible to compare spontaneous and imitative multiword utterances with respect to the development of different linguistic forms (subcategories) within each semantic–syntactic category. For example, in Peter's speech, in the category *Action-on-Affected-Object*, the subcategories were pronominal and nominal representation of affected-object. In addition to presenting the *observed* occurrence of different utterances, the *expected* occurrence within subcategories will be presented. Expected frequencies were determined from the overall proportion of different *syntactic* utterances imitated at each Time (see Table 2). The information presented here consists of the observed and expected occurrence of utterance types that were imitative or spontaneous, within categories and across time.

PETER I–VII   There were no productive categories (with productivity defined as five or more different utterances within a category) in Peter's speech samples at Times I and II. Several semantic–syntactic categories reached the criterion of productivity at Time III. As will be seen, the relative occurrence of imitative and spontaneous utterances at Time VI, when MLU was 1.75, forced the decision to consider the next sample, Time VII, when MLU was 2.39 and beyond the original limits of the study.

Four semantic–syntactic categories were Noncontrastive in Peter's speech. Table 5 shows that even for these categories there were some lexical differences in the subcategories. In addition, Peter did not develop syntactic negation in the time period discussed here. In the semantic–syntactic category Negation, only the subcategory Nonexistence was productive at Time VI, but dropped from productivity at Time VII.

Existence. In Peter's speech, reference to existence was made by utterances with a primitive form of "a" or "the" or a demonstrative pronoun (the subcategories /ə/ and "Dem" in Fig. 2) and a noun. There were few utterances with a demonstrative at Times III, IV, and V, and those that did occur were largely imitative. At Time V there were one spontaneous and 4 imitative utterances with a demonstrative. At Time VI

Table 5   Noncontrastive Semantic-Syntactic Categories: Peter, Times III-VII

Semantic-Syntactic Category	Number of Spontaneous and Imitative Utterance Types at Each time									
	III		IV		V		VI		VII	
	Sp	Im	Sp	Im	Sp	Im	Sp	Im	Sp	Im
Notice	3	1	2	1	—	2	9	4	6	3
Recurrence	15	2	14	5[a]	10	1	12	7[b]	31	3
Vocative	—	—	—	—	—	—	9	1	39	2
Manner	—	—	—	—	—	—	4	—	6	—
Action-Agent	—	—	8	3	4	1	9	4	29	7
Locative-Action-Mover	—	—	—	—	—	—	6	4	25	4

[a] Included three utterances with "too" or "some more" which did not also occur spontaneously.
[b] Included three utterances with "another" which only occurred once spontaneously, and three utterances with "too" which also occurred four times spontaneously.

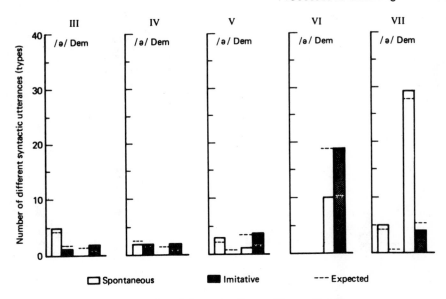

Figure 2. Existence. Peter, Times III–VII.

there were 10 spontaneous utterances with a demonstrative, but there were 19 utterances that were imitative, which greatly exceeded the expected frequency of imitative utterances given the proportion of syntactic imitation at Time VI. That is, inasmuch as 38% of all of Peter's different syntactic utterances at Time VI were imitative, the observed ratio of imitative to spontaneous occurrence was inversely

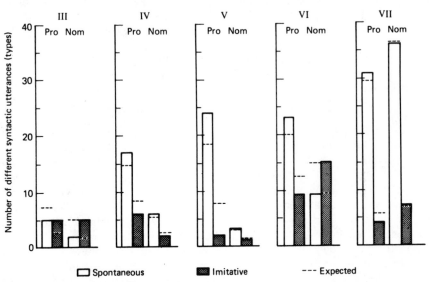

Figure 3. Action-on-Affected-Object. Peter, Times III–VII.

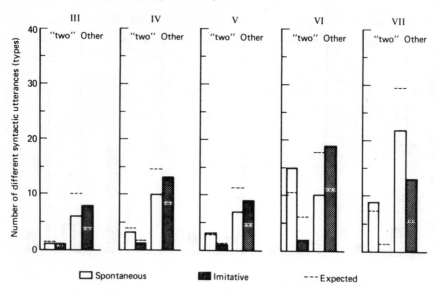

Figure 4.   Attribution, Peter, Times III–VII.

related to the expected ratio, in the Demonstrative subcategory. However, in the next sample at Time VII, the situation was reversed: only 4 utterances with a demonstrative were imitative, while 29 utterances occurred spontaneously, and the observed imitative to spontaneous ratio was in the expected direction, with the observed occurrence of imitation below expected occurrence.

Thus, there was a subcategory shift in the linguistic form of utterances specifying *Existence*, from imitative to spontaneous occurrence of demonstrative pronouns, between Times VI and VII. It can be concluded that Peter learned to use demonstrative pronouns to indicate *Existence* between Times VI and VII. The imitation data at Time VI provided evidence that he was in the process of learning the form, whereas the relation between imitative and spontaneous occurrence at Time VII indicated that he had learned it, to the extent that spontaneous use was an index of learning. Utterances with /ə/ occurred less often, and, except at Time IV, they were rarely imitative.

Action-on-Affected-Object. The most dramatic interaction between imitative and spontaneous speech took place in the category *Action-on-Affected-Object*, in which the subcategories were Pronominal ("Pro") and Nominal ("Nom") representation of Affected-Object. There were both a category shift and a subcategory shift from imitative to spontaneous occurrence. As can be seen in Fig. 3, there were 17 different utterances in the category at Time III, but there were more imitative than spontaneous utterances, and the observed ratio of imitative to spontaneous occurrence was inversely related to the expected imitative to spontaneous ratio. The category shift occurred between Time III, when it was concluded that Peter was learning to code the category, and Time IV, when it appeared that he had learned the category *Action-on-Affected-Object* since the observed and expected ratios of imitative to spontaneous occurrence were in the same direction. Subsequently, at Time V, it might be said that Peter consolidated his gains and used the pronoun "it" overwhelmingly to represent *Affected-Object* in the category *Action-on-Affected-Object*.

Attribution. The category *Attribution* (Fig. 4) presented a category shift over a longer time period, between Times III and VI. The subcategories were "two," in reference to two objects or a second object (there were a few utterances with "two" where there was not evidence of duality in the context, and these were not included in Fig. 4), and other attributive forms such as "big," "nice," "dirty," and "funny." While it was possible to conclude that Peter was learning attributive reference from Time III through Time V, the evidence of a category shift at Time VI consisted only of the fact that Peter had learned to use the word "two" to talk about exactly two objects or a second object, and he rarely imitated such utterances. However, the inverse relation between observed and expected occurrence of imitative and spontaneous utterances with other attributive forms continued from Time III through Time VI. Further, even though the observed and expected ratios of imitative to spontaneous occurrence with other attributives were in the same direction at Time VII, the observed frequency of imitative utterance types was still considerably greater than the expected frequency. It appears that, at Time VII, Peter had learned a single attributive form ("two") and no longer imitated that form, but he was still in the process of learning to use a class of other attributive forms for attributive reference at Time VII.

Locative Relations. Figures 5, 6, 7, and 8 present the interaction between spontaneous and imitative speech in the locative categories.

Whereas action verbs had been productive since Time III, locative-action verbs did not occur in multiword utterances until Time V. Utterances in the category *Place-of-Locative-Action* (with verb expressed), for example, "put there" or "put car," were

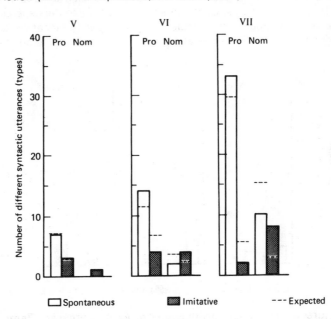

Figure 5.   Place-of-Locative Action, verb expressed. Peter, Times V–VII.

always more frequent than utterances in the category *Object-of-Locative-Action* (with verb expressed), for example, "put pretzel" or "put it." Thus, reference to affected-object was more likely to occur when Peter used an action verb than when he used a locative-action verb which could entail two complements: both affected-object and place. Both verb complements began to occur within a single utterance at Time VI, so that utterances counted at Times VI and VII in Figs. 5 and 6 were sometimes the same.

In addition to the categories *Place* (without a verb) and *Place-of-Locative-Action* (with a locative verb), there were also utterances which specified both place and affected-object with no verb expressed. Such utterances could be classified according to whether or not the locative relations between place and affected-object entailed movement—that is, the distinction between *State-Location-of-Object* (Fig. 8), for example, "chair right there," and *Action-Location-of-Object*, for example, "pencil down there" as Peter was putting a pencil on the floor. The two-place predicate complement with no verb expressed was far more frequent when the relation between place and affected object was stative than when an action (to bring about the relation) was involved. The category *Action-Location-of-Object* with no verb expressed was barely productive at Time VI and not productive at Time VII.

If there was a locative action involved, Peter expressed the locative verb (with place or affected-object) far more often than he expressed just place and affected-object. However, stative relations did not entail a verb form in Peter's utterances and he simply specified the place-object relationship. This distinction between action and stative relations does not appear to be strictly a linguistic constraint due to the absence of locative-state verbs. On the one hand, it points to the general absence in Peter's speech of the copula, which could be used to specify a locative-state relation. On the other hand, Peter did use locative-action verbs that, in the adult model, can

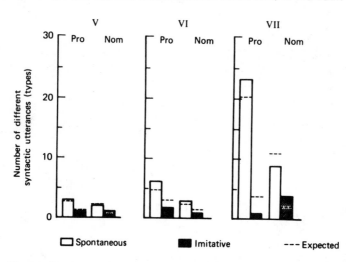

Figure 6. **Object-of-Locative-Action, verb expressed. Peter, Times V–VII.**

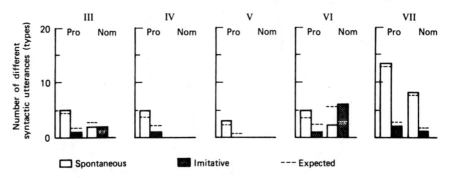

Figure 7. Place. Peter, Times III–VII.

also specify state relations. For example, one can refer to "sit" or "sitting" in both action and stative events. However, Peter did not. If he referred to the location of an object and specified both place and affected-object without a verb, the relation was a stative one rather than one entailing locative action.

New Categories at Time VI. The proportion of syntactic imitation in Peter's speech decreased markedly between Times VI and VII, (from .38 to .16). It might be argued

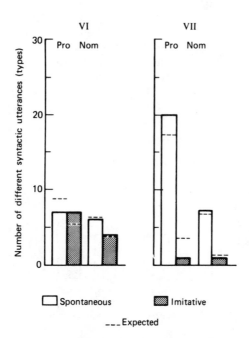

Figure 8. State-Location of Object, no verb expressed. "Pro" and "Nom" refer to Place. Peter, Times VI and VII.

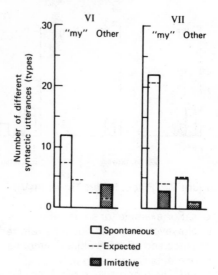

Figure 9. Possession. Peter, Times VI
and VII.

that the subcategory shifts that have been described did not have to do with semantic–syntactic learning as much as they were a function of the decrease in imitation
in general between Times VI and VII. However, as was seen with *Attribution* and
several of the locative relations, the observed frequency of imitation continued to be
greater than the expected frequency of imitation at Time VII. The interaction be-

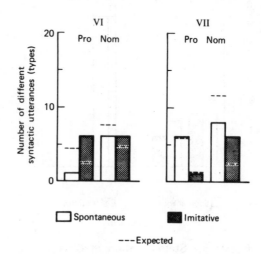

Figure 10. State-and-Causative-Object. Peter, Times VI and VII.

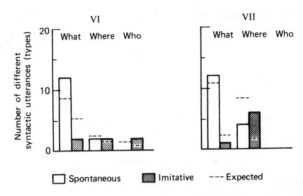

Figure 11.   Wh- Questions. Peter, Times VI and VII.

tween imitative and spontaneous speech continued with new categories that first appeared at Time VI, as can be seen in Figs. 9–11.

The data from Peter have demonstrated the interaction between imitative and spontaneous speech most explicitly: imitation occurred within semantic categories and with syntactic forms that were just emerging in grammatical competence. Peter did not imitate what he knew best and he did not imitate what he knew nothing about. Whenever imitation exceeded expectation, there were always spontaneous utterances within the same category or subcategory as well. Peter imitated utterances in just those categories which were to become fully productive at a subsequent time, but which were currently beyond his productive capacity. To that extent, imitation provided evidence of grammatical learning.

Peter imitated more than the other children. Furthermore, the Peter data were collected at three-week intervals so that it was possible to detect the developmental changes in his speech that might have been missed if data collection had been more widely spaced. However, the same interaction between imitative and spontaneous utterance types within certain categories was observed in Kathryn I and Jane I and II.

KATHRYN I   There were five semantic–syntactic categories that were Noncontrastive in Kathryn's speech. Table 6 shows that even for these categories there were lexical subcategory differences.[10] All other categories are represented in Table 7. As with Peter, the dominant semantic–syntactic category involved action. However, whereas in Peter's speech pronominal reference was always far more frequent than nominal reference and Peter progressed from pronominal to nominal reference from

---

[10] Data from 5 of the original 7.5 hr of interaction with Kathryn at Time I were processed for the following analysis, and for this reason the numbers of utterances within particular categories do not correspond to the account in Bloom (1970).

Table 6   Noncontrastive Semantic-Syntactic Categories: Kathryn, Time I

Semantic-Syntactic Category	Number of Spontaneous and Imitative Utterance Types	
	Sp	Im
Negation	8	2
State[a]	5	3
Existence[b]	24	6
Locative-State	4	3

[a]Spontaneous utterances included "want" and "tired"; imitative utterances included "happen" (2 instances) and "keep ə going."
[b]Three spontaneous utterances included "this" or "here"; all others included schwa, "/ə/".

Time III to Time VII, pronouns occurred rarely in Kathryn's speech and were imitative more often than spontaneous. Another difference between the two children was that *Action-Agent* was far more frequent at Kathryn I, when MLU was 1.32, than in

Table 7   Contrastive Semantic-Syntactic Categories: Kathryn, Time I

	Observed and Expected Occurrence of Spontaneous and Imitative Utterance Types							
	Subcategories							
	Pro				Nom			
Semantic-Syntactic Category	Sp		Im		Sp		Im	
	Obs	Exp	Obs	Exp	Obs	Exp	Obs	Exp
Action-Agent	1	2	2	1	12	8.6	1	4.4
Action-Aff. Obj.	1	2.6	3	1.4	21	19.1	8	9.9
Place	—	2	3	1	1	3.3	4.	1.7
Possession	1	2.6	3	1.4	8	9.2	6	4.8
Attribution	1	2	2	1	28	23.8	8	12.2
	"more"				"another"			
Recurrence[a]	13	8.6	—	4.4	2	4.6	5	2.4
	"Hi"				Notice verb			
Notice	4	2.6	—	1.4	3	5.9	6	3.1

[a]All occurrences of "another" and three occurrences of "more" specified another instance of an object while the first object was still present. The remaining ten occurrences of "more" specified a second object or event without the simultaneous presence of the first.

samples of Peter's speech with comparable MLU (see Bloom, Lightbown, & Hood, 1975, for further discussion of these differences).

JANE I AND II   There were four Nonconstrative Categories in Jane's speech and these are presented in Table 8. All other productive categories are represented in Fig. 12.

The data collected from Jane were the least satisfying for several reasons. First of all, her family moved away after the second session, so that it was not possible to follow development in those categories that were predominantly or only imitative at Time II. Second, even though 6 weeks elapsed between Times I and II, there was virtually no change in mean length of utterance and change in only 3 semantic–syntactic categories: the subcategory shift with *Action-on-Affected-Object,* and the appearance of two new categories at Time II, *Locative-State* and *Attribution.* Finally, there was a relatively large number of nonproductive categories—more than for Peter, Kathryn, or Eric—which left the impression that Jane had spread herself thin, trying to learn many things at once. However, as with Peter and Kathryn (at Time I), it was possible to conclude that Jane was indeed using imitation in processing information about the semantic–syntactic relations between words as she learned grammar.

ERIC I–IV   The data from Eric told a different story about the relation between imitative and spontaneous utterances: none of the semantic–syntactic categories was contrastive. As can be seen in Figs. 13 and 14, imitative occurrence in multiword utterances was relatively infrequent and essentially shadowed spontaneous occurrence. The observed and expected imitation in each category was virtually identical, in marked contrast to the differences between observed and expected imitation in the speech of the other children. This observed–expected convergence in Eric's syntactic speech was evidence that his imitative behavior was not motivated by his learning the semantic–syntactic structure of multiword utterances.

It has already been reported that Eric was apparently using imitation in the process of learning individual lexical items. It appears that Eric's imitation of multiword utterances was also lexically motivated. Individual words that occurred in imitative multiword utterances did not also occur in spontaneous multiword utterances. However,

Table 8   Noncontrastive Semantic-Syntactic Categories: Jane, Times I and II

| Semantic-syntactic category | Number of spontaneous and imitative utterance types at each time | | | |
| | I | | II | |
	Sp	Im	Sp	Im
Existence	5	—	3	—
Disappearance	2	1	4	2
Recurrence	2	3	2	3

the words in imitative multiword utterances occurred both spontaneously and imitatively as single-word utterances in the same sample. This parallels the finding that for the children whose imitation was evidence of semantic–syntactic learning, utterance types were imitative in semantic–syntactic categories only where there were spontaneous utterance types as well.

The difference between Peter and Eric in progression from imitative to spontaneous use of words reported earlier (the porgression occurred in single-word utterances for Peter and in multiword utterances for Eric) corresponded to the differences observed between them in the semantic–syntactic analysis. Peter apparently imitated words that he already knew in semantic–syntactic relations that he was in the process of learning. Eric, however, imitated words he did not yet know that occurred in the semantic–syntactic relations that he already was able to use spontaneously.

The semantic–syntactic categorization of utterances revealed that for Eric, as with the other children, imitation was never random, given the two results that (a) there was a difference between lexical items that were spontaneous and imitative in syntactic contexts, and (b) the overall proportion of imitation in his speech predicted the proportion of imitation within each semantic–syntactic category. Thus, Eric imitated new lexical items when they occurred in multiword utterances that encoded the same

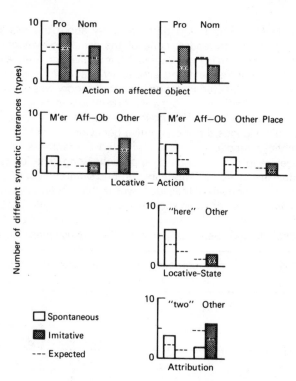

Figure 12. Semantic-syntactic categories. Jane, Times I and II.

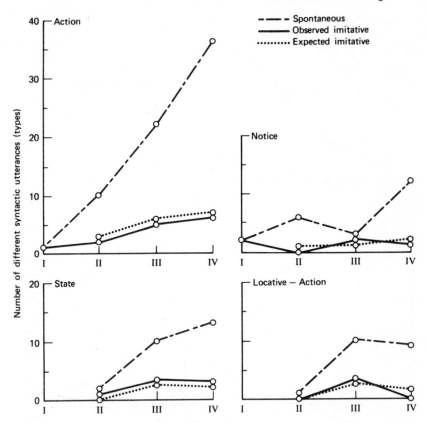

Figure 13.   Relative frequency of utterances with different verbs. Eric, Times
I–IV.

kind of knowledge about the world that was represented in his own utterances, and
it appeared that such knowledge structured his processing of linguistic and nonlinguistic information for learning new lexical items

IMITATION AND UTTERANCE LENGTH
When mean length of utterance values (for morphemes) were computed separately
for spontaneous and imitative utterances, two different trends appeared for imitating
and nonimitating children. For those samples where the overall proportion of imitation was less than .15, MLU was consistently higher for spontaneous utterances than
for imitative utterances. However, in those language samples where the overall proportion of imitation was greater than .15, the MLU of imitative utterances usually
equaled or exceeded the MLU of the spontaneous utterances. The claim that imitation had an important function in the language development of the children who
imitated does not require that imitative utterances be longer than spontaneous ones
—only that they be different and that the differences be related to developmental

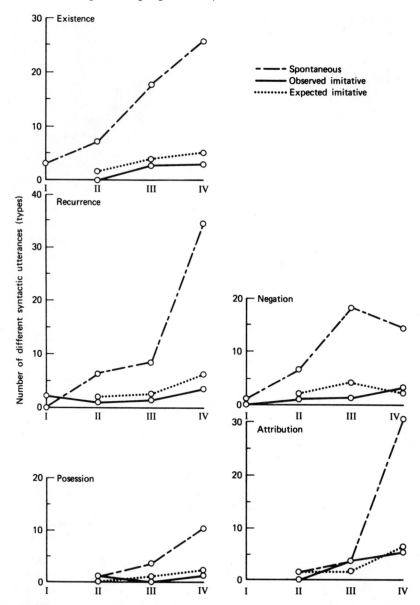

Figure 14. Relative frequency of utterances in semantic-syntactic categories without verbs. Eric, Times I–IV.

change. The lexical and semantic–syntatic analyses made it clear that these differences did exist. The longer MLU of the imitative speech simply represented a superficial index of such differences.

SUMMARY

In the syntactic speech of Kathryn at Time I, Jane, and Peter, certain categories and subcategories that were productive in spontaneous speech were imitated rarely, if at all. However, it was almost always the case that when observed imitation exceeded expected imitation within a category or subcategory, there were spontaneous utterance types as well—evidence that the children already knew something about what they were imitating. This result does not conflict with the earlier finding that different lexical items were only imitative or only spontaneous; both kinds of utterance types (lexical items and multiword) were either imitative or spontaneous, as indicated by the small number of Sp+Im in Table 2. However, the lexical analysis was based on token frequencies, whereas for multiword utterances the important analysis was the relative spontaneous and imitative occurrences of utterance types within semantic–syntactic categories. The categories included both spontaneous and imitative utterance types, but each multiword utterance type was either imitative or spontaneous.

Finally, the developmental interaction between imitative and spontaneous speech moved in the same direction—from imitative to spontaneous occurrence—for lexical items (in the speech of Peter and Eric) and grammatical structure (in the speech of Peter, Jane, and Kathryn). Once lexical items and semantic–syntactic categories and subcategories were observed to be predominantly spontaneous, they were never predominantly imitative in subsequent samples. Imitation appeared to function for learning the semantic–syntatic relations in multiword utterances for Peter, Jane, and Kathryn. However, in Eric's speech, the semantic–syntactic relations between words were not different in imitative and spontaneous utterances, and the motivation for imitation in Eric's speech was lexical. Lexical and grammatical imitation in the children's speech was developmentally progressive.

IMITATION AND LANGUAGE DEVELOPMENT

Before discussing the results of this study as evidence of information processing for language development, the results will be compared with two other studies that also examined and compared children's imitative and spontaneous utterances: Ervin-Tripp (1964) and Kemp and Dale (1973), and with other discussion of imitation in the literature.[11]

In the study by Ervin-Tripp, rules of grammar were proposed for the spontaneous utterances in the speech of five children who ranged in age from 22 to 34 months, and then the children's imitative utterances were examined to determine the extent to which they were consistent with the rules of grammar. In the speech of four of the children, both imitative and spontaneous utterances could be accounted for by the same rules. For the fifth child, imitative utterances were shorter and less complex than spontaneous utterances.[12] Ervin-Tripp concluded that imitation was not "grammati-

---

[11] Some of the issues in the present paper have also been discussed by Miyamoto (1973). Ryan (1973) has independently presented data that complement the data presented here, with strikingly similar interpretations and conclusions.

[12] If a child is imitating what he does not quite know, then his reproduction of such utterances might well be more fragmented and less "complete" than other speech, as was the case with a few of the samples from the imitating children in the present study.

cally progressive" for the five children. According to the examples of grammars, the rules on which the analysis was based were rules of *word order* in which three or more optional classes of words were ordered relative to a final required class. The optional classes included articles, demonstrative pronouns, attributives, certain verbs, and such words as "more" and "no." In some rules the final optional class was virtually identical to the required class, which included such words as noun forms and certain other attributives (for example, color names).[13] This result was consistent with the report by Brown and Fraser (1963) that both imitative and spontaneous child speech preserved the word order of the model language.

In the present study, rules of *word order* would not have differentiated between imitative and spontaneous utterances either. Demonstratives, articles, verbs, attributives, and such forms as "more" and "no" preceded object nouns in both kinds of speech. Thus, it was not so much the case that the results reported here were inconsistent with Ervin-Tripp's conclusions; rather, the analysis she reported was simply not sensitive enough to detect the differences that might have existed between the two kinds of utterances in her data.

Kemp and Dale (1973) embedded model sentences in the speech that they addressed to 30 children between the ages of 22 and 36 months during play. They interpreted two results as opposing: (1) since certain grammatical features which occurred in free speech were never imitated, they concluded that imitative speech was even less advanced than spontaneous speech; (2) on the other hand, since other grammatical features occurred in imitative utterances but not in free speech, then imitative speech could be grammatically progressive. The present study obtained similar results, but interpreted them as complementary aspects of the nature of imitation in language development.

TO IMITATE OR NOT TO IMITATE

The variation among the six children in this study with respect to *if* they imitated (their relative tendency to imitate) and *when* they imitated (the lexical and grammatical conditions that accompanied imitation) may point to at least part of the source of the confusion that has accumulated in the literature of the last century about the importance of imitation for language development. The more important theoretical issues have evolved about the central question of *why* some children imitate—how imitation may function as a process in language development.

Certain speculations that might explain why some children imitate in the first place cannot be resolved by the data or the results of this study. Such factors as parent–child interaction, personality, or intelligence might well have been important as predisposing factors that determined whether a child was or was not an imitator in the first place. As such, they would appear to be empirical issues that could be tested elsewhere. However, such factors are essentially passive influences on behavior—an individual's intelligence, personality, and parents are not self-determined. Thus, a child may not be able to control whether or not he is an imitator in the first place. But if he does imitate, it appears that *when* he will imitate and *why* are self-deter-

---

[13] More recently, Ervin-Tripp (personal communication) has reported that other grammars not discussed in the original report were more complex.

mined, to the extent that they are based upon what the child already knows and what he is in the process of learning.

IMITATION AS AN ACTIVE PROCESS

If certain model utterances had not been available for a child to imitate, then, obviously, they could not have appeared among his imitative utterances, and the fact that they did not occur would have been determined by the environment and not by the child. However, Peter had ample opportunity to imitate both pronominal and nominal reference to affected-objects at Time IV, as revealed by the following analysis. All of the *adult* utterances to Peter that (a) immediately preceded an utterance by Peter and (b) represented *Notice* or *Action-on-Affected-Object* were compared with Peter's subsequent utterances, for the first 2 hr (almost one-half) of the sample at Time IV. There were 45 adult utterances that met the criteria and 20 of these included pronouns as affected-object (2 with "one" and 18 with "it"). Peter imitated only one of these. In all other instances, he either said something related to the utterance or repeated a previous utterance. Yet in his spontaneous speech, pronominal reference occurred far more often than nominal reference. The fact that Peter did not imitate utterances with pronominal reference even though they were present in the environment was evidence that Peter determined what he did and did not imitate.

The fact that imitation is selective has been reported frequently, if not actually demonstrated, by Guillaume (1926), Valentine (1930), Jakobson (1968), Aronfreed (1969), and others. However, there have been different views of the factors that underlie the choice of what is imitated. On the one hand, if each time that a child imitates he affirms for himself the relation between a linguistic signal and its referent in a speech event, then one could say there is an intrinsic reinforcement that serves to maintain imitation behavior. In this case, the reward for imitation is learning—a conclusion that would be supported by the data presented here. On the other hand, it is frequently presumed that children repeat the speech that they hear because such behavior is rewarded by the environment. Several theories to explain language development have depended on such a chain of events whereby the child hears a stimulus, repeats it, and is reinforced by an adult in the situation who may smile, repeat it again, supply a referent, etc. (Allport, 1924; Mowrer, 1960; Jenkins & Palermo, 1964; Staats, 1971). While it may well be true that children enjoy whatever attention is given to imitating behavior, such pleasure and attention alone would not explain the systematic relationship between imitative and spontaneous utterances in the children's speech that was observed in this study.

The idea that a child's imitation is determined or shaped by reinforcement from the environment is another view of the child as essentially passive with respect to the forces that contribute to and maintain his behavior. Similarly, the view of language development that depends upon an independent cognitive structure for organizing linguistic input, such as the "language acquisition device" proposed by Chomsky (1965) and McNeill (1970), places the child in another kind of passive role. Both the behaviorist and the nativist positions result in the conclusion that the child is simply the victim of fate and circumstance in learning to talk. But, whatever the nature of the child's linguistic knowledge may be at any time, it appears that he adds to and changes that knowledge in relation to his experience. The results of this study have emphasized the active interaction of the child in language development: the children appeared to imitate as they processed linguistic and nonlinguistic input from the environment for information about language.

Piaget (1962) distinguished between early sensorimotor imitation in the first two years and later "representative" imitation that begins some time toward the end of the second year. During the sensorimotor period, according to Piaget, imitation is unconscious and comes about through the child's confusion between the movements of others and his own movements. Because the child is unable to differentiate between internal and external states, he cannot distinguish his own actions and movements from those that he sees. His sensorimotor imitations are provoked from "direct perceptions." An important change occurs at the end of the second year and continues into the early school years (to about age seven), as the reproduction of a model comes to be preceded by an "imaged representation" of it. It is this reproduction of an image of the model that is characterized by Piaget as "representative imitation" that is "deferred." Although the model is not perceptually present to the child, he necessarily has an image of the model in mind before he reproduces it.[14]

The imitation behavior in the present study would qualify as sensorimotor imitation as described by Piaget to the extent that the model utterances were perceptually present. Indeed, the operating definition of imitation depended upon "direct perception," even though perception and production were sequential (as was the case with the imitative behavior described by Piaget). However, the important result of this study of such perceptual imitation was that the children's behavior was discriminating in that they differentiated among stimuli in a highly systematic way. The imitating children discriminated, first, between their own linguistic behavior and the behavior of others and, second, among the different linguistic behaviors of others. That is, they imitated only words and structures in the speech that they heard which they appeared to be in the process of learning. They tended not to imitate words and structures that they themselves either used spontaneously and so presumably knew, or did not use spontaneously at all and so presumably did not know.

There are, to be sure, important limitations on the extent to which spontaneous use of a word or grammatical structure is an index of knowing the word or structure. However, spontaneous use provides evidence of the child's awareness of referential meanings. He uses the word or structure in reference to events that he already knows something about—events that are schematically represented in cognitive memory and coded for association with formal linguistic representations by semantic schemas, and further levels of meaning would develop as the capacities for mental representation of information increase. One might expect a child to again imitate a word that he knows only in its referential sense, when he hears it in a new sense or in a less literal or more complex reference—as in a metaphor or a more complex grammatical structure.

Behavior that occurs in the presence of a perceptual model would appear to involve altogether different processes from those involved with behavior that follows from a mental representation. If the child's behavior is based on a mental representation, then the mechanism by which the original model was represented in memory,

---

[14] Piaget discussed linguistic imitation only in the context of imitation in general as it functions in the development of symbolic thought.

as well as mechanisms of retrieval and variation of the model in the contexts of different situations, must be accounted for. Such behavior presupposes processing of the original model behavior, which is precisely what the present study has described. The interaction between imitative and spontaneous utterances within semantic–syntactic categories indicated that the children processed linguistic signals in relation to nonlinguistic states of affairs when they perceived and reproduced utterances that referred to objects, events, and relations that they knew something about. Some semantic processing of the signal had already taken place then before imitation of it occurred. Imitative behavior was not merely acoustic or an automatic echoing of random linguistic events.

When a child imitated an adult utterance he must have already processed it to the extent that he recognized that some aspect of the utterance was in that grey area of what he knew about language—it was not entirely new to him nor already in his productive competence. This level of processing (P) involved recognition of partial relationships among an aspect of utterance form, an aspect of the situation, and some information about form and content already in cognitive memory. Utterances and event contexts were processed in relation to emerging semantic–syntactic schemas. Imitating the utterance allowed the child to experience encoding a state of affairs with the perceptual support of a relevant message. Such supported encoding was a further processing (P') of linguistic form and content that added information for the mapping of conceptual schemas onto semantic–syntactic schemas in cognitive memory. Evidence of such a second level processing was the fact that spontaneous use increased as imitation decreased—evidence that such processing through imitation might have functioned in achieving spontaneous use.

There were, of course, levels of processing before the processing (P) described here. The children had to take in information about novel utterances and new situations in order to arrive at the ability to recognize their relationship to conceptual schemas (and, indeed, in order to form such conceptual schemas). A more extended theoretical discussion of how such levels of processing contribute to the development of both comprehension and production is presented in Bloom (1974).

In conclusion, it appears that when and why the imitating child would imitate depended upon what he already knew about the behavior presented to him. The important facts were that the children imitated neither linguistic signals that were already well-known to them nor structures that were completely absent from their own spontaneous speech. Peter imitated relatively new semantic–syntactic structures that included words that he used spontaneously elsewhere; Eric imitated new words only when they occurred in the same semantic–syntactic structures as were represented in his spontaneous speech. Similarly, in the study by Shipley, Smith and Gleitman (1969), the novel (nonsense) words that seemed to precipitate imitation were embedded in standard sentence frames and in familiar contexts. The conclusion by Fraser, Bellugi and Brown (1963) that imitation precedes comprehension and production in development was not supported. Rather, the results confirmed the observations of Preyer (1882), Guillaume (1926), Valentine (1930), and others that the child imitates only what he is already able to understand to some extent. Piaget (1954) observed that imitation is always a continuation of understanding.

One might explain imitation as a form of encoding that continues the processing of information that is necessary for the representation of linguistic schemas (both semantic and syntactic) in cognitive memory. In the imitation context, the child has the perceptual support of a model utterance relative to events which, while recognized, are only partially mapped onto linguistic schemas in cognitive memory. Imitating the model utterance provides experience in encoding the relevant aspects of the situation to which the utterance refers, so that the mapping or coding relation between form and content can be affirmed. Although the imitation behavior observed in this study provided evidence of such active processing of linguistic and nonlinguistic information for learning the relation between the form of speech and the nonlinguistic states of affairs to which it refers, it was not clear that the imitation behavior was necessary for such information processing. Further, it was apparent that some processing of the same kind of information input is possible without such supported encoding, certainly for the nonimitating children and perhaps for the imitating children as well.

REFERENCES

Allport, F. W. *Social psychology*. Boston: Houghton-Mifflin, 1924.

Aronfreed, J. The problem of imitation. In L. Lipsitt & H. Reese (Eds.), *Advances in child development and behavior*. Vol. 4. New York: Academic Press, 1969. Pp. 210–319.

Bellugi, U., & Brown, R. (Eds.) The acquisition of language. *Monograph of the Society for Research in Child Development*, 1964, **29.**

Bloch, O. Les premiers stades du langage de l'enfant. *Journal de Psychologie*, 1921, **18,** 693–712.

Bloom, L. *Language development: Form and function in emerging grammars*. Doctoral dissertation, Columbia University, 1968. Cambridge, MA: The MIT Press, 1970.

Bloom, L. *One word at a time: The use of single-word utterances before syntax*. The Hague: Mouton, 1973.

Bloom, L. Talking, understanding and thinking. In R. Schiefelbusch and L. Lloyd (Eds.), *Language perspective—acquisition, retardation, and intervention*. Baltimore, MD: University Park Press, 1974.

Bloom, L., Lightbrown, P., & Hood, L. Structure and variation in child language. Manuscript, 1974.

Braine, M. D. S. The acquisition of language in infant and child. In C. Reed (Ed.), *The learning of language*. New York: Appleton-Century-Crofts, 1971. Pp. 7–86.

Brown, R. The first sentences of child and chimpanzee. In R. Brown, *Psycholinguistics*. New York: Free Press, 1970. Pp. 208–234.

Brown, R., & Fraser, C. The acquisition of syntax. In C. N. Cofer & B. Musgrave (Eds.), *Verbal behavior and learning: Problems and processes*. New York: McGraw-Hill, 1963. Pp. 158–197.

Chomsky, N. Review of 'Verbal behavior' by B. F. Skinner. *Language*, 1959, **35**(1), 26–58.

Chomsky, N. *Syntactic structures*. The Hague: Mouton, 1957.

Chomsky, N. *Aspects of the theory of syntax*. Cambridge, MA: The MIT Press, 1965.

Dixon, T., & Horton, D. *Verbal behavior and general behavior theory*. Englewood Cliffs, NJ: Prentice-Hall, 1968.

Ervin-Tripp, S. Imitation and structural change in children's language. In E. H. Lenneberg (Ed.), *New directions in the study of language*. Cambridge, MA: The MIT Press, 1964. Pp. 163–189.

Fraser, C., Bellugi, U., & Brown, R. Control of grammar in imitation, comprehension and production. *Journal of Verbal Learning and Verbal Behavior*, 1963, **2,** 121–135.

Guillaume, P. *Imitation in children*. Chicago: University of Chicago Press, 1968.

Harvard University, Staff of the Computation Laboratory. *Tables of the cumulative binomial probability distribution.* Cambridge, MA: Harvard University Press, 1955.

Jakobson, R. *Child language, aphasia and phonological universals.* The Hague: Mouton, 1968.

Jenkins, J., & Palermo, D. Mediation processes and the acquisition of linguistic structure. In U. Bellugi & R. Brown (Eds.). *The acquisition of language. Monograph of the Society for Research in Child Development,* 1964, **29.**

Jespersen, O. *Language: Its nature, development, and origin.* London: George Allen and Unwin, 1922.

Kemp, J., & Dale, P. Spontaneous imitation and free speech: A developmental comparison. Paper presented at the biennial meeting of the Society for Research in Child Development, Philadelphia, April 1973.

Kirkpatrick, E. A. *Genetic psychology.* New York: Macmillan, 1909.

Leopold, W. F. *Speech development of a bilingual child.* Vol. 3. Evanston, IL: Northwestern University Press, 1949.

Lewis, M. M. *Infant speech, a study of the beginnings of language.* New York: Humanities Press, 1951.

McNeill, D. *The acquisition of language: The study of developmental psycholinguistics.* New York: Harper and Row, 1970.

Meumann, E. *Die sprache des kindes.* Zurich, 1903.

Miyamoto, J. Imitation and the learning of grammatical rules. In *Papers from the ninth regional meeting,* Chicago Linguistic Society, 1973, 398–409.

Mowrer, O. H. *Learning theory and the symbolic processes.* New York: Wiley, 1960.

Piaget, J. *The construction of reality in the child.* New York: Ballantine Books, 1954.

Piaget, J. *Play, dreams and imitation in childhood.* New York: W. W. Norton, 1962.

Preyer, W. History of the development of speech, excerpt from *Die Sprache des Kindes,* (1882). In A. Bar-Adon & W. Leopold (Eds.), *Child language: A book of readings.* Englewood Cliffs, NJ: Prentice-Hall, 1971. Pp. 29–31.

Rodd, L., & Braine, M. D. S. Children's imitations of syntactic constructions as a measure of linguistic competence. *Journal of Verbal Learning and Verbal Behavior,* 1971, **10,** 430–443.

Ryan, J. Interpretation and imitation in early language development. In R. A. Hinde and J. Stevenson-Hinde (Eds.), *Constraints on learning.* New York: Academic Press, 1973. Pp. 427–443.

Shipley, E., Smith, C., & Gleitman, L. A study in the acquisition of language: Free responses to commands. *Language,* 1969, **45,** 322–342.

Sinclair, H. Sensorimotor action patterns as a condition for the acquisition of syntax. In R. Huxley & E. Ingram (Eds.), *Language acquisition: Models and methods.* New York: Academic Press, 1971. Pp. 121–130.

Slobin, D. I. Imitation and grammatical development in children. In N. Endler, L. Boulter, & H. Osser (Eds.), *Contemporary issues in developmental psychology.* New York: Holt, Rinehart & Winston, 1968.

Slobin, D. I. (Ed.). *The ontogenesis of grammar: Some facts and several theories.* New York: Academic Press, 1971.

Slobin, D. I., & Welsh, C. A. Elicited imitation as a research tool in developmental psycholinguistics. In C. A. Ferguson & D. I. Slobin (Eds.), *Studies of child language development.* New York: Holt, Rinehart & Winston, 1973. Pp. 485–497.

Smith, F., & Miller, G. (Eds.). *The genesis of language.* Cambridge, MA: The MIT Press, 1966.

Staats, A. W. Linguistic–mentalistic theory versus an explanatory S-R learning theory of language development. In D. I. Slobin (Ed.), *The ontogenesis of grammar.* New York: Academic Press, 1971. Pp. 103–150.

Thorndike, E. L. *The original nature of man.* New York: Teachers College, Columbia University, 1913.

Valentine, C. W. The psychology of imitation with special reference to early childhood. *Journal of Psychology,* 1930, **21,** 105–132.

Mothers' Speech To Children Learning Language
Catherine E. Snow

The assumption that language acquisition is relatively independent of the amount and kind of language input must be assessed in light of information about the speech actually heard by young children. The speech of middle-class mothers to 2-year-old children was found to be simpler and more redundant than their speech to 10-year-old children. The mothers modified their speech less when talking to children whose responses they could not observe, indicating that the children played some role in eliciting the speech modifications. Task difficulty did not contribute to the mothers' production of simplified, redundant speech. Experienced mothers were only slightly better than nonmothers in predicting the speech-style modifications required by young children. These findings indicate that children who are learning language have available a sample of speech which is simpler, more redundant, and less confusing than normal adult speech.

The speech young children hear is their only source of information about the language they are to learn. As such, it must be taken into account in any attempt to explain the process of language acquisition. Despite its unquestioned importance for language learning, very little is actually known about the kind of language which is addressed to children. Developmental psycholinguists have assumed that children hear a random sample of adult utterances, characterized by all the stutters, mistakes, garbles, inconsistencies, and complexities which are common in adults' speech to other adults (Chomsky 1965, 1968; Lenneberg 1969; McNeill 1970). This assumption about the primary linguistic data has been offered as a key bit of evidence in support of the view that infants must be largely preprogrammed for the task of language learning.

Considering the theoretical importance of the child's early linguistic environment, not only to students of language acquisition, but also to those trying to explain social

From *Child Development* 1972, **43,** pp. 549–565. Reprinted by permission of the Society for Research in Child Development, Inc.

This paper is based on a doctoral dissertation submitted to McGill University. The author wishes to thank Dr. M. Sam Rabinovitch, thesis advisor, for his help, and Dr. Ellis Olim for making available the Language Styles Scoring Manual, from which several of the measures used in the present experiments were borrowed or adapted. The author was supported by a National Science Foundation graduate fellowship during the time the research was completed. Author's current address: Institute for General Linguistics, University of Amsterdam, Spui 21, Amsterdam.

class differences in linguistic ability (Bernstein 1970; Hess & Shipman 1965; Olim 1970), it seemed valuable to study the language actually heard by young children. Accordingly, the present experiments were performed in order to investigate: (a) whether the speech of mothers to children just learning to talk differed from the speech of those same mothers to older children, (b) whether speech-style modifications for young children depended on the presence of the child with the mother, as opposed to the mother's mere intention to address a 2-year-old, (c) whether the difficulty of the tasks for the child affected the mother's production of speech-style modifications, and (d) whether nonmothers differed from mothers in their ability to modify their speech for young children.

EXPERIMENTAL INVESTIGATIONS

SUBJECTS
The women who served as subjects were all college graduates who volunteered after being contacted through their alumni association. The women were told that the experiments dealt with "how children learn to talk." Apparently none of them suspected that her own speech and not the child's behavior was of primary interest. Twelve of the women tested had children in the age range 9;5 to 12;4. These children participated with their mothers in experiment 1, serving as the stimulus children for the 10-year-old condition. Twenty-four of the subjects had children ranging in age from 2;0 to 3;4. Twelve of these mothers and their children participated in experiment 1; and 12, in experiment 2. Six women who had no children and who were not frequently in the company of children participated in experiment 3.

SCORING PROCEDURE
Tape recordings of all experimental sessions were transcribed, and scoring of the following nine measures was done on the typewritten transcriptions.

1. Quantity of speech: total number of words spoken.
2. Mean length of utterance: ratio of the total number of words spoken to the total number of utterances. Utterances were scored by listening to the tapes and marking the transcriptions as indicated by the phonetic cues and pauses in the mothers' speech. Run-on sentences were scored as two or more utterances. Phrases and sentence fragments were accepted as utterances if they were characterized by a complete intonation pattern. Thus, what was scored as a complete utterance often was not a complete sentence as defined by traditional grammar.
3. Sentence complexity: ratio of the number of compound verbs plus subordinate clauses to the total number of utterances.
4. Mean preverb length: ratio of the total number of words before the main verb in all clauses to the total number of clauses. Imperatives were excluded from both these counts.

5. Incidence of utterances without verbs: ratio of the number of utterances that did not contain verbs to the total number of utterances.
6. Incidence of third-person pronouns: ratio of the total number of occurrences of the pronouns *he, she, it, they, him, her, them, his, her, hers, its, their,* and *theirs* to the total number of words.
7. Incidence of complete repetitions: ratio of the number of complete repetitions of sentences (i.e., utterances which contain both subject and verb) to the total number of utterances. Repetitions were scored only if they occurred within three utterances of the original.
8. Incidence of partial repetitions: ratio of the number of repetitions of one or more major units within an utterance (e.g., repetition of the subject phrase or a subordinate clause) or of an entire utterance without a verb to the total number of utterances. If all major units were repeated, a complete repetition was scored. If only some of the units were repeated, a partial repetition was scored. Again, the repetition was scored only if it occurred within three utterances of the original.
9. Incidence of semantic repetitions: ratio of the number of repetitions of the meaning of a previous utterance which did not include repetition of any of its grammatical units to the number of utterances. An utterance was scored as a semantic repetition only if it was a true paraphrase and did not qualify as a complete or partial repetition. The repetition was scored only if it occurred within three utterances of the original.

Measures 1–6 were simple counting procedures and were scored in all cases by the experimenter. Since measures 7, 8, and 9 involved some subjective judgment, an independent observer also scored these. The reliability coefficients for the experimenter and the independent judge ranged from .7 to .9 and were in all cases highly significant, so a mean of the two scores was assigned as the subject's score.

EXPERIMENT 1

The primary purpose of experiment 1 was to investigate whether mothers modified their speech styles when addressing young children. Second, the absence or presence of the child in the room with the mother was varied in an attempt to separate the effects of the mothers' expectations about the linguistic capabilities of young children from the effects of any implicit demands the children might make on the adult speakers.

METHOD.   Appointments were scheduled so that a mother of a 2-year-old came to the laboratory with her child at the same time as a mother of a 10-year-old came with her child. Each of the two mothers then performed three verbal tasks with both children. In addition to performing the tasks with the child of either age group actually present in the room, the mother was asked to perform the tasks while speaking into a tape recorder in the absence of the child, but as if she were speaking to a child of the appropriate age group. Thus, each mother performed the tasks four times, with an absent 2-year-old, a present 2-year-old, an absent 10-year-old, and a present 10-year-old. The three tasks consisted of (*a*) making up and telling a story to the child, based on a picture provided by the experimenter, (*b*) telling the child how to sort a number of small plastic toys in several ways, and (*c*) explaining a physical phenomenon to the child. The speech during the three tasks was pooled for scoring. Half the mothers performed the tasks first with their own children, and half performed the tasks first with a 2-year-old. All the mothers performed the absent condition for each age before the present condition for that age. The experimenter was not present during any of the testing.

RESULTS.   Each measure was analyzed separately with a three-way analysis of variance. A small number of missing scores which resulted from mechanical failure of the tape recorder or from recalcitrance among the 2-year-olds were estimated using the procedure described in Winer (1962), so that an analysis for repeated measures could be applied. Degrees of freedom were subtracted from the error terms to compensate for the effects of estimation. The groups factor (mothers of 2-year-olds versus mothers of 10-year-olds) yielded no significant differences, so the two groups will be considered together in discussion of the results. Whenever the analysis of variance showed overall significance, cell means within the presence and age factors were compared using Scheffé (1953) tests.

The analysis of variance for quantity of speech indicates that mothers talked longer when a child was present in the room and that mothers talked longer to 2-year-olds than to 10-year-olds (see Table 1). The age × presence interaction was significant, reflecting a much greater effect of the presence of the child in the 2-year-old than in the 10-year-old condition. Results of the Scheffé tests (indicated by lines between the cell means in table 1) show that the 2-year-old present condition was significantly different from all the others, and that the 10-year-old present condition was significantly different from the 10-year-old absent condition. The primary reason for quantity-of-speech differences was probably the greater difficulty of the tasks for the younger children and the greater interest of the tasks for the mothers in the present condition.

Mean length of utterance, sentence complexity, and mean preverb length are all measures of the grammatical complexity of speech. In each case, a higher score indicates more complex speech. For every measure, the absent condition elicited more complex speech than the present condition, and the 10-year-olds elicited more complex speech than the 2-year-olds. All the differences were significant except the difference between the 2-year-old and the 10-year-old conditions for mean preverb length, which approached significance. Mean preverb length and sentence complexity showed significant age × presence interactions; both these interactions reflect a much greater difference between present and absent scores in the 2-year-old than in the 10-year-old condition. Scheffé tests for all three measures show an identical pattern; there were no significant differences among the 2-year-old absent, 10-year-old absent, and 10-year-old present conditions, but all of these differed significantly from the 2-year-old present condition. On every measure of complexity, the speech produced in the 2-year-old present condition was significantly simpler than that produced in any other condition.

Table 1   Results of Three-Way Analyses of Variance and Scheffè Tests, Experiment 1

	Means		ANOVA Significant Effects		
Measures	2-Year-Olds	10-Year-Olds	Age	Presence	Age X Presence
Quantity of Speech:					
Absent	426.7	:390.0	.01	.01	.05
Present	1448.2	:861.2			
Mean length of utterance:					
Absent	9.839	11.245	.01	.01	—
Present	6.596	9.633			
Sentence complexity:					
Absent	0.473	0.543	.01	.01	.05
Present	0.189	0.464			
Mean preverb length:					
Absent	2.685	2.594	—	.01	.01
Present	2.044	2.448			
Utterances without verbs:					
Absent	0.074	0.043	.05	.01	—
Present	0.165	0.121			
Third-person pronouns:					
Absent	0.049	0.062	.01	.01	—
Present	0.039	0.051			
Complete repetitions:					
Absent	0.008	0.003	.01	.01	—
Present	0.029	0.007			
Partial repetitions:					
Absent	0.284	0.138	.01	.01	—
Present	0.157	0.105			
Semantic repetitions:					
Absent	0.059	0.032	.01	.01	.05
Present	0.136	0.049			

Note.—Scheffé test results are indicated by lines between cell means:
——, p < .01; . . . ., p < .05.

All three repetition measures showed significant age and presence effects. In all cases, mothers made more repetitions to 2-year-olds than to 10-year-olds. Also, complete repetitions and semantic repetitions occurred more frequently in the present than in the absent condition. Scheffé tests for these two repetition measures show the same pattern as for the complexity measures: more repetitions occurred in the 2-year-old present condition than in any other condition, and the other conditions did not differ from one another. This pattern is confirmed by the significant age ×

presence interaction for semantic repetitions. However, the results for the presence factor were reversed for incidence of partial repetitions; there were more partial repetitions in the absent condition than in the present condition. Scheffé tests indicate that there were more partial repetitions in the 2-year-old absent condition than in any other condition. The 2-year-old present condition also elicited more partial repetitions than the 10-year-old present condition. The production of more partial repetitions in the absent condition indicates that mothers predicted the need for this kind of repetition, though they were unable to predict the need for complete repetitions, paraphrases, or grammatical simplification. Why this should be the case is unclear.

Significantly fewer third-person pronouns were used in the present and in the 2-year-old conditions. Scheffé tests indicate that fewer third-person pronouns were used in the 2-year-old present condition than in either 10-year-old condition, and fewer were used in the 2-year-old absent than in the 10-year-old absent condition. Mothers tended to repeat nouns, especially subject and direct object nouns, when speaking to 2-year-olds rather than substituting pronouns for them.

Incidence of utterances without verbs was higher in the 2-year-old condition and in the present condition. Scheffé tests show that the 2-year-old present condition elicited more utterances without verbs than either absent condition, and the 10-year-old present condition elicited more utterances without verbs than the 10-year-old absent condition. This suggests that mothers did not maintain formal correctness in their speech to 2-year-olds. Rather, they produced sentence fragments, many of which were repetitions of phrases from preceding sentences.

Cell means for measures which showed significant groups $\times$ age interactions are given in Table 2. These interactions can perhaps best be understood as differences between mothers talking to their own children and strangers' children. The interaction for quantity of speech occurred because mothers of 2-year-olds talked more to their own children than to the older children, while mothers of 10-year-olds talked about the same amount to both groups of children. The two complexity measures, mean length of utterance and sentence complexity, reveal that mothers of 2-year-olds used less complex language when speaking to the younger children and more complex language when speaking to the older children than did the mothers of 10-year-olds. The mothers of 10-year-olds simplified their speech somewhat for 2-year-olds but also spoke more simply to the 10-year-olds than did the other group of mothers. In general, it seems that the mothers of 2-year-olds were more sensitive than the mothers of 10-year-olds to the demands for simplified speech made by 2-year-old children.

EXPERIMENT 2

Experiment 2 was performed with two purposes in mind. The first was to confirm the results found for the presence factor in experiment 1. The procedure for the absent condition was changed somewhat in an attempt to motivate the mothers maximally to produce the speech modifications. The second purpose was systematically to vary task difficulty to ensure that the differences between the 2-year-old and 10-year-old

Table 2   Cell Means for the Measures Which Showed Groups X Age
Interactions in Experiment 1

| Measures and Condition | Means | | Significance Level |
	Mothers of 2-Year-Olds	Mothers of 10-Year-Olds	
Quantity of speech:			
2-year-old	1084.7	790.2	.05
10-year-old	567.7	680.8	
Mean length of utterance:			
2-year-old	7.833	8.603	.01
10-year-old	11.399	9.479	
Sentence complexity:			
2-year-old	0.284	0.379	.01
10-year-old	0.578	0.429	

conditions found in experiment 1 were not simply a result of greater difficulty of the
tasks for the 2-year-olds.

METHOD   Each of 12 mothers performed a number of tasks with her own 2-year-old
child. In the first task, called block selection, the mother described a specific block
(chosen by the experimenter) in terms of its size, its color, and the animal(s) pictured
on it. The child had to pick out the block described from among a group of several
similar blocks. The easy level of the task consisted of finding a small block with only
one animal pictured on it from among 12 alternatives; the difficult level consisted of
finding a large block with two animals pictured on it from among 24 alternatives. In
the pattern-construction task, the mother described a pattern composed of light and
dark wooden blocks of different sizes and shapes so that the child could reproduce
the pattern with the blocks. In the easy task, the pattern consisted of five or six easily
described blocks; in the difficult task the pattern consisted of 14–16 blocks, including
shapes for which the children had no names. Each mother performed an easy and a
difficult version of each task with her child in both the absent and the present condition. To ensure maximum similarity of the absent and present conditions, the mothers
were warned that the tapes made in the absent condition would actually be played
to the children, and this was done. Half the mothers performed the absent condition
first and half performed the present condition first. The mothers scored the children's
responses in all the tasks; the experimenter was not present during the testing.

RESULTS   Each measure was analyzed separately with a two-way analysis of variance. The two tasks were analyzed separately because of the problem of ranking
difficulty within the two disparate tasks. The cell means and levels of significance for
the analyses of variance are given in Table 3.
    In general, the findings for the presence factor were the same as those of experi-

ment 1, except that some of the measures which showed an absent-present difference in experiment 1 no longer showed this difference under the more rigorous
conditions of experiment 2. As predicted from experiment 1, quantity of speech was
greater in the present condition. Significantly less complex speech occurred in the
present condition in the pattern-construction task, as reflected in mean length of
utterance and mean preverb length. For the block-selection task, however, only mean
length of utterance decreased significantly in the present condition. Results for repetition measures were similar to those obtained in experiment 1. Complete repetitions
increased in the present condition, and partial repetitions decreased. There were no
significant differences for semantic repetitions. Whereas incidence of third-person
pronouns, incidence of utterances without verbs, and incidence of semantic repetitions showed presence effects in experiment 1, these were not affected by the
absence of the child in experiment 2. Thus, it seems that experienced mothers under
properly motivating conditions can predict to some extent what kinds of speech
modifications their children will require. They can produce speech in the absent
condition which is in some ways similar to their normal speech to children, but the
presence of the child remains a potent factor in eliciting still more extensive modifications.

The difficulty factor had only scattered effects, as indicated by the fact that for any
given measure the difficulty factor was never significant for both tasks. As might be
expected, quantity of speech increased with more difficult problems. This was only
true for the pattern-construction task, however, where greater difficulty was partly a
function of the need for more steps to solve the problem. Of the speech-complexity
measures, sentence complexity increased in the difficult condition in the pattern-
construction task, and mean preverb length increased in the difficult condition in the
block-selection task. Mean length of utterance tended to increase in the difficult
condition in the pattern-construction task, but this difference did not reach statistical
significance. If the mothers in experiment 1 were responding to the children's difficulty with the tasks, they would be expected to have simplified their speech in the
difficult condition; instead they produced more complex speech in this condition,
suggesting that it was in fact the children's linguistic immaturity that was crucial in
stimulating the mothers' speech modifications.

No repetition measures showed any difficulty effects in either of the tasks. Incidence of third-person pronouns decreased in the difficult condition only in the block-
selection task. Incidence of utterances without verbs was not affected by difficulty.

The only presence × difficulty interaction effect occurred for incidence of partial
repetitions in the block-selection task. Mothers produced more partial repetitions in
the difficult condition if the child was absent, but not if the child was present to offer
some feedback about the kind of information needed.

EXPERIMENT 3

In experiment 3, the speech of highly motivated mothers in the absent condition was
compared to the speech of nonmothers who had had very little experience with
children. This was done in order to determine whether their past experience in talking
to children had taught the mothers who served as subjects in experiments 1 and 2
anything about the speech modifications that young children require.

METHOD. Nonmothers were asked to make stimulus tapes for 2-year-old children, for use in "an experiment in cognitive development." They recorded instructions, only in the absent-condition, for the same tasks as used in experiment 2. These tapes were compared to absent-condition data collected from mothers in experiment 2.

RESULTS. The most striking finding was the general absence of differences be-

Table 3   Results of Two-Way Analyses of Variance in Experiment 2

| | Means | | | | ANOVA Significant Effects | | |
| | Absent | | Present | | | | Presence X |
Measures and Task[a]	Easy	Difficult	Easy	Difficult	Presence	Difficulty	Difficulty
Quantity of speech:							
A	147.2	148.9	321.0	269.0	.05	—	—
B	181.6	631.3	398.8	889.2	.05	.01	—
Mean length of utterance:							
A	8.555	8.497	6.314	6.037	.01	—	—
B	9.851	10.180	6.497	6.749	.01	—	—
Sentence complexity:							
A	0.214	0.163	0.118	0.104	—	—	—
B	0.195	0.246	0.126	0.171	—	.05	—
Mean preverb length:							
A	2.111	2.353	2.003	2.101	—	.01	—
B	2.260	2.598	2.204	2.242	.01	—	—
Utterances without verbs:							
A	0.163	0.247	0.212	0.213	—	—	—
B	0.159	0.122	0.191	0.176	—	—	—
Third-person pronouns:							
A	0.052	0.029	0.044	0.025	—	.01	—
B	0.039	0.034	0.034	0.046	—	—	—
Complete repetitions:							
A	0.030	0.022	0.055	0.087	.05	—	—
B	0.042	0.031	0.057	0.085	.05	—	—
Partial repetitions:							
A	0.259	0.325	0.164	0.134	.01	—	.05
B	0.273	0.208	0.182	0.143	.05	—	—
Semantic repetitions:							
A	0.016	0.027	0.015	0.022	—	—	—
B	0.047	0.030	0.026	0.013	—	—	—

[a] Task A denotes the block-selection task; task B denotes the pattern-construction task.

tween the speech of mothers and nonmothers (see Table 4). Only quantity of speech, mean length of utterance, and incidence of utterances without verbs showed significant differences; in the first two cases nonmothers' scores were higher, in the last case, lower. Inspection of the protocols reveals that nonmothers' speech was more detailed, precise, and formal-sounding than mothers' speech. Nonmothers' speech was also more complex and less repetitive, but not significantly so.

The difficulty factor produced three differences. Quantity of speech increased in the difficult condition, as it had in experiment 2. Mean length of utterance was significantly greater in the difficult condition in both tasks. Comparison of easy and difficult conditions for the other complexity measures indicates that, although the differences were not significant, almost all of them were in the direction of greater complexity in the difficult condition. There were significantly more partial repetitions in the difficult condition in the block-selection task. However, in the pattern-construction task, there were fewer partial repetitions in the difficult condition, although this was not a significant difference. No other repetition measures showed any difficulty effects.

There were two significant groups × difficulty interaction effects. The increase in quantity of speech in the difficult condition in the pattern-construction task was much greater for nonmothers than for mothers. Mothers' mean length of utterance decreased slightly in the difficult condition in the block-selection task, while nonmothers' mean length of utterance increased substantially. In both cases, the difference between the conditions affected the nonmothers more than it affected the mothers.

DISCUSSION

To recapitulate the findings of the present experiments: (a) mothers' speech to young children was simpler and more redundant than their normal speech, (b) these modifications in mothers' speech styles depended to some extent on the reactions of the child being addressed, (c) task difficulty did not contribute to the mothers' production of simplified, redundant speech, and (d) experienced mothers were only slightly better than nonmothers in predicting the speech-style modifications required by young children.

The present findings strongly suggest that middle-class children such as those included in this study do not learn language on the basis of a confusing corpus full of mistakes, garbles, and complexities. They hear, in fact, a relatively consistent, organized, simplified, and redundant set of utterances which in many ways seems quite well designed as a set of "language lessons." It might be useful to explore in some detail how these speech-style modifications function as tutorial devices.

POTENTIAL VALUE OF GRAMMATICAL SIMPLIFICATION
One striking feature of mothers' speech in the presence of young children was the reduction in the length of their utterances. Since run-on sentences were scored as two or more utterances, the shorter utterances which were produced in the presence of 2-year-olds were, on the average, less elaborated than normal utterances. Elaboration can occur in many ways. Sentence complexity scores were lower in the 2-year-old present condition, indicating less use of subordinate clauses and compound verbs. Incidence of utterances without verbs was greater, indicating increased use of constructions so simple they did not even qualify as sentences. Mean preverb-

Table 4   Results of Two-Way Analyses of Variance in Experiment 3

Measures and Tasks[a]	Means				ANOVA Significant Effects		
	Mothers		Nonmothers				Groups X
	Easy	Difficult	Easy	Difficult	Groups	Difficulty	Difficulty
Quantity of Speech:							
A	147.2	148.9	192.2	157.3	—	—	—
B	181.6	631.4	472.2	1328.0	.01	.01	.05
Mean length of utterance:							
A	8.555	8.497	9.747	12.640	.05	.05	.05
B	9.851	10.180	10.008	11.242	—	.05	—
Sentence Complexity:							
A	0.214	0	.163	0.218	.267	—	—
	—			0			
B	0.195	0.246	0.327	0.341	—	—	—
Mean preverb length:							
A	2.111	2.353	2.582	2.587	—	—	—
B	2.260	2.598	2.733	2.947	—	—	—
Utterances without verbs:							
A	0.163	0.247	0.019	0.022	.01	—	—
B	0.159	0.122	0.051	0.065	.05	—	—
Third-person pronouns:							
A	0.052	0.029	0.040	0.031	—	—	—
B	0.039	0.034	0.035	0.041	—	—	—
Complete repetitions:							
A	0.030	0.022	0.014	0.014	—	—	—
B	0.042	0.031	0.011	0.016	—	—	—
Partial Repetitions:							
A	0.259	0.325	0.177	0.227	—	.01	—
B	0.273	0.208	0.227	0.178	—	—	—
Semantic repetitions:							
A	0.016	0.027	0.036	0.011	—	—	—
B	0.047	0.030	0.014	0.010	—	—	—

[a] Task A denotes the block-selection task; task B denotes the pattern-construction task.

length scores were lower, indicating less left-branching and self-embedding. It is clear that the number of words before the verb is very high in a left-branching sentence such as, "Bill who is the son of the woman who lives next door cuts my lawn." Such sentences occurred very rarely in speech to 2-year-olds. Similarly, self-embedded sentences such as, "The rat that the cat that the dog worried killed ate the malt," never occurred in speech to 2-year-olds. Whatever the specific changes leading to shorter utterances, it seems clear that, in general, these changes are correlated with grammatical (and semantic) simplicity. This means that the surface structure, which the child hears, is related by a smaller number of steps to the base structure, which must be reached if the sentence is to be interpreted correctly. Further, the child's work in searching for the major units in a sentence is considerably lightened if there are fewer minor units to process. Finally, there are fewer inflections in a shorter sentence; this may improve the chances that the child will notice, remember, and induce the rules governing the inflections that do occur.

Mothers used fewer subordinate clauses and compound verbs when speaking to young children; for example: "That's a lion. And the lion's name is Leo. Leo lives in a big house. Leo goes for a walk every morning. And he always takes his cane along." If there are fewer clauses in a sentence, then the child is faced with fewer subject-verb and subject-verb-object relations to puzzle out, and related subjects and verbs are more likely to follow one another directly. Thus, the child might discover the subject-verb-object rule for sentence production with greater ease than if he were faced with sentences composed of many interembedded clauses. Evidence presented by Slobin and Welsh (1968) suggests that children do process sentences by searching out the subject and verb. If the subejct or verb were somehow obscured in the sentences offered to their subject for imitation, she would treat the sentence as a word list. But she could extract a subject, verb, and object from a scrambled sentence if she could identify two nouns and a verb which had some semantically acceptable relationship.

Mean preverb length was shorter in speech addressed to 2-year-olds. Greater mean preverb length can result from center-embedding or left-branching; such sentences are known to be more difficult to process for children (Gaer 1969) and for adults (Miller 1962). Since the subject is normally the first element in an English sentence, greater mean preverb length would often involve separation between the subject and the verb. This kind of sentence is probably both difficult and confusing to a child who is just mastering a subject-verb rule for forming sentences. Furthermore, considering the evidence that a meaningful verb is important in making it possible for children to process sentences (Herriot 1968), sentences in which the verb is placed toward the end may be more difficult to understand.

About 16% of the utterances spoken to 2-year-olds were simple phrases, which were not produced on the basis of a subject-verb rule. This is quite a high percentage for a child who will have to deduce subject-verb rules for producing sentences. Inspection of the protocols indicates that much of the increase of utterances without verbs in the 2-year-old condition can be attributed to repetition of important phrases from preceding sentences; for example: "Put the red truck in the box now. The red truck. No, the red truck. In the box. The red truck in the box." The value of this kind of repetition for guiding the child's behavior is obvious. Grammatically, it may have yet another value. It gives information about the boundaries of units within utterances, since only complete units—noun phrases and prepositional phrases, primarily

—are repeated in this way. A major step in decoding a sentence is assigning a phrase structure to it. Information about the limits of subunits within the sentence is extremely valuable in this task.

Fewer third-person pronouns were used in speech to young children. Mothers repeated the subjects and objects of their sentences rather than substituting pronouns for them. Thus, the children were not required, in the early stages of rule formation, to deal with the difficulties of pronoun reference. Furthermore it is possible that the existence of subject-verb relations in sentences is somewhat obscured when a pronoun is substituted for the subject noun phrase, which has a more obvious semantic reference to an actor or a topic. The difficulties would be especially great for a child who is not yet sure which pronouns refer to which classes of nouns.

POTENTIAL VALUE OF REPETITION

Repetition of complete sentences was about four times as frequent for 2-year-olds as for 10-year-olds. Depending on the task, 3%–8% of the utterances that 2-year-olds heard were repeated shortly afterwards. Short-term memory limits the time available for processing input. Repetition of a sentence would give added processing time, thus increasing the child's chances of successfully processing the sentence. For example, if a child had decoded the major components of a sentence at first hearing, repetition would give him an opportunity to pay attention to the more minor constructions, such as modifiers and subordinate clauses. Perhaps the function of these unstressed constructions in long sentences first becomes obvious to the child only following repetition of the sentence.

Repetition of phrases was much more common in speech addressed to 2-year-olds. As discussed above, the repetition of noun and prepositional phrases is clearly of value, assuming that one of the child's tasks is to assign a phrase structure to what he hears. Often, when mothers repeated phrases, they used a new frame for the repeated phrase; for example: "Pick up the red one. Find the red one. Not the green one. I want the red one. Can you find the red one?" This is a valuable object lesson in the basic linguistic skill of rearranging units to form new utterances. Interestingly, it is quite similar to language games that children themselves play with their newly learned words (Weir 1962).

In experiment 1, 14% of mothers' utterances to 2-year-olds in the present condition were paraphrases of preceding utterances; for example: "Give mummy all the red toys. I would like all the things that look like this. Can you give me all the red things?" This is more than twice as many paraphrases as in the absent condition and three times as many as provided for 10-year-olds. Some of this was undoubtedly due to the child's failure to comprehend the mother's first statement. Thus, the mother was required to find a new way to say what she meant. Interestingly, the mothers did not predict this need as readily as they predicted the need for partial repetition. The ability to paraphrase represents another basic feature of language. The relationship between sound and meaning is arbitrary, and therefore several different sound signals can have the same meaning. Thus, it makes no sense to memorize sentences; new ones meaning the same thing can always be created without waste of memory stores. Hearing adults paraphrase their own utterances could be a valuable demonstration of this basic feature of language to a child whose vocabulary and grammar are still so small that he has only one way to say most things. Furthermore, if the child has figured out the meaning of the sentence, he needs less time to interpret its paraphrase and thus can spend more time decoding grammatically less important units of the paraphrase.

CONCLUSIONS

The modifications which mothers produce for young children may be valuable in at least two ways. The first value, no doubt intended by the speaker, is to keep his speech simple, interesting, and comprehensible to young children. The second value, unintended by the adult but potentially as important as the first, is that simplified speech is admirably designed to aid children in learning language. This makes it somewhat easier to understand how a child can accomplish the formidable task of learning his native language with such relative ease. The willingness of the child's parents to produce simplified and redundant speech, combined with the child's own ability to attend selectively to simple, meaningful, and comprehensible utterances (Shipley, Gleitman, & Smith 1969; Snow 1971; also see Friedlander 1968, 1970; Turnure 1971), provide the child with tractable, relatively consistent, and relevant linguistic information from which to formulate the rules of grammar.

REFERENCES

Bernstein, B. A sociolinguistic approach to socialization: with some reference to educability. In F. Williams (Ed.), *Language and poverty: perspectives on a theme*. Chicago: Markham, 1970.

Chomsky, N. *Aspects of the theory of syntax*. Cambridge: The M.I.T. Press, 1965.

Chomsky, N. *Language and mind*. New York: Harcourt, Brace & World, 1968.

Friedlander, B. Z. The effect of speaker identity, voice inflection, vocabulary, and message redundancy on infants' selection of vocal reinforcement. *Journal of Experimental Child Psychology*, 1968, **6**, 443–459.

Friedlander, B. Z. Receptive language development in infancy: issues and problems. *Merrill-Palmer Quarterly*, 1970, **16**, 7–51.

Gaer, E. P. Children's understanding and production of sentences. *Journal of Verbal Learning and Verbal Behavior*, 1969, **8**, 289–294.

Herriot, P. The comprehension of syntax. *Child Development*, 1968, **39**, 273–282.

Hess, R. D., & Shipman, V. C. Early experience and the socialization of cognitive modes in children. *Child Development*, 1965, **36**, 869–886.

Lenneberg, E H. On explaining language. *Science*, 1969, **164**, 635–643.

McNeill, D. A. *The acquisition of language: the study of developmental phycholinguistics*. New York: Harper & Row, 1970.

Miller, G. A. Some psychological studies of grammar. *American Psychologist*, 1962, **17**, 748–762.

Olim, E. Maternal language styles and the cognitive development of children. In F. Williams (Ed.), *Language and poverty: perspectives on a theme*. Chicago: Markham, 1970.

Scheffé, H. A method for judging all contrasts in the analysis of variance. *Biometrika*, 1953, **40**, 87–104.

Shipley, E. F.; Gleitman, C. S.; & Smith, L. R. A study of the acquisition of language: free responses to commands. *Language*, 1969, **45**, 322–342.

Slobin, D. I., & Welsh, C. A. Elicited imitations as a research tool in developmental psycholinguistics. Working Paper No. 10, Language-Behavior Research Laboratory, University of California at Berkeley, May 1968.

Snow, C. E. Language acquisition and mothers' speech to children. Unpublished doctoral dissertation, McGill University, 1971.

Turnure, C. Response to voice of mother and stranger by babies in the first year. *Developmental Psychology*, 1971, **4**, 182–190.

Weir, R. *Language in the crib*. The Hague: Mouton, 1962.

Winer, B. J. *Statistical principles in experimental design*. New York: McGraw-Hill, 1962.

BIBLIOGRAPHY

Berko, J. and Brown, R. Psycholinguistic research methods. In P. Mussen (Ed.), *Handbook of research methods in child development.* New York: John Wiley & Sons, 1960.

Bever, T. G., Fodor, J. A., & Weksel, W. On the acquisition of syntax: A critique of "contextual generalization." *Psychological Review,* 1965, *72,* 467-482.

Bloom, L. *Language development: Form and function in emerging grammars.* Cambridge, Massachusetts: The M.I.T. Press, 1970.

Bloom, L. One word at a time: The use of single-word utterances before syntax. The Hague: Mouton, 1973.

Bloom, L., Hood, L., and Lightbown, P. Imitation in language development: If, when and why. *Cognitive Psychology,* 1974, 6, 380–420.

Bloom, L., Miller, P., and Hood, L. Variation and reduction as aspects of competence in language development. In A. Pick (Ed.), *Minnesota Symposia on Child Psychology, Volume 9.* Minneapolis: The University of Minnesota Press, 1975.

Bowerman, M. F. *Early syntactic development: A cross-linguistic study with special reference to Finish,* Cambridge, England: Cambridge University Press, 1973.

Bowerman, M. Structural relationships in children's utterances: Syntactic or semantic? In T. Moore (Ed.), *Cognitive development and the acquisition of language.* New York: Academic Press, 1973.

Braine, M. D. S. The ontogeny of English phrase structure: The first phase. *Language,* 1963, *39,* 1–13.

Braine, M. D. S. The acquisition of language in infant and child. In C. Reed (Ed.) *The learning of language*. New York: Appleton, 1971.

Brown, R. Linguistic determinism and the part of speech. *Journal of Abnormal Social Psychology*, 1957, 55, 1–5.

Brown, R. The development of Wh-questions in child speech. *Journal of Verbal Learning and Verbal Behavior*, 1968, 7, 279–290.

Brown, R. *A first language*. Cambridge, Massachusetts: Harvard University Press, 1973.

Brown, R., Cazden, C. B., & Bellugi, U. The child's grammar from 1 to 3. In J. P. Hill (Ed.), *Minnesota symposia on child psychology*, Vol. 2. Minneapolis: University of Minnesota Press, 1969. Pp. 28–73.

Brown, R. and Fraser, C. The acquisition of syntax. In C. H. Cofer and B. Musgrave (Eds.), *Verbal behavior and learning*. New York: McGraw-Hill, 1963. Pp. 155–197.

Cazden, C. The acquisition of noun and verb inflections. *Child Development*, 1968, 39, 433–438.

Chapman, R. and Miller, J. Word order in early two and three word sentences. *Journal of Speech and Hearing Research*, 1975, 18, 355–371.

Chomsky, N. *Syntactic structures*. The Hague: Mouton, 1957.

Chomsky, N. *Aspects of the theory of syntax*. Cambridge, Massachussets: The M.I.T. Press, 1965.

Clark, E. Non-linguistic strategies and the acquisition of word meanings. *Cognition*, 1973, 2, 161–182.

Cohen, L. and Salapatek, P. (Eds.), *Infant perception: From sensation to cognition*, (Vols. I and II). New York: Academic Press, 1975.

Delack, J.B. Aspects of infant speech development in the first year of life. *Canadian Journal of Linguistics*, 1976, 21, 17–37.

de Villiers, J.G. and de Villiers, P.A. A cross-sectional study of the acquisition of grammatical morphemes. *Journal of Psycholinguistic Research*, 1973, 2, 267-278.

Drach, K. *The language of the parent: A pilot study*. In Working Paper No. 14: The structure of linguistic input to children. Language Behavior Research Laboratory, University of California at Berkeley, 1969.

Eimas, P.D., Siqueland, E.R., Jusczyk, P., and Vigorito, J. Speech perception in infants. *Science*, 1971, 171, 303–306.

Ervin-Tripp, S. Language development. In L. Hoffman and M. Hoffman (Eds.), *Review of child development research*. New York: Russell Sage Foundation, 1966.

Ervin-Tripp S. An overview of theories of grammatical development. In D. I. Slobin (Ed.), *The ontogenesis of grammar*. New York: Academic Press, 1971. Pp. 189–212.

Fillmore, C. J. The case for case. In E. Bach & R. T. Harms (Eds.), *Universals in linguistic theory*. New York: Holt, 1968.

Fillmore, C. Deixis, I. Unpublished lectures. Unpublished lectures, delivered at the University of California at Santa Cruz, 1971.

Garvey, C. Requests and responses in children's speech. *Journal of Child Language*, 1975, 2, 41–63.

Gleason, J.B. The child's learning of English morphology. *Word*, 1958, 14, 150–177.

Glucksburg, S., Krauss, R. M. & Higgins, E. T. The development of referential communication skills. *Review of Child Development Research*. Vol. 4. Chicago: University of Chicago Pres, 1975.

Guillaume, P. Les débuts de la phrase dans le langage de l'enfant. *Journal de Psychologie,* 1927, 24, 1–25. Translation by E. Clark, in C. Ferguson and D. Slobin (Eds.), *Studies of child language and development,* 1973.

Gvozdev, A. N. Voprozy izucheniia detskoi rechi. (Problems in the language development of the child). Moscow: Academy of Pediatric Science, 1961.

Halliday, M.A.K. A sociosemiotic perspective on language development. *Bulletin of the School of Oriental and African Studies,* University of London. Vol. XXXVII, part 1, 1974.

Huxley, R. The development of the correct use of subject personal pronouns in two children. In G. B. Flores d'Arcais & W. J. M. Levelt (Eds.), *Advances in psycholinguistics.* New York: American Elsevier, 1970.

Jakobson, R. *Child language, aphasia and phonological universals.* The Hague: Mouton, 1968 (originally in German, 1941).

Jesperson, O. *Language: Its nature, development, and origin.* London: Allen & Unwin, 1922, and New York: W.W. Norton, 1964.

Katz, J. J., & Postal, P. M. *An integrated theory of linguistic descriptions.* Cambridge, Massachuetts: The M.I.T. Press, 1964.

Kernan, K. T. The acquisition of language by Samoan children. Unpublished doctoral dissertation, University of California at Berkeley, 1969.

Kernan, K. T. Semantic relations and the child's acquisition of language. *Anthropological linguistics,* 1970, *12* (5), 171-187.

Leopold, W. *Speech development of a bilingual child.* Evanston, Illinois: Northwestern University (4 volumes), 1939.

Lightbown, P. Nominal and pronominal forms in the speech of three French-speaking children: A pilot study. Unpublished doctoral dissertation proposal, Teachers College, Columbia University, 1973.

Macnamara, J. Cognitive vases for language learning in infants. *Psychological Review,* 1972, 79, 1–13.

McCarthy, D. Language development in children. In L. Carmichael (Ed.), *Manual of child psychology.* New York: John Wiley & Sons, 1954.

McCawley, J. D. The role of semantics in grammar. In E. Bach & R. T. Harms (Eds.), *Universals in linguistic theory.* New York: Holt, 1968.

McNeill, D. The creation of language by children. In J. Lyons & R. J. Wales (Eds.), *Psycholinguistic papers.* Edinburgh: University of Edinburgh Press, 1966. (a)

McNeill, D. Developmental psycholinguistics. In F. Smith and G. A. Miller (Eds.), *The genesis of language: A psycholinguistic approach.* Cambridge, Massachusetts: The M.I.T. Press, 1966. (b)

McNeill, D. Language before symbols: Very early children's grammar. *Interchange,* 1970, *1* (No. 3). (a)

McNeill, D. *The acquisition of language.* New York: Harper and Row, 1970. (b)

McNeill, D. The capacity for the ontogenesis of grammar. In D. I. Slobin (Ed.) *The ontogenesis of grammar.* New York: Academic Press, 1971. Pp. 17-40.

Maratsos, M. The use of definite and indefinite reference in young children. Unpublished doctoral dissertation, Harvard University, 1971.

Miller, W. and Ervin, S.M. The development of grammar in child language. In U. Bellugi and R. Brown (Eds.), The acquisition of language. *Monographs of the Society for Research in Child Development,* 1964, No. *29,* 9-33.

Nelson, K. Structure and strategy in learning to talk. *Monographs of the Society for Research in Child Development,* 1973, *38* (1-2, Serial No. 149).

Pfuderer, C. Some suggestions for a syntactic characterization of baby talk style. In Working Paper No. 14, *The structure of linguistic input to children.* Language-Behavior Research Laboratory, University of California at Berkeley, 1969.

Schlesinger, I. M. Production of utterances and language acquisition. In D. I. Slobin (Ed.), *The ontogenesis of grammar.* New York: Academic Press, 1971.

Shipley, E., Smith, C., and Gleitman, L. A study of the acquisition of language: Free responses to commands. *Language,* 1969, 45, 322–342.

Sinclair, H. The transition from sensory-motor behavior to symbolic activity. *Interchange,* 1970, 1, 119–126.

Slobin, D. I. *Universals of grammatical development in children.* In G. B. Flores d'Arcais & W. J. M. Levelt (Eds.), *Advances in psycholinguistics.* New York: American Elsevier, 1970. Pp. 174-184.

Slobin, D. Cognitive prerequisites for the development of grammar. In C. A. Ferguson and D.I. Slobin (Eds.), *Studies of child language development.* New York: Holt Rinehart and Winston, 1973.

Smith, M. An investigation of the development of the sentence and the extent of vocabulary in young children. In B. Baldwin (Ed.), *University of Iowa studies in child welfare.* Iowa City, Iowa: University of Iowa Press.

Smith, M. Grammatical errors in the speech of preschool children. *Child Development,* 1933, 4, 182–190.

Smith, M. The influence of age, sex, and situation on the frequency, form and function of questions asked by preschool children. *Child Development,* 1934, 5, 201–213.

Snow, C. Mothers' speech to children learning language. *Child Development,* 1972, 43, 549–565.

Stern, D., Jaffe, J., Beebe, B., and Bennett, S. Vocalizing in unison and in alternation: Two modes of communication within the mother-infant dyad. In D. Aronson and R. Rieber (Eds.), *Developmental psycholinguistics and communication disorders.* Annals of the New York Academy of Sciences, 1975, 263, 89–100.

Templin, M. *Certain language skills in children.* Minneapolis: University of Minnesota Press, 1957.

Vosniadov, S. Strategies in the acquisition of Greek. Unpublished M.A. thesis, Teachers College, Columbia University, 1974.

Warden, D. The influence of context on children's use of identifying expressions and references. *British Journal of Psychology,* 1976, 67, 101–112.